READING
MASTER

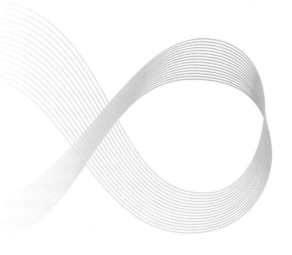

수능
고난도

STAFF

발행인 정선욱

퍼블리싱 총괄 남형주

개발 김태원 김한길 박하영 송경미

기획 · 디자인 · 마케팅 조비호 김정인 강윤정

유통 · 제작 서준성 신성철

Reading Master 수능 고난도 202406 초판 1쇄

펴낸곳 이투스에듀(주) 서울시 서초구 남부순환로 2547

고객센터 1599-3225

등록번호 제2007-000035호

ISBN 979-11-389-2478-8 [53740]

학습 목표별 수능 영어 독해의 체계적 완성

READING MASTER

Reading Master 수능 유형

수능과 내신 대비가 가능한 고등 입문 유형 학습서

수능 독해의 각 유형별 특징 및 해결 전략을 학습하고 이를 풍부한 연습 문제에 적용해보면서 전략적인 수능 대비가 가능하도록 하였습니다. 또한 앞에서 학습한 지문을 변형하여 주요 내신 출제 패턴을 학습하고 연습 문제에 적용해보면서 내신 대비까지 가능하도록 하였습니다.

Reading Master 수능 실전

2~3등급을 목표로 하는 학생들의 실전서

수능 실전 감각을 기를 수 있도록 모든 유형을 골고루 배치한 하프 모의고사 15회를 수록하여 회별로 균형 있게 다양한 유형의 독해 학습이 가능하도록 하였습니다. 또한 고난도 유형의 문제만 집중 연습할 수 있는 고난도 모의고사 5회를 수록하여 심층적인 독해 학습을 통해 고난도 문항 대비까지 가능하도록 하였습니다.

Reading Master 수능 고난도

상위권을 위한 검증된 고퀄리티의 고난도 실전서

실제 성적 데이터를 통해 검증된 고난도 우수 문항을 선별하여 회별 12문항씩 고난도 모의고사 15회를 수록하였습니다. 오답률이 높은 고난도 문항을 풀며 상위권 학생들의 집중적인 고난도 학습이 가능하도록 하였습니다. 또한 앞에서 학습한 지문을 유형을 바꾸어 출제한 REVIEW 모의고사 5회를 수록하여 복습과 테스트가 동시에 가능하도록 하였습니다.

FEATURES

PART I 고난도 모의고사

고난도 모의고사

실제 성적 데이터를 통해 검증된 정답률 60% 미만의 고난도 우수 문항을 선별하여, 고난도로 자주 출제되는 유형으로 회별 12문항씩 15회를 수록하였습니다.

정답률 & 초고난도

문항별 정답률을 표기하여 학생들이 문항을 풀면서 자신의 수준을 확인 가능하도록 하였습니다. 정답률 30%미만의 문항은 초고난도로 표기하였습니다.

부록

WORDS LIST

고난도 모의고사의 어휘를 회별로 모아 정리하여 어휘 학습의 편의성을 높였습니다.

WORDS REVIEW

각 회별 암기한 어휘를 테스트하면서 복습할 수 있도록 하였습니다.

PART Ⅱ REVIEW 모의고사

REVIEW 모의고사
PART I에서 학습한 지문을 유형을 바꾸어 출제한
REVIEW 모의고사 5회를 수록하였습니다.

정답 및 해설

지문 해석, 해설, 매력적 오답, WHY 고난도, TEXT FLOW, 구문 등을 제시하여 학습
자가 스스로 학습하기에 어려움이 없도록 상세한 풀이를 제공하였습니다.

매력적 오답 & WHY 고난도
선택률이 정답률과 비슷하거나 더 높았던 매력적 오답을 분석하여 학생들이 함정에
빠지지 않고 정답을 찾을 수 있도록 하였습니다. 또한 해당 문제가 왜 고난도 문항인
지를 해설하여 고난도 문항에 대한 이해를 돕도록 하였습니다.

TEXT FLOW
지문의 논리적 흐름을 이해할 수 있도록 지문 구조를 분석하여 요약 정리한 TEXT
FLOW를 수록하였습니다.

CONTENTS

PART II REVIEW 모의고사

부록

PART

1

고난도
모의고사

01

밑줄 친 "Develop!"이 다음 글에서 의미하는 바로 가장 적절한 것은?

We need caution. Human virtues are multileveled. That nature builds character is but half the truth and absurd if taken for the whole. That would omit all the civic virtues, without which we could not be human. Character is developed in a dialectic of nature and culture. "Man is by nature a political animal." Humans are animals who build themselves a polis, a city, and love to socialize within it. "Man is the animal for whom it is natural to be artificial." *Homo sapiens* is "the natural alien." What humans "naturally" do when they encounter nature is build a culture differentiating themselves from nature. Agriculture, business, and industry are their real vocation. Virtue has to be "cultivated," "cultured." Living with wild nature in nostalgic simplicity and frugality, these "humanists" will say, is romantic nonsense that forgets how much the human genius lies in departure from and resourceful transformation of nature. The modern word for this is "Develop!"

*dialectic: 변증법

① Learn from and get new ideas from nature!
② Change nature according to humans' will!
③ Recover from diseases and stay healthy!
④ Take environmental issues into account!
⑤ Form intimate bonds with wild animals!

02

다음 글의 주제로 가장 적절한 것은?

The critique of oral histories as subjective and inaccurate risks discarding one of their greatest values, the insight they offer into subjective experience. This does more than merely add color to history: few historians would refute, for example, that personal opinions, friendships, and dislikes can make the difference between a successful military campaign and its failure, a consensual policy or a deep political rift. Indeed, the subjectivity of the interview has the power to transform what subject matter is considered worthy of historical investigation. Thompson, for example, has drawn attention to the "transforming impact of oral history upon the history of the family," pointing out that without it, "the historian can discover very little indeed about either the ordinary family's contacts with neighbors and kin, or its internal relationships." Feminist historians have pointed out that subjective experience and emotional meaning has as much place in historical investigation as narratives of events.

*consensual: 대체로 동의하는 **rift: 균열

① difficulties of restoring losers' voices in history
② significance of oral histories in historical research
③ methods of preserving oral histories for further research
④ differences between oral histories and published records
⑤ ways historians' perspectives affect historical interpretation

03

정답률 38%

다음 글의 밑줄 친 부분 중, 어법상 틀린 것은?

Nitrogen in its gaseous form is often used in situations in which it is important ① to keep other, more reactive atmospheric gases away. It serves industry as a blanketing gas, for example, in protecting materials such as electronic components during production or storage. To prevent the oxidation of wine, wine bottles are often ② filled with nitrogen after the cork is removed. Nitrogen has recently also been used in blanketing fruit after it has been picked to protect ③ itself from rotting. Apples, for example, can be stored for up to 30 months if they are kept at low temperatures in an atmosphere of nitrogen. In addition to these applications, nitrogen is used in oil production, ④ in which it is pumped in compressed form underground to force oil to the surface. Ordinary air cannot be used for this purpose because some of the gases that make up air would react with the oil, ⑤ producing undesired by-products.

*oxidation: 산화(酸化)

04

정답률 52%

다음 글의 밑줄 친 부분 중, 문맥상 낱말의 쓰임이 적절하지 않은 것은?

One reason for stipulating a distinction between disaster-planning and disaster-response is that the unexpected may occur, ① requiring unanticipated actions and rules of action. For example, there could be a plan for the orderly evacuation of a place, but in an earthquake, exit routes might be blocked, requiring the improvisation of ② new exit routes and evacuation methods. Perhaps the preparation plan does not require helicopter rescues, but developing circumstances do, so this is ③ included in the response plan. A change like this does not entail a change in ethical principles, provided the intention that everyone be safely evacuated is present in both plans. One way to avoid apparent contradictions between preparation and response plans is to make the preparation plans ④ fixed. For example, safe evacuation of all occupants is stated as a primary goal in the preparation plan, and several exit routes are specified beforehand, but the choice of exit route is left open, to be determined by ⑤ actual circumstances.

*stipulate: 규정하다

[05~06] 다음 빈칸에 들어갈 말로 가장 적절한 것을 고르시오.

05 초고난도
정답률 27%

In times of crisis, the media react to society's need for surveillance and information by devoting massive time and energy to coverage of the crisis. All too often, though, it is difficult to gather information. Yet, it would be dysfunctional for media coverage to cease until information can be collected and verified. In order to reduce tension in society, media devote a good deal of coverage to media content intended to comfort their audience. _____ is functional for society in times of crisis. The media highlight the wisdom of leaders and the bravery of rescue workers or soldiers to reassure society that "we are all in this together" and that everything possible is being done for survival. So, although the media may be unable to fulfill surveillance and correlation needs, they are able to offer assurance and tension reduction.

*surveillance: 감시 **dysfunctional: 제 기능을 하지 않는

① Novelty seeking
② Social distancing
③ Resource sharing
④ Solidarity building
⑤ Maintaining transparency

06 초고난도
정답률 28%

Sports texts have many forms, functions, and readerships. The traditional sports report is intended to bear witness to what has occurred for those who were not present. At the most basic, denotative level it is an uncontroversial statement that, for example, Crewe Alexandra drew 0-0 with Burnley in Division Three of the English Football League at the Gresty Road Ground in front of a crowd of 2,816 cold, wet spectators. Not much human intervention is needed here: a few units of data are "sent down the wire" or entered into a computer database, producing a text that has little more cultural resonance than the shipping or stock market reports. Except that, just as those anonymous units of information have much greater importance and depth of meaning for the seafarers and "desk jockeys" who depend on them for their livelihoods, the relevant sports fan will not only invest these facts with significance, but also expect more information. Thus it is unlikely that many followers of sport will _____.

*denotative: 외연적인 **resonance: 반향(反響), 울림

① emphasize the importance of impact over facts
② regard fierce competition between players as natural
③ be satisfied for long with a simple news digest format
④ welcome any human intervention that provides details
⑤ see their favorite players in person on the field

07

다음 글에서 전체 흐름과 관계 <u>없는</u> 문장은?

Depending on what else is going on in your life, or at the moment, a particular incident might make you feel a little sad, causing the corners of your mouth to turn down. Or it might make you very sad, and your eyes might start tearing. ① Emotion states allow for a gradient of intensity of reaction to the same stimulus, depending on a spectrum of other relevant factors. ② A strange noise coming from downstairs when you'd thought you were alone might make you a little fearful if the incident happens at noon, but very afraid if it's at midnight. ③ The difference in reaction is a useful distinction based on your knowledge of the world (specifically in this case on your knowledge of when home break-ins are most likely to occur). ④ Expressing an emotion doesn't have to be something outward like slamming a door, yelling into a pillow or even telling someone about it. ⑤ It is made possible by the scalability of emotion, and not characteristic of the one-size-fits-all approach of reflexive processing.

*a gradient of: 정도가 다양한
**scalability: 점차 증가할 수 있는 성질

08 초고난도

주어진 글 다음에 이어질 글의 순서로 가장 적절한 것은?

Computer-based search tools are undoubtedly useful: *Current Contents* gives you a quick view of recently published work in journals of interest; the *Web of Science* (and similar tools) allows a rapid search for literature by authors, keywords, or tracking citations. How did we do it before the search engines were available?

(A) The big advantage of this method is that it gives you the citation structure of the field and some feel for how things have developed. A related technique searches in the opposite direction, and search engines are very helpful here.

(B) I would start by scanning through the major journals that published the topic for, say, the past five years, copying any relevant papers. To discover the older literature, I would then examine citations in these papers, inferring the important sources from the frequency and nature of the references to them.

(C) Identify a key paper on the topic published, say, 20 years ago and then look at the papers published since then that cite this paper. Sometimes, you pick up papers you would otherwise miss because they were published in unusual places or lacked obviously linked keywords or titles.

① (A) – (C) – (B)　　② (B) – (A) – (C)
③ (B) – (C) – (A)　　④ (C) – (A) – (B)
⑤ (C) – (B) – (A)

09

정답률 38%

글의 흐름으로 보아, 주어진 문장이 들어가기에 가장 적절한 곳은?

> In consequence, it is denied access to a whole domain of reality in which mankind can move freely.

Self-awareness, or reflective thought, is the main attribute distinguishing humans from animals. (①) It is the consciousness that enables us to contemplate ourselves. (②) Reflection is the power to turn one's consciousness upon oneself, to know oneself and, especially, to *know that one knows*. (③) Humans are the only creation in the universe who can be the object of their own reflection and, because of that, another world is born: an inner world, a reality in which no lower animal can ever participate. (④) Incapable of contemplating itself, or of being aware of itself as the conscious subject, not even a higher type of animal, such as a dog or cat that knows who its master is and where its food is, can know that it knows. (⑤) Systems of physics, philosophy, mathematics, and astronomy, for example, have all been constructed because of man's unique ability to reflect inwardly.

10

정답률 55%

다음 글의 내용을 한 문장으로 요약하고자 한다. 빈칸 (A), (B)에 들어갈 말로 가장 적절한 것은?

Animals with territories that take days or weeks to patrol need to advertise with something long-lasting, something that will keep on broadcasting even when they are gone. Since odors have the ability to linger, animals often anoint their territories with scent marks that other animals can read as they pass by. Animals that operate in the dark depend on sounds as well as odors, whereas day-active animals are more likely to use visual means for their messages. You'll see the most dramatic visual signals exchanged between animals of the open plains, since, in their native habitat, they have the luxury of unobstructed views. Birds in dense forests usually can't see their receivers, however, so they have perfected a rich repertoire of songs instead. Low-frequency songs are preferred, since higher frequencies tend to hit and bounce back from objects such as tree trunks. Songsters usually perch in the tree canopy, where an "acoustic window" carries their messages most effectively.

*anoint: (액체를) 바르다
**canopy: (숲의 나뭇가지들이) 지붕 모양으로 우거진 곳

⬇

> In the animal kingdom, various methods of _____(A)_____ have emerged to fit each animal's _____(B)_____ and habitat.

	(A)		(B)
①	hunting	......	physiology
②	hunting	......	lifestyle
③	protection	......	physiology
④	communication	......	personality
⑤	communication	......	lifestyle

[11~12] 다음 글을 읽고, 물음에 답하시오.

Consciousness of external events takes about half a second (500 milliseconds) to develop. Our perceived awareness of the "present" is actually an awareness of the (a)recent past, sometimes called the *remembered present*. This delay suggests that conscious awareness requires many passes of signals back and forth between widespread cortical and lower brain regions. *Consciousness of the outside world is apparently represented in the total activity of distributed cortical networks rather than any one network node or small network.* Parts of the unconscious may be viewed as incompletely formed consciousness, that is, (b)pre-conscious processes from which consciousness emerges after a few hundred milliseconds or so. Other parts of our unconscious remain forever hidden from awareness but still exert important influences on our conscious mind, affecting our choices to act in certain ways. Interactions occur in (c)both directions; the conscious mind may influence the unconscious, and vice versa.

Our unconscious actions occur much faster than our conscious actions. Initiation and guidance of voluntary acts by the unconscious is a common occurrence (d)familiar to anyone who has ever played baseball or tennis. The complex responses required in sports or playing the piano are much more involved than simple reflexes. A basketball player attempting a jump shot makes split-second adjustments according to his location, velocity, and body angle as well as to the positions of his opponents. Conscious planning of quick action in sports or playing musical instruments is typically (e)beneficial to performance; it is best if our painfully slow consciousness hands over control to the faster unconscious.

*cortical: 피질의 **node: 마디, 교점 ***velocity: 속도

11

윗글의 제목으로 가장 적절한 것은?

① The Present Is Always Formed by the Past
② The Unconscious Is a Mirror to the Conscious
③ Consciousness: Behind Time and Against Action
④ How Memories Are Formed, Stored, and Recalled
⑤ Remembered Past: A Reflection of Unexpressed Wishes

12

밑줄 친 (a)~(e) 중에서 문맥상 낱말의 쓰임이 적절하지 않은 것은?

① (a)　　② (b)　　③ (c)　　④ (d)　　⑤ (e)

01

밑줄 친 What we don't spend on the front end가 다음 글에서 의미하는 바로 가장 적절한 것은?

They say that time and money are the biggest perceived obstacles to eating well. In most cases, neither is a true obstacle. Americans spend eight hours a day in front of a screen. On average, we each spend two hours a day on the Internet — something that didn't even exist 20 years ago! But can't we find the time to plan, shop, and cook for our families? True, it might cost a little more to buy fresh meat, fish, and produce than to eat processed junk and fast food. But it doesn't have to. In fact, studies have shown that eating real food is not more expensive than eating processed food. You don't have to buy grass-fed steak (although that's ideal). You can eat well for less. To put it in perspective, Europeans spend about 20 percent of their income on food, Americans only 9 percent. What we don't spend on the front end we pay for on the back end at the drugstore and the doctor's office.

① The expense and effort we avoid on preparing real food
② The money we don't spend on junk and processed food
③ The unsatisfied desire for healthy home-cooked meals
④ The attention and time we pay to exotic healthy food
⑤ The choice we make for productivity in our work

02

다음 글의 제목으로 가장 적절한 것은?

Abstract properties of physical objects may be products of event perception. Consider notions related to substance, such as solidity and weight. These might seem to be haptic or kinesthetically known properties of objects. According to a sensation-based view, in fact, it might seem impossible that such properties could be perceived visually from reflected light; not so, however, according to an event perception view. Runeson argued that kinematic patterns in events specify the properties of objects. For example, adult participants in his experiments viewed other people lifting a covered box containing varying weights and estimated the weight on each trial. Participants' estimates were as accurate when they viewed someone else lifting the box as when they lifted it themselves. Complex relationships in the viewed biomechanical event of a person lifting something can specify material properties such as weight.

*haptic: 촉각에 의한 **kinesthetically: 운동 감각에 의한
***kinematic: 운동학적인

① Perceptions: Inferences from Haptic Feedback
② Sight Can Reveal Objects' Nonvisual Properties
③ It Takes Every Sense to Know Things Inside Out
④ Abstractions: Accessible Only Through Cognition
⑤ How to Describe the Sensory Properties of Objects

03 초고난도

정답률 17%

다음 글의 밑줄 친 부분 중, 어법상 틀린 것은?

Edison knew, as did others, that running electricity through a variety of materials could make those materials glow — a process called *incandescence* — thereby producing a light source ①that could be used as an alternative to candles and natural gas lamps. The problem was that the glowing material (the *filament*) would degrade after a short while, making its use as a household lighting device ②impractical. Not knowing any of the physical principles by which electricity destroyed the filament, Edison simply tried every material he could ③see if one would glow brightly, yet resist burning out. After trying 1,600 different materials, including cotton and turtle shell, he happened upon carbonized bamboo, which turned out to be the filament of choice (to the joy of turtles everywhere). When ④used in an air-evacuated bulb (i.e., a vacuum tube), the carbonized bamboo outshone and lasted much longer than any of the other tested filaments. Edison had his light bulb. Although tungsten soon replaced carbonized bamboo in home light bulbs, illumination by incandescence became the predominant mode of interior lighting for many decades ⑤to follow.

*incandescence: 고온 발광

04

정답률 51%

다음 글의 밑줄 친 부분 중, 문맥상 낱말의 쓰임이 적절하지 않은 것은?

Affect can be expressed through facial expressions and through modulations in the tone and prosody of the voice. These ①nonverbal aspects of language communication, in both their expression and perception, appear to be mediated predominantly by the right hemisphere. The body's posture and movement can also ②blend with the voice and facial expression in sending affective signals that are readily perceived by other people. What is striking is the finding that the ③input from the body — including signals from the muscles, bones, and viscera (such as the heart and the intestines) — is more highly integrated in the right hemisphere than in the left. In other words, the whole body is ④represented in an integrated way in the right hemisphere. Even the regulation of the body's autonomic nervous system is primarily mediated by right-brain mechanisms. The right hemisphere therefore appears to play a ⑤trivial role in mediating regulatory emotional processes, as well as in permitting the expression of emotional states and the conscious awareness of emotional experience.

*affect: 정서, 감정 **prosody: 운율(학) ***viscera: 내장(內臟)

[05~07] 다음 빈칸에 들어갈 말로 가장 적절한 것을 고르시오.

05 초고난도 〔정답률 27%〕

The people who came before you invented science because your natural way of understanding and explaining what you experience is terrible. When you have zero evidence, every assumption is basically equal. You prefer to see causes rather than effects, signals in the noise, patterns in the randomness. You prefer easy-to-understand stories, and thus turn everything in life into a narrative so that complicated problems become easy. Scientists work to remove the narrative, to boil it away, leaving behind only the raw facts. Those data sit there, naked and exposed, so they can _____. Scientists and laypeople will conjure up new stories using the data, and they will argue, but the data will not budge. They may not even make sense for a hundred years or more, but thanks to the scientific method, the stories, full of biases and fallacies, will crash against the facts and recede into history.

*conjure up: ~을 생각해 내다 **budge: 조금 움직이다
***recede: (서서히) 물러나다

① be accepted or rejected based on popularity
② play a role in making a story the best it can be
③ cause complex problems that lead to disharmony
④ unlock people's potential and boost their self-esteem
⑤ be reflected upon and rearranged by each new visitor

06 〔정답률 31%〕

In the seventeenth and eighteenth centuries, Ireland was a colony under England. This meant that England controlled all Irish resources. As in many other colonial situations — many of them British — England did not do the work of being a colonial power on its own. Middlemen were effective tools of colonization. Underneath the British but above Irish Catholics in Ireland were "the Dissenters." These Irish non-Catholic Dissenters, "who were mostly Presbyterian farmers, mechanics, and small tradesmen," helped maintain the oppressive hierarchy imposed by Britain. They saved the English labor and trouble, often receiving relatively little in return. They did gain one important benefit from their social position. Like Irish Catholics, they themselves might live in terrible conditions, but as Protestants, they could at least consider themselves part of the dominant — the better — race. In other words, in terms of their "race," _____. No matter how poor they might be, Protestants gained a psychic power from being Protestant Irish, not Catholic.

*Dissenter: 비국교도 **Presbyterian: (기독교) 장로교의

① Irish Catholics resisted their differing religious belief
② the British always considered other races to be inferior
③ colonial residents were rated by the value of their labor
④ even the dominant were divided by their economic status
⑤ all Protestants benefited from the British-imposed hierarchy

07 초고난도

To value something is to believe that it is valuable and to *care* about it. If one does not care, one does not value. Unfortunately, the nature of care is almost as ambiguous as the notion of understanding. But at least one thing is clear: care cannot be defined apart from its relation to the emotions. One might go so far as to think of care as a mere disposition to emotion. I think that this is a mistake. Since caring gives rise to a variety of different emotions, actions, and thoughts, it cannot be reduced to a mere disposition to emote. All I am confident in affirming is that our emotions depend on what we care about. For example, we only fear for that which we care about. In general, standard emotions essentially involve evaluations of the way something we care about stands to be or has been affected. But it is incoherent to think that someone could care about something and not be prone to feel fear when it is threatened, or hope when it stands to flourish. Accordingly, it is uncontroversial to suggest that our cares _____ .

*emote: 감정을 과장되게 드러내다

① are so strong that we cannot control them
② are often by-products of rational thoughts
③ do not usually contribute to emotional reactions
④ persist even as we get older and our bodies change
⑤ are sometimes revealed to us by our emotional responses

08

주어진 글 다음에 이어질 글의 순서로 가장 적절한 것은?

The most basic human instinct is the instinct for self-preservation. Criminal law recognizes this impulse and authorizes its use in the justice system via the doctrine of self-defense.

(A) Another feature of self-defense is that the strategy only wins provided the defendant can demonstrate that he exercised a necessary and proportional response. It is possible that the proportionality requirement would limit its utility for defendants in cultural defense cases.

(B) When the individual who argues self-defense acts reasonably, he will have the benefit of a complete defense to a number of crimes. For the most part, self-defense will succeed only if a defendant has a reasonable belief that the use of force is necessary. Hence the critical question in cultural defense cases will be how to judge whether a person has such a "reasonable" belief.

(C) The reason for this is that the determination of what constitutes a proportionate response would depend upon the cultural background of the person making the assessment. Presumably, the judge from the dominant culture would not view the act as a proportionate response, even if members of the defendant's cultural community agreed that it was.

*defendant: 피고(인)
**proportionality: (법의) 비례의 원칙(과잉조치 금지의 원칙)

① (A) – (C) – (B)　　② (B) – (A) – (C)
③ (B) – (C) – (A)　　④ (C) – (A) – (B)
⑤ (C) – (B) – (A)

09

글의 흐름으로 보아, 주어진 문장이 들어가기에 가장 적절한 곳은?

> Only in really abundant environments, however, particularly those with rich marine resources, can foragers live permanently in groups of several dozens or sometimes hundreds strong.

Despite disagreements on forager social organizations, the central demographic facts are not in dispute. (①) The low density of wild food resources means that most contemporary foragers spend most of their time in very small groups, usually of two to eight closely related people. (②) All, however, need to belong to much larger groups of at least five hundred people, because only these can provide a viable breeding population. (③) It is unusual for so many foragers to assemble physically, but even the smallest groups do regularly assemble in larger bands or camps of perhaps fifty-plus people, and networks of these bands/camps create genetic pools of the required size. (④) In fertile environments, people spend more of the year in these larger groups; in harsh environments, less of it. (⑤) The old foraging villages of North America's Pacific Coast, from the Chumash of Southern California to the Tlingit of the Alaska panhandle, are the best-known cases.

*forager: (먹을 것의) 채집자
**panhandle: 좁고 길게 다른 주(州)로 뻗어 있는 지역

10

다음 글의 내용을 한 문장으로 요약하고자 한다. 빈칸 (A), (B)에 들어갈 말로 가장 적절한 것은?

Films often construct idealized representations of places, weaving compelling narratives that can distort our true understanding of these places. These cinematic representations tend to amplify the extraordinary aspects of these destinations, fostering a one-dimensional view that doesn't reflect the nuanced and multifaceted reality of the real world. As a result, audiences may unknowingly develop overly optimistic or pessimistic impressions by accepting these representations as authentic reflections of the places in question. This can result in people arriving at these destinations with inflated or unjustified expectations, only to be confronted with the more imperfect reality they encounter. Similarly, films often take creative liberties to portray certain places as filled with danger, crime, or other unfavorable characteristics, causing people to have unwarranted concerns or fears about visiting these places. Consequently, while the cinematic lens is a compelling medium for storytelling, it can sometimes blur the line between fiction and reality, sowing the seeds of false impressions about places that persist long after the credits roll.

*unwarranted: 부당한

↓

> Films create ___(A)___ perceptions of places, which can lead to ___(B)___ about those locations in real life.

	(A)		(B)
①	cognitive	·····	criticisms
②	cognitive	·····	misconceptions
③	inaccurate	·····	misconceptions
④	inaccurate	·····	modifications
⑤	realistic	·····	modifications

[11~12] 다음 글을 읽고, 물음에 답하시오.

Sometimes, small things can create big problems, as is the case with the smallest of energy products: batteries. At the end of their life, batteries become an unfortunate combination of useless, worthless, and toxic. Batteries' complex chemical ingredients can be difficult to separate, and dumping them in landfills without any treatment can (a)release toxic chemicals into the environment. Recycling batteries costs at least 10 times more than burying them in a landfill. Owing to the toxic nature of battery waste, many governments have regulated their disposal at the consumer level to force recycling. Despite the fact that California, for example, (b)allows discarding batteries in household trash, Californians recycle less than 5 percent of the batteries they buy.

The government of Belgium used the threat of a high eco-tax on new batteries to (c)convince battery makers to collect and dispose of old ones. An 800-member nonprofit consortium of battery producers called Bebat handles battery collection and recycling. The program adds about 15 to 25 cents to the cost of each battery, but that cost is only about one-quarter the cost of the threatened eco-tax that battery makers would pay if they do not achieve the government's ever-increasing recycling rate targets. To achieve the required rate, Bebat (d)installed bright green collection boxes at 24,000 locations in markets, photo shops, jewelers, schools, municipal locations, and elsewhere to offer convenient battery drop-off points for consumers. The consortium also paid for public information campaigns to (e)ensure that the vast majority of consumers know about the recycling program. As of 2015, Belgians recycled an estimated 56 percent of batteries, demonstrating the potential benefits of placing an eco-tax on batteries.

*consortium: (특정 사업 수행 목적의) 컨소시엄, 협력단
**municipal: 시(립)의

11
🔎 정답률 42%

윗글의 제목으로 가장 적절한 것은?

① Conflicting Attitudes Toward Battery Recycling
② Imposition of Taxes to Increase Battery Recycling
③ Decreased Recycling Rate of Batteries and Its Causes
④ Ever-Growing Markets for Numerous Waste Batteries
⑤ Potential Risks of Dumping Batteries in Household Trash

12
🔎 정답률 37%

밑줄 친 (a)~(e) 중에서 문맥상 낱말의 쓰임이 적절하지 않은 것은?

① (a)   ② (b)   ③ (c)   ④ (d)   ⑤ (e)

01

정답률 52%

밑줄 친 sweep them under the rug가 다음 글에서 의미하는 바로 가장 적절한 것은?

Compared to the average person, writers take easily to self-transformation through language. In fact, if their publishers encourage it, some writers shed voices like old skins and leap into more crowd-pleasing selves. But for most other people — especially youth — a sudden leap into expressiveness may seem like dancing across the bowling lanes in a ballet costume. True, your inner transformations may be crying for expression, but you express one thing and (inarticulate) people suspect you of another. Originality is suspect. Soon the transformations themselves become suspect and you sweep them under the rug. From English class or an overheard remark, a new word comes to light on your tongue and feels good there. "Transcendent." You try it privately; it carries a meaning you used to grope for with phrases such as "far out" — but no one ever realized just how far out you meant. "How'd you feel when the ball landed in your mitt?" Transcendent! A transcendent moment! That's exactly what it was; but unfortunately you can never tell anyone because *that word ain't you.*

*transcendent: 초월적인 **grope: 더듬어 찾다

① give up on making others appreciate your sincerity
② deny creating pieces full of exaggerated expressions
③ avoid talking about your dream of becoming a writer
④ refrain from expressing your ideas with unusual words
⑤ hide your identity as a writer with a public-pleasing voice

02

정답률 47%

다음 글의 주제로 가장 적절한 것은?

The North America Free Trade Agreement (NAFTA) gives us the window through which to see the issues of free trade. In the U.S. and Canada, the debate over NAFTA centered mainly on jobs. How could each country open its borders to trade, and a flood of better-made and cheaper imports, without losing jobs? The leaders of the NAFTA countries realized that closing borders to trade would, in the long term, lead to a loss of competitiveness and an eventual loss of jobs for a nation that lost its ability to compete on the world markets. They realized that the world economy is not a zero-sum game, where one country's gain was another country's loss. Open markets, in the long term, would provide the incentive for producers on both sides of the border to concentrate on producing only those goods and services in which they had a competitive advantage. In addition, the constant pressure from foreign competitors would force each country to improve the quality and value of its products.

① political considerations influencing international trade contracts
② domestic job markets threatened by opening the border to trade
③ conflicts between the advocates and the opponents of free trade
④ competitive advantages achieved by focusing on chosen products
⑤ projected benefits that open markets provide to the domestic economy

03 초고난도

정답률 22%

다음 글의 밑줄 친 부분 중, 어법상 틀린 것은?

Placing organic products into the global market has a number of implications. Global markets are characterized by the strong role played by corporations in transport, handling, distribution, marketing and sales. Entering into the same markets as conventional agricultural products is likely to result in organic produce ① is subject to the same economic conditions that have shaped conventional agriculture and made sustainable practices unattractive. Organic producers competing in existing global markets will face economic incentives ② likely to erode the principles of organic farming. An emerging issue of potentially great concern is challenges brought against nations ③ whose trading preferences run counter to such groups as the World Trade Organization. Entry into global markets may offer grounds on which ④ to challenge national subsidies for conventional agriculture, but retaliatory challenges against organic farming are likely. A further concern is that global markets are uncertain and often volatile, which has the effect of ⑤ reducing the security of farming enterprises and can be added to the economic incentives for larger-scale enterprises.

*retaliatory: 보복성(의) **volatile: 불안정한

04

정답률 44%

다음 글의 밑줄 친 부분 중, 문맥상 낱말의 쓰임이 적절하지 않은 것은?

Politicians, especially those in the national spotlight, are often jokingly accused of being narcissists but, in all seriousness, their profession lends itself to this particularly ① destructive personality trait. For example, in order to be a successful candidate, you have to be unnaturally optimistic even in the face of probable defeat and possess ② high levels of self-esteem despite the constant criticism that comes with the territory. Furthermore, you are constantly given sole credit for successes — even though those successes were ③ achieved, in part, by the work of many aides and assistants. Finally, you constantly have people relying on you, believing in you, and holding you responsible as the sole ④ representative of a cause. All of this power can lead to an exaggerated sense of self-importance that can cause some individuals to believe that the world revolves around them. That's when their out-of-control behaviors become ⑤ harder to rationalize.

*narcissist: 나르시시스트(자기 도취자)
**come with the territory: 일상적인 일이다

[05-06] 다음 빈칸에 들어갈 말로 가장 적절한 것을 고르시오.

05 초고난도
정답률 27%

Competitive activities can be more than just performance showcases where the best is recognized and the rest are overlooked. The provision of timely, constructive feedback to participants on performance is an asset that some competitions and contests offer. In a sense, all competitions give feedback. For many, this is restricted to information about whether the participant is an award- or prizewinner. The provision of that type of feedback can be interpreted as shifting the emphasis to demonstrating superior performance but not necessarily excellence. The best competitions promote excellence, not just winning or "beating" others. The emphasis on superiority is what we typically see as _____. Performance feedback requires that the program go beyond the "win, place, or show" level of feedback. Information about performance can be very helpful, not only to the participant who does not win or place but also to those who do.

① fostering a harmful effect of competition
② sharing constructive feedback with performers
③ decreasing competitiveness at the stage of development
④ making participants focus on what they're good at doing
⑤ providing the opportunity to go beyond one's limitations

06
정답률 31%

The savage, like the infant, is a creature of first impressions, and obeys his impulses. Civilized people halt their first impressions, subject their impulses to examination, put it up against contrary factors, deliberate, and become master of whether to perform the act or not to perform it or to put it off. Inhibition is the mark of civilization. The mastery of civilized people, their rule over their emotions and impulses is nowhere more striking than in that blossom of civilization that we call sophistication. Perhaps a useless flower, but shimmering. The worldly-wise person is imperturbable; the most violent emotions change neither the correctness of one's shirtfront nor the grace of one's movements, neither the polish of one's smile nor the calmness of one's voice. Worldly men and women have mastered the craft of the actor and seem to play at life, _____.

*savage: 야생 상태의 사람   **shimmer: (희미하게) 반짝이다
***imperturbable: 침착한

① with their ears alert for what's alive inside of themselves
② without experiencing for themselves any real emotions
③ reliving their victories and failures with the audience
④ serving as an outlet for deep-seated human emotions
⑤ letting their violent emotions control their actions

07

정답률 56%

다음 글에서 전체 흐름과 관계 <u>없는</u> 문장은?

To the modern Western mind, it would seem a betrayal of true emotion to choose a spouse on the criteria of wealth, education, or occupational background. ① Yet when one dispassionately compares such demographic and socio-economic characteristics of spouses, one finds that the choices apparently made on the grounds of love and affection none the less show very clear social patterns. ② While rarely conscious of compromising love with extra-emotional considerations, most people marry others of the same religion, race, class, and educational background. ③ Our social groups effectively socialize us to see particular dress and hair styles, modes of demeanor and address, accents and vocabularies as being more attractive than others. ④ People tend to be attracted to mates with genetic traits they are lacking, which makes for healthier children with stronger immune systems. ⑤ Although the choice seems personal, what draws us to a certain person (or repulses us about another) is much the same as what a diligent matchmaker would bear in mind when choosing a mate for us.

*demographic: 인구학의 **demeanor: 행실, 처신
***repulse: 혐오감을 주다

08

정답률 46%

주어진 글 다음에 이어질 글의 순서로 가장 적절한 것은?

Garrison Keillor, author and host of the radio variety program *A Prairie Home Companion*, closes the news portion of every show with the line "Well, that's the news from Lake Wobegon, where all the women are strong, all the men are good-looking, and all the children are above average."

(A) For example, more than 90 percent of university professors rate themselves above average in teaching ability, and more than two-thirds believe they are among the top 25 percent. Nearly two-thirds of American drivers rate themselves as excellent or very good. Most people think they are fairer than their peers are.

(B) All of these are, of course, mathematically impossible. Moreover, studies show a fairly low correlation between people's self-evaluations and objective assessments of their work-related skills.

(C) Although it's supposed to be in Minnesota, this fictional town with its illusion of superiority could be anywhere. That's because time and time again people respond to surveys indicating that they are *above average* regardless of the skill and competence examined.

① (A) – (C) – (B) ② (B) – (A) – (C)
③ (B) – (C) – (A) ④ (C) – (A) – (B)
⑤ (C) – (B) – (A)

09 초고난도

글의 흐름으로 보아, 주어진 문장이 들어가기에 가장 적절한 곳은?

정답률 19%

> But this idea does not convince the great world leaders in science, who are very comfortable with the system of contributions as it is the one that has provided them with that leadership.

Richard Smith, director of the British Medical Journal for 13 years, says in his book that science cannot work well without methods to clarify what part of the work each contributor has done in each article. Smith proposes that journals should include a list of the co-authors with their biographies and what they have contributed to each study. (①) This relationship should be developed and agreed upon by the authors of the paper themselves. (②) However, it discourages talented young people from engaging in it. (③) The current scientist does not feel that the research is his own. (④) He or she produces scientific literature on which his or her name is written, but many times has not even written the article, or even a part of it. (⑤) In fact, it is becoming increasingly common for powerful research groups to hire specialized writers — young doctors — to whom the scientists pass the data.

*contribution: 기고(旗鼓), 기여

10

다음 글의 내용을 한 문장으로 요약하고자 한다. 빈칸 (A), (B)에 들어갈 말로 가장 적절한 것은?

정답률 57%

Typically, warfare as practiced among indigenous peoples on the periphery of industrial society is said to be highly ritualized and, as a result, reduces the number of casualties when compared with modern warfare of industrial civilization. Though there is debate about the claim, this anthropological view of the inherent sensibility of "primitive" warfare has filtered into more popular ideas. The historian of war Gwynne Dyer claims that hunting-gathering societies understand and practice war as "an important ritual, an exciting and dangerous game, and perhaps even as an opportunity for self-expression, but it is not about power in any modern sense of the word, and it is most certainly not about slaughter." Modern warfare, so this line of argument contends, is waged with violence and costs far beyond that of primitive warfare due to not only technological advances in weaponry but a de-ritualization of the practice of war. Tom Driver has suggested that the latter is partly responsible for the phenomenon of "total war," war waged with no regard for limits or constraints.

*periphery: 주변(부)

↓

Modern warfare is thought to be more ____(A)____ than "primitive" warfare because of technical advances in weaponry and the ____(B)____ of ritualization about waging a war.

	(A)		(B)
①	destructive	·····	loss
②	destructive	·····	revival
③	effective	·····	loss
④	effective	·····	ban
⑤	exhausting	·····	revival

[11~12] 다음 글을 읽고, 물음에 답하시오.

If the ethics of the study of art is to be seen in facilitating the enjoyment and understanding of art objects, as well as in finding some insight into the lives and sensibilities of the people who made and used the art, then the topic of global art history will sooner or later face the issue of universals: a concept that enjoys (a) little prestige in contemporary humanities. Appeals to "essential human conditions," a "common humanity," or an "inner spiritual core" may have (b) legitimate roles in particular kinds of rhetoric, but they provide a weak foundation for thinking about global art history. A different way of engaging universals was pursued with scientific rigor in the 1960s and 1970s but did not provide much nourishment for art history. Attempts were made to (c) objectively determine the universality of aesthetic values; the investigators typically concluded that there are some universal formal categories such as symmetry, proportion, balance, and repose, and that the aesthetic appeal of a work of art depends partly on the universals of human nature. Not surprisingly, such views were (d) always found useful for the interpretation and presentation of works of art. Many anthropologists engaged in the study of "ethnoart" (e) agreed that to understand and appreciate the aesthetic dimensions of other cultures one needs to study their images not as isolated aesthetic phenomena but rather in the context of social action and the lives of human actors.

*rhetoric: 수사학 **repose: (색채 등의) 조화

11　　　　　　　　　정답률 43%

윗글의 제목으로 가장 적절한 것은?

① Should We Pursue Aesthetic Universality in Global Art Study?
② Global Art History: A Blending of Science and Spirituality
③ What Role Does Universality Play in Keeping Society Equal?
④ Works of Art: The Main Study Materials of Anthropology
⑤ Why Is the Study of Art Necessary for Humanity?

12　　　　　　　　　정답률 33%

밑줄 친 (a)~(e) 중에서 문맥상 낱말의 쓰임이 적절하지 <u>않은</u> 것은?

① (a)　　② (b)　　③ (c)　　④ (d)　　⑤ (e)

01

정답률 51%

밑줄 친 Which cup would you rather be?가 다음 글에서 의미하는 바로 가장 적절한 것은?

Each person has a different level of adaptability to stress. Imagine a paper cup placed upside down on a table. How much weight do you think it can handle? Can I place a small paperback book on it and expect it to hold? How about a large hardcover encyclopedia? How about two, three, or four large, heavy books? Eventually the cup will succumb to the weight of the books, and it will collapse. What if I use a metal cup instead of the paper cup? Will it collapse under the same amount of weight (stress), or will it be able to hold much more weight before bending? Which cup would you rather be? A cup is inanimate, but the human body can adapt. The part of your mind that is highly sensitive to stress has the power to learn. The body's adaptation potential is what determines how much stress someone can handle before they succumb to illness.

*succumb: 굴복하다 **inanimate: 무생물의

① Would you change your personality under stress?
② How would you use stress to strengthen your health?
③ Would you like to be capable of enduring severe stress?
④ Are you going to hold on to the stress that you cannot control?
⑤ Why don't you learn from someone who's adapted to their stress?

02 초고난도

정답률 27%

다음 글의 제목으로 가장 적절한 것은?

While focusing on themselves, people become aware of internal information (anxious feelings and images), which they mistakenly take as good evidence for their worst fears. One of the most common fears is that people will see that you are anxious. People with social anxiety disorder look much less anxious than they feel, but they tend to believe that their feelings are a good indicator of how they look. Images also play a prominent role. When particularly anxious, people with social anxiety disorder report seeing themselves in their mind's eye as though from an observer's perspective. Unfortunately, what they see is not what the observer actually sees but instead is a visualization of their worst fears. So someone who is concerned about blushing may have turned a mild pink in reality, but in their mind's eye, will see themselves as beet red with large beads of sweat dripping from their forehead.

*beet: 비트(사탕무)

① The Amplifying Effect of Anxiety on Fearful Feelings
② Our Self-Images: Reflections of Our Hopes and Beliefs
③ Anxiety: The Most Powerful Motivator of Achievement
④ How Our Mind's Eye Creates a World Full of Fearful Things
⑤ Separating the Image in Our Mind's Eye from Our True Self

03

다음 글의 밑줄 친 부분 중, 어법상 틀린 것은?

Occupied time feels shorter than unoccupied time. If you are busy ①doing something while you are waiting, the time seems to go by faster. Most line waits can be made more enjoyable and made ②to feel less lengthy if guests can be distracted or diverted in some way. Disney planners are the masters of managing time waits by giving their guests something to stop ③them from thinking about the wait. If the line for a particular Walt Disney World Resort attraction has become extraordinarily long and a service failure is imminent, a strolling band or acrobats or some other distraction arrives to entertain and ④occupy the guests while they wait. For long lines, Universal Orlando Resort spaces television sets throughout the time ⑤when show a video or movie. People can watch an interesting program while moving toward the entrance to the attraction.

04

다음 글의 밑줄 친 부분 중, 문맥상 낱말의 쓰임이 적절하지 않은 것은?

Most often, "human nature" is invoked in a ①casual way to account for various behaviors we encounter. Almost anything that we regularly come across is assumed with a shrug to describe the human condition. Interestingly, the characteristics that we explain away in this fashion are almost always unsavory; an act of ②generosity is rarely dismissed on the grounds that it is "just human nature." Apart from the empirical grounds for defending such claims, though, it is important to remember that the burden of proof falls heavily on someone who ③denies that a given characteristic is part of our nature. It is he or she who must provide compelling evidence to substantiate such a belief, and not the rest of us who must prove it is not so. Anyone who offers an assertion for our consideration has such a burden, but it is that much more formidable when the claim is ④absolute: to say that a given characteristic is in our nature is to assert that it is a feature of all human beings, across all cultures and throughout human history. Moreover, it is to propose its ⑤inescapability for all humans in the future.

*invoke: 언급하다, 들다 **unsavory: 불미스러운
***formidable: 어마어마한

05 초고난도   정답률 23%

The universality of music is, perhaps, more contentious than that of language because we place greater emphasis on production than listening, with many individuals declaring themselves to be unmusical. In this regard, John Blacking's comments, made in the 1970s, on the contradiction between theory and practice in the middle-class, Western society in which he grew up, remain relevant today. Music was and remains all around us: we hear it when we eat and try to talk in restaurants and airport lounges; it is played all day long on the radio; in fact, there are few occasions when someone is not trying to fill moments of potential silence with music. Blacking remarked that 'society claims that only a limited number of people are musical, and yet it behaves as if all possessed the basic capacity without which no musical tradition can exist — the capacity to listen and distinguish patterns of sound'. He favoured the idea that there was no such thing as an unmusical human being, and noted that the existence of a Bach or a Beethoven was only possible because of _____.

*contentious: 이론의 여지가 있는

① their outstanding ability to create music
② similarities between music and language
③ the presence of a discriminating audience
④ theoretical development of music composition
⑤ a social atmosphere that rewards individual talent

06   정답률 30%

With any luck, we will realize that making waste is not the problem we must solve. If a living species does not generate waste, it is most likely dead, or at least very ill. The problem we have, and that we must address, is that we waste the waste we create. Consider that the conversion of waste into nutrients both requires and generates energy. While we are always looking for sources of energy for commercial and home applications, ecosystems never need to be wired. No member of an ecosystem needs fossil fuel or a connection to the grid to achieve output; nor is waste an outcome in natural systems. In nature, the waste of one process is always a nutrient, a material, or a source of energy for another. Everything stays in the nutrient stream. Thus the solution not only to the environmental challenges of pollution but to the economic challenges of scarcity may be found in the application of models we can observe in a natural ecosystem. Perhaps we can turn dilemma into solution by broadening our perspective and _____.

*grid: 배전망

① abandoning the concept of waste
② overcoming inefficiency in nature
③ switching to renewable energy sources
④ eliminating waste from the nutrient stream
⑤ separating environmental and economic problems

07

정답률 43%

주어진 글 다음에 이어질 글의 순서로 가장 적절한 것은?

Top-down portfolio construction starts with asset allocation. For example, an individual who currently holds all of his money in a bank account would first decide what proportion of the overall portfolio ought to be moved into stocks, bonds, and so on.

(A) On the other hand, stocks are far riskier, with annual returns that have ranged as low as –46% and as high as 55%. In contrast, Treasury bills are effectively risk-free: You know what interest rate you will earn when you buy them.

(B) In this way, the broad features of the portfolio are established. For example, while the average annual return on the common stock of large firms since 1926 has been better than 11% per year, the average return on U.S. Treasury bills has been less than 4%.

(C) Therefore, the decision to allocate your investments to the stock market or to the money market where Treasury bills are traded will have great consequences for both the risk and the return of your portfolio. A top-down investor first makes this and other crucial asset allocation decisions.

*portfolio: 포트폴리오(투자 자산 구성) **bond: 채권
***Treasury bill: 재무부 증권(재무부 발행의 단기 채권)

① (A) – (C) – (B) ② (B) – (A) – (C)
③ (B) – (C) – (A) ④ (C) – (A) – (B)
⑤ (C) – (B) – (A)

[08~09] 글의 흐름으로 보아, 주어진 문장이 들어가기에 가장 적절한 곳을 고르시오.

08

정답률 43%

The fact is that the termite mounds in western Africa are much softer, owing to larger amounts of rain, than those of eastern Africa.

Chimpanzees in some populations of eastern Africa fish for termites by probing termite mounds with small, thin sticks. Some other populations of chimpanzees in western Africa, however, simply destroy termite mounds with large sticks and attempt to scoop up the insects by the handful. (①) Field researchers such as Boesch and McGrew have claimed that specific tool-use practices such as these are "culturally transmitted" among the individuals of the various communities. (②) But there is a competing explanation that is also quite plausible. (③) The strategy of destroying the mound with a large stick is thus available only to the western populations. (④) Under this hypothesis, then, there would be group differences of behavior superficially resembling human cultural differences, but with no type of social learning involved at all. (⑤) In such cases, the "culture" is simply a result of individual learning driven by the different local ecologies of the different populations.

*termite: 흰개미 **scoop up: ~을 퍼내다
***plausible: 그럴듯한

09 초고난도

정답률 16%

As long as these are based on intercontinental tourism, doubling the income of the poorest 2.8 billion people would require a volume of air transport of 20 to 50 times total air transport in 2000.

Intercontinental travel causes the largest environmental effects. However, the total number of trips is not very large. Generally, 80% of the environmental problems are caused by only 20% of the market. Therefore, reductions may be reached without a total change of the market and compromising human needs for travel and leisure. (①) The solution will be an uncoupling of tourism growth and transport growth. (②) It is important to bear in mind that it is not the number of leisure days that has to be reduced, but the total kilometers travelled during leisure time. (③) Hence, tourism growth is not restricted, but only transport volume growth. (④) Of course, side effects must be studied, for example, the effects on the emerging tourism industry in developing countries. (⑤) This is neither sustainable nor possible.

10

정답률 58%

다음 글의 내용을 한 문장으로 요약하고자 한다. 빈칸 (A), (B)에 들어갈 말로 가장 적절한 것은?

Photographers, along with exhibit designers and museum curators, want to make viewers see things in a specific arrangement that they hope will push viewers to make certain comparisons along certain dimensions, generating particular moods. They understand that a single image is ambiguous and does not easily and unequivocally reveal "what it is about." When photographers make pictures for such other purposes as news and advertising, they usually compose them so as to exclude all "extraneous" detail, everything except the "point" of the news story or the product feature to which they want to call attention. They choose the details that surround that point carefully, to emphasize the story's main ideas or enhance the product's appeal. Pictures made for scientific purposes similarly restrict their content to what the maker (usually the author of the scientific article) wants users to know and rigorously exclude anything extraneous to that purpose.

*unequivocally: 모호하지 않게 **extraneous: 관련 없는

⬇

In exhibition, photographers plan the ____(A)____ of images to let the viewers understand the message, and in news, ads, and articles, they ____(B)____ some details to make the main idea clear.

	(A)		(B)
①	repetition	·····	explain
②	expansion	·····	compare
③	expansion	·····	repeat
④	arrangement	·····	layer
⑤	arrangement	·····	exclude

[11-12] 다음 글을 읽고, 물음에 답하시오.

For all the talk of the metaverse, the fundamental difference between the metaverse and the internet today is not quality but quantity. The metaverse threatens to add virtual reality, "augmented" reality, and NFTs to the existing potent online world, but all of the metaverse's changes will amount to the same thing: *more* data, *more* connectivity, *more* transactions, *more* complexity. The movement from Web 1.0 to Web 2.0 to the metaverse and onward has not stemmed from (a) radical new technologies. Rather, the change in online life is like the evolution of the brain, growing ever more complex until surprising new phenomena (b) emerge purely through that complexity. The metaverse, for all practical purposes, is already here, growing steadily. We lose more control to it by the day.

In addition to the creation of the metaverse, the consequences of wrapping our world in networked computation have not merely been lifestyle changes but also the steady growth of (c) autonomous networks not under the control of their corporate or governmental administrators. To understand today's world, we have to think not like a human, nor like a state, but like a server. A server — or more accurately, a collective army of servers — sees the world as computable data, floods of numbers representing every aspect of life, in quantities so great that much of the *meaning* of this data is (d) preserved, even as we feed ever more data into the system. In turn, our servers feed that data back to us, and we come to see the world the same way. Without realizing it, machines and humans are building a new world (e) together, a world we cannot control in the way we controlled the old world.

*NFT(non-fungible token): 대체 불가능한 토큰
(다른 토큰으로 대체하는 것이 불가능한 암호 화폐)

11

윗글의 제목으로 가장 적절한 것은?

① Computing Everything Made Possible by the Metaverse
② Has Virtual Reality Existed Since the Early Internet Age?
③ The Crucial Role of High-Quality Servers in Network Computing
④ The Metaverse: Not Much More Complex than the Human Mind
⑤ Out of Control: The Metaverse and the Networked Online World

12

밑줄 친 (a)~(e) 중에서 문맥상 낱말의 쓰임이 적절하지 않은 것은?

① (a)　　② (b)　　③ (c)　　④ (d)　　⑤ (e)

01

정답률 49%

밑줄 친 the deepest tragedy of their time이 다음 글에서 의미하는 바로 가장 적절한 것은?

Whenever someone is lost in waves of e-mail and information, they're often unaware of the deepest tragedy of their time. It's not the stress of dealing with so many requests and obligations (as real and challenging as that stress might be). It's that somewhere in the wash of interactions and split attentions is the missed possibility they're looking for: Meaning. Depth of experience. Connection. To quote Robert Pirsig, "The truth knocks on the door and we say, 'Go away. I'm looking for the truth.'" In the race to clean out inboxes and scratch items off the to-do list, we miss chances to find the thing we've created the inbox and to-do list for. Like an American tourist in Europe racing from site to site with barely a moment to take a picture or talk to someone not on their tour bus, we're trapped in a quantity mentality, despite our quality-based desires.

① being confined to self-serving thoughts, ignoring a larger community
② not focusing on where information has been combined and distributed
③ not seeing what we're searching for, buried in information processing
④ seeking truth in the form of abstract knowledge, not real-life wisdom
⑤ doubting their ability to produce information that is useful and meaningful

02

정답률 46%

다음 글의 주제로 가장 적절한 것은?

The increase in wealth and education in the eighteenth century was accompanied by an expansion of public interest in art, as reflected in the growth of the art market and the emergence of public exhibitions and museums. Public sales and auctions became an early venue for an art-hungry public, and dealers used new marketing strategies — shop windows, newspaper ads, and sales catalogues — to tempt the newly moneyed classes into the pleasures and social advantages of collecting. Engraving greatly extended the reach of high art, and the collecting of drawings became fashionable, but ownership of painting and sculpture required deep pockets. Speaking on behalf of those without collections of their own, critics demanded greater public access to art, and from mid-century their calls were answered. Academies sponsored regular exhibitions of their members' work, the best known being the so-called *Salon* in Paris (from 1737) and the Royal Academy exhibitions in London (from 1768).

*venue: 장소 **engraving: 판화

① the influence of eighteenth-century critics on art styles
② art types representing each class in the eighteenth century
③ monopolization of the eighteenth-century art world by the rich
④ the buildup of wealth from art trading in the eighteenth century
⑤ how the growing demand for art was met in the eighteenth century

03

다음 글의 밑줄 친 부분 중, 어법상 틀린 것은?

Solomon, in all his wisdom, would be hard-pressed to sort out the potentially destructive possibilities from the positive fruits of technological innovation. Nevertheless, each of us is asked ①to give at least implicit approval to the glorious and unsettling march of technological progress. Unfortunately, most people have only a basic understanding of the ideas and discoveries ②that will shape their own future. Even those who craft public policy regarding the financing of research are highly dependent on the recommendations of experts. The difficulty lies in knowing what questions to ask and where to turn for a ③balanced perspective. All too often scientists assume beyond their expertise and their understanding. The desire to get research funded can cloud their judgment. Hype from scientists, in the form of overly optimistic time frames for achieving the next technological breakthrough, ④encouraging both unrealistic hopes and fears regarding scientific progress. The most persuasive voices commonly are ⑤those that loudly support or loudly oppose the development of a particular technology.

*hype: (과장된) 선전

04

다음 글의 밑줄 친 부분 중, 문맥상 낱말의 쓰임이 적절하지 않은 것은?

Structural leaders develop a new model of the relationship of structure, strategy, and environment for their organizations. They focus on implementation. The right answer helps only if it can be implemented. These leaders ①emphasize rationality, analysis, logic, fact, and data. They are likely to believe strongly in the importance of clear structure and well-developed management systems. A good leader is someone who thinks clearly, makes good decisions, has good analytical skills, and can ②create structures and systems that get the job done. Structural leaders sometimes fail because they miscalculate the difficulty of putting their designs in place. They often ③overestimate the resistance that it will generate, and they take few steps to build a base of support for their innovations. In short, they are often ④undone by human resource, political, and symbolic considerations. Structural leaders do continually experiment, evaluate, and adapt, but because they fail to consider the entire environment in which they are situated, they sometimes are ⑤ineffective.

[05-06] 다음 빈칸에 들어갈 말로 가장 적절한 것을 고르시오.

05 초고난도
정답률 25%

Ideas about uncertainty are governed by the way society perceives the relationship between the present and the future. When, as today, the future is regarded as a dangerous territory, uncertainty is framed in a negative light. In such a setting, change itself is perceived as threatening. A potent undercurrent of apprehension towards change — whether technological, social or political — permeates the day-to-day affairs of the contemporary Western world. Uncertainty was at times regarded as an opportunity — that it now tends to be cast in a negative light is symptomatic of a mood of fatalism towards the challenges faced by society. This fatalistic attitude is summed up by the often-repeated catch-phrase — 'The question is "not if, but when?"' Warnings of catastrophic climate events, deadly flu epidemics or mass casualty terrorism usually conclude with this defeatist refrain, which implicitly and sometimes explicitly calls into question humanity's capacity to avoid the destructive consequences of the threats it faces. In this way, the dangers of the future _____. They demand that we ring the alarm bells while implying that there is very little that can be done to avoid the dangers that lie ahead.

*undercurrent: (부정적인 감정의) 암류(暗流)
**apprehension: 불안 ***permeate: 스며들다

① vary greatly from person to person
② acquire an immediate and intimate quality
③ are often based on misleading information
④ can be predicted and completely controlled
⑤ are not as pronounced as those from the past

06
정답률 30%

You can bend truth with statistics. There are many forms of counting up something and then reporting it as something else. The general method is _____. As personnel manager for a company that is scrapping with a union you "make a survey" of employees to find out how many have a complaint against the union. Unless the union is a band of angels with an archangel at their head you can ask and record with perfect honesty and come out with proof that the greater part of the men do have some complaint or other. You issue your information as a report that "a vast majority — 78 percent — are opposed to the union." What you have done is to add up a bunch of undifferentiated complaints and tiny gripes and then call them something else that sounds like the same thing. You haven't proved a thing, but it rather sounds as if you have, doesn't it?

*scrap with: ~와 다투다

① to report something old but make it sound new
② to ask your opponent to prove something vague
③ to pick two things that sound the same but are not
④ to use numbers to emphasize the accuracy of your report
⑤ to exaggerate tiny differences to make them sound serious

07

정답률 50%

다음 글에서 전체 흐름과 관계 <u>없는</u> 문장은?

Most modern jobs and careers fall into the category of wage labor — whether they are in private companies or public agencies, blue-collar or white-collar. The stereotype of a "worker" as someone who performs boring, unpleasant tasks on an assembly line is badly outdated. ① Workers today perform a wide variety of functions, many of them requiring advanced skills. ② But they are still workers, so long as they perform that work for someone else, in return for a wage or salary. ③ Scientists in a research laboratory; surgeons in a large hospital; engineers in a construction firm — these are all workers (although culturally, they may not like to define themselves as such). ④ Labor income includes the wages of employees and part of the income of the self-employed, the latter often being difficult to state. ⑤ They perform their labor in return for a salary, and they do not own or significantly control the organization that they work for.

08 초고난도

정답률 24%

주어진 글 다음에 이어질 글의 순서로 가장 적절한 것은?

Basically, in any multiparty trade system, there will always be imbalances, deficits, or surpluses in the monetary value of goods and services traded.

(A) These imports, if not made up for in an equal number of exports, are "paid for" by sending something else abroad — usually paper assets, such as stocks and bonds. The purchase of U.S. dollar securities is the way most countries have compensated for the imbalances in trade with the United States.

(B) When one country is experiencing an economic boom with full employment, for example, it is natural to turn to foreign producers to provide the goods and services for increased local consumption. In fact, it is the only way to increase consumption if local factories are running at full capacity — as the United States was in the late 2010s.

(C) Many countries, particularly countries in Asia and the Middle East, have used their earnings from exports to purchase trillions of dollars' worth of U.S. Treasury bonds to use as a store against future uncertainties — or to buy U.S. goods and services in the future.

*securities: 유가 증권

① (A) – (C) – (B)　　② (B) – (A) – (C)
③ (B) – (C) – (A)　　④ (C) – (A) – (B)
⑤ (C) – (B) – (A)

09

정답률 37%

글의 흐름으로 보아, 주어진 문장이 들어가기에 가장 적절한 곳은?

> The obstacle is not the child's lack of ability to count but the fact that he has to answer questions that he does not comprehend, or he does not realize what the expected answer is, until he has had some more years of practice.

The fact that the ability to count is not acquired until a child is three or four years old does not necessarily prove that the characteristic is not innate. (①) In many observations, including Piaget's experiments, counting and arithmetic were acquired together with the ability to communicate and to use a given language, generally the mother tongue. (②) It is not surprising that communicating in a given language is not an innate attribute but a learned one. (③) The ability to learn a language is an inborn characteristic, but acquiring the language itself takes several years. (④) Before the child learns a language, his arithmetic abilities do not come into play, as seen in various experiments. (⑤) It is easy to devise tests showing that understanding the question plays an important role in interpreting the results.

10

정답률 59%

다음 글의 내용을 한 문장으로 요약하고자 한다. 빈칸 (A), (B)에 들어갈 말로 가장 적절한 것은?

In student assessment, the quality of the data gathered and the conclusions and inferences drawn are influenced by the perceptions and values of the teacher involved in the inquiry. Examining the cultural background of students requires some degree of objectivity. An egocentric or ethnocentric perspective in data collection is counterproductive. You must be able to examine the cultures of your students without making value judgments based on your own personal or cultural experiences. The only legitimate reason for collecting data on the background and experiences of students is for improving classroom instruction. Teachers who are convinced that their instruction is appropriate and should not change, although it does not serve some groups of students well, and who blame the students or their life conditions for instructional failures, probably would not benefit from collecting data on their students. For these teachers, there is the probability that data collection will reinforce negative beliefs about their students.

⬇

> An examination of students' backgrounds is crucial for improving classroom instruction but it must be ___(A)___, as teachers who ___(B)___ a biased teaching style may not benefit from collecting data on their students.

	(A)		(B)
①	objective	·····	maintain
②	objective	·····	change
③	consistent	·····	hide
④	consistent	·····	reveal
⑤	organizational	·····	diversify

[11~12] 다음 글을 읽고, 물음에 답하시오.

Shifts in the ethnic composition of states do not just affect the developed world, nor do they just impact electoral politics; they are also associated with civil strife. Demography, the changes in numbers of population, has become more important in more recent times, particularly as a factor in intra-state conflict. The sheer scale of demographic change and its (a)acceleration over time is one of the reasons. As birth rates hit unprecedented highs for lengthy periods while death rates drop rapidly, populations can (b)grow fast, as did England's in the nineteenth century. Indeed, those experiencing these changes later experienced population growth that far outstripped the UK's nineteenth-century achievement. Often such growth affects one ethnic group but not another because of different social or religious practices or different levels of socio-economic development. It has become harshly apparent that demographic strength between different ethnic and social groups can (c)change with historically unprecedented speed, and this can have a dislocating and disorienting impact.

Although sometimes an *inter-state* phenomenon, these shifts are often experienced at the *intra-state* level since most states contain ethnic minorities and many of those minorities display markedly (d)identical demographic behavior from the majority. Chechens in Russia, Albanians in Serbia (or what was Serbia), and Catholics in Northern Ireland spring to mind. These are all cases where minorities have a higher birth rate than majorities, with the result being a shift in or challenge to the (e)prevailing power structure.

*intra-state: 국가 내의 **dislocate: 혼란에 빠뜨리다

11 초고난도　　　　　　　　　　정답률 26%

윗글의 제목으로 가장 적절한 것은?

① Demographics: A Determiner of Domestic Power Landscapes
② Why Minorities Show Higher Birth Rates than Majorities
③ International Conflicts Caused by Overpopulation
④ Ethnicity: A Frequent Source of Social Conflict
⑤ Population Growth: A Benefit to the Economy

12　　　　　　　　　　　　　　정답률 53%

밑줄 친 (a)~(e) 중에서 문맥상 낱말의 쓰임이 적절하지 않은 것은?

① (a)　② (b)　③ (c)　④ (d)　⑤ (e)

01

정답률 48%

밑줄 친 thank them for the disguised compliment가 다음 글에서 의미하는 바로 가장 적절한 것은?

I used to get sensitive and upset when others would criticize or insult me. I don't let this bother me anymore. In fact the more successful in life you get, the more this will happen to you. How should you react? Well, first of all, I hope this happens to you more often because it is a reflection of your success. You want this to happen more often as it is incredibly flattering. Your coworkers might develop a more condescending tone with you over the years the more successful you become as well. You almost want to reach out and thank them for the disguised compliment! Don't worry because they just feel threatened by you, which can be seen as a huge compliment. Successful people are criticized all the time. The ones who are the happiest and have the best peace of mind are those who see criticism as nothing more than a disguised compliment. So bring it on doubters of mine, and I'll show you what I can do!

*condescending: 잘난 체하는

① look down on them because of their lack of empathy
② pretend to be happy with their justified criticism of you
③ accept their concerns about your arrogance toward others
④ feel pleased by their defensive responses to your achievement
⑤ use the criticism as a guide to distinguish flattery from advice

02

정답률 43%

다음 글의 제목으로 가장 적절한 것은?

The word *algorithm*, derived from the name of a ninth-century mathematician named Abu Abdullah Muhammad ibn Mūsā Al-Khwārizmī, simply means a set of step-by-step instructions. Machine-learning algorithms, which drive much of the progress in AI today, are specifically aimed at letting systems learn from their experience instead of being guided by explicit rules. Many of them draw on ideas from the early days of AI — ideas developed long before there was enough processing power and data available to turn them from intriguing theoretical possibilities into something more practical. Indeed, some of today's greatest pragmatist triumphs have grown out of earlier purist attempts to copy human beings. For instance, many of the most capable machines today rely on what are known as "artificial neural networks," which were first built decades ago in an attempt to simulate the workings of the human brain. Today, though, there is little sense that these networks should be judged according to how closely they imitate human anatomy; instead, they are evaluated entirely pragmatically, according to how well they perform whatever tasks they are set.

① Can the Uniqueness of the Human Brain Be Perfectly Copied?
② Major Criticisms of Machine-Learning Algorithms in Technology
③ Human Neural Networks Best Suited to Learning and Application
④ Algorithmic Thinking: The Key Concept in Computational Thinking
⑤ By What Should Machine-Learning Algorithms Be Evaluated Now?

03

다음 글의 밑줄 친 부분 중, 어법상 <u>틀린</u> 것은?

A characteristic of decision making is related to the structure of the brain. *The brain cannot analyze a problem without preconceptions.* When someone is confronted with a problem or a question, a preconception is used immediately, sometimes based and dependent on ① <u>how</u> the question is worded or the information is presented. Thus, the reaction of a sick person to the doctor's prognosis ② <u>which</u> he has an 80 percent chance of recovering is different than his reaction to the news that he has a 20 percent chance of remaining sick for the rest of his life. The rational mind would recognize that an 80 percent chance of success is the same as a 20 percent chance of failure. A mind that acts only in an ③ <u>evolutionarily</u> rational way will not recognize the equivalence. That recognition is not worth the effort needed to compare and analyze the facts in every case, and we therefore cling to concepts and attitudes already ④ <u>present</u> in our brains. The popular belief that we can examine a question without preconceptions ⑤ <u>is</u> incorrect.

*prognosis: (의학) 예후, 예측

04 초고난도

다음 글의 밑줄 친 부분 중, 문맥상 낱말의 쓰임이 적절하지 <u>않은</u> 것은?

As Larry Cuban, former president of the American Educational Research Association, points out, schools have spent billions of dollars over the years on technologies that have, in fact, ① <u>changed</u> very little of how we think about an "education" in the developed world. More often than not, we ② <u>strip</u> the agency and freedoms that digital tools give to learners and creators outside of school when they bring those same tools into the building. The system of schooling that most of us are products of is based on a series of structures and efficiencies that do not work ③ <u>well</u> with the messier, less linear, more self-organized ways we can learn, create, and connect on the Internet. In fact, the system almost unwittingly ④ <u>marginalizes</u> digital technologies in schools. We relegate them to labs or libraries, or if we place them in students' hands, they're used only for discrete, narrow purposes like reading textbooks, creating documents, or taking assessments. ⑤ <u>Many</u> would argue that in schools today, we see technology primarily as an institutional teaching tool, not a personal learning tool.

*unwittingly: 부지불식간에
**relegate: (덜 중요한 위치로) 밀쳐 버리다

[05-07] 다음 빈칸에 들어갈 말로 가장 적절한 것을 고르시오.

05

정답률 38%

For years people thought that ice melting under pressure was the only reason for ice being slippery. But it turns out that the story is more complex than that, because it doesn't explain why ice is still slippery at temperatures well below its freezing point, or when the pressure isn't enough to melt it (*e.g.* ice is still slippery if you wear flat shoes, not just ice skates). It turns out that friction plays a big part — as the ice skates, skis, or glaciers slide, the friction generates heat, which melts the surface of the ice slightly. But that's still not the whole story, as it doesn't explain why ice is slippery even if you stand still. Modern analysis has shown that because the molecules at the surface of ice are inherently unstable due to the lack of molecules above them, the surface reconstructs to form a liquid-like layer. This verified the original hypothesis made by the famous physicist Michael Faraday in 1850 that all ice has an intrinsic thin layer of water at the surface. So ice is slippery due to its inherent surface water layer, which can be _____ using pressure and friction.

① detected
② eliminated
③ enhanced
④ scratched
⑤ evaporated

06 초고난도

정답률 29%

Although his philosophical approach was formed by Kant's aesthetics and epistemology in fundamental ways, Schopenhauer undertakes what he calls his "correction" of Kant: to reverse Kant's privileging of abstract thinking over perceptual knowledge, and to insist on the physiological makeup of the subject as the site on which _____. Schopenhauer's answer to the Kantian problem of *Vorstellung* (concept) removes us completely from the classical terms of the camera obscura: "What is representation? A very complicated *physiological* occurrence in an animal's brain, whose result is the consciousness of a *picture* or *image* at that very spot." What Kant called the synthetic unity of apperception, Schopenhauer unhesitatingly identifies as the human brain. Schopenhauer here is but one instance in the first half of the nineteenth century of what has been called "the physiological reinterpretation of the Kantian critique of reason." He writes, "A philosophy like the Kantian, that ignores entirely [the physiological] point of view, is one-sided and therefore inadequate. It leaves an immense gulf between our philosophical and physiological knowledge, with which we can never be satisfied."

*epistemology: 인식론 **camera obscura: 암상자(초창기 카메라)
***apperception: 통각(감각의 통합)

① reason justifies perceptual experiences
② the formation of representations occurs
③ existing abstract ideas are reinterpreted
④ appreciation for uniqueness of perception is achieved
⑤ the brain's cognitive process is delayed by the senses

07 초고난도   정답률 27%

We often choose so rapidly that it is scarcely possible to distinguish all the elements involved in the act. When we weigh the respective advantages of alternative objects or courses of action distant from us in time or space or both, we are more likely to become aware of all the factors that enter into a choice. In the first place, we try to foresee the future, and in particular how each alternative act will affect us. In this effort, we depend largely upon memory of past experiences in similar situations, because without knowledge of the past and faith in the uniformity of nature we would be at a loss to anticipate the future. In _____, we are above all interested in how it will affect our feelings, whether it will bring us pleasure or pain, joy or sorrow, satisfaction or disgust. And of course, in this phase of our deliberation, too, we are guided by recollections of similar affections. Thus the affective no less than the rational functions of the mind play important roles in each important choice we make.

① projecting ourselves into the contemplated situation
② justifying our choice by creating logical reasons
③ focusing on our present situation and emotions
④ looking at our behavior in terms of motivation
⑤ taking the perspectives of others closest to us

08   정답률 45%

주어진 글 다음에 이어질 글의 순서로 가장 적절한 것은?

Consider the process of a student learning to solve elementary algebra equations. At first, the process of keeping the equation balanced might be complicated, and the student needs to keep straight the rules for how to isolate the variable that she is solving for.

(A) If a new problem is similar to one that has been solved in the past, then she can use the same set of strategies to solve this new problem. In other words, problems that are similar are solved similarly; a problem-solver can use this assessment similarity to assist in solving problems.

(B) In other words, it is a complex problem to solve and places a significant demand on cognitive resources. Furthermore, suppose that the student is going to be learning several kinds of algebra problems: linear equations with one variable, linear equations with two variables, quadratic equations, etc.

(C) Initially, solving each kind takes effort, and keeping each kind of problem straight also takes effort. As the student acquires more skills, she begins to recognize the patterns and rules for each problem type.

*algebra: 대수학 **linear: 선형의 ***quadratic: 이차의

① (A) – (C) – (B)   ② (B) – (A) – (C)
③ (B) – (C) – (A)   ④ (C) – (A) – (B)
⑤ (C) – (B) – (A)

09

글의 흐름으로 보아, 주어진 문장이 들어가기에 가장 적절한 곳은?

> On the other hand, there are often in the same individual several originalities that are contradictory or at the very least extremely divergent.

People are both like and different from each other at the same time. It is not insofar as alike that they are individuals, but as different. Individuality is thus a differing originality, but the point is to free the originality with which each of us is born. (①) It is more or less overlaid by the mass of social similarities. (②) Many people never come to think for themselves, never liberate themselves from the settled, the banal, and the commonplace. (③) The same child shows very different aptitudes for mathematics or for music, or for the adventures of travel. (④) The best of all these originalities must be selected, the most intimate, the most powerful. (⑤) Finally, there are bad or anti-social originalities, which it is desirable not to see developed.

*banal: 평범한

10

다음 글의 내용을 한 문장으로 요약하고자 한다. 빈칸 (A), (B)에 들어갈 말로 가장 적절한 것은?

Environmentalists have long argued that population pressures are the main reasons for climate change and destruction of planetary biodiversity. Those who hold this view advocate strict control of birthrates in countries with rapid population expansion to protect limited natural resources. Yet others suggest that over-population is not the problem; rather, over-consumption in developed nations is depleting the world's resources, as well as preventing people in developing nations from accessing much-needed resources. Since 1950, the richest 20 per cent of the global population has doubled its consumption of energy, meat, forests, and metals, and quadrupled car ownership. Critics of imperialism, then, believe that population-control programs are designed to provide wealthy Western nations with uncontested access to the resources they demand. Some critics even suggest that the pervasiveness of the over-population notion legitimizes the authoritarian actions perpetuated by wealthy nations against developing nations and their people.

↓

> Contrary to environmentalists' claim that over-population is the cause of resource depletion, it is also argued that ___(A)___ in rich countries is the main cause and that the movement to control birthrates is another form of ___(B)___ .

	(A)		(B)
①	over-consumption	……	imperialism
②	over-consumption	……	protection
③	hyper-growth	……	expansion
④	resource-sharing	……	relativism
⑤	resource-sharing	……	transmission

[11-12] 다음 글을 읽고, 물음에 답하시오.

Considering pollution control based on opportunity cost raises the question of what expenditure would be needed to offset the pollution produced. In general the problem with this approach is that if the (a) value placed by the population on the effect in question is not known, then it is not known whether in fact it is worth offsetting it. In some circumstances, however, it may be clear that it is (b) worthwhile offsetting it (for instance, where air pollution damages a building and it is cheaper to repair it than to replace it, or where it destroys crops and it is known that their market value is at least as great as the cost of replacing them).

A version of this approach has become much more common in recent years as a result of developments in pollution control. It is a tendency in the face of uncertainty about the true damage costs caused by different pollutants to adopt a "precautionary principle" of (c) limiting the level of the pollutant to what is considered a safe level. In this situation, any project that pushes pollution above the limit must be balanced by another (shadow) project to offset this effect. For instance if the limit for greenhouse gas emissions that can be tolerated is known, and emissions from transport are to be allowed to rise, then other emissions must be (d) increased elsewhere. In this context, the cost of reducing greenhouse gas emissions elsewhere by one unit becomes the opportunity cost of allowing them to rise in transport. Quantification of this opportunity cost is also not without its problems; strictly it (e) requires examination of all possible ways of reducing greenhouse gas emissions elsewhere in the economy in order to identify the one with the least cost.

11

정답률 38%

윗글의 제목으로 가장 적절한 것은?

① Opportunity Costs: An Obstacle to Reducing Pollution
② Economic Approaches to Pollution: A Sure Path to Failure
③ Why Opportunity Cost Approaches Are Superior to Others
④ Costs of Greenhouse Gas Emissions: Beyond Our Imagination
⑤ Balancing Out Pollution Requires Opportunity Cost Assessments

12

정답률 58%

밑줄 친 (a)~(e) 중에서 문맥상 낱말의 쓰임이 적절하지 않은 것은?

① (a)　　② (b)　　③ (c)　　④ (d)　　⑤ (e)

01

정답률 46%

밑줄 친 I zip along the surface like a guy on a Jet Ski가 다음 글에서 의미하는 바로 가장 적절한 것은?

For me, as for others, the internet is becoming a universal medium, the conduit for most of the information that flows through my eyes and ears and into my mind. The advantages of having immediate access to such an incredibly rich store of information are many, and they've been widely described and duly applauded. "The perfect recall of silicon memory," *Wired*'s Clive Thompson has written, "can be an enormous boon to thinking." But that boon comes at a price. As the media theorist Marshall McLuhan pointed out in the 1960s, media are not just passive channels of information. They supply the stuff of thought, but they also shape the process of thought. And what the internet seems to be doing is chipping away my capacity for concentration and contemplation. My mind now expects to take in information the way the internet distributes it: in a swiftly moving stream of particles. Once I was a scuba diver in the sea of words. Now I zip along the surface like a guy on a Jet Ski.

*conduit: (정보나 물자의) 전달자 **duly: 정당하게
***boon: 혜택

① I have developed cognitive skills for critical thinking.
② I do not take the time to fully understand information.
③ I have lots of fun with so many things to enjoy online.
④ My concentration needs to improve against digital distractions.
⑤ My search skills are not good enough to find online information.

02

정답률 51%

다음 글의 주제로 가장 적절한 것은?

Social similarities, which can be of a highly varied nature — community of race, language, religion, habits, scientific culture, etc. — act as a unifying force: "birds of a feather flock together" is truly a social law. In the formation of peoples, the community of race is the fundamental force, and it can be challenged, accidentally, only by other similarities, community of religion, or of general culture. The instinct of sympathy, which pushes a person into society, is intimately tied to likenesses. This evident fact is hardly open to further explanation; it is a primary, irreducible, and permanent fact. But the result of it is that solidarity based on likenesses presents itself to us as much more acceptable than one based on division of labor; for in place of the thought of obligation, it gives rise to thoughts of sympathy. It is this that calls forth the relations of friendship and politeness, philanthropic suggestions, and charitable works. Rather than showing the need to carry out a personal duty, it furnishes us the means to continue the moral impulse of others.

① impacts of social solidarity on thoughts of sympathy
② social similarities as a source of solidarity in society
③ various criteria for categorizing social similarities
④ the relationship between sympathy and obligation
⑤ different social similarities in different cultures

03

다음 글의 밑줄 친 부분 중, 어법상 틀린 것은?

The fear of disclosure is so great in some people, termed "inhibitors" or "suppressors," ① that they avoid revealing anything negative to others. Indeed, in many subcultures, self-disclosure is actively discouraged with the child ② is told "Don't let others know your business," "Tell people only what they need to know," or "Whatever you say, say nothing." This attitude then persists into later life ③ where respect is often given to the person who "plays cards close to the chest." While in a game of poker it is wise not to disclose too much, either verbally or nonverbally, the attitude of avoiding self-disclosure can cause problems for people when they may have a need ④ to talk about personal matters. Often, before we make a deep disclosure, there is a strategic process of testing or advance pre-testing, whereby we "trail" the topic with potential confidants and ⑤ observe their reactions. If these are favorable, then we continue with the revelations; if not, we move on to a new topic.

*confidant: (비밀도 털어놓는 절친한) 친구

04

다음 글의 밑줄 친 부분 중, 문맥상 낱말의 쓰임이 적절하지 않은 것은?

In one fMRI (functional magnetic resonance imaging) study, subjects were asked to classify stimuli on one of three dimensions (color, shape, or pattern). In terms of behavior, one finding was that subjects took ① longer to classify stimuli in switch trials compared to stay trials. In terms of the brain, frontoparietal regions were ② more responsive during switch than stay trials. In fact, ③ inconsistent with the view that multitasking creates heightened neurocognitive demands, the strength of task representation in the control network was greater when subjects switched to a new task than when they stayed with the same task. This means that when we switch from one task to another, it requires more neural processing because we have to bring back to mind the new task's representation and then use it to ④ allocate attention to information that is relevant to perform the new task. As a consequence, when we switch between tasks, we ⑤ lose the benefits of automaticity and efficiency that come from staying focused on a single task.

*fMRI: 기능성 자기 공명 영상
**frontoparietal: 전두두정골(前頭頭頂骨)의

[05-06] 다음 빈칸에 들어갈 말로 가장 적절한 것을 고르시오.

05

정답률 30%

Consider a glass vase sitting on a shelf fully intact. We could conceive of the vase shattering into lots and lots of pieces, were it to be dropped on the floor. From this, you might think, we can conclude that the vase is actually fragile. That's not to say that it is actually *broken*; as we said, it's fully intact. But our act of conceiving might plausibly seem to show us something about a property that it has, namely, its fragility. Likewise, the fact that we can conceive of the mind and the body as existing separately from one another does not show that they are actually separated from one another. But our act of conceiving here too might seem to show us something about a property they have, namely, that they are _____ entities. And that's all that the dualist needs to support the claim that the mind and the body are distinct from one another. None of this shows that the Conceivability Argument is successful, but it should help to show that the argument is at least not entirely invalid.

*intact: 온전한 **entity: 실체
***Conceivability Argument: 논리적 가능성 주장

① temporary
② vulnerable
③ inseparable
④ complementary
⑤ distinguishable

06 초고난도

정답률 26%

Western social science generally endorses the idea that social scientists as scientists should adopt the *theoretical attitude* — that is, scientific contemplation at a distance. As the creator of theory, the social scientist ought to be a disinterested observer of the sociopolitical world and, in that sense, disengaged from society. Social scientists should study the workings of society dispassionately and aim only at developing and testing theoretical explanations of the way the world is. In this way of thinking, the activity of theorizing social and political life as traditionally conceived lies outside the rest of the activity of social life. Judgments about the way the sociopolitical world ought to be _____. The enterprise of social science and the individual social scientist should be value free — that is, neutral with respect to decisions about how we should live or act as humans in society.

*endorse: 지지하다

① are closely linked to reality
② are notoriously hard to explain
③ should be left to others to decide
④ do not support the theoretical attitude
⑤ are often based on subjective emotions

07

정답률 31%

다음 글에서 전체 흐름과 관계 <u>없는</u> 문장은?

Twentieth-century scientific positivism demands that we let data speak for itself. Following this demand, wherever data tells us to go, we will find truth. ① But the data that Google uses to categorize people and assign status of identity does not speak; it is evaluated and ordered by a powerful corporation in order to avoid legal culpability. ② While such data traces can provide invaluable indications of criminal activities and tendencies, making sense of all that data is becoming increasingly challenging. ③ Indeed, scholars Lisa Gitelman and Virginia Jackson argue data doesn't speak but is spoken for. ④ Data does not naturally appear in the wild; rather, it is collected by humans, manipulated by researchers, and ultimately massaged by theoreticians to explain a phenomenon. ⑤ Whoever speaks for data, then, wields the extraordinary power to frame how we come to understand ourselves and our place in the world.

*positivism: 실증주의　**culpability: 유죄

08

정답률 42%

주어진 글 다음에 이어질 글의 순서로 가장 적절한 것은?

Normative beliefs are generally viewed as resulting from social interaction. Indeed, much of the early research on normative social influence used real people in staged settings to convey information about the norm.

(A) While this traditional method is still used (and widely cited as *the* approach to normative social influence), other procedures have been employed in which normative information is conveyed through nonsocial channels.

(B) For example, Sherif's studies on the autokinetic effect used groups of participants (usually three) whose judgments on a task were publicized to the other participants. Similarly, Asch used confederates to convey normative information in his studies of conformity, as did Latané and Darley in their studies of pluralistic ignorance.

(C) That is, although seeing other people act can clearly provide information about the social norms in a given context, social interaction is not required. Individuals use a variety of cues, social and nonsocial, to draw inferences about the behavior of others.

*autokinetic effect: 자동 운동 효과　**confederate: 공모자

① (A) – (C) – (B)　　② (B) – (A) – (C)
③ (B) – (C) – (A)　　④ (C) – (A) – (B)
⑤ (C) – (B) – (A)

09 초고난도
정답률 28%

글의 흐름으로 보아, 주어진 문장이 들어가기에 가장 적절한 곳은?

In a sense, it worked, as the roads soon had fewer and smaller signs, and yet something else happened too — the spontaneous growth of weird and enormous sculptures.

In 1968, concerned officials in the state of Vermont attempted to protect the beautiful views of woodland and pasture along its highways, then being spoiled by the signs and unsightly billboards of restaurants and other businesses. (①) State lawmakers had a simple solution — a law banning all billboards and signs over a certain size. (②) To draw attention to his business, one auto dealer erected a twelve-foot, sixteen-ton gorilla clutching a real Volkswagen Beetle. (③) Not to be outdone, the owner of a carpet store built a huge ceramic teapot with steam and an enormous genie emerging from it, a roll of carpet under his arm. (④) Because these structures weren't displaying messages of any kind, the law didn't apply. (⑤) The legislature hadn't fully appreciated a notorious principle of the social world — the law of unintended consequences.

10
정답률 58%

다음 글의 내용을 한 문장으로 요약하고자 한다. 빈칸 (A), (B)에 들어갈 말로 가장 적절한 것은?

One advantage of thinking verbally is that language liberates you from the here and now. By virtue of language and meaning, you can think about possible future events, about people who are far away, about promises made in the distant past. A rat or insect essentially lives in the immediate present and can respond only on the basis of what it can see, hear, and taste. Language allows people to imagine possible events that have never occurred. This facility is powerfully helpful and liberating. As just one example, animals that have no language cannot possibly understand that some of this year's harvest has to be saved for planting next year, and they might eat their seed corn when they got hungry. They would feel better in the short run, but next year they would have nothing to plant and hence no crop at all. It is hardly an accident that our species is the only one to cultivate the land and reap the harvest, even though a great many species eat plants.

⬇

As opposed to animals, language gives humans the ability to ____(A)____ the immediate situation, which is exemplified by our engagement in ____(B)____.

	(A)		(B)
①	exploit	......	education
②	improve	......	agriculture
③	improve	......	transaction
④	transcend	......	agriculture
⑤	transcend	......	education

[11~12] 다음 글을 읽고, 물음에 답하시오.

Most athletes have developed core mental skills to a sufficient degree that they can function well in day-to-day situations or even in low-level competitive events. But when confronted with more demanding, pressure-packed situations, they may (a) fail. This can be most frustrating to athletes — and their coaches — because they know they have the potential to perform well. Not recognizing that the performance problems are due to a lack of mental skills, coaches may (b) encourage athletes to work even harder on their physical skills. A gymnast may spend extra time on an apparatus. A basketball player may spend extra time shooting free throws after practice. Distance runners may pound their bodies even harder, sometimes to the point of overtraining. Indeed, some performance problems might stem from physical issues, such as poor training or biomechanics. However, in many cases inadequate mental skills could be the cause.

A coach who is (c) aware of how to help athletes develop the necessary mental skills usually does one of three things: tries to support the athlete with empathy and encouragement; selects another athlete who may be less talented physically but can perform better under pressure; or worsens the problem by placing more pressure on the athlete to begin performing up to his or her capability. The alternative, of course, is to capitalize on advances in sport psychology. Coaches from all sports are increasingly recognizing that athletes can learn and improve the mental skills needed to (d) achieve excellence in sport. Rather than leaving development of mental skills to chance, top coaches are increasingly taking responsibility for helping their athletes develop these essential skills by (e) incorporating sport psychology into their athletes' mental training programs.

*apparatus: 기구, 기계

11
정답률 56%

윗글의 제목으로 가장 적절한 것은?

① Distorted Relationships Between Coaches and Athletes
② Physical Factors That Greatly Affect Athletes' Performance
③ Development of Sport Psychology Based on Cumulative Studies
④ Empathy and Encouragement: Always Right for Athletes in Need
⑤ Sport Psychology: The Right Thing for Athletes' Best Performance

12 초고난도
정답률 27%

밑줄 친 (a)~(e) 중에서 문맥상 낱말의 쓰임이 적절하지 않은 것은?

① (a) ② (b) ③ (c) ④ (d) ⑤ (e)

01

정답률 46%

밑줄 친 people are very much unlike rocks가 다음 글에서 의미하는 바로 가장 적절한 것은?

An obvious but often forgotten fact is that historians are people who study people and there is a problem with people. Geologists are also people but they examine rocks. The convenient thing about rocks is that they are rather predictable. Diamonds always cut glass, regardless of whether the geologist had a rough night or is in a bad mood. The point is that people are very much unlike rocks. They are unpredictable, contradictory and quite capable not only of lying to others but also to themselves. It is common for people, even historians, to confuse their own petty personal situations with the flow of history. As the British scholar A.J.P. Taylor once noted, all sorts of talk about the decline of civilization really "means that university professors used to have domestic servants and now do their own washing-up." It would be fair to note that it is not just university professors who have such tendencies.

① People's thoughts are affected by social and economic changes.
② People can be deceptive and may differ from one day to the next.
③ People frequently distort historical findings for their own interests.
④ Even theories proved by evidence can be challenged by individuals.
⑤ Firsthand accounts of people's personal lives are often lost over time.

02

정답률 52%

다음 글의 주제로 가장 적절한 것은?

I once stumbled upon the remains of an ancient tree stump that was still alive. But how could the remains have clung on to life for so long? Living cells in the tree must have food in the form of sugar, they must breathe, and they must grow, at least a little. But without leaves — and therefore without photosynthesis — that's impossible. No being on our planet can maintain a centuries-long fast, not even the remains of a tree, and certainly not a stump that has had to survive on its own. It was clear that something else was happening with this stump. It must be getting assistance from neighboring trees, specifically from their roots. Scientists investigating similar situations have discovered that assistance may either be delivered remotely by fungal networks around the root tips — which facilitate nutrient exchange between trees — or the roots themselves may be interconnected. In the case of the stump I had stumbled upon, I couldn't find out what was going on, because I didn't want to injure the old stump by digging around it, but one thing was clear: the surrounding trees were pumping sugar to the stump to keep it alive.

*stump: 그루터기 **fungal: 균(菌)의

① hierarchical structures used for survival in the forest
② why a stump without self-sufficient capability can survive
③ how living cells produce food through mutual cooperation
④ influence of fungal networks on the growth of tree species
⑤ process by which trees and animals become interdependent

03

다음 글의 밑줄 친 부분 중, 어법상 틀린 것은?

Our early human ancestors needed to keep moving and adapting to new environments, and they were well adapted to being on the move. It isn't surprising ①that some of them moved right out of Africa. Human remains older than a million years have been found (so far) near the Black Sea on the eastern edge of Europe, in China, and on the Indonesian island of Java. The presence of early human remains on Java ②suggesting that they were already making their way across Asia nearly two million years ago. To get to the island from mainland Asia today, it's necessary to cross the Strait of Malacca, which is over 500 miles wide, to get to Sumatra, and then cross another 20-mile stretch of water to get to Java. But the sea level is much lower during ice ages, ③when much more of the Earth's water is frozen into sheets of ice at the poles and on mountaintops. During the ice age that occurred around 1.9 million years ago, the sea level was 200 feet lower than it ④is today. The islands of Java and Sumatra were attached to the mainland at that time, and early humans could have simply walked to ⑤them.

04

다음 글의 밑줄 친 부분 중, 문맥상 낱말의 쓰임이 적절하지 않은 것은?

People seem to have little difficulty in accepting the ①modifiability of 'environmental' effects on human development. If a child has had bad teaching in mathematics, it is accepted that the resulting deficiency can be ②remedied by extra good teaching the following year. But any suggestion that the child's mathematical deficiency might have a genetic origin is likely to be greeted with something approaching ③despair: if it is in the genes 'it is written', it is 'determined' and nothing can be done about it: you might as well give up attempting to teach the child mathematics. This is pernicious rubbish on an almost astrological scale. Genetic causes and environmental causes are in principle no ④different from each other. Some influences of both types may be hard to reverse; others may be easy to reverse. Some may be usually hard to reverse but easy if the right agent is applied. The important point is that there is no general reason for expecting genetic influences to be any more ⑤reversible than environmental ones.

*pernicious: 유해한

[05~06] 다음 빈칸에 들어갈 말로 가장 적절한 것을 고르시오.

05 초고난도
정답률 29%

Air transportation is particularly vulnerable to weather disruptions, such as during winter when a snowstorm can create cascading effects on air services. There is a seasonality for global wind patterns. Jet streams are also a major physical component that international air carriers must take into consideration. For an aircraft, the speed of wind can affect travel time and costs. Tailwind conditions can reduce scheduled flight time by up to an hour for intercontinental flights. For instance, due to strong jet stream conditions during winter months, transatlantic flights between the American East Coast and Europe can arrive 30 to 45 minutes earlier than scheduled for eastbound flights. However, for westbound flights, unusually strong jet stream conditions will lengthen flight time and may on occasion force a flight to make an unscheduled refueling stop at intermediary airports such as Gander (Newfoundland) or Bangor (Maine). It is expected that climate change will increase the strength of the North Atlantic jet stream and could _____.

① reduce the seasonality in wind patterns in North America
② switch the direction of the headwind for eastbound flights
③ increase the strength of the tailwind for westbound flights
④ narrow the difference in eastbound and westbound flight times
⑤ lengthen westbound flights between North America and Europe

06 초고난도
정답률 26%

It is relatively easy to understand secessionist civil wars in West Africa, where ethnic groups fight to carve out their own new states. It is more difficult to understand West Africa's rebels without a cause, who want to take over the national government without a defined ideological platform, as in a nation-wide coup. The rebels claim that their aim is to introduce cleaner, fairer government, but because their own leaders are so often demonstrably corrupt, such claims appear implausible. But our interviews with the followers suggest that they are making a rational bet: either everyone will get to benefit from a fairer sharing of the spoils or at least they themselves will get to benefit because their side will have gained power and will be directing the spoils their way. Many join the rebels simply to protect their own home villages. Rebels have a very local perspective. They aim to take over national governments in the capital because this is still the way to control the distribution of the spoils. Good governance as an ideology may _____.

*secessionist: 분리 독립을 지지하는 **coup: 쿠데타
***spoils: 전리품

① lead to increased productivity of labor
② differ at national, regional, and local levels
③ put economic interest ahead of local needs
④ mean national equity or just a new set of winners
⑤ be achieved by both the creation and use of legal systems

[07~08] 주어진 글 다음에 이어질 글의 순서로 가장 적절한 것을 고르시오.

07

정답률 46%

One of the most compelling pieces of evidence for humans' apparently automatic social nature comes from Fritz Heider and Marianne Simmel's famous 1944 animation of two triangles and a circle orbiting a rectangle.

(A) A closer look at the video, and a closer reading of Heider and Simmel's article describing the phenomenon, suggests that the perception of these shapes in social terms is not automatic but must be evoked by features of the stimuli and situation. These shapes were designed to move in trajectories that specifically mimic social behavior.

(B) If the shapes' motion is altered or reversed, they fail to elicit the same degree of social responses. Furthermore, participants in the original studies of this animation were prompted to describe the shapes in social terms by the language and instructions the experimenters used. Humans may be ready and willing to view the world through a social lens, but they don't do so automatically.

(C) The animation depicts merely shapes, yet people find it nearly impossible not to interpret these objects as human actors and to construct a social drama around their movements.

*trajectory: 궤적

① (A) – (C) – (B)　　② (B) – (A) – (C)
③ (B) – (C) – (A)　　④ (C) – (A) – (B)
⑤ (C) – (B) – (A)

08

정답률 41%

Competition between the private shipping industry and the federal post office demonstrates an important tension in the management of communication infrastructure: between universal service, the expectation of basic capacities to all, and common carriage, the expectation of fair, nondiscriminatory service.

(A) But these benefits came at a price. The private expresses were cartels that avoided competition, engaged in price fixing and freight discrimination, and were in general hard to hold accountable.

(B) The private shipping company, in contrast, went everywhere, did almost anything for anybody, and was the nearest thing to a universal service company ever invented; indeed, private express shipping was often the first thing established in every new camp, especially in the Gold Rush West, where there was lucrative work to be found in transporting bullion.

(C) The US post office lacked the resources, and the infrastructure, to provide universal service to the entire nation. In general, the federal system prioritized slowly developing reliable infrastructure over speedy delivery.

*cartel: 카르텔(기업 연합) **lucrative: 수익성 좋은
***bullion: 금괴, 금

① (A) – (C) – (B)　　② (B) – (A) – (C)
③ (B) – (C) – (A)　　④ (C) – (A) – (B)
⑤ (C) – (B) – (A)

09

정답률 36%

글의 흐름으로 보아, 주어진 문장이 들어가기에 가장 적절한 곳은?

> The challenge for consultants is to identify the precise reasons for changes in intensity in individual athletes.

Intensity is now seen as being affected by many physical, psychological, and emotional factors. Lew Hardy, for example, proposed the cusp catastrophe model, which suggests that intensity possesses thought and physical components. (①) This theory asserts that declines in performance will only occur when high physical intensity and high cognitive intensity are both present. (②) When this situation arises, "catastrophe" occurs, resulting in a rapid and dramatic deterioration in athletic performance. (③) For example, a pole vaulter who worries about an upcoming meet may experience high levels of cognitive intensity, as expressed by negative thoughts and doubts about his ability to achieve his goals. (④) These worrisome thoughts are manifested in physiological experiences of overintensity, such as muscle tightness and rapid breathing, both of which may be harmful to successful performance. (⑤) Only when an athlete can identify the specific causes for changes in intensity can she then learn to control them and, thus, perform her best.

*intensity: 긴장 **cusp: 첨단, 뾰족한 끝

10

정답률 54%

다음 글의 내용을 한 문장으로 요약하고자 한다. 빈칸 (A), (B)에 들어갈 말로 가장 적절한 것은?

There is a kind of large thing that cannot be readily tested until it is fully built and tried. This is the civil engineering project — the dam, tunnel, building, bridge — whose scale is so large, whose cost is so great, and whose design is so specific to the site that the structure is unique. Because it is one of a kind, not made in a factory but constructed in place, there is no disposable example to test. Scale models may be employed for testing theories or comparing alternative designs, but no model will ever fully replicate conditions of the actual as-built structure. Even if incontrovertibly meaningful models were possible, it is not possible to model fully the natural forces of future earthquakes, wind storms, and the like to which the structure might be subjected. In short, the only way to test definitively a large civil engineering structure is to build it in anticipation of how nature will challenge it and then let nature take its course. This fact of large-scale engineering demands careful, proactive failure analyses.

*incontrovertibly: 논쟁의 여지가 없이

↓

Massive structures do not allow perfect ___(A)___ of natural forces, so the only way to test the design's validity is to ___(B)___ the structure with careful precautions.

	(A)		(B)
①	simulation	......	sample
②	simulation	......	construct
③	transformation	......	reinforce
④	penetration	......	examine
⑤	penetration	......	duplicate

[11-12] 다음 글을 읽고, 물음에 답하시오.

Economic growth is a very (a) recent phenomenon. In fact, for most of the three hundred thousand years that human beings have been around, economic life has been relatively stagnant. Our more distant ancestors simply hunted and gathered what little they needed to survive, and that was about it. But over the last few hundred years, that economic (b) inactivity came to an explosive end. The amount each person produced increased about thirteen-fold, and world output rocketed nearly three hundred-fold. Imagine that the sum of human existence was an hour long: most of this action happened in the last half-second or so, in the literal blink of an eye.

Economists tend to agree with one another that this growth was (c) propelled by sustained technological progress, though not on the reasons why it started just where and when it did — in Western Europe, toward the end of the eighteenth century. One reason may be (d) geographical: certain countries had bountiful resources, a hospitable climate, and easily traversable coastlines and rivers for trade. Another may be cultural: people in different communities, shaped by very different intellectual histories and religions, had different attitudes toward the scientific method, finance, hard work, and each other (the level of "trust" in a society is said to be important). The most common explanation of all, though, is (e) personal: certain states protected property rights and enforced the rule of law in a way that encouraged risk taking, hustle, and innovation, while others did not.

11

정답률 53%

윗글의 제목으로 가장 적절한 것은?

① Economic Theory Applies Throughout the Ages
② Unfortunate Results of Human Economic Greed
③ What Did Humans Lose Through Economic Development?
④ Economic Activity: A Mirror Reflecting Basic Human Needs
⑤ What Caused the Explosive Growth of Human Economic Activity?

12 초고난도

정답률 26%

밑줄 친 (a)~(e) 중에서 문맥상 낱말의 쓰임이 적절하지 <u>않은</u> 것은?

① (a)　　② (b)　　③ (c)　　④ (d)　　⑤ (e)

01

정답률 45%

밑줄 친 it's a mistake to assume that more is better가 다음 글에서 의미하는 바로 가장 적절한 것은?

Steven Johnson, in his 2005 book *Everything Bad Is Good for You*, contrasted the widespread, teeming neural activity seen in the brains of computer users with the much more muted activity evident in the brains of book readers. The comparison led him to suggest that computer use provides more intense mental stimulation than does book reading. The neural evidence could even, he wrote, lead a person to conclude that "reading books chronically understimulates the senses." But while Johnson's diagnosis is correct, his interpretation of the differing patterns of brain activity is misleading. It is the very fact that book reading "understimulates the senses" that makes the activity so intellectually rewarding. By allowing us to filter out distractions, to quiet the problem-solving functions of the frontal lobes, deep reading becomes a form of deep thinking. The mind of the experienced book reader is a calm mind, not a buzzing one. When it comes to the firing of our neurons, it's a mistake to assume that more is better.

*teeming: 풍부한 **frontal lobe: 전두엽

① believing that greater oral output is desirable is wrong
② signals from different sensory organs do not have the same value
③ excessive interaction with computers makes people too sensitive
④ keeping the neurons silent does not prevent us from feeling fatigue
⑤ the milder mental stimulation of reading better benefits the intellect

02

정답률 40%

다음 글의 제목으로 가장 적절한 것은?

One of the consequences of the oft-proclaimed crisis of the idea of progress is that the future becomes problematic and the present is rendered absolute. We find ourselves in a regime of historicity where the present is lord and master. This is the oppressive power of the current legislature, of the short term, consumerism, our generation, proximity, etc. This is the economy that privileges the financial sector, profits over investments, cost reductions over company cohesion. We practice an imperialism that is no longer related to space but to time, an imperialism of the present that colonizes everything. There is a colonization of the future that consists of living at its expense and an imperialism of the present that absorbs the future and feeds off it parasitically. Bertman calls it "the power of the now," the present that is not invested in any other dimension of time. This present replaces the long term with the short term, duration with immediacy, permanence with transience, memory with sensation, vision with impulse.

*proximity: 근접성 **parasitically: 기생적으로

① The Inherent Uncertainty of the Future
② The Tyranny of the Present over the Future
③ Crisis in the Present, Struggle in the Future
④ The Concept of Progress: Planning for the Future
⑤ Collaboration Between the Present and the Future

03

정답률 46%

다음 글의 밑줄 친 부분 중, 어법상 **틀린** 것은?

Rephotography is when a photographer returns to a subject that had been previously photographed and ① attempts to make the same picture again to show how time has altered the original scene. Precise records are maintained so the returning photographer can more ② easily duplicate the original scene. The original photograph and the new one are usually displayed next to each other ③ to make comparison easy. In another form of rephotography, the photographer returns to the same subject over a period of time. Examples of this would range from making a picture of yourself every day for a week to Alfred Stieglitz's photographs of Georgia O'Keeffe ④ who span decades. The relationship of the photographer and the subject is pursued over a period of time. The results should represent the broad range of visual possibilities that can be ⑤ produced from this combination due to changes in feeling, light, and mood.

04

정답률 58%

다음 글의 밑줄 친 부분 중, 문맥상 낱말의 쓰임이 적절하지 **않은** 것은?

Social lives are derived from human instincts. Human instincts include humanized instincts and dehumanized instincts. The humanized instincts are used originally involving humans. The dehumanized instincts are used originally involving nonhumans. It is quite ① common among social animals to behave differently toward animals of the same species than toward animals of different species. For example, cannibalism and killing among animals of the same species are ② rare in social animals even during fighting among animals of the same species. Fighting among animals of the same species for the purpose of domination is often ③ ritualistic and does not cause serious injury. Injuries to infant animals from animals of the same species are infrequent. On the other hand, as predators, animals kill prey of different species without ④ hesitation. As prey, an animal makes a manipulative strategy to escape from a predator of a different species. Animals make a ⑤ vague distinction between the animals of different species and animals of the same species.

*cannibalism: 식인 풍습

[05-06] 다음 빈칸에 들어갈 말로 가장 적절한 것을 고르시오.

05

정답률 32%

Why do some people engage in conspiracy theory thinking while others do not? Various psychological theories have been offered, involving factors such as inflated self-confidence or low self-esteem. A more popular consensus seems to be that conspiracy theories are a coping mechanism that some people use to deal with feelings of anxiety and loss of control in the face of large, upsetting events. The human brain does not like random events, because we cannot learn from and therefore cannot plan for them. When we feel helpless (due to lack of understanding, the scale of an event, its personal impact on us, or our social position), we may feel drawn to explanations that identify an enemy we can confront. This is not a rational process, and researchers who have studied conspiracy theories note that those who tend to "go with their gut" are the most likely to engage in conspiracy-based thinking. This is why ignorance is highly correlated with belief in conspiracy theories. When we are less able to _____, we may feel more threatened by it.

*conspiracy theory: 음모론

① maintain a skeptical attitude toward a conspiracy theory claim
② understand something on the basis of our analytical faculties
③ refuse to entertain any notion lacking credibility or evidence
④ influence others with our biased perspectives of an event
⑤ overlook or dismiss something irrelevant to our interests

06 초고난도

정답률 22%

The act of recognizing in a given situation a case of a familiar proverb can cast new light on the situation. It provides a fresh, abstract, and non-obvious viewpoint, going well beyond the situation's superficial details. Since proverbs are the labels of rather subtle and complicated categories, slapping a proverb onto a situation is a way of _____. The use of a proverb as a label is a way of making sense — albeit perhaps a biased type of sense — of what one is seeing. Applying a proverb to a freshly encountered situation results in a kind of insight that comes from filtering what one sees through the lens of the proverb, rather than from a purely logical analysis. In summary, a proverb is a convenient, concise label for a vast set of highly different situations — past, present, future, hypothetical — that are all linked to each other by analogy.

*albeit: 비록 ~일지라도 **analogy: 비유

① combining logic and emotion to change others' viewpoints
② putting new experiences into old and useless categories
③ borrowing conventional wisdom to deliver a fresh idea
④ bringing out aspects that otherwise might remain hidden
⑤ removing details that are essential to understanding a situation

07

다음 글에서 전체 흐름과 관계 <u>없는</u> 문장은?

In studying concepts we have to follow their trajectories, not only in the theoretical environment in which they "live" but also in the observational, experimental, and measuring practices associated with them. ① These practices play a significant role in the specification of the meaning of scientific concepts. ② Observation and experimentation guide the articulation of concepts, by indicating the kinds of properties that their referents should have in order to account for the observational and experimental situations attributed to them. ③ When experimenting, scientists should be aware of all potential sources of bias and undertake all possible actions to reduce and minimize deviation from the truth. ④ For instance, the articulation of the concept of the electron in the early 20th century was guided by the experimental phenomena attributed to it. ⑤ The discrete structure of the hydrogen spectrum, just to mention one example, indicated the discrete structure of the energy levels of the hydrogen atom and, thereby, the quantization of electron orbits within the atom.

*trajectory: 궤적 **discrete: 이산(離散)의, 별개의
***quantization: 양자화

08 초고난도

주어진 글 다음에 이어질 글의 순서로 가장 적절한 것은?

The advantages of musical healing over mere magic are especially tangible when viewed for their efficacy as rituals. Rituals that involve only a single individual, as in the case of the magician, do not contribute to social cohesion and do not inspire or inflame the emotions of onlookers.

(A) The rituals of musical healing, in contrast, are lavish "all-singing, all-dancing" productions with inherent crowd appeal. Even without considering the question of therapeutic efficacy, the superiority of the musical ritual is clearly evident.

(B) If ritual should be viewed as akin to a theatrical performance, then the magical spell is a play without an audience. The performer is engaged in a lonely monologue with no one to appreciate the soliloquy, no matter how moving or eloquent.

(C) Music, in contrast, is not only able to do these things but may even be the single most powerful tool we possess in achieving them. What force better contributes to group integration, ritualistic power, visionary inspiration, or emotional intensity than music?

*tangible: 분명한 **efficacy: 효험 *** soliloquy: 혼잣말

① (A) – (C) – (B) ② (B) – (A) – (C)
③ (B) – (C) – (A) ④ (C) – (A) – (B)
⑤ (C) – (B) – (A)

09 초고난도 정답률 29%

글의 흐름으로 보아, 주어진 문장이 들어가기에 가장 적절한 곳은?

> Furthermore, languages that have two terms to cover *in* and *on*, as in English, sometimes do not do so in the same way as in English.

Spatial prepositions are not only interesting in their own right, but for a number of other reasons as well. For example, they are among the hardest expressions to acquire when learning a second language. (①) This is because languages differ in the way in which they map linguistic terms onto spatial relations. (②) For instance, in Spanish there is a single word, *en*, which maps onto the meanings of both *in* and *on* in English. (③) Conversely, other languages subdivide *containment* and *support* relations more than does English. (④) For example, in Dutch there are two words corresponding to *on* in English: *aan* is used for cases such as "*The handle is on the cupboard door*," and *op* is used for cases such as "*The cup is on the table*." (⑤) In Finnish, for example, the equivalent of "*The handle is on the cupboard door*" and "*The apple is in the bowl*" are grouped together using the ending *-ssa*, whereas the ending *-lla* is used for "*The cup is on the table*."

*spatial preposition: 공간을 나타내는 전치사
**containment: 포함

10 정답률 40%

다음 글의 내용을 한 문장으로 요약하고자 한다. 빈칸 (A), (B)에 들어갈 말로 가장 적절한 것은?

One important reason, apart from costs, why legal rights must always be subject to curtailment or limitation is that rights are, in reality, legal powers that can be exercised over others. Powers can always be used for a bad purpose. Rights must be subject to constraints in order to prevent their exploitation for wrongful ends. For instance, the right to self-defense is well established in American law, but it is justifiable only because, or to the extent that, courts keep an eye out for its abuse. You cannot claim to have acted in self-defense, for example, if you were not seriously endangered. Similarly, the rights of a stockholder to sue a company's management can be used to harass and eventually to obtain a handsome bribe for dropping the case. The possibility of abusive suits must be taken into account by legislators and judges who determine the conditions under which the right to sue fails. The American legal system makes continuous remedial and compensatory adjustments to handle the unintended side effects that necessarily occur whenever the government hands individuals the discretionary right to wield the public power.

*curtailment: 축소 **discretionary: 재량의

⬇

> Legal rights, including the right to self-defense and the right of a stockholder to sue a company's management, must be ____(A)____, because they can be ____(B)____ when exerted over others.

	(A)		(B)
①	corrected	......	shared
②	corrected	......	rejected
③	restricted	......	misused
④	restricted	......	justified
⑤	abandoned	......	prejudiced

[11~12] 다음 글을 읽고, 물음에 답하시오.

Just as its name suggests, monopolistic competition is a type of market structure that blends elements of monopoly with elements of competition. Typically, the industry (a)contains a moderate to large number of sellers, whose products are differentiated rather than homogeneous. Book publishing, shoe and apparel manufacturing, and automotive repair are examples. In each of these industries there is competition because a large number of firms are selling goods or services that are close (b)substitutes for one another. But there is an element of monopoly, as well, insofar as each firm has a monopoly over its own brand, type, quality, or design. However, it is a crucial characteristic of monopolistic competition that there are enough sellers that each assumes its pricing decisions will not provoke a reaction from the others. Firms are, in other words, (c)price-dependent.

Among individual sectors of the performing arts industry, the Broadway theater can be accurately described as monopolistically competitive. Thirty or more plays and musicals open during a single season and certainly compete with each other for an audience. Yet each company clearly has a monopoly over its own show and sets prices on the assumption that its own policies will not provoke a response from competitors. If we adopt a broader definition, under which all the live performing arts make up a (d)single industry, then the industry itself, in most large cities, is monopolistically competitive: The opera company, the symphony orchestra, the dance groups, and the resident theater companies compete with each other by offering products that are (e)unique, and yet closely substitutable as forms of artistic entertainment.

*homogeneous: 동질적인

11

정답률 53%

윗글의 제목으로 가장 적절한 것은?

① Features and Examples of Monopolistic Competition
② A Short History of Monopolistic Competition Theory
③ The Explosive Growth of the Performing Arts Industry
④ Advantages and Disadvantages of Monopolistic Industry
⑤ How to Survive in a Monopolistically Competitive Market

12

정답률 35%

밑줄 친 (a)~(e) 중에서 문맥상 낱말의 쓰임이 적절하지 <u>않은</u> 것은?

① (a)　　② (b)　　③ (c)　　④ (d)　　⑤ (e)

01

정답률 43%

밑줄 친 always in quotation marks and fancy dress가 다음 글에서 의미하는 바로 가장 적절한 것은?

Preservation's act of reshaping the past according to the views of the present effectively distances the past from the present, causing it to seem like a distinct, separate realm, rather than something intimately connected with today. Recognizing the past's difference promotes its preservation, and the act of preserving it makes that difference still more apparent. Particularly in the United States, heritage is often not permitted to coexist with the present; instead it is fenced off, "always in quotation marks and fancy dress," and visited on special occasions. Setting aspects of the past off as national parks contributes to this separation, implying that history is something to be visited and viewed, rather than lived with, day to day. Similarly, as geographer Yi-Fu Tuan writes, preserving particular ways of life associated with the past "turn[s] them into figures in glass cases, labeled and categorized as in a museum" — an approach more bluntly described as "geographic taxidermy."

*set off: ~을 돋보이게 하다 **taxidermy: 박제술

① regarded as a timeless object of admiration
② poorly preserved with little detail surviving
③ made more easily accessible to all than ever
④ never seen as an integrated part of everyday life
⑤ blended into the present for a particular purpose

02

정답률 37%

다음 글의 제목으로 가장 적절한 것은?

The drive to make AI "explainable" — solemnly stated in law in the European Union's General Data Protection Regulation — demands the question be asked: Explainable to whom? Different stakeholders seek different kinds of explanations. The problem arises even with a relatively simple loan risk assessment system. Software developers and system administrators want an explanation in terms of architecture and processing parameters. A seasoned loan officer, who makes the final decision, might want to know how various factors have been weighted in the system's recommendation. An applicant who has been denied a loan wants to know precisely why — *is it my age, my race, my zip code, an inaccurate credit history*? A regulator wants to be assured that the system doesn't compromise data privacy, violate anti-discrimination laws, or leave itself open to financial fraud. A layperson, contemplating the black box problem — that many AI systems are opaque — generally, might want to know why anyone would build a machine they don't understand.

*parameter: 매개 변수 **opaque: 불투명한, 이해하기 힘든

① Risk Assessment: A Simple Task with an AI Assistant
② Various Questions from Different Users on the Workings of AI
③ How AI's Understanding of Values Is Different from Ours
④ AI Systems: Optimal Black Boxes for the Human Race
⑤ Why AI Developers Suffer from Strict Regulations

03

정답률 50%

다음 글의 밑줄 친 부분 중, 어법상 틀린 것은?

When the Roman Empire eventually collapsed, the Catholic Church became the dominant structure in Europe. The Catholic Church rejected the activities that the Roman Empire had accepted, including ① its hedonistic ways. One example of this was the fact that people ② involved in theater could not be baptized. The concept that "idleness is the great enemy of the soul" emerged, and ③ doing nothing was thought to be evil. The church wielded great influence during this time over the social order, consisting of nobility and peasants. The clergy dictated societal values, ④ whose adoption would lead to saving souls, the highest goal at the time. Although the Catholic Church influenced what were acceptable and unacceptable leisure activities, so strict ⑤ was many rules that during the end of this period the church went through a period of renaissance where individuals within the church developed different perspectives. This renaissance saw a renewed appreciation for a variety of leisure activities.

*hedonistic: 쾌락주의의 **baptize: 세례를 베풀다

04

정답률 58%

다음 글의 밑줄 친 부분 중, 문맥상 낱말의 쓰임이 적절하지 않은 것은?

The epic moments of sport, for all the ready availability of prose, poetry and the moving image, are most memorably captured by still photography. The 'frozen in time' sight of the instant of a famous victory or gesture is perhaps the most potent of all media sports texts, ① able to convey historical weight, emotion and a sense of the unique. One of the most ② memorable is the "black power" protest by Tommie Smith and John Carlos on the victory dais at the 1968 Mexico Olympics which, by the 1990s, had become incorporated into corporate leisurewear marketing campaigns as images of funky black radical chic. Like all media texts, sports photographs ③ work through a particular ordering of signs and codes that are part aesthetic, part ideological. They are not ④ biased records of events — through selection, composition and manipulation, sports photographs offer up an account of how the world is (or how the photographer thinks it should be). The most important object in sports photography is the sport's prime instrument, the human body. The bodies of sportspeople are closely ⑤ observed through striking images that draw their power.

*dais: 단상, 연단 **funky: 파격적이고 멋진
***chic: (독특한) 스타일

[05-06] 다음 빈칸에 들어갈 말로 가장 적절한 것을 고르시오.

05 초고난도 · 정답률 29%

Many authoritarian systems are characterized by the absence of civil society. This can be the specific result of those in power, who have taken steps to harass, absorb, monitor, or destroy any form of independent action outside of the state and those in power. Civil society may also have little precedent in society or be hindered by significant ethnic or other societal divisions that dissuade people from forming organizations across these institutional barriers. The result can be a society that is more familiar with viewing the state as a primary arena for social organization, or that thinks of association more in terms of mass movements and protest. Sometimes both of these go hand in hand in what is known as populism. Populism is not a specific ideology and in fact draws much of its power from an anti-institutional approach. But generally, populism carries within it the view that elites and established institutions do not fully represent the will of the people and that a new movement, free from ideology and often led by a charismatic leader, can usher in a new order. Where civil society is weak, populism may _____.

① find more fertile ground
② decrease desire for protest
③ destroy authoritarian systems
④ create tension among citizens
⑤ serve as a corrective to democracy

06 초고난도 · 정답률 20%

Aristotle, through his philosophy and natural history, had concluded that although humans and animals share many characteristics such as perception and emotion, humans alone have the capacity for logos or reason. For Aristotle this was simply a factual conclusion about the mental capabilities of animals. However, thinkers of the Stoic school made it the basis for their ethical position on animals. The Stoics saw justice as rooted in the concept of mutual 'belonging'. Some Stoics applied the notion of belonging narrowly, to ourselves and our offspring; others applied it more widely to all virtuous people, or even to all fellow humans. But the Stoics considered that no such community of belonging can exist between rational and non-rational beings. Hence, what had been for Aristotle a purely factual conclusion about the mental powers of animals was used by the Stoics as the basis for the ethical conclusion that _____.

① non-rational beings should be treated equally to rational ones
② people should not take advantage of animals for human benefit
③ humans need to extend the notion of belonging to all creatures
④ animals fall outside the sphere of human justice and moral concern
⑤ the concept of mutual belonging is applicable to humans and animals

07

정답률 32%

주어진 글 다음에 이어질 글의 순서로 가장 적절한 것은?

While continuing to grapple with local environmental problems, many cities also expect to face new challenges as a result of climate change.

(A) But cities also play a major role in increasing the risk of climate change by generating greenhouse gases, such as carbon dioxide. Since reducing emissions is costly, and the benefits of doing so are shared with the rest of the world, each city has few incentives to limit greenhouse gas production on its own. This is a classic example of the free-rider problem.

(B) In theory, cities could help head off these problems. After all, cities are leading centers of idea generation. Urban centers may incubate new technologies that could weaken the link between economic activity and greenhouse gas production.

(C) For example, coastal cities, especially those closer to the equator, will face a greater risk of flooding and extreme heat. Does Hurricane Katrina's blow to New Orleans foreshadow future urban impacts? If climate change increases the frequency and severity of natural disasters, the answer may be yes.

*grapple with: ~와 씨름하다
**foreshadow: ~의 전조가 되다

① (A) – (C) – (B)   ② (B) – (A) – (C)
③ (B) – (C) – (A)   ④ (C) – (A) – (B)
⑤ (C) – (B) – (A)

[08-09] 글의 흐름으로 보아, 주어진 문장이 들어가기에 가장 적절한 곳을 고르시오.

08

정답률 43%

She thus transforms that formerly shared portion of the world into something over which she possesses an exclusive right.

Our understanding of private property has evolved over the last 500 years. The most significant early modern theorist of private property was the philosopher John Locke. Locke argued that private ownership of property is a natural right and that it cannot be usurped arbitrarily by the state. (①) In fact, he insisted that the right to acquire and accumulate property is, like human liberty, both conceptually and historically prior to the state. (②) When an individual mixes her labor with some portion of the natural world in the pre-political "state of nature," she expresses a fundamental aspect of her own selfhood. (③) She may now use it as she sees fit — sell it, transfer it, or turn it into an asset designed to generate income, for instance. (④) Other people are barred from taking over her property without her consent. (⑤) In fact, for Locke, the basic purpose of the state is to assure that the property rights of the individual are not infringed upon by others.

*usurp: 빼앗다 **infringe upon: ~을 침해하다

09 초고난도   정답률 21%

Yet no system ought to be allowed to obscure the elemental fact that war consisted of fighting and that fighting — in other words, battle — determined the outcome of wars.

Much like his immediate predecessors, Carl von Clausewitz distinguished between tactics, which he called the art of winning battles, and strategy, which he defined as the art of using battles to gain the objectives of the campaign. More fundamentally, though, war was a duel between two independent minds. (①) Its interactive nature sharply differentiated it from other activities. (②) To paraphrase, making swords (which only involved acting upon dead matter) was one thing. (③) Using them against another swordsman who is capable of parrying one's own thrusts and replying with others of his own is quite another. (④) In a brief but brilliant discussion of the theory of war, Clausewitz acknowledges that the system offered by each of his predecessors contained some elements of truth. (⑤) No amount of fancy maneuvering could do any good unless it was backed up with a big, sharp sword.

*predecessor: 선배, 전임자   **duel: 결투
***parry: 받아넘기다   ****maneuver: 책략을 쓰다

10   정답률 43%

다음 글의 내용을 한 문장으로 요약하고자 한다. 빈칸 (A), (B)에 들어갈 말로 가장 적절한 것은?

A common experimental approach in attempting to observe the ideas and thinking of young children, particularly babies, is the use of habituation studies. Habituation is one of the simplest and most fundamental forms of human learning and involves the way in which we all show a decline of interest in, or response to, repeated or continued experience. For example, a baby may continue to turn his head and look at a rattle being shaken for some time. Over time, however, he will tend to stop turning his head, showing signs of boredom and a new stimulus may be required to restart the head turning. Such behaviour is taken to imply evidence of learning and memory. The decreased response to a stimulus can be taken to suggest that a child has a memory of what it is: "Oh, I know what that is. I've seen/heard/touched/tasted it before, so I don't need to look at it/listen to it/touch it/taste it now." When a baby is presented with an unfamiliar experience, dishabituation occurs: "I don't think I know what that is."

⬇

Babies' habituation to stimuli means that they've stopped ____(A)____ to recurrence of the stimuli; they break from habituation when given a ____(B)____ stimulus.

	(A)		(B)
①	reacting	......	complicated
②	reacting	......	novel
③	agreeing	......	conditioned
④	adjusting	......	repeated
⑤	adjusting	......	persistent

[11-12] 다음 글을 읽고, 물음에 답하시오.

A fundamental key to understanding the power of thought is realizing the role that your beliefs play. Regardless of what you believe, your beliefs determine every single experience you have in life. Moreover, your beliefs are (a) loyal to you. They are strong lures for thoughts that validate and strengthen the core belief and strong repellents for thoughts that betray the belief. As a result, you will have only those encounters that coincide with your beliefs. Change is then difficult to incorporate because you cannot bring into reality that which conflicts with your belief system. What you do not believe or what is not believable is automatically (b) disregarded. That means change cannot occur, for you are unknowingly rejecting it.

If you want to be a rock star, then you cannot have that experience if you do not believe being a rock star is an (c) option for you. While you might have thoughts of desire towards that profession, typically daydreams are neither believable to most of us, nor do they achieve the level of obsession necessary for actualization. The challenge is to build up an idea until your thoughts form an obsession within the mind. You must then embrace your idea until a belief forms that your idea is doable. At the point the belief starts to form, you will take action and your idea will (d) collapse. Unfortunately, most people never get past these hurdles because their established beliefs prevent ideas that are contrary to the belief from reaching a level of obsession. If you have ever experienced doubt, skepticism, or fear of failure, then you have experienced the process of your beliefs (e) resisting new or opposing thoughts.

11

정답률 52%

윗글의 제목으로 가장 적절한 것은?

① Your Belief System Will Vary Every Minute
② Break Free from Your Past and Move Forward
③ Change Occurs When You Believe It's Possible
④ Obsession with an Idea: A Major Barrier to Success
⑤ Enhance the Power of Thought with the Help of Others

12

정답률 55%

밑줄 친 (a)~(e) 중에서 문맥상 낱말의 쓰임이 적절하지 않은 것은?

① (a) ② (b) ③ (c) ④ (d) ⑤ (e)

01

정답률 42%

밑줄 친 sentence ourselves to idleness가 다음 글에서 의미하는 바로 가장 적절한 것은?

More often than not, our discipline fades and our mind wanders when we're not on the job. We may yearn for the workday to be over so we can start spending our pay and having some fun, but most of us fritter away our leisure hours. We avoid hard work and only rarely engage in challenging hobbies. Instead, we watch TV or go to the mall or log on to Facebook. We get lazy. And then we get bored and edgy. Disengaged from any outward focus, our attention turns inward, and we end up locked in what Emerson called the jail of self-consciousness. Jobs, even crummy ones, are "actually easier to enjoy than free time," says Csikszentmihalyi, because they have the "built-in" goals and challenges that "encourage one to become involved in one's work, to concentrate and lose oneself in it." But that's not what our deceiving minds want us to believe. Given the opportunity, we'll eagerly relieve ourselves of the rigors of labor. We'll sentence ourselves to idleness.

*fritter away: ~을 조금씩 허비해 버리다 **crummy: 형편없는

① criticize ourselves for being innately lazy
② do more mental labor and less manual labor
③ punish ourselves by voluntarily doing nothing
④ give in to our desire to keep away from all labor
⑤ lose our jobs due to drastic changes in technology

02

정답률 55%

다음 글의 주제로 가장 적절한 것은?

In a purely oral culture, thinking is governed by the capacity of human memory. Knowledge is what you recall, and what you recall is limited to what you can hold in your mind. Through the millennia of man's preliterate history, language evolved to aid the storage of complex information in individual memory and to make it easy to exchange that information with others through speech. "Serious thought," Ong writes, was by necessity "intertwined with memory systems." Diction and syntax became highly rhythmical, tuned to the ear, and information was encoded in common turns of phrase — what we'd today call clichés — to aid memorization. Knowledge was embedded in "poetry," as Plato defined it, and a specialized class of poet-scholars became the human devices, the flesh-and-blood intellectual technologies, for information storage, retrieval, and transmission. Laws, records, transactions, decisions, traditions — everything that today would be "documented" — in oral cultures had to be, as Havelock says, "composed in formulaic verse" and distributed "by being sung or chanted aloud."

*cliché: 상투적인 어구 **flesh-and-blood: 인간의
***formulaic: 상투적인 표현의

① linguistic devices for memorizing information in oral cultures
② our natural instinct to exchange information for survival
③ limitations of oral tradition in transmitting knowledge
④ importance of memory in prehistoric oral cultures
⑤ ancient scholars' efforts to improve memorization

03 초고난도

정답률 29%

다음 글의 밑줄 친 부분 중, 어법상 <u>틀린</u> 것은?

It is important to recognize the nature of mathematics and the very radical abstraction that it involves. Galileo, Descartes, Huygens and Newton all ①<u>produced</u> formulae. In other words, they were seeking to create a mathematical and abstract way of summing up physical phenomena, using mathematics to express patterns seen in nature. ②<u>What</u> it should be possible for an abstract formula to correspond to nature was a fundamental assumption made by those involved in the emerging sciences. Beneath it ③<u>lay</u> the deeper assumption that the world is a predictable and ordered place. Escaping from the earlier era of crude superstition and magic, they saw themselves emerging into a world ④<u>where</u> reason and evidence would triumph. But reason, in its purest form, is seen in logic and mathematics, and it was therefore natural ⑤<u>to expect</u> that the world would be, in principle, comprehensible in terms of 'laws of nature' which, with mathematical precision, would determine the movement of all things.

04

정답률 59%

다음 글의 밑줄 친 부분 중, 문맥상 낱말의 쓰임이 적절하지 <u>않은</u> 것은?

In seventeenth-century England, liberalism emerged at the same time as capitalism. Liberal merchants, manufacturers, financiers, and intellectuals articulated ideas that ①<u>diverged</u> from medieval Catholic theology supporting the monarchy, the mercantilist state, feudal status distinctions, and the established church. Politically, liberals ②<u>demanded</u> a more representative government based on parliamentary rule. Impersonal law, not a monarch, should undergird political authority. Economically, liberals favored greater freedom for the private entrepreneur. Individuals should have the opportunity to ③<u>pursue</u> their self-interests — wealth and social status — free from tight state controls. Classical liberals supported the expression of sacred and worldly values in different realms. The separation of church from state ④<u>restricted</u> individual freedom. Religious toleration enabled the individual to pursue salvation free from orthodox controls. In short, classical liberals ⑤<u>stressed</u> the primacy of individual freedom over the hierarchical, collectivist order linked to medieval Catholicism.

*mercantilist: 중상주의(자)의 **feudal: 봉건(제)의
***undergird: 뒷받침하다

[05~06] 다음 빈칸에 들어갈 말로 가장 적절한 것을 고르시오.

05 초고난도   정답률 29%

We mostly ignore our built landscapes because practically, _____. This aligns with our approach to other swaths of our daily experience and needs: for medical help, we go to doctors; to repair our car, we visit the auto mechanic. Most of us, implicitly or explicitly, have given up control over our built environments, having entrusted decision-making about them to experts: city council members, real estate developers, builders and contractors, product manufacturers, and designers. Most of us perceive ourselves as helpless to make changes in the built environment. This very sense of powerlessness results in a paradoxical situation: real estate developers configure new projects based on what they believe consumers want, which they assess mainly by examining what previous consumers have purchased. But when it comes to the built environment, consumers gravitate toward conventional designs without thinking very much about them. So developers continue to build what they think people want. No one steps back to consider what might serve people better, what people could like, or what they actually might need.

*swath: 영역 **configure: 구성하다

① too many professionals are involved in their designs
② we don't think commercial spaces are for personal use
③ aesthetic considerations make few functional differences
④ we have no obvious stake or influence in their production
⑤ financial gains come before our needs in their construction

06 초고난도   정답률 25%

Many young birds need to learn much by observing their parents and elders, and parrots probably need to learn more than most. That's why trying to restore parrot populations by captive breeding and reintroduction is tricky and fraught. It's not as easy as training young or orphaned creatures to recognize what is food while they're in the safety of a cage, then simply opening the door. "In a cage," Sam Williams says, "you can't train them to know where, when, and how to find that food, or about trees with good nest sites." And a landscape is complex and ever changing. "Just throwing birds out when we haven't prepared them for survival would be unethical," Williams believes. Worse, it might not work. The prospects for survival of released individuals are most severely undermined when there are no free-living elder role models. _____ frustrated attempts to reintroduce thick-billed parrots to parts of the southwestern United States where they'd been wiped out. Conservation workers could not teach the captive-raised parrots to search for and find their traditional wild foods.

*fraught: 걱정스러운

① High-density rearing in training sites
② A generational break in cultural traditions
③ A constant lack of food in natural settings
④ Unjustified violence involved in captive breeding
⑤ The presence of peer pressure in socialization process

07

정답률 58%

다음 글에서 전체 흐름과 관계 <u>없는</u> 문장은?

In sports, attendance is nearly always (98-99 percent of the time) with at least one other person. The sports fan pays a price for the right to enjoy an emotional experience with others. ① The fan goes to the game to be with others, to share the experience in this social exchange. ② More broadly speaking, unlike most other retail settings, large crowds have positive psychological effects. ③ No line at the grocery checkout will make most shoppers happy, but no line to see a ballgame is a definite hint to a fan either that this is a terrible sporting event or that the fan has arrived at the stadium on the wrong date. ④ The potential benefits of sport participation do not happen automatically; coaches must structure players' sport experience to help players gain these psychological benefits. ⑤ The excitement of the competition and the aura of the star power of the players on the team are such that the experience is best enjoyed in the presence of others.

*aura: 기운, 매력

08

정답률 34%

주어진 글 다음에 이어질 글의 순서로 가장 적절한 것은?

A chorus of voices in moral philosophy has lately been raised in protest against ethical theorists' recurrent tendency to ignore the importance of context. Objections have been directed, for instance, against theorists whose love of simplicity and order blinds them to the rich diversity of the moral landscape.

(A) Those who lack moral knowledge will stumble about blindly, like novice hikers outfitted with GPS who discover that they are in fact poorly if expensively equipped to find their way. However good your map, it can't keep you from getting lost if you don't know where you are.

(B) Other objections have been raised against the arrogance that mere possession of a moral theory is sufficient for moral knowledge. However adequate a set of moral principles might be, after all, someone who doesn't notice what is salient in a situation won't know what to apply the principles to.

(C) By these voices, we're reminded that theory isn't supposed to confine everything into a few favorite categories; proposals that prune and consolidate the explanatory concepts of ethics too radically will end up leaving out important phenomena or rendering them unrecognizable.

*novice: 초보자 **salient: 가장 중요한
***prune: 가지치기하다

① (A) – (C) – (B)   ② (B) – (A) – (C)
③ (B) – (C) – (A)   ④ (C) – (A) – (B)
⑤ (C) – (B) – (A)

09

글의 흐름으로 보아, 주어진 문장이 들어가기에 가장 적절한 곳은?

> That is, advertising is as likely to be about maintaining or protecting market share (or "brand loyalty") as increasing it.

From an economic perspective, television advertising is seen as creating demand for consumer goods, allowing for the widespread proliferation of product names and brands. (①) Indeed, without advertising it would be difficult for consumers to negotiate supermarket shelves containing dozens or even hundreds of varieties of the same product. (②) While many scholars see advertising as playing a key role in the development of a capitalist consumer economy, the evidence suggests that the degree to which TV advertising raises aggregate market consumption is inconclusive at best. (③) As a consequence, the costs of advertising a product are generally not recuperated through economies of scale in increased production. (④) Accordingly, the costs of advertising are generally passed on to the consumer. (⑤) The consumer is, in effect, paying for the advertising campaign used to influence their purchase.

*proliferation: 확산   **aggregate: 총계의
***recuperate: 회수하다

10

다음 글의 내용을 한 문장으로 요약하고자 한다. 빈칸 (A), (B)에 들어갈 말로 가장 적절한 것은?

An important response to statistical illiteracy is to give the public more numbers. Patients have a right to learn how big benefits and harms of a treatment are. Qualitative risk terms are notoriously unclear. There are attempts to standardize verbal expressions, such as the EU guideline for drug labels and package leaflets, where specific terms are defined for frequency intervals. However, people seem to overestimate the frequencies of side effects based on those labels. Moreover, terms such as "unlikely" are interpreted differently from context to context. For example, more severe side effects are estimated to occur less frequently than less severe side effects described by the same qualitative term. Patients tend to overestimate risks when disclosed verbally and are less likely to comply if information is given numerically. But research suggested that, for both written and verbal information, patients had a more accurate perception of risk when it was presented in numbers as opposed to words. Therefore, risk should always be specified numerically.

⬇

Patients may mentally ___(A)___ risks when qualitative risk terms are presented verbally and will have a more accurate perception of the terms if they are given to patients with ___(B)___.

	(A)		(B)
①	doubt	......	examples
②	overlook	......	figures
③	overlook	......	symbols
④	exaggerate	......	figures
⑤	exaggerate	......	examples

[11~12] 다음 글을 읽고, 물음에 답하시오.

Aboriginal foragers represent a domestic mode of production, where production decisions are made at the household level with minimal outside pressure. Aborigines did not use labor, technology, and resources to their maximum productive potential, choosing instead to maximize their leisure, sharing, and ceremonial activities above purely material concerns. The relative uniformity and durability of their forager system suggests that Aborigines had designed a sustainable (a)no-growth culture, whether intentionally or not. Aborigines did not "invest" surplus production in either supporting larger populations or expanding economic production; instead they directed it into activities that helped individuals build their social and cultural capital in ways that also benefited society as a whole and contributed to the (b)reproduction of the culture. Food sharing, ceremonial feasting, and leisure provided growth-reducing effects and helped Aborigines avoid the dilemma of endless cycles of population growth and subsistence intensification. When people shared food, there was little incentive to produce beyond their (c)immediate needs.

(d)Limited material production by Aborigines can be partially understood as the outcome of cost-benefit decisions given forager technology. The more hours per day foragers work, the less efficient their efforts become, because their prey becomes scarcer relative to the number of people to be fed. Computer simulations show that relatively low work effort actually produces the largest sustainable human population and the (e)minimal return for forager effort. It may seem counterintuitive, but increased effort in the form of longer hours spent foraging appears to only reduce efficiency because of resource depletion.

*Aborigine: 호주 원주민 **subsistence: 부양

11

윗글의 제목으로 가장 적절한 것은?

① Why Didn't Aborigines Produce Surplus Food?
② The Cultural Capital: The Base for Economic Prosperity
③ How Population Growth Affected Aboriginal Economies
④ Aborigines' Intensification of Efforts to Increase Returns
⑤ Agriculture: The Answer to Resource Depletion for Aborigines

12

밑줄 친 (a)~(e) 중에서 문맥상 낱말의 쓰임이 적절하지 않은 것은?

① (a)   ② (b)   ③ (c)   ④ (d)   ⑤ (e)

01

밑줄 친 eying breakfast and dinner가 다음 글에서 의미하는 바로 가장 적절한 것은?

Some important dynamics have reduced the need for lawyers and intensified competition for the legal work that remains. Technology is partly responsible, displacing demand for many lawyers' services. For attorneys serving individual clients, online document preparation services are acquiring an increasing share of the legal market. For attorneys in virtually all areas of legal practice, the traditional "artisan" model of lawyering is being replaced by commoditized legal work, and the broader economy's relentless pressure toward more for less will intensify this trend. Technology-driven legal service providers aren't just eating big law firm's lunch; they are eying breakfast and dinner as well. So too, corporate clients, who are facing increased pressures in their own markets, have responded by reducing legal costs. Businesses have moved more routine work in-house and parceled out more projects based on short-term competitive considerations rather than long-term lawyer-client relationships.

*commoditize: 상품화하다 **relentless: 가차 없는

① demanding increased fees for routine work
② deciding the quality of legal services based on fees
③ developing new technologies for free legal services
④ aiming to take over the entire traditional legal market
⑤ seeking opportunities to collaborate with traditional firms

02

다음 글의 제목으로 가장 적절한 것은?

We want desperately to be mentally engaged. We hate feeling bored. And yet, we also try to avoid the feeling of mental strain, which can arise when performing demanding tasks. Boredom and mental strain can push us toward easy ways of engaging that require little skill and arguably do not enrich our lives in any way — scrolling mindlessly through Facebook or Instagram, playing video games, watching Netflix, etc. These easy engagement outlets can control us for hours on end. Devices that have been very carefully crafted to attract and hold our attention, to optimally challenge us so that we are free of boredom and mental strain, surround us no matter where we turn. It's so easy to slip into the machine zone. We don't need much skill to get started, and before we know it, an hour has gone by or we have developed an addiction. Or, even worse, we have ignored our bodily needs to the point of putting our lives in danger — dead with the game console still in our hands.

① Boredom and Overload End Up Leading to Machine Addiction
② Mental Strain: The Very Motivator for Better Technology
③ Digital Entertainment Connects Us to Our Neighbors
④ The Better Technology, the Better Human Cognition
⑤ Technological Developments Bring Forth Boredom

03

정답률 42%

다음 글의 밑줄 친 부분 중, 어법상 **틀린** 것은?

Keep in mind that more innovation is not necessarily better. Some proponents of innovation have ①been carried away in their apparent zeal regarding innovation; they have recommended that all businesses strive for significant, continual doses of innovation, especially radical, game-changing innovation. This is simply not true. Every organization that intends to survive beyond the next two product life cycles ②needs healthy infusions of innovation and must invest to get them. This does not mean ③that an organization needs constant blockbuster or breakthrough innovations, though. It is hard to imagine an organization that could effectively harness a constant supply of breakthrough radical innovations, each of ④them would cause significant change in its business and technology base. That level of change might bedevil the competition, but it would also break the back of the innovating organization, considering the huge costs of developing ⑤such a flow of innovations, coupled with the huge tensions and destabilizations created in the organization by the constant, radical change.

*zeal: 열정 **harness: 활용하다 ***bedevil: 괴롭히다

04

정답률 57%

(A), (B), (C)의 각 네모 안에서 문맥에 맞는 낱말로 가장 적절한 것은?

We see life in two ways: the stories we tell ourselves about ourselves, and the stories about ourselves that are true. Not to say that the stories we tell ourselves about ourselves are false, they are often shaped by our character. In sociological theory, the Interactionist Perspective says that social interaction is a cooperative activity about impression (A) formation / dissolution . There are two types of impressions: the ones we "give," and the ones we "give off." The impressions we give are controllable (more or less), such as diction and body language; whereas, the impressions we "give off" are more or less (B) conscious / subconscious and uncontrollable. The impressions we "give" are not necessarily fiction, however they can be distorted or exaggerated because we have control over them. The stories we tell ourselves about ourselves are the stories we "give," so to speak. The stories about ourselves that are invariably true are the ones we "give off," (C) constrained / unconstrained by distortion or exaggeration.

	(A)	(B)	(C)
①	formation	conscious	constrained
②	formation	subconscious	unconstrained
③	dissolution	conscious	unconstrained
④	formation	subconscious	constrained
⑤	dissolution	subconscious	constrained

[05~07] 다음 빈칸에 들어갈 말로 가장 적절한 것을 고르시오.

05 초고난도   정답률 29%

Some thinkers imagine that the goal in war or battle is to kill all of one's enemies. That is wrong, as the philosopher Elaine Scarry explained in her thoughtful book, *The Body in Pain*. War stems from incompatible ideas. Two countries have different ideas about where the border should be drawn, or how they should be treated by each other, or which one has the best political or economic or religious system. Faced with disagreement, they are willing to put some of their people's lives and limbs, and some of their wealth, in jeopardy so as to force the other to agree. The opponents likewise think they'd rather risk some of their people and their resources in order to win the argument. During the battles, both sides lose people and other resources (blood and treasure, in the usual phrase) in service of the ideas they favor. Almost no battles or wars are pursued until one side is totally wiped out. Rather, at some point, one side decides that it would rather give up on some of its ideas than lose any more of its lives and wealth. It _____.

*jeopardy: 위험

① yields   ② appears
③ persists   ④ disagrees
⑤ dominates

06   정답률 31%

Even as it overloads us, email is useful in helping work move forward, in assessing the pulse of an organization, and in receiving the opinions, suggestions, and ideas of fellow workers. To sustain these benefits, while increasing my own productivity, I have constructed an array of on-screen "push buttons." When I click on a button, it inserts a preset note informing the recipient of my conclusion or question, forwards the annotated message to my assistant or the person who emailed me the message, and removes the mail from the incoming message list — all with one click. I have different buttons that say nicely, "Yes, I'll do it," "No," "You handle it," "Let's talk," and so on. I have been able to reply to enough messages via these push buttons to reduce my per-message average to less than one minute. No doubt, future email software will include such capabilities to help _____. Of course, these techniques do not eliminate the fundamental problem. They just delay its onset.

*annotated: 주석이 달린

① shrink our email load
② evaluate the urgency of an email
③ increase interpersonal interaction
④ speed up our real-time predictions
⑤ block emails from unknown senders

07 초고난도   정답률 22%

As runners, there's one thing we should keep in mind. When we _____, we may find it hard to motivate ourselves without an event on the schedule. Our training might be overly focused on the demands of race day at the expense of our long-term growth as a runner and human. We may try to cram in more long runs or vert (vertical elevation gain) than is helpful or healthy because we are fixated on overcoming our perceived biggest weakness. We may even reach the point where we find ways to insert additional training or ignore our plan, claiming innocence and inadvertent mistakes, when we know deep down it was intentional. Any setback feels like a catastrophe. The smallest steps backward make us sink into serious regression without a consistent base of training to lean on. We might tell ourselves that once we achieve the next outcome, we will stop these behaviors, but they can become addictive and difficult to stop.

*cram: 밀어 넣다   **inadvertent: 의도치 않은
***regression: 퇴보

① don't overcome our weaknesses
② aren't invested in the long term
③ encounter unexpected distractions
④ experience small setbacks too often
⑤ don't try to change training schedules

08   정답률 40%

주어진 글 다음에 이어질 글의 순서로 가장 적절한 것은?

It was only 50 years ago that humanity began to extend its presence into space — first with robots, then with animals and finally with humans.

(A) It is not surprising, therefore, to find that such possibilities have been discussed by every human civilization and culture, primitive or advanced, as far back as we have written records. Even before these thoughts were given a name, such extraterrestrial wonderings found their outlet through myths, cave paintings, fictional literature, music and poetry, then later through films and TV shows.

(B) However, considering the size of the universe and the growing number of promising sites on many worlds where life might quite like to snuggle up, the search has barely begun. When we finally find life on another world — and we will — it will be one of the most significant cultural events in human history, having a profound impact on the question of our origins.

(C) This tentative expansion of our species towards other worlds has been made possible by the development of technology, which has finally started to reach a level that can complement and support our imagination and desire for exploration.

*extraterrestrial: 외계의   **snuggle up: 바싹 파고들다
***tentative: 시험적인

① (A) – (C) – (B)   ② (B) – (A) – (C)
③ (B) – (C) – (A)   ④ (C) – (A) – (B)
⑤ (C) – (B) – (A)

09 초고난도

정답률 24%

글의 흐름으로 보아, 주어진 문장이 들어가기에 가장 적절한 곳은?

> Zebra finches use the right hemisphere to process information about the harmonics in individual syllables of songs to which the bird is listening, and the left hemisphere to process information about the whole song.

Lateralization of the brain in songbirds seems to be an essential part of their ability to recognize familiar songs sung by other birds and to produce their own songs. (①) Although the same set of song nuclei is present in both hemispheres of the songbird's brain, only the set of song nuclei in the left hemisphere controls singing. (②) This dominance of the left hemisphere for song control has been found in all species of songbirds studied so far, except the zebra finch. (③) In this species, the right hemisphere plays a greater role in the production of song, although the left hemisphere still has some role. (④) The song nuclei are used not only to produce song but also to perceive song, and this perception of song is different in the left and right hemispheres. (⑤) In other words, the right hemisphere attends to the details of a song, whereas the left hemisphere listens to the entire song and so is used to discriminate between familiar and unfamiliar songs.

*harmonics: 배음(倍音)
**lateralization: (대뇌의) 좌우의 기능 분화, 측면화
***nucleus: 핵(pl. nuclei)

10

정답률 52%

다음 글의 내용을 한 문장으로 요약하고자 한다. 빈칸 (A), (B)에 들어갈 말로 가장 적절한 것은?

Although the aim of a prophecy is to remove uncertainty about the future, uncertainty in the form of randomness is frequently the mechanism used to generate prophecies. The random way in which tea leaves and yarrow stalks fall illustrates this. It's as if the randomness serves as a doorway to the powers divulging the "information." Théphile Gautier had a nice way of describing it. He said, "Chance is perhaps the pseudonym of God when he didn't want to sign." The tea-leaves and yarrow-stalks examples also show that often a special type of knowledge is required to interpret the supernatural messages. Indeed, mystics, priests, prophets, and oracles maintain their positions in societies in part thanks to their unique intermediary role as the only people able to understand the messages passed down from above. When the German priests of Tacitus's time made choices by randomly choosing bark strips inscribed with runes, and the Jews made important decisions by drawing lots, the random procedures apparently gave an opportunity for the will of the superior being to manifest itself. The Bible says, "The lot is cast into the lap, but its every decision is from the Lord."

*yarrow: 서양톱풀   **divulge: (비밀 등을) 알려 주다
***pseudonym: 필명

⬇

Possessing the special knowledge to interpret ___(A)___ messages in random events enabled a few chosen individuals to ___(B)___ their position in society.

(A)	(B)
① manipulated	...... hold
② manipulated	...... reject
③ ancient	...... change
④ divine	...... hold
⑤ divine	...... change

[11-12] 다음 글을 읽고, 물음에 답하시오.

Schadenfreude, the experience of pleasure in the pain of other people, is distinctly related to envy, as several studies have demonstrated. When we envy someone, we are (a)prone to feel excitement, even joy, if they experience a setback or suffer in some way. But it would be wise to practice instead the opposite, what the philosopher Friedrich Nietzsche called *Mitfreude* — "joying with." As he wrote, "The serpent that stings us means to hurt us and rejoices as it does so; the lowest animal can imagine the pain of others. But to imagine the joy of others and to rejoice at it is the highest privilege of the highest animals."

This means that instead of merely congratulating people on their good fortune, something easy to do and easily forgotten, you must instead actively try to feel their joy, as a form of empathy. This can be somewhat (b)natural, as our first tendency is to feel a pang of envy, but we can train ourselves to imagine how it must feel to others to experience their happiness or satisfaction. This not only (c)cleans our brain of ugly envy but also creates an unusual form of rapport. If we are the targets of *Mitfreude*, we feel the other person's genuine excitement at our good fortune, instead of just hearing words, and it (d)induces us to feel the same for them. Because it is such a rare occurrence, it contains great power to bond people. And in (e)internalizing other people's joy, we increase our own capacity to feel this emotion in relation to our own experiences.

*serpent: (특히 크고 독이 있는) 뱀 **pang: 고통

---

11 정답률 67%

윗글의 제목으로 가장 적절한 것은?

① Can Empathy Truly Be Taught?
② Is Envy a Source of Inspiration or Conflict?
③ Feel Joy at the Joy of Others, Not at Their Pain
④ Sharing Emotions: A Difference Between Animals and Humans
⑤ Competition, Not Cooperation, as a Basis for Human Relationships

12 정답률 43%

밑줄 친 (a)~(e) 중에서 문맥상 낱말의 쓰임이 적절하지 않은 것은?

① (a)   ② (b)   ③ (c)   ④ (d)   ⑤ (e)

01

정답률 38%

밑줄 친 to be safe than sure가 다음 글에서 의미하는 바로 가장 적절한 것은?

What if pain is intense and no meaningful damage occurred? Is that pain truthful? This paradox of the veracity of pain's role, *damage is about to occur*, is just what stinging insects exploit. When a person steps on a bee, the sting it delivers to the sole elicits pain, and lifting the foot is a response that benefits the bee. Has meaningful physical damage to the person been done by this sting? Often, the answer is no. Stinging insects are masters at exploiting this weakness to their benefit in the honesty of the pain signal. To stinging insects, we might simply be fools who fall for the trick. To us, it is better to be safe than sure; thus, we believe the signal is true. If the damage were real, the downside cost could far outweigh any benefit obtained by ignoring the pain. Why take a risk? In life's risk-benefit equation, the risk often dwarfs any potential benefit. Herein lies the psychology of pain. Unless the animal or human can know that a rainbow of benefit is awaiting on the far side of the pain, natural psychology dictates not to chase the rainbow.

*veracity: 진실성 **elicit: 유발하다

① to doubt the honesty of the pain signal
② to assume that pain will lead to damage
③ not to blindly accept the truthfulness of pain
④ to maximize the benefit by ignoring the pain
⑤ not to fall for insects' trick of exploiting pain

02

정답률 50%

다음 글의 제목으로 가장 적절한 것은?

Research repeatedly shows that dissenters have "hidden" influence. In general, they change attitudes in private more than in public. They change minds — even if those in the majority don't realize it or choose not to acknowledge the influence. We see this pattern in many of our studies using mock jury deliberations. If the dissenter doesn't compromise, agreement is rarely reached. The majority will not budge. They just get irritated. However, the repeated pattern is a change in attitudes, even just ten minutes later and despite no movement during the deliberation. Participants often don't acknowledge this change directly, but if the researcher changes the phrasing of the question, their response reflects the change in their attitudes. The researcher can ask a million "what-if" questions, such as, "What if the plaintiff asked for double the amount of money?" This gives the majority cover: they can change their minds without acknowledging having been persuaded by the dissenter.

*dissenter: 반대자, 불찬성자 **budge: 의견을 바꾸다
***plaintiff: 원고

① The Impact of Dissent: More Than It Seems
② Hidden Assumptions Concerning Majority Rule
③ When Dissent Is Useless: The Stubborn Majority
④ Only Conflicts When There Are Many Dissenters
⑤ Compromise as an Effective Problem-Solving Tool

03 초고난도 · 정답률 22%

다음 글의 밑줄 친 부분 중, 어법상 틀린 것은?

Perhaps more than any other species, humans simply love one another a surprising amount of the time. They love enough to give others their time and energy and even their lives. It is common to see people using their resources, and whatever other influence they gain from their rank, ① to help those who are not kin and who could not possibly help them personally. Scientists now offer an explanation for this type of selfless love. They have shown that very often groups survive better if they have ② mostly altruistic members. In the old days altruistic behavior — behavior ③ that helped everyone survive — meant sharing your meat. Today group survival is about teamwork on the job and family loyalty at home. Altruism can be passed down genetically or culturally as moral values, but ④ whatever it happens, it helps survival. Groups ⑤ made up entirely of freeloaders and obsessive rankers are less likely to make it to the next generation.

04 · 정답률 43%

(A), (B), (C)의 각 네모 안에서 문맥에 맞는 낱말로 가장 적절한 것은?

Chronic stress affects how the brain processes threats. A person's fear response involves multiple parts of the brain, including the amygdala, which helps (A) detect / overlook noticeable threats in the environment and generate feelings of fear and anxiety, and the prefrontal cortex and other areas, which modulate a person's reaction to bring it in line with reality. When a person is in a state of emotional regulation, these responses are (B) balanced / unbalanced . But prolonged stress increases the activity of the amygdala, facilitating the growth of neurons in this region while diminishing the strength of the prefrontal cortex. This throws off one's ability to regulate emotions. While fear has a role in policing (it's reasonable to feel terrified if one is first on the scene of a shooting by a criminal), a chronically stressed police officer may be (C) faster / slower to feel and respond to fear. Because heightened activity in the amygdala and a weaker response from the prefrontal cortex are also associated with aggression, the officer could also be more prone to violence.

*amygdala: (뇌의) 편도체 **prefrontal cortex: 전두엽 피질
***area: (특수한 기능을 갖춘) 뇌피질부(腦皮質部)

	(A)		(B)		(C)
①	detect	……	balanced	……	faster
②	detect	……	unbalanced	……	faster
③	detect	……	balanced	……	slower
④	overlook	……	unbalanced	……	faster
⑤	overlook	……	unbalanced	……	slower

[05-06] 다음 빈칸에 들어갈 말로 가장 적절한 것을 고르시오.

05

정답률 31%

It is through language that all organizations form and teach their dominant ideas, values, and norms. Ideas are made from the words within the language learned. The emphases in the language create the emphases in the ideas. Thus, in a capitalist society we are likely to use certain words over and over: *competition, free enterprise, profit, individual effort, private property*, and *marketplace*. Around these words will grow a set of ideas that are reinforced over and over. We may have ideas concerning socialism, but such ideas are reinforced less — unless, of course, they are used negatively in relation to our commitment to capitalism. Political leaders know that the use of words is an important way to influence people's thinking: Words are carefully chosen in order to gain support. "War on terrorism," "evil societies," and "preemptive war" are all phrases used by leaders to help us "understand" and support the policies toward those we wish to battle. "Death taxes," "secularists," "fascists," "liberal professors," and "evolutionists" are phrases used to _____ .

* preemptive: 선제의 ** secularist: 세속주의자
*** fascist: 파시즘 신봉자

① show how important it is for politicians to make policies based on facts

② encourage political leaders to work for the common good of the society

③ demonstrate that compromise is always the key to productivity in politics

④ influence us to swallow simple explanations about highly complex issues

⑤ criticize the society for its unjust and unequal distribution of opportunities

06 초고난도

정답률 16%

The division between large cities and rural areas is central to the cultural and political conflicts that are reshaping democracies around the world. While economic factors are important here (major metropolises have become engines of growth, while small towns and rural territories struggle), there is an arguably more important split in how recognition is distributed. All too often, communities that are distant from metropolitan centers have been treated as having nothing of interest to say. Their knowledge and culture have not been valued by major media outlets, universities, or expert institutions, but rather they've been passive recipients of handouts and information. Ecological emergency and the dawn of the Anthropocene potentially changes this: those who live and work with nature, rather than accumulating facts and theories about nature from afar, have know-how that could become increasingly valuable as nature becomes more politically problematic. In parallel to "citizen science," _____ will be both necessary and politically beneficial.

* Anthropocene: 인류세(인류로 인한 지구온난화 및 생태계 침범을 특징으로 하는 현재의 지질학적 시기)

① exposing the vast majority of urban citizens to rural culture

② blurring or erasing the line between large cities and rural areas

③ encouraging more people to leave cities and live in the countryside

④ figuring out how cities are using technology to solve their problems

⑤ harnessing the nonexpert knowledge scattered across rural populations

07

정답률 58%

다음 글에서 전체 흐름과 관계 <u>없는</u> 문장은?

As the world becomes increasingly connected, the importance of anthropology also increases. For example, in recent times, anthropologists have been able to make important contributions to helping people suffering from epidemics, natural disasters, and conflict. ① They do this in multiple ways, including using their cultural knowledge to help those suffering as well as educating those seeking to provide aid. ② This is especially important, for example, in areas where Indigenous peoples may mistrust or not understand modern medicines and health facilities, and where the people may have a general mistrust of governments or foreigners. ③ Anthropologists can work in educating or serving as mediators between those providing and those receiving aid. ④ They know that a comprehensive understanding of both human biology and human culture includes knowledge of the evolution of primates and the behavior of nonhuman primates. ⑤ Anthropologists can mitigate potential misunderstandings, and they also recognize, through the holistic perspective, that even emergency aid can have profound effects on other aspects of a culture.

*mitigate: 완화시키다 **holistic: 전체론적인

08

정답률 35%

주어진 글 다음에 이어질 글의 순서로 가장 적절한 것은?

When the topic turns to the unconscious mind, differences between Freudian and Darwinian thought persist; and some of the difference revolves around the function of pain.

(A) Freud cited this remark as evidence of the Freudian tendency "to ward off from memory that which is unpleasant." This tendency was for Freud a broad and general one, found among the mentally healthy and ill alike, and central to the dynamics of the unconscious mind.

(B) But there is one problem with this supposed generality: sometimes painful memories are the very hardest to forget. Indeed, Freud acknowledged, only a few sentences after citing Darwin's golden rule, that people had mentioned this to him, stressing in particular the painfully persistent recollection of grievances or humiliations.

(C) Recall Darwin's "golden rule": to immediately write down any observation that seemed inconsistent with his theories — "for I had found by experience that such facts and thoughts were far more apt to escape from the memory than favourable ones."

① (A) – (C) – (B)　　② (B) – (A) – (C)
③ (B) – (C) – (A)　　④ (C) – (A) – (B)
⑤ (C) – (B) – (A)

09 초고난도   정답률 29%

글의 흐름으로 보아, 주어진 문장이 들어가기에 가장 적절한 곳은?

> This may be less clear today, since contemporary society is characterized by the fragmentation of older taste cultures and the proliferation of new ones.

Musical judgments are never made in complete isolation. The formation of "taste cultures" has always been socially defined. Participation in certain genres of music was historically determined by a person's social position, not by a purely independent aesthetic choice. (①) Indeed, from a sociological perspective, taste is always a social category rather than an aesthetic one; it refers to the way we use cultural judgments as social "currency," to mark our social positions. (②) In this context, cultural transactions take place with increasing rapidity — hence the heating up of the cultural economy and its rapid turnover of new products. (③) Not only are taste cultures themselves shifting, but people now tend to move between them with greater ease. (④) These factors contribute to a sense of the relativity of any single position. (⑤) Contemporary musical choices are plural as never before, and the effect of that plurality is inevitably to confirm that, in matters of musical judgment, the individual can be the only authority.

*proliferation: 확산

10   정답률 47%

다음 글의 내용을 한 문장으로 요약하고자 한다. 빈칸 (A), (B)에 들어갈 말로 가장 적절한 것은?

Berkeley researcher Mary Main developed an interview called the "Adult Attachment Interview." In this interview, Main scored how people told the story of their childhoods, and whether or not these childhoods were painful and traumatic. She was less interested in the content of the stories than in how the stories were told. People who were able to tell coherent stories about their traumatic childhood were observed to be very different kinds of parents than people who had the same amount of childhood trauma but were somehow not done with it. They were anxious, preoccupied, dismissing, or simply incoherent in their account of these childhood events. When studying the babies of these two types of parents, Mary Main discovered an amazing effect. The people who were somehow done with the trauma, who could tell a coherent story about it, who were not disorganized and flooded with emotion while telling the story, had infants who were securely attached. On the other hand, the people who were not done with the trauma, who could not tell a coherent story about it, who were disorganized and flooded with emotion while telling the story, had infants who were insecurely attached.

⬇

> Mary Main found out that whether or not parents ___(A)___ childhood trauma had an effect on the level of ___(B)___ infants felt in their attachment to their parents.

	(A)		(B)
①	experienced	······	security
②	experienced	······	maturity
③	forgot	······	responsibility
④	overcame	······	responsibility
⑤	overcame	······	security

[11~12] 다음 글을 읽고, 물음에 답하시오.

Humans are usually stuck in a bad pattern that would take an enormous amount of effort to change. Organizations have the (a)same problem. I know a company with a long history that was struggling. Although it was agreed that the problems were temporary and the market would eventually correct itself, in the short term, the company was facing disaster. An influential executive was positive the answer was layoffs. He was articulate and compelling about the need to use them. Anything less (b)lacked courage and business acumen. The slash and burn option began to emerge as synonymous with visionary and bold.

However, another executive was troubled by this view and asked human resources to trace how the company had handled (c)adverse conditions in the past. They went back to records of the Depression and found that, during that whole period, the company had not laid off a single worker. They had reduced salaries, cut hours of work, and lowered benefits but no one had lost their job. When this was presented, several managers who had been silent until then spoke. The Depression story reminded them of who they were as a company, that they had a long tradition of working with their employees through adversity. By (d)connecting with their own history and tradition, they were able to break out of the pattern of assuming layoffs were the only option. However, they would not have been able to do so unless a dissenter had pointed out that they were in a bad pattern. Sometimes (e)disagreement is the major problem in an organization.

*business acumen: 뛰어난 사업 감각
**slash and burn: 마구 해를 입히는

11

정답률 76%

윗글의 제목으로 가장 적절한 것은?

① A Hot Issue in Business: Hiring and Firing
② Break Out of a Bad Pattern for Problem-Solving
③ Employee Empowerment as a Form of Leadership
④ A Driving Force in Organizations: Mutual Consent
⑤ Develop Quick Decision-Making Skills for Success

12

정답률 44%

밑줄 친 (a)~(e) 중에서 문맥상 낱말의 쓰임이 적절하지 않은 것은?

① (a)   ② (b)   ③ (c)   ④ (d)   ⑤ (e)

01

정답률 38%

밑줄 친 the "slippery slope" argument가 다음 글에서
의미하는 바로 가장 적절한 것은?

One of the things I would most like to do
is eliminate the "slippery slope" argument
from neuroethical discussions. This has been a
centerpiece of many arguments in the council's
various reports. By arguing extremes, to which
the slippery slope will take us, ethicists play on
the public's fears and suggest that if we give
scientists an inch, they'll take a mile. The truth is,
most of these arguments are the stuff of science
fiction. Take the "humanzee" example — the
fear that scientists would cross a human with a
chimpanzee using modern genetic manipulations.
You present the humanzee as a possibility, and
suddenly everyone's afraid of letting scientists
grow human stem cells in mice — research that
might lead to cures for Parkinson's, Alzheimer's,
and other diseases. Yet the 'humanzee' is an odd
and dated strawman to invoke, and it is difficult
to find any well-regarded commentator — from
the academic sphere or otherwise — proposing
that neuroscientific developments should work
towards anything remotely comparable to this
example.

*strawman: 하찮은 논의[인물]

① the fallacy that is based on an appeal to
emotion
② a set of unknown truths that are soon to be
revealed
③ an educational theory rejected by contemporary
scientists
④ a controversial but irrefutable opinion
supported by the majority
⑤ an overstated claim that something will have
undesirable consequences

02

정답률 57%

다음 글의 주제로 가장 적절한 것은?

The way we interact in the world can be divided
between two views of reality, one a view of the
mind we call mindsight, the other a view into the
physical nature of the world of objects. Modern
life often depends more on physical sight rather
than on honoring the mental inner view. This lack
of focus on the inner subjective world is a concern
because not seeing the mind can lead to people
treating others without respect or compassion.
Since the experiences we have shape who we are,
at home with family or friends, at school with
teachers and peers, and in our interactions with
the larger social world of culture and society,
how we attend to those experiences can promote
mindsight or discourage it. So if most of these
experiences are externally focused, harnessing
only our physical-object perceptual system, then
we won't be developing our skills to see and
shape the personal world of our inner and our
interpersonal life.

*mindsight: 정신에 대한 주의집중

① roles of our social experiences in forming our
inner world
② reasons for not matching one's self-image to
social norms
③ dangers of not focusing on our subjective
mental experiences
④ respect and compassion as the products of
social interactions
⑤ frustration caused by the gap between the inner
and outer world

03

정답률 49%

다음 글의 밑줄 친 부분 중, 어법상 틀린 것은?

For brains, everything is noise at first. Then brains notice the patterns in the static, and they move up a level, ① noticing patterns in how those patterns interact. Then they move up another level, and on and on it goes. Layers of pattern recognition built on top of simpler layers ② become a rough understanding of what to expect from the world around us, and their interactions become our sense of cause and effect. The roundness of a ball, the hard edge of a table, the soft elbow of a stuffed animal, each object excites certain neural pathways and not others, and each exposure strengthens their connections until the brain comes to expect those elements of the world and becomes better at making sense of ③ themselves in context. Likewise, as causes ④ regularly lead to effects, our innate pattern recognition takes notice and forms expectations — Mom will come when I cry at night; mashed potatoes will make me happy; bees hurt when they sting. We start our lives filled with unpredictable chaos, but our regular perceptions become the expectations we use ⑤ to turn that chaos into predictable order.

04

정답률 39%

다음 글의 밑줄 친 부분 중, 문맥상 낱말의 쓰임이 적절하지 않은 것은?

In the 1960s, philosopher Hubert Dreyfus argued that "computers need bodies in order to be intelligent." This position has a corollary; whatever intelligence machines may ① achieve, it will never be the kind that people have because no body given to a machine will be a human body. Therefore, the machine's intelligence, no matter how interesting, will be ② alien. Neuroscientist Antonio Damasio takes up this argument from a different research tradition. For Damasio, all thinking and all emotion is embodied. The absence of emotion ③ reduces the scope of rationality because we literally think with our feelings. Damasio insists that there is no mind/body dualism, no ④ split between thought and feeling. When we have to make a decision, brain processes that are shaped by our body guide our reasoning by remembering our pleasures and pains. This can be ⑤ rejected as an argument for why robots will never have humanlike intelligence: they have neither bodily feelings nor feelings of emotion.

*corollary: 당연한 귀결

[05-06] 다음 빈칸에 들어갈 말로 가장 적절한 것을 고르시오.

05 초고난도   정답률 29%

A major concern expressed by many critics of genetic patenting is that patents covering elements of life forms may give individuals, companies, or governments greatly expanded powers over human individuals and human societies. For instance, if a farmer wants access to the best crops and in fact needs the best crops simply to compete with his neighbors and remain a viable farmer, and those crops are all covered by patents owned by companies, has he become economically weaker than during the days when crops were covered by far fewer legal restrictions? Some critics suggest the situation of many relatively poor and weak people such as farmers in a technologically advanced and patent-dominated area is similar to that of serfs in the medieval world. They rely utterly on the lordly authorities to be allowed to subsist on their humble plot. Rather than giving them more useful tools, the patent-controlled innovations _____. Patents, to these critics, can drive people such as farmers to subordination to companies that will allow them just enough profit within the system to survive, but not enough to flourish.

*viable: 독자 생존 가능한 **serf: 농노
***subsist on: ~으로 연명하다

① motivate them to make drastic changes to their environment
② provide a fundamental solution to a particular problem
③ limit their concerns to virtual spaces, not real-life ones
④ strip away almost all of their ability to be independent
⑤ tolerate harsh conditions that are hard to survive

06 초고난도   정답률 26%

When we offer a commentary upon a poem, which has been constructed as an object rather than by an arrangement of words with meanings or referents, we produce a form of interpretation because we are translating what is implicit in the poem into the explicitness of commentary. Such commentary is usually tied to the particular interests and vocabularies of a time and place. In order to transcend the tendency of each most recent and fashionable discipline to convert the poem to its terms and purposes, literary criticism needs a hypothesis of its own, which _____.
This does not mean that literature is unrelated to other systems of symbolism. It can enter into any kind of relationship to them, but literature as a system remains a hypothetical creation of criticism. Northrop Frye's explanatory analogy is mathematics, a self-enclosed system that enters into relationships with other systems, always on its own terms.

*transcend: 넘어서다, 초월하다

① presumably would lead to an autonomous critical language
② inevitably should be proved by a close analysis of the work
③ eventually could influence the contemporary interpretation
④ necessarily should be suggested with historical authority
⑤ frequently would depend on other critics' commentaries

[07-08] 주어진 글 다음에 이어질 글의 순서로 가장 적절한 것을 고르시오.

07

정답률 48%

Eligibility for some policy programs is determined by whether a measurable characteristic of a person is above or below a specific cut-off point.

(A) Suppose, though, that instead of comparing the health of everyone above $20,000 with the health of everyone below $20,000, we compare the outcomes for those who were just *barely* eligible to those who just *barely* missed being eligible for the program. This is an attractive strategy because while households well above and below $20,000 differ from each other, households earning $20,001 are likely to be similar to those earning $19,999.

(B) For example, the government might make public health insurance available only to households whose annual incomes are below $20,000. An observational study that compared health outcomes of those who received the public health insurance to those who did not would likely be biased because the two groups differ in many ways.

(C) This approach is called regression-discontinuity analysis. The fundamental assumption that must be met for this approach to replicate an experiment is that the characteristics of those who just barely missed eligibility are the same on average as those who just barely made it.

*eligibility: 자격
**regression-discontinuity: 회귀−불연속

① (A) – (C) – (B)　　② (B) – (A) – (C)
③ (B) – (C) – (A)　　④ (C) – (A) – (B)
⑤ (C) – (B) – (A)

08

정답률 41%

If a target population of a survey covers a wide geographical area, then a simple random sample may have selected respondents in quite different parts of the country. If the method employed to collect the data is of the face-to-face interview type, then clearly a great deal of travelling could be involved.

(A) It is important that the random final sample chosen from each area is the same proportion of the population or bias towards certain areas could result. As it is, bias is likely to occur as a result of similarity of responses from people within the same area, but this is the price you pay for reduced travelling time.

(B) To overcome this problem, the area to be surveyed is divided into smaller areas and a number of these smaller areas randomly selected. If desired, the smaller areas chosen could themselves be divided into smaller districts and a random number of these selected.

(C) This procedure is continued until the area is small enough for a simple random sample (or a stratified sample) to be selected. The final sample should consist of respondents concentrated into a small number of areas.

*stratified sample: 층화 표본(모집단을 가장 잘 대표하는 표본)

① (A) – (C) – (B)　　② (B) – (A) – (C)
③ (B) – (C) – (A)　　④ (C) – (A) – (B)
⑤ (C) – (B) – (A)

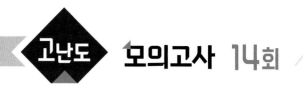

09 초고난도   정답률 20%

글의 흐름으로 보아, 주어진 문장이 들어가기에 가장 적절한 곳은?

> If, on the other hand, you happen to casually see a newspaper lying on a table as you pass by, you might see that it is covered with words, but you won't necessarily notice the words themselves.

When you focus conscious attention on reading these sentences, the unconscious parts that are gating visual inflows allow your conscious intent to override their narrowing of the sensory gates. They no longer act to gate inputs as they normally do. (①) In consequence the words on this page begin to stand out as individual identities. (②) At an unconscious level you have gated them out. (③) Similarly, if you casually opened a book and glanced at a page, though you might "see" the words, you would not necessarily be actively attentive to them as individuals or to the meanings inside them. (④) The incoming visual messages — in this instance, the meanings in the words and sentences — are "gated" because the unconscious parts of you have determined they are not, at that moment in time, important enough to pay attention to. (⑤) This keeps you oriented to the surface of the visual world.

10   정답률 46%

다음 글의 내용을 한 문장으로 요약하고자 한다. 빈칸 (A), (B)에 들어갈 말로 가장 적절한 것은?

Consider windmills. In the U.S. they have been estimated to kill at least 45,000 birds and bats each year. That sounds like a lot of birds and bats. To place that number in perspective, consider that pet cats that are allowed to wander in and out of their owners' houses have been measured to kill an average of more than 300 birds per year per cat. If the U.S. population of outdoor cats is estimated at about 100 million, then cats can be calculated to kill at least 30 billion birds per year in the U.S., compared to the mere 45,000 birds and bats killed per year by windmills. That windmill toll is equivalent to the work of just 150 cats. One could thus argue that, if we are seriously concerned about U.S. birds and bats, we should focus our attention on cats, rather than on windmills. In further defense of windmills over cats, please reflect that cats don't repay us for the damage they do to our birds by providing us with energy, unpolluted air, and relief from global warming, while windmills do provide all of those things.

⬇

> Compared to pet cats, windmills have a ___(A)___ of impact on birds and bats that is far less ___(B)___.

	(A)		(B)
①	variety	......	measurable
②	variety	......	sustainable
③	duration	......	significant
④	level	......	significant
⑤	level	......	sustainable

[11~12] 다음 글을 읽고, 물음에 답하시오.

What images come to mind when you think of the US Thanksgiving holiday? While Pilgrims, Native Americans, the Macy's Thanksgiving Day Parade, and American football likely figure prominently, turkey with all the trimmings springs to mind for many. The ample meal is based on the US Thanksgiving story. According to tradition, the winter of 1621 was (a) devastating for the Pilgrims of Plymouth Colony. Had it not been for the Native Americans, who shared their food, hunting methods, and knowledge of local foods and growing techniques, the Pilgrims would have perished. After a successful fall harvest, the Pilgrims (b) celebrated with their Native American friends by sharing a feast and giving thanks to God. This story, however, is more myth than reality, as historians, social scientists, and food scholars explain. More accurately, the Thanksgiving tradition was invented to promote American national solidarity following the Civil War.

According to Siskind, participating in the Thanksgiving ritual "transforms a collection of immigrants into Americans by connecting them to a cultural history stretching back to the 'founding' of the country." This founding story, in which Pilgrims and Native Americans supposedly shared their (c) abundant harvest in a feast, is largely invented; that is, the tradition is based on a culturally constructed and idealized version of the first Thanksgiving. Invented traditions like these (d) defeat at least three important purposes. First, they symbolize social cohesion and create a strong collective identity. Second, invented traditions establish new social institutions and legitimize existing ones. Finally, invented traditions socialize individuals into the shared norms and values of the group practicing them. Thanksgiving is an important invented tradition grounding the present in an invented past, symbolizing national unity, and (e) reaffirming a distinct national identity based on the institution of the family.

11

정답률 46%

윗글의 제목으로 가장 적절한 것은?

① What Americans Mainly Do on Thanksgiving Day
② The Many Variations of the Thanksgiving Tradition
③ The Meaning of Thanksgiving for Native Americans
④ The Reasons for Increasingly Simplified Thanksgiving Rituals
⑤ Thanksgiving Holiday: An Invented Tradition for National Identity

12

정답률 62%

밑줄 친 (a)~(e) 중에서 문맥상 낱말의 쓰임이 적절하지 않은 것은?

① (a)   ② (b)   ③ (c)   ④ (d)   ⑤ (e)

01 초고난도

정답률 28%

밑줄 친 not want the lid to be lifted가 다음 글에서 의미하는 바로 가장 적절한 것은?

We do not like being told what to do. We want to enjoy our lives, and we want to enjoy them with a good conscience. People who disturb that equilibrium make us uncomfortable, so moralists are often uninvited guests at the feast, and we have a multitude of defenses against them. Analogously, some individuals can insulate themselves from a poor physical environment, for a time. They may profit by creating one. The owner can live upwind of his chemical factory, and the logger may know that the trees will not give out until after he is dead. Similarly, individuals can insulate themselves from a poor moral environment, or profit from it. Just as some trees flourish by depriving others of nutrients or light, so some people flourish by depriving others of their due. The Western white male may flourish because of the inferior economic or social status of people who are not Western, or white, or male. Insofar as we are like that, we will <u>not want the lid to be lifted</u>.

*equilibrium: 평형 (상태)

① avoid having our moral shortcomings revealed
② reflect on ourselves rather than blame others
③ hate the feeling that we are being patronized
④ criticize acts that undermine social balance
⑤ find reasons to justify our lack of action

02

정답률 49%

다음 글의 제목으로 가장 적절한 것은?

Imagine taking a certain road home every day after work for many years until one day the road that takes you home collapses, and that route is no longer available for you to take. If you live in an area where many roads have been built over time, the collapse of one road will not prevent you from reaching your destination, because you can take an alternative route to reach your home. But if that is the only way that exists to your home, or the only way you know, then you have a problem. In the same way, if one pathway in the brain has decayed and is no longer available for accessing memories or information, a multilingual has other pathways that have been built over time as a result of the links between words, memories, and experiences accumulated in the other languages or across two or more languages.

① The Power of Multilingualism in Diversifying Cognitive Pathways
② The Advantage of Many Roads: Insurance Against Congestion
③ Skills Needed to Bridge the Gap Between Languages in Use
④ The Collapse of a Familiar Route: A Commuting Challenge
⑤ The Multilingual Brain: Too Many Ways to Communicate

03

정답률 54%

다음 글의 밑줄 친 부분 중, 어법상 틀린 것은?

Despite the richness and depth of his explanations throughout his writings, especially in the book *The Feeling of What Happens*, Damasio struggles in his attempts ① to explain how consciousness occurs and the central role that feeling plays in that occurrence. That struggle is attributable, to a large extent, to the fact that we do not have language available to conceptualize the specificities of this phenomenon, and perhaps we may never have it, given the shortcomings of language to express ② what is above and beyond language. Not everything in our experience, after all, can be represented accurately by language, something music educators, and educators in the other arts, ③ knowing full well. We certainly experience feeling and consciousness, just as we certainly experience music. Putting those experiences into the representations language is capable of mediating can be very frustrating and unsatisfying ④ because of the disparities between language and felt, aware experience. Nevertheless, several insights ⑤ that Damasio offers from his brain studies clarify how music works and how we might be more effective in teaching it.

*disparity: 차이

04

정답률 39%

다음 글의 밑줄 친 부분 중, 문맥상 낱말의 쓰임이 적절하지 않은 것은?

Hitting baseballs or playing musical instruments requires intricate control of muscles carrying out complex tasks in a series of steps. Yet they occur automatically in experienced players, outside of ① awareness. These tasks require a part of the mind that we cannot be fully aware of, but one that still exerts critical influence on thoughts and actions. Creativity also appears to ② originate with unconscious mental processes; solutions to difficult problems may appear to "pop out of nowhere" after an incubation period in the unconscious. Intuitive feelings or hunches are apparently based on the unconscious sensing something without common ③ reasoning. Acting without good reason might seem like a dubious life strategy; however, we encounter many fuzzy situations where choices must be made with very ④ limited information. If our source of intuition is actually an experienced unconscious, following hunches seems to constitute a strategy far ⑤ inferior to random choices.

*incubation period: 잠복기

[05-06] 다음 빈칸에 들어갈 말로 가장 적절한 것을 고르시오.

05 초고난도   정답률 29%

One reason that people sometimes favor relativism — even simple relativism — over objective theories of truth is the sense that relativism encourages greater tolerance. The thought that there is Truth out there with a capital "T" often goes together, relativists have pointed out, with the conviction that some people have privileged access to the truth and others don't. Just this sentiment was the hallmark of nineteenth-century Western colonialism, when missionaries worked with the armies and police of colonial governments to force people to believe, or at least say they believed, what the colonialists wanted them to. But if there is no such thing as objective truth, then no one occupies a privileged position on the truth. We can no longer justify forcing people to believe in our gods by saying that we know the truth and they don't. _____ the idea of objective truth seems to encourage a more tolerant outlook on life.

① Testing   ② Welcoming
③ Developing   ④ Abandoning
⑤ Remembering

06 초고난도   정답률 24%

Suppose that we can identify a human group homogeneous enough to count as a biological subpopulation of the human race. Invariably, the variation among persons within the group _____. Take the much-debated IQ difference between blacks and whites in the United States. The *average* performance of African-Americans may fall below that of Americans of European ancestry; even so, the range in IQ scores within each subpopulation is so wide that millions of whites will be intellectually inferior to millions of blacks. To offer an extreme case, the mean difference did not prevent the emergence in the 1930s of a nine-year-old girl of purely African ancestry with an IQ of 200. That was better than more than 99% of the white children of her generation. And she achieved this score notwithstanding the intimidating handicaps that black Americans had to face when she was growing up.

*homogeneous: 동질적인

① rarely reflects the gender composition of the members of that population
② increasingly diminishes as education extends its influence over the entire group
③ turns out to have something to do with social factors rather than biological ones
④ amply exceeds the differences between that population and other human populations
⑤ is remarkably small compared to the variations between different biological subpopulations

07

주어진 글 다음에 이어질 글의 순서로 가장 적절한 것은?

Ironically, science both appeals to the data of the senses and simultaneously rejects them as being unreliable. In the first place, sense data are measured.

(A) However, we have shown that knowledge of measurables is as inextricably bound to the senses as is seeing color. In fact, the measurable qualities are based on what are, in a way, the most personally directed of the senses.

(B) Only sense experience amenable to measurement is therefore incorporated into science. That which is not measurable, that which is in essence qualitative, is taken to be mere subjective sensation. Measurable qualities are endowed with an objective reality presumed to be independent of the senses.

(C) They are the ones that tell us about our own bodies. Based on what we know of the world through our senses, we can see that choosing to limit science only to those experiences that are measurable is a wholly arbitrary choice within the framework of the nature of sense experience.

*inextricably: 불가분하게 **amenable to: ~할 수 있는

① (A) – (C) – (B)   ② (B) – (A) – (C)
③ (B) – (C) – (A)   ④ (C) – (A) – (B)
⑤ (C) – (B) – (A)

[08~09] 글의 흐름으로 보아, 주어진 문장이 들어가기에 가장 적절한 곳을 고르시오.

08

For example, much research in the Status Characteristics Theory tradition finds that group members base status allocation on characteristics like gender, race, social class, and physical attractiveness, assuming that these characteristics are associated with general competence, even when they are not.

High-status group members' duties and responsibilities can be social in nature; for example, they are often expected to inspire their group, keep the peace among its members, and facilitate communication between individuals. However, in most group settings they also must understand the technical problems faced by the group. (①) Having task competent people in charge helps groups perform better. (②) Therefore, many groups prioritize task competence over other factors like social skills when allocating influence. (③) On a team of engineers, for example, technical ability would likely be seen as more important than the ability to communicate. (④) However, groups often fail to base their status hierarchies on differences in task competence. (⑤) Similarly, individuals higher in self-confidence are also more likely to be selected as leaders, though self-confidence is not highly predictive of actual abilities.

09

정답률 43%

To appreciate this point, suppose that in a congested city, Mary can expect to commute at a speed of just 15 miles per hour.

Achieving higher speeds in cities would facilitate climate change adaptation because people will have a greater choice of neighborhoods. If Mary is willing to commute for thirty minutes one way and she can travel at 40 miles per hour, then she can look for a place to live in a 20-mile radius around her place of work. (①) The area of a circle with a radius of 20 miles equals 3.14×400, or more than 1,200 square miles! (②) Such a huge area provides ample opportunities for Mary to find the neighborhood that matches her desires. (③) With a thirty-minute commute, she will be able to look for housing only in a 7.5-mile radius of her place of work, and this circle's area equals 3.14×7.5×7.5=176 square miles. (④) This is a much smaller area in which to search. (⑤) By having a larger set of residential opportunities, each household will have a greater chance of finding a climate-resilient area.

*congested: 혼잡한 **radius: 반경, 반지름
***ample: 충분한

10

정답률 52%

다음 글의 내용을 한 문장으로 요약하고자 한다. 빈칸 (A), (B)에 들어갈 말로 가장 적절한 것은?

Historians prefer the past tense, but verb tense is often the subject of some confusion. This is largely because scholars who write about literature have a different set of conventions. A literary critic might write "In *Black Boy*, Richard Wright speaks eloquently and forcefully against American racism and capitalism." Wright's words ring just as true today as they did in 1937 when he wrote them. For the purposes of writing about literature, the present tense conveys that the author's idea is still valid today. Literary classics have a powerful effect on readers today, but historians want to place Wright's novel within the context of his life and times. Wright does not really speak today — he died in 1960. He wrote *Black Boy* during the Great Depression. At the time, readers interpreted Wright's work differently than they do today. Using the present tense confuses the chronology of Wright's life and times, while using the past tense enables writers to arrange one event in relationship to another.

⬇

While literary critics prefer the present tense because it gives an author's idea a sense of _____(A)_____, historians prefer the past tense because it puts emphasis on the _____(B)_____ of events.

	(A)		(B)
①	control	......	importance
②	immediacy	......	sequence
③	immediacy	......	importance
④	accomplishment	......	origin
⑤	accomplishment	......	sequence

[11~12] 다음 글을 읽고, 물음에 답하시오.

A good deal of empirical evidence supports the view that emotions, whether positive or negative, tend to be socially shared, and that the social sharing of emotions results in a strong emotional impact on the exposed person. An emotional experience (a)provokes a person to talk about it with others, as those affected attempt to understand and learn more about their experience. The more intense the personal emotions, the more likely it is that we will share them with others. Talking about an event is a form of rehearsal that may (b)aid memory because talking or translating an experience into language, seen as the social mechanism guiding memories, can help to organize and assimilate the event in people's minds. Language — as the primary symbol system that defines the framework for individuals' memories — is therefore "the (c)vehicle for important cognitive, and learning processes following an emotional upheaval." The more an event provokes an emotion, the more it elicits social sharing and distinctly vivid, precise, (d)concrete memories of the event. This type of memory, known as flashbulb memory, is seen as being qualitatively different from ordinary memories and as superior in terms of time because this type of memory is assumed to be clearer and (e)more affected by time than other memories. Being a result of a surprising and emotionally intense event, a flashbulb memory is likely to be long-lasting.

*upheaval: 격변

11

윗글의 제목으로 가장 적절한 것은?

① Past Experience Creates Our Personalities
② The Power of Language: How It Shapes Reality
③ Flashbulb Memory: Not a Precise Record of History
④ Socially Shared Emotion as an Activator of Memory
⑤ The Benefits of Emotion in Learning a New Language

12

밑줄 친 (a)~(e) 중에서 문맥상 낱말의 쓰임이 적절하지 <u>않은</u> 것은?

① (a) ② (b) ③ (c) ④ (d) ⑤ (e)

PART

REVIEW
모의고사

01

04회 10번 요약문

다음 글의 주제로 가장 적절한 것은?

Photographers, along with exhibit designers and museum curators, want to make viewers see things in a specific arrangement that they hope will push viewers to make certain comparisons along certain dimensions, generating particular moods. They understand that a single image is ambiguous and does not easily and unequivocally reveal "what it is about." When photographers make pictures for such other purposes as news and advertising, they usually compose them so as to exclude all "extraneous" detail, everything except the "point" of the news story or the product feature to which they want to call attention. They choose the details that surround that point carefully, to emphasize the story's main ideas or enhance the product's appeal. Pictures made for scientific purposes similarly restrict their content to what the maker (usually the author of the scientific article) wants users to know and rigorously exclude anything extraneous to that purpose.

*unequivocally: 모호하지 않게 **extraneous: 관련 없는

① the power of photography in advertising and graphic design
② the intentional arrangement of visual content in photography
③ the role of photographers in a news story or a product feature
④ the technical challenge of arranging photographs to form a story
⑤ the emotional effects of viewing pictures of natural environments

02

01회 01번 함축 의미

다음 글의 밑줄 친 부분 중, 어법상 틀린 것은?

We need caution. Human virtues are multileveled. That nature builds character is but half the truth and absurd if ① taken for the whole. That would omit all the civic virtues, without ② which we could not be human. Character is developed in a dialectic of nature and culture. "Man is by nature a political animal." Humans are animals who build ③ themselves a polis, a city, and love to socialize within it. "Man is the animal for whom it is natural to be artificial." *Homo sapiens* is "the natural alien." What humans "naturally" do when they encounter nature ④ is build a culture differentiating themselves from nature. Agriculture, business, and industry are their real vocation. Virtue has to be "cultivated," "cultured." ⑤ Live with wild nature in nostalgic simplicity and frugality, these "humanists" will say, is romantic nonsense that forgets how much the human genius lies in departure from and resourceful transformation of nature. The modern word for this is "Develop!"

*dialectic: 변증법

03

02회 07번 빈칸

다음 글의 밑줄 친 부분 중, 문맥상 낱말의 쓰임이 적절하지 않은 것은?

To value something is to believe that it is valuable and to care about it. If one does not care, one does not value. Unfortunately, the nature of care is almost as ① ambiguous as the notion of understanding. But at least one thing is clear: care cannot be defined apart from its relation to the emotions. One might go so far as to think of care as a mere disposition to emotion. I think that this is a ② mistake. Since caring gives rise to a variety of different emotions, actions, and thoughts, it cannot be reduced to a mere disposition to emote. All I am confident in affirming is that our emotions depend on what we care about. For example, we only ③ fear for that which we care about. In general, standard emotions essentially involve evaluations of the way something we care about stands to be or has been affected. But it is ④ incoherent to think that someone could care about something and not be prone to feel fear when it is threatened, or hope when it stands to flourish. Accordingly, it is ⑤ controversial to suggest that our cares are sometimes revealed to us by our emotional responses.

＊emote: 감정을 과장되게 드러내다

[04-06] 다음 빈칸에 들어갈 말로 가장 적절한 것을 고르시오.

04

03회 09번 문장 삽입

Richard Smith, director of the British Medical Journal for 13 years, says in his book that science cannot work well without methods to clarify what part of the work each contributor has done in each article. Smith proposes that journals should include a list of the co-authors with their biographies and what they have contributed to each study. This relationship should be developed and agreed upon by the authors of the paper themselves. But this idea does not convince the great world leaders in science, who are very comfortable with the system of contributions as it is the one that has provided them with that leadership. However, it discourages talented young people from engaging in it. The current scientist does not feel that _____. He or she produces scientific literature on which his or her name is written, but many times has not even written the article, or even a part of it. In fact, it is becoming increasingly common for powerful research groups to hire specialized writers — young doctors — to whom the scientists pass the data.

＊contribution: 기고(旗鼓), 기여

① the research is his own
② the payment is sufficient
③ the leaders work with them
④ the community values collaboration
⑤ the subject is related to their specialty

05

08회 10번 요약문

There is a kind of large thing that cannot be readily tested until it is fully built and tried. This is the civil engineering project — the dam, tunnel, building, bridge — whose scale is so large, whose cost is so great, and whose design is so specific to the site that the structure is unique. Because it is one of a kind, not made in a factory but constructed in place, there is no disposable example to test. Scale models may be employed for testing theories or comparing alternative designs, but no model will ever fully replicate conditions of the actual as-built structure. Even if incontrovertibly meaningful models were possible, it is not possible to model fully the natural forces of future earthquakes, wind storms, and the like to which the structure might be subjected. In short, the only way to test definitively a large civil engineering structure is to build it in anticipation of how nature will challenge it and then let nature take its course. This fact of large-scale engineering demands _____.

*incontrovertibly: 논쟁의 여지가 없이

① careful, proactive failure analyses
② sufficient space in storage facilities
③ real-world testing before actual use
④ pre-made models with safety features
⑤ collaborative, ongoing funding resources

06

14회 09번 문장 삽입

When you focus conscious attention on reading these sentences, the unconscious parts that are gating visual inflows allow your conscious intent to override their narrowing of the sensory gates. They no longer act to gate inputs as they normally do. In consequence the words on this page begin to stand out as individual identities. If, on the other hand, you happen to casually see a newspaper lying on a table as you pass by, you might see that it is covered with words, but you won't necessarily notice the words themselves. At an unconscious level you have gated them out. Similarly, if you casually opened a book and glanced at a page, though you might "see" the words, you would not necessarily be actively attentive to them as individuals or to the meanings inside them. The incoming visual messages — in this instance, the meanings in the words and sentences — are "gated" because the unconscious parts of you have determined they are not, at that moment in time, important enough to pay attention to. This _____.

① elevates your awareness of subconscious visual cues
② keeps you oriented to the surface of the visual world
③ distracts your conscious focus from surrounding details
④ triggers heightened emotional responses to visual stimuli
⑤ facilitates neural processing of visual inputs at multiple stages

07

05회 02번 주제

다음 글에서 전체 흐름과 관계 <u>없는</u> 문장은?

The increase in wealth and education in the eighteenth century was accompanied by an expansion of public interest in art, as reflected in the growth of the art market and the emergence of public exhibitions and museums. ① Public sales and auctions became an early venue for an art-hungry public, and dealers used new marketing strategies — shop windows, newspaper ads, and sales catalogues — to tempt the newly moneyed classes into the pleasures and social advantages of collecting. ② Engraving greatly extended the reach of high art, and the collecting of drawings became fashionable, but ownership of painting and sculpture required deep pockets. ③ In the West, however, by the mid-18th century the development of academies for painting and sculpture established a sense that highly functional works were "art." ④ Speaking on behalf of those without collections of their own, critics demanded greater public access to art, and from mid-century their calls were answered. ⑤ Academies sponsored regular exhibitions of their members' work, the best known being the so-called Salon in Paris (from 1737) and the Royal Academy exhibitions in London (from 1768).

*venue: 장소　**engraving: 판화

[08~09] 주어진 글 다음에 이어질 글의 순서로 가장 적절한 것을 고르시오.

08

11회 01번 함축 의미

More often than not, our discipline fades and our mind wanders when we're not on the job. We may yearn for the workday to be over so we can start spending our pay and having some fun, but most of us fritter away our leisure hours.

(A) But that's not what our deceiving minds want us to believe. Given the opportunity, we'll eagerly relieve ourselves of the rigors of labor. We'll sentence ourselves to idleness.

(B) Jobs, even crummy ones, are "actually easier to enjoy than free time," says Csikszentmihalyi, because they have the "built-in" goals and challenges that "encourage one to become involved in one's work, to concentrate and lose oneself in it."

(C) We avoid hard work and only rarely engage in challenging hobbies. Instead, we watch TV or go to the mall or log on to Facebook. We get lazy. And then we get bored and edgy. Disengaged from any outward focus, our attention turns inward, and we end up locked in what Emerson called the jail of self-consciousness.

*fritter away: ~을 조금씩 허비해 버리다
**crummy: 형편없는

① (A) – (C) – (B)　　② (B) – (A) – (C)
③ (B) – (C) – (A)　　④ (C) – (A) – (B)
⑤ (C) – (B) – (A)

09

09회 04번 어휘

Social lives are derived from human instincts. Human instincts include humanized instincts and dehumanized instincts. The humanized instincts are used originally involving humans. The dehumanized instincts are used originally involving nonhumans.

(A) Fighting among animals of the same species for the purpose of domination is often ritualistic and does not cause serious injury. Injuries to infant animals from animals of the same species are infrequent.

(B) On the other hand, as predators, animals kill prey of different species without hesitation. As prey, an animal makes a manipulative strategy to escape from a predator of a different species. Animals make a clear distinction between the animals of different species and animals of the same species.

(C) It is quite common among social animals to behave differently toward animals of the same species than toward animals of different species. For example, cannibalism and killing among animals of the same species are rare in social animals even during fighting among animals of the same species.

*cannibalism: 식인 풍습

① (A) – (C) – (B)   ② (B) – (A) – (C)
③ (B) – (C) – (A)   ④ (C) – (A) – (B)
⑤ (C) – (B) – (A)

[10~11] 글의 흐름으로 보아, 주어진 문장이 들어가기에 가장 적절한 곳을 고르시오.

10

08회 02번 주제

It was clear that something else was happening with this stump.

I once stumbled upon the remains of an ancient tree stump that was still alive. But how could the remains have clung on to life for so long? Living cells in the tree must have food in the form of sugar, they must breathe, and they must grow, at least a little. (①) But without leaves — and therefore without photosynthesis — that's impossible. (②) No being on our planet can maintain a centuries-long fast, not even the remains of a tree, and certainly not a stump that has had to survive on its own. (③) It must be getting assistance from neighboring trees, specifically from their roots. (④) Scientists investigating similar situations have discovered that assistance may either be delivered remotely by fungal networks around the root tips — which facilitate nutrient exchange between trees — or the roots themselves may be interconnected. (⑤) In the case of the stump I had stumbled upon, I couldn't find out what was going on, because I didn't want to injure the old stump by digging around it, but one thing was clear: the surrounding trees were pumping sugar to the stump to keep it alive.

*stump: 그루터기   **fungal: 균(菌)의

11

05회 04번 어휘

They often underestimate the resistance that it will generate, and they take few steps to build a base of support for their innovations.

Structural leaders develop a new model of the relationship of structure, strategy, and environment for their organizations. They focus on implementation. The right answer helps only if it can be implemented. These leaders emphasize rationality, analysis, logic, fact, and data. (①) They are likely to believe strongly in the importance of clear structure and well-developed management systems. (②) A good leader is someone who thinks clearly, makes good decisions, has good analytical skills, and can create structures and systems that get the job done. (③) Structural leaders sometimes fail because they miscalculate the difficulty of putting their designs in place. (④) In short, they are often undone by human resource, political, and symbolic considerations. (⑤) Structural leaders do continually experiment, evaluate, and adapt, but because they fail to consider the entire environment in which they are situated, they sometimes are ineffective.

12

11회 11~12번 장문

다음 글의 내용을 한 문장으로 요약하고자 한다. 빈칸 (A), (B)에 들어갈 말로 가장 적절한 것은?

Aboriginal foragers represent a domestic mode of production, where production decisions are made at the household level with minimal outside pressure. Aborigines did not use labor, technology, and resources to their maximum productive potential, choosing instead to maximize their leisure, sharing, and ceremonial activities above purely material concerns. The relative uniformity and durability of their forager system suggests that Aborigines had designed a sustainable no-growth culture, whether intentionally or not. Aborigines did not "invest" surplus production in either supporting larger populations or expanding economic production; instead they directed it into activities that helped individuals build their social and cultural capital in ways that also benefited society as a whole and contributed to the reproduction of the culture. Food sharing, ceremonial feasting, and leisure provided growth-reducing effects and helped Aborigines avoid the dilemma of endless cycles of population growth and subsistence intensification. When people shared food, there was little incentive to produce beyond their immediate needs.

⬇

Aboriginal foragers, while ___(A)___ a culture that did not emphasize growth, directed surplus production towards building social and cultural capital, ___(B)___ a mode of production where they produced more than they needed.

	(A)		(B)
①	imagining	······	avoiding
②	practicing	······	developing
③	practicing	······	avoiding
④	rejecting	······	developing
⑤	rejecting	······	questioning

01

10회 09번 문장 삽입

밑줄 친 a big, sharp sword가 다음 글에서 의미하는 바로 가장 적절한 것은?

Much like his immediate predecessors, Carl von Clausewitz distinguished between tactics, which he called the art of winning battles, and strategy, which he defined as the art of using battles to gain the objectives of the campaign. More fundamentally, though, war was a duel between two independent minds. Its interactive nature sharply differentiated it from other activities. To paraphrase, making swords (which only involved acting upon dead matter) was one thing. Using them against another swordsman who is capable of parrying one's own thrusts and replying with others of his own is quite another. In a brief but brilliant discussion of the theory of war, Clausewitz acknowledges that the system offered by each of his predecessors contained some elements of truth. Yet no system ought to be allowed to obscure the elemental fact that war consisted of fighting and that fighting — in other words, battle — determined the outcome of wars. No amount of fancy maneuvering could do any good unless it was backed up with a big, sharp sword.

*predecessor: 선배, 전임자 **duel: 결투
***parry: 받아넘기다 ****maneuver: 책략을 쓰다

① a vast and expansive control of territory
② a sophisticated and advanced storage facility
③ a cunning and strategic battlefield commander
④ a strong and effective military force or capability
⑤ a high and advantageous ground from which to attack

02

02회 09번 문장 삽입

다음 글의 주제로 가장 적절한 것은?

Despite disagreements on forager social organizations, the central demographic facts are not in dispute. The low density of wild food resources means that most contemporary foragers spend most of their time in very small groups, usually of two to eight closely related people. All, however, need to belong to much larger groups of at least five hundred people, because only these can provide a viable breeding population. It is unusual for so many foragers to assemble physically, but even the smallest groups do regularly assemble in larger bands or camps of perhaps fifty-plus people, and networks of these bands/camps create genetic pools of the required size. In fertile environments, people spend more of the year in these larger groups; in harsh environments, less of it. Only in really abundant environments, however, particularly those with rich marine resources, can foragers live permanently in groups of several dozens or sometimes hundreds strong. The old foraging villages of North America's Pacific Coast, from the Chumash of Southern California to the Tlingit of the Alaska panhandle, are the best-known cases.

*forager: (먹을 것의) 채집자
**panhandle: 좁고 길게 다른 주(州)로 뻗어 있는 지역

① the economic and social challenges faced by foragers in modern times
② the environmental factors that explain the evolution of foraging technique
③ the impact of environmental and demographic factors on forager societies
④ the social organization and demographic characteristics of forager societies
⑤ the difference between structures of ancient forager societies and modern ones

03

14회 10번 요약문

다음 글의 제목으로 가장 적절한 것은?

Consider windmills. In the U.S. they have been estimated to kill at least 45,000 birds and bats each year. That sounds like a lot of birds and bats. To place that number in perspective, consider that pet cats that are allowed to wander in and out of their owners' houses have been measured to kill an average of more than 300 birds per year per cat. If the U.S. population of outdoor cats is estimated at about 100 million, then cats can be calculated to kill at least 30 billion birds per year in the U.S., compared to the mere 45,000 birds and bats killed per year by windmills. That windmill toll is equivalent to the work of just 150 cats. One could thus argue that, if we are seriously concerned about U.S. birds and bats, we should focus our attention on cats, rather than on windmills. In further defense of windmills over cats, please reflect that cats don't repay us for the damage they do to our birds by providing us with energy, unpolluted air, and relief from global warming, while windmills do provide all of those things.

① Keeping Pet Cats and Birds: A Risky Situation
② Cats and Wind Turbines: A Bird's Two Greatest Fears
③ Birds and Bats: The Latest Victims of Powerful Windmills
④ Windmills: Worth More than Their Impact on Birds and Bats
⑤ Conservation: A Balancing Act Between Nature and Technology

04

02회 08번 순서 배열

다음 글의 밑줄 친 부분 중, 어법상 틀린 것은?

The most basic human instinct is the instinct for self-preservation. Criminal law recognizes this impulse and authorizes ① its use in the justice system via the doctrine of self-defense. When the individual who argues self-defense acts ② reasonably, he will have the benefit of a complete defense to a number of crimes. For the most part, self-defense will succeed only if a defendant has a reasonable belief that the use of force is necessary. Hence the critical question in cultural defense cases will be how to judge whether a person has such a "reasonable" belief. Another feature of self-defense is ③ that the strategy only wins provided the defendant can demonstrate that he exercised a necessary and proportional response. It is possible that the proportionality requirement would limit its utility for defendants in cultural defense cases. The reason for this is that the determination of what constitutes a proportionate response would depend upon the cultural background of the person ④ making the assessment. Presumably, the judge from the dominant culture would not view the act as a proportionate response, even if members of the defendant's cultural community agreed that it ⑤ did.

＊defendant: 피고(인)
＊＊proportionality: (법의) 비례의 원칙(과잉조치 금지의 원칙)

05

01회 06번 빈칸

다음 글의 밑줄 친 부분 중, 문맥상 낱말의 쓰임이 적절하지 않은 것은?

Sports texts have many forms, functions, and readerships. The traditional sports report is intended to bear witness to what has occurred for those who were not ①present. At the most basic, denotative level it is an ②uncontroversial statement that, for example, Crewe Alexandra drew 0-0 with Burnley in Division Three of the English Football League at the Gresty Road Ground in front of a crowd of 2,816 cold, wet spectators. Not much human ③intervention is needed here: a few units of data are "sent down the wire" or entered into a computer database, producing a text that has little more cultural resonance than the shipping or stock market reports. Except that, just as those anonymous units of information have much ④greater importance and depth of meaning for the seafarers and "desk jockeys" who depend on them for their livelihoods, the relevant sports fan will not only invest these facts with significance, but also expect more information. Thus it is ⑤likely that many followers of sport will be satisfied for long with a simple news digest format.

*denotative: 외연적인 **resonance: 반향(反響), 울림

[06-08] 다음 빈칸에 들어갈 말로 가장 적절한 것을 고르시오.

06

07회 09번 문장 삽입

In 1968, concerned officials in the state of Vermont attempted to protect the beautiful views of woodland and pasture along its highways, then being spoiled by the signs and unsightly billboards of restaurants and other businesses. State lawmakers had a simple solution — a law banning all billboards and signs over a certain size. In a sense, it worked, as the roads soon had fewer and smaller signs, and yet something else happened too — the spontaneous growth of weird and enormous sculptures. To draw attention to his business, one auto dealer erected a twelve-foot, sixteen-ton gorilla clutching a real Volkswagen Beetle. Not to be outdone, the owner of a carpet store built a huge ceramic teapot with steam and an enormous genie emerging from it, a roll of carpet under his arm. Because these structures weren't displaying messages of any kind, the law didn't apply. The legislature hadn't fully appreciated a notorious principle of the social world — the law of _____.

① deliberate actions
② legislative oversight
③ proportional response
④ regulatory compliance
⑤ unintended consequences

07

09회 03번 어법

Rephotography is when a photographer returns to a subject that had been previously photographed and attempts to make the same picture again to show how time has altered the original scene. Precise records are maintained so the returning photographer can more easily duplicate the original scene. The original photograph and the new one are usually displayed next to each other to make comparison easy. In another form of rephotography, the photographer returns to the same subject over a period of time. Examples of this would range from making a picture of yourself every day for a week to Alfred Stieglitz's photographs of Georgia O'Keeffe that span decades. The relationship of the photographer and the subject is pursued over a period of time. The results should _____ that can be produced from this combination due to changes in feeling, light, and mood.

① demonstrate the consistent visual stagnation
② represent the broad range of visual possibilities
③ highlight the subject's future qualities and perspectives
④ convey the static variations of technological information
⑤ pose a variety of questions about the unrelated environment

08

06회 03번 어법

A characteristic of decision making is related to the structure of the brain. *The brain cannot analyze a problem without preconceptions.* When someone is confronted with a problem or a question, a preconception is used immediately, sometimes based and dependent on how the question is worded or the information is presented. Thus, the reaction of a sick person to the doctor's prognosis that he has an 80 percent chance of recovering is different than his reaction to the news that he has a 20 percent chance of remaining sick for the rest of his life. The rational mind would recognize that an 80 percent chance of success is the same as a 20 percent chance of failure. A mind that acts only in an evolutionarily rational way will not recognize the equivalence. That recognition is not worth the effort needed to compare and analyze the facts in every case, and we therefore _____. The popular belief that we can examine a question without preconceptions is incorrect.

*prognosis: (의학) 예후, 예측

① prioritize objective analysis over subjective preconceptions
② overlook the effect of external factors on decision making
③ cling to concepts and attitudes already present in our brains
④ minimize the role of intuition in the decision-making process
⑤ acknowledge the limitations of purely rational decision making

[09-10] 주어진 글 다음에 이어질 글의 순서로 가장 적절한 것을 고르시오.

09

03회 04번 어휘

Politicians, especially those in the national spotlight, are often jokingly accused of being narcissists but, in all seriousness, their profession lends itself to this particularly destructive personality trait.

(A) All of this power can lead to an exaggerated sense of self-importance that can cause some individuals to believe that the world revolves around them. That's when their out-of-control behaviors become easier to rationalize.

(B) For example, in order to be a successful candidate, you have to be unnaturally optimistic even in the face of probable defeat and possess high levels of self-esteem despite the constant criticism that comes with the territory.

(C) Furthermore, you are constantly given sole credit for successes — even though those successes were achieved, in part, by the work of many aides and assistants. Finally, you constantly have people relying on you, believing in you, and holding you responsible as the sole representative of a cause.

*narcissist: 나르시시스트(자기 도취자)
**come with the territory: 일상적인 일이다

① (A) – (C) – (B)   ② (B) – (A) – (C)
③ (B) – (C) – (A)   ④ (C) – (A) – (B)
⑤ (C) – (B) – (A)

10

04회 08번 문장 삽입

Chimpanzees in some populations of eastern Africa fish for termites by probing termite mounds with small, thin sticks. Some other populations of chimpanzees in western Africa, however, simply destroy termite mounds with large sticks and attempt to scoop up the insects by the handful.

(A) The fact is that the termite mounds in western Africa are much softer, owing to larger amounts of rain, than those of eastern Africa. The strategy of destroying the mound with a large stick is thus available only to the western populations.

(B) Field researchers such as Boesch and McGrew have claimed that specific tool-use practices such as these are "culturally transmitted" among the individuals of the various communities. But there is a competing explanation that is also quite plausible.

(C) Under this hypothesis, then, there would be group differences of behavior superficially resembling human cultural differences, but with no type of social learning involved at all. In such cases, the "culture" is simply a result of individual learning driven by the different local ecologies of the different populations.

*termite: 흰개미 **scoop up: ~을 퍼내다
***plausible: 그럴듯한

① (A) – (C) – (B)   ② (B) – (A) – (C)
③ (B) – (C) – (A)   ④ (C) – (A) – (B)
⑤ (C) – (B) – (A)

[11~12] 글의 흐름으로 보아, 주어진 문장이 들어가기에 가장 적절한 곳을 고르시오.

11

02회 06번 빈칸

They did gain one important benefit from their social position.

In the seventeenth and eighteenth centuries, Ireland was a colony under England. This meant that England controlled all Irish resources. As in many other colonial situations — many of them British — England did not do the work of being a colonial power on its own. Middlemen were effective tools of colonization. Underneath the British but above Irish Catholics in Ireland were "the Dissenters." (①) These Irish non-Catholic Dissenters, "who were mostly Presbyterian farmers, mechanics, and small tradesmen," helped maintain the oppressive hierarchy imposed by Britain. (②) They saved the English labor and trouble, often receiving relatively little in return. (③) Like Irish Catholics, they themselves might live in terrible conditions, but as Protestants, they could at least consider themselves part of the dominant — the better — race. (④) In other words, in terms of their "race," all Protestants benefited from the British-imposed hierarchy. (⑤) No matter how poor they might be, Protestants gained a psychic power from being Protestant Irish, not Catholic.

*Dissenter: 비국교도 **Presbyterian: (기독교) 장로교의

12

06회 07번 빈칸

In projecting ourselves into the contemplated situation, we are above all interested in how it will affect our feelings, whether it will bring us pleasure or pain, joy or sorrow, satisfaction or disgust.

We often choose so rapidly that it is scarcely possible to distinguish all the elements involved in the act. (①) When we weigh the respective advantages of alternative objects or courses of action distant from us in time or space or both, we are more likely to become aware of all the factors that enter into a choice. (②) In the first place, we try to foresee the future, and in particular how each alternative act will affect us. (③) In this effort, we depend largely upon memory of past experiences in similar situations, because without knowledge of the past and faith in the uniformity of nature we would be at a loss to anticipate the future. (④) And of course, in this phase of our deliberation, too, we are guided by recollections of similar affections. (⑤) Thus the affective no less than the rational functions of the mind play important roles in each important choice we make.

01

12회 03번 어법

다음 글의 주제로 가장 적절한 것은?

Keep in mind that more innovation is not necessarily better. Some proponents of innovation have been carried away in their apparent zeal regarding innovation; they have recommended that all businesses strive for significant, continual doses of innovation, especially radical, game-changing innovation. This is simply not true. Every organization that intends to survive beyond the next two product life cycles needs healthy infusions of innovation and must invest to get them. This does not mean that an organization needs constant blockbuster or breakthrough innovations, though. It is hard to imagine an organization that could effectively harness a constant supply of breakthrough radical innovations, each of which would cause significant change in its business and technology base. That level of change might bedevil the competition, but it would also break the back of the innovating organization, considering the huge costs of developing such a flow of innovations, coupled with the huge tensions and destabilizations created in the organization by the constant, radical change.

① the differences between gradual innovations and radical ones
② the misconception of continuous radical innovation for success
③ the strategies for managing constant innovation in organizations
④ the financial and managerial benefits of constant radical innovation
⑤ the necessary resources to consistently implement radical innovations

02

08회 07번 순서 배열

다음 글의 밑줄 친 부분 중, 어법상 **틀린** 것은?

One of the most compelling pieces of evidence for humans' apparently automatic social nature comes from Fritz Heider and Marianne Simmel's famous 1944 animation of two triangles and a circle orbiting a rectangle. The animation depicts merely shapes, yet people find ①it nearly impossible not to interpret these objects as human actors and to construct a social drama around their movements. A closer look at the video, and a closer reading of Heider and Simmel's article describing the phenomenon, ②suggesting that the perception of these shapes in social terms is not automatic but must be evoked by features of the stimuli and situation. These shapes were designed to move in trajectories that specifically ③mimic social behavior. If the shapes' motion is altered or reversed, they fail to elicit the same degree of social responses. Furthermore, participants in the original studies of this animation were prompted to describe the shapes in social terms by the language and instructions ④that the experimenters used. Humans may be ready and willing to view the world through a social lens, but they don't do ⑤so automatically.

*trajectory: 궤적

03

08회 05번 빈칸

다음 글의 밑줄 친 부분 중, 문맥상 낱말의 쓰임이 적절하지 않은 것은?

Air transportation is particularly vulnerable to weather disruptions, such as during winter when a snowstorm can create cascading effects on air services. There is a ① seasonality for global wind patterns. Jet streams are also a major physical component that international air carriers must take into consideration. For an aircraft, the speed of wind can affect travel time and costs. Tailwind conditions can ② reduce scheduled flight time by up to an hour for intercontinental flights. For instance, due to strong jet stream conditions during winter months, transatlantic flights between the American East Coast and Europe can arrive 30 to 45 minutes ③ earlier than scheduled for eastbound flights. However, for westbound flights, unusually strong jet stream conditions will ④ shorten flight time and may on occasion force a flight to make an unscheduled refueling stop at intermediary airports such as Gander (Newfoundland) or Bangor (Maine). It is expected that climate change will ⑤ increase the strength of the North Atlantic jet stream and could lengthen westbound flights between North America and Europe.

[04-06] 다음 빈칸에 들어갈 말로 가장 적절한 것을 고르시오.

04

15회 07번 순서 배열

Ironically, science both appeals to the data of the senses and simultaneously rejects them as being unreliable. In the first place, sense data are measured. Only sense experience amenable to measurement is therefore incorporated into science. That which is not measurable, that which is in essence qualitative, is taken to be mere subjective sensation. Measurable qualities are endowed with an objective reality presumed to be independent of the senses. However, we have shown that knowledge of measurables is as inextricably bound to the senses as is seeing color. In fact, the measurable qualities are based on what are, in a way, the most personally directed of the senses. They are the ones that tell us about our own bodies. Based on what we know of the world through our senses, we can see that choosing to limit science only to those experiences that are measurable is a wholly _____ choice within the framework of the nature of sense experience.

*amenable to: ~할 수 있는 **inextricably: 불가분하게

① rational　　　　　② arbitrary
③ conscious　　　　④ purposeful
⑤ economical

05

11회 08번 순서 배열

A chorus of voices in moral philosophy has lately been raised in protest against ethical theorists' recurrent tendency to _____. Objections have been directed, for instance, against theorists whose love of simplicity and order blinds them to the rich diversity of the moral landscape. By these voices, we're reminded that theory isn't supposed to confine everything into a few favorite categories; proposals that prune and consolidate the explanatory concepts of ethics too radically will end up leaving out important phenomena or rendering them unrecognizable. Other objections have been raised against the arrogance that mere possession of a moral theory is sufficient for moral knowledge. However adequate a set of moral principles might be, after all, someone who doesn't notice what is salient in a situation won't know what to apply the principles to. Those who lack moral knowledge will stumble about blindly, like novice hikers outfitted with GPS who discover that they are in fact poorly if expensively equipped to find their way. However good your map, it can't keep you from getting lost if you don't know where you are.

*prune: 가지치기하다　**salient: 가장 중요한　***novice: 초보자

① ignore the importance of context
② justify contemporary moral theory
③ reflect the nuances of moral dilemmas
④ highlight the complexities of ethical issues
⑤ discredit the effect of individual perspectives

06

13회 01번 함축 의미

What if pain is intense and no meaningful damage occurred? Is that pain truthful? This paradox of the veracity of pain's role, *damage is about to occur*, is just what stinging insects exploit. When a person steps on a bee, the sting it delivers to the sole elicits pain, and lifting the foot is a response that benefits the bee. Has meaningful physical damage to the person been done by this sting? Often, the answer is no. Stinging insects are masters at exploiting this weakness to their benefit in the honesty of the pain signal. To stinging insects, we _____.
To us, it is better to be safe than sure; thus, we believe the signal is true. If the damage were real, the downside cost could far outweigh any benefit obtained by ignoring the pain. Why take a risk? In life's risk-benefit equation, the risk often dwarfs any potential benefit. Herein lies the psychology of pain. Unless the animal or human can know that a rainbow of benefit is awaiting on the far side of the pain, natural psychology dictates not to chase the rainbow.

*veracity: 진실성　**elicit: 유발하다

① might simply be fools who fall for the trick
② consider ourselves indifferent to their tactics
③ understand the complexities of pain perception
④ can be seen to paralyze their cunning strategies
⑤ are equipped with sensors to detect their threats

07

09회 06번 빈칸

다음 글에서 전체 흐름과 관계 <u>없는</u> 문장은?

The act of recognizing in a given situation a case of a familiar proverb can cast new light on the situation. It provides a fresh, abstract, and non-obvious viewpoint, going well beyond the situation's superficial details. ① Since proverbs are the labels of rather subtle and complicated categories, slapping a proverb onto a situation is a way of bringing out aspects that otherwise might remain hidden. ② The use of a proverb as a label is a way of making sense — albeit perhaps a biased type of sense — of what one is seeing. ③ Applying a proverb to a freshly encountered situation results in a kind of insight that comes from filtering what one sees through the lens of the proverb, rather than from a purely logical analysis. ④ The difference is that a proverb is a fixed expression, while a proverbial phrase permits alterations to fit the grammar of the context. ⑤ In summary, a proverb is a convenient, concise label for a vast set of highly different situations — past, present, future, hypothetical — that are all linked to each other by analogy.

*albeit: 비록 ~일지라도 **analogy: 비유

[08-09] 주어진 글 다음에 이어질 글의 순서로 가장 적절한 것을 고르시오.

08

01회 03번 어법

Nitrogen in its gaseous form is often used in situations in which it is important to keep other, more reactive atmospheric gases away.

(A) Nitrogen has recently also been used in blanketing fruit after it has been picked to protect it from rotting. Apples, for example, can be stored for up to 30 months if they are kept at low temperatures in an atmosphere of nitrogen.

(B) It serves industry as a blanketing gas, for example, in protecting materials such as electronic components during production or storage. To prevent the oxidation of wine, wine bottles are often filled with nitrogen after the cork is removed.

(C) In addition to these applications, nitrogen is used in oil production, in which it is pumped in compressed form underground to force oil to the surface. Ordinary air cannot be used for this purpose because some of the gases that make up air would react with the oil, producing undesired by-products.

① (A) – (C) – (B) ② (B) – (A) – (C)
③ (B) – (C) – (A) ④ (C) – (A) – (B)
⑤ (C) – (B) – (A)

09

13회 05번 빈칸

It is through language that all organizations form and teach their dominant ideas, values, and norms. Ideas are made from the words within the language learned. The emphases in the language create the emphases in the ideas.

(A) We may have ideas concerning socialism, but such ideas are reinforced less — unless, of course, they are used negatively in relation to our commitment to capitalism. Political leaders know that the use of words is an important way to influence people's thinking: Words are carefully chosen in order to gain support.

(B) Thus, in a capitalist society we are likely to use certain words over and over: *competition, free enterprise, profit, individual effort, private property,* and *marketplace.* Around these words will grow a set of ideas that are reinforced over and over.

(C) "War on terrorism," "evil societies," and "preemptive war" are all phrases used by leaders to help us "understand" and support the policies toward those we wish to battle. "Death taxes," "secularists," "fascists," "liberal professors," and "evolutionists" are phrases used to influence us to swallow simple explanations about highly complex issues.

*preemptive: 선제의 **secularist: 세속주의자
***fascist: 파시즘 신봉자

① (A) – (C) – (B)　　② (B) – (A) – (C)
③ (B) – (C) – (A)　　④ (C) – (A) – (B)
⑤ (C) – (B) – (A)

[10-11] 글의 흐름으로 보아, 주어진 문장이 들어가기에 가장 적절한 곳을 고르시오.

10

04회 07번 순서 배열

In contrast, Treasury bills are effectively risk-free: You know what interest rate you will earn when you buy them.

Top-down portfolio construction starts with asset allocation. For example, an individual who currently holds all of his money in a bank account would first decide what proportion of the overall portfolio ought to be moved into stocks, bonds, and so on. (①) In this way, the broad features of the portfolio are established. (②) For example, while the average annual return on the common stock of large firms since 1926 has been better than 11% per year, the average return on U.S. Treasury bills has been less than 4%. (③) On the other hand, stocks are far riskier, with annual returns that have ranged as low as –46% and as high as 55%. (④) Therefore, the decision to allocate your investments to the stock market or to the money market where Treasury bills are traded will have great consequences for both the risk and the return of your portfolio. (⑤) A top-down investor first makes this and other crucial asset allocation decisions.

*Treasury bill: 재무부 증권(재무부 발행의 단기 채권)
**portfolio: 포트폴리오(투자 자산 구성) ***bond: 채권

11

13회 10번 요약문

> The people who were somehow done with the trauma, who could tell a coherent story about it, who were not disorganized and flooded with emotion while telling the story, had infants who were securely attached.

Berkeley researcher Mary Main developed an interview called the "Adult Attachment Interview." In this interview, Main scored how people told the story of their childhoods, and whether or not these childhoods were painful and traumatic. (①) She was less interested in the content of the stories than in how the stories were told. (②) People who were able to tell coherent stories about their traumatic childhood were observed to be very different kinds of parents than people who had the same amount of childhood trauma but were somehow not done with it. (③) They were anxious, preoccupied, dismissing, or simply incoherent in their account of these childhood events. (④) When studying the babies of these two types of parents, Mary Main discovered an amazing effect. (⑤) On the other hand, the people who were not done with the trauma, who could not tell a coherent story about it, who were disorganized and flooded with emotion while telling the story, had infants who were insecurely attached.

12

05회 09번 문장 삽입

다음 글의 내용을 한 문장으로 요약하고자 한다. 빈칸 (A), (B)에 들어갈 말로 가장 적절한 것은?

The fact that the ability to count is not acquired until a child is three or four years old does not necessarily prove that the characteristic is not innate. In many observations, including Piaget's experiments, counting and arithmetic were acquired together with the ability to communicate and to use a given language, generally the mother tongue. It is not surprising that communicating in a given language is not an innate attribute but a learned one. The ability to learn a language is an inborn characteristic, but acquiring the language itself takes several years. Before the child learns a language, his arithmetic abilities do not come into play, as seen in various experiments. The obstacle is not the child's lack of ability to count but the fact that he has to answer questions that he does not comprehend, or he does not realize what the expected answer is, until he has had some more years of practice. It is easy to devise tests showing that understanding the question plays an important role in interpreting the results.

↓

The _____(A)_____ in counting ability is attributed not to a lack of innate capability, but rather to the child's need for language development to fully _____(B)_____ arithmetic tasks.

	(A)		(B)
①	delay	......	avoid
②	delay	......	comprehend
③	change	......	expect
④	difference	......	comprehend
⑤	difference	......	expect

01

📍14회 05번 빈칸

다음 글의 주제로 가장 적절한 것은?

A major concern expressed by many critics of genetic patenting is that patents covering elements of life forms may give individuals, companies, or governments greatly expanded powers over human individuals and human societies. For instance, if a farmer wants access to the best crops and in fact needs the best crops simply to compete with his neighbors and remain a viable farmer, and those crops are all covered by patents owned by companies, has he become economically weaker than during the days when crops were covered by far fewer legal restrictions? Some critics suggest the situation of many relatively poor and weak people such as farmers in a technologically advanced and patent-dominated area is similar to that of serfs in the medieval world. They rely utterly on the lordly authorities to be allowed to subsist on their humble plot. Rather than giving them more useful tools, the patent-controlled innovations strip away almost all of their ability to be independent. Patents, to these critics, can drive people such as farmers to subordination to companies that will allow them just enough profit within the system to survive, but not enough to flourish.

*viable: 독자 생존 가능한 **serf: 농노
***subsist on: ~으로 연명하다

① legal and policy measures in the area of genetic patenting
② genetic patenting that makes the poor and weak subordinated
③ strategies for farmers to navigate patent-controlled innovations
④ the effects of genetic patenting on social and economic strength
⑤ benefits of genetic patenting for small and medium-sized companies

02

📍14회 03번 어법

다음 글의 제목으로 가장 적절한 것은?

For brains, everything is noise at first. Then brains notice the patterns in the static, and they move up a level, noticing patterns in how those patterns interact. Then they move up another level, and on and on it goes. Layers of pattern recognition built on top of simpler layers become a rough understanding of what to expect from the world around us, and their interactions become our sense of cause and effect. The roundness of a ball, the hard edge of a table, the soft elbow of a stuffed animal, each object excites certain neural pathways and not others, and each exposure strengthens their connections until the brain comes to expect those elements of the world and becomes better at making sense of them in context. Likewise, as causes regularly lead to effects, our innate pattern recognition takes notice and forms expectations — Mom will come when I cry at night; mashed potatoes will make me happy; bees hurt when they sting. We start our lives filled with unpredictable chaos, but our regular perceptions become the expectations we use to turn that chaos into predictable order.

① Analyzing the Mechanisms of Brain Adaptation
② Exploring the Depths of Cognitive Interpretation
③ Taming the Wild: How Our Minds Find Patterns
④ From Chaos to Order: The Brain's Predictive Dance
⑤ Solving Problems: Decoding Regular Brain Patterns

03

12회 10번 요약문

다음 글의 밑줄 친 부분 중, 어법상 틀린 것은?

Although the aim of a prophecy is to remove uncertainty about the future, uncertainty in the form of randomness is frequently the mechanism used to generate prophecies. The random way ① in which tea leaves and yarrow stalks fall illustrates this. It's as if the randomness serves as a doorway to the powers ② divulging the "information." Théphile Gautier had a nice way of describing it. He said, "Chance is perhaps the pseudonym of God when he didn't want to sign." The tea-leaves and yarrow-stalks examples also show that often a special type of knowledge ③ is required to interpret the supernatural messages. Indeed, mystics, priests, prophets, and oracles maintain their positions in societies in part thanks to their unique intermediary role as the only people ④ able to understand the messages passed down from above. When the German priests of Tacitus's time made choices by randomly choosing bark strips inscribed with runes, and the Jews made important decisions by drawing lots, the random procedures apparently gave an opportunity for the will of the superior being to manifest ⑤ it. The Bible says, "The lot is cast into the lap, but its every decision is from the Lord."

*yarrow: 서양톱풀 **divulge: (비밀 등을) 알려 주다
***pseudonym: 필명

04

02회 10번 요약문

다음 글의 밑줄 친 부분 중, 문맥상 낱말의 쓰임이 적절하지 않은 것은?

Films often construct idealized representations of places, weaving compelling narratives that can distort our true understanding of these places. These cinematic representations tend to ① amplify the extraordinary aspects of these destinations, fostering a one-dimensional view that doesn't reflect the nuanced and multifaceted reality of the real world. As a result, audiences may unknowingly develop ② overly optimistic or pessimistic impressions by accepting these representations as authentic reflections of the places in question. This can result in people arriving at these destinations with inflated or unjustified expectations, only to be confronted with the more ③ imperfect reality they encounter. Similarly, films often take creative ④ liberties to portray certain places as filled with danger, crime, or other unfavorable characteristics, causing people to have unwarranted concerns or fears about visiting these places. Consequently, while the cinematic lens is a compelling medium for storytelling, it can sometimes ⑤ clarify the line between fiction and reality, sowing the seeds of false impressions about places that persist long after the credits roll.

*unwarranted: 부당한

[05-07] 다음 빈칸에 들어갈 말로 가장 적절한 것을 고르시오.

05

15회 08번 문장 삽입

High-status group members' duties and responsibilities can be social in nature; for example, they are often expected to inspire their group, keep the peace among its members, and facilitate communication between individuals. However, in most group settings they also must understand the technical problems faced by the group. Having task competent people in charge helps groups perform better. Therefore, many groups prioritize task competence over other factors like social skills when _____. On a team of engineers, for example, technical ability would likely be seen as more important than the ability to communicate. However, groups often fail to base their status hierarchies on differences in task competence. For example, much research in the Status Characteristics Theory tradition finds that group members base status allocation on characteristics like gender, race, social class, and physical attractiveness, assuming that these characteristics are associated with general competence, even when they are not. Similarly, individuals higher in self-confidence are also more likely to be selected as leaders, though self-confidence is not highly predictive of actual abilities.

① ranking expertise
② evaluating aptitude
③ allocating influence
④ gauging proficiency
⑤ fostering collaboration

06

09회 02번 제목

One of the consequences of the oft-proclaimed crisis of the idea of progress is that the future becomes problematic and the present is rendered absolute. We find ourselves in a regime of historicity where the present is lord and master. This is the oppressive power of the current legislature, of the short term, consumerism, our generation, proximity, etc. This is the economy that privileges the financial sector, profits over investments, cost reductions over company cohesion. We practice an imperialism that is no longer related to space but to time, an imperialism of the present that colonizes everything. There is a colonization of the future that consists of living at its expense and an imperialism of the present that _____. Bertman calls it "the power of the now," the present that is not invested in any other dimension of time. This present replaces the long term with the short term, duration with immediacy, permanence with transience, memory with sensation, vision with impulse.

*proximity: 근접성

① blinds us from possibilities for positive change
② absorbs the future and feeds off it parasitically
③ regains the past and thereby changes the future
④ makes our future worthy, prosperous and successful
⑤ assimilates the past and flourishes from it symbiotically

07

13회 04번 어휘

Chronic stress affects how the brain processes threats. A person's fear response involves multiple parts of the brain, including the amygdala, which helps detect noticeable threats in the environment and generate feelings of fear and anxiety, and the prefrontal cortex and other areas, which modulate a person's reaction to bring it in line with reality. When a person is in a state of emotional regulation, these responses are balanced. But prolonged stress increases the activity of the amygdala, facilitating the growth of neurons in this region while diminishing the strength of the prefrontal cortex. This throws off one's ability to regulate emotions. While fear has a role in policing (it's reasonable to feel terrified if one is first on the scene of a shooting by a criminal), a chronically stressed police officer may be faster to feel and respond to fear. Because heightened activity in the amygdala and a weaker response from the prefrontal cortex are also associated with aggression, the officer _____.

*amygdala: (뇌의) 편도체 **prefrontal cortex: 전두엽 피질
***area: (특수한 기능을 갖춘) 뇌피질부(腦皮質部)

① would likely justify his actions later
② would likely resolve conflicts better
③ could also be more prone to violence
④ could exceed the scope of the permit
⑤ may exhibit heightened mutual empathy

08

02회 11~12번 장문

다음 글에서 전체 흐름과 관계 없는 문장은?

Sometimes, small things can create big problems, as is the case with the smallest of energy products: batteries. At the end of their life, batteries become an unfortunate combination of useless, worthless, and toxic. ① Batteries' complex chemical ingredients can be difficult to separate, and dumping them in landfills without any treatment can release toxic chemicals into the environment. ② Recycling batteries costs at least 10 times more than burying them in a landfill. ③ While there are some drawbacks, recycling batteries helps to prevent them from contaminating soil, water sources and harming wildlife with toxins such as lead, nickel and cadmium. ④ Owing to the toxic nature of battery waste, many governments have regulated their disposal at the consumer level to force recycling. ⑤ Despite the fact that California, for example, prohibits discarding batteries in household trash, Californians recycle less than 5 percent of the batteries they buy.

[09~10] 주어진 글 다음에 이어질 글의 순서로 가장 적절한 것을 고르시오.

09

07회 11~12번 장문

Most athletes have developed core mental skills to a sufficient degree that they can function well in day-to-day situations or even in low-level competitive events. But when confronted with more demanding, pressure-packed situations, they may fail.

(A) Indeed, some performance problems might stem from physical issues, such as poor training or biomechanics. However, in many cases inadequate mental skills could be the cause.

(B) A gymnast may spend extra time on an apparatus. A basketball player may spend extra time shooting free throws after practice. Distance runners may pound their bodies even harder, sometimes to the point of overtraining.

(C) This can be most frustrating to athletes — and their coaches — because they know they have the potential to perform well. Not recognizing that the performance problems are due to a lack of mental skills, coaches may encourage athletes to work even harder on their physical skills.

*apparatus: 기구, 기계

① (A) – (C) – (B) ② (B) – (A) – (C)
③ (B) – (C) – (A) ④ (C) – (A) – (B)
⑤ (C) – (B) – (A)

10

07회 02번 주제

Social similarities, which can be of a highly varied nature — community of race, language, religion, habits, scientific culture, etc. — act as a unifying force: "birds of a feather flock together" is truly a social law.

(A) It is this that calls forth the relations of friendship and politeness, philanthropic suggestions, and charitable works. Rather than showing the need to carry out a personal duty, it furnishes us the means to continue the moral impulse of others.

(B) In the formation of peoples, the community of race is the fundamental force, and it can be challenged, accidentally, only by other similarities, community of religion, or of general culture. The instinct of sympathy, which pushes a person into society, is intimately tied to likenesses.

(C) This evident fact is hardly open to further explanation; it is a primary, irreducible, and permanent fact. But the result of it is that solidarity based on likenesses presents itself to us as much more acceptable than one based on division of labor; for in place of the thought of obligation, it gives rise to thoughts of sympathy.

① (A) – (C) – (B) ② (B) – (A) – (C)
③ (B) – (C) – (A) ④ (C) – (A) – (B)
⑤ (C) – (B) – (A)

[11-12] 글의 흐름으로 보아, 주어진 문장이 들어가기에 가장 적절한 곳을 고르시오.

11

09회 05번 빈칸

This is why ignorance is highly correlated with belief in conspiracy theories.

Why do some people engage in conspiracy theory thinking while others do not? Various psychological theories have been offered, involving factors such as inflated self-confidence or low self-esteem. (①) A more popular consensus seems to be that conspiracy theories are a coping mechanism that some people use to deal with feelings of anxiety and loss of control in the face of large, upsetting events. (②) The human brain does not like random events, because we cannot learn from and therefore cannot plan for them. (③) When we feel helpless (due to lack of understanding, the scale of an event, its personal impact on us, or our social position), we may feel drawn to explanations that identify an enemy we can confront. (④) This is not a rational process, and researchers who have studied conspiracy theories note that those who tend to "go with their gut" are the most likely to engage in conspiracy-based thinking. (⑤) When we are less able to understand something on the basis of our analytical faculties, we may feel more threatened by it.

*conspiracy theory: 음모론

12

05회 10번 요약문

The only legitimate reason for collecting data on the background and experiences of students is for improving classroom instruction.

In student assessment, the quality of the data gathered and the conclusions and inferences drawn are influenced by the perceptions and values of the teacher involved in the inquiry. (①) Examining the cultural background of students requires some degree of objectivity. (②) An egocentric or ethnocentric perspective in data collection is counterproductive. (③) You must be able to examine the cultures of your students without making value judgments based on your own personal or cultural experiences. (④) Teachers who are convinced that their instruction is appropriate and should not change, although it does not serve some groups of students well, and who blame the students or their life conditions for instructional failures, probably would not benefit from collecting data on their students. (⑤) For these teachers, there is the probability that data collection will reinforce negative beliefs about their students.

01

09회 01번 함축 의미

다음 글의 제목으로 가장 적절한 것은?

Steven Johnson, in his 2005 book *Everything Bad Is Good for You*, contrasted the widespread, teeming neural activity seen in the brains of computer users with the much more muted activity evident in the brains of book readers. The comparison led him to suggest that computer use provides more intense mental stimulation than does book reading. The neural evidence could even, he wrote, lead a person to conclude that "reading books chronically understimulates the senses." But while Johnson's diagnosis is correct, his interpretation of the differing patterns of brain activity is misleading. It is the very fact that book reading "understimulates the senses" that makes the activity so intellectually rewarding. By allowing us to filter out distractions, to quiet the problem-solving functions of the frontal lobes, deep reading becomes a form of deep thinking. The mind of the experienced book reader is a calm mind, not a buzzing one. When it comes to the firing of our neurons, it's a mistake to assume that more is better.

*teeming: 풍부한 **frontal lobe: 전두엽

① The Neurological Benefits of Intense Mental Stimulation
② Rethinking Mental Engagement: The Value of Deep Thinking
③ E-Book vs Physical Book Reading: Different Emotional Effects
④ The Pitfalls of Overstimulation: A Closer Look at Brain Activity
⑤ The Intellectual Rewards of Understimulated Senses in Book Reading

02

06회 04번 어휘

다음 글의 밑줄 친 부분 중, 어법상 틀린 것은?

As Larry Cuban, former president of the American Educational Research Association, points out, schools have spent billions of dollars over the years on technologies that have, in fact, changed very little of ① how we think about an "education" in the developed world. More often than not, we strip the agency and freedoms that digital tools ② give to learners and creators outside of school when they bring those same tools into the building. The system of schooling that most of us are products of ③ being based on a series of structures and efficiencies that do not work well with the messier, less linear, more self-organized ways we can learn, create, and connect on the Internet. In fact, the system almost unwittingly marginalizes digital technologies in schools. We relegate them to labs or libraries, or if we place them in students' hands, they're ④ used only for discrete, narrow purposes like reading textbooks, creating documents, or taking assessments. Few would argue that in schools today, we see technology ⑤ primarily as an institutional teaching tool, not a personal learning tool.

*unwittingly: 부지불식간에
**relegate: (덜 중요한 위치로) 밀쳐 버리다

03

11회 05번 빈칸

다음 글의 밑줄 친 부분 중, 문맥상 낱말의 쓰임이 적절하지 <u>않은</u> 것은?

We mostly ignore our built landscapes because practically, we have no obvious stake or influence in their production. This ① aligns with our approach to other swaths of our daily experience and needs: for medical help, we go to doctors; to repair our car, we visit the auto mechanic. Most of us, implicitly or explicitly, have given up control over our built environments, having ② entrusted decision-making about them to experts: city council members, real estate developers, builders and contractors, product manufacturers, and designers. Most of us perceive ourselves as ③ helpful to make changes in the built environment. This very sense of powerlessness results in a ④ paradoxical situation: real estate developers configure new projects based on what they believe consumers want, which they assess mainly by examining what previous consumers have purchased. But when it comes to the built environment, consumers gravitate toward conventional designs without thinking very much about them. So developers ⑤ continue to build what they think people want. No one steps back to consider what might serve people better, what people could like, or what they actually might need.

*swath: 영역   **configure: 구성하다

[04-06] 다음 빈칸에 들어갈 말로 가장 적절한 것을 고르시오.

04

07회 04번 어휘

In one fMRI (functional magnetic resonance imaging) study, subjects were asked to classify stimuli on one of three dimensions (color, shape, or pattern). In terms of behavior, one finding was that subjects took longer to classify stimuli in switch trials compared to stay trials. In terms of the brain, frontoparietal regions were more responsive during switch than stay trials. In fact, consistent with the view that multitasking creates heightened neurocognitive demands, the strength of task representation in the control network was greater when subjects switched to a new task than when they stayed with the same task. This means that when we switch from one task to another, it requires more neural processing because we have to bring back to mind the new task's representation and then use it to allocate attention to information that is relevant to perform the new task. As a consequence, when we switch between tasks, we lose the benefits of _____ that come from staying focused on a single task.

*fMRI: 기능성 자기 공명 영상
**frontoparietal: 전두두정골(前頭頭頂骨)의

① regulation and stability
② clarity and transparency
③ flexibility and adaptability
④ automaticity and efficiency
⑤ consolidation and retention

05

07회 08번 순서 배열

Normative beliefs are generally viewed as resulting from social interaction. Indeed, much of the early research on normative social influence used real people in staged settings to convey information about the norm. For example, Sherif's studies on the autokinetic effect used groups of participants (usually three) whose judgments on a task were publicized to the other participants. Similarly, Asch used confederates to convey normative information in his studies of conformity, as did Latané and Darley in their studies of pluralistic ignorance. While this traditional method is still used (and widely cited as *the* approach to normative social influence), other procedures have been employed in which normative information is conveyed through nonsocial channels. That is, although _____ can clearly provide information about the social norms in a given context, social interaction is not required. Individuals use a variety of cues, social and nonsocial, to draw inferences about the behavior of others.

*autokinetic effect: 자동 운동 효과 **confederate: 공모자

① seeing other people act
② analyzing historical data
③ interpreting cultural symbols
④ observing social media trends
⑤ monitoring public announcements

06

02회 01번 함축 의미

They say that time and money are the biggest perceived obstacles to eating well. In most cases, neither is a true obstacle. Americans spend eight hours a day in front of a screen. On average, we each spend two hours a day on the Internet — something that didn't even exist 20 years ago! But can't we find the time to plan, shop, and cook for our families? True, it might cost a little more to buy fresh meat, fish, and produce than to eat processed junk and fast food. But it doesn't have to. In fact, studies have shown that _____. You don't have to buy grass-fed steak (although that's ideal). You can eat well for less. To put it in perspective, Europeans spend about 20 percent of their income on food, Americans only 9 percent. What we don't spend on the front end we pay for on the back end at the drugstore and the doctor's office.

① a balanced diet requires cooking skills that many people lack
② maintaining a healthy diet is costlier than common medicines
③ it's nice to prepare a dish with one or two specialty ingredients
④ eating real food is not more expensive than eating processed food
⑤ fresh ingredients have a better taste than their processed counterparts

07

07회 06번 빈칸

다음 글에서 전체 흐름과 관계 없는 문장은?

Western social science generally endorses the idea that social scientists as scientists should adopt the theoretical attitude — that is, scientific contemplation at a distance. As the creator of theory, the social scientist ought to be a disinterested observer of the sociopolitical world and, in that sense, disengaged from society. ① Social scientists should study the workings of society dispassionately and aim only at developing and testing theoretical explanations of the way the world is. ② In this way of thinking, the activity of theorizing social and political life as traditionally conceived lies outside the rest of the activity of social life. ③ Judgments about the way the sociopolitical world ought to be should be left to others to decide. ④ The social world thus modelled is a sociopolitical world: Individuals and classes spend a great deal of time and energy in competition and cooperation. ⑤ The enterprise of social science and the individual social scientist should be value free — that is, neutral with respect to decisions about how we should live or act as humans in society.

*endorse: 지지하다

[08-09] 주어진 글 다음에 이어질 글의 순서로 가장 적절한 것을 고르시오.

08

04회 06번 빈칸

With any luck, we will realize that making waste is not the problem we must solve. If a living species does not generate waste, it is most likely dead, or at least very ill.

(A) No member of an ecosystem needs fossil fuel or a connection to the grid to achieve output; nor is waste an outcome in natural systems. In nature, the waste of one process is always a nutrient, a material, or a source of energy for another. Everything stays in the nutrient stream.

(B) The problem we have, and that we must address, is that we waste the waste we create. Consider that the conversion of waste into nutrients both requires and generates energy. While we are always looking for sources of energy for commercial and home applications, ecosystems never need to be wired.

(C) Thus the solution not only to the environmental challenges of pollution but to the economic challenges of scarcity may be found in the application of models we can observe in a natural ecosystem. Perhaps we can turn dilemma into solution by broadening our perspective and abandoning the concept of waste.

*grid: 배전망

① (A) – (C) – (B)   ② (B) – (A) – (C)
③ (B) – (C) – (A)   ④ (C) – (A) – (B)
⑤ (C) – (B) – (A)

09

08회 06번 빈칸

It is relatively easy to understand secessionist civil wars in West Africa, where ethnic groups fight to carve out their own new states

(A) But our interviews with the followers suggest that they are making a rational bet: either everyone will get to benefit from a fairer sharing of the spoils or at least they themselves will get to benefit because their side will have gained power and will be directing the spoils their way.

(B) Many join the rebels simply to protect their own home villages. Rebels have a very local perspective. They aim to take over national governments in the capital because this is still the way to control the distribution of the spoils. Good governance as an ideology may mean national equity or just a new set of winners.

(C) It is more difficult to understand West Africa's rebels without a cause, who want to take over the national government without a defined ideological platform, as in a nation-wide coup. The rebels claim that their aim is to introduce cleaner, fairer government, but because their own leaders are so often demonstrably corrupt, such claims appear implausible.

*secessionist: 분리 독립을 지지하는 **spoils: 전리품
***coup: 쿠데타

① (A) – (C) – (B) ② (B) – (A) – (C)
③ (B) – (C) – (A) ④ (C) – (A) – (B)
⑤ (C) – (B) – (A)

[10-11] 글의 흐름으로 보아, 주어진 문장이 들어가기에 가장 적절한 곳을 고르시오.

10

07회 10번 요약문

Language allows people to imagine possible events that have never occurred.

One advantage of thinking verbally is that language liberates you from the here and now. By virtue of language and meaning, you can think about possible future events, about people who are far away, about promises made in the distant past. (①) A rat or insect essentially lives in the immediate present and can respond only on the basis of what it can see, hear, and taste. (②) This facility is powerfully helpful and liberating. (③) As just one example, animals that have no language cannot possibly understand that some of this year's harvest has to be saved for planting next year, and they might eat their seed corn when they got hungry. (④) They would feel better in the short run, but next year they would have nothing to plant and hence no crop at all. (⑤) It is hardly an accident that our species is the only one to cultivate the land and reap the harvest, even though a great many species eat plants.

11

A related technique searches in the opposite direction, and search engines are very helpful here.

Computer-based search tools are undoubtedly useful: *Current Contents* gives you a quick view of recently published work in journals of interest; the *Web of Science* (and similar tools) allows a rapid search for literature by authors, keywords, or tracking citations. How did we do it before the search engines were available? (①) I would start by scanning through the major journals that published the topic for, say, the past five years, copying any relevant papers. (②) To discover the older literature, I would then examine citations in these papers, inferring the important sources from the frequency and nature of the references to them. (③) The big advantage of this method is that it gives you the citation structure of the field and some feel for how things have developed. (④) Identify a key paper on the topic published, say, 20 years ago and then look at the papers published since then that cite this paper. (⑤) Sometimes, you pick up papers you would otherwise miss because they were published in unusual places or lacked obviously linked keywords or titles.

12

다음 글의 내용을 한 문장으로 요약하고자 한다. 빈칸 (A), (B)에 들어갈 말로 가장 적절한 것은?

While focusing on themselves, people become aware of internal information (anxious feelings and images), which they mistakenly take as good evidence for their worst fears. One of the most common fears is that people will see that you are anxious. People with social anxiety disorder look much less anxious than they feel, but they tend to believe that their feelings are a good indicator of how they look. Images also play a prominent role. When particularly anxious, people with social anxiety disorder report seeing themselves in their mind's eye as though from an observer's perspective. Unfortunately, what they see is not what the observer actually sees but instead is a visualization of their worst fears. So someone who is concerned about blushing may have turned a mild pink in reality, but in their mind's eye, will see themselves as beet red with large beads of sweat dripping from their forehead.

⬇

People with social anxiety disorder often ___(A)___ their internal sensations and images, leading them to ___(B)___ that others perceive them as more anxious than they actually appear.

	(A)		(B)
①	avoid	......	prove
②	avoid	......	doubt
③	overlook	......	believe
④	overestimate	......	doubt
⑤	overestimate	......	believe

부록

WORDS LIST

01
multileveled 다층적인
omit 제외하다, 빼먹다
civic 시민의
by nature 본래
polis 도시 국가
artificial 인위적인
alien 이방인
differentiate 구별하다
vocation 천직
nostalgic 향수를 불러일으키는
frugality 검소함
genius 비범한 재능
departure 이탈, 벗어남
resourceful 수완 좋은

02
critique 비평
subjective 주관적인
discard 버리다
refute 부인하다, 반박하다
investigation 연구, 조사
kin 친족
narrative 서술

03
nitrogen 질소
atmospheric 대기의
blanket 뒤덮다
component 부품, 요소
rot 부패하다, 썩다
application 활용, 이용, 적용
compress 압축하다
make up ~을 구성하다
by-product 부산물

04
distinction 구별, 구분
action 조치, 행동
orderly 질서 있는
evacuation 대피
improvisation 즉흥성
rescue 구조
develop 전개되다
entail 수반하다
ethical 윤리적인
provided 만일 ~이라면
apparent 명백한

contradiction 모순
state 진술하다
primary 주요한
specify 명시하다

05
devote (노력 등을) 쏟다[할애하다]
massive 막대한
coverage 보도, 방송
cease 중단되다, 중단시키다
a good deal of 많은 양의
highlight 강조하다
rescue worker 구조 대원
reassure 안심시키다
correlation 상호 관계, 연관성

06
bear witness to ~을 증언하다
uncontroversial 논란의 여지가 없는
spectator 관중
intervention 개입
anonymous 익명의
seafarer 선원, 뱃사람
desk jockey 사무직원
livelihood 생계
invest A with B A에게 B를 부여하다

07
incident 사건
reaction 반응
stimulus 자극
a spectrum of (정도가) 다양한 일련의
fearful 겁나는
home break-in 가택 침입
outward 외부를 향한
slam 쾅 닫다
pillow 베개
one-size-fits-all 일률적인
reflexive 반사적인

08
literature 문헌
track 추적하다
citation 인용, 인용구, 인용문
scan through ~을 대강 훑어보다
relevant 관련된, 적절한
infer 유추하다
frequency 빈도

reference 참조 문헌
lack (~이) 없다

09
mankind 인류
self-awareness 자기 인식
reflective 성찰하는, 깊이 생각하는
contemplate 깊이 생각하다

10
patrol 돌아다니다
odor 냄새
linger 남다, 계속되다
scent 냄새, 향기
have the luxury 호사를 누리다
unobstructed 가로막히지 않은
dense 울창한
frequency 주파수
trunk 나무줄기
perch (새가) 앉다

11-12
consciousness 의식
millisecond 밀리초(1000분의 1초)
awareness 인식
apparently 분명히
distribute 분산하다
pre-conscious 전의식의
emerge 생겨나다
exert 발휘하다, 행사하다
vice versa 역도 또한 마찬가지인
initiation 시작, 개시
occurrence 생기는 일
reflex 반사 작용
involved 복잡한
split-second 순간적인
adjustment 조절, 조정
opponent 상대편
beneficial 이로운
painfully 극도로
hand over ~을 건네주다

WORDS LIST

01
obstacle 장애물
produce 농산물
front end 초반
back end 말미, 말기

02
abstract 추상적인
property 특성
perception 인식, 지각
notion 개념
solidity 단단함
reflect 반사하다
specify 구체적으로 말하다, 명시하다
estimate 추산[추정]하다; 추산[추정]
biomechanical 생체 역학의

03
filament 필라멘트
degrade 훼손되다, 질을 저하시키다
impractical 비실용적인
turtle shell 거북이 등껍질
happen upon ~을 우연히 발견하다
carbonized bamboo 탄화 대나무
air-evacuated 공기를 뺀
outshine ~보다 더 밝게 빛나다
light bulb 전구
illumination 조명
predominant 지배적인

04
modulation 조정, 조절
nonverbal 비언어적인
mediate 조정하다, 중재하다
predominantly 대부분, 대개
hemisphere (뇌의) 반구
blend (뒤)섞이다
striking 놀라운, 눈에 띄는
finding (조사·연구 등의) 결과
input 정보, 투입
intestine 장(腸)
integrate 통합하다
represent 나타내다, 표현하다
regulation 조절, 규제
autonomic nervous system 자율
신경계
awareness 인식

05
randomness 무작위
boil ~ away ~을 증발시키다
raw 가공하지 않은
naked 무방비 상태의, 벌거벗은
layperson 비전문가(pl. laypeople)
fallacy 오류
reflect upon ~을 숙고하다

06
colony 식민지
middleman 중개인
underneath ~의 아래에
tradesman 소매상인
oppressive 억압적인
hierarchy 위계질서
impose 강요하다
dominant 지배적인
psychic 정신적인

07
ambiguous 모호한, 애매한
disposition 성향, 기질
give rise to ~을 낳다
affirm 단언하다
stand to ~할 것 같다
incoherent 일관성이 없는
prone to ~하는 경향이 있는
flourish 번성하다
uncontroversial 논란의 여지가 없는

08
self-preservation 자기 보존
authorize 허가하다
justice 사법, 정의
doctrine 원칙, 교리, 주의
self-defense 정당방위
exercise 행사하다
proportionate response 비례적 대응
assessment 판단, 평가

09
abundant 풍요로운
marine 해양의
permanently 영구적으로
strong (인원이) ~명에 달하는
demographic 인구 통계의

viable 독자적으로 생존 가능한
breeding population 번식 집단
assemble 모이다

10
idealized 이상화된
representation 묘사, 표현
weave 엮다
compelling 흥미를 돋우는, 설득력 있는
narrative 이야기
distort 왜곡하다
amplify 증폭시키다
foster 조장하다
nuanced 미묘한
multifaceted 다면적인
reflection (거울 등에 비친) 모습[상]
inflated 부풀려진
unjustified 정당하지 않은
blur 모호하게 만들다
credits (보통 복수로) 크레디트(영화 등에서
제작에 참여한 사람과 배우의 이름을 언급하는
부분)

11~12
worthless 가치 없는
toxic 독성이 있는
ingredient 성분
dump 버리다
landfill 매립지
disposal 처리
discard 버리다, 폐기하다
convince 설득하다
dispose of ~을 처리하다
install 설치하다
demonstrate 증명하다

WORDS LIST

01
compared to ~와 비교하여
take to ~에 대한 능력을 발전시키다
shed 벗어 버리다
leap into ~로 뛰어들다
sudden 갑작스러운
expressiveness 풍부한 표현력
inarticulate 알아들을 수 없는
overhear 우연히 듣다

02
debate 토론
mainly 주로
border 국경
import 수입품
competitiveness 경쟁력
eventual 궁극적인
incentive 장려책, 인센티브
constant 지속적인
pressure 압박

03
implication 영향, 의미, 함축
conventional agriculture 관행 농업(화학 비료와 유기 합성 농약을 사용하여 작물을 재배하는 기존의 농업 형태)
erode 무너뜨리다, 침식하다
emerging 새롭게 부상하는, 새로 떠오르는
trading preference 무역 편애(국제 간 상품 수출입에 있어 특정 국가의 상품을 선호하는 것)
run counter to ~에 역행하다, ~을 거스르다
subsidy 보조금

04
spotlight 주목
be accused of ~이라는 이유로 비난받다
in all seriousness 진정[진심]으로
lend oneself to ~에 기여하다, ~에 도움이 되다
in the face of ~에도 불구하고
self-esteem 자존감
aide 보좌관
exaggerated 과장된
self-importance 자만(심), 자존, 거만
revolve 돌다, 회전하다
out-of-control 통제 불능의
rationalize 합리화하다

05
showcase (사람의 재능·사물의 장점 등을 알리는) 공개 행사, 진열장
provision 제공, 공급
constructive 건설적인
emphasis 강조(점), 주안점
foster 조장[조성]하다

06
impulse 충동
civilized 문명화된
halt 중지시키다
subject ~ to ... ~을 …에 맡기다
deliberate 숙고하다
put off ~을 연기하다
striking 두드러진, 현저한
sophistication 교양, 세련
worldly-wise 세상 물정에 밝은
polish 광택
craft 기술, 기교

07
betrayal 배신
spouse 배우자
dispassionately 냉정하게
compromise 타협하다
effectively 사실상, 효과적으로
socialize 사회화하다
address 호칭
matchmaker 중매인

08
portion 부분
correlation 상관관계
evaluation 평가
superiority 우월감, 우월성
time and time again 몇 번이고 계속해서
competence 역량

09
contribution 기고, 기여
clarify 명확하게 설명하다
co-author 공동 저자
biography 전기
engage in ~에 참여하다
specialized 전문화된

10
warfare 전쟁, 전투
indigenous people 토착 민족
ritualize 의식화하다
casualty 사상자
inherent 본질적인
filter into ~에 스며들다
slaughter 살육
contend 주장하다
wage (전쟁 등을) 수행하다, 벌이다
with no regard for ~을 배려하지 않고
constraint 제약

11~12
ethics 윤리(학)
insight 통찰력
sensibility 감성
universal 보편적인 것
prestige 위신
contemporary 현대의
humanities 인문학
legitimate 정당한
nourishment 양분, 영양
aesthetic 미적인
investigator 연구자
typically 일반적으로
symmetry 대칭
proportion 비율
presentation 표현
anthropologist 인류학자
ethnoart 민족 미술
dimension 차원
isolated 고립된

WORDS LIST

01
adaptability 적응력
upside down 거꾸로
handle 견디다, 대처하다
paperback 종이 표지의, 페이퍼백의
hardcover 단단한 표지의, 하드커버의
encyclopedia 백과사전
collapse 무너지다
bend 구부러지다
sensitive 민감한
determine 결정하다

02
internal 내적인
disorder 장애
indicator 지표
prominent 두드러진
blush 얼굴이 붉어지다
beads of sweat 땀방울

03
occupied 바쁜
lengthy 지루한
distract 분산시키다
divert 주의를 다른 곳으로 돌리다
extraordinarily 엄청나게
imminent 임박한
stroll 순회공연하다
acrobat 곡예사
distraction 오락거리
space ~에 일정한 간격으로 두다

04
assume (태도를) 취하다
shrug (어깨를) 으쓱하기
generosity 관대함
dismiss 일축하다, 묵살하다
empirical 실증적인
burden of proof 입증의 책임
substantiate 증명하다, 입증하다
assertion 주장
assert 단언하다
inescapability 피할 수 없음

05
universality 보편성, 일반성
declare 단언하다, 선언하다
unmusical 음악적 소양이 없는
in this regard 이런 면에서
contradiction 모순, 반박
capacity 능력, 용량
discriminating 분별 있는

06
address (문제를) 다루다
conversion 변환, 전환
nutrient 영양분, 영양소
commercial 상업용의
application 사용, 적용
ecosystem 생태계
wire 전선을 연결하다
output 생산물
scarcity 희소성
observe 관찰하다
dilemma 난제, 딜레마
perspective 관점
inefficiency 비효율성

07
top-down 하향식의, 톱다운의(위에서
아래로 향하는)
asset 자산
allocation 배분, 배치
account 계좌
proportion 정도, 비율
return 수익률, 수익
effectively 실질적으로, 사실상
broad 전반적인
establish 수립하다, 확립하다
crucial 매우 중요한

08
mound 둔덕, 작은 언덕
population 개체군
probe 탐지하다, 조사하다
community (동물의) 군집
competing 상충하는, 대립하는
hypothesis 가설
superficially 표면적으로
ecology 생태

09
intercontinental 대륙 간의
reduction 절감, 감소
compromise 손상하다
uncouple 분리하다
bear in mind that ~을 명심하다
restrict 제한하다
side effect 부작용
emerging 신흥의, 최근 생겨난
sustainable 지속 가능한

10
curator 큐레이터, (박물관·도서관 등의)
관리자
arrangement 배열, 배치
dimension 관점, 차원
ambiguous 모호한, 불확실한
rigorously 엄격히, 엄밀히

11~12
fundamental 근본적인
virtual reality 가상현실
augmented 증강된
potent 강력한
amount to ~에 이르다
connectivity 연결성
transaction 거래
onward 계속 이어서 나아가는
stem from ~에서 비롯되다
radical 급진적인
emerge 나타나다
for all practical purposes 실제로
consequence 결과
autonomous 자율적인
administrator 관리자
computable 계산 가능한
flood 홍수
aspect 측면

01
unaware of ~을 알지 못하는
deal with ~을 다루다
obligation 의무
quote 말을 인용하다
inbox 받은 편지함
scratch ~ off ~을 지우다
mentality 사고방식

02
accompany 동반하다
expansion 확장
emergence 출현
auction 경매
strategy 전략
tempt 유혹하다
moneyed 부유한
speak on behalf of ~을 대변하다
critic 비평가

03
hard-pressed (~을 하는 데) 애를 먹는
sort out ~을 선별하다
destructive 파괴적인
innovation 혁신
nevertheless 그럼에도 불구하고
implicit 암묵적인
approval 승인
unsettling (마음을) 불안하게 하는
march 행진
craft 공들여 만들다
finance 자금을 공급하다
perspective 시각, 관점
expertise 전문 기술
optimistic 낙관적인
breakthrough 돌파구
persuasive 설득력 있는
oppose 반대하다

04
implementation 이행, 시행
emphasize 강조하다
rationality 합리성
miscalculate 오판하다
put ~ in place ~을 제자리에 놓다
resistance 저항
undo 실패하게 만들다

05
be regarded as ~으로 간주되다
territory 영역, 영토
threatening 위협적인
contemporary 현대의
symptomatic 징후[증상]를 보이는
fatalism 숙명[운명]론
catch-phrase 유명 문구, 선전 구호
flu epidemic 유행성 독감
defeatist 패배주의적인, 패배주의자의
refrain 자주 반복되는 어구[말], 후렴
implicitly 암시적으로
explicitly 명시적으로
call ~ into question ~에 의문을 제기하다
ring the alarm bell(s) 비상벨을 울리다

06
count up ~을 다 세어 내다
personnel 인사과
archangel 천사장, 대천사(大天使)
come out with ~을 발표하다[말하다]
a bunch of 많은
undifferentiated 구별되지 않은, 획일적인
gripe 불평

07
agency 기관
stereotype 고정 관념
assembly 조립
in return for ~에 대한 대가로
laboratory 실험실
surgeon 외과 의사

08
multiparty 다자의
imbalance 불균형
deficit 적자
surplus 잉여금
monetary 화폐의
asset 자산
bond 채권
compensate for ~을 보충하다
at full capacity 전면 가동으로
earnings 수입, 소득
Treasury (미국) 재무부

09
acquire 습득하다
arithmetic 산수
innate 타고난, 선천적인
attribute 속성
inborn 타고난
come into play 작동하기 시작하다
devise 고안하다

10
inference 추론
inquiry 조사, 탐구
objectivity 객관성
egocentric 자기중심적인
ethnocentric 민족 중심적인
counterproductive 역효과를 낳는
legitimate 정당한, 합법적인
probability 가능성
reinforce 강화하다

11-12
ethnic 민족의
electoral 선거의
civil strife 사회적 갈등
demography 인구 변동
sheer 순전한
unprecedented 전례 없는, 유례가 없는
outstrip 앞지르다
harshly (불쾌할 정도로) 분명히, 엄격히
disorient 어리둥절하게 하다
markedly 눈에 띄게, 현저하게

WORDS LIST

01
sensitive 예민한
insult 모욕하다
reflection 반영
flattering 기분 좋게 해 주는, 으쓱하게 하는
tone 어조

02
derived from ~에서 유래된
instruction 지시 사항, 지시
draw on ~에 의존하다
intriguing 흥미로운
theoretical 이론적인, 이론의
triumph 승리
anatomy (해부학적) 구조

03
preconception 선입관(념), 예상
confront 직면시키다
immediately 즉시
rational 이성적인, 합리적인
equivalence 동등함
cling to ~을 고수하다, ~에 집착하다

04
strip 박탈하다, 벗기다
agency 힘, 작용, 대리(권)
messy 다루기 힘든, 더러운
linear 1차원의, 선형적인, 직선의
marginalize 하찮은 존재로 만들다, 무시하다
discrete 별개의, 분리된
institutional 제도적인, 기관의

05
freezing point 어는점
friction 마찰
glacier 빙하
inherently 본질적으로
reconstruct 구조를 조정하다
verify 사실임을 입증하다, 증명하다
physicist 물리학자
intrinsic 고유한, 본질적인
layer 층

06
aesthetics 미학
undertake 착수하다
reverse 뒤집다
privilege 특권을 부여하다
abstract 추상적인
perceptual 지각의
physiological 생리적인, 생리학의
makeup 구성
complicated 복잡한
occurrence 발생하는 것, 존재
consciousness 인식, 의식
synthetic 종합적인
unhesitatingly 서슴없이, 재빠르게
reinterpretation 재해석
critique 비판, 비평
inadequate 부적절한
immense 헤아릴 수 없는
gulf 틈, 격차
satisfy 만족시키다

07
distinguish 구별하다
weigh 평가하다
course of action 행동 방침
uniformity 한결같음, 균일성
at a loss 어쩔 줄을 모르는
deliberation 숙고
recollection 회상
affection 정서, 감정
no less than ~에 못지않게
contemplate 심사숙고하다

08
equation 방정식, 등식
keep straight ~을 명확히 이해하다
isolate 분리하다
variable 변수
assessment 평가
significant 상당한
cognitive 인지적인, 인식의
initially 처음에

09
originality 독창성
contradictory 모순된
at the very least 적어도
divergent 서로 다른
insofar as ~인 정도에서
individuality 개성
overlay 덧입히다
commonplace 흔한
aptitude 적성
intimate 친밀한

10
population pressure 인구압, 인구 과잉
planetary 지구의, 행성의
advocate 옹호하다
deplete 고갈시키다
quadruple 네 배로 만들다; 네 배의
imperialism 제국주의
pervasiveness 만연, 넘침
legitimize 정당화[합법화]하다
perpetuate 지속하게 하다, 영속시키다

11-12
opportunity cost 기회비용
expenditure 지출
offset 상쇄하다
crop 작물
market value 시장 가치
uncertainty 불확실성
precautionary 예방(책)의
quantification 수량화, 정량화
examination 검사

WORDS LIST

01
applaud 찬사를 보내다
recall 기억(력)
at a price 대가를 치르고
chip away ~을 조금씩 깎아 내다
contemplation 숙고
distribute 배포하다
zip (어떤 방향으로) 쌩 하고 가다

02
similarity 유사성
community 공통성, 공유
sympathy 공감, 동정
intimately 밀접하게
likeness 유사성
irreducible 더는 줄일 수 없는
permanent 영구적인
solidarity 결속, 연대
division of labor 노동의 분업
obligation 의무
call forth ~을 불러일으키다
philanthropic 박애의
charitable 자선의
furnish 제공하다
means 수단
moral 도덕의
impulse 충동

03
disclosure 노출, 공개
inhibitor 억제자
suppressor 억압자
persist into ~까지 지속되다
play cards close to the chest 비밀을 지키다
verbally 말로, 언어적으로
strategic 전략적인
advance 사전의
favorable 호의적인
revelation 드러냄

04
subject 피실험자
classify 분류하다
stimulus 자극(pl. stimuli)
dimension 차원
switch 전환(하다)
responsive 반응적인

heightened 높인, 증가된
neurocognitive 신경 인지적인
representation 표현, 재현
allocate 할당하다
automaticity 자동성

05
conceive of ~을 상상하다
shatter 깨지다
fragile 깨지기 쉬운
plausibly 그럴듯하게
property 속성
dualist 이원론자
invalid 무효한

06
theoretical 이론적인
contemplation 심사숙고
disinterested 사심 없는, 객관적인
disengaged 떨어져 있는
dispassionately 냉정하게
conceive 생각하다
enterprise 일, 계획
value free 가치 판단의 영향을 받지 않는
neutral 중립적인
with respect to ~과 관련하여

07
categorize 분류하다
assign 부여하다
status 지위, 신분
identity 신분, 정체성
corporation 법인, 회사
legal 법률상의
trace 흔적, 자취
invaluable 매우 귀중한
indication 암시
criminal 범죄의
tendency 경향
make sense of ~을 파악하다
manipulate 처리하다, 조작하다
ultimately 궁극적으로
massage 조작하다
theoretician 이론가
phenomenon 현상
frame 틀을 잡다

08
normative 규범의
staged 연출된
setting 환경
procedure 절차
channel 경로, 통로
publicize 공개하다, 알리다
conformity 순응(성)
pluralistic 다원적인

09
spontaneous 자연스러운, 자발적인
weird 이상한
sculpture 조각품
pasture 목초지
spoil 훼손하다
unsightly 보기 흉한
ban 금지하다
clutch 움켜쥐다
outdo 능가하다
legislature 입법 기관

10
liberate 자유롭게 하다
by virtue of ~ 덕분에
immediate 즉각적인, 눈앞의
crop (농)작물
cultivate 경작하다

11-12
gymnast 체조 선수
pound 세게 치다
stem from ~에서 비롯되다
inadequate 부적절한
empathy 공감
alternative 대안
capitalize on ~을 이용하다
incorporate 포함시키다

WORDS LIST

01
geologist 지질학자
predictable 예측 가능한
contradictory 모순된
petty 사소한
civilization 문명
domestic 가정의

02
stumble upon ~을 우연히 발견하다
remains 잔해
cling on to ~을 붙잡다, ~에 매달리다
photosynthesis 광합성
fast 단식
investigate 조사하다
remotely 원격으로
facilitate 용이하게 하다
nutrient 영양소
interconnected 상호 연결된, 상호 연관된
pump 퍼붓다, 주입하다
hierarchical 계층적인, 계급의
self-sufficient 자급할 수 있는
mutual 상호 간의

03
adapt to ~에 적응하다
pole 극지방

04
modifiability 수정 가능성
deficiency 결손, 결함
might as well ~하는 편이 낫다
rubbish 말도 안 되는 소리, 쓰레기
astrological 점성술의
in principle 원칙적으로
agent 동인(動因)

05
vulnerable 취약한
disruption 장애
cascading effect 폭포 효과
seasonality 계절성
jet stream 제트 기류
component 요소
take ~ into consideration ~을 고려하다
tailwind 뒤바람, 순풍
intercontinental 대륙 간의
transatlantic 대서양 횡단의

eastbound 동쪽으로 가는
westbound 서쪽으로 가는
lengthen 연장시키다
on occasion 때로
refueling 연료 보급의
intermediary 기착지의, 중간에 있는

06
carve out ~를 개척하다
rebel 반군, 반역자
cause 대의명분, 정당한 이유
ideological 이념적인, 사상적인
demonstrably 명백하게, 논증할 수 있게
corrupt 부패한
claim 주장, 요구, 권리
implausible 타당하지 않은
suggest 암시하다, 시사하다
make a bet 내기를 하다
take over ~을 장악하다, ~을 탈취하다
distribution 분배
governance 통치 (방식), 관리(법)

07
automatic 자동인
orbit 주위를 돌다
perception 지각
evoke 환기시키다
mimic 모방하다
elicit 이끌어 내다
prompt 유도하다
depict 묘사하다

08
federal 연방의
infrastructure 기반 시설
basic capacity 기본 수용력
common carriage 공공 운송
nondiscriminatory 차별 없는
freight 화물
discrimination 차별
accountable 책임이 있는
prioritize 우선시하다
reliable 신뢰할 수 있는

09
consultant 상담사
identify 파악하다
catastrophe 재앙
component 요소
assert 주장하다
cognitive 인지적인
deterioration 저하, 타락
pole vaulter 장대높이뛰기 선수
meet (운동) 경기
worrisome 걱정스러운
manifest 나타내다
physiological 생리적인
overintensity 과도한 긴장

10
civil engineering 토목 공학
one of a kind 유일한 것, 독특한 것
disposable 1회용의, 마음대로 쓰고 버리는
replicate 복제하다
as-built 지어진 것처럼
and the like 그와 유사한 것
definitively 명확하게, 결정적으로
proactive 사전 대책을 강구하는

11-12
stagnant 침체된
ancestor 조상
inactivity 휴지, 무활동
in the blink of an eye 눈 깜짝할 사이에
literal 말 그대로의
propel 추진하다
sustained 지속적인
geographical 지리적인
bountiful 풍부한
hospitable 쾌적한
traversable 횡단할 수 있는
intellectual 지적인
enforce 시행하다
hustle 정력적 활동

WORDS LIST

01
muted 조용한
intense 집중적인
chronically 오랜 시간에 걸쳐, 만성적으로
diagnosis 진단
interpretation 해석
rewarding 도움이 되는, 보람 있는
distraction 산만하게 하는 것

02
render 만들다
regime 체제
oppressive 억압적인
legislature 입법 기관, 입법부
consumerism 소비 지상주의
privilege 특권을 주다
cohesion 화합, 유대
imperialism 제국주의
colonize 식민지화하다
at one's expense 스스로 희생하여
immediacy 즉각성
transience 일시성

03
rephotography 재촬영
subject 피사체
alter 변화시키다
maintain 유지하다
duplicate 복제하다
comparison 비교
span (얼마의 기간에) 걸치다
mood 분위기

04
be derived from ~에서 비롯되다
instinct 본능
dehumanized 비인간화된
domination 지배
ritualistic 의례적인
infrequent 잦지 않은, 뜸한
predator 포식자
manipulative 교묘하게 다루는

05
factor 요인
inflated 부풀려진
self-esteem 자존감
consensus 합의

cope 대처하다
mechanism 메커니즘, 작동 기제
upsetting 혼란스럽게 하는
random 무작위의
impact 영향
feel drawn to ~에 마음이 끌리다
confront 맞서다, 직면하다
gut 직감
be correlated with ~와 관련되어 있다

06
proverb 속담
cast light on ~의 이해에 도움을 주다
abstract 추상적인
non-obvious 자명하지 않은
superficial 피상적인
subtle 미묘한
complicated 복잡한
slap A onto B A를 B에 적용하다
insight 통찰(력)
analysis 분석
concise 간결한
hypothetical 가상의, 가설적인

07
theoretical 이론의
experimental 실험의
associated with ~과 관련된
specification 상술(詳述)
articulation 표현
property 특성, 속성
referent 지시 대상
account for ~을 설명하다
attributed to ~에 기인하는
bias 편향
minimize 최소화하다
deviation 이탈, 일탈
electron 전자
hydrogen 수소
orbit 궤도

08
ritual 의식
inflame 격앙시키다
onlooker 구경꾼
lavish 호화로운
inherent 고유의
therapeutic 치료의

superiority 우월성
evident 분명한
akin 유사한
theatrical 연극의, 극장의
spell 주문
monologue 독백
eloquent 웅변적인
integration 통합
inspiration 영감
intensity 강도

09
linguistic 언어적인
conversely 정반대로, 역으로
subdivide 세분하다
corresponding to ~에 상응하는
equivalent 상응하는 것

10
constraint 제약
exploitation 불법 이용, 착취
keep an eye out for ~을 감시하다
sue 고소하다
harass 괴롭히다
handsome 상당한
bribe 뇌물
drop a case 소송을 취하하다
abusive 남용[악용]하는
legislator 입법자
remedial 개선적인, 보충적인
compensatory 보완적인, 보상의
adjustment 조정
wield (권력·권위를) 행사하다

11-12
monopolistic 독점적인
blend 혼합하다
moderate 중간 정도의, 보통의
substitute 대체물
provoke 불러일으키다

WORDS LIST

01
preservation 보존
reshape 고쳐 만들다
effectively 사실상
distance 떼어 놓다
distinct 별개의
realm 영역
intimately 밀접하게
apparent 뚜렷한
heritage 유산
coexist 공존하다
fence off ~을 울타리로 구분하다
contribute to ~의 원인이 되다
imply 암시하다
figure 형상
categorize 분류하다
approach 접근법
bluntly 직설적으로

02
solemnly 엄숙하게
stakeholder 이해 당사자
assessment 평가
architecture 컴퓨터 시스템의 구성
seasoned 경험 많은
weight 가중치를 주다
zip code 우편 번호
regulator 규제 기관
anti-discrimination law 차별 금지법
fraud 사기
layperson 일반인

03
nobility 귀족
peasant 소작농
clergy 성직자
dictate 좌우하다, 지배하다
societal 사회의
adoption 채택
go through ~을 경험하다[겪다]
renewed 새로운
appreciation 이해, 평가

04
epic 장대한, 서사시적인
for all ~에도 불구하고
prose 산문
still photography (영화 선전용) 스틸 사진
potent 강력한

incorporate 포함하다, 통합하다
ideological 이념적인
composition 구성
manipulation 조작, 조종
account 설명
prime 주요한
instrument 도구

05
authoritarian 권위주의적인
harass 박해하다
monitor 감시하다
barrier 장벽, 장애(물)
dissuade 만류하다
mass movement 대중 운동
protest 항의, 시위
go hand in hand 서로 협조하다
usher in ~을 안내하다

06
perception 지각, 인식
factual 사실적인, 사실의
ethical 윤리적인, 윤리의
mutual 상호의
belonging 소속
notion 개념
offspring 자손
virtuous 덕망 있는

07
carbon dioxide 이산화탄소
emission 배출(물)
free-rider 무임승차자
head off ~을 막다
incubate 육성하다
equator 적도
flooding 홍수

08
transform 바꾸다
exclusive 전적인
theorist 이론가
ownership 소유권
arbitrarily 자의적으로
conceptually 개념상으로
prior to ~ 이전에
selfhood 자아
asset 자산

bar A from -ing A가 ~하는 것을 금지하다
consent 동의

09
obscure 가리다
elemental 근본적인
consist of ~로 구성되다
outcome 결과
immediate 직속의, 직접적인
distinguish 구별하다
tactic 전술
strategy 전략
objective 목적
campaign 전쟁, 군사 작전
differentiate 구별하다
paraphrase 다른 말로 나타내다
swordsman 검투사, 검객
thrust 찌르기
reply 응수하다
brief 간결한
brilliant 명석한, 재기발랄한
acknowledge 인정하다

10
habituation 습관화
rattle 딸랑이
dishabituation 탈습관화
recurrence 반복

11-12
lure 유혹(하는 것), 미끼
validate 검증하다, 입증하다
strengthen 강화하다
repellent 반발력, 물리치는 것
coincide with ~과 일치하다
incorporate 포함[통합]하다
disregard 무시하다
obsession 집념, 집착
actualization 현실화
embrace 받아들이다
doable 실행할 수 있는
collapse 무너지다
hurdle 장애물
skepticism 회의(론)

WORDS LIST

01
discipline 규율
fade 약화되다, 시들다
on the job 일하는 중인
yearn for ~을 갈망하다
edgy 초조해하는
disengage 벗어나게 하다, 철수하다
self-consciousness 자의식
built-in 내재된
deceive 기만하다, 속이다
relieve ~ of ... ~에게서 …을 덜어 내다
rigor 고됨
idleness 나태, 게으름

02
purely 완전히, 순전히
oral 구술의
millennium 천 년간(pl. millennia)
preliterate 문자 이전의
storage 저장
by necessity 필요에 의해서
intertwine 밀접하게 관련짓다
diction 화법
tune (~에 맞게) 조정하다
encode 부호화하다, (부호로) 입력하다
turn (특별한) 표현, 말투
embed 내재화하다, 끼워 넣다
verse 구절
chant 연호하다

03
radical 근본적인, 기초적인
abstraction 추상 관념, 추출
formula (수학) 공식, 화학식
sum up ~을 압축하다
phenomenon 현상(pl. phenomena)
correspond to ~와 부합하다, ~와 상응하다
assumption 가정
emerging 신생의
ordered 질서 정연한, 정돈된
crude 조잡한
superstition 미신
triumph 승리하다
comprehensible 이해될 수 있는
precision 정확성, 정확도

04
liberalism 자유주의
capitalism 자본주의
articulate 명확히 표현하다
diverge 벗어나다, 갈라지다
medieval 중세의
theology 신학
monarchy 군주제
representative 대표성 있는, 대표하는
parliamentary rule 의회 통치
impersonal 개인과 상관없는, 비인격적인
entrepreneur 기업가
sacred 신성한
worldly 세속적인
separation 분리
toleration 관용
salvation 구원
orthodox 정통의, 보수적인
primacy 으뜸, 최고
collectivist 집단주의적인, 집단주의(자)의

05
align with ~와 일치하다
explicitly 명시적으로
entrust 맡기다
city council 시 의회
real estate 부동산
contractor 토건업자, (건축 등의) 청부업자
paradoxical 역설적인
assess 평가하다
gravitate toward ~로 끌리다
conventional 전통적인, 관습적인

06
restore 복원하다
captive breeding 포획 번식
reintroduction 재도입
orphaned 고아가 된
unethical 비윤리적인
undermine 훼손하다
thick-billed parrot 큰부리앵무새

07
broadly speaking 개략적으로[대체로] 말하자면
retail 소매의

08
recurrent 반복되는
objection 이의, 반대
simplicity 단순성
landscape 환경, 풍경
stumble 발을 헛디디다
outfit 장착하다
consolidate 강화하다, 굳건히 하다
radically 과격하게, 근본적으로
render (어떤 상태가 되게) 만들다

09
share 점유율
negotiate 협상하다, 뚫고 나가다
capitalist 자본주의의, 자본주의적인
inconclusive 결정적이지 않은
at best 좋게 봐도, 기껏해야
in effect 사실상

10
illiteracy 잘못 사용하는 것, 문맹
qualitative 질적인
notoriously 악명 높게
standardize 표준화하다
verbal 언어의, 말의
overestimate 과대평가하다
disclose 제공하다, 공개하다
comply 따르다, 순응하다
numerically 수치로, 숫자로
as opposed to ~ 대신에, ~이 아니라

11-12
forager 수렵 채집인
domestic 가내의, 가정의
minimal 최소의
maximum 최대한(도)
ceremonial 의례(상)의
relative 상대적인
uniformity 일관성
durability 영속성, 내구성
sustainable 지속 가능한
surplus 잉여(의)
reproduction 재생산
intensification 증대
incentive 유인, 동기
scarce 부족한, 희귀한
counterintuitive 직관에 어긋나는
depletion 고갈

01
dynamics 역학
intensify 강화하다, 심화시키다
displace 대체하다, 추방하다
service (의사, 변호사 등의 전문적) 업무
attorney 변호사
artisan 장인
corporate 기업의
in-house 사내로, 사내에서
parcel out ~을 나눠 맡기다

02
desperately 필사적으로
engaged 활동하고 있는, 바쁜
strain 피로(감), 긴장, 부담
boredom 지루함
arguably 거의 틀림없이
outlet 배출구
on end 계속
craft (손으로 공들여) 만들다
optimally 최적으로
addiction 중독
game console 게임기

03
proponent 지지자, 옹호자
carry away ~을 도취시키다
dose (어느 정도의) 양
game-changing 판도를 바꾸는
infusion 주입, 투입, 고취
breakthrough 획기적인
coupled with ~과 더불어
tension 긴장
destabilization 불안정

04
sociological 사회학의, 사회학적인
interactionist 상호 작용주의적인
perspective 관점
cooperative 협력적인
distort 왜곡하다
exaggerate 과장하다
invariably 언제나

05
stem from ~에서 비롯되다
incompatible 양립할 수 없는
disagreement 불일치
lives and limbs 생명과 신체
wipe out ~을 전멸시키다

06
even as ~하는 바로 그 순간에
overload 과부하가 걸리게 하다
assess 평가하다
pulse (일반적인) 경향
recipient 수신자
forward 전송하다
eliminate 제거하다
fundamental 근본적인
onset 시작

07
overly 지나치게
fixate (병적으로) 집착하게 하다
perceive 인식하다
elevation 고도
vertical 수직
innocence 결백
intentional 의도적인
setback 퇴보, 차질
catastrophe 재앙
consistent 일관된
addictive 중독성이 있는

08
civilization 문명
primitive 원시적인
outlet 배출구, 발산 수단
cave painting 동굴 벽화
considering ~을 고려할 때
promising 기대되는, 장래성 있는
profound 지대한, 엄청난
origin 기원, 출처
expansion 확장
complement 보완하다

09
zebra finch 금화조(錦華鳥)
hemisphere (뇌의) 반구
syllable 음절
dominance 우위
attend to ~을 처리하다
discriminate 구별하다

10
prophecy 예언
randomness 무작위
mechanism 기제
stalk 줄기
illustrate 분명히 보여 주다
interpret 해석하다
supernatural 초자연적인
mystic 신비주의자
oracle 제사장, 신탁
intermediary 중개의
inscribe 새기다
manifest 나타내다
lap 무릎

11-12
prone to ~하는 경향이 있는
setback 좌절
rapport 친밀한 관계

WORDS LIST

01
intense 심한, 강렬한
truthful 진실한, 정말의
stinging 침을 쏘는
exploit 이용하다
sting 침 (쏘기)
sole 발바닥
to one's benefit ~에게 이롭게
fall for ~에 속아 넘어가다
downside 부정적인
outweigh 더 크다
equation 방정식
dwarf 축소하다, 작게 하다
potential 잠재적인
herein 여기에
dictate 지시하다

02
acknowledge 인정하다
mock jury 모의 배심원단
deliberation 심의, 검토

03
resource 자산, 자원
kin 친족
selfless 이타적인
altruistic 이타적인
loyalty 충성
altruism 이타주의
freeloader 무임승차자
obsessive ranker 지위에 집착하는 사람

04
chronic 만성의
process 처리하다
involve 수반하다
generate 유발하다, 만들어 내다
modulate 조정하다
regulation 조절, 규제
prolonged 장기간의
facilitate 촉진하다
region (인체의) 부위, 구역
diminish 감소시키다
throw off ~을 없애다
police 치안을 유지하다
aggression 공격성
prone to ~에 취약한, ~을 당하기 쉬운

05
dominant 지배적인
enterprise 기업(체)
property 재산
commitment 헌신, 전념

06
rural 시골의
reshape 재편하다
metropolis 대도시
arguably 거의 틀림없이
territory 지역, 영토
split 분열, 분리
media outlet (신문·방송 등의) 매스컴
passive 수동적인
recipient 수신자
ecological 생태학적인, 생태적인
afar 멀리
problematic 문제가 있는
parallel 평행한, 병행하는
harness 활용[이용]하다
scatter 흐트러뜨리다

07
anthropology 인류학
epidemic 전염병
indigenous 토착의
mediator 중재자
comprehensive 포괄적인
primate 영장류

08
persist 지속되다
revolve around ~을 중심으로 돌다
cite 인용하다
ward off ~을 멀리하다, ~을 가까이 오지 못하게 하다
dynamics 역학
generality 일반론
recollection 기억
grievance 불만
humiliation 굴욕
inconsistent 불일치한

09
contemporary 현대의
fragmentation 해체, 단편화
formation 형성

aesthetic 미적인
transaction 거래
rapidity 속도
plurality 다양성
turnover (상품·자금의) 회전율
plural 다양한
inevitably 필연적으로

10
attachment 애착
traumatic 충격이 큰, 매우 충격적인
coherent 일관성 있는
trauma 충격적인 경험
preoccupied 정신이 팔린, 사로잡힌
dismissing 일축하는
disorganized 정리가 안 된, 흐트러진
infant 유아
insecurely 불안하게

11-12
enormous 엄청난
temporary 일시적인
influential 영향력 있는
layoff (일시적인) 해고
articulate 명확한, 잘 표현하는
compelling 설득력 있는
synonymous with ~와 동의어인
visionary 선견지명 있는
trace 추적하다
adverse 역경의
the Depression (미국의) 대공황
benefit 수당
dissenter 반대자

WORDS LIST

01
eliminate 없애다
manipulation 조작
invoke (근거·이유로 인물·이론·예 등을) 들다[언급하다]
commentator 논평자
remotely 아주 조금
comparable 유사한, 비슷한
work towards ~을 얻으려고 노력하다

02
object 사물, 물건
subjective 주관적인
compassion 연민, 동정심
peer 또래
attend to ~에 주의를 기울이다
discourage 좌절하게 하다
externally 외적으로

03
static (수신기의) 잡음
recognition 인식
interaction 상호 작용
edge 가장자리
stuffed animal 봉제 인형
neural 신경의
pathway 경로
innate 내재된
mashed potato 으깬 감자
chaos 혼돈

04
neuroscientist 신경 과학자
argument 주장, 논거
embody 합체시키다, 구현하다
scope 범위
rationality 합리성
literally 말 그대로
mind/body dualism 심신 이원론
reasoning 추론

05
genetic patenting 유전자 특허
expanded 확대된
restriction 제한
medieval 중세
lordly 영주의, 귀족의
humble 보잘것없는

plot 작은 땅
subordination to ~에의 종속
flourish 번창하다

06
commentary 해설
arrangement 배열, 배합
referent 지칭, 지시 대상
interpretation 해석
translate 번역하다
implicit 암시적인
explicitness 명시성
interest 관심사
discipline (학문) 분야
convert 전환하다
purpose 목적
criticism 비평
unrelated to ~과 연관이 없는
symbolism 상징적 표현
hypothetical 가설적인, 가설의
explanatory 설명하는
analogy 비유
self-enclosed 자체 완결적인, 자체적으로 테두리가 정해진
autonomous 독자적인, 자체적인

07
measurable 측정 가능한
cut-off point 기준점, 구분점
barely 간신히
eligible 자격을 갖춘
observational 관찰의
biased 편향된
analysis 분석
replicate an experiment 실험을 되풀이하다

08
target population 대상 모집단
random 무작위의
respondent 응답자
employ 사용하다
involve 수반하다
proportion 비율
bias 치우침, 편향
result 생기다
similarity 유사성
overcome 극복하다

district 구역
procedure 절차

09
casually 무심코
gate 통제하다; (관)문
inflow 유입(량)
override 무시하다, 중단시키다
stand out 눈에 띄다
glance 대충 훑어보다, 힐끗 보다

10
estimate 추산하다
toll 대가
equivalent to ~와 동일한
in defense of ~을 변호하여
repay 보상하다, 갚다

11-12
pilgrim 순례자
prominently 두드러지게
trimming 곁들이는 음식
ample 풍성한
devastating 지독한, 파괴적인
Plymouth Colony 플리머스 식민지(Pilgrim Fathers가 1620년 Massachusetts 주에 건설했던 식민지)
perish 소멸하다, 죽다
feast 만찬, 연회
solidarity 결속, 연대
the Civil War (미국의) 남북 전쟁
ritual 의식
immigrant 이주민
founding 건국
abundant 풍성한, 풍요로운
constructed 구성된
idealized 이상화된
cohesion 응집력
legitimize 합법화하다
ground 근거시키다
reaffirm 재확인하다
distinct 뚜렷한

WORDS LIST

01

with a good conscience 정정당당하게,
양심에 거리끼는 바 없이
feast 축제, 연회
analogously 유사하게
insulate 분리[격리]시키다
upwind 바람과 반대 방향으로
logger 벌목꾼
give out 동이 나다, 바닥이 나다
deprive ~ of ... ~에게서 …을 빼앗다
due 몫, 마땅히 받아야 할 것
insofar as ~하는[인] 한
lift the lid 뚜껑을 들어올리다, (불쾌하거나
충격적인 사실을) 폭로하다

02

collapse 붕괴되다; 붕괴
route 경로
destination 목적지
alternative 다른, 대안적인
pathway 길, 경로
decay 쇠퇴하다, 썩다
access 접근하다
multilingual 다국어 사용자
accumulate 축적하다

03

be attributable to ~에서 기인하다
conceptualize 개념화하다
specificity 특수성
shortcoming 단점
mediate 전달하다
clarify 명확하게 하다

04

intricate 복잡한
exert 미치다, 발휘하다
critical 중대한, 결정적인
originate with ~에서 비롯되다
intuitive 직관적인
hunch 예감, 직감
apparently ~인 것 같이
common 통례적인, 일반적인
dubious 의심스러운
encounter 직면하다
fuzzy 애매한, 불분명한
constitute 구성하다

05

relativism 상대주의
objective 객관적인
tolerance 관용
capital 대문자
conviction 확신
privileged 특권적인, 특권을 가진
hallmark 특징
colonialism 식민주의
missionary 선교사
justify 정당화하다
outlook on life 인생관

06

count as ~로 간주하다
subpopulation 하위 집단
invariably 반드시
variation 차이
ancestry 가계(家系), 혈통
inferior 열등한
mean 평균의
notwithstanding ~에도 불구하고
intimidating 위협적인
amply 크게

07

simultaneously 동시에
unreliable 신뢰할 수 없는
measure 측정하다
directed 규제된, 유도된
incorporate 포함하다
in essence 본질적으로
endow 부여하다
presume 추정하다
independent of ~와 무관한, ~의 영향을
받지 않는
arbitrary 자의적인

08

allocation 할당
characteristic 특징
prioritize 우선시하다
hierarchy 계층 구조

09

commute 통근하다
adaptation 적응
residential 주거의
resilient 회복력이 있는

10

convention 관행
eloquently 유창하게
forcefully 강력하게
racism 인종 차별주의
capitalism 자본주의
context 상황, 맥락
the Great Depression (1930년대 미국
의) 대공황
chronology 연대기
arrange 배열하다

11-12

a good deal of 많은 양의, 다량의
empirical 경험적인, 경험의
provoke 자극하다, 생기게 하다
intense 강렬한, 강력한
assimilate 완전히 이해하다, 동화하다
elicit 이끌어 내다
distinctly 명백하게, 뚜렷하게
vivid 생생한
precise 정확한
concrete 구체적인
flashbulb memory 섬광 기억

READING
MASTER

WORDS REVIEW

A 다음 영어 단어에 해당하는 우리말 뜻을 빈칸에 쓰시오.

01 artificial _____

02 discard _____

03 evacuation _____

04 differentiate _____

05 contemplate _____

06 reflexive _____

07 exert _____

08 distinction _____

09 beneficial _____

10 coverage _____

11 atmospheric _____

12 frugality _____

B 다음 우리말과 의미가 같도록 빈칸에 알맞은 말을 [보기]에서 골라 쓰시오. (필요시 형태를 변형할 것)

┌─ 보기 ───┐
correlation   subjective   linger   opponent   relevant
└──┘

01 A basketball player attempting a jump shot makes split-second adjustments according to his location, velocity, and body angle as well as to the positions of his _____.

점프 슛을 시도하는 농구 선수는 상대편들의 위치는 물론 자신의 위치, 속도, 몸 각도에 따라 순간적으로 조절한다.

02 Although the media may be unable to fulfill surveillance and _____ needs, they are able to offer assurance and tension reduction.

비록 대중 매체가 감시와 상호 관계의 욕구는 충족시킬 수 없을지라도, 확신을 주고 긴장감을 감소시킬 수는 있다.

03 Feminist historians have pointed out that _____ experience and emotional meaning has as much place in historical investigation as narratives of events.

여성주의 역사가들은 주관적인 경험과 감정적인 의미는 역사적인 연구에서 사건의 서술만큼이나 중요한 지위를 차지한다고 지적해 왔다.

04 I would start by scanning through the major journals that published the topic for the past five years, copying any _____ papers.

나는 지난 5년간 해당 주제를 발표한 주요 저널을 대강 훑어보며 관련된 논문은 무엇이나 복사하는 것으로 시작할 것이다.

05 Since odors have the ability to _____, animals often anoint their territories with scent marks that other animals can read as they pass by.

냄새는 오래 남을 수 있기 때문에, 동물들은 흔히 다른 동물들이 지나갈 때 읽을 수 있는 냄새 자취를 자신들의 영역에 바른다.

C 다음 네모 안에서 문맥에 맞는 말을 고르시오.

01 It is a(n) [controversial / uncontroversial] statement that the use of fossil fuels contributes to environmental degradation and climate change.

02 Social media platforms allow users to remain [identified / anonymous], providing a sense of privacy and freedom in expression.

WORDS REVIEW

A 다음 영어 단어에 해당하는 우리말 뜻을 빈칸에 쓰시오.

01 illumination _____ 07 abstract _____

02 mediate _____ 08 foster _____

03 obstacle _____ 09 blur _____

04 raw _____ 10 affirm _____

05 compelling _____ 11 install _____

06 authorize _____ 12 integrate _____

B 다음 우리말과 의미가 같도록 빈칸에 알맞은 말을 [보기]에서 골라 쓰시오.

┌─ 보기 ───┐
specify   incoherent   impractical   oppressive   distort
└──┘

01 Complex relationships in the viewed biomechanical event of a person lifting something can _____ material properties such as weight.

사람이 무언가를 들어올리는 것을 보는 생체 역학적 일의 복잡한 관계는 무게 같은 물질적인 특성을 구체적으로 말해 줄 수 있다.

02 These Irish non-Catholic Dissenters helped maintain the _____ hierarchy imposed by Britain.

이 비가톨릭교도인 아일랜드 비국교도들은 영국에 의해 강요된 억압적인 위계질서를 유지하는 것을 도왔다.

03 Films often construct idealized representations of places, weaving compelling narratives that can _____ our true understanding of these places.

영화는 흔히 장소에 대한 이상화된 묘사를 구성하는데, 이러한 장소에 대한 우리의 진정한 이해를 왜곡할 수 있는 흥미를 돋우는 이야기를 엮어 낸다.

04 The problem was that the glowing material would degrade after a short while, making its use as a household lighting device _____.

문제는 발광 물질이 잠시 후에 훼손되어 가정용 조명기기로서 그것을 사용하는 것을 비실용적으로 만들 것이라는 점이었다.

05 It is _____ to think that someone could care about something and not be prone to feel fear when it is threatened.

누군가가 어떤 것에 관해 관심을 가질 수 있으면서 그것이 위협을 받을 때 두려움을 느끼지 않는 경향이 있을 수 있다고 생각하는 것은 일관성이 없는 일이다.

C 다음 네모 안에서 문맥에 맞는 말을 고르시오.

01 The painting's ambiguous / apparent colors and shapes allowed for multiple interpretations, sparking lively debates among art critics.

02 The crowd's cheers amplified / reduced the energy of the stadium, sparking a strong excitement that spread throughout the entire arena.

WORDS REVIEW

A 다음 영어 단어에 해당하는 우리말 뜻을 빈칸에 쓰시오.

01 provision _____

02 compromise _____

03 erode _____

04 aesthetic _____

05 eventual _____

06 deliberate _____

07 prestige _____

08 constraint _____

09 legitimate _____

10 correlation _____

11 ritualize _____

12 competence _____

B 다음 우리말과 의미가 같도록 빈칸에 알맞은 말을 [보기]에서 골라 쓰시오. (필요시 형태를 변형할 것)

/ 보기 /

| compared to | with no regard for | accused of | in the face of | run counter to |

01 An emerging issue of potentially great concern is challenges brought against nations whose trading preferences _____ such groups as the World Trade Organization.

잠재적으로 큰 우려가 될 수 있는 새롭게 부상하는 문제는 (국가의) 무역 편애가 세계무역기구와 같은 단체에 역행하는 국가들에 제기되는 어려움이다.

02 In order to be a successful candidate, you have to be unnaturally optimistic even _____ probable defeat.

성공적인 후보자가 되기 위해, 여러분은 심지어 패배가 있을 것 같음에도 불구하고 이상할 정도로 낙관적이어야 한다.

03 _____ the average person, writers take easily to self-transformation through language.

보통 사람들과 비교하여, 작가들은 언어를 통해 자기 변형에 대한 능력을 쉽게 발전시킨다.

04 Politicians, especially those in the national spotlight, are often jokingly _____ being narcissists.

정치인, 특히 전국적인 주목을 받는 정치인은 흔히 농담 삼아 나르시시스트라는 이유로 비난을 받는다.

05 Tom Driver has suggested that the latter is partly responsible for the phenomenon of "total war," war waged _____ limits or constraints.

Tom Driver는 후자가 '전면전', 즉 한계나 제약을 전혀 배려하지 않고 행해지는 전쟁이라는 현상에 대해 부분적으로 책임이 있다는 것을 시사해 왔다.

C 다음 네모 안에서 문맥에 맞는 말을 고르시오.

01 The sudden / gradual change in temperature from hot to cold can cause bursts and leaks that require immediate repair.

02 Constructive / Destructive feedback from mentors or supervisors can help employees refine their skills and enhance their performance in the workplace.

WORDS REVIEW

A 다음 영어 단어에 해당하는 우리말 뜻을 빈칸에 쓰시오.

01 discriminating _____
02 intercontinental _____
03 conversion _____
04 lengthy _____
05 transaction _____
06 prominent _____
07 autonomous _____
08 indicator _____
09 adaptability _____
10 assertion _____
11 probe _____
12 dimension _____

B 다음 우리말과 의미가 같도록 빈칸에 알맞은 말을 [보기]에서 골라 쓰시오.

/ 보기 /
contradiction   collapse   fundamental   substantiate   imminent

01 Eventually the cup will succumb to the weight of the books, and it will _____.

결국 그 컵은 책의 무게에 굴복하고 그것은 무너질 것이다.

02 If the line for a particular attraction has become extraordinarily long and a service failure is _____, a strolling band or acrobats arrive to entertain the guests while they wait.

만약 인기를 끄는 특정한 것의 줄이 엄청나게 길어지고 서비스 차질이 임박해 있다면, 순회공연 밴드나 곡예사가 와서 고객들이 기다리는 동안 그들을 즐겁게 해 준다.

03 For all the talk of the metaverse, the _____ difference between the metaverse and the internet today is not quality but quantity.

메타버스에 대한 이야기에도 불구하고 오늘날 메타버스와 인터넷의 근본적인 차이점은 질이 아니라 양이다.

04 It is he or she who must provide compelling evidence to _____ such a belief, and not the rest of us who must prove it is not so.

그런 믿음을 입증하기 위해 설득력 있는 근거를 제공해야 하는 사람은 바로 그나 그녀이고 그렇지 않다는 것을 증명해야 하는 사람도 우리 중 나머지가 아니다.

05 In this regard, John Blacking's comments, made in the 1970s, on the _____ between theory and practice in the middle-class, Western society in which he grew up, remain relevant today.

이런 면에서 John Blacking이 자신이 성장한 서양 중산층 사회의 이론과 실제 사이의 모순에 대해 1970년대에 했던 논평은 오늘날에도 여전히 타당하다.

C 다음 네모 안에서 문맥에 맞는 말을 고르시오.

01 The implementation of rainwater harvesting systems has helped alleviate water abundance / scarcity in some communities by storing rainfall for future use.

02 The field of renewable energy engineering focuses on developing sustainable / temporary energy sources such as solar, wind, and geothermal power to meet the world's growing energy needs.

WORDS REVIEW

A 다음 영어 단어에 해당하는 우리말 뜻을 빈칸에 쓰시오.

01 persuasive _____
02 contemporary _____
03 emergence _____
04 demography _____
05 territory _____
06 perspective _____
07 breakthrough _____
08 attribute _____
09 reinforce _____
10 expertise _____
11 monetary _____
12 assembly _____

B 다음 우리말과 의미가 같도록 빈칸에 알맞은 말을 [보기]에서 골라 쓰시오. (필요시 형태를 변형할 것)

───| 보기 |───
call into question   come into play   speak on behalf of   compensate for

01 Warnings of catastrophic climate events usually conclude with this defeatist refrain, which _____ humanity's capacity to avoid the destructive consequences of the threats it faces.

대재앙의 기후와 관련된 사건에 대한 경고는 대개 이 패배주의적인 자주 반복되는 어구로 끝을 맺는데, 그것은 인류가 직면하는 위협의 파괴적인 결과를 피할 수 있는 인류의 능력에 의문을 제기한다.

02 _____ those without collections of their own, critics demanded greater public access to art, and from mid-century their calls were answered.

자신만의 수집품이 없는 사람들을 대변하여, 비평가들은 예술에 대한 대중의 더 큰 접근성을 요구했고, 세기 중반부터 그들의 요구가 받아들여졌다.

03 The purchase of U.S. dollar securities is the way most countries have _____ the imbalances in trade with the United States.

미국의 유가 증권을 구입하는 것은 대부분의 국가가 미국과의 무역에서 불균형을 보충해 온 방법이다.

04 Before the child learns a language, his arithmetic abilities do not _____, as seen in various experiments.

다양한 실험에서 보이듯 어린이가 언어를 배우기 전에, 그의 산수 능력은 작동하기 시작하지 않는다.

C 다음 네모 안에서 문맥에 맞는 말을 고르시오.

01 The warning label on the medication bottle should implicitly / explicitly list possible side effects and detailed dosage instructions.

02 The scientist hypothesized that the innate / trained behavior of migratory birds is influenced by genetic tendencies inherited from their ancestors.

WORDS REVIEW

A 다음 영어 단어에 해당하는 우리말 뜻을 빈칸에 쓰시오.

01	sensitive	_____	07	intimate	_____
02	individuality	_____	08	advocate	_____
03	reverse	_____	09	confront	_____
04	offset	_____	10	variable	_____
05	perceptual	_____	11	marginalize	_____
06	verify	_____	12	uniformity	_____

B 다음 우리말과 의미가 같도록 빈칸에 알맞은 말을 [보기]에서 골라 쓰시오. (필요시 형태를 변형할 것)

보기
discrete   intrinsic   immense   deplete   divergent

01 It leaves a(n) _____ gulf between our philosophical and physiological knowledge, with which we can never be satisfied.

그것은 우리의 철학적인 지식과 생리학적인 지식 사이에 헤아릴 수 없는 틈을 남기는데, 우리는 그것에 대해 절대 만족할 수 없다.

02 There are often in the same individual several originalities that are contradictory or at the very least extremely _____.

동일한 개인 내에 모순되거나 적어도 매우 서로 다른 몇 가지 독창성이 있는 경우가 흔히 있다.

03 If we place them in students' hands, they're used only for _____, narrow purposes like reading textbooks, creating documents, or taking assessments.

우리가 그것들을 학생들의 손에 맡기면, 그것들은 교과서 읽기, 문서 만들기, 혹은 평가받기와 같은 별개의 한정된 목적에만 사용된다.

04 This verified the original hypothesis made by the famous physicist Michael Faraday in 1850 that all ice has a(n) _____ thin layer of water at the surface.

이것은 1850년 유명한 물리학자 Michael Faraday가 세운 모든 얼음은 표면에 고유한 얇은 물의 층을 가지고 있다는 최초의 가설이 사실임을 입증했다.

05 Others suggest that over-consumption in developed nations is _____ the world's resources.

다른 이들은 선진국에서의 과소비가 세계의 자원을 고갈시키고 있다고 말한다.

C 다음 네모 안에서 문맥에 맞는 말을 고르시오.

01 Despite his best intentions, his explanation of the complex theory was adequate / inadequate and left his audience confused.

02 In mathematics, theoretical / practical concepts such as infinity and imaginary numbers allow us to explore abstract ideas beyond tangible quantities.

WORDS REVIEW

A 다음 영어 단어에 해당하는 우리말 뜻을 빈칸에 쓰시오.

01 allocate _____

02 by virtue of _____

03 similarity _____

04 ultimately _____

05 spontaneous _____

06 procedure _____

07 empathy _____

08 plausibly _____

09 capitalize on _____

10 verbally _____

11 alternative _____

12 charitable _____

B 다음 우리말과 의미가 같도록 빈칸에 알맞은 말을 [보기]에서 골라 쓰시오. (필요시 형태를 변형할 것)

보기
cultivate   furnish   conceive   manipulate   distribute

01 My mind now expects to take in information the way the internet _____ it: in a swiftly moving stream of particles.

이제 내 마음은 인터넷이 정보를 배포하는 방식, 즉 빠르게 움직이는 (정보) 조각의 흐름으로 정보를 받아들이기를 기대한다.

02 Data does not naturally appear in the wild; rather, it is collected by humans, _____ by researchers, and ultimately massaged by theoreticians.

데이터는 자연적으로 야생에서 나타나는 것이 아니라, 오히려 인간에 의해 수집되고, 연구자에 의해 처리되며, 궁극적으로는 이론가에 의해 조작된다.

03 Rather than showing the need to carry out a personal duty, it _____ us the means to continue the moral impulse of others.

그것은 자신의 본분을 수행할 필요성을 보여 주기보다 다른 사람의 도덕적 충동을 지속하는 수단을 우리에게 제공한다.

04 In this way of thinking, the activity of theorizing social and political life as traditionally _____ lies outside the rest of the activity of social life.

이런 사고방식에서, 전통적으로 생각되었던 사회 · 정치적 삶을 이론화하는 활동은 사회적 삶의 활동의 나머지 밖에 존재한다.

05 It is hardly an accident that our species is the only one to _____ the land and reap the harvest, even though a great many species eat plants.

아주 많은 종들이 식물을 먹기는 하겠지만, 우리 종이 땅을 경작해 수확물을 거두는 유일한 종이라는 것은 거의 우연이 아니다.

C 다음 네모 안에서 문맥에 맞는 말을 고르시오.

01 The medical facility maintains strict confidentiality policies to ensure the privacy of patient information and prevent unauthorized concealment / disclosure .

02 The museum's collection of rare artifacts is dispensable / invaluable and offers a glimpse into history that cannot be found anywhere else.

WORDS REVIEW

A 다음 영어 단어에 해당하는 우리말 뜻을 빈칸에 쓰시오.

01 lengthen _____　07 domestic _____

02 manifest _____　08 governance _____

03 disposable _____　09 proactive _____

04 modifiability _____　10 elicit _____

05 depict _____　11 federal _____

06 bountiful _____　12 prioritize _____

B 다음 우리말과 의미가 같도록 빈칸에 알맞은 말을 [보기]에서 골라 쓰시오.

/ 보기 /
vulnerable　implausible　deterioration　facilitate　replicate

01 Air transportation is particularly _____ to weather disruptions.

항공 운송은 기상 장애에 특히 취약하다.

02 When this situation arises, "catastrophe" occurs, resulting in a rapid and dramatic _____ in athletic performance.

이러한 상황이 발생하면 '재앙'이 일어나 운동 수행에서 빠르고도 급격한 저하라는 결과로 이어진다.

03 Scientists have discovered that assistance may either be delivered remotely by fungal networks around the root tips — which _____ nutrient exchange between trees — or the roots themselves may be interconnected.

과학자들은 나무 사이의 영양소 교환을 용이하게 하는 뿌리 끝 주변의 균 네트워크에 의해 원격으로 지원이 전달될 수 있거나 뿌리 자체가 상호 연결될 수도 있다는 것을 발견했다.

04 The rebels claim that their aim is to introduce cleaner, fairer government, but because their own leaders are so often demonstrably corrupt, such claims appear _____.

반군들은 자신의 목표가 더 깨끗하고 더 공정한 정부를 도입하는 것이라고 주장하지만, 그들 자신의 지도자들이 너무 자주 명백하게 부패해 있기 때문에 그러한 주장은 타당하지 않아 보인다.

05 Scale models may be employed for testing theories or comparing alternative designs, but no model will ever fully _____ conditions of the actual as-built structure.

이론을 실험하거나 대안적인 설계를 비교하기 위해 축소판 모델이 사용될 수도 있지만, 어떠한 모델도 지어진 실제 건축물의 조건을 절대 완전히 복제하지 못할 것이다.

C 다음 네모 안에서 문맥에 맞는 말을 고르시오.

01 The automatic / manual dog feeder ensured that my dog was well fed even when I was away by dispensing food at scheduled intervals.

02 Despite legislative efforts to fight against equality / discrimination, subtle biases still influence how people are hired, denying some groups an equal chance at employment.

WORDS REVIEW

A 다음 영어 단어에 해당하는 우리말 뜻을 빈칸에 쓰시오.

01 chronically   _____   07 regime   _____

02 comparison   _____   08 composition   _____

03 consensus   _____   09 superficial   _____

04 articulation   _____   10 integration   _____

05 wield   _____   11 monopolistic   _____

06 inflame   _____   12 colonize   _____

B 다음 우리말과 의미가 같도록 빈칸에 알맞은 말을 [보기]에서 골라 쓰시오. (필요시 형태를 변형할 것)

| 보기 |
| inspiration   distraction   deviation   exploitation   cohesion |

01 When experimenting, scientists should be aware of all potential sources of bias and undertake all possible actions to reduce and minimize _____ from the truth.

실험을 할 때, 과학자들은 가능한 모든 편향의 원천을 인지하고, 진실로부터의 이탈을 줄이고 최소화하기 위해 가능한 모든 조치를 취해야 한다.

02 Rights must be subject to constraints in order to prevent their _____ for wrongful ends.

권리는 부당한 목적을 위한 그것의 불법 이용을 막기 위해 제약을 받아야 한다.

03 This is the economy that privileges the financial sector, profits over investments, cost reductions over company _____.

이것은 금융 부문에, 투자보다는 수익에, 회사의 화합보다는 비용 절감에 특권을 주는 경제이다.

04 What force better contributes to group integration, ritualistic power, visionary _____, or emotional intensity than music?

어떤 힘이 음악보다 그룹 통합, 의식적 힘, 꿈같은 영감 또는 감정적 강도에 더 잘 기여할까?

05 By allowing us to filter out _____, to quiet the problem-solving functions of the frontal lobes, deep reading becomes a form of deep thinking.

우리를 산만하게 하는 것들을 거르도록 허용하고 전두엽의 문제 해결 기능을 진정시킴으로써, 깊은 독서는 깊은 사색의 한 형태가 된다.

C 다음 네모 안에서 문맥에 맞는 말을 고르시오.

01 The concise / lengthy summary at the beginning of the book provided readers with a clear roadmap and allowed them to grasp the key points without getting lost in a sea of words.

02 The company prioritizes the well-being of its employees. Similarly / Conversely, its competitor prioritizes maximizing productivity at all costs.

WORDS REVIEW

A 다음 영어 단어에 해당하는 우리말 뜻을 빈칸에 쓰시오.

01 realm _____   07 heritage _____

02 harass _____   08 differentiate _____

03 rational _____   09 incubate _____

04 lure _____   10 embrace _____

05 arbitrarily _____   11 domination _____

06 head off _____   12 bluntly _____

B 다음 우리말과 의미가 같도록 빈칸에 알맞은 말을 [보기]에서 골라 쓰시오. (필요시 형태를 변형할 것)

/ 보기 /
| obscure | distance | seasoned | dissuade | dictate |

01 A(n) _____ loan officer, who makes the final decision, might want to know how various factors have been weighted in the system's recommendation.

최종 결정을 내리는 경험 많은 대출 직원은 그 시스템의 추천에서 다양한 요인들에 가중치가 주어진 방식을 알고 싶을 수도 있다.

02 Yet no system ought to be allowed to _____ the elemental fact that war consisted of fighting and that fighting determined the outcome of wars.

그러나 어떠한 체제도 전쟁은 싸움으로 구성되며, 그 싸움이 전쟁의 결과를 결정한다는 근본적인 사실을 가리도록 허용되어서는 안 된다.

03 Civil society may be hindered by significant ethnic or other societal divisions that _____ people from forming organizations across these institutional barriers.

시민 사회는 이 제도적 장벽을 넘어 사람들이 조직을 형성하지 못하도록 만류하는 중요한 민족적 또는 다른 사회적 분열에 의해 방해받을 수 있다.

04 The clergy _____ societal values, whose adoption would lead to saving souls, the highest goal at the time.

성직자들이 사회의 가치를 좌우했는데, 그 가치의 채택은 그 당시 최고의 목표였던 영혼 구원으로 이어질 것이었다.

05 Preservation's act of reshaping the past according to the views of the present effectively _____ the past from the present.

현재의 관점에 따라 과거를 고쳐 만드는 보존 행위는 사실상 과거를 현재에서 떼어 놓는다.

C 다음 네모 안에서 문맥에 맞는 말을 고르시오.

01 The policeman's [corrupt / virtuous] conduct restored faith in the justice system and earned the admiration of the public.

02 Before implementing the new policy, the company required written [consent / dissent] from all employees.

WORDS REVIEW

A 다음 영어 단어에 해당하는 우리말 뜻을 빈칸에 쓰시오.

01 deceive _____   07 orthodox _____

02 recurrent _____   08 intertwine _____

03 toleration _____   09 align with _____

04 emerging _____   10 scarce _____

05 comply _____   11 inconclusive _____

06 uniformity _____   12 entrust _____

B 다음 우리말과 의미가 같도록 빈칸에 알맞은 말을 [보기]에서 골라 쓰시오. (필요시 형태를 변형할 것)

┌─ 보기 ───┐
│ disengage   undermine   embed   articulate   consolidate │
└──┘

01 Liberal merchants, manufacturers, financiers, and intellectuals _____ ideas that diverged from medieval Catholic theology.

자유주의 상인, 제조업자, 금융가, 그리고 지식인은 중세 가톨릭 신학에서 벗어난 사상을 명확히 표현했다.

02 Proposals that prune and _____ the explanatory concepts of ethics too radically will end up leaving out important phenomena or rendering them unrecognizable.

너무 과격하게 윤리학의 설명적인 개념을 가지치기하고 강화하는 제안들이 결국 중요한 현상들을 제외하거나 혹은 그것을 인식할 수 없게 만들 것이다.

03 _____ from any outward focus, our attention turns inward, and we end up locked in what Emerson called the jail of self-consciousness.

우리의 주의는 외부로의 집중에서 벗어나 내부로 향하고, 우리는 결국 Emerson이 자의식의 감옥이라고 말한 것에 감금된다.

04 Knowledge was _____ in "poetry," as Plato defined it, and a specialized class of poet-scholars became the human intellectual technologies for information storage, retrieval, and transmission.

지식은 플라톤이 정의한 대로 '시'에 내재되었고, 시인-학자라는 전문화된 계층이 정보 저장, 검색, 전달을 위한 인간의 지적 기술이 되었다.

05 The prospects for survival of released individuals are most severely _____ when there are no free-living elder role models.

방생된 개체들의 생존에 대한 전망은 자유롭게 사는 어른 역할 모델이 없을 경우 가장 심각하게 훼손된다.

C 다음 네모 안에서 문맥에 맞는 말을 고르시오.

01 The executive's tendency to [underestimate / overestimate] market demand led to overproduction and excess inventory, which ultimately hurt the company's bottom line.

02 As the priest performed the [sacred / worldly] ritual, the people watched in awe, sensing the profound meaning of the ceremonial gestures.

WORDS REVIEW

A 다음 영어 단어에 해당하는 우리말 뜻을 빈칸에 쓰시오.

01 strain _____

02 breakthrough _____

03 incompatible _____

04 fixate _____

05 inscribe _____

06 syllable _____

07 intensify _____

08 optimally _____

09 destabilization _____

10 invariably _____

11 vertical _____

12 prophecy _____

B 다음 우리말과 의미가 같도록 빈칸에 알맞은 말을 [보기]에서 골라 쓰시오.

/ 보기 /

| infusion | supernatural | dominance | arguably | addictive |

01 Every organization that intends to survive beyond the next two product life cycles needs healthy _____ of innovation and must invest to get them.

제품 수명 주기가 두 번 지난 이후에도 생존하고자 하는 모든 조직은 건전한 혁신의 주입들이 필요하고, 그것들을 얻기 위해 투자해야 한다.

02 We might tell ourselves that once we achieve the next outcome, we will stop these behaviors, but they can become _____ and difficult to stop.

우리는 다음 결과를 달성하면 우리가 이러한 행동을 멈출 것이라고 스스로에게 말할 수도 있지만, 그것들은 중독성이 생겨서 멈추기 어려울 수 있다.

03 Boredom and mental strain can push us toward easy ways of engaging that require little skill and _____ do not enrich our lives in any way.

지루함과 정신적 피로는 우리를 기술이 거의 필요하지 않고 거의 틀림없이 우리의 삶을 결코 풍요롭게 하지 않는 쉬운 방식의 활동으로 이끌 수 있다.

04 This _____ of the left hemisphere for song control has been found in all species of songbirds studied so far, except the zebra finch.

노래 조절에 대한 좌반구의 이러한 우위는 금화조를 제외한 지금까지 연구된 모든 지저귀는 새의 종에서 발견되었다.

05 The tea-leaves and yarrow-stalks examples also show that often a special type of knowledge is required to interpret the _____ messages.

찻잎과 서양톱풀 줄기의 예는 또한 초자연적인 메시지를 해석하기 위해서는 자주 특별한 종류의 지식이 필요하다는 것을 보여 준다.

C 다음 네모 안에서 문맥에 맞는 말을 고르시오.

01 Throughout history, many great leaders have emerged as proponents / opponents of peace, striving to resolve conflicts through diplomacy rather than violence.

02 Archaeologists have shed light on early human civilization by uncovering modern / primitive tools dating back thousands of years.

WORDS REVIEW

A 다음 영어 단어에 해당하는 우리말 뜻을 빈칸에 쓰시오.

01	downside	_____	07	intense	_____
02	fragmentation	_____	08	prolonged	_____
03	attachment	_____	09	inevitably	_____
04	visionary	_____	10	modulate	_____
05	recollection	_____	11	ecological	_____
06	adverse	_____	12	harness	_____

B 다음 우리말과 의미가 같도록 빈칸에 알맞은 말을 [보기]에서 골라 쓰시오. (필요시 형태를 변형할 것)

---- 보기 ----

| epidemic | coherent | recipient | indigenous | deliberation |

01 This is especially important in areas where _____ peoples may mistrust or not understand modern medicines and health facilities.

이것은 토착 부족들이 현대 의약품과 의료 시설을 불신하거나 이해하지 못할 수도 있는 지역에서 특히 중요하다.

02 However, the repeated pattern is a change in attitudes, even just ten minutes later and despite no movement during the _____.

하지만 반복되는 패턴은 심의 중 불과 10분 후에 그리고 아무런 움직임이 없음에도 불구하고 태도에서 변화가 있다.

03 Their knowledge and culture have not been valued by major media outlets, universities, or expert institutions, but rather they've been passive _____ of handouts and information.

그들의 지식과 문화는 주요 매스컴, 대학교, 또는 전문 기관에 의해 가치 있게 여겨진 것이 아니라 오히려 유인물과 정보의 수동적인 수신자들이었다.

04 People who were able to tell _____ stories about their traumatic childhood were observed to be very different kinds of parents than people who had the same amount of childhood trauma but were somehow not done with it.

자신의 매우 충격적인 어린 시절에 관해 일관성 있는 이야기를 할 수 있었던 사람들은 같은 양의 어린 시절의 충격적인 경험을 가지고 있지만 어쩐지 그것을 마무리하지 못했던 사람들과는 매우 다른 종류의 부모가 된 것으로 관찰되었다.

05 In recent times, anthropologists have been able to make important contributions to helping people suffering from _____, natural disasters, and conflict.

최근에 인류학자들은 전염병들, 자연재해, 그리고 내전으로 고통받고 있는 사람들을 돕는 데 중요한 기여를 해 올 수 있었다.

C 다음 네모 안에서 문맥에 맞는 말을 고르시오.

01 The pain from the injury [increased / diminished] with each passing day, thanks to diligent physical therapy and rehabilitation.

02 [Altruistic / Self-centered] individuals often volunteer their time and resources to support charitable causes in their communities.

WORDS REVIEW

A 다음 영어 단어에 해당하는 우리말 뜻을 빈칸에 쓰시오.

01 medieval _____   07 commentary _____
02 override _____   08 proportion _____
03 perish _____   09 convert _____
04 prominently _____   10 ample _____
05 compassion _____   11 employ _____
06 referent _____   12 invoke _____

B 다음 우리말과 의미가 같도록 빈칸에 알맞은 말을 [보기]에서 골라 쓰시오.

보기
comparable   subordination   explanatory   rationality   solidarity

01 It is difficult to find any well-regarded commentator proposing that neuroscientific developments should work towards anything remotely _____ to this example.
인정받는 논평자가 신경 과학의 발전이 이 사례와 아주 조금 유사한 것을 얻으려고 노력해야 한다고 제안하는 것을 발견하기는 어렵다.

02 The absence of emotion reduces the scope of _____ because we literally think with our feelings.
우리는 말 그대로 우리의 느낌과 함께 사고하기 때문에 감정의 부재는 합리성의 범위를 축소시킨다.

03 Northrop Frye's _____ analogy is mathematics, a self-enclosed system that enters into relationships with other systems, always on its own terms.
Northrop Frye가 설명하는 비유는 수학인데, 그것은 항상 그 자체의 용어를 가지고 다른 체계와 관계를 맺는 자체 완결적인 체계이다.

04 Patents can drive people to _____ to companies that will allow them just enough profit within the system to survive, but not enough to flourish.
특허란 사람들을 그들로 하여금 살아남기 위해 체제 안에서 겨우 충족될 만큼만의 이익을 허용하지만 번창할 정도로 충분하지 않은 수익을 허용할 회사에의 종속으로 몰아넣을 수 있다.

05 More accurately, the Thanksgiving tradition was invented to promote American national _____ following the Civil War.
더 정확하게, 추수 감사절 전통은 남북 전쟁 이후에 미국의 국가적 결속을 증진하기 위해 만들어졌다.

C 다음 네모 안에서 문맥에 맞는 말을 고르시오.

01 Farmers, if eligible / ineligible , can apply for subsidies that help increase agricultural productivity and sustainability.

02 Permissions / Restrictions on travel to certain regions due to political instability have had a negative economic impact on the tourism industry and local livelihoods.

WORDS REVIEW

A 다음 영어 단어에 해당하는 우리말 뜻을 빈칸에 쓰시오.

01	eloquently	_____	07	analogously	_____
02	mediate	_____	08	exert	_____
03	invariably	_____	09	insulate	_____
04	concrete	_____	10	residential	_____
05	mean	_____	11	elicit	_____
06	endow	_____	12	intimidating	_____

B 다음 우리말과 의미가 같도록 빈칸에 알맞은 말을 [보기]에서 골라 쓰시오. (필요시 형태를 변형할 것)

┌─ 보기 /─────────────────────────────────┐
│ intricate   arbitrary   decay   assimilate   conceptualize │
└──┘

01 If one pathway in the brain has _____, a multilingual has other pathways that have been built over time as a result of the links between words, memories, and experiences accumulated in the other languages.

뇌의 한 경로가 쇠퇴한 경우에, 다국어 사용자는 다른 언어에서 축적된 단어, 기억, 경험 간의 연결로 인해 시간이 지남에 따라 구축된 다른 경로를 가지고 있다.

02 That struggle is attributable, to a large extent, to the fact that we do not have language available to _____ the specificities of this phenomenon.

그 고군분투는 대체로 우리에게 이 현상의 특수성을 개념화할 수 있는 언어가 없다는 사실에 기인한다.

03 We can see that choosing to limit science only to those experiences that are measurable is a wholly _____ choice within the framework of the nature of sense experience.

우리는 과학을 측정할 수 있는 그런 경험으로만 한정하기로 선택하는 것은 감각 경험의 본질이라는 틀 내에서 내린 완전히 자의적인 선택이라는 것을 이해할 수 있다.

04 Talking or translating an experience into language, seen as the social mechanism guiding memories, can help to organize and _____ the event in people's minds.

기억을 안내하는 사회적 메커니즘으로 여겨지는, 경험을 말하거나 언어로 옮기는 것은 사람들의 마음속에서 그 사건을 조직화하고 완전히 이해하는 것을 도울 수 있다.

05 Hitting baseballs or playing musical instruments requires _____ control of muscles carrying out complex tasks in a series of steps.

야구공을 치거나 악기를 연주하는 것은 일련의 단계 속에서 복잡한 작업을 수행하는 근육의 복잡한 조절을 필요로 한다.

C 다음 네모 안에서 문맥에 맞는 말을 고르시오.

01 The boy recovered from the disease much faster than expected, thanks to his resilient / vulnerable immune system.

02 The superior / inferior quality of the product was directly responsible for the increase in customer complaints and the subsequent decline in sales.

김종석 보습학원	심효령 삼부가람학원	이혜린 스카이영어학원	박진경 제이즈잉글리쉬	최유송 목동 씨앤씨학원
김지영 김지영영어	안수정 궁극의 사고	임정연 안은경영어학원	박찬경 펜타곤영어	최정문 한성학원
김하나 하나로운영어	오봉주 새미래영수학원	장혜인 민락능률이엠학원	박현서 e. Class	최형미 전문과외
김희정 탑에이스학원	유수민 대치이강	정승덕 학장중학교	반향진 세레나영어수학	최희재 표현학원
노태경 윙스잉글리쉬	윤영숙 전문과외	정영훈 제이앤씨영어전문학원	배지원 빛나는영어교습소	표효진 전문과외
문창숙 지앤비(GnB)스페셜입시학원	이보배 비비영어교습소	채지영 리드앤톡영어도서관학원	배현경 전문과외	하다님 연세 마스터스 학원
민승규 민승규영어학원	이성구 청명대입학원	최승빈 다온학원	백미선 최종호영어학원	한성호 티포인트에듀
박고은 스테듀입시학원	임혜주 파라곤어학원	최우성 초이English&Pass	백희영 서초토피아어학원	한인혜 레나잉글리쉬
박라율 열공열강영어수학학원	장유리 삼성영어셀레나 도안학습관	최이내 전문과외	신경훈 탑앤탑수학영어학원	한혜주 함영원입시전문학원
박소현 워싱턴어학원	장윤정 이지탑학원	탁아진 에이블영어국어학원	심나현 성북메가스터디	허미영 삼성영어 창일교실 학원
박예빈 영재키움영어수학전문학원	정예슬 소로영어	하현진 브릿츠영어학원	안미영 스카이플러스학원	홍대균 홍대균 영어
박지환 전문과외	정윤희 Alex's English		양하나(바이올렛) 목동 씨앤씨	홍영민 성북상상학원
방성모 방성모영어학원	정현지 전문과외	서울	엄태엽 대치차오름학원	황선애 앤스영어학원
백재인 에소테리카 영어학원	정혜수 쌜리영어	가혜림 위즈스터디	오유림 헬리오 오샘 영어	황혜진 이루다 영어
서정인 서울입시학원	최성호 에이스영어교습소	강경표 최선어학원 중계캠퍼스	오은경 전문과외	
신혜경 전문과외	한형식 서대전여자고등학교	강은 더이룸학원	용혜영 SWEET ENGLISH 영어전문 공부방	세종
심경아 전문과외	허욱 Ben class(전문과외)	강이권 네오어학원	유경미 서울	강홍구 세종시 더올림 입시학원
엄재경 하이엔드영어학원	황지현 공부자존감영어입시학원	강준수 전문과외	유연이 오세용학원	김세인 이룸영어교습소
우유진 이듀 잉글리쉬		강현숙 토피아어학원 중계지점	유은주 리프영어	방종영 세움학원
원현지 원샘영어교습소	부산	강호영 인투엠학원	윤성 대치동 새움학원	성민진 EiE 반곡 캠퍼스
유경아 티나잉글리시	강민주 에듀플렉스 명륜점	공진 리더스	윤은미 CnT영어학원	손대령 강한영어학원
유지연 에스피영어	고경원 JS영수학원	김경수 탑킴입시컨설팅진학지도	이계훈 이지영어학원	안성주 더타임학원
윤이강 윤이강 영어학원	김경희 거제동 니키영어	김명열 대치명인학원 은평캠퍼스	이남규 전문과외	
이가나 이나영어교실	김대영 엘리트에듀 학원	김미은 오늘도맑음 영어교습소	이명순 Top Class 영어	울산
이근성 헬렌영어학원	김도담 도담한영어교실	김미정 전문과외	이상윤 주연학원	강상배 전문과외
이동현 쌤마스터입시학원	김도윤 코어영어교습소	김배성 정명영어교습소	이석원 지구촌고등학교	김경수 핀포인트영어학원
이미경 전문과외	김동혁 코어영어수학전문학원	김상희 스카이플러스학원	이선미 범블비 영어 교습소	김경현 에린영어
이샛별 전문과외	김동휘 장정호 영어전문학원	김선경 마크영어학원	이선정 제이나영어학원	김문정 천곡고려학원
이수희 이온영어학원	김미혜 더멘토영어교습소	김성근 더원잉글리시	이성택 엠아이씨영어학원	김은주 공부발전소학원
이승현 학문당입시학원	김소림 엘라영어학원	김성연 대치청출어람학원	이수정 영샘영어	김주희 하이디영어교습소
이지현 지니영어	김소연 전문과외	김승환 Arnold English	이승혜 스텔라 영어	김한중 스마트영어전문학원
이헌욱 이헌욱 영어학원	김은정 클라라 잉글리쉬	김영재 제니퍼영어 교습소	이승회Edward 임팩트7영어학원 목동	서예원 해법멘토영어수학학원
이현지 리즈영어	김재경 탑클래스영어학원	김용봉 SKY PLUS 학원	2단지 고등관	송회철 꿈꾸는고래학원
인솔내 제인영어학당	김진규 의문을열다	김은영 LCA 영어학원	이연주 Real Iris Class	엄여은 준쌤영어교습소
임형주 사범대단과학원	김효은 김효은 영수 전문학원	김은정 전문과외	이은선 드림영어하이수학학원	윤주이 고도영어학원
전윤애 올리영어교습소	남재호 제니스학원	김은진 ACE영어교습소	이은영 한국연예예술학교	이서경 이서경영어학원
전윤영 뮤엠영어 경동초점	류미향 류미향입시영어	김정민 W영어	이자임 자몽영어교습소	이수현 제이엘영어학원
전지영 제이제이영어	문희진 베아투스학원	김종현 김종현영어	이정혜 수시이룸교육	이승준 전문과외
정대웅 유신학원	박미지 MJ영어학원	김지윤 비타윤영어	이지윤 전문과외	이은민 스마트영어전문학원
정용희 에스피영어학원	박수진 제이엔씨 영어학원	김태성 전문과외	이철웅 비상하는 또또학원	이재은 잉크영어학원
진보라 메이킹어학원	박인혜 정철어학원	김현지 전문과외	이혜정 이루리학원	임재희 임재희영어전문학원
최효진 너를 위한 영어	박정아 전문과외	김혜영 스터디원	이희영 이샘아카데미 영어교습소	정은선 한국esl어학원
한정아 능인고등학교	박지우 영어를 ON하다	나명은 전문과외	임광영 러셀 메가스터디	정혜미 전문과외
황윤슬 사적인영어	박지은 박지은영어전문과외방	노현희 전문과외	임서우 형설학원	조승현 스마트영어전문학원
	박창헌 오늘도,영어그리고수학	도선혜 중계동 영어	임소례 윤선생영어교실우리집앞신내키움	조충일 YBM 잉글루 울산언양 제1학원
대전	배슬기 전문과외	류하영 유니스영어	영어교습소	최아현 jp영어학원
Tony Park Tony Park English	배찬원 에이플러스 영어	맹혜선 휘경여자고등학교	임은옥 전문과외	한건수 한스영어
고우리 영어의꿈	백은비 비앙카 영어 교습소	명가은 명가은 영어하다 학원	임해림 그레이스학원	허부배 비즈단과학원
김근범 딱쌤학원	변혜련 전문과외	문명기 문명기 영어학원	장서인 함께 자라는 스마트올클래스	
김기형 상승학원	성장우 전문과외	문슬기 문쌤 전문영어과외	전지영 탑클래스영수학원	인천
김민정 전문과외	손소희 에스 잉글리쉬 사이언스	박기철 한진연 입시전략연구소	정경록 미즈원어학원	강재민 스터디위드제이쌤
김아영 전문과외	송석준 스카이영수전문학원	박남규 알짜영어교습소	정연우 전문과외	김미경 김선생영어/수학교실
김영철 빅뱅잉글리시리더스	송초롱 최상위영어교습소	박미애 명문지혜학원	정유하 크라센어학원	김민영 YBM Homeschool 영종자이센터
김주리 위드제이영어	안정희 GnB어학원양성캠퍼스	박미정 위드멘토학원	정재욱 씨알학원	김민정 김민영어
김현지 영어과외	예다슬 전문과외	박병석 주영학원	조길영 이앤조영어	김서애 제이플러스영어
나규성 대전 비전21학원	오세창 범석반석단과학원	박선경 씨투엠학원	조미영 튼튼영어마스터클럽구로학원	김선나 지니어스영어학원
남영종 엠베스트SE학원 대전 전민점	오지은 이루다영어	박소영 JOY	조미지 책읽는영어교습소 제니쌤영어	김영태 에듀타학원
노지혜 제일학원	옥지윤 더센텀영어학원	박소하 전문과외	조민석 더원영수학원	김영호 조주석수학&영어클리닉학원
노현서 앨리글리쉬아카데미	윤지영 잉글리쉬무무영어교습소	박솔이 Sole English	조봉현 대치명인학원 중계캠퍼	김옥경 잉글리쉬 베이
박난경 제일학원	윤진희 위니드영어전문교습소	박승규 이지수능교육	채보경 개인과외	김주영 아너스영어학원
박성희 청담프라임학원	이미정 탑에듀영어교습소	박정미 드림영어 하이수학학원	채상우 클레스영어	김지연 송도탑영어학원
박정민 율영수학원	이상석 엠베스트se 공부습관365 학원	박정효 성북메가스터디학원	채에스더 문래중학교 방과후	김현미 송도탑영어학원
박지현 더브라이트학원	이순실 하단종로엠학원	박준용 G1230학원	최미림 밀리에듀영어학원	김현섭 전문과외
박효진 박효진 영어	이영준 개금국제어학원	박지훈 청담어학원	최민주 전문과외	김현준 JKD영어전문학원

나일지	두드림하이학원	조예진	에이펙스 영어학원
문지현	전문과외	조형진	대니아빠앤디영어교습소
박가람	전문과외	최미화	MH노블영어학원
박나혜	TOP과외	최석원	전주에듀캠프학원
박민아	하이영어 공부방	한주훈	알파스터디영어수학전문학원
박승민	대치세정학원	황보희	에임드영수학원
박주현	Ashley's English Corner		
신나리	이루다교육학원	**제주**	
신은주	명문학원	Brian T.K	Top Class Academy
신현경	GMI 어학원	고보경	제주여자고등학교
오희정	더제니스엣지영어학원	고승용	진정성학원제주노형센터
윤효주	잉글리시브릿지	김진재	함성소리학원
윤희영	세실영어	김평호	서이현아카데미학원
이가희	S&U영어	김현정	유비고영어학원
이미선	고품격EMEDU	문재웅	문&YES 중고등 내신수능 영어
이수진	전문과외	배동환	뿌리와샘
이영태	인천부흥고등학교	이승우	늘다올 학원
이은정	인천논현고등학교	이윤아	에이투지어학원
이진희	이진희영어	이재철	함성소리학원
장승혁	지엘학원	임정열	엑셀영어
전혜원	제일고등학교	정승현	J's English
정도영	스테디 잉글리시	지광미	지샘입시영어학원
정춘기	정상어학원		
조윤정	인천이음중학교	**충남**	
최민솔	영웅아카데미	강유안	전문과외
최민지	빅뱅영어	고유미	고유미영어
최수련	업앤업영어교습소	김인영	더오름영어
최창영	학산에듀넷	김일환	김일환어학원
최하은	정철어학원	김창현	타임영어학원
홍영주	홍이어쎈영어	박서현	TIE고려대어학원
		박재영	로제타스톤 영어교실
전남		박희진	박쌤영어과외
강용문	강용문영수입시전문	우경희	우쌤클라쓰
김숙진	지니쌤 공부방	윤현미	비비안의 잉글리쉬 클래스
김아름	전문과외	이규현	글로벌학원
김은정	BestnBest 공부방	이상진	마틴영어학원
김임열	태강수학영어학원	이영롱	대승학원
김재원	나주혁신위즈수학영어학원	이종화	오름에듀
박민지	벨라영어	임진주	원더크라운영어학원
박주형	해룡고등학교	장성은	상승기류
배송이	JH공터영어전문학원	장완기	장완기학원
손성호	아름다운 11월학원	정래	(주)탑씨크리트교육
양명승	엠에스어학원	조남진	천안 불당PYO영어국어학원
오은주	순천금당고등학교	채은주	위너스 학원
이상호	스카이입시학원		
이용	해룡고등학교	**충북**	
이정원	앤더슨 영어학원	김보경	더시에나영어학원
조소을	수잉글리쉬	박광수	폴인어학원
차형진	상아탑학원	박수열	전문과외
		박현자	박쌤영어
전북		신유정	비타민 영어클리닉
길지만	비상잉글리시아이영어학원	안지영	전문과외
김나은	애플영어학원	양미정	전문과외
김보경	최영훈영수학원	양미진	JEC지니영어교실
김설아	전주 에듀캠프학원	윤선아	타임즈영어학원
김수정	베이스탑영어	윤홍석	대학가는길
김예원	옥스포드 어학원	이경수	더애스에이티영수단과학원
김예진	카일리영어학원	이재욱	대학 가는 길 학원
이경훈	리더스영수전문학원	이재은	파머스영어와이즈톡학원
이수정	씨에이엔영어학원	조현국	업클래스학원
이진주	전문과외	하선빈	어썸영어수학학원
이한결	DNA영어학원		
이효상	에임하이영수학원		
장길호	장길호영어학원		

READING MASTER

수능 고난도

정답 및 해설

이투스북

READING MASTER

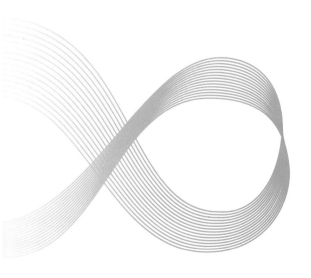

수능 고난도

정답 및 해설

고난도 모의고사 01회

| 01 ② | 02 ② | 03 ③ | 04 ④ | 05 ④ | 06 ③ |
| 07 ④ | 08 ② | 09 ⑤ | 10 ⑤ | 11 ③ | 12 ⑤ |

01
정답 ②

우리는 신중함이 필요하다. 인간의 미덕은 다층적이다. 자연이 인격을 형성한다는 것은 절반의 진실에 불과하고, 그것을 전부라고 받아들이면 어리석은 것이다. 그것은 모든 시민적 덕성을 제외할 것인데, 그것 없이 우리는 인간일 수 없을 것이다. 인격은 자연과 문화의 변증법에서 발달된다. "인간은 본래 정치적 동물이다." 인간은 스스로 도시 국가인 도시를 세우고 그 안에서 사회화하는 것을 좋아하는 동물이다. "인간은 인위적이 되는 것이 자연스러운 동물이다." '호모 사피엔스'는 '타고난 이방인'이다. 인간이 자연과 만날 때 '자연스럽게' 하는 것은 자신을 자연과 구별하는 문화를 만드는 것이다. 농업, 상업, 그리고 산업이 그들의 진정한 천직이다. 미덕은 '함양되고,' '키워져야' 한다. 향수를 불러일으키는 소박함과 검소함 속에서 야생적인 자연과 함께 산다는 것은, 인간의 비범한 재능이 얼마나 많이 자연으로부터의 이탈 및 수완 좋은 자연의 변형에서 발견되는지를 망각하는 낭만적이고 터무니없는 생각이라고 이러한 '인문주의자들'은 말할 것이다. 이것에 대한 현대어는 "개발하라!"이다.

해설
인간은 자연과 만났을 때 자연과 구별되는 자신의 문화를 만들어 온 존재이고 인간의 비범한 재능은 자연을 수완 좋게 변형시키는 데 있다고 서술하고 있으므로, 밑줄 친 부분이 의미하는 바로 가장 적절한 것은 ② '인간의 의지에 따라 자연을 바꾸라!'이다.
① 자연에서 배우고 새로운 아이디어를 얻어라!
③ 질병에서 회복하고 건강하라!
④ 환경 문제를 고려하라!
⑤ 야생 동물과 친밀한 유대감을 형성하라!

TEXT FLOW

> 도입 인간의 인격은 자연과 문화의 변증법에서 발달함
> 부연 인간은 자연과 만났을 때 자신을 자연과 구별하는 문화를 만들어 온 존재임
> 결론 인간의 재능은 자연을 수완 좋게 변형시키는 데 있음

구문
• [That nature builds character] is **but** half the truth and absurd [if taken for the whole].
: 첫 번째 [ ]는 접속사 That이 이끄는 명사절로 문장의 주어이다. but은 부사로 only의 뜻이다. 두 번째 [ ]는 if it is taken for the whole에서 it is가 생략된 형태이다.
• [What humans "naturally" do {when they encounter nature}] is [**build** a culture {differentiating themselves from nature}].
: 첫 번째 [ ]는 관계대명사 What이 이끄는 명사절로 문장의 주어이고, 그

안의 { }는 때를 나타내는 부사절이다. 두 번째 [ ]는 주격 보어 역할을 하는 원형부정사구이고, 그 안의 { }는 a culture를 수식하는 현재분사구이다. 「what/all+주어+동사」가 주어일 때는 주격 보어로 to부정사의 to가 생략된 원형부정사(build)를 쓰기도 한다.

02
정답 ②

구전된 역사 자료가 주관적이고 부정확하다는 비평은 그것들(역사 자료)의 가장 큰 가치 중 하나, 즉 그것들이 주관적인 경험에 제공하는 통찰을 버리는 위험을 무릅쓰는 것이다. 이것은 그저 역사에 색채를 더하는 것 이상이며, 예를 들어 개인적인 의견, 친분, 그리고 반감이 성공적인 군사 작전과 그것의 실패, 대체로 동의하는 정책이나 깊은 정치적인 균열 사이에 차이를 만들어 낼 수 있다는 것을 부인하는 역사가는 거의 없을 것이다. 정말로, 면담의 주관성은 어떤 주제가 역사적인 연구를 할 가치가 있다고 여길지를 바꿀 힘이 있다. 예를 들어, Thompson은 '구전된 역사 자료가 가족의 역사에 미치는 변화의 영향력'에 주목해 왔으며 그것이 없다면 '역사가는 평범한 가족이 이웃과 친족과 가지는 접촉이나 혹은 그것(가족)의 내적인 관계에 대해 정말로 거의 아무것도 알아낼 수 없다'고 지적했다. 여성주의 역사가들은 주관적인 경험과 감정적인 의미는 역사적인 연구에서 사건의 서술만큼이나 중요한 지위를 차지한다고 지적해 왔다.

해설
구전된 역사 자료는 역사를 보는 관점에 대한 통찰을 줄 수 있으며 그것이 사건의 서술만큼이나 중요한 가치를 가진다는 내용이므로, 글의 주제로 가장 적절한 것은 ② '역사 연구에서 구전된 역사 자료의 중요성'이다.
① 역사에서 패자의 목소리를 회복하는 어려움
③ 추가적인 연구를 위해 구전된 역사 자료를 보존하는 방법
④ 구전된 역사 자료와 출판된 기록의 차이
⑤ 역사학자들의 관점이 역사적 해석에 영향을 미치는 방법

TEXT FLOW

> 도입 구전된 역사 자료는 주관적인 경험이 제공하는 통찰을 줌
> 부연 면담의 주관성은 역사적인 연구를 할 가치가 있는 문제를 바꿀 힘이 있음
> 예시 Thompson은 구전된 역사 자료가 가족의 역사에 미치는 변화의 영향력에 주목함
> 결론 구전된 역사 자료는 사건의 서술만큼이나 중요한 지위를 차지함

구문
• [The critique of oral histories as subjective and inaccurate] risks [discarding one of their greatest values, {the insight they offer into subjective experience}].
: 첫 번째 [ ]는 문장의 주어이고 두 번째 [ ]는 risks의 목적어이다. { }는 one of their greatest values를 설명하는 동격어구이다.

03
정답 ③

기체 형태의 질소는 다른, 더 반응성이 있는 대기 가스가 가까이 오지 못하게

하는 것이 중요한 상황에서 자주 사용된다. 예를 들어, 그것은 생산 또는 보관 중인 전자 부품 같은 재료를 보호하는 데 있어 블랭킷 가스로서 산업에 도움이 된다. 포도주의 산화를 막기 위해 포도주병은 코르크가 제거된 후에 자주 질소로 채워진다. 최근에 질소는 또한 과일을 딴 후에 부패로부터 보호하기 위해 과일을 뒤덮는 데 사용되어 왔다. 예를 들어 사과는 공기가 질소로만 된 곳에서 낮은 온도로 유지되면 30개월까지 저장될 수 있다. 이런 활용 이외에 질소는 원유 생산에도 사용되는데, 원유를 표면에 올라오게 하기 위해 압축된 형태로 펌프를 통해 질소를 땅속으로 보낸다. 보통의 공기는 이 목적으로 사용될 수 없는데, 이는 공기를 구성하는 기체들 중 일부가 원유와 반응하여 원하지 않는 부산물을 만들어 낼 것이기 때문이다.

해설

③ to protect 이하는 to부정사구로 목적의 의미를 가지는데, protect의 행위를 하는 주체는 fruit이 아니라 Nitrogen이므로, 재귀대명사 itself를 대명사 it으로 고쳐야 한다.
① 관계절 안에서 it은 가주어이고 to keep 이하가 진주어이므로, to keep은 어법상 적절하다.
② wine bottles는 fill의 행위를 당하는 대상이므로, 수동의 의미를 나타내는 과거분사 filled는 어법상 맞는 표현이다.
④ in which 이하는 oil production을 부연 설명하는 관계절이며 완전한 형태의 절이므로, in which는 어법상 적절하다.
⑤ producing은 결과를 나타내는 분사구문으로 some of the gases that make up air would react with the oil 전체를 부연 설명한다. producing은 which produces 또는 and it produces의 의미이다.

TEXT FLOW

도입	질소는 더 반응성 있는 대기 가스가 가까이 오지 못하게 하는 상황에서 사용됨
예시	전자 부품을 보호하는 블랭킷 가스, 포도주 산화와 과일 부패를 막는 용도로 사용됨
부연	질소는 원유 생산에도 사용됨

04
정답 ④

재난-계획과 재난-대응의 구별을 규정하는 한 가지 이유는 예상치 못한 일이 발생해서 예상치 못한 조치와 행동 규칙이 요구될 수도 있기 때문이다. 예를 들어, 한 장소로부터 질서 있는 대피를 위한 계획이 있을 수도 있지만, 지진이 났을 때 출구 경로가 차단되어 새로운 출구 경로와 대피 방법의 즉흥성이 필요할 수도 있다. 어쩌면 준비 계획은 헬기 구조를 필요로 하지 않을 수도 있지만 전개되는 상황에는 필요하고, 따라서 이것이 대응 계획에 포함된다. 모든 사람이 안전하게 대피해야 한다는 의도가 두 계획에 존재한다면, 이와 같은 변화는 윤리적 원칙의 변화를 수반하지 않는다. 준비 계획과 대응 계획 사이의 명백한 모순을 피하기 위한 한 가지 방법은 준비 계획을 고정되도록(→ 개괄적으로) 만드는 것이다. 예를 들어, 준비 계획에서 모든 거주자의 안전한 대피가 주요 목표로 진술되어 있으며, 몇 가지 출구 경로가 사전에 명시되어 있지만, 출구 경로의 선택은 열려 있어서 실제 상황에 의해 결정된다.

해설

준비 계획과 대응 계획 사이의 명백한 모순을 피하기 위한 한 가지 방법의 예는 몇 개의 출구 경로를 사전에 명시해 놓고 출구 경로의 선택은 열어 놓는다는 것이다. 즉 준비 계획을 포괄적으로 만드는 것이므로 ④의 'fixed(고정된)'를 'general(개괄적인)'과 같은 낱말로 바꾸어야 한다.

TEXT FLOW

도입	재난-계획과 재난-대응의 구별을 규정하는 이유는 예상치 못한 조치와 규칙이 요구될 수 있기 때문임
부연	준비 계획에는 필요하지 않은 것이 전개되는 상황상 필요하고, 이것이 대응 계획에 포함됨
결론	준비 계획과 대응 계획의 모순을 피하기 위해 준비 계획을 개괄적으로 만들어야 함

구문

• A change like this does not entail a change in ethical principles, **provided** the intention [that everyone be safely evacuated] is present in both plans.
: provided는 '만일 ~이라면'의 뜻을 가진 접속사이고 provided 다음에는 that이 생략되어 있다. [ ]는 주어 the intention의 구체적인 내용을 설명하는 동격절이다.

05
정답 ④

위기의 시기에, 대중 매체는 그 위기를 보도하는 데 막대한 시간과 에너지를 쏟음으로써 감시와 정보에 대한 사회의 욕구에 반응한다. 그럼에도 많은 경우 정보를 수집하는 것이 어렵다. 하지만 정보를 수집하고 확인할 수 있을 때까지 대중 매체의 보도가 중단되는 것은 제 기능을 하지 않는 것일 것이다. 사회의 긴장감을 줄이기 위해서, 대중 매체는 시청자에게 위안을 주려는 의도의 미디어 콘텐트에 많은 양의 보도를 할애한다. 연대 의식 구축은 위기의 시기에 사회를 위한 기능적 역할을 한다. 대중 매체는 '우리는 모두 이 안에 함께 있다' 그리고 생존을 위해 가능한 모든 것이 행해지고 있다고 사회를 안심시키기 위해 지도자의 지혜 및 구조 대원이나 군인들의 용기를 강조한다. 따라서 대중 매체가 감시와 상호 관계의 욕구는 충족시킬 수 없을지라도, 확신을 주고 긴장감을 감소시킬 수는 있다.

해설

위기의 시기에 대중 매체가 무엇을 해야 하는지에 관한 글이다. 대중 매체는 불안해하는 사람들에게 모두가 이 위기의 시기를 함께 헤쳐 나간다는 메시지를 주면서 시청자를 위로하고 긴장감을 감소시키는 역할을 한다고 했으므로, 빈칸에 들어갈 말로 가장 적절한 것은 ④ '연대 의식 구축'이다.
① 참신함 추구
② 사회적 거리두기
③ 자원 공유
⑤ 투명성 유지하기

TEXT FLOW

도입	위기의 시대에 대중 매체는 감시와 정보에 대한 사회의 욕구에 반응함
부연	대중 매체는 사회의 긴장감을 줄이고 시청자에게 위안을 주려는 의도의 콘텐트에 많은 양의 보도를 할애함
결론	대중 매체는 확신을 주고 긴장감을 감소시키는 역할을 함

구문

• The media **highlight** the wisdom of leaders and the bravery of rescue workers or soldiers [**to reassure** society {that "we are all in this together"} and {that everything possible is being done for survival}].
: The media 다음에는 단수 동사나 복수 동사 모두 올 수 있는데, 이 문장에서는 복수 동사 highlight가 쓰였다. [ ]는 목적을 나타내는 부사적 용

법의 to부정사구이고, 그 안의 두 개의 { }는 and로 연결되어 reassure 의 간접 목적어 역할을 하는 명사절이다.

06

스포츠 텍스트에는 많은 형태, 기능, 독자층이 있다. 전통적인 스포츠 보도는 현장에 참석하지 않은 사람들을 위해 일어난 일을 증언하기 위한 것이다. 가장 기본적이고 외연적인 수준에서, 예를 들어 Gresty Road Ground에서 2,816명의 춥고 비에 젖은 관중이 지켜보는 가운데, 영국 축구 3부 리그에서 Crewe Alexandra가 Burnley와 0대 0으로 비겼다는 것은 논란의 여지가 없는 진술이다. 여기에는 사람의 개입이 많이 필요하지 않다. 즉, 몇 단위의 데이터가 '유선으로 전송'되거나 컴퓨터 데이터베이스에 입력되어, 해운이나 주식 시장 보고서보다 더 문화적 반향(反響)이 거의 없는 텍스트를 생성한다. 다만, 그러한 익명의 정보 단위가 그것에 생계를 의존하는 선원이나 '사무직원'에게는 훨씬 더 중요하고 깊은 의미를 갖는 것처럼, 관련 스포츠 팬은 이러한 사실에 의미를 부여할 뿐만 아니라 더 많은 정보를 기대할 것이다. 따라서 많은 스포츠 추종자들이 단순한 뉴스 요약 형식에 오랫동안 만족할 것 같지는 않다.

해설
스포츠 텍스트는 사람의 많은 개입이 필요 없는, 논란의 여지가 없는 진술도 있지만, 관련된 스포츠 팬은 정보 단위에 의미를 부여할 뿐만 아니라 더 많은 정보를 기대할 것이라는 내용의 글이다. 따라서 빈칸에 들어갈 말로 가장 적절한 것은 ③ '단순한 뉴스 요약 형식에 오랫동안 만족할'이다.
① 사실보다 영향력의 중요성을 강조할
② 선수 간의 치열한 경쟁을 당연한 것으로 여길
④ 상세한 정보를 제공하는 어떤 이의 개입이든 환영할
⑤ 그들이 좋아하는 선수들을 경기장에서 직접 볼

❓ WHY 고난도
지문의 문장이 길고 복잡한 구조로 이루어져 있어 문장 해석이 쉽지 않고, 빈칸이 있는 문장에서 부정의 의미를 갖는 unlikely에 유의해 답을 선택해야 하는 고난도 문제이다.

TEXT FLOW
도입	스포츠 텍스트는 사람의 개입이 필요하지 않고 논란의 여지가 없는 진술임
전환	관련된 스포츠 팬은 이러한 사실에 의미를 부여하고 더 많은 정보를 기대함
결론	스포츠 팬들은 단순한 뉴스 요약 형식에 만족하지 않음

구문
• At the most basic, denotative level **it** is an uncontroversial statement [that, for example, Crewe Alexandra drew 0-0 {**with** Burnley in Division Three of the English Football League at the Gresty Road Ground **in front of a crowd of 2,816 cold, wet spectators**}].
: it은 가주어이고, 진주어는 [ ]이다. 그 안의 { }는 「with + 명사(구) + 부사(구)」로 부대상황을 나타낸다.

07

여러분의 삶에서 혹은 현재에 다른 무슨 일이 일어나는지에 따라 특정한 사건은 여러분을 약간 슬프게 해 여러분의 입꼬리가 아래로 처지게 할 수도 있다. 혹은 그것이 여러분을 매우 슬프게 할 수도 있어서 여러분의 눈에는 눈물이 고이기 시작할 수도 있다. 감정 상태는 다양한 일련의 다른 관련된 요인에 따라 같은 자극에 대해 정도가 다양한 강도의 반응을 허용한다. 혼자 있다고 생각할 때 아래층에서 나는 낯선 소리는, 정오에 그 사건이 발생하면 약간 겁나게 할 수도 있지만, 한밤중이라면 매우 두렵게 할 수도 있다. 반응의 차이는 세상에 대한 여러분의 지식에 근거한(특히 이 경우 언제 가택 침입이 일어날 가능성이 가장 높은가에 대한 여러분의 지식에 근거한) 유용한 구분이다. (감정을 표현하는 것은 문을 쾅 닫거나, 베개에 대고 소리를 치거나, 심지어 그것에 대해 누군가에게 말하는 것처럼 외부를 향한 것일 필요는 없다.) 그것은 감정이 점차 증가할 수 있는 성질에 의해 가능해지며, 반사적으로 처리할 수 있는 일률적인 접근 방식을 특징으로 하지 않는다.

해설
감정 상태는 다양한 관련 요인에 대한 판단에 따라 다양한 반응을 허용하게 되는데, 이러한 반응은 세상에 대한 지식에 근거하는 것이라는 내용의 글이다. 그러므로 감정을 표현하는 방식에 관한 내용의 ④는 글의 흐름과 관계가 없다.

TEXT FLOW
도입	감정 상태는 다양한 관련 요인에 따른 자극에 대해 다양한 강도의 반응을 허용함
주제	이러한 반응은 세상에 대한 지식에 근거한 유용한 구분임
부연	이는 반사적인 접근이 아닌 감정이 점차 증가할 수 있는 성질에 의해 가능함

구문
• [A strange noise {coming from downstairs when you'd thought you were alone}] might make you a little fearful if the incident happens at noon, but **very afraid** if it's at midnight.
: [ ]는 문장의 주어이고 { }는 A strange noise를 수식하는 현재분사구이다. very afraid 앞에는 반복되는 어구 make you가 생략되었다.

08

컴퓨터 기반의 검색 도구는 의심의 여지없이 유용하여, 'Current Contents'는 여러분이 관심 있는 저널의 최근 출판물을 빠르게 살펴볼 수 있게 해 주고, 'Web of Science'(그리고 이와 유사한 도구)는 저자, 키워드, 또는 인용구 추적으로 문헌을 신속하게 검색하게 해 준다. 검색 엔진을 사용할 수 있기 전에는 우리는 어떻게 그것을 했을까? (B) 나는 가령 지난 5년간 해당 주제를 발표한 주요 저널을 대강 훑어보며 관련된 논문은 무엇이나 복사하는 것으로 시작할 것이다. 그런 다음에 나는 더 오래된 문헌을 찾아내기 위해 이들 논문 속의 인용문들을 검토하고, 그 인용문들에 대한 참조 문헌의 빈도와 성향으로부터 중요한 자료를 유추할 것이다. (A) 이 방법의 큰 장점은 그 분야의 인용 구조를 제공하고 상황이 어떻게 발전해 왔는지 어느 정도 감을 잡을 수 있게 해 준다는 것이다. 한 가지 관련된 기법은 반대 방향으로 검색하는데, 이 부분에서 검색 엔진이 큰 도움이 된다. (C) 가령 20년 전에 발표된 해당 주제에 대한 핵심 논문을 찾고 나서 이 논문을 인용하는, 그때 이후로 발표된 논문을 살펴보라. 때로는 그것들이 특이한 장소에서 발표되었거나 명백하게 연관된 키워드나 제목이 없기 때문에, 그렇게 하지 않으면 놓칠 수 있을 논문을 획득하게 된다.

검색 엔진의 유용성에 대해 언급한 후, 그것이 없을 때는 검색을 어떻게 했을지 의문을 제기하는 주어진 글 다음에, 검색 엔진이 없을 때 했던 방법으로 관심 주제를 발표한 주요 저널을 훑어보고, 관련 논문을 복사하고, 논문 속 인용구로부터 주요 자료를 유추한 방식을 언급한 (B)가 와야 한다. 이어서 (B)에서 언급된 방법의 장점을 The big advantage of this method로 시작하여 소개하는 (A)가 온 다음, (A)의 마지막 문장에서 언급된 검색 엔진의 유용성에 대한 사례를 제시하는 (C)가 마지막에 오는 것이 글의 순서로 가장 적절하다.

❌ 매력적인 오답 주의!
⑤ (B)에서 (A)로의 연결은 잘 이해했으나, 주어진 문장 마지막에 검색 엔진을 사용하기 전에 했던 방법에 대한 질문에 이어지는 내용을 단순히 20 years ago로 판단하여 (C)로 선택한 것으로 보인다. [선택률 41%]

TEXT FLOW

도입	검색 엔진이 없을 때는 지난 5년간의 주요 저널을 훑어보고, 인용문을 검토하여 중요한 자료를 유추했음
부연	장점은 인용 구조를 제공하고 상황이 어떻게 발전했는지 감을 잡을 수 있게 해 줌
결론	반대로 검색할 때는 검색 엔진이 큰 도움이 됨

구문
• [Identify a key paper on the topic {published, say, 20 years ago}] and [then look at the papers published since then {that cite this paper}].
: 두 개의 [ ]는 동사원형으로 시작하는 명령문이며 and로 연결되어 있다. 첫 번째 [ ]에서 on the topic은 목적어 a key paper를 수식하는 전치사구이고, { }는 a key paper on the topic을 수식하는 과거분사구이다. 두 번째 [ ]에서 published since then은 the papers를 수식하는 과거분사구이며, { }는 the papers published since then을 수식하는 관계절이다.

09   정답 ⑤

자기 인식, 즉 성찰적 사고는 인간을 동물과 구별하는 주된 속성이다. 그것은 우리가 스스로를 깊이 생각할 수 있게 해 주는 의식이다. 성찰은 자신의 의식을 자신에게 돌리고, 자신을 알고, 특히 '자신이 알고 있다는 것을 아는' 힘이다. 인간은 자기 자신의 성찰의 대상이 될 수 있는 우주에서 유일한 창조물이며, 그것 때문에 하등 동물이 결코 참여할 수 없는 실재로서 내면의 세계인 또 다른 세계가 탄생한다. 스스로를 깊이 생각할 수 없어서, 또는 스스로가 의식이 있는 주체임을 인식하지 못하므로, 심지어 자신의 주인이 누구이며 음식이 어디에 있는지 아는 개나 고양이와 같은 지능이 더 높은 종류의 동물도 자신이 알고 있다는 것을 알 수 없다. 그 결과, 인류가 자유롭게 움직일 수 있는 실재라는 전체 영역에 대한 접근이 거부된다. 예를 들어 물리학, 철학, 수학, 천문학의 체계는 모두 내적으로 성찰하는 인간의 고유한 능력 때문에 구축되어 왔다.

결과를 나타내는 연결어구 In consequence로 시작하는 주어진 문장은 그것은 인류가 자유롭게 움직일 수 있는 전체 영역에 접근하지

못한다는 내용으로, a whole domain of reality in which mankind can move freely의 예를 Systems of physics, philosophy, mathematics, and astronomy, for example, ~로 드는 문장 앞인 ⑤에 들어가는 것이 가장 적절하다. 주어진 문장의 it은 ⑤ 앞 문장의 a higher type of animal, ~ its food is를 가리킨다.

TEXT FLOW

도입	성찰적 사고는 인간을 동물과 구별하는 주된 속성임
부연	그것 때문에 동물이 참여할 수 없는 내면의 세계가 탄생함
결론	인류가 자유롭게 움직일 수 있는 실재라는 전체 영역에 대한 접근이 거부됨

구문
• Reflection is the power [to turn one's consciousness upon oneself], [to know oneself] and, especially, [to *know that one knows*].
: 세 개의 [ ]가 the power를 수식하는 형용사적 용법의 to부정사구이며, and에 의해 병렬 구조를 이룬다.

• [Incapable of contemplating itself, or {of being aware of itself as the conscious subject}], not even a higher type of animal, such as a dog or cat that knows who its master is and where its food is, can know that it knows.
: [ ]는 As it is incapable of contemplating itself, or as it is *incapable* of being aware of itself as the conscious subject의 부사절을 분사구문으로 바꾼 것으로, 그 안의 { }는 반복되어 사용되는 incapable이 생략되었다.

10   정답 ⑤

돌아다니는 데 여러 날이나 여러 주가 걸리는 영역을 가진 동물들은 오래 지속되는 어떤 것, 즉 그들이 가고 나서까지도 계속 널리 자신을 알려 줄 어떤 것을 가지고 알릴 필요가 있다. 냄새는 오래 남을 수 있기 때문에, 동물들은 흔히 다른 동물들이 지나갈 때 읽을 수 있는 냄새 자취를 자신들의 영역에 바른다. 어두운 곳에서 활동하는 동물들은 냄새뿐만 아니라 소리에 의존하지만, 낮에 활동하는 동물들은 자신들의 메시지를 위해 시각적 수단을 사용할 가능성이 더 크다. 여러분은 가장 극적인 시각적 신호들이 탁 트인 평원의 동물들 사이에서 교환되는 것을 보게 될 것인데, 그들의 토착 서식지에서는 가로막히지 않은 시야라는 호사를 누리기 때문이다. 하지만 울창한 숲속의 새들은 보통 자신들의 수신자를 볼 수 없기 때문에, 그들은 대신에 풍성한 노래 목록을 완성했다. 저주파의 노래가 선호되는데, 고주파의 노래는 나무줄기 같은 물체에 부딪혀서 되돌아오기 쉽기 때문이다. 노래하는 새들은 대개 (숲의) 나뭇가지들이 지붕 모양으로 우거진 곳에 앉는데, 그곳에서는 '음향 창'이 그들의 메시지를 가장 효과적으로 전달한다.
➡ 동물의 왕국에서, 각 동물의 생활 방식과 그것의 서식지에 적합하도록 다양한 의사소통 수단이 나타났다.

동물들이 자신들의 특성과 서식지 및 생활 방식에 적합한 의사소통 수단을 만들어 냈다는 내용의 글이므로, 요약문의 빈칸 (A), (B)에 들어갈 말로는 ⑤ 'communication(의사소통) – lifestyle(생활 방식)'이 가장 적절하다.
① 사냥 – 생리   ② 사냥 – 생활 방식
③ 보호 – 생리   ④ 의사소통 – 특성

구문

• You'll see the most dramatic visual signals [exchanged between animals of the open plains], since, in their native habitat, they have the luxury of unobstructed views.
: [ ]는 the most dramatic visual signals를 수식하는 과거분사구이다.

11-12

정답 11 ③   12 ⑤

외부 사건에 대한 의식은 생기는 데 약 0.5초(500밀리초)가 걸린다. '현재'에 대한 우리의 인지된 인식은 사실상 때로는 '기억된 현재'라고 불리는 최근의 과거에 대한 인식이다. 이런 지연은 의식적인 인식이 광범위한 피질 대뇌 영역과 하부 대뇌 영역 간에 오가는 많은 신호 전달을 요구한다는 것을 보여 준다. '외부 세계에 대한 의식은 분명히 그 어떤 하나의 신경망 마디나 작은 신경망이라기보다 분산된 피질 신경망의 전체 활동으로 나타난다.' 무의식의 일부는 불완전하게 형성된 의식, 즉 수백 밀리초 정도 후에 생겨나는 의식의 원천인 전의식 과정으로 간주될 수도 있다. 무의식의 다른 일부는 영원히 인식으로부터 계속 숨겨져 있지만 여전히 우리의 의식적인 마음에 중요한 영향을 발휘하여, 특정한 방식으로 행동하려는 우리의 선택에 영향을 준다. 상호작용은 양방향으로 일어나, 의식적인 마음이 무의식에 영향을 미칠 수도 있고, 그 역도 또한 마찬가지이다.

우리의 무의식적인 행동은 우리의 의식적인 행동보다 훨씬 더 빨리 일어난다. 무의식에 의한 자발적인 행동의 시작과 안내는 야구나 테니스를 해 본 적이 있는 사람은 누구에게나 친숙한 흔히 생기는 일이다. 스포츠나 피아노 연주에 필요한 복잡한 반응은 단순한 반사 작용보다 훨씬 더 많은 것이 복잡하다. 점프 슛을 시도하는 농구 선수는 상대편의 위치는 물론 자신의 위치, 속도, 몸 각도에 따라 순간적으로 조절한다. 스포츠나 악기 연주에서 신속한 행동을 의식적으로 계획하는 것은 일반적으로 수행에 이로우며(→ 불리하며), 우리의 극도로 느린 의식이 더 빠른 무의식에 통제력을 건네주는 경우가 최선이다.

해설

11 외부 사건에 대한 의식은 그 사건보다 약 0.5초 늦게 생기므로, 스포츠나 악기 연주의 경우에 신속한 행동을 의식적으로 계획하면 수행에 불리하다는 내용의 글이다. 따라서 글의 제목으로 가장 적절한 것은 ③ '의식: 시간에 늦고 행동에 불리하다'이다.
① 현재는 항상 과거에 의해 형성된다
② 무의식은 의식의 거울이다
④ 기억은 어떻게 형성되고 저장되고 상기되는가
⑤ 기억된 과거: 표현되지 않은 소망의 반영

12 스포츠나 피아노 연주처럼 단순한 반사 작용보다 훨씬 더 복잡한 반응이 관련되는 경우 의식적인 계획은 행동을 느리게 하므로 수행에 이롭지 않고 불리할 것이라는 흐름이다. 따라서 ⑤의 'beneficial(이로운)'을 'detrimental(불리한)'과 같은 낱말로 바꾸어야 한다.

구문

• A basketball player [attempting a jump shot] makes split-second adjustments [**according to** his location, velocity, and body angle **as well as to** the positions of his opponents].
: 첫 번째 [ ]는 A basketball player를 수식하는 현재분사구이다. 두 번째 [ ]에서 as well as 다음에 전치사 to를 쓴 것은 앞의 according에 연결되기 때문이다.

고난도 모의고사 **02**회

| 01 ① | 02 ② | 03 ③ | 04 ⑤ | 05 ⑤ | 06 ⑤ |
| 07 ⑤ | 08 ② | 09 ⑤ | 10 ③ | 11 ② | 12 ② |

01 정답 ①

사람들은 시간과 돈이 잘 먹는 데 가장 큰 장애물로 인식된다고 말한다. 대부분의 경우, 둘 다 진정한 장애물이 아니다. 미국인들은 화면 앞에서 하루에 여덟 시간을 보낸다. 평균적으로, 우리 각각은 하루에 두 시간을 인터넷에 쓰는데, 그것은 20년 전에는 존재하지조차 않았던 것이다! 그렇지만 우리가 가족을 위해 계획을 세우고, 장을 보고, 요리를 할 시간은 낼 수 없는 것인가? 가공된 정크 푸드와 패스트푸드를 먹는 것보다 신선한 육류, 생선, 그리고 농산물을 사는 데는 돈이 약간 더 들 것이라는 것은 사실이다. 하지만 그럴 필요는 없다. 사실, 연구들은 진정한 식품을 먹는 것이 가공식품을 먹는 것보다 더 비싸지 않다는 것을 보여 주었다. 여러분은 풀을 먹인 스테이크를 사야 할 필요는 없다(비록 그것이 이상적일지라도). 여러분은 더 적은 돈으로 잘 먹을 수 있다. 전체적인 시야로 보면, 유럽인들은 소득의 20퍼센트 정도를 음식에 사용하고, 미국인들은 9퍼센트만 사용한다. 초반에 쓰지 않는 것을 우리는 말미에 약국과 병원에서 지불한다.

해설
미국인들은 양질의 음식을 준비하기 위해 응당 사용해야 할 시간과 돈을 사용하지 않고 정크 푸드와 패스트푸드를 먹는데, 결국 건강을 해쳐서 약국과 병원에서 그만큼의 시간과 돈을 사용한다는 맥락이다. 따라서 밑줄 친 부분이 의미하는 바로 ① '우리가 진정한 식품을 준비하는 데 피하는 비용과 노력'이 가장 적절하다.
② 우리가 정크 푸드와 가공식품에 쓰지 않는 돈
③ 건강한 집밥에 대한 만족스럽지 못한 욕구
④ 이국적인 건강식에 우리가 쏟는 관심과 시간
⑤ 우리가 작업에서 생산성을 위해 내리는 선택

TEXT FLOW

도입	시간과 돈은 잘 먹는 데 진정한 장애물이 아님
전개 1	인터넷에는 두 시간을 쓰는데 가족을 위해 요리할 시간은 낼 수 없는가?
전개 2	연구는 더 적은 돈으로 잘 먹을 수 있음을 보여 줌
결론	초반에 쓰지 않는 돈을 말미에 약국과 병원에 지불함

구문
• [What we don't spend on the front end] we **pay for** on the back end at the drugstore and the doctor's office.
: [ ]는 동사 pay for의 목적어이다. 동사의 목적어를 강조하기 위해 문장의 앞에 쓸 때 주어와 동사는 도치되지 않는다.

02 정답 ②

물체의 추상적 특성은 일어나는 일에 대한 지각의 결과일 수 있다. 단단함과 무게 같은 물질과 관련된 개념을 고려해 보라. 이들은 촉각이나 운동 감각에 의해 알려지는 물체의 특성인 것처럼 보일 수도 있다. 사실, 감각 기반의 관점에 따르면 반사된 빛에서 그런 특성이 시각적으로 인식될 수 있다는 것은 불가능해 보일 수도 있지만, 일어나는 일의 지각이라는 관점에 따르면 그렇지 않다. Runeson은 일어나는 일의 운동학적 방식이 물체의 속성을 구체적으로 말해 준다고 주장했다. 예를 들어, 그의 실험에 참여한 성인들은 다른 사람들이 여러 무게의 추가 들어 있는 뚜껑이 닫힌 상자를 들어올리는 것을 보고 매번 시도할 때마다 그 무게를 추산했다. 참가자들이 다른 사람이 상자를 들어올리는 것을 보았을 때 그들이 한 추산은 자신들이 그 상자를 직접 들어올릴 때만큼 정확했다. 사람이 무언가를 들어올리는 것을 보는 생체 역학적 일의 복잡한 관계는 무게 같은 물질적인 특성을 구체적으로 말해 줄 수 있다.

해설
단단함과 무게 같은 물체의 추상적 특성이 시각적으로 인식될 수 있다는 내용의 글이다. 따라서 글의 제목으로 가장 적절한 것은 ② '보는 것이 사물의 비시각적 특징을 드러낼 수 있다'이다.
① 지각: 촉각 반응에 의한 추론
③ 사물을 속속들이 알기 위해서는 모든 감각이 필요하다
④ 추상화: 인지를 통해서만 접근 가능하다
⑤ 사물의 감각적 특성을 묘사하는 방법

TEXT FLOW

주제	물체의 추상적 특성은 일어나는 일에 대한 지각의 결과일 수 있음
부연	일어나는 일의 운동학적 방식이 물체의 속성을 구체적으로 말해 줌
예시	실험에서 참여자들은 다른 사람들이 상자를 들어올리는 것을 보고 정확하게 무게를 추산함

구문
• For example, adult participants in his experiments **viewed** other people [lifting a covered box {containing varying weights}] and estimated the weight on each trial.
: [ ]는 동사 viewed의 목적격 보어로 쓰였고, { }는 a covered box를 수식하는 현재분사구이다.

• Participants' estimates were **as accurate** [when they viewed someone else lifting the box] **as** [when they lifted it themselves].
: 두 개의 [ ]가 as accurate ~ as에 의해 서로 비교되고 있다.

03 정답 ③

다른 사람들과 마찬가지로, 에디슨은 '고온 발광'이라고 불리는 과정, 즉 다양한 물질을 통해 흐르는 전기는 그 물질들이 빛을 내게 할 수 있고 그럼으로써 양초와 천연 가스등의 대안으로 사용될 수 있는 광원(光源)을 만들 수 있다는 것을 알고 있었다. 문제는 발광 물질(필라멘트)이 잠시 후에 훼손되어 가정용 조명기기로서 그것을 사용하는 것을 비실용적으로 만들 것이라는 점이었다. 전기가 필라멘트를 파괴하는 물리적 원리에 관해 전혀 알지 못했기 때문에 에디슨은 어떤 물질이 밝게 빛을 내면서도 다 타 버리지 않고 견디는지를 알아보기 위해서 그야말로 자신이 시도해 볼 수 있는 모든 물질을 시도해 보았다. 면화와 거북이 등껍질을 포함하여 1,600가지 다른 물질을 시도해 본 후에 그는 우연히 탄화 대나무를 발견했는데, (각처에 사는 거북이에게는 기쁜 일이었겠는데) 그것이 선택할 수 있는 필라멘트임이 밝혀졌다. 공기를 뺀 전구(즉 진공관)에서 사용될 때, 탄화 대나무는 시험된 다른 필라멘트 중 어떤 것보다 더 밝게 빛났고 훨씬 더 오래 지속되었다. 에디슨은 자신의 전구를 갖

게 되었다. 비록 텅스텐이 금방 가정용 전구에서 탄화 대나무를 대체했지만, 고온 발광에 의한 조명은 향후 수십 년 동안 실내조명의 지배적인 방식이 되었다.

해설

③ 문장 성분이 모두 존재하는 완전한 문장으로, see 앞의 he could는 목적격 관계대명사가 생략되어 every material을 수식하는 관계절이다. 따라서 see는 목적을 나타내는 to부정사구가 되어야 하므로 to see로 고쳐야 한다.

① could be used 이하의 주어 역할을 하면서 a light source를 수식하는 관계사가 필요하므로, that은 어법상 적절하다.

② making 다음에 목적어인 its use as a household lighting device가 이어지고 그 다음에 목적격 보어 역할을 하는 형용사가 필요하므로, impractical은 어법상 적절하다.

④ 주절의 the carbonized bamboo를 의미상의 주어로 하는 분사구문으로, When과 used 사이에 주어인 it(= the carbonized bamboo) was가 생략된 것으로 이해할 수 있으므로, used는 어법상 적절하다.

⑤ many decades를 수식하는 형용사적 용법의 to부정사구 to follow는 어법상 적절하다.

⑦ WHY 고난도

문장 해석에 유의하지 않으면 every material을 수식하는 관계절인 he could에 see가 이어진다고 착각할 수 있는 고난도 문제이다.

TEXT FLOW

도입	에디슨은 '고온 발광' 과정을 통해 양초, 천연 가스등의 대안 광원을 만들 수 있음을 알고 있었음
반전	문제는 필라멘트가 금방 훼손되어 비실용적이라는 점이었음
부연	에디슨은 1,600가지 물질을 시도했음
결론	더 밝게 빛나고 더 오래 지속되는 탄화 대나무를 발견함

구문

• Edison knew, **as did others**, that running electricity through a variety of materials could make those materials glow — a process called *incandescence* — thereby producing a light source that could be used as an alternative to candles and natural gas lamps.

: as did others는 as others knew에서 knew가 대동사 did로 바뀐 다음에 주어와 대동사 did가 도치된 형태이다. as나 than 다음에서 주어와 조동사(또는 be동사)가 흔히 도치된다.

04
정답 ⑤

정서는 얼굴 표정을 통해, 그리고 목소리의 어조와 운율의 조정을 통해 표현될 수 있다. 언어 의사소통의 이 비언어적인 측면은, 그것의 표현과 인식 둘 다 대부분 우뇌에 의해 조정되는 것처럼 보인다. 몸의 자세와 움직임 또한 다른 사람들에 의해 쉽게 인식되는 정서적인 신호를 보낼 때 목소리 및 얼굴 표정과 뒤섞일 수도 있다. 놀라운 점은, 근육, 뼈, 그리고 (심장과 장(腸) 같은) 내장(內臟)에서 오는 신호를 포함하여, 몸으로부터의 정보가 좌뇌보다 우뇌에서 더 많이 통합된다는 연구 결과이다. 다시 말해, 몸 전체가 우뇌에서 통합된 방식으로 나타난다. 몸의 자율 신경계의 조절조차도 주로 우뇌 구조에 의해 조정된다. 그러므로 우뇌는 감정 상태의 표현과 감정 경험의 의식적 인식을 허용하는 데뿐만 아니라, 감정을 조절하는 과정을 조정하는 데도 사소

한(→ 중요한) 역할을 하는 것으로 보인다.

해설

언어 의사소통의 비언어적인 측면은 표현과 인식 둘 다 대부분 우뇌에 의해 조정되는 것처럼 보이고, 몸으로부터 오는 정보도 좌뇌보다는 우뇌에서 더 많이 통합된다는 내용이므로, ⑤의 'trivial(사소한)'을 'major(중요한)'와 같은 낱말로 바꾸어야 한다.

TEXT FLOW

도입	의사소통의 비언어적인 측면은 표현, 인식 모두 우뇌에 의해 조정되는 것처럼 보임
전개	몸의 신호와 몸으로부터의 정보, 즉 몸 전체가 우뇌에서 더 많이 통합됨
결론	우뇌는 감정 표현과 인식을 허용하고, 감정을 조절하는 과정을 조정하는 역할도 함

구문

• [What is striking] is the finding [that **the input** {from the body —including signals from the muscles, bones, and viscera (such as the heart and the intestines) —} is more highly integrated in the right hemisphere than in the left].

: 첫 번째 [ ]는 문장의 주어이고 the finding이 보어이다. 두 번째 [ ]는 the finding의 구체적인 내용을 설명하는 동격이고, that절의 주어는 the input이고 동사는 is이다. { }는 주어 the input을 수식하는 전치사구이다.

05
정답 ⑤

여러분 이전에 세상을 살았던 사람들은 여러분이 경험하는 것을 이해하고 설명하는 자연적인 방식이 형편없기 때문에 과학을 발명했다. 증거가 없을 때, 모든 추정은 기본적으로 동일하다. 여러분은 결과보다는 원인을, 소음 속에서 신호를, 무작위 속에서 패턴을 보는 것을 선호한다. 여러분은 쉽게 이해할 수 있는 이야기를 더 좋아해서, 복잡한 문제가 쉬워질 수 있도록 삶의 모든 것을 이야기로 전환한다. 과학자들은 이야기를 제거하려고, 즉 그것을 증발시켜 오로지 가공하지 않은 사실만 남기기 위해 노력한다. 그러한 자료들은 무방비 상태로 노출된 채 존재해서 각각의 새로운 참관자에 의해 숙고되고 재조정될 수 있다. 과학자들과 비전문가들은 그 자료를 이용해서 새로운 이야기를 생각해 낼 것이고 논쟁을 벌이겠지만, 그 자료는 조금도 움직이지 않을 것이다. 그것들은 심지어 백 년 이상이 지나도 이해되지 않을 수도 있지만, 과학적 방법 덕분에, 편견과 오류로 가득 찬 그 이야기들은 사실과 충돌하고 역사 속으로 (서서히) 물러날 것이다.

해설

사람들이 경험을 통해 만드는 이야기는 오류로 가득 차 있고, 과학이 편견과 오류로 가득 찬 그 이야기를 제거하여 가공하지 않은 사실만을 그대로 제시한다는 내용의 글이다. 빈칸 앞 문장에서는 과학자들이 사람들의 이야기를 제거하여 가공되지 않은 사실만 남기려고 한다고 했고, 빈칸 다음 문장에서는 과학자들과 비전문가들이 그런 자료를 이용해서 새로운 이야기를 생각해 내지만 그것은 편견과 오류로 가득한 이야기일 것이라는 내용이 이어지고 있으므로, 빈칸에 들어갈 말로 가장 적절한 것은 ⑤ '각각의 새로운 참관자에 의해 숙고되고 재조정될'이다.

① 인기에 따라 받아들여지거나 거절당할
② 이야기를 최고가 될 수 있게 만드는 역할을 할
③ 부조화를 가져오는 복잡한 문제를 일으킬

④ 사람들의 잠재력을 열고 그들의 자존감을 높여 줄

구문

• Those data **sit** there, [naked and exposed], so they can be **reflected upon** and rearranged by each new visitor.
: data는 일상 영어에서는 단수 취급을 하고 학술적인 영어에서는 복수 취급을 하는데 여기서는 복수 취급을 해서 복수 동사 sit이 쓰였다. [ ]는 주격 보어 역할을 한다. reflected upon은 구동사로, 수동태로 쓰일 때 전치사를 생략하지 않는다.

06　　　　　　　　　　　　　　　　　정답 ⑤

17세기와 18세기에 아일랜드는 잉글랜드의 식민지였다. 이것은 잉글랜드가 모든 아일랜드의 자원을 통제했다는 것을 의미했다. 그중 많은 수가 영국령이었던 많은 다른 식민지의 상황에서처럼, 잉글랜드는 잉글랜드 자체가 식민지 권력이 되는 일을 하지 않았다. 중개인은 식민화의 효과적인 도구였다. '비국교도들'은 영국인 아래에 있었지만 아일랜드 가톨릭교도 위에 있었다. '대개 장로교 농부, 기술자, 그리고 소규모 소매상인'이던 이 비가톨릭교도인 아일랜드 비국교도들은 영국에 의해 강요된 억압적인 위계질서를 유지하는 것을 도왔다. 그들은 종종 비교적 거의 아무것도 대가로 받지 않고 잉글랜드인들이 노동과 골칫거리를 면하게 해 주었다. 그들은 자신들의 사회적 지위로부터 아주 중요한 한 가지 혜택을 받았다. 아일랜드 가톨릭교도처럼, 그들 자신도 가혹한 환경에서 살아갈 수도 있었지만, 개신교도로서, 그들은 최소한 자신이 지배적인, 즉 더 나은 민족이라고 여길 수 있었다. 다시 말해, 그들이 생각하는 '민족'이라는 관점에서 모든 개신교도는 영국인이 강요한 위계질서로부터 혜택을 받았다. 아무리 가난할지라도, 개신교도는 가톨릭교도가 아니라 아일랜드 개신교도가 되는 것으로부터 정신적인 힘을 얻었다.

해설

잉글랜드의 식민지였던 아일랜드에서 비국교도가 잉글랜드 지배의 중개인 역할을 했는데 그들은 아일랜드 가톨릭교도보다 자신들이 더 나은 민족이라고 여기는 이득을 얻었다는 내용이 앞서 제시되고, 빈칸 뒤에서 그것을 a psychic power라 언급했으므로, 빈칸에 들어갈 말로 가장 적절한 것은 ⑤ '모든 개신교도는 영국인이 강요한 위계질서로부터 혜택을 받았다'이다.
① 아일랜드 가톨릭교도는 그들의 다른 종교적 믿음에 저항했다
② 영국인들은 항상 다른 인종들을 열등하다고 여겼다
③ 식민지 주민들은 그들의 노동의 가치에 의해 평가되었다
④ 지배적인 사람들조차도 그들의 경제적 지위에 의해 분열되었다

구문

• [Underneath the British but above Irish Catholics in Ireland] were "the Dissenters."
: 전치사구인 [ ]가 문장 앞에 나와서 주어 "the Dissenters"와 동사 were가 도치된 형태이다.

07　　　　　　　　　　　　　　　　　정답 ⑤

어떤 것을 가치 있게 여기는 것은 그것이 가치 있다고 믿고 그것에 '관심을 갖는' 것이다. 관심을 갖지 않으면 어떤 것을 가치 있게 여기지 않는다. 불행하게도, 관심의 본질은 이해의 개념만큼이나 거의 모호하다. 그러나 적어도 한 가지는 분명한데, 관심은 그것이 감정과 갖는 관계를 떠나서는 정의될 수 없다는 것이다. 심지어 관심을 감정에 대한 단순한 성향이라고 생각할 수도 있다. 나는 이것이 오류라고 생각한다. 관심을 가지는 것이 다양한 다른 감정, 행동, 생각을 낳기 때문에, 그것은 감정을 과장되게 드러내는 단순한 성향으로 환원될 수 없다. 내가 자신 있게 단언할 수 있는 것은 우리의 감정은 우리가 무엇에 관심을 가지느냐에 달려 있다는 것이다. 예를 들어, 우리는 우리가 관심을 가지고 있는 것에 대해서만 두려워한다. 일반적으로, 보통의 감정은 우리가 관심을 가지고 있는 어떤 것이 영향을 받을 것 같거나, 영향을 받아 온 방식에 대한 평가를 본질적으로 포함한다. 그러나 누군가가 어떤 것에 관해 관심을 가질 수 있으면서 그것이 위협을 받을 때 두려움을 느끼지 않거나 그것이 번성할 것 같을 때 희망을 느끼지 않는 경향이 있을 수 있다고 생각하는 것은 일관성이 없는 일이다. 따라서 우리의 관심사가 때때로 우리의 감정적인 반응에 의해 우리에게 드러난다는 것을 말하는 것은 논란의 여지가 없다.

해설

우리가 어떤 것을 가치 있게 여기면 그것에 관심을 갖게 되는데, 관심을 갖는 것은 감정과의 관계를 떠나서는 정의될 수 없다는 내용의 글이다. 중반 이후에 필자는 우리의 감정은 우리가 무엇에 관심을 가지느냐에 달려 있다고 했고, 그에 대한 예를 든 후 Accordingly로 결론을 제시하고 있으므로, 빈칸에 들어갈 말로 가장 적절한 것은 ⑤ '때때로 우리의 감정적인 반응에 의해 우리에게 드러난다'이다.
① 너무 강력해서 우리가 그것들을 통제할 수 없다
② 흔히 이성적인 생각의 산물인 경우가 있다
③ 보통 감정적인 반응에 기여하지 않는다
④ 우리가 나이가 들고 몸이 변해도 지속된다

구문

• In general, standard emotions essentially involve evaluations of the way [something {we care about} stands to be or has been affected].
: [ ]는 the way를 수식하는 관계절이고, 그 안의 { }는 something을 수식하는 관계절이다. stands to be 다음에는 affected가 생략되었다.

08

인간의 가장 기본적인 본능은 자기 보존을 위한 본능이다. 형법은 이러한 충동을 인정하고 정당방위의 원칙을 통해 사법 제도에서 그것의 사용을 허용한다. (B) 정당방위를 주장하는 개인이 합리적으로 행동할 때, 그는 다수의 범죄에 대해 완전하게 방어하게 되는 이점을 얻을 것이다. 대부분의 경우, 피고가 무력 사용이 필요하다는 합리적인 믿음을 가질 경우에만 정당방어가 성공할 것이다. 그러므로 문화적 방어 사건에서 중요한 문제는 누군가가 그러한 '합리적' 믿음을 가지고 있는지를 어떻게 판단하는지가 될 것이다. (A) 정당방위의 또 다른 특징은 피고인이 필요하고 비례적인 대응을 행사했다는 것을 입증할 수 있어야만 그 전략이 이긴다는 것이다. 비례의 원칙 요건이 문화적 방어 사건의 피고에 대한 그것의 효용을 제한할 가능성이 있다. (C) 이에 대한 이유는 무엇이 비례적 대응에 해당하는지에 대한 판단은 평가를 하는 사람의 문화적 배경에 따라 다를 것이기 때문이다. 짐작건대, 피고의 문화계 구성원들이 그것이 그렇다고 동의할지라도, 지배 문화권 출신의 판사는 그 행위를 비례적 대응으로 보지 않을 수 있을 것이다.

해설

자기 보존 본능은 인간의 가장 기본적인 본능이므로, 형법은 정당방위 원칙을 통해 사법 제도에서 정당방위의 사용을 허용한다는 내용의 주어진 글 다음에는, 정당방위가 성공하는 경우는 피고가 무력 사용이 필요하다는 합리적인 믿음을 가질 경우에만 그렇다는 내용의 (B)가 온 후, Another feature of self-defense로 정당방위의 또 다른 특징을 기술하는 (A)가 온 다음, 마지막으로 피고인이 필요하고 비례적인 대응을 행사했다는 것이 입증되어야 하는 이유를 The reason for this ~로 기술하는 (C)가 마지막으로 오는 것이 글의 순서로 가장 적절하다.

TEXT FLOW

도입	형법은 자기 보존을 위한 본능에 의한 충동을 인정하고, 정당방위 원칙을 통해 허용함
전개 1	피고가 무력 사용이 필요하다는 합리적인 믿음을 가질 경우에만 정당방어가 성공함
전개 2	피고가 필요하고 비례적인 대응을 행사했다는 것을 입증해야 전략이 이김

구문

• Another feature of self-defense is [that the strategy only wins {**provided** the defendant can demonstrate that he exercised a necessary and proportional response}].
: [ ]는 주격 보어 역할을 하는 명사절이다. 그 안의 { }는 '만약 ~이라면'을 뜻하는 접속사 provided가 이끄는 조건절이다.

09

채집자의 사회적인 조직에 대한 이견에도 불구하고, 핵심적인 인구 통계적 사실은 논란의 여지가 없다. 야생 식량 자원의 낮은 밀도는 대부분의 현대 채집자들이 대개 가까운 친척인 2명에서 8명으로 이루어진 매우 작은 집단 안에서 자신들의 시간의 대부분을 보낸다는 것을 의미한다. 그러나 모든 사람들은 최소한 500명으로 이루어진 훨씬 더 큰 집단에 속해야 하는데, 이러한 집단만이 독자적으로 생존 가능한 번식 집단을 제공하기 때문이다. 그렇게 많은 채집자들이 물리적으로 모이는 것은 드문 일이지만, 아무리 가장 작은 집단이라도 아마도 50명이 넘는 사람들로 이루어진 더 큰 모임이나 캠프에서 주기적으로 모이며 이러한 모임/캠프 네트워크는 요구되는 크기의 유전

자 풀을 만든다. 풍요로운 환경에서는 사람들은 이러한 더 큰 집단 안에서 연중 더 많은 시간을 보내고, 가혹한 환경에서는 연중 더 적은 시간을 보낸다. 그러나 정말 풍요로운 환경, 특히 해양 자원이 풍부한 환경에서만, 채집자들은 수십 명, 간혹 수백 명에 달하는 집단으로 영구적으로 살아갈 수 있다. 남캘리포니아의 Chumash로부터 알래스카의 좁고 길게 다른 주로 뻗어 있는 지역의 Tlingit에 이르기까지, 북아메리카 태평양 연안의 오래된 채집자 마을이 가장 잘 알려진 사례이다.

해설

주어진 문장은 채집자들이 정말 풍요로운 환경에서는 영구적으로 살아갈 수 있다는 내용이다. ⑤ 앞에서 환경의 풍요로움의 정도에 따라 집단 안에서 보내는 시간이 다르다는 내용으로 풍요로운 환경과 가혹한 환경을 비교하고, ⑤ 뒤에서는 채집자들이 정착한 마을의 사례가 제시되므로, 주어진 문장이 들어가기에 가장 적절한 곳은 ⑤이다.

> ⊗ **매력적인 오답 주의!**
>
> ④ 뒤의 문장의 fertile environments라는 단편적인 어구를 근거로 주어진 문장의 abundant environments와 연결하여 선택한 것으로 보인다.
>
> [선택률 37%]

TEXT FLOW

도입	야생 식량 자원의 낮은 밀도는 작은 집단에서 자신들의 시간을 대부분 보낸다는 것을 의미함
전환	더 큰 집단만이 독자적으로 생존 가능한 번식 집단을 제공함
부연	풍요로운 환경에서는 사람들이 더 큰 집단 안에서 더 많은 시간을 보내고, 가혹한 환경에서는 더 적은 시간을 보냄

구문

• [Only in really abundant environments], however, particularly **those** with rich marine resources, can foragers live permanently in groups of several dozens or sometimes hundreds strong.
: Only를 수반한 부사구 [ ]가 문장 앞에 나와서 주어 foragers와 조동사 can이 도치된 형태이다. those는 the environments를 대신하는 대명사이다.

• In fertile environments, people spend more of the year in these larger groups; in harsh environments, **less of it**.
: less of it은 people spend less of it(= the year) in these larger groups에서 반복되는 부분이 생략되고 남은 형태이다.

10

영화는 흔히 장소에 대한 이상화된 묘사를 구성하는데, 이러한 장소에 대한 우리의 진정한 이해를 왜곡할 수 있는 흥미를 돋우는 이야기를 엮어 낸다. 영화의 이러한 묘사는 이러한 목적지의 매우 색다른 측면을 증폭시켜, 현실 세계의 미묘하고 다면적인 현실을 반영하지 않는 일차원적인 시각을 조장하는 경향이 있다. 그 결과, 관람객은 이러한 묘사를 해당 장소의 진정한 모습으로 그대로 받아들여 자신도 모르게 지나치게 낙관적이거나 비관적인 인상을 갖게 될 수도 있다. 이로 인해 사람들은 부풀려지거나 정당하지 않은 기대감을 가지고 목적지에 도착했다가 자신들이 마주하는 더 불완전한 현실에 직면할 수 있다. 마찬가지로, 영화는 자주 창의적인 자유를 발휘하여 특정 장소를 위험, 범죄 또는 기타 불리한 특성이 가득한 곳으로 묘사하여, 사람들이 이러한 장소를 방문하는 것에 대해 부당한 우려나 두려움을 갖게 한다. 따라서 영화

의 렌즈는 스토리텔링을 위한 흥미를 돋우는 매체이지만, 때때로 허구와 현실의 경계를 모호하게 만들어, 크레디트가 올라가고 나서도 오랫동안 지속되는, 장소에 대한 잘못된 인상의 씨앗을 심을 수 있다.

➡ 영화는 장소에 대한 부정확한 인식을 만들어 내어, 실생활에서 그런 장소에 대한 오해를 초래할 수 있다.

해설

영화는 흔히 어떤 장소를 지나치게 낙관적이거나 비관적으로 표현하여, 관람객이나 실제 방문객이 그 장소에 대한 잘못된 인상을 가지게 할 수 있다는 내용의 글이다. 따라서 요약문의 빈칸 (A), (B)에 들어갈 말로는 ③ 'inaccurate(부정확한) – misconceptions(오해)'가 가장 적절하다.

① 인지적인 – 비평　　　　　② 인지적인 – 오해
④ 부정확한 – 변형　　　　　⑤ 사실적인 – 변형

TEXT FLOW

도입	영화의 이상화된 묘사는 장소에 대한 우리의 이해를 왜곡하는 경향이 있음
부연	관람객은 그 장소에 대해 지나치게 낙관적이거나 비관적인 인상을 가질 수 있음
결론	영화의 렌즈는 허구와 현실의 경계를 모호하게 만들어 장소에 대한 잘못된 인상을 가지게 할 수 있음

구문

• This can result in [**people** arriving at these destinations with inflated or unjustified expectations, **only to** be confronted with the more imperfect reality they encounter].
: [ ]는 전치사 in의 목적어 역할을 하는 동명사구로, people은 이 동명사구의 의미상의 주어이다. only to는 '~했으나 결과는 …하다'는 의미로 결과가 실망스럽거나 놀라운 감정을 동반할 때 사용한다.

11-12

정답 11 ② 12 ②

때때로, 가장 작은 에너지 제품인 배터리가 그러하듯이, 작은 것들이 큰 문제를 일으킬 수 있다. 수명이 다하면, 배터리는 쓸모없고, 가치 없고, 독성이 있는 불행한 조합이 된다. 배터리의 복잡한 화학 성분은 분리하기 어려울 수 있고, 아무런 처리 없이 그것을 매립지에 버리는 것은 독성 화학 물질을 자연 환경으로 방출할 수 있다. 배터리를 재활용하는 것은 그것을 매립지에 묻는 것보다 적어도 10배가 넘는 비용이 든다. 배터리 폐기물의 독성 때문에, 많은 정부가 재활용을 강제하기 위해 소비자 수준에서 그것들의 처리를 규제해 왔다. 예를 들어, 캘리포니아가 가정용 쓰레기에 배터리를 버리는 것을 허용한다(→ 금지한다)는 사실에도 불구하고, 캘리포니아 사람들은 자신들이 구입하는 배터리의 5퍼센트 미만을 재활용한다.
벨기에 정부는 새 배터리에 높은 환경세를 부과하겠다는 위협을 이용하여 배터리 제조업체들이 오래된 배터리를 회수하고 폐기하도록 설득했다. Bebat이라 불리는 800명의 회원으로 구성된 비영리 배터리 생산업체 컨소시엄이 배터리 수거 및 재활용을 처리한다. 그 프로그램은 각 배터리의 비용에 약 15에서 25센트를 추가하지만, 그 비용은 배터리 제조업체들이 계속 증가하는 정부의 재활용률 목표를 달성하지 못할 경우 지불하게 될 위협적인 환경세 비용의 약 4분의 1에 불과하다. 요구되는 비율을 달성하기 위해, Bebat은 시장, 사진관, 보석상, 학교, 시립 소유지 및 그 밖의 24,000곳에 밝은 녹색 수거 박스를 설치하여 소비자들에게 배터리를 편리하게 갖다 놓는 지점을 제공했다. 컨소시엄은 또한 대다수의 소비자들이 재활용 프로그램에 대해 확실히 알 수 있도록 공공 정보 캠페인 비용도 지불했다. 2015년 현재, 벨기에

사람들은 배터리의 약 56퍼센트를 재활용했고, 그것은 배터리에 대한 환경세 부과의 잠재적 이익을 증명했다.

해설

11 배터리 폐기물의 독성은 자연 환경에 치명적인데도 불구하고 배터리 재활용 비율이 너무 낮은 상황에서, 벨기에 정부가 배터리에 환경세를 부과함으로써 배터리 재활용을 증가시켰다는 내용이므로, 글의 제목으로 가장 적절한 것은 ② '배터리 재활용을 증가시키기 위한 세금 부과'이다.
① 배터리 재활용에 대한 상반된 태도
③ 줄어든 배터리 재활용률과 그 원인
④ 끊임없이 커지는 수많은 폐배터리 시장
⑤ 가정용 쓰레기에 버려지는 배터리의 잠재적 위험성

12 배터리 폐기물의 독성 때문에 많은 정부가 재활용을 강제하기 위해 소비자 수준에서 그것들의 처리를 규제해 왔다고 했으므로, ②의 'allows(허용하다)'는 'prohibits(금지하다)'와 같은 낱말로 바꾸어야 한다.

TEXT FLOW

도입	수명이 다한 배터리는 분리하거나 매립지에 버리는 것이 어려움
부연	배터리 폐기물의 독성 때문에 많은 정부가 재활용을 강제해 옴
예시 1	캘리포니아는 가정용 쓰레기에 배터리를 버리는 것을 금지하지만, 배터리의 5퍼센트 미만을 재활용함
예시 2	벨기에는 비영리 배터리 생산업체 컨소시엄이 배터리 수거, 재활용을 처리하고, 배터리 수거 박스를 설치하고, 공공 정보 캠페인을 함으로써 배터리의 약 56퍼센트를 재활용함

구문

• As of 2015, Belgians recycled an estimated 56 percent of batteries, **demonstrating** the potential benefits of placing an eco-tax on batteries.
: demonstrating은 앞 문장 전체를 의미상의 주어로 하는 분사구문이며 which demonstrated로 바꾸어 쓸 수 있다.

고난도 모의고사 03회

| 01 ④ | 02 ⑤ | 03 ① | 04 ⑤ | 05 ① | 06 ② |
| 07 ④ | 08 ④ | 09 ② | 10 ① | 11 ① | 12 ④ |

01

정답 ④

보통 사람들과 비교하여, 작가들은 언어를 통해 자기 변형에 대한 능력을 쉽게 발전시킨다. 사실상, 만일 그들의 출판사가 그것을 권장한다면, 몇몇 작가들은 오래된 피부 같은 문체(어조)를 벗어 버리고 더욱 대중을 즐겁게 하는 자신으로 뛰어든다. 하지만 대부분의 다른 사람, 특히 젊은이들에게는 풍부한 표현력 속으로 갑작스럽게 뛰어드는 것은 발레 의상을 입고 볼링장을 가로지르며 춤을 추는 것 같을 것이다. 정말로, 여러분의 내적인 변화는 표현을 진심으로 바라고 있을 수도 있지만, 여러분이 어떤 것을 표현하면 (알아들을 수 없는) 사람들은 여러분이 다른 사람이라고 의심한다. 독창성은 의구심이다. 곧 그 변화 자체가 의구심이 되고 여러분은 <u>그것을 카펫 아래에 쓸어 넣는다</u>. 영어 수업이나 우연히 들은 말에서, 새로운 말이 바로 여러분의 혀 위에서 살아나고 거기에서 좋은 느낌이 든다. '초월적인.' 여러분은 그 말을 혼자 시도해 본다. 그것은 여러분이 전에 '극단적인'과 같은 어구들과 함께 찾았지만 아무도 여러분이 얼마나 엄청나다고 말하는지를 전혀 알아차리지 못했던 의미를 지닌다. "공이 여러분의 글러브에 날아왔을 때 여러분이 어떤 기분일까?" 초월적이다! 초월적인 순간이다! 그것이 바로 그런 느낌이었지만, 유감스럽게도 여러분은 '그 단어가 여러분이 (익숙하게 사용하는 것이) 아니라서' 절대 아무에게도 말할 수 없다.

해설
작가와 비교해서 보통 사람들은 언어를 통해 스스로를 바꾸는 것에 능숙하지 않으며 설령 표현력 있는 사람이 되고 싶어도 한 번도 써 본 적 없는 멋진 표현은 어색해서 사용하는 것을 삼간다는 맥락이므로, 밑줄 친 부분이 글에서 의미하는 바로 가장 적절한 것은 ④ '익숙하지 않은 말로 자신의 생각을 표현하는 것을 삼간다'이다.
① 다른 사람들이 자신의 진정성을 높이 평가하는 것을 포기한다
② 과장된 표현으로 가득한 작품을 만드는 것을 거부한다
③ 작가가 되려는 자신의 꿈에 대해 말하는 것을 피한다
⑤ 대중을 즐겁게 하는 표현을 가진 작가로서의 자신의 신분을 숨긴다

TEXT FLOW

도입	작가는 언어를 통한 자기 변형에 능함
반전	대부분의 사람들은 풍부한 표현력을 갑자기 갖추려고 하면 사람들의 의구심을 사게 됨
부연	'초월적인'이라는 단어를 사용하고 싶지만, 익숙하게 사용하는 것이 아니라서 아무에게도 말할 수 없음

구문

- [True, your inner transformations may be crying for expression], but you express one thing and (inarticulate) people suspect you of another.
  : [ ]는 It is true that your inner transformations may be crying for expression에서 It is와 that이 생략되고 True,만 남은 형태이다. 「True, ... but」은 '~은 사실이지만'의 뜻으로 쓰이는 관용 표현이다.

02

정답 ⑤

북미 자유 무역 협정(NAFTA)은 우리에게 자유 무역의 사안들을 볼 수 있는 창을 제공한다. 미국과 캐나다에서, 북미 자유 무역 협정에 대한 토론은 주로 일자리에 주안점을 두었다. 어떻게 각각의 국가는 일자리를 잃지 않고도 무역과 더 잘 만들어진, 더 값싼 수입품의 홍수에 국경을 개방할 수 있을까? 북미 자유 무역 협정 국가의 지도자들은 무역에 국경을 닫는 것은 장기적으로 세계 시장에서 경쟁할 능력을 잃은 국가의 경쟁력 손실과 일자리의 궁극적인 손실을 초래한다는 것을 깨달았다. 그들은 세계 경제가 한 국가가 이득을 보게 되면 다른 한 국가는 손해를 보게 되는 제로섬 게임이 아니라는 것을 깨달았다. 장기적으로는 개방된 시장이 국경 양쪽의 생산자들에게 자신들이 경쟁력을 가진 재화와 용역만 생산하는 데 집중할 장려책을 제공할 것이었다. 게다가, 외국의 경쟁자로부터 오는 지속적인 압박은 각국이 자국 제품의 질과 가치를 개선할 수밖에 없도록 할 것이었다.

해설
북미 자유 무역 협정을 통해, 일자리를 유지하면서도 상품의 시장 개방을 통해 제로섬 게임이 아닌 상생 및 발전을 도모할 수 있다는 내용의 토론이 진행되었다는 내용이므로, 글의 주제로 가장 적절한 것은 ⑤ '개방된 시장이 국내 경제에 제공하는 예상되는 이점'이다.
① 국제 무역 계약에 영향을 미치는 정치적인 고려
② 무역에 국경을 개방함으로써 위협받는 국내 고용 시장
③ 자유 무역 옹호자와 반대자 사이의 갈등
④ 선택된 상품에 주력함으로써 달성되는 경쟁 우위

TEXT FLOW

도입	북미 자유 무역 협정에 대한 토론은 주로 일자리에 중점을 둠
전개	각각의 국가는 어떻게 일자리를 잃지 않고 무역과 더 좋은 수입품에 국경을 개방할까?
부연 1	무역에 국경을 닫는 것은 장기적으로 국가 경쟁력 및 일자리의 손실을 초래함
부연 2	외국 경쟁자로부터의 압박으로 제품의 질과 가치를 개선할 수밖에 없음

구문

- Open markets, in the long term, would **provide** the incentive **for** producers on both sides of the border [to concentrate on producing only those goods and services {in which they had a competitive advantage}].
  : 'B에게 A를 제공하다'를 뜻하는 「provide A for B」가 쓰였다. [ ]는 the incentive를 수식하는 to부정사구로 길어서 for producers on both sides of the border 뒤로 간 형태이다. 그 안의 { }는 those goods and services를 수식하는 관계절이다.

03

정답 ①

유기농 제품을 세계 시장에 내놓는 것은 여러 가지 영향을 미친다. 세계 시장의 특징은 운송, 출하, 유통, 마케팅 그리고 판매에서 기업이 큰 역할을 한다는 것이다. 관행 농산물과 동일한 시장에 진입하는 것은 유기농 농산물로 하여금 관행 농업을 형성하고 지속 가능한 관행들을 매력이 없는 것으로 만들었던 것과 똑같은 경제적 상황에 처할 수 있게 하는 결과를 가져올 가능성이 있다. 기존 세계 시장에서 경쟁하는 유기농 생산자들은 유기 농업의 원칙을 무너뜨릴 가능성이 있는 경제적 인센티브에 직면하게 될 것이다. 잠재적으로

큰 우려가 될 수 있는 새롭게 부상하는 문제는 (국가의) 무역 편애가 세계 무역 기구와 같은 단체에 역행하는 국가들에 제기되는 어려움이다. 세계 시장 진출은 관행 농업에 대한 국가 보조금에 이의를 제기할 근거를 제공할 수도 있지만, 유기 농업에 대한 보복성 도전이 있을 가능성도 있다. 추가적인 우려는 세계 시장이 불확실하고 자주 불안정하다는 것인데, 이는 농업 기업의 안전성을 약화시키는 결과를 낳아, 더 큰 규모의 기업에 대한 경제적 인센티브에 추가될 수 있다.

해설

① 문장의 주어인 동명사구(Entering ~ products)와 술어 동사 is가 이미 앞에 나와 있고 organic produce는 전치사 in의 목적어 역할을 하는 동명사구의 의미상의 주어 역할을 해야 하므로 is는 being으로 고쳐야 한다. 전치사 in 다음에는 주어(organic produce)와 동사(is)가 오는 절이 올 수 없다는 점에 유의한다.
② economic incentives를 수식하는 형용사구를 이끄는 likely는 어법상 적절하다.
③ nations를 수식하는 소유격 관계대명사 whose는 어법상 적절하다.
④ on which we can challenge의 의미를 to부정사구로 표현할 수 있으므로, to challenge는 어법상 적절하다.
⑤ 전치사 of의 목적어 역할을 하는 명사구를 이끌면서 목적어(the security of farming enterprises)를 취하는 동사의 역할을 해야 하므로, 동명사 reducing은 어법상 적절하다.

? WHY 고난도

문장이 길고 구조가 복잡하여 주어와 동사의 파악이 쉽지 않고, is가 뒤에 나오는 subject to에 자연스럽게 연결되는 동사로 착각할 수 있는 고난도 문제이다.

TEXT FLOW

주제	유기농 제품을 세계 시장에 내놓는 것의 영향들
부연 1	관행 농업을 매력 없게 만들었던 것과 같은 상황에 처할 수 있음
부연 2	유기 농업에 대한 보복성 도전이 있을 수 있음
부연 3	세계 시장의 불확실성으로 농업 기업의 안전성을 약화시킬 수 있음

구문

• A further concern is [that {global markets are uncertain and often volatile}, **which** has the effect of reducing the security of farming enterprises and can be added to the economic incentives for larger-scale enterprises].
: [ ]는 주격 보어 역할을 하는 명사절이다. 그 안의 { }는 관계대명사 which의 선행사이다.

04

정답 ⑤

정치인, 특히 전국적인 주목을 받는 정치인은 흔히 농담 삼아 나르시시스트라는 이유로 비난을 받지만, 진정으로, 그들의 직업이 특히 이 파괴적인 성격 특성에 기여한다. 예를 들면, 성공적인 후보자가 되기 위해, 여러분은 심지어 패배가 있을 것 같음에도 불구하고 이상할 정도로 낙관적이어야 하며 (정치인에게) 일상이 된 지속적인 비난에도 불구하고 높은 수준의 자존감을 지니고 있어야 한다. 게다가, 여러분은 비록 성공이 부분적으로 많은 보좌관과 조력자의 노력에 의해 성취된 것임에도 불구하고 성공에 대한 인정을 계속 혼자 받는다. 마지막으로, 여러분은 끊임없이 사람들이 여러분에게 의지하고, 여러분을 믿으며, 어떤 대의명분의 유일한 대표로서 여러분에게 책임을 묻게 한다. 이 모든 힘은 어떤 사람들이 세상이 자신을 중심으로 돌아간다고 믿게 하는, 과장된 자만심으로 이어질 수 있다. 바로 그때 자신들의 통제 불능의 행동은 합리화하기가 <u>더 어려워(→ 더 쉬워)</u>진다.

해설

나르시시스트적인 성격으로 비난받는 정치인은 모든 것이 자신을 중심으로 돌아간다고 믿게 하는 과장된 자만심을 가질 수 있다는 점에서 자신들의 통제 불능의 행동을 합리화하기가 더 쉽다는 내용의 글이다. 따라서 ⑤의 'harder(더 어려운)'를 'easier(더 쉬운)'와 같은 낱말로 바꾸어야 한다.

TEXT FLOW

주제	정치인은 나르시시스트라는 이유로 비난을 받지만, 직업이 이 성격 특성에 기여함
부연 1	항상 낙관적이어야 하고, 지속적인 비난에도 높은 수준의 자존감을 지녀야 함
부연 2	성공이 보좌관과 조력자의 노력에 의한 것임에도 인정은 혼자 받음
부연 3	모든 것이 자신을 중심으로 돌아간다고 믿는 자만심과 통제 불능의 행동은 합리화하기 더 쉬워짐

구문

• Finally, you constantly **have people** [**relying** on you], [**believing** in you], and [**holding** you responsible as the sole representative of a cause].
: 「have+사람+-ing」는 '사람이 ~하게 만들다'의 의미이다. 세 개의 목적격 보어 [ ]가 and로 연결된 형태이다.

05

정답 ①

경쟁을 벌이는 활동은 최고는 인정받고 나머지는 무시되는, 단지 수행 기량을 보여 주는 공개 행사 그 이상일 수 있다. 참가자에게 수행 기량에 대한 시기적절하고 건설적인 피드백을 제공하는 것은 일부 대회와 경연이 제공하는 자산이다. 어떤 의미에서 모든 대회는 피드백을 제공한다. 많은 경우에, 이것은 참가자가 상을 받았는지에 관한 정보에 제한된다. 그러한 유형의 피드백을 제공하는 것은 반드시 탁월함이 아니라 우월한 수행 기량을 보여 주는 것으로 강조점을 이동하는 것으로 해석될 수 있다. 최고의 대회는 단순히 승리하는 것이나 다른 사람을 '패배시키는 것'이 아니라, 탁월함을 장려한다. 우월성에 대한 강조는 우리가 일반적으로 경쟁의 해로운 효과를 조장하는 것이라고 간주하는 것이다. 수행 기량에 대한 피드백은 프로그램이 '이기거나, 입상하거나, 또는 보여 주는' 수준의 피드백을 넘어설 것을 요구한다. 수행 기량에 관한 정보는 이기지 못하거나 입상하지 못하는 참가자뿐만 아니라 이기거나 입상하는 참가자에게도 매우 도움이 될 수 있다.

해설

경쟁을 벌이는 활동에서 우월성(superiority)은 다른 참가자와의 비교에 중점을 두어 최고는 인정하고 나머지는 무시하는 것이므로, 기량 자체의 탁월함을 강조하는 건설적인 피드백에 중점을 두어야 한다는 내용의 글이다. 따라서 빈칸에 들어갈 말로 가장 적절한 것은 ① '경쟁의 해로운 효과를 조장하는 것'이다.
② 건설적인 피드백을 수행자와 공유하는 것
③ 개발 단계에서의 경쟁력을 저하하는 것

④ 참가자들이 자신이 잘하는 일에 집중하도록 하는 것
⑤ 자신의 한계를 넘어설 수 있는 기회를 제공하는 것

⊗ **매력적인 오답 주의!**

② 빈칸에는 주제에 반대되는 The emphasis on superiority에 대한 진술이 들어가야 하는데, 빈칸이 있는 문장을 제대로 해석하지 않고 주제에 해당하는 진술을 선택한 것으로 보인다. [선택률 40%]

TEXT FLOW

도입	수행 기량에 대한 시기적절하고 건설적인 피드백을 제공하는 것은 대회가 제공하는 자산임
반전	대회의 많은 경우 참가자가 상을 받았는지에 관한 정보에만 제한됨
부연	우월성을 강조하는 것은 경쟁의 해로운 효과를 조장하는 것임
결론	수행 기량에 대한 피드백은 모든 참가자에게 도움이 됨

구문

• Performance feedback requires [that the program **go** beyond the "win, place, or show" level of feedback].
: [ ]는 requires의 목적어 역할을 하는 명사절이고, requires가 '요구'를 나타내므로 that절에는 should가 생략된 동사원형 go가 쓰였다.

06
정답 ②

야생 상태의 사람은 유아처럼 첫인상에 지배되는 존재이고 자신의 충동을 따른다. 문명인은 자신의 첫인상을 중지시키고, 자신의 충동을 검토에 맡기며, 반대되는 요소에 견주어 보고, 숙고하고, 그 행동을 할 것인지 하지 않을 것인지, 아니면 그것을 연기할 것인지의 달인이 된다. 억제는 문명의 표지이다. 문명인의 통달, 그들의 자기 감정과 충동에 대한 통제가 우리가 교양이라고 부르는 문명의 개화에서보다 더 두드러지는 곳은 없다. 어쩌면 쓸모없지만 반짝이는 꽃이다. 세상 물정에 밝은 사람은 침착하여, 가장 격렬한 감정도 셔츠 앞면의 단정함도, 몸동작의 우아함도, 미소의 광택도, 목소리의 차분함도 바꾸지 못한다. 세상 경험이 많은 남녀는 배우의 기술을 통달했고, 스스로 어떠한 실제 감정도 전혀 경험하지 않고 인생을 연기하는 것 같다.

해설

유아와 같이 자신의 충동을 따르는 사람들과 달리 문명인은 자신의 감정과 충동을 지배하며 스스로에 대한 억제가 가능한 교양을 갖춘 사람들이라는 내용이므로, 빈칸에 들어갈 말로 가장 적절한 것은 ② '스스로 어떠한 실제 감정도 전혀 경험하지 않고'이다.
① 자기 안에 살아 있는 것에 그들의 귀를 기울이고
③ 그들의 승리와 실패를 관객과 함께 되살리면서
④ 심층적인 인간 감정의 배출구로서의 역할을 하면서
⑤ 폭력적인 감정이 그들의 행동을 통제하도록 하면서

TEXT FLOW

도입	야생 상태의 사람과는 달리 문명인은 자신의 충동을 검토하고 숙고함
부연	문명인의 자기 감정과 충동에 대한 통제가 교양이라고 부르는 문명의 개화에서 두드러짐
결론	세상의 기술을 통달한 남녀는 인생을 연기하는 것 같음

구문

• [The mastery of civilized people, their rule over their emotions and impulses] is nowhere more striking than in that blossom of civilization [that we call sophistication].
: 첫 번째 [ ]는 문장의 주어이며 그 안에 세 개의 명사구가 and로 연결되어 있다. 두 번째 [ ]는 civilization을 수식하는 관계절이다.

07
정답 ④

현대 서구인의 생각에는, 부, 교육, 또는 직업 배경의 기준으로 배우자를 선택하는 것이 진정한 감정에 대한 배신으로 보일 것이다. 그러나 배우자의 그러한 인구학적이고 사회·경제적인 특성을 냉정하게 비교할 때, 겉으로 보기에 사랑과 애정에 근거한 선택이 그럼에도 불구하고 매우 분명한 사회적 패턴을 보여 준다는 것을 알게 된다. 감정 이외의 고려 사항과 사랑을 타협한다는 것을 거의 의식하지 못하지만, 대부분의 사람들은 같은 종교, 인종, 계급, 교육 배경을 가진 사람들과 결혼한다. 우리의 사회 집단은 사실상 특정한 옷차림과 머리 모양, 행실과 호칭 방식, 억양과 어휘를 다른 것보다 더 매력적인 것으로 보도록 우리를 사회화한다. (사람들은 자신들에게 부족한 유전적 특징을 가진 짝에게 끌리는 경향이 있는데, 그것은 더 강한 면역 체계를 가진 더 건강한 자녀를 갖는 데 도움이 된다.) 그 선택이 개인적인 것으로 보이긴 하지만, 우리를 특정 사람에게로 끌어당기는 (또는 다른 사람에 대해 우리에게 혐오감을 주는) 것은 우리를 위해 짝을 고를 때 부지런한 중매인이 염두에 두는 것과 거의 같은 것이다.

해설

현대 서구인에게는 배우자를 부, 교육, 또는 직업 배경의 기준으로 선택하는 것이 진정한 감정에 대한 배신으로 보이겠지만, 대부분의 사람들이 배우자로 같은 종교, 인종, 계급, 교육 배경을 가진 사람을 선택한다는 내용의 글이다. 따라서 사람은 자신에게 부족한 유전적 특성을 가진 짝에게 끌리는 영향이 있고, 이러한 특성은 더 건강한 자녀를 갖는 데 도움이 된다는 내용의 ④는 전체 글의 흐름과 관계가 없다.

TEXT FLOW

도입	부, 교육, 직업 배경의 기준으로 배우자를 선택하는 것이 감정에 대한 배신으로 느껴짐
반전	사람들은 배우자로 같은 종교, 인종, 계급, 교육 배경을 가진 사람을 선택함
부연	우리는 특정한 옷차림과 행실 등을 더 매력적으로 보도록 사회화되어서 특정 사람에게 끌리는 것임

구문

• People tend to be attracted to mates [with genetic traits {they are lacking}], **which** makes for healthier children with stronger immune systems.
: [ ]는 mates를 수식하는 전치사구이고, { }는 genetic traits를 수식하는 관계절이다. which의 선행사는 앞 문장 전체이므로 단수 동사 makes가 쓰였다.

08
정답 ④

라디오 버라이어티 프로그램 'A Prairie Home Companion'의 작가이자 진행자인 Garrison Keillor는 모든 프로그램의 뉴스 부분을 "자,

모든 여성은 강하고, 모든 남성이 잘생겼으며, 모든 아이가 평균 이상인 Lake Wobegon에서 온 뉴스입니다."라는 말을 하면서 끝맺는다. (C) Minnesota에 있는 것으로 가정되고 있지만, 우월감의 환상을 가진 이 허구의 마을은 어디에나 있을 수 있다. 이는 사람들이 몇 번이고 계속해서 자신들은 조사된 기술과 역량에 상관없이 '평균 이상'이라는 것을 나타내는 설문 조사에 응답하기 때문이다. (A) 예를 들어, 90퍼센트 이상의 대학교수들은 스스로를 교수 능력이 평균 이상이라고 평가하며, 3분의 2가 넘는 수가 자신들이 상위 25퍼센트에 속한다고 믿는다. 미국 운전자의 거의 3분의 2는 스스로를 탁월하거나 매우 뛰어나다고 평가한다. 대부분의 사람들은 자신들이 동료들보다 더 공정하다고 생각한다. (B) 물론 이 모든 것들은 수학적으로 불가능하다. 더욱이, 연구는 사람들의 자기 평가와 자신들의 업무 관련 기술에 대한 객관적 평가 사이의 상당히 낮은 상관관계를 보여 준다.

해설
라디오 버라이어티 프로그램 'A Prairie Home Companion'의 Garrison Keillor는 프로그램의 뉴스 부분을 우월감이 담긴 멘트로 마무리한다는 내용의 주어진 글 다음에는, 이러한 곳이 어디에나 있을 수 있으며, 이러한 우월감의 이유는 계속해서 설문 조사에서 자신의 기술과 역량에 상관없이 자신들을 평균 이상이라고 답했기 때문이라는 내용의 (C)가 온 다음, 평균 이상이라고 응답한 예시가 담긴 (A)가 온다. 이어서 이러한 예를 All of these로 받아서 이는 수학적으로 불가능하고, 이에 대한 부연 설명을 추가하는 (B)가 오는 것이 글의 순서로 가장 적절하다.

TEXT FLOW

도입	라디오 프로그램의 뉴스 부분을 우월감이 담긴 멘트로 마무리함
전개	사람들은 설문 조사에서 자신들이 '평균 이상'이라고 답함
예시	대부분의 대학교수와 미국 운전자는 스스로를 탁월하다고 평가하며, 사람들은 동료들보다 자신이 더 공정하다고 생각함
결론	자기 평가와 객관적 평가 사이의 상당히 낮은 상관관계를 보여 줌

구문
• That's because time and time again people respond to surveys [indicating {that they are *above average*} regardless of the skill and competence examined].
: [ ]는 surveys를 수식하는 현재분사구이며, 그 안의 { }는 indicating의 목적어 역할을 하는 명사절이다.

09   정답 ②

13년 동안 영국 의학 저널의 책임자인 Richard Smith는 자신의 저서에서, 각각의 기고자가 각각의 소논문에서 어떤 부분의 일을 수행했는지를 명백하게 설명해 주는 방법 없이는 과학이 잘 작동될 수 없다고 말한다. Smith는 공동 저자들의 목록이 그들의 전기 및 그들이 각 연구에 기고한 내용과 함께 저널에 포함되어야 한다고 제안한다. 이 관계는 논문 저자 당사자들에 의해 전개되고 동의되어야 한다. 그러나 이 생각은 과학의 위대한 세계 지도자들을 설득하지 못하는데, 그들은 자신들에게 그 지도력을 제공해 온 것이 바로 그 기고 시스템이기 때문에 그 시스템에 매우 만족해한다. 그러나 그것[기고 시스템]은 재능 있는 젊은이들이 그것에 참여하는 것을 단념시킨다. 현재의 과학자는 연구가 자기 자신의 것이라고 느끼지 않는다. 그 과학자는 자신의 이름이 쓰인 과학 문헌을 만들지만, 많은 경우 심지어 그 글을 쓴 적도 없거나 그 글의 일부도 쓰지 않았다. 사실, 힘 있는 연구 집단이 과학자들이 데이터를 넘기는 전문 작가, 즉 젊은 박사들을 고용하는 것이 점점 더 흔해지고 있다.

해설
But으로 시작하는 주어진 문장의 this idea는 저널에 공동 저자들의 전기와 그들이 각 연구에 기고한 내용에 대한 목록이 포함되어야 한다는 Smith의 제안을 가리키고, ② 다음의 두 개의 it은 주어진 문장의 the system of contributions를 가리키는 것이 문맥상 자연스러우므로, 주어진 문장이 들어가기에 가장 적절한 곳은 ②이다.

TEXT FLOW

도입	Richard Smith는 각각의 기고자가 소논문에서 어떤 일을 수행했는지 설명해야 한다고 주장함
반전	세계 지도자들은 자신들에게 지도력을 제공한 지금의 기고 시스템에 만족함
부연 1	지금의 기고 시스템은 재능 있는 젊은이들이 참여하는 것을 단념시킴
부연 2	힘 있는 연구 집단이 젊은 박사를 고용하는 것이 더욱 흔해짐

구문
• But this idea does not convince the great world leaders in science, [who are very comfortable with the system of contributions] [as **it is** the one **that** has provided them with that leadership].
: 첫 번째 [ ]는 계속적 용법의 관계대명사 who가 이끄는 절로, 선행사는 the great world leaders in science이다. 두 번째 [ ]는 이유를 나타내는 부사절로, 「it is ~ that ...」 강조구문이 사용되어 주어 the one(=the system of contributions)이 강조되었다. 「provide A with B」는 'A에게 B를 주다'라는 의미이다.

10   정답 ①

전형적으로, 산업 사회의 주변부에 있는 토착 민족들 사이에서 행해진 것과 같은 전쟁은 산업 문명의 현대적인 전쟁과 비교할 때 매우 의식적으로 행해진다고 하고, 그 결과 사상자의 수를 줄인다. 그 주장에 관한 논쟁은 있지만, '원시적인' 전쟁의 본질적인 감성에 대한 이런 인류학적인 견해는 더 대중적인 생각에 스며들어 왔다. 전쟁 역사가인 Gwynne Dyer는 수렵 · 채집하는 사회는 전쟁을 '중요한 의식이자, 흥미롭고 위험한 게임, 그리고 어쩌면 심지어 자기 표현을 위한 기회라고 이해하고 수행하지만, 그것은 그 말의 어떤 현대적인 의미에서 힘에 관한 것이 아니고, 그것은 절대로 틀림없이 살육에 관한 것은 아니다'라고 주장한다. 그래서 이 계통의 논의가 주장하는 바에 따르면, 현대적인 전쟁은 무기의 기술적 진보뿐만 아니라 전쟁 수행의 탈의식화 때문에, 원시적인 전쟁의 희생을 훨씬 뛰어넘는 폭력과 희생으로 행해진다. Tom Driver는 후자가 '전면전', 즉 한계나 제약을 전혀 배려하지 않고 행해지는 전쟁이라는 현상에 대해 부분적으로 책임이 있다는 것을 시사해 왔다.

➡ 현대의 전쟁은 '원시적인' 전쟁보다 더 <u>파괴적</u>이라고 여겨지는데, 무기에 있어서의 기술적 발전 및 전쟁을 벌이는 것과 관련한 의식화의 <u>상실</u> 때문이다.

해설
토착 민족들 사이의 전쟁은 매우 의식화되어 있어서 현대적인 전쟁에 비해 사상자의 수가 적지만, 현대적인 전쟁은 무기의 기술적 진보와 의식으로서의 전쟁 수행이 사라지면서 폭력과 대규모 희생으로 행해진다는 내용의 글이다. 따라서 요약문의 빈칸 (A), (B)에 들어갈 말로는 ① 'destructive(파괴적인) – loss(상실)'가 가장 적절하다.
② 파괴적인 – 회복   ③ 효과적인 – 상실
④ 효과적인 – 금지   ⑤ 소모적인 – 회복

도입	토착 민족들의 전쟁은 매우 의식적으로 행해져 사상자의 수가 적음
부연	수렵·채집 사회는 전쟁을 중요한 의식으로 이해하고 살육에 관한 것은 아니라고 주장함
전환	현대적인 전쟁은 무기의 기술적 진보와 전쟁 수행의 탈의식화로 폭력과 대규모 희생으로 행해짐

구문

• Tom Driver has suggested [that the latter is partly responsible for the phenomenon of "total war,"] [war waged with no regard for limits or constraints].

: 첫 번째 [ ]는 has suggested의 목적어 역할을 하는 명사절이고, 두 번째 [ ]는 바로 앞의 total war와 동격 관계이다.

11-12
정답 11 ① 12 ④

만약 미술 연구의 윤리를 미술품을 만들고 사용한 사람들의 삶과 감성에 대한 약간의 통찰력을 찾는 것에서뿐만 아니라 미술품을 즐기고 이해하는 것을 촉진하는 것에서 보고자 한다면, 세계 미술사의 주제는 조만간 보편적인 것들에 대한 문제, 즉 현대 인문학에서 거의 위신을 누리지 못하는 개념에 직면할 것이다. '본질적인 인간 조건', '공통적인 인간성' 또는 '내부에 있는 정신적 핵심'에 대한 호소는 특정 종류의 수사학에서는 정당한 역할을 할 수도 있지만, 그것들은 세계 미술사에 대해 생각하기에는 약한 기반을 제공한다. 보편적 특성을 끌어들이는 다른 방식이 1960년대와 1970년대에 과학적 정밀함으로 추구되었지만, 미술사에 많은 양분을 제공하지는 못했다. 미적 가치의 보편성을 객관적으로 결정하기 위한 시도가 있었으며, 연구자들은 일반적으로 대칭, 비율, 균형, 조화와 같은 보편적인 형식 범주가 있으며 미술 작품의 미적 매력은 부분적으로 인간 본성의 보편성에 달려 있다고 결론 내렸다. 놀랄 것도 없이, 그러한 견해는 예술 작품의 해석과 표현에 유용한 것으로 항상 생각되었다(→ 거의 생각되지 않았다). '민족 미술'에 대한 연구에 종사하는 많은 인류학자들은 다른 문화의 미적 차원을 이해하고 감상하기 위해서는 그들의 이미지를 고립된 미적 현상으로서가 아니라 오히려 사회적 행동과 인간 행위자의 삶의 맥락에서 연구할 필요가 있다고 동의했다.

해설

11 미술품의 가치를 이해하기 위해서 보편적인 기준을 정하려는 시도가 있었지만 그것은 세계 미술사에 많은 양분을 주지 못했으며, 보편적인 기준이 아니라 사회적 행동과 인간 행위자의 삶의 맥락에서 미술을 이해할 필요가 있음을 설명하는 글이다. 따라서 글의 제목으로 가장 적절한 것은 ① '세계 미술 연구에서 미적 보편성을 추구해야 하는가?'이다.
② 세계 미술사: 과학과 영성의 융합
③ 보편성은 사회를 평등하게 유지하는 데 어떤 역할을 하는가?
④ 미술 작품: 인류학의 주요 연구 자료
⑤ 예술 연구가 인류에게 필요한 이유는 무엇인가?

12 미적 가치의 보편성을 객관적으로 결정하기 위한 시도가 있었지만, 미술사에 많은 영향을 주지 못했다는 내용이므로, 그러한 관점은 유용한 것으로 드러나지 못했다는 맥락이 되어야 한다. 그러므로 ④의 'always(항상)'는 'seldom(거의 ~ 않는)'과 같은 낱말로 바꾸어야 한다.

도입	세계 미술사는 보편성의 문제에 직면함
전개 1	보편적 특성을 끌어들이는 시도가 과학적으로 추구되었지만, 미술사에 자양분을 제공하지는 못함
전개 2	미적 가치와 미적 매력에 대한 견해는 유용한 것으로 여겨지지 지 않음
결론	다른 문화의 미적 차원을 감상하기 위해서는 사회적 행동과 삶의 맥락에서 이해해야 함

구문

• [If the ethics of the study of art **is to** be seen {in facilitating the enjoyment and understanding of art objects}, **as well as** {in finding some insight into the lives and sensibilities of the people who made and used the art}], then ~.

: [ ]는 if가 이끄는 조건절이고, then 이하는 주절이다. if절에 쓰인 「be+to부정사」는 의도를 나타내며 '~하고자 한다면'으로 해석한다. 두 개의 { }는 「B as well as A」 구문의 B와 A에 해당한다.

고난도 모의고사 **04회**

01 ③	02 ①	03 ⑤	04 ③	05 ③	06 ①
07 ②	08 ③	09 ⑤	10 ⑤	11 ⑤	12 ④

01
정답 ③

스트레스에 대한 적응력의 수준은 사람마다 각각 다르다. 탁자에 거꾸로 놓인 종이컵을 상상해 보라. 여러분은 그것이 얼마나 많은 무게를 견딜 수 있다고 생각하는가? 내가 작은 종이 표지의 책을 그 위에 올려 놓고 그것이 버틸 것으로 기대할 수 있을까? 큰 단단한 표지의 백과사전은 어떤가? 둘, 셋, 혹은 넷의 크고 무거운 책은 어떤가? 결국 그 컵은 책의 무게에 굴복하고 그것은 무너질 것이다. 내가 종이컵 대신 금속 컵을 사용하면 어떻게 될까? 그것은 같은 양의 무게(스트레스) 아래에서 무너질 것인가 아니면 구부러지기 전까지 훨씬 더 많은 무게를 버틸 수 있을 것인가? 여러분은 어떤 컵이 되고 싶은가? 컵은 무생물이지만, 인간의 신체는 적응할 수 있다. 스트레스에 매우 민감한 여러분의 정신의 부분은 배울 힘을 갖추고 있다. 신체의 적응 잠재력은 사람들이 병에 굴복하기까지 얼마나 많은 스트레스에 대처할 수 있는지를 결정하는 것이다.

해설
사람마다 스트레스에 대한 다른 적응력 수준을 가지며, 종이컵처럼 약한 적응력을 가진 사람도 있고 금속 컵처럼 강한 적응력을 가진 사람도 있다고 언급하며, 스트레스에 대한 적응력을 키우는 것이 필요하다고 제시하므로, 밑줄 친 부분이 글에서 의미하는 바로 가장 적절한 것은 ③ '여러분은 심한 스트레스를 견딜 수 있기를 바라는가?'이다.
① 여러분은 스트레스를 받으면 성격이 변하는가?
② 건강을 강화하기 위해 스트레스를 어떻게 사용하겠는가?
④ 여러분은 통제할 수 없는 스트레스를 붙잡고 있을 것인가?
⑤ 스트레스에 적응한 사람에게서 배우는 게 어떤가?

TEXT FLOW
도입	스트레스에 대한 적응력은 사람마다 다름
예시	종이컵은 작은 무게에도 무너질 것이고, 금속 컵은 훨씬 더 많은 무게를 버틸 것임
부연	사람의 신체는 적응할 수 있고, 스트레스에 민감한 정신도 배울 힘이 있음
결론	신체의 적응 잠재력은 얼마나 많은 스트레스에 대처할 수 있는지 결정하는 것임

구문
• [The body's adaptation potential] is [what determines how much stress someone can handle before they succumb to illness].
: 첫 번째 [ ]는 주어이고 두 번째 [ ]는 주격 보어 역할을 하는 명사절이다.

02
정답 ①

자신들에게 집중할 때, 사람들은 (불안한 감정과 이미지 같은) 내적인 정보를 인식하게 되는데, 그들은 그것들을 자신들의 최악의 공포에 대한 충분한 증거라고 잘못 받아들인다. 가장 흔한 공포 중 하나는 여러분이 불안하다는 것을 사람들이 알게 될 거라는 것이다. 사회적 불안 장애를 가진 사람들은 그들이 느끼는 것보다 훨씬 덜 불안해 보이지만, 그들은 자신들의 감정이 자신들이 어떻게 보이는지에 대한 좋은 지표라고 믿는 경향이 있다. 이미지 또한 두드러진 역할을 한다. 특히 불안할 때 사회적 불안 장애를 가진 사람들은 마치 관찰자의 시각에서 보듯 자신들의 마음속 눈으로 스스로를 본다고 보고한다. 유감스럽게도, 그들이 보는 것은 관찰자가 사실상 보는 것이 아니라 대신에 자신들의 최악의 공포가 시각화된 것이다. 그러므로 얼굴이 붉어지는 것에 대해 우려하는 사람은 실제로 약간 분홍빛이 되었을지도 모르지만, 그들의 마음속 눈에서는 자신들이 비트 같은 붉은색이며 자신들의 이마로부터 큰 땀방울이 뚝뚝 떨어지고 있는 것으로 보일 것이다.

해설
실제 겉으로 보이는 것보다 마음속의 눈으로 본 자신이 훨씬 더 불안해 보이며 사람들은 내적인 정보를 과대평가하여 자신의 공포에 대한 증거라고 받아들인다는 내용이므로, 글의 제목으로 가장 적절한 것은 ① '불안이 두려운 기분에 미치는 증폭 효과'이다.
② 우리의 자아상: 희망과 신념의 반영
③ 불안감: 가장 강력한 성취동기
④ 마음속 눈은 어떻게 무서운 것들로 가득한 세상을 만드는가
⑤ 마음속 눈에 비친 이미지와 진짜 자아 분리하기

⊗ 매력적인 오답 주의!
④ 글 전체의 의미를 이해하기보다 지문의 anxious feelings, worst fears, anxiety disorder, mind's eye 등의 단편적인 어휘나 표현을 근거로 선택한 것으로 보인다. [선택률 29%]

TEXT FLOW
주제	자신에게 집중할 때, 사람들은 내적 정보를 인지하면서 그것들을 공포에 대한 증거라고 잘못 받아들임
부연 1	자신이 불안하다는 것을 사람들이 알게 될 것이라는 공포가 있음
부연 2	자신들의 마음속 눈으로 스스로를 보면서 실제가 아닌 최악의 공포가 시각화됨
예시	실제로는 분홍빛이 된 얼굴이지만, 마음속 눈에서는 붉은색으로 보임

구문
• [When particularly anxious], people with social anxiety disorder **report** seeing themselves in their mind's eye [as though from an observer's perspective].
: 첫 번째 [ ]는 시간의 부사절로 When they are particularly anxious에서 「대명사 주어+be동사」가 생략된 형태이다. 이어지는 주절의 동사는 report이며, 두 번째 [ ]는 as though seeing themselves from an observer's perspective에서 반복되는 어구 seeing themselves가 생략된 형태이다.

03
정답 ⑤

바쁘게 보내는 시간은 바쁘게 보내지 않는 시간보다 더 짧게 느껴진다. 기다리는 동안 여러분이 뭔가를 하느라 바쁘면, 그 시간이 더 빠르게 흘러가는 것처럼 보인다. 고객들이 어떤 식으로든 주의가 분산되거나 다른 곳으로 돌려질 수 있으면, 대부분의 줄 대기 시간을 더 즐겁게 그리고 덜 지루하게 느껴

지게 만들 수 있다. Disney 기획자들은 고객들에게 그 기다림에 대해 생각하는 것을 멈추게 할 어떤 것을 제공함으로써 대기 시간을 관리하는 달인들이다. 만약 Walt Disney World Resort에서 인기를 끄는 특정한 것의 줄이 엄청나게 길어지고 서비스 차질이 임박해 있다면, 순회공연 밴드나 곡예사 혹은 다른 오락거리가 와서 고객들이 기다리는 동안 그들을 즐겁게 해 주고 주의를 끈다. 긴 줄을 위해서, Universal Orlando Resort는 줄곧 비디오나 영화를 보여 주는 텔레비전 수상기를 일정한 간격으로 둔다. 사람들은 인기를 끄는 것의 입구 쪽으로 이동하면서 재미있는 프로그램을 볼 수 있다.

해설

⑤ show a video or movie에서 show의 주어 역할을 하면서 선행사를 수식하는 관계대명사의 역할을 하는 표현이 필요한데, 관계절 안의 동사가 show이므로 the time이 관계절의 수식을 받는 선행사가 될 수 없다. throughout the time은 전치사구로 '줄곧'이라는 뜻이고, show의 주어역할을 하는 선행사는 television sets가 되어야 어법상 문제가 없는 구조가 되므로, when은 which[that]로 고쳐야 한다.
① '~하느라 바쁜'이라는 뜻은 「be busy + -ing」로 쓰므로, doing은 어법상 적절하다.
② 목적어와 목적격 보어(동사원형)를 취하는 사역동사 make가 수동태가 될 때, 동사원형의 형태였던 목적격 보어는 to부정사로 쓰이므로, to feel은 어법상 적절하다.
③ stop의 행위를 하는 것은 something이고, stop의 행위를 당하는 대상은 their guests이므로, 대명사 them은 어법상 적절하다.
④ and로 대등하게 연결되어 entertain과 병렬 구조를 이루므로, occupy는 어법상 적절하다.

TEXT FLOW

도입	기다리는 동안 원가를 하느라 바쁘면, 시간이 빠르게 흘러가는 것처럼 느껴짐
부연	고객의 주의가 다른 곳으로 돌려지면, 대기 시간이 덜 지루하게 느껴지게 만들 수 있음
예시 1	Disney는 순회공연 밴드, 곡예사, 오락거리로 고객을 즐겁게 해 주고 주의를 끔
예시 2	Universal Orlando Resort는 텔레비전 수상기를 일정한 간격으로 둠

04
정답 ③

매우 자주, '인간의 본성'은 우리가 마주치는 다양한 행동을 설명하는 부담 없는 방식으로 언급된다. 우리가 정기적으로 마주치는 거의 모든 것이 어깨를 으쓱하는 행동을 취해 그 인간적 상황을 설명하려 한다. 흥미롭게도, 우리가 이런 방식으로 설명해 버리는 특징들은 거의 항상 불미스러운 일들인데, 관대함의 행위는 그것이 '그저 인간의 본성'이라는 근거로 일축되는 경우가 거의 없다. 그렇지만, 그러한 주장을 방어하기 위한 실증적인 근거와는 별개로, 특정한 특징이 우리 본성의 일부라고 반대하는(→ 단언하는) 사람에게 입증의 책임이 무겁게 지워진다는 것을 기억하는 것은 중요하다. 그런 믿음을 입증하기 위해 설득력 있는 근거를 제공해야 하는 사람은 바로 그나 그녀이고 그렇지 않다는 것을 증명해야 하는 사람도 우리 중 나머지가 아니다. 우리에게 고려해 보라고 주장하는 사람은 그러한 책임을 가지지만, 그 주장이 절대적일 때 그것은 더욱 더 어마어마하다. 어떤 특징이 우리의 본성이라고 말하는 것은 그것이 모든 문화에 걸쳐 그리고 인간 역사를 통틀어 모든 인간의 특징이라고 단언하는 것이다. 게다가, 그것은 미래의 모든 인간도 피할 수 없음을 제안하는 것이다.

해설

부정적인 어떤 특징이 인간의 본성이라고 아주 쉽게 말하지만 긍정적인 특징이 인간의 본성이라고 말하는 경우는 매우 드물며, 심지어 그렇게 말하려면 그 믿음을 입증하기 위해 설득력 있는 근거를 제공할 책임을 지게 된다는 맥락이므로, ③의 'denies(반대하다)'를 'asserts(단언하다)'와 같은 낱말로 바꾸어야 한다.

TEXT FLOW

도입	'인간의 본성'은 우리가 마주치는 다양한 행동을 설명하기 위해 자주 언급됨
전개	이런 방식으로 설명해 버리는 특징들은 거의 불미스러운 것들임
주제	특정한 특징이 우리 본성의 일부라고 주장하기 위해서는 설득력 있는 근거를 제공해야 함
부연	어떤 특징이 우리의 본성이라고 말하는 것은 모든 문화와 인간 역사를 통틀어 단언하는 것이고, 미래의 인간도 포함하는 것임

구문

• [It is he or she **who** must provide compelling evidence {to substantiate such a belief}], and [not the rest of us **who** must prove it is not so].
: 첫 번째 [ ]는 「It is ~ who ....」 강조구문이 쓰여 주어 he or she가 강조되었다. 그 안의 { }는 목적을 나타내는 to부정사구이다. 두 번째 [ ]도 주어 not the rest of us를 강조하는 「It is ~ who ....」 강조구문이고, 반복을 피하기 위해 it is가 생략되었다.

05
정답 ③

음악의 보편성은 아마도 언어의 보편성보다 이론의 여지가 더 많을 것인데, 그 이유는 많은 사람이 스스로 음악적 소양이 없다고 단언하는 가운데, 우리가 듣는 것보다 만들어 내는 것을 더 강조하기 때문이다. 이런 면에서 John Blacking이 자신이 성장한 서양 중산층 사회의 이론과 실제 사이의 모순에 대해 1970년대에 했던 논평은 오늘날에도 여전히 타당하다. 음악은 우리 주변 어디에나 있었고 여전히 그러하다. 즉 우리는 음식점과 공항 라운지에서 밥을 먹고 이야기하려고 할 때 음악을 들으며, 음악은 라디오에서 온종일 연주되고, 사실 누군가가 잠재적인 침묵의 순간을 음악으로 채우려 하지 않는 경우는 거의 없다. Blacking은 '사회는 제한된 수의 사람들만 음악적 소양이 있다고 주장하지만, 그것이 없으면 음악적 전통이 존재할 수 없는 기본적인 능력, 즉 소리의 패턴을 듣고 구별할 수 있는 능력을 모두가 소유하고 있는 것처럼 움직인다.'라고 말했다. 그는 음악적 소양이 없는 인간 같은 것은 없다는 생각에 찬성했고 바흐나 베토벤과 같은 음악가의 존재는 <u>분별 있는 청중의 존재</u> 때문에만 가능했다고 말했다.

해설

많은 사람이 스스로 음악을 모른다고 하며 음악의 보편성에 대해 의문을 품지만, 사실 항상 음악을 듣고 음악을 위한 기본 능력인 소리의 패턴 분별 능력을 가지고 있기에 음악은 보편적이라고 할 수 있으며, 바흐나 베토벤 같은 음악가가 존재할 수 있었던 것은 그런 음악가의 음악을 들을 수 있는 청중이 있었기 때문이라는 내용의 글이므로, 빈칸에 들어갈 말로 가장 적절한 것은 ③ '분별 있는 청중의 존재'이다.
① 그들의 뛰어난 음악 창작 능력
② 음악과 언어의 유사점
④ 음악 작곡의 이론적 발전
⑤ 개인의 재능을 보상하는 사회적인 분위기

지문에 드러난 음악적 소양에 대한 사회와 Blacking의 상반된 주장을 명확하게 파악하고 있지 않으면, 잘못된 주장의 근거로 빈칸에 들어갈 말을 선택할 수 있는 고난도 문제이다.

TEXT FLOW

도입	음악의 보편성은 이론의 여지가 많은데, 많은 사람이 스스로 음악적 소양이 없다고 단언하고, 음악을 만들어 내는 것을 강조하기 때문임
전개 1	음악은 우리 주변 어디에나 있음
전개 2	모든 사람이 소리의 패턴을 듣고 구별할 수 있는 능력이 있으므로 음악적 소양이 없는 사람은 없음

구문

• In this regard, John Blacking's comments, [made in the 1970s], [on the contradiction between theory and practice in the middle-class, Western society {in which he grew up}], remain relevant today.

: 첫 번째 [ ]와 두 번째 [ ]는 각각 John Blacking's comments를 수식하는 과거분사구와 전치사구이다. 두 번째 [ ] 안의 { }는 the middle-class, Western society를 수식하는 관계절이다.

06   정답 ①

운이 조금이라도 있다면, 우리는 폐기물을 만드는 것이 우리가 풀어야 할 문제가 아니라는 것을 깨달을 것이다. 만약 살아 있는 어떤 종이 폐기물을 발생시키지 않는다면, 그것은 아마도 죽은 것이거나 적어도 매우 아픈 것이다. 우리에게 있고 우리가 다뤄야 할 문제는 우리가 만들어 내는 폐기물을 허비한다는 것이다. 폐기물을 영양분으로 변환하는 것은 에너지를 필요로 하기도 하고 발생시키기도 한다는 것을 생각해 보라. 우리는 항상 상업용 및 가정용 기기를 위한 에너지원을 찾고 있지만, 생태계는 결코 전선을 연결할 필요가 없다. 생태계의 어느 구성원도 생산물을 내기 위해 화석 연료나 배전망 연결을 필요로 하지 않고, 자연 체계에서는 또한 폐기물이 결과물도 아니다. 자연에서는, 한 공정의 폐기물은 항상 다른 공정을 위한 영양분, 재료, 혹은 에너지원이다. 모든 것이 영양분 흐름 속에 머문다. 따라서 오염의 환경 문제뿐만 아니라 희소성의 경제 문제에 대한 해결책은 자연 생태계에서 관찰할 수 있는 모델의 적용에서 찾을 수 있을 것이다. 어쩌면 우리는 우리의 관점을 넓히고 폐기물의 개념을 버림으로써 난제를 해결책으로 바꿀 수 있다.

해설

생태계에서는 어떤 공정의 폐기물이 항상 다른 공정을 위한 영양분, 재료, 혹은 에너지원이 되기 때문에 생태계의 모델을 적용하면 환경 문제와 경제 문제가 모두 해결될 수 있다는 내용의 글이다. 따라서 우리가 당면한 문제의 해결책에 해당하는 빈칸에 들어갈 말로 가장 적절한 것은 ① '폐기물의 개념을 버림'이다.
② 자연의 비효율성을 극복함
③ 재생 가능한 에너지원으로 전환함
④ 영양분 흐름에서 폐기물을 제거함
⑤ 환경 문제와 경제 문제를 분리함

TEXT FLOW

도입	우리는 우리가 만들어 낸 폐기물을 허비하고 있음
전환	생태계에서는 어떤 공정의 폐기물이 항상 다른 공정을 위한 영양분, 재료, 에너지원임
결론	생태계의 모델을 적용하여 환경과 경제 문제를 해결할 수 있음

구문

• The problem [we have], and [that we must address], is [that we **waste** the **waste** we create].

: 첫 번째 [ ]와 두 번째 [ ]는 The problem을 수식하는 관계절이고 we have 앞에는 목적격 관계대명사 that이 생략되었다. 세 번째 [ ]는 보어 역할을 하는 명사절로, 그 안의 첫 번째 waste는 '허비하다'라는 뜻의 동사이고 두 번째 waste는 '폐기물'이라는 뜻의 명사이다.

07   정답 ②

하향식 포트폴리오 구성은 자산 배분으로 시작된다. 예를 들어, 현재 자신의 모든 돈을 은행 계좌에 보유한 사람은 전체 포트폴리오의 어느 정도가 주식, 채권 등으로 이동되어야 하는지를 먼저 결정할 것이다. (B) 이런 방식으로, 포트폴리오의 전반적인 특징이 수립된다. 예를 들어, 1926년부터 대기업의 보통 주식의 평균 연간 수익률은 1년에 11퍼센트보다 더 높았던 반면, 미국 재무부 단기 채권의 평균 수익은 4퍼센트 미만이었다. (A) 반면, 주식은 범위가 −46퍼센트만큼이나 낮고 55퍼센트만큼이나 높았던 연 수익률 때문에 훨씬 더 위험스럽다. 이와 대조적으로, 재무부 증권은 실질적으로 위험이 없는데, 여러분은 그것을 살 때 얼마의 이자를 벌어들일지 안다. (C) 따라서 투자금을 주식 시장이나 재무부 증권이 거래되는 화폐 시장에 배분하는 결정은 여러분의 포트폴리오의 위험과 수익 둘 다에 큰 영향을 미칠 것이다. 하향식 투자자는 먼저 이것과 기타 매우 중요한 자산 배분 결정을 내린다.

해설

하향식 포트폴리오 구성을 언급하고, 이러한 방식으로 주식, 채권 등으로 돈을 배분하려는 사례를 드는 주어진 글 다음에는, In this way로 그것을 받아, 우선 대기업의 보통 주식과 재무부 단기 채권의 수익률에 관해 언급하는 (B)가 온 후, 주식의 수익률 범위와 재무부 증권의 특징에 관해 더 자세히 언급한 (A)가 온 다음, (B)와 (A)에 따라 자산의 배분은 수익과 위험 둘 다에 영향을 미치며, 하향식 투자자는 먼저 이것과 기타 매우 중요한 자산 배분을 결정한다고 언급한 (C)가 마지막에 오는 것이 글의 순서로 가장 적절하다.

TEXT FLOW

도입	하향식 포트폴리오 구성은 자산 배분으로 시작됨
예시	은행 계좌에 있는 돈은 어느 정도가 주식, 채권 등으로 이동되어야 할지 결정될 것임
부연	대기업의 보통 주식과 재무부 단기 채권의 수익률
결론	투자금 배분 결정은 포트폴리오의 위험과 수익 둘 다에 영향을 미침

구문

• On the other hand, stocks are **far** riskier, **with** annual returns [that have ranged as low as –46% and as high as 55%].

: far는 '훨씬'의 의미로 비교급 riskier를 강조한다. with는 '~ 때문에'의 의미이다. [ ]는 annual returns를 수식하는 관계절이다.

08

정답 ③

동부 아프리카의 일부 개체군의 침팬지는 작고 가는 막대기로 흰개미 둔덕을 탐지하여 흰개미를 잡는다. 그러나 서부 아프리카의 일부 다른 침팬지 개체군은 큰 막대기로 흰개미 둔덕을 파괴하여 그 곤충을 한 움큼 퍼내려고 시도한다. Boesch와 McGrew 같은 현장 연구자들은 이와 같은 특정한 도구 사용 관행이 다양한 군집의 개체 사이에서 '문화적으로 전수된'다고 주장했다. 하지만 또한 꽤 그럴듯한 상충하는 설명이 있다. 사실은 서부 아프리카의 흰개미 둔덕이 더 많은 양의 비로 인해 동부 아프리카의 흰개미 둔덕보다 훨씬 더 부드럽다는 것이다. 따라서 큰 막대기로 둔덕을 파괴하는 전략은 서부 개체군에서만 이용 가능하다. 그러므로 이 가설에 따르면, 표면적으로는 인간의 문화적 차이와 비슷하지만, 어떤 유형의 사회적 학습도 전혀 개입되지 않은, 행동의 집단적 차이가 존재할 것이다. 그러한 경우에 '문화'는 단순히 서로 다른 개체군의 서로 다른 지역 생태에 의해 주도되는 개별 학습의 결과일 뿐이다.

해설

주어진 문장은 서부 아프리카의 흰개미 둔덕이 동부 아프리카의 흰개미 둔덕보다 훨씬 더 부드럽다는 내용으로, ③ 뒤 문장의 서부 침팬지 개체군만이 큰 막대기로 흰개미 둔덕을 파괴할 수 있다는 내용의 원인에 해당한다. 따라서 주어진 문장이 들어가기에 가장 적절한 곳은 ③이다.

TEXT FLOW

도입	동부 아프리카 침팬지는 작고 가는 막대기로 흰개미를 잡고, 서부 침팬지는 큰 막대기로 흰개미를 잡음
주장	이와 같은 특정한 도구 사용 관행은 문화적으로 전수된다고 주장함
반전	하지만 서부 아프리카의 흰개미 둔덕이 동부 아프리카의 둔덕보다 많은 양의 비로 인해 더 부드러움
부연	행동의 집단적 차이는 다른 개체군의 다른 지역 생태에 의해 주도되는 개별 학습의 결과임

구문

- The fact is [that the termite mounds in western Africa are much softer, owing to larger amounts of rain, than **those** of eastern Africa].
  : [ ]는 주격 보어 역할을 하는 명사절이다. those는 the termite mounds를 받는 대명사이다.

09

정답 ⑤

대륙 간 여행은 가장 커다란 환경적 영향을 초래한다. 하지만 총 여행 횟수는 그리 크지 않다. 일반적으로 환경 문제의 80%는 그 시장의 20%에 의해서만 유발된다. 따라서 시장의 완전한 변화와 여행 및 여가에 대한 인간의 요구를 손상하지 않고도 절감에 도달할 수 있다. 그 해결책은 관광 성장과 운송 성장을 분리하는 것일 것이다. 감소되어야 하는 것은 여가 일수가 아니라, 여가 시간 동안 여행하는 총 킬로미터 수라는 것을 명심하는 것이 중요하다. 따라서 관광 증가는 제한되지 않고 운송량 증가만 제한될 뿐이다. 물론, 가령 개발 도상국의 신흥 관광 산업에 미치는 영향 같은 부작용은 연구되어야 한다. 이것들이 대륙 간 관광을 기반으로 하는 한, 극빈층 28억 명의 소득을 두 배로 늘리는 것은 2000년의 전체 항공 운송량의 20배에서 50배의 항공 운송량을 필요로 할 것이다. 이것은 지속 가능하지도 않고 가능하지도 않다.

해설

주어진 문장은 ⑤ 바로 앞 문장의 사례에 해당하고 ⑤ 바로 뒤 문장의 This가 가리키는 것이 주어진 문장의 주절의 내용에 해당하므로, 주어진 문장이 들어가기에 가장 적절한 곳은 ⑤이다.

TEXT FLOW

도입	대륙 간 여행은 커다란 환경적 영향을 초래하지만 이를 절감할 해결책이 있음
전개	해결책은 관광 성장과 운송 성장을 분리하는 것임
부연	감소되어야 할 것은 여행하는 총 킬로미터 수이므로 운송량 증가만 제한됨
예시	개발 도상국의 신흥 관광 산업에 미치는 영향과 같은 부작용도 연구되어야 함

구문

- It is important to bear in mind [that **it is** not the number of leisure days **that** has to be reduced, but the total kilometers travelled during leisure time].
  : [ ]는 bear in mind의 목적어 역할을 하는 명사절이고, not the number of leisure days를 강조하는 「it is ~ that ....」 강조구문이 쓰였다.

10

정답 ⑤

전시 디자이너, 미술관 큐레이터와 마찬가지로 사진작가들도 관람객이 사물을 특정한 관점을 따라 특정한 비교를 하도록 촉진하여 특별한 기분을 만들어 내기를 바라는 명확한 배열 속에서 보기를 원한다. 그들은 단일 이미지가 불확실하며 '그것이 무엇에 관한 것인지'를 쉽게 그리고 모호하지 않게 드러내지 않는다는 점을 알고 있다. 사진작가들이 뉴스와 광고 같은 다른 목적을 위해 사진을 제작할 때는, 대체로 모든 '관련 없는' 세부 사항, 즉 그들이 주의를 끌기를 원하는 뉴스 이야기의 '핵심'이나 제품의 특징을 제외한 모든 것을 전부 배제하도록 사진을 구성한다. 그들은 그 이야기의 핵심적인 아이디어를 강조하거나 그 제품의 매력을 향상하기 위해 요점과 밀접한 관련이 있는 세부 사항을 주의 깊게 선택한다. 과학적인 목적을 위해 제작된 사진들도 이와 비슷하게 제작자(대체로 그 과학 논문의 저자)가 사용자들이 알기를 바라는 점에 그 사진의 내용물을 제한하고 그 목적과 관련 없는 것은 무엇이든지 엄격히 배제한다.

➡ 사진작가들은 전시회에서 다수의 이미지의 배치를 계획해서 관람객들이 메시지를 이해하도록 하며, 뉴스, 광고, 논문에서는 요지를 분명하게 하기 위해 몇몇 세부 사항을 배제한다.

해설

사진작가들은 전시회에서는 단일 이미지를 제시하는 것이 아니라 사물을 특정한 관점에 따라 배열하여 관객을 유도하고자 하며, 뉴스 또는 광고 등의 목적을 위해서는 관련 없는 세부 사항을 배제하여 핵심을 보여 주려 한다는 내용이므로, 요약문의 빈칸 (A), (B)에 들어갈 말로는 ⑤ 'arrangement(배치) – exclude(배제하다)'가 가장 적절하다.
① 반복 – 설명하다
② 확대 – 비교하다
③ 확대 – 반복하다
④ 배치 – 겹겹이 쌓다

구문

- Pictures [made for scientific purposes] similarly **restrict** their content **to** [what the maker (usually the author of the scientific article) wants users to know] and rigorously **exclude** anything extraneous to that purpose.

: 첫 번째 [ ]는 Pictures를 수식하는 과거분사구이다. 「restrict A to B」는 'A를 B로 제한하다'의 의미로, 두 번째 [ ]는 B에 해당한다. exclude는 and로 연결되어 restrict와 병렬 구조를 이룬다.

11~12

정답 11 ⑤ 12 ④

메타버스에 대한 이야기에도 불구하고 오늘날 메타버스와 인터넷의 근본적인 차이점은 질이 아니라 양이다. 메타버스는 기존의 강력한 온라인 세계에 가상 현실, '증강' 현실, 대체 불가능한 토큰을 추가한다고 위협하지만, 메타버스의 모든 변화는 '더 많은' 데이터, '더 많은' 연결성, '더 많은' 거래, '더 많은' 복잡성이라는 동일한 결과에 이를 것이다. 웹 1.0에서 웹 2.0, 메타버스, 그리고 계속 이어서 나아가는 이동은 급진적인 신기술에서 비롯된 것이 아니다. 오히려 온라인 생활의 변화는 뇌의 진화와 비슷해, 점점 더 복잡해지다가 순전히 그 복잡성을 통해 놀랍고 새로운 현상이 나타나게 된다. 실제로 메타버스는 이미 여기 존재하며 꾸준히 성장하고 있다. 우리는 날이 갈수록 그것에 대한 통제력을 잃어 가고 있다.

메타버스의 탄생뿐만 아니라, 우리의 세상을 네트워크화된 컴퓨터 조작으로 감싼 결과는 생활 방식의 변화뿐만 아니라 기업이나 정부 관리자의 통제 하에 놓이지 않는 자율적인 네트워크의 꾸준한 성장이었다. 오늘날의 세상을 이해하려면 우리는 인간이나 국가가 아니라 서버처럼 생각해야 한다. 서버, 더 정확하게는 서버 집합체는 세상을 계산 가능한 데이터, 삶의 모든 측면을 나타내는 숫자의 홍수로 보는데 그러한 숫자는 양이 너무 커서 우리가 시스템에 계속 더 많은 데이터를 주입하는 동안에도 이 데이터의 '의미' 대부분이 보존된다(→ 사라진다). 결국 우리의 서버가 그 데이터를 다시 우리에게 주입하고, 우리는 같은 방식으로 세상을 바라보게 된다. 깨닫지 못하는 사이에 기계와 인간은 새로운 세상을 함께 만들어 가고 있으며, 그 세상은 우리가 옛 세상을 통제했던 방식으로는 통제할 수 없는 세상이다.

해설

11 메타버스를 비롯한 인터넷 세상은 점점 더 복잡해지면서 순전히 스스로 진화하고 자율적인 네트워크를 발전시켜 우리가 이전 세상을 통제하던 방식으로는 통제할 수 없는 세상이 되어 가고 있다는 내용이므로, 글의 제목으로 가장 적절한 것은 ⑤ '통제 불능: 메타버스와 네트워크로 연결된 온라인 세상'이다.
① 메타버스에 의해 가능해진 모든 것을 계산하기
② 가상 현실은 초기 인터넷 시대부터 존재해 왔는가?
③ 네트워크 컴퓨팅에서 고품질 서버의 중요한 역할
④ 메타버스: 인간의 마음보다 훨씬 더 복잡하지 않은 것

12 서버는 세상을 계산 가능한 데이터, 수많은 숫자로만 보기 때문에 우리가 서버에 공급하는 데이터의 의미는 상실되고 그들이 우리에게 다시

보내는 데이터를 통해 우리가 세상을 바라보게 된다는 맥락이므로, ④의 'preserved(보존된)'를 'lost(사라진)'와 같은 낱말로 바꾸어야 한다.

구문

- **For all** the talk of the metaverse, [the fundamental difference between the metaverse and the internet today] is [**not** quality **but** quantity].

: For all은 '~에도 불구하고'의 의미로 In spite of나 Despite로 바꾸어 쓸 수 있다. 첫 번째 [ ]는 문장의 주어이고, 두 번째 [ ]는 주격 보어로 「not A but B」의 구문이 사용되었다.

고난도 모의고사 05회

01 ③	02 ⑤	03 ④	04 ③	05 ②	06 ③
07 ④	08 ②	09 ⑤	10 ①	11 ①	12 ④

01
정답 ③

누군가가 이메일과 정보의 파도에 빠져 있을 때마다, 그들은 흔히 그들 시대의 가장 깊은 비극을 알지 못한다. 그것은 (그 스트레스가 실제적이고 매우 힘들 수도 있겠지만) 매우 많은 요청과 의무를 다루어야 하는 스트레스는 아니다. 그것은 상호 작용과 분산된 주의력의 너울 어디에선가 그들이 찾고 있는 놓쳐 버린 가능성, 즉 의미, 경험의 깊이, 연결이 있다는 것이다. Robert Pirsig의 말을 인용하면, "진리가 문을 두드리는데, 우리는 '저리 가. 나는 진리를 찾고 있단 말이야.'라고 말한다." 받은 편지함을 정리하고 할 일 목록에서 항목을 지우려는 경쟁에서, 우리는 그것을 위해 만든 받은 편지함과 할 일 목록에 있는 어떤 것을 찾는 기회를 놓친다. 유럽의 미국 관광객이 사진을 찍거나 관광버스에 타지 않은 누군가에게 말을 걸 틈도 거의 없이 이곳저곳을 질주하는 것처럼, 품질에 기반한 욕망에도 불구하고 우리는 양의 사고방식에 갇혀 있다.

해설
이메일과 정보의 파도에 빠지게 되면 받은 편지함을 정리하고 할 일 목록에서 항목을 지우는 일에만 몰두하게 되어, 즉 양의 사고방식에 갇혀서 정작 찾고 있는 것을 찾지 못하게 된다는 내용의 글이므로, 밑줄 친 부분이 의미하는 바로 가장 적절한 것은 ③ '정보 처리에 몰두한 채, 우리가 찾고 있는 것을 보지 못하는 것'이다.
① 더 큰 공동체를 무시하고 자기 잇속만 차리는 것
② 정보가 결합되고 배포된 위치에 초점을 맞추지 않는 것
④ 실생활의 지혜가 아닌 추상적인 지식의 형태로 진리를 추구하는 것
⑤ 유용하고 의미 있는 정보를 생산할 수 있는 그들의 능력을 의심하는 것

TEXT FLOW
도입	이메일과 정보의 파도에 빠지게 되면, 의미, 경험의 깊이, 연결의 가능성을 놓치게 됨
부연	받은 편지함을 정리하고 할 일 목록에서 항목을 지우는 일에 몰두해 정작 찾고자 하는 것을 찾지 못함
결론	품질에 기반한 욕망에도 불구하고 우리는 양의 사고방식에 갇혀 있음

구문
• It's [that {somewhere in the wash of interactions and split attentions} is the missed possibility {they're looking for}: Meaning. Depth of experience. Connection.]
: [ ]는 주격 보어 역할을 하는 명사절이다. 그 안의 첫 번째 { }는 부사구이고 문장 앞에 쓰여 뒤에 주어 the missed possibility와 동사 is가 도치되었다. 두 번째 { }는 the missed possibility를 수식하는 관계절이다.

02
정답 ⑤

18세기 부와 교육의 증가는 예술 시장의 성장과 공공 전시회 및 박물관의 출현에 반영된 것처럼 예술에 대한 대중 관심의 확장을 동반했다. 공개 판매와 경매는 예술품에 굶주린 대중을 위한 초창기 장이 되었고, 딜러들은 상점 창문, 신문 광고, 판매 카탈로그 등 새로운 마케팅 전략을 사용하여 새로운 부유층을 수집의 즐거움과 사회적 이점으로 유혹했다. 판화는 고급 예술의 범위를 크게 확장했고 그림 수집이 유행했지만 그림과 조각품을 소유하려면 큰 돈이 필요했다. 자신만의 수집품이 없는 사람들을 대변하여, 비평가들은 예술에 대한 대중의 더 큰 접근성을 요구했고, 세기 중반부터 그들의 요구가 받아들여졌다. 예술원은 회원들의 작품을 정기적으로 전시하는 전시회를 후원했는데, 가장 잘 알려진 전시회는 파리의 '살롱'(1737년부터)과 런던의 왕립 예술원 전시회(1768년부터)였다.

해설
18세기 부와 교육의 증가로 인해 예술에 대한 확장된 대중의 관심은 공개 판매 및 경매, 예술품 수집, 대중의 접근성을 높인 전시회 출현 등 일련의 과정을 통해 충족되었음을 설명하는 글이다. 그러므로 글의 주제로 가장 적절한 것은 ⑤ '18세기에 예술에 대한 늘어난 수요가 충족된 방식'이다.
① 예술 양식에 대한 18세기 비평가들의 영향
② 18세기에 각 계층을 대표하는 예술 유형
③ 부유층에 의한 18세기 예술계의 독점
④ 18세기에 예술품 거래로 인한 부의 축적

TEXT FLOW
주제	18세기 부와 교육의 증가는 예술에 대한 대중 관심의 확장을 동반했음
예시 1	공개 판매, 경매, 예술품 수집으로 새로운 부유층을 유혹함
예시 2	예술원은 대중의 접근성을 높인 전시회를 후원함

구문
• Academies sponsored regular exhibitions of their members' work, [the best known being the so-called Salon in Paris (from 1737) and the Royal Academy exhibitions in London (from 1768)].
: [ ]는 앞 문장을 부연 설명하는 분사구문이고, the best known이 의미상의 주어이다. the best known 다음에는 반복을 피하기 위해 regular exhibitions of their members' work가 생략되었다.

03
정답 ④

Solomon은 자신의 모든 지혜로도 기술 혁신의 긍정적인 결실에서 파괴적 잠재성이 있는 가능성을 선별하는 데 애를 먹을 것이다. 그럼에도 불구하고, 우리들 각자는 기술 발전의 영광스럽고도 불안하게 하는 행진에 대해 최소한 암묵적인 승인을 보내도록 요구받는다. 유감스럽게도, 사람들 대부분은 그들 자신의 미래를 만들어 갈 생각과 발견에 대해 기초적인 이해만을 하고 있을 뿐이다. 연구 자금 공급과 관련한 공공 정책을 세밀하게 만드는 사람들조차 전문가들의 추천에 매우 의존한다. 어려움은 균형 잡힌 시각을 위해 어떤 질문을 하고 어디에 의존할 것인가를 아는 데 있다. 너무나 자주 과학자들은 자신들의 전문 기술과 자신들의 이해를 넘어서 추정한다. 연구에 자금 지원을 받고자 하는 욕구는 그들의 판단을 흐릴 수 있다. 그 다음의 기술적 돌파구 달성에 대한 지나치게 낙관적인 시간의 틀의 형태를 하고 있는 과학자들의 과장된 선전은 과학 발전에 관해 비현실적인 희망과 공포를 부추긴다. 가장 설득력 있는 주장은 흔히 특정한 기술의 발전을 큰 목소리로 지지하거나 큰 목소리로 반대하는 주장이다.

해설

④ 문장의 주어는 Hype ~ breakthrough이며, 이와 연결되는 술어 동사가 필요하므로 분사인 encouraging은 적절치 않고, encourages로 바꿔야 한다.

① ask는 목적격 보어로 to부정사를 취하며 수동태일 때 to부정사는 그대로 쓰이므로, to give는 어법상 적절하다.

② the ideas and discoveries를 수식하며 관계절에서 주어 역할을 하므로, 관계대명사 that을 쓰는 것은 어법상 적절하다.

③ perspective는 동사 balance의 동작 대상이고 수동의 의미가 되어 과거분사 balanced의 수식을 받는 것이 적절하므로, 과거분사 balanced는 어법상 적절하다.

⑤ the voices를 대신하는 대명사이므로, 복수 대명사인 those를 쓰는 것은 어법상 적절하다.

TEXT FLOW

도입	우리는 기술 발전에 암묵적인 승인을 보내도록 요구받음
전개 1	우리는 그러한 발전에 대해 기초적인 이해만을 하고 있고, 전문가들의 추천에 매우 의존함
전개 2	과학자들은 자신들의 이해를 넘어서 추정하고, 과장된 선전으로 과학 발전에 대해 비현실적인 희망과 공포를 부추김

04
정답 ③

구조적 지도자들은 자신들의 조직을 위해 구조, 전략 및 환경의 관계에 대한 새로운 모델을 개발한다. 그들은 이행에 초점을 맞춘다. 정답은 그것이 이행될 수 있을 경우에만 도움이 될 뿐이다. 이러한 지도자들은 합리성, 분석, 논리, 사실, 자료를 강조한다. 그들은 분명한 구조와 잘 개발된 관리 시스템의 중요성을 강하게 믿을 가능성이 높다. 훌륭한 지도자는 명료하게 생각하고, 현명한 결정을 내리며, 좋은 분석 기술을 가지고, 일을 완수할 수 있는 구조와 시스템을 만들 수 있는 사람이다. 구조적 지도자들은 자신들의 설계를 제자리에 놓는 것의 어려움을 오판하기 때문에 때때로 실패한다. 그들은 그것이 만들어 낼 저항을 흔히 과대평가하고(→ 과소평가하고) 자신들의 혁신에 대한 지지 기반을 구축하기 위한 조치를 취하지 않는다. 요약하면, 그들은 인적 자원, 정치적, 상징적 고려 사항 때문에 흔히 실패하게 된다. 구조적 지도자들은 지속적으로 실험하고 평가하며 적응하지만, 자신들이 위치한 전체 환경을 고려하지 못하기 때문에 때때로 그들은 비효율적이다.

해설

구조적 지도자들은 조직의 구조와 전략 및 환경의 관계에 대해 새로운 모델을 개발하는데, 이 지도자들은 분명한 구조와 관리 시스템의 중요성을 믿지만 자신들이 만든 설계를 제자리에 놓을 때 생길 수 있는 어려움을 오판하기 때문에 때때로 실패한다는 맥락이 되어야 자연스러우므로, ③의 'overestimate(과대평가하다)'는 'underestimate(과소평가하다)'와 같은 낱말로 바꾸어야 한다.

TEXT FLOW

도입	구조적 지도자들은 조직의 구조, 전략 및 환경의 관계에 대한 새로운 모델을 개발함
부연	그들은 분명한 구조와 잘 개발된 관리 시스템의 중요성을 믿음
반전	자신들의 설계를 제자리에 놓는 것의 어려움을 오판하여 때때로 실패함
결론	그들은 실험하고 평가하며 적응하지만, 전체 환경을 고려하지 못하여 때로 비효율적임

구문

• Structural leaders **do** continually experiment, evaluate, and adapt, but because they fail to consider the entire environment [in which they are situated], they sometimes are ineffective.

: do는 동사 experiment, evaluate, adapt를 강조하는 조동사이다. [ ]는 the entire environment를 수식하는 관계절이다.

05
정답 ②

불확실성에 대한 생각은 사회가 현재와 미래의 관계를 인식하는 방식에 의해 지배된다. 오늘날과 같이 미래가 위험한 영역으로 간주될 때, 불확실성은 부정적인 시각으로 표현된다. 그런 환경에서는 변화 자체가 위협적인 것으로 인식된다. 기술적이든, 사회적이든 또는 정치적이든, 변화에 대한 불안의 강력한 암류(暗流)는 현대 서구 세계의 일상적인 일들에 스며든다. 불확실성은 때때로 기회로 여겨졌는데, 지금 그것이 부정적인 시각으로 비춰지는 경향이 있다는 것은 사회가 직면한 난제에 대한 숙명론적 분위기의 징후를 보인다. 이러한 숙명론적인 태도는 '문제는 '(변화 발생의) 여부가 아니라 시점'이다'라는 자주 언급되는 유명한 문구로 요약된다. 대재앙의 기후와 관련된 사건, 치명적인 유행성 독감 또는 대량 살상 테러에 대한 경고는 대개 이 패배주의적인 자주 반복되는 어구로 끝을 맺는데, 그것은 암시적으로 그리고 때로는 명시적으로 인류가 직면하는 위협의 파괴적인 결과를 피할 수 있는 인류의 능력에 의문을 제기한다. 이렇게 해서 미래의 위험은 즉각적이고 친밀한 특성을 획득한다. 그것(미래의 위험)은 우리가 앞에 놓여 있는 위험을 피하기 위해 할 수 있는 일이 거의 없다는 것을 암시하면서 우리에게 비상벨을 울릴 것을 요구한다.

해설

인류가 직면한 미래의 불확실성으로 인한 변화를 피하기 위해 할 수 있는 일이 거의 없다고 생각하면서 숙명론적인 태도를 가지게 되며, 변화에 대한 불안의 강력한 암류(暗流)가 현대 세계의 일상적인 일들에 스며들어 있다는 내용의 글이다. 따라서 빈칸에 들어갈 말로 가장 적절한 것은 ② '즉각적이고 친밀한 특성을 획득한다'이다.

① 사람마다 천차만별이다
③ 오해의 소지가 있는 정보를 기반으로 하는 경우가 많다
④ 예측 가능하고 완전히 제어할 수 있다
⑤ 예전의 그것들만큼 뚜렷하지 않다

TEXT FLOW

도입	불확실성은 미래가 위험하다고 느껴지면 부정적인 시각으로 표현됨
부연	그런 환경에서는 변화에 대한 불안의 암류가 현대 세계의 일상적인 일들에 스며들어 있음
전개	부정적인 시각으로 보는 불확실성은 사회가 직면한 난제에 대한 숙명론적 분위기를 보임
결론	미래의 위험은 인류가 직면하는 위협의 결과를 피하기 위해 할 수 있는 일이 거의 없음을 암시함

구문

• Uncertainty was at times regarded as an opportunity — [that it now tends to be cast in a negative light] is symptomatic of a mood of fatalism towards the challenges [faced by society].

: 첫 번째 [ ]는 주어 역할을 하는 명사절이고, 두 번째 [ ]는 the challenges를 수식하는 과거분사구이다.

- Warnings of catastrophic climate events, deadly flu epidemics or mass casualty terrorism usually conclude with this defeatist refrain, [which implicitly and sometimes explicitly **calls** into question humanity's capacity {to avoid the destructive consequences of the threats it faces}].
  : [ ]는 앞 문장의 내용을 부연 설명하는 계속적 용법의 관계절이다. which 의 선행사는 앞 문장 전체이므로 단수 동사 calls가 쓰였다. 그 안의 { }는 humanity's capacity를 수식하는 to부정사구이다.

06 정답 ③

여러분은 통계 수치로 사실을 왜곡할 수 있다. 뭔가를 다 세어 내고 그런 다음 그것을 다른 것으로 보고하는 여러 가지 형태가 있다. 일반적인 방법은 같은 것처럼 들리지만 그렇지 않은 두 가지를 골라내는 것이다. 노동조합과 다투고 있는 회사의 인사과 관리자로 여러분은 얼마나 많은 사람이 노동조합에 대해 불만을 가지고 있는지를 알아려고 직원들에 대해 '조사를 수행'한다. 노동조합이 천사장이 우두머리인 천사들의 집단이 아닌 이상 여러분은 완전히 정직하게 질문하고 기록한 다음 사람들 대다수가 정말로 한두 가지의 불만을 가지고 있다는 증거를 발표한다. 여러분은 "대다수, 즉 78퍼센트가 노동조합에 대해 반대한다."라는 보고서로 여러분의 정보를 내보낸다. 여러분이 한 것은 구별되지 않은 많은 불만과 사소한 불평을 모두 더한 다음 그것을 같은 것처럼 들리는 다른 것으로 선언한 것이다. 여러분은 한 가지도 증명하지 않았지만, 마치 다소 증명한 것처럼 들린다, 그렇지 않은가?

해설
통계를 사용하여 사실을 왜곡할 수 있는 것의 사례로 노동조합에 대한 직원들의 사소한 불만들을 모아, 마치 직원 대다수가 노동조합을 반대하는 것처럼 보고하는 것을 들어 사실상 다른 것을 마치 같은 것인 양 발표하는 방식에 대해 언급하고 있으므로, 빈칸에 들어갈 말로 가장 적절한 것은 ③ '같은 것처럼 보이지만 그렇지 않은 두 가지를 골라내는 것'이다.
① 오래된 것을 보고하지만 새것처럼 들리는 것
② 여러분의 상대에게 모호한 것을 증명해 달라고 요청하는 것
④ 보고서의 정확성을 강조하기 위해 숫자를 사용하는 것
⑤ 그것들을 심각하게 보이도록 작은 차이점을 과장하는 것

TEXT FLOW
도입	통계 수치로 사실을 왜곡할 수 있음
예시	한두 가지의 불만을 모아서 마치 직원 대다수가 노동조합을 반대하는 것처럼 보고함
결론	구별되지 않은 불만과 불평을 모두 더한 다음 같은 것처럼 들리는 다른 것으로 선언한 것임

구문
- [Unless the union is a band of angels {with an archangel at their head}] you can ask and record **with perfect honesty** and come out with proof [that the greater part of the men do have some complaint or other].
  : 첫 번째 [ ]는 조건의 부사절이고, 그 안의 { }는 a band of angels를 수식하는 전치사구이다. 「with+추상 명사」는 부사(구)로 바꾸어 쓸 수 있으며 perfectly honestly의 의미이다. 두 번째 [ ]는 proof의 동격절이다.

07 정답 ④

대부분의 현대 직업과 경력은, 그것이 사기업에 있든 공공 기관에 있든, 육체 노동이든 정신 노동이든, 임금 노동의 범주에 들어간다. 조립 라인에서의 지루하고 불쾌한 과업을 수행하는 사람으로서의 '노동자'에 대한 고정 관념은 매우 시대에 뒤떨어진 것이다. 오늘날의 노동자는 매우 다양한 기능을 수행하며, 그것들 중 많은 기능은 고급 기술을 필요로 한다. 그러나 임금이나 급여를 대가로 다른 사람을 위해 일하는 한 그들은 여전히 노동자이다. (문화적으로 자신을 그렇게 정의하는 것을 좋아하지 않을 수도 있지만) 연구실의 과학자, 큰 병원의 외과 의사, 건설 회사의 공학자, 이들은 모두 노동자이다. (근로 수입은 피고용인으로서의 급여와 자영업 수입의 일부를 포함하는데, 후자는 흔히 명시하기 어렵다.) 그들은 급여에 대한 대가로 자신의 노동을 수행하며, 자신이 일하는 조직을 소유하거나 크게 통제하지 않는다.

해설
임금 노동의 범주에 관해 설명하는 글로, 노동자는 급여에 대한 대가로 노동을 수행하며, 조직을 소유하거나 통제하지 않음을 설명하고 있으므로, 근로 수입의 정의와 자영업 수입 명시의 어려움을 언급하는 ④는 글의 전체 흐름과 관계가 없다.

TEXT FLOW
도입	대부분의 현대 직업과 경력은 임금 노동의 범주에 들어감
부연 1	오늘날 노동자는 다양한 기능을 수행하고, 고급 기술을 필요로 하고, 임금을 대가로 일함
부연 2	노동자는 급여에 대한 대가로 일을 하고, 조직을 소유하거나 통제하지 않음

구문
- Workers today perform a wide variety of functions, [**many of them** requiring advanced skills].
  : [ ]는 분사구문으로 many of them이 의미상의 주어이다.

- Labor income includes the wages of employees and part of the income of the self-employed, [**the latter** often being difficult to state].
  : [ ]는 분사구문으로 the latter가 의미상의 주어이다. the latter는 the income of the self-employed를 지칭한다.

08 정답 ②

근본적으로, 어떤 다자 무역 체제에서든, 교역되는 상품과 용역의 화폐 가치에서 항상 불균형, 적자, 잉여금이 있기 마련이다. (B) 예를 들어, 한 국가가 완전 고용의 경제적 호황을 누리고 있을 때, 그 지역의 늘어난 소비에 대한 상품과 용역의 제공을 외국의 제조업자들에게 의존하는 것은 자연스럽다. 사실상, 그것이 2010년대 후반 미국에서처럼 현지의 공장들이 전면 가동되고 있을 때 소비를 늘릴 유일한 길이다. (A) 이러한 수입은 동일한 수의 수출에 의해 보충되지 않는다면 뭔가 다른 것, 즉 대체로 주식과 채권 같은 종이 자산을 해외로 보냄으로써 '지불된다.' 미국의 유가 증권을 구입하는 것은 대부분의 국가가 미국과의 무역에서 불균형을 보충해 온 방법이다. (C) 많은 국가, 특히 아시아와 중동의 국가가 수출로 벌어들인 자신들의 수입을 미래의 불확실성에 대한 비축 자산으로 사용하거나 혹은 미래에 미국의 상품과 용역을 사기 위해 수조 달러 상당의 미국 국채를 구입하는 데 사용해 왔다.

해설

근본적으로 무역에서는 불균형, 적자, 잉여금이 발생한다는 내용의 주어진 글 다음에는, 한 나라의 내수 경제가 호황일 때, 그 소비 수요를 위해 외국의 제조업자들로부터 물건을 수입해야 하는 상황이 제시되고 그 예로 미국을 소개한 (B)가 온 후, 이렇게 수입이 발생하고 동일액의 수출이 없을 경우 종이 자산으로 지불해야 하는 상황을 미국을 예로 들어 설명하는 (A)가 온다. 이어서 미국과의 무역 적자 발생 시를 대비하여 미국 국채를 비축해 두는 아시아와 중동 국가들의 상황을 설명한 (C)가 오는 것이 글의 순서로 가장 적절하다.

⊗ 매력적인 오답 주의!

③ (A)의 These imports는 (B)의 to turn to foreign producers를 가리키는데 언급된 위치상 연결이 쉽지 않기 때문에 상대적으로 쉽게 눈에 띄는 (C)의 마지막에 언급된 buy U.S. goods and services로 잘못 판단하여 선택한 것으로 보인다. [선택률 39%]

TEXT FLOW

도입	근본적으로 무역에서는 불균형, 적자, 잉여금이 발생함
예시	미국의 경우처럼 국가가 경제적 호황을 누릴 때, 그 소비 수요를 외국의 제조업자에게 의존하고 이러한 수입이 수출에 의해 보충되지 않으면 종이 자산으로 지불함
부연	많은 국가가 수출로 번 수입을 나중을 위해 비축 자산으로 사용하거나 미국 국채를 구입함

구문

• In fact, it is the only way to increase consumption if local factories are running at full capacity — as the United States **was** in the late 2010s.
: was running at full capacity에서 running at full capacity가 앞에 나왔기 때문에 반복을 피하기 위해 생략되고 was만 남은 형태이다.

09 정답 ⑤

아이가 서너 살이 되기 전까지는 세는 능력이 습득되지 못한다는 사실이 그 특징이 타고나는 것이 아니라는 것을 반드시 증명하는 것은 아니다. Piaget의 실험을 포함한 많은 관찰에서, 세기와 산수는 의사소통하는 능력 및 대체로 모국어인 주어진 언어를 사용하는 능력과 함께 습득되었다. 주어진 언어로 의사소통하는 것이 타고난 속성이 아니고 학습된 것이라는 것은 놀랄 일이 아니다. 언어를 배우는 능력은 타고난 특징이지만 그 언어 자체를 습득하는 것에는 여러 해가 걸린다. 다양한 실험에서 보이듯, 어린이가 언어를 배우기 전에, 그의 산수 능력은 작동하기 시작하지 않는다. 아이의 세는 능력 부족이 장애가 아니라 그가 몇 년 동안의 연습을 더 하기 전까지는 그가 이해하지 못하는 질문에 대답해야 한다든가, 혹은 기대되는 대답이 무엇인지를 그가 깨닫지 못한다는 사실이다. 질문을 이해하는 것이 결과를 분석하는 데 중요한 역할을 한다는 것을 보여 주는 검사를 고안하는 것은 쉽다.

해설

주어진 문장은 아이가 질문을 이해하지 못해 대답을 못하는 것이 세는 능력과 산수 능력을 측정하는 것을 어렵게 한다는 내용이므로, 아이가 언어 능력을 습득하기 전까지 산수 능력이 작동하지 않는다는 내용과 질문의 이해가 결과의 분석에 영향을 미치는 것을 보여 주는 검사를 고안하는 것은 쉽다는 내용을 연결할 수 있는 ⑤에 들어가야 자연스럽다.

TEXT FLOW

도입	아이가 서너 살이 되기 전까지는 세는 능력이 습득되지 못함
주제	세기와 산수는 의사소통하는 능력 및 모국어 사용 능력과 함께 습득됨
부연	언어를 습득하는 것에 여러 해가 걸리고, 언어를 배우기 전에 산수 능력은 작동하지 않음
결론	세는 능력 부족이 아니라 질문을 이해하지 못해 대답을 못하기 때문임

구문

• [The fact {that the ability to count is not acquired until a child is three or four years old}] does **not necessarily** prove [that the characteristic is not innate].
: 첫 번째 [ ]는 주어이고, 그 안의 { }는 The fact의 동격절이다. 두 번째 [ ]는 prove의 목적어 역할을 하는 명사절이다. not necessarily는 부분 부정으로 '반드시 ~인 것은 아니다'를 뜻한다.

10 정답 ①

학생 평가에서 수집된 데이터의 품질과 도출된 결론 및 추론은 조사에 참여하는 교사의 인식과 가치관에 의해 영향을 받는다. 학생의 문화적 배경을 조사하려면 어느 정도의 객관성이 필요하다. 데이터 수집 시 자기중심적이거나 민족 중심적인 관점은 역효과를 낳는다. 자신의 개인적 또는 문화적 경험에 근거하여 가치 판단을 내리지 않고 학생의 문화를 조사할 수 있어야 한다. 학생의 배경과 경험에 대한 데이터를 수집하는 유일하게 정당한 이유는 교실 수업을 개선하기 위해서이다. 자신의 수업이 일부 학생 집단에 잘 맞지 않는데도 그것이 적절하고 변경해서는 안 된다고 확신하고, 수업 실패의 원인을 학생이나 학생의 생활 환경 탓으로 돌리는 교사는 학생에 대한 데이터를 수집하는 것이 아마 도움이 되지 않을 것이다. 이러한 교사에게는 데이터 수집이 자신의 학생에 대한 부정적인 믿음을 강화할 가능성이 있다.

➡ 학생들의 배경 조사는 교실 수업을 개선하는 데 매우 중요하지만 이것은 객관적이어야 하는데, 왜냐하면 편향된 교육 방식을 유지하는 교사들이 학생들에 대한 데이터를 수집하는 것으로부터 이익을 얻지 못할 수 있기 때문이다.

해설

교사가 학생들의 문화적 배경 데이터를 수집하는 것은 교실 수업을 개선하기 위해서인데, 이는 교사가 편견 없이 객관성을 유지할 때에만 효과가 있을 것이라는 내용의 글이다. 따라서 요약문의 빈칸 (A), (B)에 들어갈 말로는 ① 'objective(객관적인) - maintain(유지하다)'이다.
② 객관적인 – 변화하다   ③ 일관된 – 감추다
④ 일관된 – 드러내다   ⑤ 조직적인 – 다양화하다

TEXT FLOW

도입	학생 평가에서 수집된 데이터는 교사의 인식과 가치관에 의해 영향을 받음
주장	학생의 문화적 배경을 조사하려면 객관성이 필요함
부연	학생의 배경과 데이터를 수집하는 이유는 교실 수업을 개선하기 위함
결론	편향된 교육 방식을 가진 교사에게는 데이터를 수집하는 것이 도움이 되지 않음

구문

• Teachers [who are convinced that their instruction is appropriate and should not change, although it does not serve some groups of students well], and [who blame the students or their life conditions for instructional failures], probably would not benefit from collecting data on their students.

: 두 개의 [ ]는 and로 연결되어 Teachers를 수식하는 관계절이고, would not benefit가 서술어이다.

11~12

정답 11 ① 12 ④

국가의 민족적 구성의 변화는 선진국들에게 영향을 미치거나 선거 정치에 영향을 미칠 뿐만 아니라 또한 사회적 갈등에도 연관되어 있다. 인구 변동, 즉 인구수의 변화는, 더욱 최근에 특히 국가 내의 갈등 요소로 더 중요해져 왔다. 인구 변동의 순전한 규모와 시간의 경과에 따른 그것의 가속이 그 이유 중 하나이다. 19세기 영국의 인구가 그랬던 것처럼, 출생률이 오랫동안 전례 없는 최고치를 기록하는 반면 사망률이 급속하게 떨어질 때 인구는 빠르게 증가할 수 있다. 사실, 이러한 변화를 경험하던 사람들은 19세기 영국의 성취를 훨씬 앞지른 인구 증가를 나중에 경험했다. 자주 그러한 증가는 한 민족 집단에 영향을 미치지만, 서로 다른 사회적 혹은 종교적 관행이나 서로 다른 사회 경제적 발전 수준 때문에 다른 인구 집단에는 영향을 미치지 않는다. 다른 민족 집단과 사회적 집단 사이의 인구의 세력이 역사적으로 유례가 없는 속도로 변화할 수 있으며, 이것이 혼란에 빠뜨리고 어리둥절하게 하는 영향을 미칠 수 있다는 것이 분명히 명백해졌다.

간혹 '국제적인' 현상이기도 하지만, 대부분의 국가들이 민족적인 소수 집단을 가지고 있으며 그러한 소수 집단 중 많은 수가 다수 집단과는 눈에 띄게 동일한(→ 다른) 인구 행동 양식을 보여 주기 때문에 이러한 변화는 자주 '국내' 수준에서 경험된다. 러시아의 체첸인, 세르비아(혹은 과거의 세르비아)의 알바니아인, 북아일랜드의 가톨릭교도가 떠오른다. 이들은 모두 다수 집단보다 소수 집단이 더 높은 출생률을 보이는 경우이며 지배적인 권력 구조의 변화나 그에 대한 도전이라는 결과를 낳는다.

해설

11 국가의 민족 구성 인구 변화는 인구 증가 및 감소에 따라 일어나는데 이것은 한 집단 내에서 일어나는 것으로 국내 권력 지형에 큰 영향을 미치고 때로는 갈등의 요인이 된다는 내용의 글이므로, 글의 제목으로 가장 적절한 것은 ① '인구 변동: 국내 권력 지형을 결정하는 것'이다.
② 소수 집단이 다수 집단보다 더 높은 출산율을 보이는 이유
③ 인구 과잉으로 인한 국제적 갈등
④ 민족성: 잦은 사회적 갈등의 원인
⑤ 인구 증가: 경제에 미치는 이익

(✗) 매력적인 오답 주의!

② 글 전체를 아우르는 내용을 가장 잘 표현한 선택지를 고르지 않고, 두 번째 단락의 인구 변동의 예로 언급된 '소수 집단이 다수 집단보다 더 높은 출생률을 보이는 경우'를 근거로 선택한 것으로 보인다. [선택률 32%]

12 소수 민족 집단의 인구 변동은 다수 집단과 다른 방식으로 나타날 수 있으며, 이의 결과로 국내의 권력 지형에 큰 변화가 올 수 있다는 맥락이며, 그 사례로 러시아의 체첸인, 세르비아(혹은 과거의 세르비아)의 알바니아인, 북아일랜드의 가톨릭교도 집단이 제시되고 있으므로 ④의 'identical(동일한)'을 'different(다른)'와 같은 낱말로 바꾸어야 한다.

TEXT FLOW

도입	인구 변동은 국가 내의 사회적 갈등 요소임
예시	19세기 영국의 인구 변동
전개	국가마다 민족적인 소수 집단이 있고 그들은 다수 집단과 다른 행동 양식을 보이기 때문에 이러한 변화는 주로 국내 수준에서 많이 경험됨
결론	소수 집단의 인구 변동으로 국내 권력 지형에 큰 영향을 미칠 수 있음

구문

• Shifts in the ethnic composition of states do **not just** affect the developed world, **nor** do they **just** impact electoral politics; they are **also** associated with civil strife.

: 'A뿐만 아니라 B도'의 뜻을 갖는 「not just A but also B」 구문이 쓰였다. 세미콜론(;)은 but 대신에 사용되었다.

• These are all cases [where minorities have a higher birth rate than majorities, with the result being a shift in or challenge to the prevailing power structure].

: [ ]는 all cases를 수식하는 관계절인데 선행사가 장소가 아니라 case, situation일 때도 관계부사 where를 사용한다.

고난도 모의고사 06회

01 ④	02 ⑤	03 ②	04 ⑤	05 ③	06 ②
07 ①	08 ③	09 ③	10 ①	11 ⑤	12 ④

01 정답 ④

나는 다른 사람이 나를 비판하거나 모욕하면 예민해지고 화를 내고는 했다. 나는 이것에 더는 신경 쓰지 않는다. 사실 여러분이 삶에서 더 성공할수록, 이런 일이 여러분에게 더 많이 일어날 것이다. 여러분은 어떻게 반응해야 하는가? 음, 우선 그것이 여러분의 성공의 반영이기 때문에 나는 이런 일이 여러분에게 더 자주 일어나기를 바란다. 그것은 매우 기분 좋은 일이기에 여러분은 이런 일이 더 자주 일어나기를 원한다. 여러분이 또한 더 성공을 거둘수록 동료들이 여러분에게 수년간 더 잘난 체하는 어조를 나타낼 수도 있다. 여러분은 손을 뻗어 그 위장된 칭찬에 대해 그들에게 감사해야 한다! 그들은 그저 여러분에게 위협감을 느끼는 것일 뿐이고 그것은 엄청난 칭찬으로 보일 수 있기 때문에 걱정하지 말라. 성공한 사람들은 항상 비난받는다. 가장 행복하고 최고의 정신적인 평화를 가진 사람은 비판이 위장된 칭찬에 지나지 않음을 아는 사람들이다. 그러니 나에 대해 의심하는 자들이여, 덤벼라, 그러면 나는 내가 할 수 있는 것을 보여 줄 것이다!

해설

자신의 성취에 대한 타인의 비판은 자신의 성취에 대한 칭찬의 위장된 표현임을 깨닫고, 이에 예민해지거나 화를 낼 필요가 없으며 오히려 기뻐하라는 내용이므로, 밑줄 친 부분이 글에서 의미하는 바로 가장 적절한 것은 ④ '자신의 성취에 대한 그들의 방어적인 반응에 기뻐하다'이다.
① 그들의 공감 부족 때문에 그들을 무시하다
② 자신에 대한 그들의 정당한 비판에 행복한 척하다
③ 다른 사람에 대한 자신의 오만함에 대해 그들의 염려를 받아들이다
⑤ 그 비평을 아첨과 충고를 구별하는 길잡이로 사용하다

TEXT FLOW

도입	다른 사람이 자신을 비판하거나 모욕하는 일은 더 성공할수록 더 많이 일어날 것임
반전	동료들의 잘난 체하는 어조는 자신에게 위협감을 느끼는 것이고 위장된 칭찬임
결론	위장된 칭찬임을 알면 행복하고 정신적인 평화를 가질 수 있음

구문

• You almost **want to** reach out and thank them for the disguised compliment!
: want to는 충고나 조언을 할 때 사용하는 표현으로 '~해야 한다'의 의미이다.

02 정답 ⑤

Abdallah Muhammad ibn Mūsā Al-Khwārizmī라고 불리는 9세기 수학자의 이름에서 유래된 '알고리즘'이라는 단어는 단순히 단계별 지시 사항의 집합을 의미한다. 오늘날 인공 지능에서의 발전의 많은 부분을 견인하는 기계 학습 알고리즘은 명시적인 규칙에 의해 인도되는 것이 아니라, (프로그램화된) 시스템이 경험에서 배우도록 하는 것을 구체적인 목표로 한다. 그중 다수는 인공 지능 초창기의 생각들에 의존하고 있는데, 그 생각은 흥미로운 이론적 가능성에서 더 실용적인 어떤 것으로 바꾸기 위해 이용 가능한 충분한 처리 능력과 데이터가 있기 훨씬 전에 개발되었다. 실제로, 오늘날의 가장 위대한 실용주의적 승리의 일부는 인간을 모방하려는 이전의 순수주의적인 시도에서 성장했다. 예를 들어, 오늘날 가장 유능한 기계 중 다수는 '인공 신경망'으로 알려져 있는 것에 의존하는데, 그것은 인간 두뇌의 작용을 흉내 내기 위해 수십 년 전에 처음 만들어졌다. 하지만, 오늘날 이 신경망이 인간의 해부학적 구조를 얼마나 자세하게 모방하는가에 따라 평가되어야 한다는 것은 거의 의미가 없다. 대신, 그것은 자신에게 부과된 어떤 과제든 얼마나 잘 수행하는지에 따라 전적으로 실용적으로 평가된다.

해설

알고리즘(algorithm)은 초기에 인간의 두뇌를 모방한 인공 신경망으로 알려져 있었지만, 오늘날에는 그것이 인간의 해부학적 구조를 얼마나 자세하게 모방하는가가 아니라, 얼마나 과제를 잘 처리하느냐에 따라 평가된다는 내용의 글이다. 따라서 글의 제목으로 가장 적절한 것은 ⑤ '오늘날 기계 학습 알고리즘은 무엇에 의해 평가되어야 하는가?'이다.
① 인간 두뇌의 고유성이 완벽하게 복제될 수 있는가?
② 기술에 있어 기계 학습 알고리즘의 주요한 비판
③ 학습과 응용에 가장 적합한 인간 신경망
④ 알고리즘적 사고: 컴퓨팅 사고의 핵심 개념

TEXT FLOW

도입	오늘날 인공 지능에서의 기계 학습 알고리즘은 시스템이 경험에서 배우는 것을 목표로 함
부연	오늘날 가장 위대한 실용주의적 승리의 일부는 인간을 모방하려는 이전의 순수주의적인 시도에서 성장함
예시	가장 유능한 기계 중 다수는 인간 두뇌의 작용을 흉내 내기 위해 수십 년 전에 처음 만들어진 '인공 신경망'에 의존함
결론	인공 신경망은 부과된 과제를 얼마나 잘 수행하는지에 따라 실용적으로 평가됨

구문

• The word *algorithm*, [derived from the name of a ninth-century mathematician named Abu Abdullah Muhammad ibn Mūsā Al-Khwārizmī], simply means a set of step-by-step instructions.
: [ ]는 문장의 주어 The word *algorithm*을 수식하는 과거분사구이다.

03 정답 ②

의사 결정의 한 가지 특징은 뇌의 구조와 관련이 있다. '뇌는 선입관 없이는 문제를 분석할 수 없다.' 누군가 한 가지 문제나 질문에 직면했을 때, 선입관은 때로는 질문이 표현되거나 정보가 제시되는 방식에 기초하고 의존하여 즉시 사용된다. 따라서 회복 가능성이 80%라는 의사의 예후에 대한 환자의 반응은 평생 아픈 채로 있을 확률이 20%라는 소식에 대한 그의 반응과 다르다. 이성적인 사고는 80%의 성공 확률과 20%의 실패 확률을 동일하게 인식할 것이다. 진화적으로 이성적인 방식으로만 행동하는 정신은 동등함을 인식하지 못할 것이다. 그러한 인식은 모든 경우에 사실을 비교하고 분석하는 데 필요한 노력의 가치가 없으므로 우리는 이미 뇌에 존재하는 개념과 태도를 고수한다. 선입관 없이 우리가 질문을 검토할 수 있다는 일반적인 믿음은 잘못된 것이다.

해설

② 뒤에 완전한 절이 이어지므로 관계대명사는 올 수 없고, the doctor's prognosis에 대한 내용의 동격절이 이어져야 하므로, which를 동격의 명사절을 이끄는 접속사 that으로 고쳐야 한다.
① 전치사 on의 목적어 역할을 하는 명사절을 이끄는 의문사 how는 어법상 적절하다.
③ 형용사 rational을 수식하는 부사 evolutionarily는 어법상 적절하다.
④ concepts and attitudes를 수식하는 형용사구를 이끄는 형용사 present는 어법상 적절하다.
⑤ 문장의 핵심 주어 The popular belief(단수)에 연결된 술어 동사로 단수 동사 is는 어법상 적절하다.

TEXT FLOW

도입	뇌는 선입관 없이는 문제를 분석할 수 없음
부연	선입관은 질문 표현 방식이나 제시되는 정보에 의존하여 즉시 사용됨
예시	회복 가능성이 80%라는 의사의 예후에 대한 환자의 반응과 평생 아픈 채로 있을 확률이 20%라는 소식에 대한 그의 반응은 다름
결론	동등함을 인식하지 못하고, 이미 뇌에 존재하는 개념과 태도를 고수함

구문

• Thus, the reaction of a sick person to the doctor's prognosis [that he has an 80 percent chance of recovering] is different than his reaction to the news [that he has a 20 percent chance of remaining sick for the rest of his life].
: 첫 번째 [ ]는 the doctor's prognosis와 동격을 이루는 명사절이고, 두 번째 [ ]는 the news와 동격을 이루는 명사절이다.

04   정답 ⑤

미국 교육 학회의 전 회장 Larry Cuban이 지적하듯이, 학교는 선진 세계의 '교육'에 대해 우리가 생각하는 방식을 사실상 거의 아무것도 바꾸지 못한 기술에 수년간 수십억 달러를 써 왔다. 자주, 우리는 디지털 도구가 학교 밖의 학습자와 창작자에게 제공하는 힘과 자유를 그들이 똑같은 그 도구를 (학교) 건물 내로 가져올 때는 박탈해 버린다. 우리 대부분이 그것의 결과물인 학교 교육 체제는 우리가 인터넷에서 배우고, 창작하고, 연결할 수 있는 더 다루기 힘들고, 덜 1차원적이고, 더 자기 조직적인 방법들과 잘 어울리지 않는 일련의 구조와 효율성에 바탕을 두고 있다. 사실, 그 체제는 학교에서 디지털 기술을 거의 부지불식간에 하찮은 존재로 만든다. 우리는 그것들을 실험실이나 도서관으로 밀쳐 버리는데, 다시 말해 학생들의 손에 맡기면, 그것들은 교과서 읽기, 문서 만들기, 혹은 평가받기와 같은 별개의 한정된 목적에만 사용된다. 오늘날의 학교에서 우리가 기술을 개인적인 학습 도구가 아니라 주로 제도적인 교육 도구로 간주한다고 주장하는 사람이 많을(→ 거의 없을) 것이다.

해설

선진국의 학교에서 지난 수년간 기술에 수십억 달러를 썼지만, 그 디지털 기술은 개인적인 학습 도구로만 쓰이고 있을 뿐, 제도적인 교육 도구로 간주되지 않고 있는 실정이라는 내용의 글이다. 따라서 ⑤의 'Many(많은)'는 'Few(거의 없는)'와 같은 낱말로 바꾸어야 한다.

? WHY 고난도

very little, not 등의 부정어와 함께 있는 문장에 선택지가 있거나, strip이나 marginalize와 같은 난이도 있는 어휘가 선택지로 쓰여 정답 파악이 쉽지 않은 고난도 문제이다.

TEXT FLOW

도입	선진 세계의 교육은 우리의 사고방식을 아무것도 바꾸지 못한 기술에 수년간 수십억 달러를 썼음
부연	학교에서는 디지털 도구와 기술을 하찮은 존재로 만들고 한정된 목적으로만 사용함
결론	오늘날 기술을 제도적인 교육 도구로 간주한다고 주장하는 사람은 거의 없음

구문

• The system of schooling [that most of us are products of] is based on a series of structures and efficiencies [that do not work well with the messier, less linear, more self-organized ways {we can learn, create, and connect on the Internet}].
: 첫 번째 [ ]는 주어 The system of schooling을 수식하는 관계절이다. 두 번째 [ ]는 a series of structures and efficiencies를 수식하는 관계절이고, 그 안의 { }는 the messier, less linear, more self-organized ways를 수식하는 관계절이다.

05   정답 ③

오랫동안 사람들은 압력이 가해져 얼음이 녹는 것이 얼음이 미끄러운 유일한 이유라고 생각했다. 그러나 이야기는 그것보다 더 복잡한 것으로 밝혀졌는데, 그것이 왜 얼음이 어는점보다 훨씬 낮은 온도에서도, 또는 압력이 그것을 녹일 정도로 충분하지 않을 때도(예를 들어, 스케이트만이 아니라 평평한 신발을 신어도 얼음이 여전히 미끄러운 경우처럼) 여전히 미끄러운지를 설명하지 않기 때문이다. 마찰이 큰 역할을 하는 것으로 밝혀졌는데, 즉 스케이트, 스키, 혹은 빙하가 미끄러지면서 마찰이 열을 발생시키고 그것이 얼음 표면을 살짝 녹인다. 그러나 가만히 서 있어도 얼음이 미끄러운 이유를 설명하지 않기 때문에, 여전히 그 설명이 전부는 아니다. 현대의 분석은 얼음 표면의 분자들이 그것들 위에 분자들이 없어서 본질적으로 불안정하기 때문에, 표면이 구조를 조정하여 액체와 유사한 층을 형성한다는 것을 보여 주었다. 이것은 1850년 유명한 물리학자 Michael Faraday가 세운 모든 얼음은 표면에 고유한 얇은 물의 층을 가지고 있다는 최초의 가설이 사실임을 입증했다. 그러므로 얼음은 고유한 표면의 물 층 때문에 미끄러운데, 이는 압력과 마찰을 이용해 강화될 수 있다.

해설

얼음이 미끄러운 것은 압력이 가해져 얼음이 녹기 때문이거나 마찰에 의해 생긴 열로 인해 얼음 표면이 살짝 녹기 때문이라는 것이 설명의 전부는 아니며, 물리학자 Michael Faraday의 가설대로 모든 얼음에 고유한 얇은 물의 층이 있기 때문이라는 내용의 글이다. 얼음의 고유한 표면의 물 층 때문에 미끄러운데 여기에 압력과 마찰이 가해져서 더 미끄러워진다는 맥락이므로, 빈칸에 들어갈 말로 가장 적절한 것은 ③ '강화될'이다.
① 감지될   ② 제거될
④ 긁힐   ⑤ 증발시킬

도입	사람들은 압력이 가해져 얼음이 녹는 것이 얼음이 미끄러운 이유라고 생각했음
전개 1	얼음이 어는점보다 낮은 온도이거나 압력이 얼음을 녹일 정도로 충분하지 않아도 미끄러운 이유는 마찰이 큰 역할을 함
전개 2	가만히 서 있어도 얼음이 미끄러운 이유는 얼음 표면의 분자들은 불안정해서 액체와 유사한 층을 형성한다는 것을 알아냄
결론	얼음은 고유한 표면의 물 층 때문에 미끄럽고, 이는 압력과 마찰에 의해 강화됨

구문

• For years people thought [that {ice melting under pressure} was the only reason for {ice being slippery}].
: [ ]는 thought의 목적어 역할을 하는 명사절이다. 그 안의 두 개의 { }는 ice를 의미상의 주어로 하는 동명사구이다.

• This verified the original hypothesis [made by the famous physicist Michael Faraday in 1850] [that all ice has an intrinsic thin layer of water at the surface].
: 첫 번째 [ ]는 the original hypothesis를 수식하는 과거분사구이고, 두 번째 [ ]는 the original hypothesis와 동격인 명사절이다.

06 정답 ②

그의 철학적 접근이 근본적인 방식에서는 칸트의 미학과 인식론에 의해 형성되기는 했지만, 쇼펜하우어는 자신이 칸트의 '수정'이라고 부르는 것에 착수하는데, 그것은 칸트가 지각에 의한 지식보다 추상적 지식에 특권을 부여한 것을 뒤집어 주체의 생리적 구성이 재현 형성이 발생하는 장소라 주장하는 것이었다. 칸트 추종자의 'Vorstellung'(개념) 문제에 대한 쇼펜하우어의 대답은 우리를 암상자의 고전적인 관점(사진의 시각적 객관성)으로부터 완전히 분리시킨다. 즉 "재현이란 무엇인가? 그것은 동물의 뇌에서 발생하는 매우 복잡한 '생리적인' 것으로, 그것의 결과가 바로 그 장소의 '그림'이나 '이미지'의 인식이다."라는 것이다. 칸트가 통각의 종합적 실체라고 부른 것을, 쇼펜하우어는 서슴없이 인간의 두뇌라고 인식한다. 여기에서 쇼펜하우어는 '칸트의 이성 비판에 대한 생리학적인 재해석'이라고 불린 19세기 전반의 한 가지 사례일 뿐이다. 그는 "완전히 (생리학적인) 관점을 무시하는 칸트주의와 같은 철학은 일방적이며 따라서 부적절하다. 그것은 우리의 철학적인 지식과 생리학적인 지식 사이에 헤아릴 수 없는 틈을 남기는데, 우리는 그것에 대해 절대 만족할 수 없다."라고 쓴다.

해설

쇼펜하우어는 칸트의 생각을 수정하고자 했는데, 그것은 지각에 의한 지식보다 추상적 지식에 특권을 부여하고자 했던 칸트의 생각을 뒤집어 주체의 생리적인 구성이 재현이 발생되고 구성되는 곳이라고 주장했다는 내용 다음에 쇼펜하우어의 재현에 대한 견해가 제시되면서, 쇼펜하우어는 재현이 두뇌에서 발생하는 것이며 따라서 생리학적 관점을 무시하는 칸트주의는 적절치 않다고 주장했다는 내용이 제시되어 있으므로, 빈칸에 들어갈 말로 가장 적절한 것은 ② '재현 형성이 발생하는'이다.
① 이성이 지각적 경험을 정당화하는
③ 기존의 추상적인 아이디어를 재해석하는
④ 인식의 고유성에 대한 진가를 얻는
⑤ 뇌의 인지적인 과정이 감각에 의해 지연되는

③ 글의 소재가 추상적이어서 내용 파악이 쉽지 않아 쇼펜하우어의 주장이 아닌 칸트의 주장에 사용된 단어를 근거로 선택한 것으로 보인다. [선택률 27%]

도입	쇼펜하우어는 주체의 생리적인 구성이 재현이 발생하는 장소라고 주장함
부연	재현은 뇌에서 발생하는 복잡한 생리적인 것으로, 그 결과가 이미지의 인식이라고 함
결론	그는 생리학적인 관점을 무시하는 칸트주의는 일방적이고 부적절하다고 주장함

구문

• [What Kant called the synthetic unity of apperception], Schopenhauer unhesitatingly identifies as the human brain.
: [ ]는 동사 identifies의 목적어로 강조를 위해 문장 앞에 왔다. 이와 같이 목적어가 문장 앞으로 나갈 때는 주어와 동사의 도치가 일어나지 않는다.

07 정답 ①

우리는 흔히 너무 빨리 선택해서 그 행동에 관련된 모든 요소들을 거의 구별할 수 없다. 우리가 시간이나 공간, 또는 그 둘 모두에서 우리와 멀리 떨어져 있는 대체물이나 행동 방침 각각의 장점을 평가할 때, 우리는 선택에 관여하는 모든 요소들을 알게 될 가능성이 더 많다. 우선, 우리는 미래를, 그리고 특히 각각의 대체 행동이 우리에게 어떻게 영향을 미칠지 예측하려고 한다. 이러한 노력에서 우리는 비슷한 상황의 과거 경험에 대한 기억에 크게 의존하는데, 왜냐하면 과거에 대한 지식과 본성의 한결같음에 대한 신뢰가 없다면 우리는 미래를 예측하기가 막막할 것이기 때문이다. 심사숙고된 상황에 우리 자신을 투영할 때, 우리는 무엇보다도 그것이 우리에게 즐거움이나 고통, 기쁨이나 슬픔, 만족이나 혐오감 어느 것을 가져다주든, 그것이 우리의 감정에 어떻게 영향을 미칠지에 관심이 있다. 그리고 물론, 우리가 숙고하는 이런 단계에서도, 우리는 비슷한 정서의 회상에 의해 인도된다. 따라서 정신의 합리적 기능 못지않은 정서적 기능이 우리가 하는 각각의 중요한 선택에서 중요한 역할을 한다.

해설

시간이나 공간, 또는 그 둘 모두에서 현재 우리와 멀리 떨어져 있는 대체물이나 행동 방침을 심사숙고함으로써 그런 각각의 행동이 우리에게 정서적으로 어떻게 영향을 미칠지 예측하려고 한다는 내용이므로, 빈칸에 들어갈 말로 가장 적절한 것은 ① '심사숙고된 상황에 우리 자신을 투영할'이다.
② 타당한 이유를 만들어 우리의 선택을 정당화할
③ 우리의 현재 상황과 감정에 초점을 맞출
④ 우리의 행동을 동기 부여의 관점에서 볼
⑤ 우리와 가장 가까운 다른 사람들의 관점을 취할

도입	우리는 시간이나 공간에서 떨어진 대체물이나 행동 방침의 장점을 더 잘 알게 됨
부연 1	우리는 비슷한 상황의 과거 경험에 대한 기억에 의존하여 미래를 예측하고자 함
부연 2	심사숙고하면서 우리는 그 각각의 행동이 감정에 어떻게 영향을 미칠지 관심이 있음
결론	정신의 합리적 기능과 정서적 기능 모두 선택에서 중요한 역할을 함

- In the first place, we try to foresee the future, and in particular [how each alternative act will affect us].
  : [ ]는 앞의 the future와 함께 foresee의 목적어이다.

- Thus [**the affective** no less than the rational **functions of the mind**] play important roles in each important choice we make.
  : [ ]는 문장의 주어이고, 주어의 핵인 the affective는 the affective functions of the mind가 반복을 피해 생략된 형태로 복수 동사 play가 쓰였다.

08　정답 ③

학생이 기본적인 대수학 방정식을 푸는 법을 배우는 과정을 생각해 보라. 처음에는 방정식의 균형을 유지하는 과정이 복잡할 수 있으며, 학생은 자신이 풀고 있는 변수를 분리하는 방법에 대한 규칙을 명확히 이해하고 있어야 한다. (B) 다시 말해서, 그것은 풀기에 복잡한 문제이며 인지 자원을 상당히 요구한다. 게다가, 그 학생이 여러 유형의 대수학 문제, 예를 들어 변수가 하나인 선형 방정식, 변수가 두 개인 선형 방정식, 이차 방정식 등을 학습할 것이라고 가정해 보라. (C) 처음에는 각 유형의 문제를 푸는 데 노력이 필요하고 각 유형의 문제를 명확히 이해하는 데도 또한 노력이 필요하다. 그 학생이 더 많은 기술을 습득함에 따라 각 문제 유형의 패턴과 규칙을 인식하기 시작한다. (A) 새로운 문제가 과거에 풀었던 것과 유사하면, 그 학생은 이 새로운 문제를 풀기 위해 같은 전략을 사용할 수 있다. 다시 말해서, 비슷한 문제는 비슷하게 해결되며, 문제 해결자는 문제 해결에 도움을 받기 위해 이러한 평가 유사성을 사용할 수 있다.

해설

학생이 기본적인 대수학 방정식을 푸는 법을 배우는 과정에서, 처음에는 복잡할 수 있어 명확한 이해가 필요하다는 주어진 글 다음에는, In other words로 연결하여 그것은 복잡한 문제이며 인지 자원이 상당히 요구된다고 하면서 여러 유형의 대수학 문제를 푸는 경우를 가정하도록 제시한 (B)가 온 후, 처음에는 각 유형의 문제를 푸는 데 노력이 필요하지만 점차 각 문제 유형의 패턴과 규칙을 인식하기 시작한다는 내용의 (C)가 온 다음, 새 문제가 과거에 풀었던 문제와 유사하면 같은 전략을 사용하여 문제를 해결할 수 있다는 내용인 (A)가 마지막에 오는 것이 글의 순서로 가장 적절하다.

TEXT FLOW

주제	대수학 방정식을 푸는 법
방법 1	자신이 풀고 있는 변수를 분리하는 방법에 대한 규칙을 이해해야 함
방법 2	각 유형의 문제를 명확히 이해하는 데도 노력이 필요함
방법 3	각 문제 유형의 패턴과 규칙을 인식하여 새로운 문제에서 같은 전략을 사용함

구문

- Consider the process of [**a student** learning to solve elementary algebra equations].
  : [ ]는 전치사 of의 목적어 역할을 하는 동명사구이며, a student는 동명사구의 의미상의 주어이다.

- If a new problem is similar to **one** [that has been solved in the past], then she can use the same set of strategies to solve this new problem.
  : [ ]은 a problem을 받는 부정대명사 one을 수식하는 관계절이다.

09　정답 ③

사람들은 동시에 서로 비슷하기도 하고 서로 다르기도 하다. 그들이 개인이라는 것은 비슷한 정도에서가 아니라 다른 정도에서이다. 따라서 개성은 상이한 독창성이지만, 요점은 우리 각자가 가지고 태어나는 독창성을 자유롭게 하는 것이다. 그것에는 어느 정도 다수의 사회적 유사성이 덧씌워진다. 많은 사람이 결코 독자적으로 생각하지 않고, 정해진 것, 평범한 것, 그리고 흔한 것에서 결코 자신을 벗어나게 하지 않는다. 반면에 동일한 개인 내에 모순되거나 적어도 매우 서로 다른 몇 가지 독창성이 있는 경우가 흔히 있다. 동일한 아이가 수학이나 음악, 혹은 여행의 모험에 대해 매우 다른 적성을 보인다. 이러한 모든 독창성 중에서 최고의 것, 즉 가장 친밀한 것, 가장 강력한 것이 선택되어야 한다. 마지막으로, 나쁘거나 반사회적인 독창성이 있는데, 그것이 계발되는 것은 안 보는 것이 바람직하다.

해설

On the other hand로 시작하는 주어진 문장은 동일한 개인에게 서로 다른 몇 가지 독창성이 있다는 내용이므로, 이 사례에 해당하는 내용인 ③ 앞에 들어가는 것이 가장 자연스럽다. 따라서 주어진 문장이 들어가기에 가장 적절한 곳은 ③이다.

TEXT FLOW

도입	개성은 상이한 독창성이고, 요점은 가지고 태어나는 독창성을 자유롭게 하는 것임
부연	많은 사람이 정해진 것에서 잘 벗어나지 않음
반전	동일한 개인 내에 서로 다른 독창성이 있는 경우가 있음
결론	이러한 독창성 중 최고의 것, 즉 친밀하고 강력한 것이 선택되어야 함

구문

- **It is** not insofar as alike **that** they are individuals, but [as different].
  : 「it is ~ that ....」 강조구문이 쓰여 not insofar as alike가 강조되었다. [ ]는 insofar as different에서 insofar가 생략된 형태이다.

- The best of all these originalities must be selected, [the most intimate], [the most powerful].
  : 두 개의 [ ]는 주어 The best of all these originalities와 동격의 관계이며 주어가 길어지는 것을 피하기 위해 문장 뒤에 쓰였다.

10　정답 ①

환경론자들은 인구압이 기후 변화 및 지구의 생물 다양성 파괴의 주요 원인이라고 오랫동안 주장해 왔다. 이런 견해를 가진 사람들은 제한된 천연자원을 보호하기 위해 인구 팽창이 빠른 나라들에서의 엄격한 출생률 통제를 옹호한다. 그러나 다른 이들은 인구 과잉이 문제가 아니며, 오히려 선진국에서의 과소비가 세계의 자원을 고갈시키고 있고, 또한 개발도상국의 사람들이 매우 필요한 자원을 이용하는 것을 방해하고 있다고 말한다. 1950년 이후 세계 인구의 가장 부유한 20퍼센트가 에너지, 육류, 삼림, 금속의 소비를 두 배로 늘렸고 자동차 소유도 네 배로 늘렸다. 그래서 제국주의를 비판하는 사람들은 인구 통제 프로그램이 부유한 서양 국가들에게 그들이 필요로 하는 자원에 대한 경쟁이 없는 이용을 제공하도록 고안되었다고 믿는다. 일부 비판가들은 심지어 인구 과잉이라는 개념의 만연이 부유한 국가들이 개발도상국과 그 국민들에 대해 지속하는 권위주의적인 행동을 정당화한다고 말한다.

➡ 인구 과잉이 자원 고갈의 원인이라는 환경론자들의 주장과는 반대로, 부유한 나라들에서의 과소비가 주된 원인이며 출생률을 통제하려는 움직임이 또 다른 형태의 제국주의라고도 주장되고 있다.

해설
제한된 천연자원의 보호를 위해 출생률 통제를 통한 인구 팽창 완화를 주장하는 환경론자들의 주장과 달리, 실은 인구 과잉이 아니라 선진국에서의 과소비가 문제이며, 인구 통제 프로그램을 통해 서양의 부유국들이 자원에 대한 경쟁 없는 이용이 가능해졌고, 그것이 부유국의 권위주의적 행동을 정당화하는 개념이라는 제국주의 비판론자의 의견을 제시하고 있다. 따라서 요약문의 빈칸 (A), (B)에 들어갈 말로는 ① 'over-consumption(과소비) - imperialism(제국주의)'이 가장 적절하다.

② 과소비 – 보호　　　　③ 초급성장 – 팽창
④ 자원 공유 – 상대주의　　⑤ 자원 공유 – 전파

TEXT FLOW

도입	환경론자들은 인구압이 환경 파괴의 원인이고, 출생률 통제를 옹호함
반전	다른 이들은 선진국에서의 과소비가 세계의 자원을 고갈시키고 있다고 주장함
부연	비판가들은 인구 통제 프로그램으로 서양 국가들이 자원을 경쟁 없이 이용 가능하고, 권위주의적 행동을 정당화한다고 함

구문
• [Those who hold this view] advocate strict control of birthrates in countries [with rapid population expansion] [to protect limited natural resources].
: 첫 번째 [ ]는 문장의 주어, 두 번째 [ ]는 countries를 수식하는 전치사구, 세 번째 [ ]는 목적을 나타내는 to부정사구이다.

11~12
정답 11 ⑤　12 ④

기회비용에 기반하여 오염 관리를 고려하는 것은 발생되는 오염을 상쇄하는 데에 어떤 지출이 필요하게 될 것인지에 대한 의문을 제기한다. 일반적으로 이러한 접근법의 문제는 만일 해당 효과에 대중이 두는 가치가 알려지지 않는다면, 사실상 그것이 비용을 상쇄할 가치가 있는지 알 수 없다는 것이다. 그러나 (예를 들어, 공기 오염이 건물을 손상하는데, 그것을 교체하는 것보다는 수리하는 것이 더 싸거나 혹은 그것이 작물을 파괴하고 그것(작물)의 시장 가치가 최소한 그것을 대체하는 비용만큼 크다는 것이 알려져 있는 것과 같은) 몇몇 상황에서는 그것이 비용을 상쇄할 가치가 있다는 것이 분명할 수도 있다.

이 접근법의 한 버전은 오염 관리의 발전 결과로 최근 몇 년 사이에 훨씬 더 흔해졌다. 그것은 다양한 오염 물질에 의해 유발되는 진정한 손상 비용의 불확실성에 직면하여 안전한 수준이라고 여겨지는 정도로 오염 물질의 수준을 제한하는 '예방 원칙'을 채택하는 경향이다. 이 상황에서, 오염을 제한선 위로 밀어 올리는 어떠한 프로젝트도 이러한 효과를 상쇄하는 다른 (그림자) 프로젝트에 의해 그 균형이 맞춰져야 한다. 예를 들어 만일 용인될 수 있는 온실

가스 배출이 알려지고, 교통수단으로부터의 배출이 상승하도록 허용된다면, 다른 곳에서 다른 배출이 증가되어야(→ 감소되어야) 한다. 이러한 맥락에서, 다른 곳에서 한 단위의 온실가스 배출을 줄이는 비용은 그것이 교통수단에서 증가하도록 허용하는 기회비용이 된다. 이러한 기회비용의 수량화 또한 문제가 없는 것은 아니다. 엄밀히 말해, 그렇게 하려면 가장 적은 비용이 발생하는 곳을 파악하기 위해 경제의 다른 곳의 모든 가능한 온실 가스 감축 방법을 검토하는 것이 필요하다.

해설
11 오염 관리에서 기회비용 접근법은 발생된 오염을 상쇄하려면 얼마만큼의 지출이 필요할지에 대한 의문을 제기하는데, 이 비용이 명확할 수도 있고 불명확할 수도 있지만, 요즘은 예방 원칙을 채택하는 경향이 흔하며 이 비용을 가장 경제적으로 상쇄할 방안을 파악하기 위한 검토가 필요하다는 내용이므로, 글의 제목으로 가장 적절한 것은 ⑤ '오염을 상쇄시키는 것은 기회비용 평가를 필요로 한다'이다.
① 기회비용: 오염 감소의 장애물
② 오염에 대한 경제적 접근: 확실한 실패의 길
③ 기회비용 접근이 다른 것들보다 월등한 이유
④ 온실가스 배출 비용: 상상을 초월함

12 오염을 제한선 위로 밀어 올리는 어떤 프로젝트도 다른 프로젝트에 의해 상쇄되어야 하며, 교통수단으로부터 배출 상승이 허용되면 다른 곳에서는 배출이 감소되어야 한다는 맥락이므로, ④의 'increased(증가하다)'를 'reduced(감소되다)'와 같은 낱말로 바꾸어야 한다.

TEXT FLOW

도입	오염 관리에서 기회비용 접근법은 오염을 상쇄하려면 어떤 지출이 필요할지의 의문을 제기함
전환	요즘은 안전한 수준으로 오염 물질을 제한하는 예방 원칙을 채택하는 경향이 있음
부연	오염을 제한선 위로 올리는 어떤 프로젝트도 다른 프로젝트에 의해 균형이 맞춰져야 함
결론	이 비용을 가장 경제적으로 상쇄할 수 있는 법을 검토해야 함

구문
• [Considering pollution control based on opportunity cost] raises the question of [what expenditure would be needed {to offset the pollution produced}].
: 첫 번째 [ ]는 문장의 주어이다. 두 번째 [ ]는 the question과 동격을 이루는 명사절이고, 그 안의 { }는 목적을 나타내는 to부정사구이고, produced는 the pollution을 수식하는 과거분사이다.

고난도 모의고사 **07회**

| 01 ② | 02 ② | 03 ② | 04 ③ | 05 ⑤ | 06 ③ |
| 07 ② | 08 ② | 09 ② | 10 ④ | 11 ⑤ | 12 ③ |

01 정답 ②

다른 사람들에게와 같이, 나에게 인터넷은 보편적인 매체, 즉 내 눈과 귀를 통해 내 마음속으로 흘러드는 대부분의 정보의 전달자가 되고 있다. 엄청나게 풍부한 정보 저장소에 즉시 접근할 수 있다는 것의 장점은 여러 가지인데, 그것들은 널리 설명되고 정당하게 찬사를 받아 왔다. 'Wired'의 Clive Thompson은 "실리콘 메모리의 완벽한 기억력은 사고력에 거대한 혜택이 될 수 있다."라고 썼다. 하지만 그러한 혜택에는 대가가 따른다. 미디어 이론가인 Marshall McLuhan이 1960년대에 지적했듯이, 미디어는 단순히 수동적인 정보 전달 채널이 아니다. 그것들은 생각할 거리를 제공할 뿐만 아니라 사고 과정을 형성하기도 한다. 그리고 인터넷이 하고 있는 것처럼 보이는 것은 집중과 숙고를 위한 나의 능력을 조금씩 깎아 내는 것이다. 이제 내 마음은 인터넷이 정보를 배포하는 방식, 즉 빠르게 움직이는 (정보) 조각의 흐름으로 정보를 받아들이기를 기대한다. 한때 나는 말의 바다 안에 있는 스쿠버 다이버였다. 이제 나는 제트 스키를 타는 사람처럼 수면 위를 쌩 하고 간다.

해설
인터넷을 통해 풍부한 정보 저장소에 즉시 접근할 수 있다는 장점은 찬사를 받아 왔지만, 인터넷은 집중하고 숙고하는 능력을 약화시킨다는 내용의 글이다. 빠르게 움직이는 정보를 받아들이지만 집중하고 숙고하는 능력이 약화된 모습을 제트 스키를 타는 사람에 비유하고 있으므로, 밑줄 친 부분이 글에서 의미하는 바로 가장 적절한 것은 ② '나는 정보를 완전히 이해하는 데 시간을 들이지 않는다.'이다.
① 나는 비판적 사고를 위한 인지 능력을 키웠다.
③ 나는 온라인에서 즐길 수 있는 많은 것들로 재미있는 시간을 갖는다.
④ 디지털 방해에 맞서 나의 집중력을 향상시켜야 한다.
⑤ 나의 검색 기술은 온라인 정보를 찾기에 충분하지 않다.

TEXT FLOW

도입	인터넷은 보편적인 매체로 대부분의 정보의 전달자가 되고 있음
전개 1	풍부한 정보 저장소에 즉시 접근할 수 있다는 장점이 있음
전개 2	집중과 숙고를 위한 우리의 능력을 조금씩 약화시키는 단점이 있음

구문
• For me, as for others, the internet is becoming a universal medium, [the conduit for most of the information {that flows through my eyes and ears and into my mind}].
: [ ]는 a universal medium과 동격을 이루는 명사구이고, 그 안의 { }는 the information을 수식하는 관계절이다.

• And [what the internet seems to be doing] is [chipping away my capacity for concentration and contemplation].
: 첫 번째 [ ]는 문장의 주어이고 두 번째 [ ]는 is의 주격 보어인 동명사구이다.

02 정답 ②

인종, 언어, 종교, 관습, 과학 문화 등의 공통성과 같이 매우 다양한 특성을 가질 수 있는 사회적 유사성은 통합의 힘으로 작용한다. 즉 '유유상종'은 정확히 사회 법칙이다. 민족의 구성에서 인종의 공통성은 근본적인 힘이며, 그것은 다른 유사성, 즉 종교나 일반 문화의 공통성에 의해서만 때때로 이의가 제기될 수 있다. 한 사람을 사회로 진입하게 하는 공감의 본능은 유사성과 밀접하게 결부되어 있다. 이 명백한 사실은 더 설명의 여지가 거의 없는데, 그것은 기본적이고, 더는 줄일 수 없으며, 영구적인 사실이다. 그러나 그 결과, 유사성에 근거한 결속은 노동의 분업에 근거한 결속보다 우리에게 훨씬 더 수용 가능한 것으로 나타나는데, 그것은 의무 대신 공감이라는 생각을 불러일으키기 때문이다. 우정과 공손함의 관계, 박애적 제안, 자선 사업을 불러일으키는 것이 바로 이것이다. 그것은 자신의 본분을 수행할 필요성을 보여 주기보다 다른 사람의 도덕적 충동을 지속하는 수단을 우리에게 제공한다.

해설
다양할 수 있는 사회적 유사성이 사회적 결속을 위한 통합의 힘으로 작용한다는 내용의 글이므로, 글의 주제로 가장 적절한 것은 ② '사회 내 결속의 원천으로서의 사회적 유사성'이다.
① 사회적 연대가 공감의 사고에 미치는 영향
③ 사회적 유사성을 분류하는 다양한 기준
④ 공감과 의무의 관계
⑤ 다른 문화에서의 다양한 사회적 유사성

TEXT FLOW

도입	다양할 수 있는 사회적 유사성은 통합의 힘으로 작용함
부연	공감의 본능은 유사성과 밀접하게 결부되어 있음
결론	유사성에 근거한 결속은 훨씬 더 수용 가능한데, 이는 의무 대신 공감이라는 생각을 불러일으키기 때문임

구문
• **It is** this **that** calls forth the relations of friendship and politeness, philanthropic suggestions, and charitable works.
: 「it is ~ that ....」 강조구문이 쓰여 주어 this가 강조되었다.

03 정답 ②

'억제자' 또는 '억압자'라고 일컬어지는 일부 사람들에게는 노출에 대한 두려움이 너무 커서, 그들은 부정적인 어떤 것도 다른 사람에게 드러내는 것을 피한다. 실제로, 많은 소문화권에서 아이에게 '다른 사람들이 네 일을 알게 하지 말아라', '그들이 알 필요가 있는 것만을 사람들에게 말해라' 또는 '네가 무슨 말을 하든, 아무 말도 하지 말아라'와 같은 말을 하며 자기 노출이 적극적으로 만류된다. 그런 다음 이러한 태도는 이후의 삶까지 지속되는데, 그때는 '비밀을 지키는' 사람에게 흔히 존경이 주어진다. 포커 게임에서는 말에 의해서든 말이 아닌 것에 의해서든 너무 많은 것을 노출하지 않는 것이 현명하지만, 자기 노출을 피하는 태도는 개인적인 문제에 관해 이야기할 필요가 있을 수도 있을 때는 사람들에게 문제를 일으킬 수 있다. 흔히, 우리가 자세히 노출하기 전에, 조사 또는 사전 예비 조사의 전략적 과정이 있는데, 그 과정에 의해 우리는 잠재적인 친구와 그 주제를 '추적하고' 그들의 반응을 관찰한다. 이 반응이 호의적이면 우리는 계속해서 (우리를) 드러내고, 그렇지 않으면 새로운 주제로 넘어간다.

해설

② the child 앞에 전치사 with가 있으므로, with가 있는 분사구문의 형태를 취해야 한다. 따라서 is를 being으로 고쳐야 한다. the child와 is told 가 각각 주어와 술어 동사가 되면 명사(구)를 뒤에 취하는 전치사 with와 함께 올 수 없기 때문에, the child is told ~는 어법상 틀린 구조가 된다.
① '너무 ~해서 …하다'의 의미를 가지는 「so ~ that …」 구문으로 that 은 어법상 적절하다. 앞뒤로 콤마가 있는 termed "inhibitors" or "suppressors"는 some people을 부연 설명하는 분사구이므로 that과 연결해서 생각하면 안 된다.
③ later life를 수식하는 관계절을 이끄는 관계부사 where는 어법상 적절하다.
④ a need를 수식하는 to부정사구를 이끄는 to talk은 어법상 적절하다.
⑤ and에 의해 "trail"과 병렬 구조를 이루어야 하므로, observe는 어법상 적절하다.

TEXT FLOW

도입	노출에 대한 두려움이 커서 어떤 것도 다른 사람에게 드러내지 않는 사람들이 있음
부연	이러한 태도로 비밀을 지키는 사람에게 존경이 주어짐
반전	개인적인 문제에 관해 이야기할 필요가 있을 때는 문제가 될 수 있음

04 정답 ③

한 fMRI(기능성 자기 공명 영상) 연구에서, 피실험자들은 세 가지 차원(색상, 모양, 또는 패턴) 중 하나에 대한 자극을 분류하도록 요청받았다. 행동 측면에서, 한 가지 연구 결과는 피실험자들은 머무름 실험에 비해 전환 실험에서 자극을 분류하는 데 더 오래 걸린다는 것이었다. 뇌의 측면에서, 전두두정골(前頭頭頂骨) 영역이 머무름 실험보다 전환 실험 동안 더 반응적이었다. 사실, 다중 작업이 신경 인지적 요구를 높인다는 견해와 일관되지 않게(→ 일관되게), 피실험자가 같은 과제에 머무를 때보다 새로운 과제로 전환할 때 제어 회로망의 과제 표현 강도가 더 컸다. 이것은 우리가 하나의 과제에서 다른 과제로 전환할 때 더 많은 신경 처리가 요구되는데, 그 이유는 우리가 새로운 과제의 표현을 다시 머리에 상기시킨 다음 그것을 이용하여 새로운 과제를 수행하기 위해 관련된 정보에 주의력을 할당해야 하기 때문이다. 그 결과, 과제 사이를 전환할 때, 우리는 단일 작업에 집중력을 유지하는 데서 오는 자동성과 효율성의 이점을 잃는다.

해설

피실험자가 과제 사이를 전환할 때는 새로운 과제 수행과 관련된 정보에 주의력을 할당해야 해서 뇌에 더 많은 신경 처리가 요구된다는 내용의 글이다. 따라서 ③의 'inconsistent(일관되지 않은)'를 'consistent(일관된)'와 같은 낱말로 바꾸어야 한다.

TEXT FLOW

도입	연구의 피실험자들은 전환 실험에서 자극을 분류하는 데 더 오래 걸림
전개	다중 작업이 신경 인지적 요구를 높임
부연	많은 신경 처리가 요구되고, 새로운 과제를 다시 머리에 상기하고 주의력을 할당해야 하기 때문임
결론	과제 사이를 전환할 때 단일 작업에 집중력을 유지하는 데서 오는 자동성과 효율성을 잃음

구문

• In fact, [consistent with the view {that multitasking creates heightened neurocognitive demands}], [the strength of task representation in the control network was greater {when subjects switched to a new task} than {when they stayed with the same task}].
: 첫 번째 [ ]는 being이 생략된 분사구문이고, 그 안의 { }는 the view와 동격인 명사절이다. 두 번째 [ ]는 주절이고 그 안의 두 개의 { }는 than에 의해 서로 비교되고 있다.

05 정답 ⑤

선반 위에 완전히 온전한 상태로 놓여 있는 유리 꽃병을 생각해 보라. 그 꽃병이 바닥에 떨어진다면 수많은 조각으로 산산조각이 날 것이라고 상상할 수 있다. 이를 통해 여러분은 그 꽃병이 실제로 깨지기 쉽다는 결론을 내릴 수 있다고 생각할지도 모른다. 그 말은 그것이 실제로 '깨졌다'라고 말하는 것이 아니라, 앞서 말했듯이 그것은 완전히 온전하다. 하지만 우리가 상상하는 행위는 꽃병이 가지고 있는 속성, 즉 깨지기 쉽다는 속성을 우리에게 그럴듯하게 보여 주는 것처럼 보일 수 있다. 마찬가지로, 우리가 마음과 몸이 서로 분리되어 존재하는 것으로 상상할 수 있다는 사실이 실제로 그것이 서로 분리되어 있다는 것을 보여 주지는 않는다. 그러나 여기서도 우리가 상상하는 행위는 그것들이 가지고 있는 속성, 즉 구별 가능한 실체라는 것을 우리에게 보여 주는 것처럼 보일 수 있다. 그리고 마음과 몸이 서로 구별된다는 주장을 뒷받침하기 위해 이원론자가 필요한 것은 그것뿐이다. 이것 중 어느 것도 논리적 가능성 주장이 성공적이라는 것을 보여 주는 것은 아니지만, 적어도 그 주장이 완전히 무효하지 않다는 것을 보여 주는 데는 도움이 될 것이다.

해설

선반 위에 있는 꽃병이 떨어진다면 깨져서 산산조각이 날 것이라고 상상한다고 해서 그것이 실제로 깨지는 것은 아니며, 단지 상상함으로써 그것이 깨지기 쉬운 속성을 가지고 있다는 것을 알게 되는 것처럼, 마음과 몸이 분리되어 있다고 우리가 상상하더라도 그것이 서로 분리되어 있는 것은 아니며, 다만 분리될 수 있다는 속성을 보여 주는 것이라는 내용의 글이다. 그러므로 빈칸에 들어갈 말로 가장 적절한 것은 ⑤ '구별 가능한'이다.
① 일시적인 ② 연약한
③ 불가분한 ④ 상호 보완적인

TEXT FLOW

도입	선반 위에 있는 꽃병이 떨어지면 깨져서 산산조각이 날 것이라고 상상한다고 해서 실제로 깨진 것은 아님
부연	그러나 꽃병이 깨지기 쉬운 속성을 가지고 있다는 것을 알 수 있게 해 줌
전환	마음과 몸이 분리되어 존재하는 것으로 상상한다고 해서 분리되어 있음을 보여 주지는 않음
결론	그러나 그것들이 구별 가능한 실체라는 속성을 알 수 있음

구문

• We could conceive of the vase shattering into lots and lots of pieces, [were it to be dropped on the floor].
: [ ]는 조건절에서 if가 생략되어 주어 it과 동사 were가 도치된 형태이다.

06

서양의 사회 과학은 과학자로서 사회 과학자들이 '이론적인 태도', 즉 거리를 두고 과학적으로 심사숙고하는 태도를 채택해야 한다는 생각을 대체로 지지한다. 이론의 창시자로서, 사회 과학자는 사회·정치적 세계에 대해 사심 없는 관찰자가 되어야 하며, 그런 의미에서 사회로부터 떨어져 있어야 한다. 사회 과학자는 사회의 활동을 냉정하게 연구해야 하며, 세계가 존재하는 방식에 대한 이론적 설명을 개발하고 시험하는 것만을 목표로 두어야 한다. 이런 사고방식에서, 전통적으로 생각되었던 사회·정치적 삶을 이론화하는 활동은 사회적 삶의 활동의 나머지 밖에 존재한다. 사회·정치적 세계가 존재해야 하는 방식에 관한 판단은 다른 사람들이 결정할 수 있도록 맡겨져야 한다. 사회 과학의 일과 개별적인 사회 과학자는 가치 판단의 영향을 받지 않아야 한다. 즉 우리가 사회에서 인간으로서 어떻게 살거나 행동해야 할지에 관한 결정과 관련하여 중립적이어야 한다.

해설
서양의 사회 과학자는 사회·정치 세계에 대해 사심 없는 관찰자가 되어 사회로부터 떨어져 있는 상태로 연구에 임해야 한다는 내용의 글이다. 따라서 사회 과학자는 사회에서 인간으로서 어떻게 살거나 행동해야 할지에 관한 결정과 관련하여 중립적이어야 하므로, 사회·정치적 세계가 존재해야 하는 방식에 관한 판단은 그들이 해야 할 몫이 아니다. 그러므로 빈칸에 들어갈 말로 가장 적절한 것은 ③ '다른 사람들이 결정할 수 있도록 맡겨져야'이다.
① 현실과 밀접한 관계가 있어야
② 설명하기 힘들 정도로 악명이 높아야
④ 이론적 태도를 지지하지 않아야
⑤ 종종 주관적인 감정에 근거해야

TEXT FLOW
도입	서양에서는 사회 과학자들이 이론적인 태도를 채택해야 한다는 생각을 지지함
부연	그들은 사회로부터 떨어져 있어야 하고, 사회·정치적 세계에 관한 판단은 다른 사람에게 맡겨야 함
결론	사회에서 인간으로 어떻게 살거나 행동해야 할지에 관한 결정과 관련하여 중립적이어야 함

구문
• Western social science generally endorses the idea [that social scientists as scientists should adopt the theoretical attitude — that is, {scientific contemplation at a distance}].
: [ ]는 the idea의 동격절이고, 그 안의 { }는 that is가 분명히 밝혀 주듯이 the theoretical attitude와 동격이다.

07

20세기의 과학적 실증주의는 데이터가 스스로 말하게 해야 한다고 요구한다. 이런 요구를 따를 때, 데이터가 가라고 하는 곳에서는 어디에서나, 우리는 진실을 찾게 될 것이다. 하지만 구글이 사람들을 분류하고 신분의 지위를 부여하는 데 사용하는 데이터는 말하지 않고, 법률상의 유죄를 피하기 위해 강력한 법인에 의해 평가되고 정리된다. (그런 데이터 흔적이 범죄 활동과 경향의 매우 귀중한 암시를 제공할 수 있지만, 그런 모든 데이터를 파악하는 것이 점점 어려워지고 있다.) 사실, 학자 Lisa Gitelman과 Virginia Jackson은 데이터는 말하는 것이 아니라, 대변된다고 주장한다. 데이터는 자연적으로 야생에서 나타나는 것이 아니라, 오히려 인간에 의해 수집되고,

연구자에 의해 처리되며, 궁극적으로는 현상을 설명하기 위해 이론가에 의해 조작된다. 따라서 데이터를 대변하는 사람은 누구나 우리가 우리 자신과 세계에서의 우리 위치를 어떻게 이해하게 되는지에 대해 틀을 잡는 놀라운 힘을 발휘한다.

해설
데이터 자체가 스스로를 대변하는 것이 아니라 데이터를 다루는 사람들에 의해 수집되고 처리됨으로써 그들을 대변한다는 내용의 글이다. 따라서 데이터 흔적을 통해 범죄 활동과 경향에 대한 정보를 얻는다고 서술하는 내용의 ②는 글의 전체 흐름과 관계가 없다.

TEXT FLOW
도입	20세기의 과학적 실증주의는 데이터가 스스로 말하게 해야 한다고 요구함
반전	데이터는 말하는 것이 아니라 대변됨
부연	데이터는 인간에 의해 수집되고 처리되며, 현상을 설명하기 위해 조작됨
결론	데이터를 대변하는 사람은 우리 자신과 세계에서의 우리 위치를 어떻게 이해하게 되는지에 대한 틀을 잡음

구문
• Data does not naturally appear in the wild; rather, it is [collected by humans], [manipulated by researchers], and [ultimately massaged by theoreticians to explain a phenomenon].
: 세 개의 [ ]는 and에 의해 병렬 구조로 연결되어 is에 이어진다.

08

규범적 믿음은 일반적으로 사회적 상호 작용에서 비롯되는 것으로 여겨진다. 실제로, 규범의 사회적 영향에 대한 초기 연구의 많은 부분은 규범에 대한 정보를 전달하기 위해 연출된 환경에서 실제 인물을 이용했다. (B) 예를 들어, 자동 운동 효과에 관한 Sherif의 연구는 한 과제에 대한 그들의 평가 결과가 다른 참가자들에게 공개되는 (보통 3명의) 참가자 집단을 이용했다. 마찬가지로, Asch는 자신의 순응성 연구에서 규범적 정보를 전달하기 위해 공모자를 이용했는데, 그것은 Latané와 Darley이 다원적 무지에 대한 연구에서 그랬던 것과 마찬가지였다. (A) 이러한 전통적 방법이 여전히 사용되고 (그리고 규범의 사회적 영향에 대한 '유일한' 접근법으로 널리 인용되고) 있지만, 규범적 정보가 비사회적 경로를 통해 전달되는 다른 절차들이 채택되어 왔다. (C) 즉, 다른 사람들이 행동하는 것을 보는 것이 특정한 맥락에서 사회적 규범에 관한 정보를 명확하게 제공할 수 있지만, 사회적 상호 작용은 요구되지 않는다. 개인은 다른 이들의 행동에 관한 추론을 이끌어 내기 위해 사회적, 비사회적인 다양한 신호를 이용한다.

해설
규범적 믿음은 사회적 상호 작용에서 비롯되는 것으로 여겨져서, 규범의 사회적 영향에 대한 초기 연구 대부분은 연출된 환경에서 실제 인물을 이용했다는 내용의 주어진 글 다음에는, For example로 여러 연구자들이 그런 환경에서 실험을 했다는 내용이 제시되는 (B)가 온 후, 주어진 문장과 (B)에서 언급한 내용을 this traditional method로 지칭하고 그 전통적 방법이 여전히 사용되지만, 규범적 정보가 비사회적 경로를 통해서도 전달되는 절차들이 있다는 내용의 (A)가 온 다음, 마지막으로 (A)에 대한 부연 설명을 That is로 제시하는 (C)가 오는 것이 글의 순서로 가장 적절하다.

도입	규범적 믿음에 대한 초기 연구 대부분은 연출된 환경에서 실제 인물을 이용했음
반전	규범적 정보가 비사회적 경로를 통해서도 전달되는 절차가 있음
결론	개인은 다른 이들의 행동에 관한 추론을 이끌어 내기 위해 사회적, 비사회적 신호를 모두 이용함

구문

• **While** this traditional method is still used (and widely cited as *the* approach to normative social influence), other procedures have been employed [in which normative information is conveyed through nonsocial channels].

: While은 여기에서 although의 의미로 쓰였다. [ ]는 other procedures를 수식하는 관계절인데 주어가 길어지는 것을 피하기 위해 문장 뒤에 쓰였다.

09 정답 ②

1968년, Vermont 주의 관련 공무원들은 고속도로를 따라 펼쳐진 삼림과 목초지의 아름다운 경관을 보호하려는 시도를 했는데, 당시 고속도로는 식당과 기타 업체들의 간판과 보기 흉한 광고판에 의해 훼손되고 있었다. 주 의회 의원들은 간단한 해결책을 가지고 있었는데 그것은 일정한 크기 이상의 모든 광고판과 간판을 금지하는 법이었다. 길에는 곧 간판의 수가 더 적어지고 크기도 더 작아졌기 때문에 어떤 의미에서 그것은 효과가 있었지만, 또한 다른 무엇인가가, 즉 이상하고 거대한 조각품들이 많아지는 일이 자연스럽게 발생했다. 자신의 사업에 대한 관심을 끌기 위해, 한 자동차 판매상은 진짜 Volkswagen Beetle을 움켜쥔 12피트 16톤의 고릴라를 세웠다. 이에 뒤질세라, 양탄자 가게 주인은 김이 나오는 거대한 도자기 찻주전자와 그 찻주전자에서 나와 겨드랑이에 양탄자 한 롤을 끼고 있는 거대한 지니를 세웠다. 이런 구조물들은 어떤 종류의 메시지도 표시하지 않고 있었기 때문에, 법이 적용되지 않았다. 입법 기관은 사회적 세계의 악명 높은 원칙, 즉 의도하지 않은 결과의 법칙을 완전히 이해하지 못했던 것이다.

해설

주어진 문장은 길에는 간판의 수가 더 적어지고 크기도 더 작아져서 그것이 효과가 있었지만, 또한 이상하고 거대한 조각품들이 많아지는 일이 발생했다는 내용이므로, 자동차 판매상이 자신의 사업에 대한 관심을 끌기 위해 Volkswagen Beetle을 움켜쥔 12피트 16톤의 고릴라를 세웠다는 내용 앞인 ②에 들어가는 것이 가장 적절하다.

⊗ 매력적인 오답 주의!

④ 주어진 문장 앞부분의 In a sense, it worked를 제대로 보지 않고, 단지 뒷부분의 sculptures만으로 these structures와 연결 지어 선택한 것으로 보인다. [선택률 38%]

도입	Vermont 주에서 경관 보호 차원으로 일정한 크기 이상의 광고판과 간판을 금지함
부연	간판의 수는 적어지고 크기는 작아졌지만, 이상하고 거대한 조각품이 많아지는 일이 발생함
예시	자동차 판매상은 차를 움켜쥔 고릴라, 양탄자 가게 주인은 거대한 지니를 세움
결론	입법 기관은 의도하지 않은 결과의 법칙을 이해하지 못했던 것임

구문

• Not to be outdone, the owner of a carpet store built [a huge ceramic teapot with steam] and [an enormous genie {emerging from it}, {a roll of carpet under his arm}].

: 두 개의 [ ]는 and로 연결된 built의 목적어이다. 두 번째 [ ] 안의 첫 번째 { }는 an enormous genie를 수식하는 현재분사구이다. 두 번째 { }는 부대상황을 나타내는 「with+명사+전치사구」의 구문으로 with a roll of carpet under his arm에서 전치사 with가 생략된 형태이다.

10 정답 ④

언어적으로 생각하는 것의 한 가지 이점은 언어가 지금 여기에서 여러분을 자유롭게 해 준다는 것이다. 언어와 의미 덕분에, 여러분은 가능한 미래의 사건에 관해, 멀리 떨어져 있는 사람들에 관해, 먼 과거에 했던 약속에 관해 생각할 수 있다. 쥐나 곤충은 본질적으로 즉각적인 현재에 살고 있으며, 그것이 보고 듣고 맛볼 수 있는 것에 기초해서만 대응할 수 있다. 언어는 사람들이 한 번도 일어나지 않았던 가능한 사건들을 상상할 수 있게 해 준다. 이 기능은 매우 도움이 되고 자유롭게 해 준다. 단 하나의 예로, 언어가 없는 동물들은 올해 수확물의 일부를 내년에 심기 위해 남겨 두어야 한다는 것을 도저히 이해할 수 없어서, 배가 고프면 자신들의 씨앗용 옥수수를 먹을 것이다. 그들은 단기적으로는 기분이 좋아지겠지만, 내년에는 심을 것이 없어 농작물이 전혀 없을 것이다. 아주 많은 종들이 식물을 먹기는 하겠지만, 우리 종이 땅을 경작해서 수확물을 거두는 유일한 종이라는 것은 거의 우연이 아니다.

➡ 동물과는 대조적으로, 언어는 인간에게 눈앞의 상황을 초월할 수 있는 능력을 부여하는데, 이에 대한 전형적인 사례는 우리가 농업에 종사하는 것에서 잘 나타난다.

해설

언어적으로 생각하는 것은 인간을 현재만 생각하는 상태로부터 자유롭게 했고, 그 덕분에 인간은 동물과 달리 씨앗을 심고 나중에 수확할 수 있는 농업에 종사할 수 있게 되었다는 내용의 글이다. 따라서 요약문의 빈칸 (A), (B)에 들어갈 말로는 ④ 'transcend(초월하다) – agriculture(농업)'가 가장 적절하다.

① 이용하다 – 교육
② 개선하다 – 농업
③ 개선하다 – 거래
⑤ 초월하다 – 교육

도입	언어적으로 생각하는 것은 현재에서 자유롭게 해 준다는 것임
부연	언어는 사람들이 한 번도 일어나지 않았던 가능한 사건들을 상상할 수 있게 해 줌
예시	언어가 없는 동물들은 배가 고프면 씨앗용 옥수수를 먹어서 내년에는 심을 것이 없음
결론	인간은 동물과 달리 농업에 종사할 수 있음

구문

• As just one example, animals [that have no language] **cannot possibly** understand [that some of this year's harvest has to be saved for planting next year], and ~.

: 첫 번째 [ ]는 animals를 수식하는 관계절이고, 두 번째 [ ]는 understand의 목적어 역할을 하는 명사절이다. cannot possibly는 '도저히 ~할 수 없다'는 의미이다.

11-12

대부분의 운동선수들은 그날그날의 상황이나, 심지어 낮은 수준의 경쟁 경기에서도 잘 기능할 수 있을 정도의 충분한 핵심 정신력을 개발해 왔다. 그러나 더 부담이 크고 압박감이 가득한 상황에 직면하게 되면, 그들은 실패할 수도 있다. 이는 운동선수와 그들의 코치들에게 매우 좌절감을 줄 수 있는데, 왜냐하면 그들은 자신들이 좋은 성적을 낼 잠재력을 가지고 있다는 것을 알고 있기 때문이다. 경기력의 문제가 정신적인 능력 부족 때문이라는 것을 인식하지 못한 채, 코치들은 운동선수들이 자신의 신체 능력을 훨씬 더 열심히 연마하도록 다그칠 수도 있다. 체조 선수는 기구에서 추가적인 시간을 보낼 수도 있다. 농구 선수는 연습 후에 자유투를 쏘는 데 추가적인 시간을 보낼 수도 있다. 장거리 달리기 선수들은 때로 과훈련이라고 할 수 있을 정도까지 훨씬 더 격렬하게 뛸 수도 있다. 실제로, 일부 경기력 문제는 형편없는 훈련이나 생체 역학과 같은 신체적 문제에서 비롯될 수도 있다. 그러나 많은 경우에 부적절한 정신력이 그 원인일 수 있다.

운동선수가 필요한 정신력을 기르도록 도울 방법을 <u>알고 있는(→ 알지 못하는)</u> 코치는 보통 세 가지 중 하나를 하는데, 공감과 격려로 운동선수를 지원하려고 노력하고, 신체적으로 재능은 덜 갖추었지만 압박감 하에서 더 경기력을 잘 보여 줄 수 있는 또 다른 운동선수를 선발하거나, 운동선수가 자신의 최대 능력까지 경기력을 보이기 시작하도록 운동선수에게 더 많은 압박을 가함으로써 문제를 악화시키는 것이다. 물론 대안은 스포츠 심리학의 발전을 이용하는 것이다. 모든 스포츠의 코치들은 운동선수들이 스포츠에서 탁월한 기량을 성취하는 데 필요한 정신 능력을 배우고 향상할 수 있다는 것을 점점 더 인식하고 있다. 정신력 개발을 운에 맡기는 것이 아니라, 최고의 코치들은 스포츠 심리학을 그들 운동선수들의 정신 훈련 프로그램에 포함시킴으로써 운동선수들이 이러한 필수적인 능력을 개발하도록 돕는 데 대한 책임을 점점 더 많이 지고 있다.

해설

11 운동선수들에게 경기력 문제가 발생할 때는 그들의 탁월한 기량을 개발하기 위해서 신체 능력을 기르는 것이 아니라 스포츠 심리학을 이용하여 적절한 정신 훈련 프로그램을 받을 수 있도록 해야 한다는 내용의 글이므로, 글의 제목으로 가장 적절한 것은 ⑤ '스포츠 심리학: 운동선수들의 최고의 경기력을 위한 바로 그것'이다.
① 코치와 선수 간의 왜곡된 관계
② 선수들의 경기력에 가장 영향을 미치는 신체적 요인
③ 누적 연구에 기반한 스포츠 심리학의 발달
④ 공감과 격려: 도움이 필요한 선수들에겐 항상 옳음

12 선수들의 경기력에 문제가 생기는 것은 신체적 문제뿐만 아니라 정신력에도 기인하는데, 이어지는 세 가지 방법은 운동선수가 필요한 정신력을 기르도록 도울 방법을 모르는 코치에 대한 내용이다. 따라서 ③의 'aware(알고 있는)'를 'unaware(알지 못하는)'와 같은 낱말로 바꾸어야 한다.

❓ WHY 고난도

후반부에 시간에 쫓기는 수험생들이 문장 전체의 흐름을 파악하지 않고 선택지를 포함한 문장 안에서의 의미만으로 적절하다고 판단할 수 있는 고난도 문제이다.

도입	운동선수들은 정신력을 개발해 왔지만, 실패할 경우 좌절감을 느낄 수 있음
부연	경기력의 문제가 정신적인 능력 부족임을 인식하지 못하고, 신체 능력을 더 연마함
예시	정신력을 기를 방법을 모르는 코치는 다른 방법들로 문제를 악화시킴
결론	스포츠 심리학으로 정신력 개발을 하고, 정신 훈련 프로그램을 포함하여 능력을 개발하도록 도와야 함

구문

• Coaches from all sports are increasingly recognizing [that athletes can learn and improve the mental skills {needed ⟨to achieve excellence in sport⟩}].
: [ ]는 동사 are recognizing의 목적어 역할을 하는 명사절이며, 그 안의 { }는 the mental skills를 수식하는 과거분사구이다. ⟨ ⟩는 목적을 나타내는 to부정사구이다.

고난도 모의고사 08회

01 ②	02 ②	03 ②	04 ⑤	05 ⑤	06 ④
07 ④	08 ⑤	09 ⑤	10 ②	11 ⑤	12 ⑤

01
정답 ②

너무나 명백하지만 자주 잊히는 사실은 역사가들이 사람들을 연구하는 사람들이고 사람들에게는 문제가 있다는 점이다. 지질학자들도 역시 사람들이지만 그들은 암석을 조사한다. 암석과 관련한 편리한 점은 그것들이 예측 가능한 편이라는 점이다. 지질학자가 힘든 밤을 보냈든 기분이 나쁘든 관계없이, 다이아몬드는 항상 유리를 자른다. 중요한 점은 사람들은 암석과 매우 다르다는 것이다. 그들은 예측 불가능하고 모순되어 있으며 다른 사람에게뿐 아니라 자신에게 거짓말하는 것도 상당히 잘할 수 있다. 사람들이, 심지어 역사가들조차 자신의 사소한 개인적인 상황을 역사의 흐름과 혼동하는 것은 흔한 일이다. 영국 학자인 A.J.P. Taylor가 언젠가 말했듯, 문명의 쇠퇴에 대한 온갖 종류의 말은 사실상 '대학 교수들이 전에는 가정에 하인들이 있었지만 지금은 자신들이 빨래를 한다는 것을 의미한다.' 그러한 경향을 가진 사람이 대학 교수만은 아니라고 말하는 것이 공정하겠다.

해설
인간은 암석처럼 예측 가능하지 않아서 일관성이 없고, 일반인뿐 아니라 역사가들조차 개인적인 상황을 역사의 흐름과 혼동한다는 내용의 글이므로, 밑줄 친 부분이 의미하는 바로 가장 적절한 것은 ② '사람들은 기만적일 수 있으며 하루하루 다를 수도 있다.'이다.
① 사람들의 생각은 사회적이고 경제적인 변화에 영향을 받는다.
③ 사람들은 자신의 이익을 위해 자주 역사적인 발견을 왜곡한다.
④ 증거로 증명된 이론일지라도 개인에 의해 이의가 제기될 수 있다.
⑤ 사람들의 개인적인 삶에 관한 직접적인 설명은 종종 시간이 지남에 따라 사라진다.

TEXT FLOW

도입	암석은 예측 가능한 편이지만, 사람들은 암석과 매우 다름
부연 1	사람들은 예측 불가능하고 모순되어 있고 거짓말에 능함
부연 2	심지어 역사가들조차 흔히 개인적인 상황과 역사의 흐름을 혼동함

구문
• It would be fair to note [that **it is** not just university professors **who** have such tendencies].
: [ ]는 note의 목적어 역할을 하는 명사절이고, 그 안에 「it is ~ who ....」 강조구문이 쓰여 not just university professors가 강조되었다.

02
정답 ②

나는 전에 여전히 살아 있는 아주 오래된 나무 그루터기 잔해를 우연히 발견했다. 그런데 어떻게 그 잔해는 그렇게 오랜 시간 삶을 붙잡고 있을 수 있었을까? 나무에 살아 있는 세포는 당분의 형태로 식량을 가지고 있어야 하고, 숨을 쉬어야 하며, 적어도 조금은 자라야 한다. 하지만 잎이 없이는, 그래서 광합성이 없이는 그것은 불가능하다. 지구상에 존재하는 어떤 생명체도 수세기

동안 단식을 유지할 수 없으며, 심지어 나무의 잔해조차도 그렇지 못하며, 스스로 살아남아야 했던 그루터기도 분명 그렇지 못하다. 이 그루터기에 뭔가 다른 일이 일어나고 있는 것이 분명했다. 그것은 이웃 나무들, 특히 그들의 뿌리에서 도움을 받고 있는 것이 틀림없다. 유사한 상황을 조사 중인 과학자들은 나무 사이의 영양소 교환을 용이하게 하는 뿌리 끝 주변의 균 네트워크에 의해 원격으로 지원이 전달될 수 있거나 뿌리 자체가 상호 연결될 수도 있다는 것을 발견했다. 내가 우연히 발견한 그루터기의 경우, 오래된 그루터기 둘레를 파서 그것을 다치게 하고 싶지 않았기 때문에, 나는 무슨 일이 일어나고 있는지 알 수 없었지만, 한 가지는 분명했으니, 그것은 주변의 나무들이 그루터기가 살아남게 하려고 그 그루터기에게 당분을 퍼붓고 있었다는 것이다.

해설
잎이 없어 스스로 살아남을 수 없는 아주 오래된 그루터기가 생명을 유지할 수 있는 것은 주변 나무들의 뿌리 끝 주변의 균 네트워크에 의해 영양소가 원격으로 전달되거나 주변 나무들과 뿌리 자체가 상호 연결되어 당분을 공급받기 때문임을 설명하는 글이다. 그러므로 글의 주제로 가장 적절한 것은 ② '자급 능력이 없는 그루터기가 살아남을 수 있는 이유'이다.
① 숲에서 생존하기 위해 사용되는 계층적 구조
③ 살아 있는 세포가 상호 협력을 통해 먹이를 생산하는 방법
④ 나무 종의 성장에 미치는 균류 네트워크의 영향
⑤ 나무와 동물이 상호 의존적이 되는 과정

TEXT FLOW

주제	오래된 나무 그루터기의 잔해는 어떻게 살아남을 수 있었을까?
부연	나무 세포는 당분 식량을 가지고, 숨을 쉬고, 자라야 하는데 잎이 없이는 불가능함
반전	이웃 나무들의 뿌리 끝 주변의 균 네트워크에 의해 영양소가 원격으로 전달되거나 주변 나무들과 뿌리 자체가 상호 연결될 수 있음을 발견함

구문
• No **being** on our planet can maintain a centuries-long **fast**, [not even the remains of a tree], and certainly [not a stump {that has had to survive on its own}].
: being은 동명사가 아니라 '생명체, 생물'의 의미이고 fast도 단식이라는 의미의 명사이다. 두 개의 [ ]는 can maintain a centuries-long fast가 반복되어 생략된 형태이다. 두 번째 [ ] 안의 { }는 a stump를 수식하는 관계절이다.

03
정답 ②

우리의 초기 인류 조상들은 계속 이동하며 새로운 환경에 적응해야 했고, 그들은 이동하는 것에 잘 적응했다. 그들 중 일부가 바로 아프리카에서 이동한 것은 놀라운 일이 아니다. 유럽 동쪽 끝의 흑해 근처, 중국, 인도네시아 자바 섬에서 100만 년이 넘는 인류의 유골이 (지금까지) 발견되어 왔다. 자바 섬에 초기 인류의 유골이 있다는 것은 그들이 거의 200만 년 전에 이미 아시아를 횡단하여 이동하고 있었다는 것을 보여 준다. 오늘날 아시아 본토에서 그 섬으로 가려면 폭이 500마일이 넘는 말라카 해협을 건너, 수마트라에 도착한 다음, 다시 20마일의 바다를 건너 자바 섬에 도착해야 한다. 하지만 빙하기에는 해수면이 훨씬 더 낮은데, 그때는 지구의 훨씬 더 많은 물이 극지방과 산 정상에서 얼음판으로 얼게 된다. 약 190만 년 전에 발생한 빙하기에는 해수면이 지금보다 200피트 더 낮았다. 당시 자바 섬과 수마트라 섬은 본토에 붙어 있었고, 초기 인류는 그냥 걸어서 그곳에 갈 수 있었을 것이다.

해설

② 문장의 주어 The presence of ~ on Java의 동사 자리이므로, suggesting은 술어 동사 suggests로 고쳐야 한다. that 이하는 목적어 역할을 하는 명사절이다.

① It은 가주어이고 that 이하는 진주어이므로, 진주어를 이끄는 접속사 that은 어법상 적절하다.

③ ice ages를 부연 설명하는 관계절을 이끄는 관계부사 when은 어법상 적절하다.

④ 앞에 나온 과거시제의 was와 대구를 이루어 현재시제로 쓰인 is는 어법상 적절하다.

⑤ The islands of Java and Sumatra를 지칭하는 복수 대명사 them은 어법상 적절하다.

TEXT FLOW

도입	초기 인류 조상은 계속 이동하며 새로운 환경에 적응하고 이동하는 것에 잘 적응했음
부연 1	자바 섬에서 발견된 초기 인류의 유골은 200만 년 전에 이미 아시아를 횡단했다는 것을 알 수 있음
부연 2	아시아에서 자바 섬까지는 해협과 바다를 건너야 하는데, 초기 인류는 걸어서 갈 수 있었음

04

정답 ⑤

사람들이 인간의 발달에 미치는 '환경적' 영향에 대한 수정 가능성을 받아들이는 데는 별 어려움이 없는 것처럼 보인다. 만약 어떤 아이가 수학에서 좋지 못한 가르침을 받았다면, 그 결과로 생긴 결손은 다음 해에 추가적인 훌륭한 가르침으로 고쳐질 수 있다고 받아들여진다. 하지만 그 아이의 수학적 결함에 유전적 원인이 있을 수 있다는 어떤 의견이라도 절망에 가까운 것으로 반응을 보일 가능성이 있는데, 그것이 유전자에 있는 것이라면, '그것은 (이미) 쓰여 있고', 그것은 '결정되어' 있으며, 그것에 대해 아무것도 할 수 있는 것이 없으므로, 여러분은 그 아이에게 수학을 가르치려고 애쓰는 것을 포기하는 편이 낫다는 것이다. 이것은 거의 점성술만큼이나 유해한 말도 안 되는 소리이다. 유전적 원인과 환경적 원인은 원칙적으로 전혀 서로 다르지 않다. 두 유형 모두의 어떤 영향은 되돌리기 어려울 수 있으며, 어떤 다른 영향은 되돌리기 쉬울 수 있다. 어떤 것들은 대개 되돌리기 어렵지만, 적절한 동인(動因)이 적용된다면 쉬울 수 있다. 요점은 유전의 영향이 환경의 영향보다 조금이라도 더 되돌릴 수 있을(→ 되돌릴 수 없을) 것이라고 예상할 보편적인 이유가 전혀 없다는 것이다.

해설

유전과 환경의 원인이 전혀 다르지 않으며 그 영향은 적절한 동인이 적용된다면 되돌리기 쉬워서 유전적 영향이 환경의 영향보다 되돌릴 수 없다고 예상할 보편적인 이유가 전혀 없다는 내용이 자연스러우므로, ⑤ 'reversible(되돌릴 수 있는)'은 'irreversible(되돌릴 수 없는)'과 같은 낱말로 바꾸어야 한다.

❓ WHY 고난도

앞의 진술과 상반된 진술의 기점이 되는 This is pernicious rubbish on an almost astrological scale.의 의미를 파악하지 못하면 바로 뒤에 나오는 ④를 정답으로 선택할 함정이 있는 고난도 문제이다.

TEXT FLOW

도입	사람들은 인간의 발달에 미치는 환경적 영향에 대한 수정 가능성은 잘 받아들임
전환	하지만 유전적 원인이 있을 수 있다는 의견에는 절망함
반전	유전적 원인과 환경적 원인은 다르지 않음
결론	유전의 영향도 적절한 동인이 적용된다면 되돌리기 쉬움

구문

• But any suggestion [that the child's mathematical deficiency might have a genetic origin] is likely to be greeted with something [approaching despair]: ~.

: 첫 번째 [ ]는 any suggestion과 동격인 명사절이고 두 번째 [ ]는 something을 수식하는 현재분사구이다.

05

정답 ⑤

항공 운송은 눈보라가 항공 운수에 폭포 효과를 미칠 수 있는 겨울 동안과 같은 기상 장애에 특히 취약하다. 지구의 바람 패턴에는 계절성이 있다. 제트 기류 또한 국제 항공사들이 고려해야 하는 주요 물리적 요소이다. 항공기에 있어서, 바람의 속도는 이동 시간과 비용에 영향을 미칠 수 있다. 대륙 간 비행에 있어서 뒤바람이 부는 조건은 예정된 비행시간을 1시간까지 단축할 수 있다. 예를 들어, 겨울철의 강한 제트 기류 조건 때문에, 미국 동부 해안과 유럽 간 대서양 횡단 비행은 동쪽으로 가는 비행에 있어 예정된 것보다 30분에서 45분 더 일찍 도착할 수 있다. 그러나 서쪽으로 가는 비행에 있어서, 비정상적으로 강한 제트 기류 조건은 비행시간을 연장시킬 것이고 때로 항공편이 어쩔 수 없이 Gander(Newfoundland)나 Bangor(Maine) 같은 기착지 공항에서 예정에 없던 연료 보급 착륙을 하도록 할 수 있다. 기후 변화는 북대서양 제트 기류의 강도를 높일 것이며 북미와 유럽 간의 서쪽으로 가는 비행시간을 연장할 수 있을 것으로 예상된다.

해설

겨울철의 강한 북대서양 제트 기류 때문에 대서양 횡단 비행이 동쪽으로 갈 때는 비행시간이 단축되지만, 서쪽으로 갈 때는 비행시간이 연장된다는 내용의 글이다. 기후 변화로 인해 북대서양 제트 기류가 더 강해지면 비행시간에 미치는 현재의 영향이 더 커질 것이라는 흐름이므로, 빈칸에 들어갈 말로 가장 적절한 것은 ⑤ '북미와 유럽 간의 서쪽으로 가는 비행시간을 연장할'이다.

① 북미의 바람 패턴의 계절성을 감소시킬
② 역풍의 방향을 동쪽으로 바꿀
③ 서쪽으로 가는 비행기의 순풍의 세기를 높일
④ 동쪽 방향과 서쪽 방향의 비행시간 차이를 좁힐

TEXT FLOW

도입	항공 운송은 겨울 동안 기상 장애에 특히 취약함
부연	항공기에 있어서 바람의 속도는 이동 시간과 비용에 영향을 미침
예시 1	겨울철 강한 제트 기류는 미국과 유럽 간의 동쪽으로 가는 비행에 있어서 시간을 단축시킴
예시 2	서쪽으로 가는 비행은 비행시간을 연장시키거나 연료 보급 착륙을 할 수 있음

구문

• Air transportation is particularly vulnerable to weather

disruptions, [such as during winter {when a snowstorm can create cascading effects on air services}].
: [ ]는 weather disruptions의 구체적인 예를 나타내며, 그 안의 { }는 winter를 수식하는 관계절이다.

06

분리 독립을 지지하는 서아프리카에서의 내전은 비교적 쉽게 이해할 수 있는데, 이곳에서 민족 집단은 자신의 새로운 국가를 개척하기 위해 싸운다. 대의명분이 없는 서아프리카의 반군들은 이해하기가 더 어려운데, 이들은 국가 규모의 쿠데타에서처럼, 정해진 이념적 강령 없이 국가 정부를 장악하고 싶어 한다. 반군들은 자신의 목표가 더 청렴하고 더 공정한 정부를 도입하는 것이라고 주장하지만, 그들 자신의 지도자들이 너무 자주 명백하게 부패해 있기 때문에 그러한 주장은 타당하지 않아 보인다. 하지만 추종자들과 함께한 우리의 인터뷰는 그들이 합리적인 내기를 하고 있다는 것을 암시한다. 즉, 더 공평하게 전리품을 나눔으로써 모든 사람이 이익을 얻거나, 그들의 편이 권력을 얻어서 전리품을 그들 방식대로 관리할 것이기 때문에 적어도 그들 자신이 이익을 얻을 것이다. 많은 이들은 그저 자신의 고향 마을을 지키기 위해 반란군에 가담한다. 반군들은 굉장히 지역적인 관점을 가지고 있다. 그들은 수도에서 국가 정부를 장악하는 것을 목표로 하는데, 왜냐하면 이것이 여전히 전리품의 분배를 통제하는 방법이기 때문이다. 이념으로서 훌륭한 통치는 국가적 공평, 혹은 그저 일련의 새로운 승리자들을 의미할지도 모른다.

해설
서아프리카에서 반군들이 내전을 일으키는 이유에 관한 글인데, 더 청렴하고 더 공정한 정부를 도입하고자 한다는 표면적 주장과는 달리, 실제로는 더 공평하게 전리품을 나눔으로써 모든 사람이 이익을 얻거나, 자신이 가담한 쪽이 권력을 얻어서 적어도 (승리한) 자신들이라도 이익을 얻을 수 있기 때문에 그렇게 한다는 내용이다. 따라서 빈칸에 들어갈 말로 가장 적절한 것은 ④ '국가적 공평, 혹은 그저 일련의 새로운 승리자들을 의미할'이다.
① 노동력의 생산성 향상으로 이어질
② 국가, 지역 및 지역 수준에 따라 다를
③ 현지의 요구보다 경제적 이익을 앞세울
⑤ 법률 제도의 창설과 이용에 의해 달성될

⊗ 매력적인 오답 주의!
② 글 전체의 의미를 이해하기보다 글 후반부의 문장 Rebels have a very local perspective.를 근거로 선택한 것으로 보인다. [선택률 31%]

TEXT FLOW

도입	서아프리카의 반군들은 자신의 목표가 공정한 정부를 도입하는 것이라고 주장함
부연	자신의 지도자들이 너무 부패해 있기 때문에 그 주장은 타당하지 않음
결론	실제로는 더 공평하게 전리품을 나누어 자신들의 편이 권력을 얻고 이익을 얻기 위함임

구문
• **It** is relatively easy [to understand secessionist civil wars in West Africa], [where ethnic groups fight to carve out their own new states].
: It은 가주어이고 첫 번째 [ ]는 진주어인 to부정사구이다. 두 번째 [ ]는 West Africa를 부연 설명하는 관계절이다.

07

겉보기에는 자동인 것 같은 인간의 사회적인 본성에 대한 가장 흥미로운 증거 가운데 하나는 한 직사각형의 주위를 도는 두 개의 삼각형과 한 개의 원을 다룬 Fritz Heider와 Marianne Simmel의 1944년의 유명한 만화 영화에서 나온다. (C) 그 만화 영화는 그저 모양들만을 묘사하지만, 사람들은 이러한 물체들을 인간 배우로 이해하고 그것들의 움직임을 중심으로 하여 사회적인 드라마를 구성하지 않는 것이 거의 불가능하다고 느낀다. (A) 그 비디오를 더 면밀히 보고, 그 현상을 묘사하는 Heider와 Simmel의 소논문을 더 면밀히 읽으면, 이 모양들을 사회적인 방식으로 지각하는 것은 자동적인 것이 아니고 자극과 상황의 특징에 의해 환기된 것임에 틀림없다는 것을 시사한다. 이러한 모양들은 사회적인 행동을 구체적으로 모방하는 궤적으로 움직이도록 고안되었다. (B) 만일 그 모양들의 움직임이 변화되거나 뒤바뀌면, 그것들은 같은 수준의 사회적인 반응을 이끌어내지 못한다. 게다가 이 만화 영화의 원래 연구의 참가자들은 그 모양을 실험자들이 사용하는 언어와 지시에 의해 사회적인 방식으로 묘사하도록 유도되었다. 인간은 사회적인 렌즈를 통해 세상을 볼 준비가 되어 있고 기꺼이 그렇게 할 수도 있지만, 그들은 자동으로 그렇게 하지는 않는다.

해설
직사각형 주위를 도는 두 개의 삼각형과 한 개의 원을 다룬 만화 영화가 인간의 사회적인 본성에 대한 흥미로운 증거를 제시한다는 내용의 주어진 글 다음에는, 주어진 글의 만화 영화를 The animation으로 받아 그 만화 영화를 볼 때 사람들은 자연스럽게 사회적인 드라마를 구성한다는 내용의 (C)가 온 후, (C)의 내용을 확장하면서 이러한 모양을 사회적 방식으로 자동으로 지각하는 것이 아니라 사회적인 행동을 모방하도록 고안된 것이라는 내용의 (A)가 온 다음, (A)의 These shapes를 the shapes'로 받아 이러한 모양의 움직임이 바뀌면 같은 반응을 이끌어내지 못하며 연구 참가자들은 그 모양을 사회적 방식으로 묘사하도록 유도된 것이라는 내용의 (B)가 오는 것이 글의 순서로 가장 적절하다.

TEXT FLOW

도입	직사각형 주위를 도는 두 개의 삼각형과 한 개의 원을 다룬 만화 영화가 인간의 사회적인 본성에 대한 증거를 제시함
부연 1	그 만화 영화를 볼 때 사람들은 사회적인 드라마를 구성함
부연 2	모양들을 자동으로 지각하는 것이 아니라 자극과 상황의 특징에 의해 환기된 것임
결론	이 만화 영화의 연구 참가자들은 그 모양을 사회적 방식으로 묘사하도록 유도되었음

구문
• The animation depicts merely shapes, yet people find **it** nearly impossible **not** [to interpret these objects as human actors] and [to construct a social drama around their movements].
: it은 find의 가목적어이고, and로 연결된 두 개의 [ ]가 진목적어이다. 두 개의 [ ]는 and로 연결되어 not에 이어진다.

08

민간 운송 업체와 연방 우체국 사이의 경쟁은 통신 기반 시설의 관리에서 중요한 긴장, 즉 보편적인 서비스, 모두에 대한 기본적인 수용력 기대 및 공공 운송, 공정하고 차별 없는 서비스에 대한 기대 사이의 긴장을 생생히 보여 준다. (C) 미국 우체국은 전국에 보편적인 서비스를 제공할 자원과 기반 시설이 부족했다. 일반적으로, 연방 시스템은 빠른 운송보다 신뢰할 수 있는 기반 시설을 천천히 개발하는 것을 우선시했다. (B) 반면 민간 운송 회사들은 어느 곳이나 갔고, 누구를 위해서든 거의 모든 일을 했고, 그간 만들어진 것들 중에서 보편적인 서비스 회사에 가장 가까운 것이었으며, 민간 특급 운송은 모든 새로운 캠프, 특히 금괴를 운반할 때 발견되는 수익성 좋은 일이 있었던 골드러시를 겪는 서부에서 자주 최초로 설립되는 것이었다. (A) 그러나 이러한 이득은 대가가 따랐다. 민간 특급은 경쟁을 피하고, 가격 담합과 화물 차별에 관여하며, 일반적으로 책임을 묻기 어려운 카르텔이었다.

해설
민간 운송 업체와 연방 우체국 사이의 경쟁을 기술하는 주어진 글 다음에는, 연방 우체국의 상황과 우선순위를 설명하는 (C)가 온 다음, 그와 대조적인 민간 운송 회사들의 영업에 관하여 설명하는 (B)가 온 후, 민간 운송 회사들의 단점을 언급하며 (B)에서 제시한 장점과 비교하는 맥락의 (A)가 오는 것이 글의 순서로 가장 적절하다.

TEXT FLOW

도입	민간 운송 업체와 연방 우체국 사이의 경쟁이 있음
전개 1	미국 우체국은 빠른 운송보다 신뢰할 수 있는 시설을 천천히 개발함
전개 2	민간 운송 회사는 보편적인 서비스 회사에 가까웠고, 금괴를 운반하는 수익성 좋은 일이었음
부연	민간 운송 회사의 단점은 책임을 묻기 어려운 카르텔임

구문
• The private expresses were cartels [that {avoided competition}, {engaged in price fixing and freight discrimination}, and {were in general hard to hold accountable}].
: [ ]는 cartels를 수식하는 관계절로 그 안의 세 개의 { }가 and에 연결되어 병렬 구조를 이룬다.

09
정답 ⑤

긴장은 오늘날 많은 신체적, 심리적, 그리고 감정적 요소에 의해 영향을 받는 것으로 여겨진다. 예를 들어, Lew Hardy는 재앙의 첨단 모델을 제안했는데, 그것은 긴장이 생각과 신체적인 요소를 가지고 있다는 것을 보여 준다. 이 이론은 (운동) 수행의 저하는 높은 신체적인 긴장과 높은 인지적인 긴장이 둘 다 존재할 때만 발생한다고 주장한다. 이러한 상황이 발생하면 '재앙'이 일어나 운동 수행에서 빠르고도 급격한 저하라는 결과로 이어진다. 예를 들어, 다가오는 경기를 두려워하는 장대높이뛰기 선수는 목표를 달성하는 자신의 능력에 대한 부정적인 생각과 의혹으로 표현되는 높은 수준의 인지적인 긴장을 경험할 수도 있다. 이러한 걱정스러운 생각들은 근육의 경직과 빠른 호흡 같은 과도한 긴장의 생리적 경험으로 나타나는데, 그것들은 둘 다 성공적인 수행에 해로울 수 있다. 상담사의 난제는 개별 선수에게서 긴장의 변화가 생긴 정확한 이유를 파악하는 것이다. 선수가 긴장의 변화의 특정한 원인을 파악할 때만 그 선수는 그것을 통제하고 이에 따라 최상의 수행을 하는 방법을 배울 수 있게 된다.

해설
주어진 문장은 상담사는 개별 선수가 긴장의 변화를 겪는 정확한 이유를 파악 도전에 직면한다는 내용인데, ⑤ 앞의 내용은 과도한 긴장은 성공적인

수행에 해로운 생리적인 현상을 초래할 수 있다는 것이고, ⑤ 뒤의 내용은 긴장의 변화의 원인을 파악해야 그 변화를 통제하고 수행을 잘할 수 있다는 것이므로, 주어진 문장이 ⑤에 들어가야 긴장의 변화에 대한 파악에서 통제의 학습으로 글이 자연스럽게 이어질 수 있다.

TEXT FLOW

도입	높은 신체적 긴장과 높은 인지적 긴장이 둘 다 존재할 때 운동 수행의 저하가 발생함
예시	다가오는 경기를 두려워하는 선수는 높은 인지적 긴장으로 근육의 경직과 빠른 호흡 같은 생리적 경험을 나타냄
부연	선수는 긴장의 원인을 파악해야 통제하고 최상의 수행을 하는 방법을 배울 수 있음

구문
• [Only when an athlete can identify the specific causes for changes in intensity] can she then learn to control them and, thus, perform her best.
: Only를 수반한 부사절 [ ]가 강조되어 문장 앞으로 오면서 주어 she와 조동사 can이 도치되었다.

10
정답 ②

완전히 건설되어 시험되기 전까지는 쉽게 검증될 수 없는 종류의 큰 것이 있다. 이것은 댐, 터널, 건물, 다리와 같은 토목 공학 프로젝트들인데, 그것들은 규모가 너무나 크고 비용이 너무나 거대하며, 디자인이 그 장소에 너무나 특화되어 있어서 그 건축물은 고유하다. 그것이 공장에서 만들어지는 것이 아니라 한 장소에 건설되는 유일한 것이어서, 검사할 만한 1회용 표본이 없다. 이론을 실험하거나 대안적인 설계를 비교하기 위해 축소판 모델이 사용될 수도 있지만, 어떠한 모델도 지어진 실제 건축물의 조건을 절대 완전히 복제하지 못할 것이다. 이론의 여지가 없이 의미 있는 모델들이 가능하다 해도, 그 건축물이 영향을 받을 미래의 지진, 폭풍, 그와 유사한 것들이 가진 자연력을 완전히 모델링하는 것은 불가능하다. 요컨대, 거대한 토목 공학 건축물을 명확하게 검증하는 유일한 방법은 자연이 그것을 어떻게 시험할 것인지를 예상하며 건설하고 자연이 그렇게 하도록 내버려 두는 것이다. 거대한 규모의 토목 공학 공사에 대한 이러한 사실은 주의 깊고, 사전 대책을 강구하는 실패 분석을 필요로 한다.

➡ 거대한 건축물들은 자연력에 대한 완벽한 시뮬레이션을 허용하지 않으므로, 그 디자인의 유효성을 검사하는 유일한 방법은 주의 깊은 사전 대책과 함께 그 건축물을 건설하는 것뿐이다.

해설
거대한 건축물들은 어떠한 수학적 모델이나 모형으로도 미리 검증하고 분석하기 어렵기 때문에 그 디자인의 유효성을 검사하려면 결국 충분한 사전 대책을 세운 후에 건설해서 자연 속에서 그것이 어떻게 견디는지를 보는 것뿐이라는 내용이므로, 요약문의 빈칸 (A), (B)에 들어갈 말로는 ② 'simulation(시뮬레이션) – construct(건설하다)'가 가장 적절하다.
① 시뮬레이션 – 견본을 만들다
③ 변화 – 강화하다
④ 간파 – 검사하다
⑤ 간파 – 복제하다

도입	거대한 건축물들은 쉽게 검증될 수 없음
부연	축소판 모델을 사용해도, 자연력을 완전히 모델링하는 것은 불가능함
결론	검사 방법은 사전 대책을 세운 후에 건설하고 자연 속에서 어떻게 견디는지를 보는 것임

구문

• This is the civil engineering project — [the dam, tunnel, building, bridge] — whose scale is **so** large, whose cost is **so** great, and whose design is **so** specific to the site **that** the structure is unique.
: [ ]는 the civil engineering project의 구체적인 예를 나타내는 동격 어구이다. 세 개의 so는 that과 연결되어 '너무 ~해서 …하다'의 의미를 나타낸다.

11~12

정답 11 ⑤   12 ⑤

경제 성장은 매우 최근의 현상이다. 사실, 인류가 살아온 30만 년의 대부분 기간 동안, 경제 생활은 비교적 침체되어 있었다. 우리의 더 먼 조상들은 단지 살아남기 위해 얼마 없지만 필요한 모든 것을 사냥하고 채집했을 뿐이며, 그 정도가 다였다. 하지만 지난 몇백 년 동안, 그 경제적 휴지는 완전히 끝났다. 한 개인이 생산하는 양은 약 13배 증가했고, 세계 생산량은 거의 300배 증가했다. 인간 존재의 합이 한 시간이라고 상상해 보면, 대부분의 이러한 활동은 마지막 0.5초 정도에, 즉 말 그대로 눈 깜짝할 사이에 일어났다.
경제학자들은 이러한 성장이, 단지 그것이 시작된 곳과 시기에 그것이 시작되었던 이유에 대해서는 아니더라도, 18세기 말로 향하던 서유럽에서 지속적인 기술적 진보에 의해 추진되었다는 데 서로 동의하는 경향이 있다. 한 가지 이유는 지리적 이유일 수 있는데, 일부 국가들은 풍부한 자원, 쾌적한 기후, 그리고 무역을 위해 쉽게 횡단할 수 있는 해안과 강을 가지고 있었기 때문이다. 또 다른 이유는 문화일 수 있는데, 매우 다른 지적 역사와 종교에 의해 형성된 서로 다른 공동체의 사람들이 과학적인 방법, 재정, 근면, 그리고 서로(한 사회에서 '신뢰'의 수준은 중요하다고 한다)에 대해 다른 태도를 가지고 있었다. 그러나 가장 일반적인 설명은 개인적인(→ 제도적인) 것이다. 어떤 국가는 재산권을 보호하고 위험 감수, 정력적 활동, 혁신을 장려하는 방식으로 법의 지배를 시행한 반면, 다른 국가는 그렇지 않았다.

해설

11 첫 번째 단락에서 경제 성장은 매우 최근의 현상이라고 말하고 있고, 두 번째 단락에서는 그 다양한 원인들에 대해 말하고 있으므로, 글의 제목으로 가장 적절한 것은 ⑤ '무엇이 인간 경제 활동의 폭발적인 성장을 야기했는가?'이다.
① 전 시대에 걸쳐 적용되는 경제 이론
② 인간의 경제적 탐욕의 불행한 결과
③ 인간은 경제 발전을 통해 무엇을 잃었는가?
④ 경제 활동: 인간의 기본적 욕구를 반영한 거울

12 두 번째 단락의 내용은 경제적 활동이 폭발적으로 성장한 다양한 원인에 대해 설명하고 있으며, (e) 뒤에 국가적 차원에서 경제적 활동을 장려한다는 내용이 이어지고 있으므로, ⑤의 'personal(개인적인)'은 'institutional(제도적인)'과 같은 낱말로 바꾸어야 한다.

도입	경제 성장은 매우 최근의 현상임
원인 1	지리적 이유 – 풍부한 자원, 쾌적한 기후, 무역에 용이한 해안과 강
원인 2	문화적 이유 – 서로 다른 공동체가 과학적인 방법, 재정 등에 대해 다른 태도를 가지고 있음
원인 3	제도적인 이유 – 국가적 차원에서 경제적 활동을 장려하는 법을 시행함

구문

• Economists tend to agree with one another [that this growth was propelled by sustained technological progress, {though not on the reasons why it started just where and when it did} — in Western Europe, toward the end of the eighteenth century].
: [ ]는 agree의 목적어 역할을 하는 명사절이다. 그 안의 { }는 though this growth was not propelled on the reasons ~에서 this growth was propelled가 생략된 부사절이다.

고난도 모의고사 09회

01 ⑤	02 ②	03 ④	04 ⑤	05 ②	06 ④
07 ③	08 ⑤	09 ⑤	10 ③	11 ①	12 ③

01

정답 ⑤

Steven Johnson은 2005년에 낸 자신의 저서 'Everything Bad Is Good for You'에서 컴퓨터 사용자들의 뇌에서 보이는 광범위한 풍부한 신경 활동을 책을 읽는 사람들의 뇌에서 분명하게 보이는 훨씬 더 조용한 활동과 대조했다. 그 비교는 그로 하여금 컴퓨터 사용이 독서보다 정신에 대한 더 집중적인 자극을 제공한다고 말하게 만들었다. 그는 신경에서 보이는 증거에 의하면 심지어 '독서는 오랜 시간에 걸쳐 감각을 덜 자극한다'라는 결론을 내리도록 이끌 수도 있다고 썼다. 그러나 비록 Johnson의 진단이 정확하기는 하지만, 서로 다른 뇌의 활동에 대한 그의 해석은 오해의 소지가 있다. 그 활동을 그토록 지적으로 도움이 되게 만들어 주는 것은 독서가 '감각을 덜 자극한다'는 바로 그 사실이다. 우리가 산만하게 하는 것들을 거르고 전두엽의 문제 해결 기능을 진정시키도록 해 줌으로써, 깊은 독서는 깊은 사색의 한 형태가 된다. 경험이 많은 독서가의 정신은 고요한 정신이며 시끄러운 것이 아니다. 우리의 뉴런 발화에 관한 한, 더 많은 것이 더 좋다고 추정하는 것은 오류이다.

해설

Steven Johnson의 견해와는 달리, 독서의 약한 자극이 전두엽의 문제 해결 기능을 진정시킴으로써 깊은 사색을 가능하게 하기 때문에 지적으로 도움이 된다는 내용이므로, 밑줄 친 부분이 글에서 의미하는 바로 가장 적절한 것은 ⑤ '독서의 부드러운 정신적 자극은 지적 능력에 더 유익하다'이다.
① 더 많은 구두 산출량이 바람직하다고 믿는 것은 잘못되었다
② 다른 감각 기관의 신호는 같은 가치를 가지지 않는다
③ 컴퓨터와의 지나친 상호 작용은 사람들을 너무 예민하게 만든다
④ 신경 세포를 고요하게 유지하는 것은 우리가 피로를 느끼는 것을 막지 못한다

TEXT FLOW

도입	Steven Johnson은 컴퓨터 사용자들의 뇌와 책을 읽는 사람들의 뇌 활동을 대조함
부연	컴퓨터 사용이 독서보다 정신에 대한 더 집중적인 자극을 제공한다고 말함
반전	독서가 '감각을 덜 자극한다'는 그 사실이 우리를 지적으로 만들어 주는 것임
결론	뉴런 발화에 있어서는 더 많은 것이 꼭 더 좋은 것은 아님

구문

• Steven Johnson, in his 2005 book *Everything Bad Is Good for You*, **contrasted** [the widespread, teeming neural activity {seen in the brains of computer users}] **with** [the much more muted activity {evident in the brains of book readers}].
: 'A와 B를 대조하다'를 뜻하는 「contrast A with B」가 쓰였고, 두 개의 [ ]는 각각 A, B에 해당한다. 첫 번째 [ ] 안의 { }는 the widespread, teeming neural activity를 수식하고, 두 번째 [ ] 안의 { }는 the much more muted activity를 수식한다.

• It is [the very fact {that book reading "understimulates the senses"}] that makes the activity so intellectually rewarding.
: 「it is ~ that ...」 강조구문이 사용되어 주어 [ ]가 강조되었다. [ ] 안의 { }는 the very fact의 동격절이다.

02

정답 ②

진보라는 개념에 대해 자주 선언되는 위기의 결과 중 하나는 미래는 문제적이 되고 현재가 절대적인 것이 된다는 것이다. 우리는 현재가 군주이자 주인인 역사성의 체제에 우리 자신이 있다는 것을 발견한다. 이것은 현 입법 기관, 단기, 소비 지상주의, 우리 세대, 근접성 등의 억압적인 힘이다. 이것은 금융 부문에, 투자보다는 수익에, 회사의 화합보다는 비용 절감에 특권을 주는 경제이다. 우리는 더는 공간과 관련이 없고 시간과 관련이 있는 제국주의, 즉 모든 것을 식민지화하는 현재의 제국주의를 실천한다. 스스로를 희생하는 삶으로 이루어진 미래에 대한 식민지화와 그 미래를 흡수해 그것을 기생적으로 먹고 사는 현재의 제국주의가 있다. Bertman은 그것을 '지금의 힘', 즉 시간의 어떤 다른 차원에 투자되지 않는 현재의 힘이라고 부른다. 이러한 현재가 장기를 단기로, 지속성을 즉각성으로, 영구성을 일시성으로, 기억을 감각으로, 비전을 충동으로 대체한다.

해설

진보에 대한 생각의 위기에 따른 결과 중 하나는 현재가 절대적인 것이 되어, 미래와 관련된 모든 것을 식민지화하는 현재의 제국주의라는 내용이므로, 글의 제목으로 가장 적절한 것은 ② '미래에 대한 현재의 횡포'이다.
① 미래의 내재적 불확실성
③ 현재의 위기, 미래의 투쟁
④ 진보의 개념: 미래를 위한 계획
⑤ 현재와 미래 간의 협력

TEXT FLOW

도입	진보의 개념에 대한 위기는 미래는 문제적이 되고 현재가 절대적이 되는 것임
부연	우리는 현재가 주인이고 모든 것을 식민지화하는 현재의 제국주의를 실천함
결론	이러한 현재가 장기를 단기로, 지속성을 즉각성으로, 영구성을 일시성으로 대체함

구문

• One of the consequences of the oft-proclaimed crisis of the idea of progress is [that {the future becomes problematic} and {the present is rendered absolute}].
: [ ]는 주격 보어 역할을 하는 명사절이고, 두 개의 절 { }가 and로 연결되어 that에 이어진다.

03

정답 ④

재촬영은 시간이 어떻게 원래 장면을 변화시켰는지 보여 주기 위해 사진작가가 이전에 찍었던 피사체로 돌아가 똑같은 사진을 다시 만들려고 시도하는 때이다. 돌아가는 사진작가가 원래 장면을 더 쉽게 복제할 수 있도록 정확한 기록이 유지된다. 원본 사진과 새로운 사진은 비교하기 쉽도록 보통 서로 나란히 전시된다. 또 다른 형태의 재촬영에서 사진작가는 일정 기간 동안 똑같은 피사체로 돌아온다. 이것의 예는 일주일 동안 매일 여러분 자신의 사

진을 찍는 것에서부터 수십 년에 걸쳐 Georgia O'Keeffe를 찍은 Alfred Stieglitz의 사진에 이르기까지 다양할 것이다. 사진작가와 피사체의 관계는 일정 기간 동안 추구된다. 그 결과는 느낌, 빛, 분위기의 변화로 인해 이 조합에서 생길 수 있는 광범위한 시각적 가능성을 나타낼 것이다.

해설

④ 관계절 안의 술어 동사 span의 주어의 핵은 Georgia O'Keeffe가 아니라 photographs이므로, who를 that이나 which로 바꾸어야 한다.
① returns와 and로 연결되어 when절의 주어인 a photographer의 술어 역할을 하고 있으므로, attempts는 어법상 적절하다.
② 비교급 more와 함께 쓰여 duplicate를 수식하는 부사 easily는 어법상 적절하다.
③ 목적을 나타내는 to부정사구를 이끄는 to make는 어법상 적절하다.
⑤ 관계절의 수식을 받는 the broad range of visual possibilities는 produce의 행위를 당하는 대상이므로, be 다음에 쓰여 수동태를 이루는 과거분사 produced는 어법상 적절하다.

TEXT FLOW

도입	재촬영은 시간이 어떻게 장면을 변화시켰는지 보여 주기 위해 이전에 찍었던 피사체로 똑같은 사진을 다시 만드는 것임
부연	원본 사진과 새로운 사진은 비교하기 위해 나란히 전시됨
전환	또 다른 형태의 재촬영은 일정 기간 동안 똑같은 피사체로 돌아옴
결론	그 결과 느낌, 빛, 분위기 변화의 조합으로 광범위한 시각적 가능성을 나타내게 됨

04

사회생활은 인간의 본능에서 비롯된다. 인간의 본능은 인간화된 본능과 비인간화된 본능을 포함한다. 인간화된 본능은 원래 인간적인 것과 관련되어 이용된다. 비인간화된 본능은 원래 비인간적인 것과 관련되어 이용된다. 사회적 동물 사이에서는 같은 종의 동물에게 다른 종의 동물에게와 다르게 행동하는 것이 꽤 흔한 일이다. 예를 들어, 식인 풍습과 같은 종의 동물들 사이의 살상은 심지어 같은 종들 간에 싸우는 중에도 사회적 동물에는 드문 일이다. 지배의 목적으로 같은 종의 동물들 간에 싸우는 것은 의례적인 경우가 흔하고 심각한 부상을 입히지 않는다. 같은 종의 동물들로 인한 동물들의 새끼에 대한 해악은 잦은 일이 아니다. 반면에, 포식자로서 동물은 주저 없이 다른 종의 먹잇감을 죽인다. 먹잇감으로서 동물은 다른 종의 포식자로부터 탈출하기 위해 교묘하게 다루는 전략을 세운다. 동물은 다른 종의 동물과 같은 종의 동물 사이를 불분명하게(→ 분명하게) 구별한다.

해설

사회생활은 인간의 본능에서 비롯되며, 사회적 동물 사이에서는 같은 종의 동물에게 다른 종의 동물에게와 다르게 행동하는 것이 꽤 흔한 일이라는 내용의 글로, 동물은 다른 종의 동물과 같은 종의 동물 사이를 분명하게 구별한다는 내용이 되어야 자연스러우므로, ⑤의 'vague(불분명한)'를 'clear(분명한)'와 같은 낱말로 바꾸어야 한다.

TEXT FLOW

도입	사회생활은 인간의 본능에서 비롯됨
전개	사회적 동물 사이에는 같은 종의 동물에게 다른 종의 동물에게와 다르게 행동하는 것이 흔함
예시	같은 종의 동물들 사이의 싸움과 살상은 드물지만, 포식자로서 주저 없이 다른 종의 먹잇감은 죽임

결론	동물은 다른 종의 동물과 같은 종의 동물 사이를 분명하게 구별함

구문

• **It** is quite common among social animals [to behave **differently** toward animals of the same species **than** toward animals of different species].
: It은 가주어이고, [ ]가 진주어이다. differently than은 differently from의 의미로 미국식 영어에서 종종 사용된다.

05
정답 ②

왜 어떤 사람들은 음모론적 사고를 하는데 다른 사람들은 그렇지 않을까? 부풀려진 자신감이나 낮은 자존감 같은 요인과 관련된 다양한 심리적인 이론이 제시되어 왔다. 음모론은 몇몇 사람이 거대하고도 혼란스럽게 하는 사건에 직면하여 불안과 통제력 상실의 느낌을 다루기 위해 사용하는 대처 메커니즘이라는 것이 더 대중적인 합의인 것 같다. 인간의 뇌는 무작위적인 사건을 좋아하지 않는데, 그것은 우리가 그것으로부터 배울 수 없고 따라서 그것을 계획할 수 없기 때문이다. (이해 부족, 사건의 규모, 그것의 개인적 영향 또는 우리의 사회적 지위로 인해) 우리가 무력감을 느낄 때, 우리는 우리가 맞설 수 있는 적을 정의하는 설명에 마음이 끌릴 수 있다. 이것은 이성적인 과정이 아니며, 음모론을 연구한 연구자들은 '직감을 따르는' 경향이 있는 사람들이 음모론에 기반한 사고를 할 가능성이 가장 높다고 지적한다. 이것이 바로 무지가 음모론에 대한 믿음과 매우 관련되어 있는 이유이다. 우리가 자신의 분석적인 능력에 기반하여 무언가를 이해할 수 있는 능력이 더 적으면, 우리는 그것에 의해 더 큰 위협을 느낄 수도 있다.

해설

음모론적 사고를 하는 이유는 불안과 통제력 상실의 느낌을 다루기 위한 대처 메커니즘이 발동되기 때문이며, 이것은 이성적인 과정이 아니어서 무지가 음모론에 대한 믿음과 매우 관련되어 있다는 내용이므로, 빈칸에는 앞의 less에 유의하여 불안과 통제력 상실, 비이성적, 무지 등과 상반되는 맥락의 말이 와야 한다. 따라서 빈칸에 들어갈 말로 가장 적절한 것은 ② '자신의 분석적인 능력에 기반하여 무언가를 이해할'이다.
① 음모론 주장에 대해 회의적인 태도를 유지할
③ 신뢰성이나 증거가 부족한 어떠한 생각도 품는 것을 거부할
④ 사건에 대한 우리의 편향된 시각으로 다른 사람들에게 영향을 미칠
⑤ 자신의 이익과 무관한 것을 간과하거나 무시할

TEXT FLOW

도입	음모론은 사건에 직면하여 불안과 통제력 상실의 느낌을 다루기 위한 대처 메커니즘임
부연 1	우리가 무력감을 느낄 때, 우리는 우리가 맞설 수 있는 적을 정의하는 설명에 마음이 끌림
부연 2	무지가 음모론에 대한 믿음과 매우 관련이 있음
결론	자신의 능력에 기반하여 분석하고 이해할 수 있는 능력이 적을수록 더 큰 위협을 느낌

구문

• Various psychological theories have been offered, [involving factors such as inflated self-confidence or low self-esteem].
: [ ]는 Various psychological theories를 수식하는 현재분사구이며, 주어가 길어지는 것을 피하기 위해 문장의 뒤에 쓰였다.

정답 및 해설 **43**

친숙한 속담의 사례를 주어진 상황에서 인식하는 행동은 그 상황의 새로운 이해에 도움을 줄 수 있다. 그것은 상황의 피상적인 세부 사항을 훨씬 넘어서는 신선하고, 추상적이며, 자명하지 않은 관점을 제공한다. 속담은 다소 미묘하고 복잡한 범주의 표지이므로, 속담을 상황에 적용하는 것은 그렇지 않으면 숨겨져 있을 수도 있는 측면을 끌어내는 방법이다. 비록 어쩌면 편향된 종류의 이해일지라도, 속담을 표지로 이용하는 것은 보고 있는 것을 이해하는 방식이다. 갓 마주한 상황에 속담을 적용하면 순전히 논리적인 분석이 아니라 보는 것을 속담의 렌즈를 통해 걸러내는 데서 나오는 일종의 통찰력을 얻게 된다. 요약하자면, 속담은 서로 비유로 모두 연결되어 있는 과거, 현재, 미래, 가상 등 일련의 매우 다양한 상황에 대한 편리하고도 간결한 표지이다.

해설

친숙한 속담의 사례를 주어진 상황에 적용하는 것은 신선하고, 추상적이며, 자명하지 않은 관점을 제공하고, 보고 있는 것을 속담의 렌즈를 통해 걸러내는 데서 나오는 통찰력을 얻게 된다는 내용이므로, 빈칸에 들어갈 말로 가장 적절한 것은 ④ '그렇지 않으면 숨겨져 있을 수도 있는 측면을 끌어내는'이다.
① 다른 사람들의 관점을 바꾸기 위해 논리와 감정을 결합하는
② 오래되고 쓸모없는 범주에 새로운 경험을 넣는
③ 새로운 아이디어를 전달하기 위해 통념을 빌리는
⑤ 상황을 이해하는 데 필수적인 세부 사항을 제거하는

⚡ WHY 고난도

주제문에 사용된 표현 일부를 putting new experiences, deliver a fresh idea 등으로 패러프레이징하여 구성한 매력적 오답이 있는 고난도 문제이다.

TEXT FLOW

도입	친숙한 속담의 사례를 주어진 상황에서 인식하는 행동은 그 상황의 이해를 도움
부연 1	속담을 상황에 적용하는 것은 그렇지 않으면 숨겨져 있을 수도 있는 측면을 끌어내는 방법임
부연 2	또한 속담의 렌즈를 통해 걸러내는 데서 나오는 일종의 통찰력을 얻게 됨
결론	속담은 서로 비유로 연결된 다양한 상황에 대한 간결한 표지임

구문

• [The act of {recognizing ⟨in a given situation⟩ a case of a familiar proverb}] can cast new light on the situation.
: [ ]는 문장의 주어이며, 그 안의 { }는 The act와 동격 관계의 명사구이다. ⟨ ⟩는 recognizing과 목적어 a case of a familiar proverb 사이에 삽입된 부사구이다.

개념을 연구할 때, 우리는 그 개념이 '살고 있는' 이론적 환경뿐만 아니라, 그것과 관련된 관찰, 실험, 그리고 측정 관행에서도 그것의 궤적을 따라가야 한다. 이러한 관행은 과학적 개념의 의미를 상술(詳述)하는 데 중요한 역할을 한다. 관찰과 실험은 그것에 기인하는 관찰 및 실험 상황을 설명하기 위해 그것의 지시 대상이 가져야 할 특성의 종류를 나타냄으로써 개념의 표현을 유도한다. (실험을 할 때, 과학자들은 모든 잠재적인 편향의 원천을 인지하고, 진실로부터의 이탈을 줄이고 최소화하기 위해 가능한 모든 조치를 취해야 한

다.) 예를 들어, 20세기 초 전자 개념의 표현은 그것에 기인하는 실험적 현상에 의해 유도되었다. 한 가지 예만 언급하자면, 수소 스펙트럼의 이산 구조는 수소 원자의 에너지 수준의 이산 구조를 나타냈는데, 그렇게 함으로써 원자 내 전자 궤도의 양자화를 나타냈다.

해설

개념을 연구할 때는 그 개념의 이론적 환경뿐만 아니라 그 개념과 관련된 관찰, 실험, 측정 관행에서도 그것의 궤적을 따라가야 한다는 내용의 글이므로, 실험을 할 때 모든 잠재적인 편향의 원천을 인지하고, 진실로부터의 이탈을 줄이고 최소화하기 위해 가능한 모든 조치를 취해야 한다는 내용의 ③은 전체 글의 흐름과 관계가 없다.

TEXT FLOW

주제	개념을 연구할 때, 그 개념의 이론적 환경뿐만 아니라 관찰, 실험, 측정 관행에서도 개념의 궤적을 따라가야 함
부연	관찰과 실험은 그것의 지시 대상이 가져야 할 특성을 나타냄으로써 개념의 표현을 유도함
예시	20세기 초 전자 개념의 표현은 그것에 기인하는 실험적 현상에 의해 유도되었음

구문

• Observation and experimentation guide the articulation of concepts, **by** indicating the kinds of properties [that their referents should have {in order to account for the observational and experimental situations ⟨attributed to them⟩}].
: by 이하는 앞 문장을 수식하는 전치사구로, [ ]는 the kinds of properties를 수식하는 관계절이고, 그 안의 { }는 목적을 나타내는 to부정사구이다. ⟨ ⟩는 the observational and experimental situations를 수식하는 과거분사구이다.

단순한 마술에 비해 음악적인 치유의 장점은 의식으로서의 효능으로 볼 때 특히 분명하다. 마술사의 경우처럼, 단 한 명의 개인만을 수반하는 의식은 사회적 유대에 기여하지 않으며 구경꾼의 감정을 고무하거나 격앙시키지 않는다. (C) 반대로 음악은 이러한 것들을 할 수 있을 뿐만 아니라 그것들을 성취하는 데 있어서 우리가 소유한 단 하나의 가장 강력한 도구일 수도 있다. 어떤 힘이 음악보다 그룹 통합, 의식적 힘, 꿈같은 영감 또는 감정적 강도에 더 잘 기여할까? (B) 의식을 연극 공연과 유사하게 봐야 한다면, 마법의 주문은 관객 없는 연극이다. 그 연기자는 아무리 감동적이거나 웅변적이든, 그 혼잣말을 감상할 사람이 아무도 없이 외로운 독백을 하고 있다. (A) 반대로, 음악적 치유의 의식은 고유의 집단적 매력을 지닌 '모두 노래하고, 모두 춤추는' 호화로운 제작물이다. 치료 효능의 문제를 고려하지 않더라도 음악 의식의 우월성은 분명히 드러난다.

해설

마술과는 다른 음악적 치유의 장점을 언급하며, 단 한 명의 개인만을 수반하는 마술사의 의식은 사회적 유대에 기여하지 않는다는 주어진 글 다음에는, 그와 반대로 음악은 통합에 기여할 수 있다는 (C)가 온 후, 앞선 내용을 보다 더 구체화해, 의식을 연극 공연에 비유하여 마법 주문을 관객 없는 연극이라고 하며 마법의 한계를 언급하는 (B)가 온 다음, 반대로 음악 의식은 '모두 노래하고, 모두 춤추는' 제작물이라며 음악 의식의 우월성을 언급하는 (A)가 마지막에 오는 것이 글의 순서로 가장 적절하다.

단순히 지시어나 대명사의 의미를 규명해서 해결하기보다는 단락 간 의미의
유사성, 논리적 흐름 등을 고려해야 풀 수 있는 고난도 문제이다.

TEXT FLOW

도입	마술에 비해 음악적인 치유의 장점은 의식으로서의 효능으로 볼 때 분명함
부연	마술사처럼 한 명의 개인을 수반하는 의식은 사회적 유대에 기여하지 않고 구경꾼의 감정을 고무하지 않지만, 음악은 그렇게 할 수 있음
비유	마법의 주문은 관객 없는 연극이고, 음악 의식은 '모두 노래하고 모두 춤추는' 제작물임
결론	음악 의식의 우월성이 분명함

구문

• The performer is engaged in a lonely monologue [with no one to appreciate the soliloquy], [no matter how moving or eloquent].

: 첫 번째 [ ]는 부대 상황을 나타내는 전치사구이다. 두 번째 [ ]는 no matter how moving or eloquent it is에서 it is가 생략된 양보절이다.

09
정답 ⑤

공간을 나타내는 전치사는 그 자체로도 흥미로울 뿐 아니라 다른 많은 이유로도 흥미롭다. 예를 들어, 그것들은 제2언어를 공부할 때 습득하기 가장 힘든 표현들에 속한다. 이것은 언어가 공간의 관계에 언어적인 용어를 배치하는 방식이 서로 다르기 때문이다. 예를 들어, 스페인어에는 영어의 'in'과 'on' 두 가지 의미를 다 보여 주는 하나의 단어 'en'이 있다. 정반대로, 다른 언어들은 '포함'과 '지탱'의 관계를 영어에서보다 더 세분한다. 예를 들어, 네덜란드어에는 영어의 'on'에 상응하는 두 개의 단어가 있는데, 'aan'은 '손잡이가 찬장 문에(on) 달려 있다'와 같은 경우에 사용되고 'op'은 '컵이 탁자 위에(on) 있다'와 같은 경우에 사용된다. 게다가, 영어에서처럼 'in'과 'on'을 다루는 두 개의 용어를 가진 언어들은 가끔 영어에서와 같은 방식으로 그렇게 하지 않는다. 예를 들어, 핀란드어에서 '손잡이가 찬장 문에(on) 달려 있다'와 '그릇 안에(in) 사과가 있다'에 상응하는 것이 한데 묶여 접미사 '-ssa'로 끝나는 반면, '컵이 탁자 위에(on) 있다'에는 접미사 '-lla'가 사용된다.

해설

주어진 문장은 영어에서처럼 'in'과 'on'을 다루는 용어가 모두 있는 언어라 할지라도 영어와 다른 방식으로 그것을 쓰는 때가 있다는 내용이다. ⑤ 뒤에 이어지는 핀란드어가 바로 그 사례에 해당하므로, 주어진 문장은 ⑤에 들어가는 것이 가장 적절하다.

TEXT FLOW

주제	공간을 나타내는 전치사는 습득하기 힘든 표현에 속함
예시 1	스페인어 'en'은 영어의 'in'과 'on' 두 가지를 다 보여 주는 단어임
예시 2	네덜란드어에는 영어의 'on'에 상응하는 단어로 'aan'과 'op' 두 단어가 있음
전개	영어처럼 'in'과 'on'이 있는 언어라도 같은 방식으로 사용하지 않음
예시 3	핀란드어에서는 영어의 'on'과 'in'을 묶어서 접미사 '-ssa', 'on'은 '-lla'가 사용됨

구문

• This is because languages differ in the way [in which they map linguistic terms onto spatial relations].

: [ ]는 the way를 수식하는 관계절이다.

10
정답 ③

비용을 제외하고, 법적 권리가 항상 축소나 제한의 대상이 되어야 하는 한 가지 중요한 이유는 권리가 실제로 다른 사람들에게 행사될 수 있는 법적 권한이기 때문이다. 권한은 항상 나쁜 목적으로 사용될 수 있다. 권리는 부당한 목적을 위한 그것의 불법 이용을 막기 위해 제약을 받아야 한다. 예를 들어, 정당방위에 대한 권리는 미국 법에서 잘 규정되어 있지만, 그것은 오로지 법원이 그것의 남용을 감시하고 있기 때문에, 또는 법원이 그것의 남용을 감시하고 있는 한에서만 정당하다. 예를 들어, 심각한 위험에 처하지 않았다면 여러분은 정당방위였음을 주장할 수 없다. 마찬가지로, 주주가 회사의 경영진을 고소할 수 있는 권리는 괴롭히기 위해서, 그리고 결국 소송 취하에 대한 상당한 뇌물을 얻기 위해 사용될 수 있다. 남용 소송의 가능성은 소송을 제기할 권리가 무산되는 조건을 결정하는 입법자와 판사들에 의해 고려되어야 한다. 미국의 법체계는 정부가 개인에게 공권력을 행사할 수 있는 재량권을 줄 때마다 필연적으로 발생하는 의도치 않은 부작용을 처리하기 위해 지속적으로 개선적이고 보완적 조정을 한다.

➡ 정당방위에 대한 권리와 회사 경영진을 고소할 수 있는 주주의 권리를 포함한 법적 권리는 제한되어야 하는데, 왜냐하면 그것들이 다른 사람들에게 행사될 때 오용될 수 있기 때문이다.

해설

정당방위권과 회사 경영진을 고소할 수 있는 주주의 권리 같은 법적 권리는 다른 사람들에게 행사될 수 있는 법적 권한으로, 나쁜 목적으로 사용될 수 있기 때문에 축소 또는 제한되어야 한다는 내용의 글이다. 따라서 요약문의 빈칸 (A), (B)에 들어갈 말로는 ③ 'restricted(제한되다) – misused(오용되다)'가 가장 적절하다.

① 바로잡다 – 공유되다
② 바로잡다 – 거부되다
④ 제한되다 – 정당화되다
⑤ 포기되다 – 편향되다

TEXT FLOW

주제	법적 권리가 제한의 대상이 되어야 하는 이유는 권리가 실제로 다른 사람들에게 행사될 수 있는 법적 권한이기 때문임
예시 1	정당방위는 법원이 그것의 남용을 감시하고 있어서 심각한 위험에 처하지 않으면 주장할 수 없음
예시 2	주주가 회사의 경영진을 고소할 수 있는 권리도 입법자와 판사들에 의해 고려됨
결론	미국은 개인에게 공권력을 행사할 수 있는 재량권에 대해 발생하는 부작용을 처리하기 위해 보완적 조정을 함

구문

• You cannot claim **to have acted** in self-defense, for example, if you were not seriously endangered.

: 현재 시제 claim보다 더 먼저 발생한 과거의 내용이므로 완료 부정사 to have acted를 사용했다.

구문

• However, **it** is a crucial characteristic of monopolistic competition [that there are enough sellers {that each assumes its pricing decisions will not provoke a reaction from the others}].

: it은 가주어이고 [ ]가 진주어이다. { }는 enough와 함께 사용되어 '~할 정도로 충분한'의 의미를 나타낸다.

그 이름이 시사하듯이, 독점 경쟁은 독점의 요소와 경쟁의 요소가 혼합된 시장 구조의 일종이다. 전형적으로, 그 산업은 중간 정도의 수에서부터 많은 수의 판매자들을 포함하고 있는데, 그들의 상품은 동질적이라기보다는 차별화된다. 도서 출판, 신발 및 의류 제조, 자동차 수리가 그 예이다. 이러한 각각의 산업에서 많은 수의 회사들이 서로의 비슷한 대체물인 제품이나 서비스를 판매하고 있기 때문에 경쟁이 있다. 그러나 각 회사가 자체 브랜드, 유형, 품질, 또는 디자인에 대한 독점을 갖고 있는 한 독점의 요소 또한 존재한다. 그러나 각 판매자의 가격 결정이 다른 판매자들로부터 반응을 불러일으키지 않을 것이라고 가정할 정도로 충분한 판매자가 있다는 것이 독점 경쟁의 매우 중요한 특징이다. 다시 말해서, 회사는 가격에 의존한다(→ 가격에 의존하지 않는다).

공연 예술 산업의 개별 부문 중에서, 브로드웨이 극장은 독점적으로 경쟁력이 있다고 정확히 묘사될 수 있다. 30편 이상의 연극과 뮤지컬이 단일 시즌 동안 열리고, 분명히 관객을 위해 서로 경쟁한다. 그러나 각 회사는 분명히 자체의 쇼에 대한 독점을 갖고 있고 그 자체의 정책이 경쟁자들로부터 반응을 불러일으키지 않을 것이라는 가정 하에 가격을 책정한다. 만약 우리가 모든 라이브 공연 예술이 단일한 산업을 구성하는 더 넓은 정의를 채택한다면, 대부분의 대도시에서 그 산업 자체는 독점적으로 경쟁력이 있다. 즉 오페라단, 교향악단, 무용단, 상주 극단 회사는 독특하지만 예술 오락 형태로서 비슷하게 대체 가능한 상품을 제공함으로써 서로와 경쟁한다.

해설

11 독점 경쟁은 독점의 요소와 경쟁의 요소가 혼합된 시장 구조의 일종으로, 도서 출판, 신발 및 의류 제조, 자동차 수리가 그것에 속하고, 두 번째 문단에서도 공연 예술 및 정의를 더 넓게 할 경우 오페라단, 교향악단, 무용단, 상주 극단 회사 역시도 독점 경쟁에 속한다는 것을 기술하며, 이 산업들 각각에서 많은 수의 회사가 서로의 비슷한 대체물로서의 제품이나 서비스를 판매하고 다른 경쟁자들과 가격 면에서 독립적인 특징을 가지고 있다는 내용이므로, 글의 제목으로 가장 적절한 것은 ① '독점 경쟁의 특징 및 사례'이다.
② 독점 경쟁 이론의 짧은 역사
③ 공연 예술 산업의 폭발적 성장
④ 독점 산업의 장단점
⑤ 독점 경쟁 시장에서 살아남는 법

12 독점 경쟁 관계에 있는 판매자들은 자신들의 가격 결정이 다른 판매자들로부터 반응을 불러일으키지 않을 것이라는 가정 하에 충분한 판매자가 있다는 것이 독점 경쟁의 특징이라고 했으므로, 회사는 가격에 의존하지 않는다는 것을 알 수 있다. 따라서 ③의 'price-dependent(가격에 의존하는)'를 'price-independent(가격에 의존하지 않는)'와 같은 낱말로 바꾸어야 한다.

TEXT FLOW

도입	독점 경쟁은 독점 요소와 경쟁의 요소가 혼합된 시장 구조의 일종임
전개 1	이 산업은 서로 비슷한 제품, 서비스를 판매하고 있어서 경쟁이 있고 상품은 차별화됨
전개 2	그러나 각 회사가 자체 브랜드, 디자인 등에 독점을 가지고 있고, 가격에 의존하지 않음
예시	브로드웨이 극장, 교향악단, 오페라단, 무용단, 상주 극단 회사는 독점적으로 경쟁력이 있음

고난도 모의고사 10회

| 01 ④ | 02 ② | 03 ⑤ | 04 ④ | 05 ① | 06 ④ |
| 07 ⑤ | 08 ③ | 09 ⑤ | 10 ② | 11 ③ | 12 ④ |

01
정답 ④

현재의 관점에 따라 과거를 고쳐 만드는 보존 행위는 사실상 과거를 현재에서 떼어 놓아서, 과거를 현재와 밀접하게 연결된 것이 아니라 별개의 분리된 영역처럼 보이게 한다. 과거의 차이점을 인식하는 것은 그것의 보존을 촉진하고, 그것을 보존하는 행위는 그 차이점을 훨씬 더 뚜렷하게 만든다. 특히 미국에서 유산은 흔히 현재와 공존하는 것이 허용되지 않고, 그 대신 울타리로 구분되어 '항상 따옴표와 화려한 복장을 걸치고 있고', 특별한 경우에 방문을 받는다. 과거의 모습을 국립 공원으로 돋보이게 하는 것은 이런 분리의 원인이 되고 그것은 역사는 나날이 더불어 살아가기보다는 방문하고 보아야 하는 것임을 암시한다. 마찬가지로, 지리학자 Yi-Fu Tuan이 쓰는 것처럼, 과거와 관련된 특정한 삶의 방식을 보존하는 것은 '박물관에서처럼 그것들을 라벨이 붙여져서 분류된 유리 상자 속의 형상으로 변환'하는데, 이는 더 직설적으로 '지리학적 박제술'이라고 묘사되는 접근법이다.

해설
현재의 관점에 따라 역사를 고치는 행위로 인해 과거가 현재와 분리된 별개의 영역처럼 보이게 된다는 내용의 글이다. 따라서 밑줄 친 부분의 의미로 가장 적절한 것은 ④ '결코 일상생활의 통합된 일부로서 간주되지 않고'이다.
① 영원한 동경의 대상으로 간주되는
② 거의 남아 있지 않은 세부 사항의 보존 상태가 나쁜
③ 그 어느 때보다도 모두에게 더 쉬운 접근이 가능하도록 한
⑤ 특정한 목적을 위해 현재에 융합된

TEXT FLOW
도입	현재의 관점에 따라 과거를 고치는 행위는 이를 별개의 분리된 영역처럼 보이게 함
부연 1	미국에서 유산은 현재와 공존하지 않고 구분되어 특별한 경우에 방문을 받음
부연 2	국립 공원으로 만드는 것도 분리에 기여함
부연 3	과거의 특정한 삶의 방식을 보존하는 것은 지리학적 박제술이라고 묘사되는 접근법임

구문
• [Preservation's act of {reshaping the past according to the views of the present}] effectively distances the past from the present, **causing** it [to seem like {a distinct, separate realm}, **rather than** {something intimately connected with today}].
: 첫 번째 [ ]는 문장의 주어이며, 그 안의 { }는 Preservation's act와 동격 관계의 명사구이다. causing은 앞 문장 전체를 의미상의 주어로 하는 분사구문으로 which causes로 바꾸어 쓸 수 있다. 두 번째 [ ]는 causing의 목적격 보어인 to부정사구이고, 그 안의 두 개의 { }는 'B보다는 오히려 A'를 의미하는 「A rather than B」 구문의 A, B에 해당되며 병렬 구조를 이루고 있다.

02
정답 ②

인공 지능을 유럽 연합의 일반 개인정보 보호 규정에서 법으로 엄숙하게 명시된 '설명 가능하게' 만들겠다는 단체 운동은 '누구에게 설명 가능하게인가?'라는 질문을 하도록 요구한다. 다양한 이해 당사자들은 다양한 종류의 설명을 찾는다. 문제는 비교적 간단한 대출 위험 평가 시스템에서조차 발생한다. 소프트웨어 개발자들과 시스템 운영자들은 컴퓨터 시스템의 구성과 처리 매개 변수 측면에서 설명을 원한다. 최종 결정을 내리는 경험 많은 대출 직원은 그 시스템의 추천에서 다양한 요인들에 가중치가 주어진 방식을 알고 싶을 수도 있다. 대출을 거절당한 신청자는 정확하게 왜 그런지, '그것이 자신의 나이, 성별, 우편 번호, 잘못된 신용 기록 때문인지' 알고 싶어 한다. 규제 기관은 그 시스템이 데이터 사생활 보호를 손상하거나, 차별 금지법을 위반하거나, 금융 사기에 노출되게 하지 않은 상태라는 것을 확인하고자 한다. 일반인은 많은 인공 지능 체계가 불투명하다는 블랙박스 문제를 숙고하면서, 대체로 왜 누군가가 자신들이 이해할 수 없는 기계를 만들려 하는지 알고자 할 수도 있다.

해설
다양한 이해 당사자들이 인공 지능에 대해 각자의 업무나 이해와 관련하여 많은 것을 알고 싶어 한다는 요지의 글로, 대출 위험 평가 시스템의 예를 통해 이를 설명하고 있다. 소프트웨어 개발자, 시스템 운영자, 대출 직원, 대출 신청자, 규제 기관, 일반인은 인공 지능으로부터 각기 다른 설명을 원한다고 했으므로, 글의 제목으로 가장 적절한 것은 ② '인공 지능 작업에 대한 서로 다른 사용자들의 다양한 질문'이다.
① 위험 평가: 인공 지능 비서를 통한 간단한 작업
③ 가치에 대한 인공 지능의 이해는 우리와 어떻게 다른가
④ 인공 지능 시스템: 인류를 위한 최적의 블랙박스
⑤ 인공 지능 개발자들이 엄격한 규제에 시달리는 이유

TEXT FLOW
도입	인공 지능을 누구에게 설명 가능하게 만들 것인가?
주제	다양한 이해 당사자들은 다양한 종류의 설명을 찾음
예시	대출 위험 평가 시스템에서도 소프트웨어 개발자, 시스템 운영자, 대출 직원, 대출 신청자, 규제 기관, 일반인 모두 각기 다른 설명을 원함

구문
• The drive to make AI "explainable" — [solemnly stated in law in the European Union's General Data Protection Regulation]—demands [the question **be** asked: Explainable to whom?]
: 첫 번째 [ ]는 "explainable"을 구체적으로 설명하는 과거분사구이다. 두 번째 [ ]는 demands의 목적어 역할을 하는 명사절이고, demands가 '요구'를 나타내므로 should가 생략된 동사원형 be가 쓰였다.

03
정답 ⑤

로마 제국이 마침내 몰락했을 때, 가톨릭교회는 유럽에서 지배적인 구조가 되었다. 가톨릭교회는 로마 제국의 쾌락주의적인 풍습을 포함해서 로마 제국이 받아들였던 활동들을 거부했다. 이것의 한 예는 극문학에 관련된 사람은 세례를 받을 수 없다는 사실이었다. '나태는 영혼의 커다란 적이다'라는 개념이 생겨났고, 아무것도 하지 않는 것은 악하다고 여겨졌다. 이 시기에 교회는 귀족과 소작농으로 구성된 사회 질서에 큰 영향력을 행사했다. 성직자들이

사회의 가치를 좌우했는데, 그 가치의 채택은 그 당시 최고의 목표였던 영혼 구원으로 이어질 것이었다. 가톨릭교회가 무엇이 허용 가능하고 허용 가능하지 않은 여가 활동인지에 영향을 주긴 했지만, 많은 규칙이 매우 엄격해서 이 시기가 끝날 때 교회는 교회 내의 사람들이 다른 관점을 갖게 된 르네상스 시기를 경험했다. 이 르네상스 시기에는 다양한 여가 활동에 대한 새로운 이해가 일어났다.

해설

⑤ 주절에서 주어와 동사가 도치된 형태이고 many rules가 주어이므로 was를 복수형 동사 were로 바꿔야 한다.

① its는 The Catholic Church를 가리키므로 단수 소유 대명사 its는 적절하다.

② 문장의 동사는 was이므로, involved는 문장 내에서 people을 수식하는 분사임을 알 수 있다. 문맥상 사람들이 '관련된' 것이므로 수동을 의미하는 과거분사 involved는 적절하다.

③ 앞의 접속사 and로 연결되는 절의 주어를 이끄는 동명사 doing은 적절하다.

④ 앞의 societal values를 선행사로 취하여 부연 설명을 하고 adoption과 결합하여 문맥상 '가치의 채택'을 의미하며 절의 주어 역할을 해야 하므로 소유격 관계대명사 whose는 적절하다.

TEXT FLOW

도입	로마 제국이 몰락하여 지배적인 구조가 된 가톨릭교회는 로마 제국의 모든 활동을 거부했음
예시	극문학에 관련된 사람은 세례를 받을 수 없었음
전개 1	교회가 사회 질서에 큰 영향을 미치고, 성직자가 사회의 가치를 좌우했음
전개 2	규칙들이 엄격해서 이 시기가 끝날 때 교회는 르네상스 시기를 경험하게 됨

04
정답 ④

스포츠의 장대한 순간들은 신문, 시, 동영상의 준비된 이용 가능성에도 불구하고, 스틸 사진에 의해 가장 기억에 남게 포착된다. 유명한 승리나 몸짓의 순간에 대한 '시간이 정지된' 모습은 아마도 모든 미디어 스포츠 텍스트 중 가장 강력할 것이며, 역사적 무게, 감정, 유일무이하다는 느낌을 전달할 수 있다. 가장 기억할 만한 것들 중 하나는 Tommie Smith와 John Carlos가 1968년 멕시코 올림픽의 승리 단상에서 벌인 '블랙 파워' 시위로, 그것은 1990년대까지 파격적이고 멋진 흑인의 래디컬 시크(진보적이고 독창적인 패션 스타일)의 이미지로 기업의 레저웨어 홍보 캠페인에 포함되었었다. 모든 미디어 텍스트와 마찬가지로, 스포츠 사진은 부분적으로는 심미적이고, 부분적으로는 이념적인 기호와 코드의 특정 배치를 통해 작동한다. 그것은 사건에 대한 편향된(→ 순수한) 기록이 아닌데, 즉 스포츠 사진은 선택, 구성, 조작을 통해 세상이 어떤지(또는 사진작가가 세상이 어떠해야 한다고 생각하는지)에 대한 설명을 제공한다. 스포츠 사진에서 가장 중요한 대상은 스포츠의 주요 도구인 신체이다. 운동선수들의 신체는 그들의 힘을 끌어내는 인상적인 이미지를 통해 면밀히 관찰된다.

해설

스포츠 사진은 선택, 구성, 조작을 통해 세상이 어떤지 또는 사진작가가 세상이 어떠해야 한다고 생각하는지에 대한 설명을 제공하는 것, 즉 편견이 들어간 기록이라는 내용으로, ④ 앞에 not이 있다는 점에 유의해야 한다. 따라서 ④의 'biased(편향된)'를 'innocent(순수한)'와 같은 낱말로 바꾸어야 한다.

TEXT FLOW

도입	스포츠의 장대한 순간들은 스틸 사진에 의해 가장 기억에 남게 포착됨
부연	스포츠 사진은 심미적이고, 이념적인 기초와 코드의 특정 배치를 통해 작동함
결론	스포츠 사진은 선택, 구성, 조작을 통해 세상이 어떠해야 한다고 생각하는지에 대한 설명을 제공함

구문

• One of the most memorable is the "black power" protest [by Tommie Smith and John Carlos on the victory dais at the 1968 Mexico Olympics] [which, by the 1990s, had become incorporated into corporate leisurewear marketing campaigns as images of funky black radical chic].

: 첫 번째 [ ]는 the "black power" protest를 수식하는 전치사구이다. 두 번째 [ ]는 the "black power" protest를 수식하는 관계절이다.

05
정답 ①

많은 권위주의적인 체제의 특징은 시민 사회의 부재이다. 이것은 권력을 잡고 있는 사람들의 특정한 성과일 수 있는데, 그들은 국가와 권력자 밖에 있는 어떤 형태의 독립적인 행동을 박해하고, 흡수하고, 감시하거나 파괴하는 조치를 취해 왔다. 시민 사회는 또한 사회에서 선례가 거의 없거나 이 제도적 장벽을 넘어 사람들이 조직을 형성하지 못하도록 만류하는 중요한 민족적 또는 다른 사회적 분열에 의해 방해받을 수 있다. 그 결과는 국가를 사회적 조직의 주요 무대로 보는 것에 더 익숙하거나, 연합을 대중 운동과 항의라는 측면에서 더 많이 생각하는 사회가 될 수 있다. 때때로 이 두 가지 모두 포퓰리즘이라고 알려져 있는 것에서 서로 협조한다. 포퓰리즘은 특정 이념이 아니며, 사실 반제도적 접근법에서 그 힘의 상당 부분을 이끌어 낸다. 그러나 일반적으로, 포퓰리즘은 엘리트 계층과 기존 제도가 국민의 의사를 온전히 대변하지는 못하며, 이념이 없고 카리스마 있는 지도자가 흔히 이끄는 새로운 운동이 새로운 질서를 안내할 수 있다는 견해를 그 안에 담고 있다. 시민 사회가 취약한 곳에서는 포퓰리즘이 더 비옥한 땅을 찾을 수도 있다.

해설

권위주의적인 체제는 국가와 권력자 밖에 있는 독립적인 행동을 억압한다. 그곳에서 포퓰리즘은 엘리트 계층과 기존 제도에 반대하면서 국민의 의사를 대변하는 카리스마 있는 지도자가 나타나 새로운 질서를 안내한다는 견해를 포함하므로, 빈칸에 들어갈 말로 가장 적절한 것은 ① '더 비옥한 땅을 찾을'이다.

② 항의에 대한 욕망을 줄일
③ 권위주의적인 체제를 파괴할
④ 시민들 사이에서 긴장감을 불러일으킬
⑤ 민주주의의 교정책 역할을 할

TEXT FLOW

도입	권위주의적인 체제의 특징은 시민 사회의 부재임
부연	국가를 사회적 조직의 무대로 보고, 연합을 대중 운동과 항의라는 측면에서 생각함
전환	포퓰리즘은 반제도적 접근법에서 힘을 이끌어 냄
결론	시민 사회가 취약한 곳에서 포퓰리즘은 새 지도자가 새로운 질서를 안내할 수 있음

• But generally, populism carries within it the view [that elites and established institutions do not fully represent the will of the people] and [that a new movement, {free from ideology and often led by a charismatic leader}, can usher in a new order].
: 두 개의 [ ]는 the view와 동격 관계인 명사절이다. { }는 a new movement를 수식한다.

06
정답 ④

자신의 철학과 자연사를 통해 아리스토텔레스는 인간과 동물이 지각과 감정 같은 많은 특성을 공유하긴 하지만, 인간만이 로고스, 즉 이성의 능력을 가진다는 결론을 내렸었다. 아리스토텔레스에게 이것은 단순히 동물의 정신 능력에 대한 사실적인 결론이었다. 하지만 스토아학파의 철학자들은 그것을 동물에 대한 자신들의 윤리적 입장의 토대로 삼았다. 스토아학파의 철학자들은 정의를 상호 '소속'이라는 개념에 뿌리를 둔 것으로 간주했다. 스토아학파의 어떤 철학자들은 소속 개념을 우리 자신과 우리 자손에게 좁게 적용했고, 다른 철학자들은 그것을 더 넓게 덕망 있는 모든 사람들, 혹은 심지어 모든 동료 인간에게 적용했다. 그러나 스토아학파 철학자들은 그런 소속 집단이 이성적 존재와 비이성적 존재 사이에 존재할 수 없다고 생각했다. 이런 이유로, 아리스토텔레스에게는 동물의 정신 능력에 대한 전적으로 사실적인 결론이었던 것이 스토아학파 철학자들에 의해 동물은 인간의 정의와 도덕적 관심의 영역 범위에 포함되지 않는다는 윤리적 결론의 토대로 사용되었다.

해설
동물에게는 이성의 능력이 없다는 아리스토텔레스의 결론을 토대로 스토아학파 철학자들이 이성적 존재와 비이성적 존재 사이에는 상호 소속 개념을 적용할 수 없으므로 인간을 대상으로 하는 윤리가 동물에게는 적용되지 않는다고 생각했다는 내용의 글이다. 따라서 빈칸에 들어갈 말로 가장 적절한 것은 ④ '동물은 인간의 정의와 도덕적 관심의 영역 범위에 포함되지 않는다'이다.
① 비이성적인 존재는 이성적인 존재와 동등하게 대우되어야 한다
② 사람들은 인간의 이익을 위해 동물을 이용해서는 안 된다
③ 인간은 모든 생명체에 속한다는 개념을 확장할 필요가 있다
⑤ 상호 소속의 개념은 인간과 동물에게 적용 가능하다

⚲ WHY 고난도
글의 소재가 추상적이고 빈칸이 있는 문장을 포함해 전체적으로 문장이 길고 구조가 복잡하여 핵심 내용 파악이 쉽지 않았을 고난도 문제이다.

TEXT FLOW

도입	인간만이 이성의 능력을 갖고 있다는 아리스토텔레스의 주장은 동물의 정신 능력에 대한 사실적인 결론으로 여겨짐
전개	스토아학파는 이 주장을 동물에 대한 윤리적 입장으로 삼음
부연	스토아학파는 정의를 '소속' 개념에 근거한 것으로 이해하여 이성적 존재와 비이성적 존재 사이에 소속 집단이 존재할 수 없다고 봄
결론	아리스토텔레스의 동물의 정신 능력에 대한 사실적인 결론이 스토아학파에 의해 동물은 인간의 정의와 도덕적 관심의 영역 범위에 포함되지 않는다는 윤리적 결론의 토대로 사용됨

구문
• Hence, [what had been for Aristotle a purely factual conclusion about the mental powers of animals] was used by the Stoics as the basis for the ethical conclusion [that animals fall outside the sphere of human justice and moral concern].
: 첫 번째 [ ]는 문장의 주어이고, 두 번째 [ ]는 the ethical conclusion과 동격 관계를 이루는 명사절이다.

07
정답 ⑤

많은 도시가 지역 환경 문제와 계속해서 씨름하는 동안, 또한 기후 변화로 인한 새로운 어려운 문제에 직면할 것을 예상한다. (C) 예를 들어 해안 도시, 특히 적도에 더 가까운 도시는 홍수와 폭염의 더 큰 위험에 직면할 것이다. Hurricane Katrina가 New Orleans를 강타한 것이 미래의 도시에 미칠 영향의 전조가 되는 것일까? 기후 변화가 자연재해의 빈도와 심각성을 증가시킨다면, 그 대답은 '그렇다'일 수도 있다. (B) 이론적으로는 도시가 이러한 문제를 막는 데 도움이 될 수 있다. 결국 도시는 아이디어 창출의 중심지이다. 도심지는 경제 활동과 온실가스 생산 사이의 연결 고리를 약화할 수 있는 새로운 기술을 육성할 수도 있다. (A) 그러나 도시는 또한 이산화탄소와 같은 온실가스를 발생시킴으로써 기후 변화의 위험을 증가시키는 데도 주요한 역할을 한다. 온실가스 배출을 줄이는 데는 비용이 많이 들고, 그렇게 하는 것의 이점이 세계의 다른 나라들과 공유되기 때문에, 각 도시가 자체적으로 온실가스 배출을 제한할 유인책이 거의 없다. 이것이 무임승차자 문제의 전형적인 예이다.

해설
많은 도시가 기후 변화로 인한 새로운 어려운 문제에 직면할 것이라는 내용의 주어진 글 다음에는, For example로 그 예를 드는 (C)가 와야 한다. 그 다음에는 (C)에 제시된 문제를 these problems로 지칭하여 도시가 이러한 문제를 막는 데 도움이 될 수도 있다는 내용의 (B)가 온 다음, But으로 시작해 (B)와 상반되는 내용, 즉 도시가 또한 이산화탄소와 같은 온실가스를 발생시킴으로써 기후 변화의 위험을 증가시키는 데도 주요한 역할을 한다는 내용의 (A)가 오는 것이 글의 순서로 가장 적절하다.

TEXT FLOW

도입	기후 변화가 자연재해의 빈도와 심각성을 증가시킬 수도 있음
전개	도시가 이러한 문제를 막는 데 도움이 될 수 있음
부연	경제 활동과 온실가스 생산 사이의 연결 고리를 약화할 기술을 육성할 수 있음
반전	그러나 도시는 온실가스를 발생시키기도 하고, 온실가스 배출을 줄이는 데 비용이 많이 들어서 배출을 제한할 유인책이 거의 없음

구문
• Urban centers may incubate new technologies [that could weaken the link **between** economic activity **and** greenhouse gas production].
: [ ]는 new technologies를 수식하는 관계절이고, 그 안에 'A와 B 사이에'라는 의미의 「between A and B」가 쓰였다.

08
정답 ③

사유 재산에 대한 우리의 이해는 지난 500년에 걸쳐 발달했다. 사유 재산에 대한 초기 근대의 가장 중요한 이론가는 철학자 John Locke였다. Locke

는 자산의 개인적인 소유권은 자연권이며 국가가 자의적으로 빼앗을 수 없다고 주장했다. 사실, 그는 자산을 습득하고 축적하는 권리는 인간의 자유처럼 개념상으로 그리고 역사적으로 국가 이전에 존재한다고 주장했다. 개인이 정치 이전의 '자연의 상태'에 있는 자연 세계의 어떤 일부에 자신의 노동을 결합시킬 때, 그 사람은 자신의 근본적인 자아의 측면을 표현하는 것이다. 따라서 그 사람은 이전에는 공유되던 세상의 일부를 자신이 전적인 권리를 소유하는 뭔가로 바꾸는 것이다. 그 사람은 이제 그것을 자신이 생각하기에 적절한 방식대로 사용할 수 있는데, 예를 들어 그것을 팔거나, 넘겨주거나, 수입을 만들어 내도록 고안된 자산으로 전환할 수 있다. 그 사람의 동의 없이 그 사람의 자산을 점유하는 것은 금지된다. 사실, Locke에게 있어서, 국가의 기본적인 목적은 개인의 자산권이 다른 사람들에 의해 침해되지 않도록 보장하는 것이다.

해설

주어진 문장은 어떤 사람이 이전에는 공유되던 세상의 일부를 자신의 권한 하에 두게 된다는 내용이다. ③의 앞선 내용은 자연 세계의 어떤 일부에 노동을 결합시키면 자아의 표현이 된다는 것이므로 주어진 문장이 ③에 들어가야 그것이 소유권과 연결되고, ③ 뒤에 이어지는 소유권의 구체적인 내용과 행사 방식에 관한 설명으로 이어질 수 있으므로, 주어진 문장이 들어가기에 가장 적절한 곳은 ③이다.

TEXT FLOW

도입	Locke는 자산의 개인적인 소유권은 자연권이며 국가가 빼앗을 수 없다고 주장함
부연 1	자산을 습득하고 축적하는 권리는 역사적으로 국가 이전에 존재한다고 주장함
부연 2	이전에 공유되던 세상의 일부를 전적인 권리를 소유하는 무언가로 바꾸는 것임
결론	국가의 기본적인 목적은 개인의 자산권이 다른 사람들에 의해 침해되지 않도록 보장하는 것임

구문

• In fact, he insisted [that the right {to acquire and accumulate property} **is**, like human liberty, both conceptually and historically prior to the state].
: [ ]는 insisted의 목적어 역할을 하는 명사절이고, { }는 that절의 주어 the right를 수식하는 형용사적 용법의 to부정사구이다. insisted가 '요구'가 아닌 '주장'을 나타내고, that절의 내용이 신념(의견)이므로 현재 시제의 동사 is가 쓰였다.

09 　　　　　　　정답 ⑤

자신의 직속 선임자들과 매우 비슷하게, Carl von Clausewitz는 자신이 전투에 이기는 기술이라 부른 전술과 전쟁의 목적을 달성하기 위해 전투를 활용하는 기술이라고 정의한 전략을 구별했다. 그러나 더욱 근본적으로, 전쟁이란 두 명의 독립된 인간 사이의 결투였다. 그것의 상호 작용적인 본성은 그것을 다른 활동들과 뚜렷이 구분 지었다. 다른 말로 나타내면, (생명이 없는 물질에 행동을 가하는 것만이 수반되는) 검을 만드는 것과 누군가의 찌르기를 받아넘기고 자신의 찌르기로 응수할 수 있는 다른 검투사에 대항해 그것을 사용하는 것은 전혀 별개의 일이었다. 전쟁의 이론에 관한 간결하지만 명석한 논의에서, Clausewitz는 자신의 선임자 각각에 의해 제안된 체제는 사실의 일부 요소를 포함하고 있었다는 점을 인정한다. 그러나 어떠한 체제도 전쟁은 싸움으로 구성되며, 그 싸움, 다시 말해 전투가 전쟁의 결과를 결정한다는 근본적인 사실을 가리도록 허용되어서는 안 된다. 크고도 날카로운 검으로 뒷받침되지 않는다면 환상적인 조종이 아무리 많아도 전혀 효력을 발휘할 수 없을 것이다.

해설

주어진 문장은 앞부분의 내용으로부터 초점을 전환하여 어떠한 체제도 전쟁은 싸움으로 구성되고 전투가 전쟁의 결과를 결정한다는 사실을 가려서는 안 된다고 서술하고 있으므로, 주어진 문장이 ⑤에 들어가야 ⑤ 앞 문장에 있는 the system을 주어진 문장의 no system으로 받고, ⑤ 뒤의 문장에서 unless ~ sword가 주어진 문장의 fighting을 가리키게 되어 글이 자연스럽게 이어질 수 있다.

⊗ 매력적인 오답 주의!

④ 다음 문장에 언급된 the system이 주어진 문장의 no system을 가리키는 것으로 판단하여 선택한 것으로 보인다. [선택률 42%]

TEXT FLOW

도입	전투에 이기는 전술과 전투를 활용하는 전략을 구별했음
전개	근본적으로 전쟁은 두 명의 독립된 인간 사이의 상호 작용적인 결투임
결론	전쟁은 싸움으로 구성되고, 전투가 전쟁의 결과를 결정한다는 사실을 가리면 안 됨

구문

• To paraphrase, making swords (which only involved acting upon dead matter) **was one thing**. Using them against another swordsman [who is capable of {parrying one's own thrusts} and {replying with others of his own}] **is** quite **another**.
: 두 문장은 'A와 B는 별개의 일이다.'를 의미하는 「A is one thing. B is another.」 구문이 쓰였다. 첫 번째 문장의 ( )는 swords를 수식하는 관계절이다. 두 번째 문장의 [ ]는 another swordsman을 수식하는 관계절이고, 그 안의 두 개의 { }는 and로 연결된 전치사 of의 목적어 역할의 동명사구이다.

10 　　　　　　　정답 ②

어린아이들, 특히 아기들의 생각과 사고를 관찰하려고 시도할 때 일반적인 실험적 접근은 습관화 연구의 사용이다. 습관화는 인간 학습의 가장 단순하고 가장 기본적인 형태 중 하나이며, 우리 모두가 반복되고 계속되는 경험에 대한 관심 혹은 반응의 감소를 보여 주는 방식을 포함한다. 예를 들어, 한 아기는 계속해서 고개를 돌려 흔들리는 딸랑이를 한동안 볼지 모른다. 하지만 시간이 흐르면서, 그는 머리를 돌리는 것을 멈추고 지루함의 징후를 보이는 경향이 있을 것이고, 머리를 돌리는 것을 다시 시작하기 위해 새로운 자극이 필요할지도 모른다. 그러한 행동은 학습과 기억의 증거를 암시하는 것으로 여겨진다. 자극에 대한 감소된 반응은 아기가 그것이 무엇인지에 대한 기억을 가지고 있다는 것을 암시하는 것으로 여겨질 수 있는데, 그것은 바로 "아, 나는 그것이 무엇인지 알고 있어. 나는 전에 그것을 보고/듣고/만지고/맛본 적이 있어서 나는 이제 그것을 보고/듣고/만지고/맛볼 필요가 없어요."이다. 아기에게 낯선 경험이 제시되면 "나는 그게 뭔지 모르는 것 같아요."와 같은 탈습관화가 일어난다.

➡ 자극에 대한 아기들의 습관화는 그들이 자극의 반복에 대해 반응하는 것을 멈췄다는 것을 의미하며, 그들은 새로운 자극이 주어지면 습관화에서 다시 벗어난다.

아기들의 생각과 사고를 연구하는 실험에서 아기들은 고개를 돌려 흔들리는 딸랑이를 보게 되지만, 시간이 흐르면서 고개를 돌리지 않으면서 지루함의 징후를 보인다. 이러한 반응의 감소는 습관화에 의한 것으로 아이가 반복된 자극에 반응하는 것을 멈추었다는 것을 의미하며, 낯선 자극을 제시하면 탈습관화가 일어남을 설명하는 글이다. 그러므로 요약문의 빈칸 (A), (B)에 들어갈 말로는 ② 'reacting(반응하는 것) – novel(새로운)'이 가장 적절하다.
① 반응하는 것 – 복잡한
③ 동의하는 것 – 조절된
④ 적응하는 것 – 반복되는
⑤ 적응하는 것 – 계속적인

TEXT FLOW

도입	아기들의 생각과 사고를 관찰하기 위한 실험적인 접근은 습관화 연구의 사용임
예시	아기들은 흔들리는 딸랑이를 고개를 돌려 보게 되지만, 시간이 흐르면서 고개를 돌리지 않고 지루함의 징후를 보임
부연 1	이러한 반응의 감소는 자극에 대한 아기들의 습관화를 보여 줌
부연 2	다시 낯선 경험이 제시되면 탈습관화가 일어남

구문

• Habituation **is** one of the simplest and most fundamental forms of human learning and **involves** the way [in which we all show a decline **of** {interest in}, or {response to}, repeated or continued experience].
: is와 involves는 and로 연결되어 주어 Habituation에 이어지는 동사이다. [ ]는 the way를 수식하는 관계절이고 그 안의 두 개의 { }는 or로 연결된 전치사 of의 목적어이다. 두 개의 { } 안의 전치사 in과 to의 목적어는 repeated or continued experience이다.

11~12

정답 11 ③ 12 ④

생각의 힘을 이해하는 근본적인 열쇠는 여러분의 신념이 하는 역할을 깨닫는 것이다. 여러분이 무엇을 믿든지 간에, 여러분의 신념은 인생에서 하는 일체의 경험을 결정한다. 게다가, 여러분의 신념은 여러분에게 충실하다. 그것은 핵심 신념을 검증하고 강화하는 생각에 대한 유혹이며, 신념을 배반하는 생각에 대해 강하게 반발하는 힘이다. 결과적으로, 여러분은 자신의 신념과 일치하는 그런 만남만을 갖게 될 것이다. 그럴 경우 여러분이 자신의 신념 체계와 충돌하는 것을 현실로 가져올 수 없기 때문에 변화를 포함하는 것이 어렵다. 여러분이 믿지 않는 것이나 믿을 수 없는 것은 무의식적으로 무시된다. 그것은 여러분이 자신도 모르게 그것을 거부하고 있기 때문에, 변화가 일어날 수 없다는 것을 의미한다.
여러분이 록 스타가 되고 싶다면, 록 스타가 되는 것이 자신에게 있어 선택 사항이라고 여러분이 믿지 않는다면 그런 경험을 가질 수 없다. 여러분이 그 직업을 향한 욕망에 대해 생각을 가지고 있을 수도 있지만, 전형적으로 백일몽은 우리 대부분에게 신뢰를 주지 않으며, 그것은 현실화에 필요한 집념의 수준을 달성하지도 못한다. 여러분의 생각이 마음속에 집념을 형성할 때까지 아이디어를 쌓는 것이 어려운 일이다. 그러면 여러분은 자신의 생각이 실행 가능하다는 믿음이 형성될 때까지 자신의 생각을 받아들여야 한다. 믿음이 형성되기 시작하는 그 시점에서, 여러분은 행동을 취할 것이고 여러분의 생각은 무너질(→ 실현될) 것이다. 불행히도, 대부분의 사람들은 이러한 장애물을 결코 넘지 못하는데, 왜냐하면 그들의 확립된 신념은 신념에 반하는 아이디어들이 집념의 수준에 도달하는 것을 막기 때문이다. 이제까지 의심, 회의

론, 또는 실패에 대한 두려움을 경험해 본 적이 있다면, 여러분은 자신의 신념이 새롭거나 반대되는 생각에 저항하는 과정을 경험한 것이다.

11 본인이 가진 생각에 대한 신념이 형성되지 않으면 어떠한 변화도 일어나지 않는다는 것이 첫 번째 문단의 주제이고, 두 번째 문단에서 첫 번째 문장의 주제를 뒷받침하는 예를 든 후 어떤 생각이 실현 가능하다고 믿을 때 행동을 취하게 되고 이로 인해 생각이 실현될 것이라는 내용이 이어지므로, 글의 제목으로 가장 적절한 것은 ③ '그것이 가능하다고 여러분이 믿을 때 변화가 일어난다'이다.
① 여러분의 신념 체계는 매 순간 달라질 것이다
② 자신의 과거에서 벗어나 앞으로 나아가라
④ 아이디어에 대한 집념: 성공의 주요 장벽
⑤ 다른 사람들의 도움으로 사고력을 강화하라

12 어떤 생각이 실행 가능하다는 믿음이 형성되면, 즉 집념이 쌓이면 변화가 일어나고 생각은 현실로 나타날 것이라는 맥락이므로, ④의 'collapse(무너지다)'를 'materialize(실현되다)'와 같은 낱말로 바꾸어야 한다.

TEXT FLOW

도입	생각의 힘을 이해하는 근본적인 열쇠는 신념이 하는 역할을 깨닫는 것임
전개	신념이 형성되지 않으면 변화가 일어날 수 없음
예시	록 스타가 되는 것이 자신의 선택 사항이라고 믿지 않는다면 이뤄지지 않을 것임
결론	그 생각이 실행 가능하다는 믿음을 형성해야만 행동을 취할 것이고 생각은 실현될 것임

구문

• Change is then difficult to incorporate because you cannot **bring into reality** [that which conflicts with your belief system].
: [ ]는 bring의 목적어 역할을 하는 명사절인데 목적어가 길고 전치사구인 into reality가 짧아서 문장의 뒤에 쓰였다.

• You must then embrace your idea until **a belief** forms [that your idea is doable].
: [ ]는 a belief와 동격인 명사절인데 주어가 길어지는 것을 방지하기 위해 동사 뒤에 쓰였다.

고난도 모의고사 11회

01 ④	02 ①	03 ②	04 ④	05 ④	06 ②
07 ④	08 ⑤	09 ③	10 ④	11 ①	12 ⑤

01 정답 ④

우리는 일을 하지 않으면 우리의 규율이 약화되고 우리의 마음이 방황하는 경우가 아주 많다. 우리는 월급을 쓰면서 재미있게 놀기 시작할 수 있도록 근무일이 끝나기를 갈망할 수도 있지만, 우리 대부분은 여가 시간을 조금씩 허비해 버린다. 우리는 힘든 일을 피하며, 도전적인 취미에 참여하는 경우는 매우 드물다. 그 대신에 우리는 TV를 보거나 쇼핑몰에 가거나 페이스북에 접속한다. 우리는 게을러진다. 그리고 나서 우리는 지루해하고 초조해한다. 우리의 주의는 외부로의 집중에서 벗어나 내부로 향하고, 우리는 결국 Emerson이 자의식의 감옥이라고 말한 것에 감듬된다. Csikszentmihalyi는 심지어 형편없는 일자리조차도 '자신의 일에 몰두하고, 자신을 그 일에 집중하고 몰입하도록 부추기는' '내재된' 목표와 과제를 가지고 있기 때문에, '실제로 여가 시간보다 더 즐기기 쉽다'고 말한다. 하지만 그것은 우리의 기만하는 마음이 우리가 믿기를 원하는 바가 아니다. 기회가 주어지면, 우리는 간절히 자신에게 노동의 고됨을 덜어 낼 것이다. 우리는 자신에게 나태를 선고할 것이다.

해설
우리는 일을 하지 않는 여가 시간에 힘든 일을 피하고 도전적인 취미에도 참여하지 않으며 우리의 삶에서 노동의 고됨을 덜어 내려고 한다는 내용의 글이므로, 밑줄 친 부분이 의미하는 바로 가장 적절한 것은 ④ '모든 노동을 멀리하려는 우리의 욕구에 굴복할'이다.
① 천성적으로 게으르다고 스스로를 비난할
② 정신노동은 더 하고 육체노동은 덜 할
③ 자발적으로 아무것도 하지 않음으로써 스스로에게 벌을 줄
⑤ 기술의 급격한 변화로 인해 일자리를 잃을

TEXT FLOW
도입	우리는 일을 하지 않으면 규율이 약화되고 마음이 방황하는 경우가 많음
부연 1	우리는 힘든 일을 피하고, 도전적인 취미에 참여하는 경우는 매우 드묾
부연 2	기회가 되면 우리는 자신에게서 노동의 고됨을 덜어 내려 함

구문
• We may yearn **for** the workday [**to** be over] [**so** we **can** start spending our pay and having some fun], but most of us fritter away our leisure hours.
: 첫 번째 [ ]는 yearn의 목적어로 쓰인 to부정사구이고, for the workday는 to부정사구의 의미상의 주어이다. 두 번째 [ ]는 '(주어가) ~할 수 있도록'을 의미하는 「so (that)+주어+can」 구문이 쓰인 부사절이다.

02 정답 ①

완전한 구술 문화에서, 사고는 인간의 기억력에 의해 지배된다. 지식은 기억해 내는 것이고, 기억하는 것은 마음속에 간직할 수 있는 것으로 한정된다. 수천 년간의 문자 이전의 인류 역사 동안 내내 언어는 개인의 기억 속에 복잡한 정보를 저장하는 것을 돕고, 말을 통해 다른 사람들과 그 정보를 교환하는 것을 용이하게 하도록 진화했다. '중대한 생각'은 필요에 의해 '기억 체계와 밀접하게 관련'되었다고 Ong은 쓰고 있다. 화법과 구문은 매우 리드미컬해져서 귀에 맞게 조정되었고, 정보는 기억을 돕기 위해 오늘날 우리가 상투적인 어구라고 부를 흔한 구절 표현으로 부호화되어 있다. 지식은 플라톤이 정의한 대로 '시'에 내재되었고, 시인-학자라는 전문화된 계층이 정보 저장, 검색, 전달을 위한 인간 장치, 즉 인간의 지적 기술이 되었다. 법률, 기록, 거래, 결정, 전통과 같이 오늘날에는 '문서화'될 모든 것이 Havelock의 말처럼 구술 문화에서는 '상투적인 표현의 구절로 구성되어' '크게 노래되거나 연호됨으로써' 전파되어야 했다.

해설
구술 문화에서 정보를 쉽게 기억해서 전달하도록 하기 위해 여러 다양한 언어적인 장치가 고안되었다는 내용이므로, 글의 주제로 가장 적절한 것은 ① '구술 문화에서 정보를 기억하기 위한 언어적 장치'이다.
② 생존을 위해 정보를 교환하려는 우리의 타고난 본능
③ 지식을 전달하는 데 있어서 구전의 한계
④ 선사시대 구술 문화에서 기억의 중요성
⑤ 암기력 향상을 위한 고대 학자들의 노력

TEXT FLOW
도입	완전한 구술 문화에서 사고는 인간의 기억력에 의해 지배됨
부연	화법과 구문은 귀에 맞게 조정되고, 정보는 기억을 돕기 위해 구절 표현으로 부호화됨
결론	오늘날 문서화될 모든 것이 구술 문화에서는 구절과 노래로 전파되어야 했음

구문
• Through the millennia of man's preliterate history, language evolved [to aid the storage of complex information in individual memory] and [to make it easy to exchange that information with others through speech].
: 두 개의 [ ]는 목적을 나타내는 부사적 용법의 to부정사구이다.

03 정답 ②

수학의 본질과 수학이 수반하는 바로 그 근본적인 추상 관념을 인식하는 것은 중요하다. Galileo, Descartes, Huygens, 그리고 Newton 모두 수학 공식을 만들어 냈다. 다시 말해, 그들은 자연에서 보이는 패턴을 표현하기 위해 수학을 이용하여 물리적 현상을 압축해 주는 수학적이고 추상적인 방법을 창조하고자 했던 것이다. 추상적인 공식이 자연과 부합할 수 있어야 한다는 것은 신생 과학에 관련된 사람들에 의해 만들어진 근본적인 가정이었다. 그런 생각의 저변에는 세상이 예측 가능하고 질서 정연한 곳이라는 더 깊은 가정이 깔려 있었다. 조잡한 미신과 마법의 초기 시대에서 벗어나, 그들은 이성과 증명이 승리할 세계 속으로 자신들이 모습을 드러내는 것을 보았다. 그런데 가장 순수한 형태의 이성은 논리와 수학에서 발견되며, 따라서 원론적으로 세상은 수학적 정확성을 가지고 만물의 움직임을 결정지을 '자연법칙'이라는 관점에서 이해될 수 있을 것으로 기대하는 것은 당연한 일이었다.

해설
② 문장의 술어 동사는 was이고 그 앞이 주어 역할을 하는 명사절이어야 하

는데, 그 안에 가주어 it, 진주어 to correspond to nature, 그리고 to부정사구의 의미상의 주어 역할을 하는 for an abstract formula가 모두 있다. 따라서 명사절에 문장의 구성 요소가 빠진 것이 없으므로, 관계대명사 What은 접속사 That으로 고쳐야 한다.

① 과거의 일에 대한 서술이므로 주어 Galileo, Descartes, Huygens and Newton의 술어 동사 produced는 어법상 적절하다.

③ 부사구 Beneath it이 문두에 오면서 주어(the deeper assumption that the world is a predictable and ordered place)와 동사(lay)가 도치된 구조이다. lay는 자동사 lie의 과거형으로 어법상 적절하다.

④ a world를 수식하는 관계절을 이끄는 관계부사 where는 어법상 적절하다.

⑤ 가주어 it 다음에 진주어를 이끄는 to부정사구가 있어야 하므로, to expect는 어법상 적절하다.

⊗ **매력적인 오답 주의!**

③ 문두에 위치한 부사구 Beneath it의 it을 주어로, lie의 과거형 lay가 아닌 '놓다'를 의미하는 lay를 동사로 착각하여 수일치를 묻는 문제로 여겨 선택한 것으로 보인다. [선택률 48%]

TEXT FLOW

도입	수학의 본질과 수학이 수반하는 근본적인 추상 관념을 인식하는 것이 중요함
부연 1	수학자들은 자연에서 보이는 패턴을 표현하고, 물리적 현상을 압축하는 추상적인 방법을 창조하고자 수학 공식을 만들어 냄
부연 2	세상이 예측 가능하고 질서 정연한 곳이라는 가정이 깔려 있음
결론	따라서 세상은 '자연법칙'의 관점에서 이해되길 기대하는 것이 당연한 일이었음

04

정답 ④

17세기 잉글랜드에서, 자유주의가 자본주의와 동시에 나타났다. 자유주의 상인, 제조업자, 금융가, 그리고 지식인은 군주제, 중상주의 국가, 봉건적 지위 구분, 기성 교회를 뒷받침하는 중세 가톨릭 신학에서 벗어난 사상을 명확히 표현했다. 정치적으로, 자유주의자들은 의회 통치에 기초한 더 대표성 있는 정부를 요구했다. 군주가 아닌, 특정 개인과 상관없는 법이 정치적 권위를 뒷받침해야 한다. 경제적으로, 자유주의자들은 민간 기업가에 대한 더 큰 자유를 선호했다. 개인들은 엄격한 국가 통제에서 벗어나, 자기 이익, 즉 부와 사회적 지위를 추구할 기회를 가져야 한다. 고전 자유주의자들은 서로 다른 영역에서 신성하고 세속적인 가치관의 표현을 지지했다. 교회와 국가의 분리는 개인적 자유를 제한했다(→ 극대화했다). 종교적 관용은 개인이 보수적인 통제에서 벗어나 구원을 추구할 수 있게 했다. 요약하면, 고전적 자유주의자들은 중세 가톨릭과 연계된 위계적이고 집단주의적인 질서보다 개인의 자유가 으뜸인 것을 강조했다.

해설

17세기 잉글랜드에서 자본주의와 함께 자유주의가 나타나면서 중세 가톨릭의 통제에서 벗어나, 정치적, 경제적으로 위계적이며 집단주의적인 질서보다 개인의 자유가 강조되게 되었다는 내용이므로, ④의 'restricted(제한했다)'를 'maximized(극대화했다)'와 같은 낱말로 바꾸어야 한다.

TEXT FLOW

도입	17세기 잉글랜드의 자유주의는 중세 가톨릭 신학에서 벗어난 사상을 명확히 표현했음
부연 1	정치적으로 의회 통치에 기초한 대표적인 정부를 요구했음
부연 2	경제적으로 민간 기업가에 대한 자유를 선호하고, 개인은 부와 사회적 지위를 추구할 기회를 가져야 했음
결론	교회와 국가의 분리는 개인의 자유를 극대화했음

구문

• Religious toleration **enabled** the individual [to pursue salvation {free from orthodox controls}].

: [ ]는 enabled의 목적격 보어인 to부정사구이고, 그 안의 { }는 salvation을 수식한다.

05

정답 ④

우리는 우리의 건설된 풍경을 대체로 무시하는데 왜냐하면 사실상 우리가 그것들의 생성에 명백한 지분이나 영향력이 전혀 없기 때문이다. 이것은 우리의 일상 경험과 필요의 다른 영역에 대한 우리의 접근 방식과 일치하여, 의학적 도움을 위해서는 의사에게 가고, 차를 수리하기 위해서는 자동차 정비사를 방문한다. 우리 대부분은 암시적으로든 명시적으로든, 건설된 환경에 대한 통제권을 포기하고, 그것들에 대한 의사 결정권을 시 의회 의원, 부동산 개발업자, 건설업자와 토건업자, 제품 제조업자, 그리고 설계사와 같은 전문가들에게 맡겨 왔다. 우리 대부분은 건설된 환경에 변화를 가져오는 데 자신들이 무력하다고 인식한다. 바로 이런 무력감은 역설적인 상황을 초래한다. 즉 부동산 개발업자들은 소비자들이 원하는 것이라 믿는 것을 기반으로 새로운 프로젝트를 구성하는데, 그들은 그것을 주로 이전 소비자들이 무엇을 구입했는지 살펴봄으로써 평가한다. 그러나 건설된 환경에 관한 한, 소비자들은 전통적인 디자인에 대해 별로 생각하지 않고 그것에 끌린다. 그러므로 개발업자들은 사람들이 원한다고 생각하는 것을 계속해서 건설한다. 무엇이 사람들에게 더 나을지, 사람들이 무엇을 좋아할 수 있을지, 혹은 그들이 실제로 무엇을 필요로 할지 한발 물러나 생각해 보는 사람은 아무도 없다.

해설

우리는 의사나 자동차 수리공에게 의료와 수리를 맡기듯, 건설된 풍경에 대한 통제권을 전문가들에게 맡기지만, 전문가들은 과거에 소비자들이 선택했던 것을 근거로 풍경을 설계하므로 결국 전통적인 설계를 답습하게 된다는 내용이다. 이에 따라 소비자가 건설된 풍경을 무시하는 이유는 그것에 대한 의사 결정 권한과 통제권이 없어서라는 추론이 가능하므로, 빈칸에 들어갈 말로 가장 적절한 것은 ④ '우리가 그것들의 생성에 명백한 지분이나 영향력이 전혀 없기'이다.

① 너무 많은 전문가들이 그것들의 디자인에 참여하기
② 우리는 상업 공간이 개인적인 용도라고 생각하지 않기
③ 심미적인 고려는 기능적인 차이를 거의 만들지 않기
⑤ 그것들의 건설에서 우리의 필요보다 재정적인 이익이 우선이기

도입	우리는 풍경의 생성에 지분과 영향력이 없으므로 건설된 풍경을 대체로 무시함
전개 1	그것들에 대한 의사 결정권을 전문가들에게 맡겨 옴
전개 2	이러한 무력감은 역설적인 상황을 초래함
부연	부동산 개발업자들은 사람들이 원한다고 생각하는 것을 건설하지만, 실제로 무엇을 좋아하고 필요로 할지 생각해 보는 사람은 없음

도입	어린 새들은 어른들을 관찰함으로써 많은 것을 배우기 때문에 포획 번식과 재도입에 의한 앵무새의 개체수 복원 시도는 걱정스러움
부연 1	인간의 훈련만으로는 충분하지 않음
부연 2	방생된 개체의 생존에 대한 전망은 자유롭게 사는 어른 모델이 없을 경우 가장 심하게 훼손됨
결론	문화적 전통의 세대 단절은 큰부리앵무새 재도입의 시도를 좌절시켰음

구문

• ~: real estate developers configure new projects [based on what they believe consumers want], [which they assess mainly by examining what previous consumers have purchased].

: 첫 번째 [ ]는 new projects를 수식하는 과거분사구이고, 두 번째 [ ]는 what they believe consumers want를 부가적으로 설명하는 계속적 용법의 관계절이다.

구문

• It's not as easy as **training** young or orphaned creatures [to recognize what is food {while they're in the safety of a cage}], then [simply opening the door].

: 첫 번째 [ ]는 training의 목적격 보어인 to부정사구이고, 그 안의 { }는 부사절이다. 두 번째 [ ]는 then으로 연결되어 as easy as에 이어진다.

06　　　　　　　　　　　　　　　　　정답 ②

많은 어린 새들은 자기 부모와 어른들을 관찰함으로써 많은 것을 배울 필요가 있고, 앵무새들은 아마도 대부분의 어린 새들보다 더 많은 것을 배울 필요가 있을 것이다. 그것이 포획 번식과 재도입에 의해 앵무새의 개체수를 복원하려는 시도가 까다롭고 걱정스러운 이유이다. 그것은 어리거나 고아가 된 생물들이 새장의 안전 속에 있을 때 무엇이 먹이인지를 인식하도록 훈련시킨 다음, 그냥 문을 열어 주는 것처럼 간단하지 않다. "새장 안에서는 그것들이 그 먹이를 어디에서, 언제, 어떻게 찾아야 하는지를, 또는 둥지를 짓기에 좋은 곳을 가진 나무에 관해 가르칠 수 없다."라고 Sam Williams는 말한다. 그리고 풍경은 복잡하고 끊임없이 변한다. "새들을 생존에 대비시키지도 못했는데 그것들을 그냥 밖으로 내던지는 것은 비윤리적일 것이다."라고 Williams는 믿는다. 더 나쁘게도, 그것은 효과가 없을 수도 있다. 방생된 개체들의 생존에 대한 전망은 자유롭게 사는 어른 역할 모델이 없을 경우 가장 심하게 훼손된다. 문화적 전통의 세대 단절은 큰부리앵무새가 전멸되었던 미국 남서부 일부 지역에 그것을 재도입하려는 시도를 좌절시켰다. 보존 일을 하는 사람들은 포획되어 길러진 앵무새들에게 전통적인 야생 먹이를 탐색하고 찾게끔 가르칠 수 없었다.

해설

포획되어 새장에 갇힌 새들은 관찰하면서 배울 부모와 어른이 없기 때문에 인간의 훈련만으로는 야생에서 생존할 기술을 배우지 못한다는 내용의 글이다. 문맥상 큰부리앵무새를 미국 남서부 일부 지역에 재도입하려던 것을 좌절시켰던 원인에 해당하는 내용이 빈칸에 와야 하므로, 빈칸에 들어갈 말로 가장 적절한 것은 ② '문화적 전통의 세대 단절'이다.
① 교육 현장에서의 고밀도 사육
③ 자연환경에서 지속적인 먹이 부족
④ 포획 번식과 관련된 부당한 폭력
⑤ 사회화 과정에서 또래 압력의 존재

⟨?⟩ WHY 고난도

포획 번식과 재도입을 통해 앵무새의 개체수를 복원하려는 시도가 실패한 근본적인 원인을 찾아 빈칸에 넣어야 하는데, 정답 선택지가 함축적인 표현이고, 예로 들었던 food를 활용한 선택지도 있어 정답을 고르기 쉽지 않았을 고난도 문제이다.

07　　　　　　　　　　　　　　　　　정답 ④

스포츠에서, 참석은 거의 항상(98~99퍼센트의 경우로) 적어도 한 명의 다른 사람과 함께 이루어진다. 스포츠 팬은 다른 사람들과 함께 감정적인 경험을 즐길 권리를 위해서 비용을 지불한다. 그 팬은 다른 사람들과 함께 있기 위해서, 이 사회적인 교류에서 경험을 공유하기 위해서 경기에 간다. 보다 개략적으로 말하자면, 다른 대부분의 소매 환경과는 달리 수많은 군중은 긍정적인 심리적 영향을 미친다. 식료품 잡화점 계산대에 줄이 없는 것은 대부분의 쇼핑객을 행복하게 만들겠지만, 야구 경기를 보려는 줄이 없다는 것은 팬에게 이것이 끔찍한 스포츠 행사이거나 혹은 그 팬이 잘못된 날짜에 경기장에 도착했다는 분명한 징후이다. (스포츠 참여의 잠재적인 이점은 자동적으로 발생하는 것이 아닌데, 코치들은 선수들이 이러한 심리적 이점을 얻는 데 도움이 되도록 선수들의 스포츠 경험을 구조화해야 한다.) 경쟁의 흥분과 선수의 스타 파워가 팀에서 가지는 기운은 너무나 커서 그 경험은 다른 사람들이 있을 때 가장 잘 즐길 수 있다.

해설

스포츠에서 경기에 참석하는 것은 다른 사람과 함께하기 위함이며, 수많은 군중 사이에 있다는 점이 스포츠를 더욱 즐길 수 있게 한다는 내용의 글이므로, 코치들은 선수들이 스포츠 참여의 잠재적 심리적 이점을 얻는 데 도움이 되도록 선수들의 스포츠 경험을 구조화해야 한다는 내용의 ④는 글의 전체 흐름과 관계가 없다.

도입	스포츠에서 경기에 참석하는 것은 다른 사람들과 함께 즐기기 위함임
부연	다른 소매 환경과 달리 수많은 군중은 긍정적인 심리적 영향을 미침
결론	경쟁의 흥분과 선수의 스타 파워가 팀에서 가지는 기운은 그 경험이 다른 사람들이 있는 가운데서 가장 잘 즐길 수 있는 것임

구문

• ~, but no line to see a ballgame is a definite hint to a fan **either** [that this is a terrible sporting event] **or** [that the fan has arrived at the stadium on the wrong date].

: 두 개의 [ ]는 a definite hint와 동격 관계의 명사절로, 「either A or B」에 의해 병렬 구조를 이룬다.

08 정답 ⑤

맥락의 중요성을 무시하는 윤리학 이론가들의 반복되는 경향에 반대하여 최근 도덕 철학에서 다수의 목소리가 울려 나오고 있다. 예를 들어, 단순성과 질서에 대한 애정 때문에 도덕적 환경의 풍부한 다양성을 보지 못하는 이론가들에 대해 이의가 제기되고 있다. (C) 이러한 목소리로, 이론이 모든 것을 몇 개의 선호되는 부류로 한정해서는 안 된다는 것을, 너무 과격하게 윤리학의 설명적인 개념을 가지치기하고 강화하는 제안들이 결국 중요한 현상들을 제외하거나 혹은 그것들을 인식할 수 없게 만들 것이라는 점이 우리에게 상기된다. (B) 단순히 도덕적 이론을 소유한 것이 도덕적인 지식으로서 충분하다는 오만함에 대해 다른 이의가 제기되어 왔다. 일련의 도덕적인 원칙이 아무리 적절할지라도, 결국 한 상황에서 무엇이 가장 중요한지 인식하지 못하는 사람은 그 원칙을 어디에 적용할지 알 수 없을 것이다. (A) 도덕적인 지식이 없는 사람은, 비싸긴 하지만, 길을 찾기에는 보잘것없는 장비를 갖추었다는 것을 알게 되는 GPS를 장착한 초보 등산객처럼, 무턱대고 여기저기 발을 헛디딜 것이다. 여러분의 지도가 아무리 좋아도, 여러분이 어디에 있는지 모른다면 그것은 여러분이 길을 잃는 것을 막아 줄 수 없다.

해설
단순성과 질서를 너무 중시하여 맥락의 다양성을 보지 못하는 위험에 관해 언급하고 있는 주어진 글 다음에는, 주어진 글의 내용을 these voices(이러한 목소리)로 받아 개념을 가지치기하면 중요한 현상을 제외할 위협이 있다는 내용의 (C)가 온 후, 제기된 다른 이의를 언급하면서 도덕적 이론을 소유하는 것만으로는 충분하지 않고 그것을 어디에 적용할지를 알아야 한다는 내용의 (B)가 온다. 이어서 그 예로 도덕적 지식이 없는 사람은 GPS를 장착한 초보 등산객과 같은 위험에 빠지게 된다는 내용의 (A)가 마지막에 오는 것이 글의 순서로 가장 자연스럽다.

TEXT FLOW
도입	단순성과 질서를 중시하여 도덕적 환경의 다양성을 보지 못하는 이론가들에 대한 이의가 제기됨
부연	개념을 가지치기하면 중요한 현상은 제외될 수 있음
결론	도덕적인 원칙이 적절하여도, 결국 그 원칙을 어디에 적용할지를 알아야 함

구문
• Those who lack moral knowledge will stumble about blindly, like novice hikers [outfitted with GPS] [who discover that they are in fact poorly {if expensively} equipped to find their way].
: 첫 번째 [ ]는 novice hikers를 수식하는 과거분사구이다. 두 번째 [ ]는 novice hikers outfitted with GPS를 수식하는 관계절이고, 그 안의 { }는 if they are expensively equipped에서 반복되는 they are equipped가 생략된 부사절이며 if는 although의 의미이다.

09 정답 ③

경제적인 관점에서, 텔레비전 광고는 소비재에 대한 수요를 창출하여 상품명과 브랜드의 광범위한 확산을 가능하게 하는 것으로 여겨진다. 실제로, 광고가 없다면 소비자들은 수십, 심지어 수백 가지 각양각색의 같은 제품이 들어 있는 슈퍼마켓 진열대와 협상하는 것이(진열대에 있는 물건 중 어느 것을 살 것인지를 결정하는 것이) 어려울 것이다. 많은 학자들이 광고가 자본주의 소비자 경제 발전에서 핵심적인 역할을 한다고 여기지만, 그 증거는 TV 광고가 시장의 총소비를 증가시키는 정도는 좋게 봐도 결정적이지 않다는 것을 시사한다. 즉, 광고는 시장 점유율(또는 '브랜드 로열티')을 증가시키는 것만큼이나 그것을 유지하거나 보호하는 것과 관련이 있을 가능성이 있다. 결과적으로 제품 광고 비용은 증가된 생산 규모의 경제를 통해 회수되지 않는 것이 일반적이다. 따라서 광고 비용은 일반적으로 소비자에게 전가된다. 소비자는 사실상 그들의 구매에 영향을 미치는 데 사용되는 광고 캠페인에 돈을 지불하고 있다.

해설
주어진 문장은 광고가 시장 점유율을 증가시키는 것만큼이나 그것을 유지하거나 보호하는 것과 관련이 있을 가능성이 있다는 내용이다. 이 문장은 ③의 앞 문장 중 the degree to which TV advertising raises aggregate market consumption is inconclusive at best를 부연 설명해 주는 역할을 하고 있으므로 주어진 문장이 들어가기에 가장 적절한 곳은 ③이다.

TEXT FLOW
도입	텔레비전 광고는 소비재에 대한 수요를 창출하여 상품명과 브랜드의 확산을 가능하게 함
전개	TV 광고가 시장의 총소비를 증가시키는 데에는 결정적이지는 않음
부연	광고는 시장 점유율을 증가시키는 것만큼이나 유지하고 보호하는 것과 관련되어 있음
결론	소비자는 사실상 광고 캠페인에 돈을 지불하고 있는 것임

구문
• While many scholars ~, the evidence suggests [that the degree {to which TV advertising raises aggregate market consumption} is inconclusive at best].
: While은 Although의 의미이다. [ ]는 suggests의 목적어 역할을 하는 명사절이고, 그 안의 { }는 that절의 주어 the degree를 수식하는 관계절이다. suggests가 '제안하다'가 아니라 '시사하다'의 의미로 쓰였으므로 that절의 동사는 is가 쓰였다.

10 정답 ④

통계를 잘못 사용하는 것에 대한 중요한 대응은 대중에게 더 많은 숫자를 주는 것이다. 환자들은 치료의 좋은 점과 나쁜 점이 얼마나 큰지 알 권리가 있다. 질적 위험 용어는 불명확한 것으로 악명이 높다. 의약품 라벨 및 포장재 인쇄물용으로 빈도 간격에 대한 특정한 용어를 정의하는 유럽 연합(EU)의 지침처럼, 언어 표현을 표준화하려는 시도가 있다. 그러나 사람들은 그러한 라벨에 근거한 부작용의 빈도를 과대평가하는 것처럼 보인다. 게다가, '가능성 낮음'과 같은 용어는 맥락마다 다르게 해석된다. 예를 들어, 더 심각한 부작용은 동일한 질적 용어로 기술된 덜 심각한 부작용보다 덜 자주 발생하는 것으로 추정된다. 환자들은 언어로 공개될 때 위험을 너무 크게 생각하는 경향이 있으며, 정보가 수치적으로 제공되면 그것을 따를 가능성이 낮다. 하지만 서면 정보와 언어 정보 모두에서, 환자들은 그것이 언어 대신에 수치로 제시될 때 위험에 대한 더 정확한 인식을 가지고 있다고 연구는 시사했다. 그러므로 위험은 항상 숫자로 명시되어야만 한다.
➡ 환자는 질적 위험 용어가 언어적으로 제시되었을 때 정신적으로 위험을 과장할 수도 있으며, 그것들이 환자에게 수치로 제공되었을 때 용어를 더

정확하게 인식할 것이다.

해설

환자들은 질적 위험 용어가 언어로 제시될 때 그것을 과대평가하기 때문에, 그들이 위험에 대해 명확하게 인식할 수 있도록 수치로 제시되어야 한다는 내용이므로, 요약문의 빈칸 (A), (B)에 들어갈 말로는 ④ 'exaggerate(과장하다) – figures(수치)'가 가장 적절하다.
① 의심하다 – 예시 ② 간과하다 – 수치
③ 간과하다 – 부호 ⑤ 과장하다 – 예시

TEXT FLOW

도입	통계를 잘못 사용하는 것에 대한 중요한 대응은 더 많은 숫자를 주는 것임
전개 1	질적 위험 용어는 불명확함
전개 2	사람들은 라벨에 근거한 부작용의 빈도를 과대평가하고, 같은 용어도 맥락마다 다르게 해석됨
결론	수치로 제시될 때 위험에 대한 더 정확한 인식을 가지게 되므로 숫자로 명시되어야 함

구문

• For example, more severe side effects are estimated to occur less frequently than less severe side effects [described by the same qualitative term].
: [ ]는 less severe side effects를 수식하는 과거분사구이다.

11~12

정답 11 ① 12 ⑤

호주 원주민 수렵 채집인들은 가내 생산 방식의 표본인데, 이 방식에서는 최소의 외부 압력으로 가구 수준에서 생산 결정이 내려진다. 호주 원주민들은 노동, 기술, 자원을 그것들의 생산 가능한 최대한도까지 사용하지 않고, 그 대신 순전히 물질적인 관심사보다 자신들의 여가, 공유, 의례 활동을 극대화하기로 선택했다. 그들의 수렵 채집 체계의 상대적 일관성과 영속성은 호주 원주민들이 의도적이든 아니든 지속 가능한 성장 없는 문화를 고안해 냈다는 것을 말한다. 호주 원주민들은 잉여 생산물을 더 많은 인구를 부양하거나 경제적 생산을 증대하는 데 '투자'하지 않고, 그 대신 그것을 또한 사회 전체의 이익이 되고 문화의 재생산에 기여하는 방식으로 사람들이 자신들의 사회문화 자본을 구축하게 돕는 활동으로 돌렸다. 식량 공유, 의례상의 축제, 그리고 여가는 성장을 줄이는 효과를 제공했고, 호주 원주민들이 인구 증가와 부양 증대의 끝없는 순환의 딜레마를 피하는 데 도움이 되었다. 사람들이 식량을 공유했을 때는, 자신들의 당면한 필요를 제외하고는 생산하게 하는 유인이 거의 없었다.
호주 원주민들에 의해 제한된 물질 생산은 부분적으로는 수렵 채집 기술을 고려할 때 비용과 편익의 결정의 결과로 이해될 수 있다. 수렵 채집인들이 하루에 많은 시간을 일할수록 그들의 노력의 효율성은 더 떨어지는데, 이는 먹여야 하는 사람의 수에 비해 그들이 모으는 식량이 더 부족해지기 때문이다. 컴퓨터 시뮬레이션은 상대적으로 적은 작업 노력이 실제로 최대치의 지속 가능한 인구를 생겨나게 하고 수렵 채집 노력에 대한 최소의(→ 최상의) 보상을 산출한다는 것을 보여 준다. 그것이 직관에 어긋나는 것처럼 보일 수도 있지만, 수렵 채집에 쓰이는 더 긴 시간의 형태로 증가된 노력은 자원 고갈 때문에 효율성을 감소시킬 뿐인 것처럼 보인다.

해설

11 호주 원주민들이 지속 가능한 문화를 만들 수 있었던 것은 물질 생산보다는 여가, 공유, 의례 활동에 집중했기 때문이었다는 내용이므로, 글의 제목으로 가장 적절한 것은 ① '호주 원주민들은 왜 잉여 식량을 생산하지 않았는가?'이다.
② 문화 수도: 경제적 번영의 기반
③ 인구 증가가 호주 원주민 경제에 미친 영향
④ 호주 원주민들의 수익을 높이기 위한 노력 강화
⑤ 농업: 호주 원주민들의 자원 고갈에 대한 해답

12 수렵 채집인들이 더 많은 시간을 일할수록 먹여야 하는 사람의 수에 비해 그들의 식량은 더 부족해지기 때문에, 상대적으로 적은 작업 노력을 기울여야 실제로 최대치의 지속 가능한 인구와 수렵 채집 노력에 대한 최상의 보상이 가능하게 된다는 맥락이다. 따라서 ⑤의 'minimal(최소의)'을 'best(최상의)'와 같은 낱말로 바꾸어야 한다.

TEXT FLOW

도입	호주 원주민 수렵 채집인들은 가내 생산 방식의 표본임
전개 1	그들은 물질 생산보다는 여가, 공유, 의례 활동을 극대화하기로 선택함
전개 2	제한된 물질 생산은 수렵 채집 기술에 주어지는 비용과 편익의 결정의 결과로 이해될 수 있음
부연	하루에 더 많은 시간을 일할수록 먹여야 하는 사람의 수에 비해 모으는 식량이 더 부족해지기 때문임

구문

• Aborigines did not "invest" surplus production in **either** [supporting larger populations] **or** [expanding economic production]; instead they directed it into activities [that helped individuals build their social and cultural capital in ways {that also benefited society as a whole and contributed to the reproduction of the culture}].
: 첫 번째 [ ]와 두 번째 [ ]는 전치사 in의 목적어인 동명사구로, 「either A or B」 구문으로 연결되어 병렬 구조를 이루고 있다. 세 번째 [ ]는 activities를 수식하는 관계절이고, 그 안의 { }는 ways를 수식하는 관계절이다.

고난도 모의고사 12회

| 01 ④ | 02 ① | 03 ④ | 04 ② | 05 ① | 06 ① |
| 07 ② | 08 ⑤ | 09 ⑤ | 10 ④ | 11 ③ | 12 ② |

01
정답 ④

몇 가지 중요한 역학으로 인해 변호사의 필요성이 줄어들고 남아 있는 법률 업무에 대한 경쟁을 강화해 왔다. 기술이 부분적으로 원인이며, 많은 변호사 업무의 수요를 대체하고 있다. 개인 고객을 위해 일하는 변호사의 경우, 온라인 문서 준비 업무가 법률 시장에서 점점 더 많은 점유율을 확보하고 있다. 거의 모든 법률 업무 분야의 변호사들에게 있어, 전통적인 변호사직 '장인' 모델은 상품화된 법률 업무로 대체되고 있으며, 더 적은 비용으로 더 많은 성과를 내야 한다는 경제 전반의 가차 없는 압박은 이러한 추세를 강화할 것이다. 기술이 주도하는 법률 서비스 제공 업체들은 대형 로펌의 점심을 먹을 뿐만 아니라 아침과 저녁에도 눈독을 들이고 있다. 마찬가지로 각자의 시장에서 커지는 압박에 직면한 기업 고객들도 법률 비용을 줄이는 방식으로 대응해 왔다. 기업들은 더 일상적인 업무를 사내로 옮기고, 변호사와 고객 간의 장기적인 관계보다는 단기적인 경쟁력이 있는 고려 사항들을 기반으로 더 많은 사업을 분배하고 있다.

해설
온라인 법률 서비스 제공 업체들이 전통적인 '장인' 모델에 근거하여 운용되는 기존의 법률 회사들의 업무를 대체하며 더 많은 점유율 확보와 함께 기존 법률 회사의 거의 모든 서비스를 대체하려고 시도하고 있다는 맥락이므로, 밑줄 친 부분이 글에서 의미하는 바로 가장 적절한 것은 ④ '전통적인 법률 시장 전체를 장악하는 것을 목표로 하고'이다.
① 일상적인 업무에 대한 인상된 수수료를 요구하고
② 수수료를 기반으로 법률 서비스 품질을 결정하고
③ 무료 법률 서비스를 위한 새로운 기술을 개발하고
⑤ 전통적인 회사와 협력할 수 있는 기회를 모색하고

TEXT FLOW

도입	몇몇 이유로 변호사의 필요성이 줄어들고 법률 업무에 대한 경쟁을 강화해 옴
부연 1	온라인 문서 준비 업무가 전통적인 법률 회사의 업무를 대체하고, 이러한 추세는 강화되고 있음
부연 2	기업 고객들도 법률 비용을 줄이는 방식으로 대응해서 더 많은 사업을 분배하고 있음

구문
• Technology-driven legal service providers are**n't just** eating big law firm's lunch**;** they are eying breakfast and dinner **as well**.
: 'A뿐만 아니라 B도'를 의미하는 「not just A but B also」 구문이 쓰였다. 세미콜론(;)이 but을 대신하고 있고, as well은 also를 대신하고 있다.

02
정답 ①

우리는 필사적으로 정신적으로 활동하고 있기를 원한다. 우리는 지루함을 느끼는 것을 싫어한다. 그럼에도 불구하고, 우리는 또한 정신적 피로감도 피하려고 노력하는데, 그것은 힘든 일을 수행할 때 발생할 수 있다. 지루함과 정신적 피로는 우리를 기술이 거의 필요하지 않고 거의 틀림없이 우리의 삶을 결코 풍요롭게 하지 않는 쉬운 방식의 활동, 즉 아무 생각 없이 Facebook이나 Instagram을 스크롤하고, 비디오 게임을 하고, Netflix를 보는 등의 활동으로 이끌 수 있다. 이런 쉬운 활동 배출구는 몇 시간 동안 계속 우리를 통제할 수 있다. 우리의 관심을 끌어서 붙잡아 두도록, 우리가 지루함과 정신적 피로가 없도록 우리에게 최적으로 도전할 수 있게 매우 조심스럽게 만들어진 장치들이 우리가 어디로 향하든 우리를 둘러싸고 있다. 기계 구역으로 빠져드는 것은 매우 쉽다. 시작하는 데 우리에게 많은 기술이 필요하지 않고, 우리가 알기도 전에, 한 시간이 지났거나 우리에게 중독이 생겼다. 혹은 설상가상으로, 우리는 자신의 생명을 위험에 빠뜨릴 정도로, 즉 게임기를 여전히 우리 양손에 쥔 채 죽을 정도로, 신체적 필요를 무시했다.

해설
우리가 지루함과 정신적 피로 둘 다를 피하려고 한 결과, 시작하는 데 기술이 거의 필요하지 않고 우리 삶에 무익한 기계 중독에 빠지게 되었다는 내용의 글이다. 따라서 글의 제목으로 가장 적절한 것은 ① '지루함과 과부하가 결국 기계 중독으로 이어진다'이다.
② 정신적 피로감: 더 나은 기술을 위한 매우 중요한 동기 부여자
③ 디지털 엔터테인먼트는 우리를 이웃과 연결한다
④ 더 나은 기술, 더 나은 인간 인지
⑤ 기술의 발전은 지루함을 자아낸다

TEXT FLOW

도입	우리는 지루함과 정신적 피로를 모두 피하려고 노력함
전개	지루함과 정신적 피로는 우리를 쉬운 활동 배출구의 활동으로 이끌 수 있음
부연	이것들은 우리의 관심을 최대한 붙잡아 두어, 기계 중독에 빠지기 쉽게 함

구문
• Boredom and mental strain can push us toward [easy ways of engaging {that require little skill and arguably do not enrich our lives in any way}] — [scrolling mindlessly through Facebook or Instagram, playing video games, watching Netflix, etc].
: 첫 번째 [ ] 안의 { }는 easy ways of engaging을 수식하는 관계절이다. 두 번째 [ ]는 첫 번째 [ ]의 예를 구체적으로 나타내는 동격어구이다.

03
정답 ④

더 많은 혁신이 반드시 더 좋은 것은 아니라는 것을 명심하라. 일부 혁신 지지자들은 혁신에 대한 자신들의 분명한 열의에 도취되었는데, 그들은 모든 기업이 상당하고 지속적인 양의 혁신, 특히 급진적이며 판도를 바꾸는 혁신을 얻으려고 노력해야 한다고 권고해 왔다. 이것은 전혀 사실이 아니다. 제품 수명 주기가 두 번 지난 이후에도 생존하고자 하는 모든 조직은 건전한 혁신의 주입이 필요하고, 그것을 얻기 위해 투자해야 한다. 하지만 이것은 조직이 끊임없는 블록버스터급이거나 획기적인 혁신을 필요로 한다는 것을 의미하는 것은 아니다. 획기적이고 급진적인 혁신의 지속적인 공급을 효과적으로 활용할 수 있는 조직을 상상하기는 어려운데, 그런 혁신은 각각 그 조직의 사업과 기술 기반에 상당한 변화를 초래할 것이다. 그런 수준의 변화는 경쟁사를 괴롭힐 수도 있지만, 그것은 또한 지속적이고 급진적인 변화로 인해 조직에서

발생하는 엄청난 긴장 및 불안정과 더불어, 그런 혁신의 흐름을 개발하는 데 드는 막대한 비용을 고려할 때, 혁신하는 조직의 근간을 무너뜨릴 것이다.

해설

④ 앞 문장과 이어 줄 접속사가 필요하므로, breakthrough radical innovations를 받는 대명사의 역할을 하면서 접속사의 역할도 하는 관계대명사 which가 와야 한다.
① Some proponents of innovation은 동사 carry away의 대상에 해당하므로 수동태로 표현된 been carried는 어법상 적절하다.
② 주어가 Every organization이므로 단수형 동사 needs는 어법상 적절하다.
③ mean의 목적어 역할을 하는 명사절을 이끄는 접속사 that은 어법상 적절하다.
⑤ 명사구 a flow of innovations를 앞에서 한정하는 such는 어법상 적절하다.

TEXT FLOW

도입	혁신 지지자들은 기업이 급진적이고 판도를 바꾸는 혁신을 해야 한다고 권고함
반론	획기적이고 급진적인 혁신의 지속적인 공급은 상당한 변화를 초래하고 이를 효과적으로 활용하기 어려움
결론	이러한 변화는 경쟁사를 괴롭히거나 조직에 긴장 및 불안정과 더불어 막대한 비용이 들 수 있음

04
정답 ②

우리는 인생을 두 가지 방식으로 바라보는데, 그것은 우리가 우리 자신에 관해 스스로에게 하는 이야기와 진실된 우리 자신에 관한 이야기이다. 우리가 우리 자신에 관해 스스로에게 하는 이야기가 거짓이라고 말할 수는 없지만, 그것들은 흔히 우리의 성격에 의해 형성된다. 사회학 이론에서 상호 작용주의적 관점은 사회적 상호 작용이 인상 형성에 관한 협력적 활동이라고 말한다. 인상에는 두 가지 유형이 있는데, 그것은 우리가 '주는' 인상과 우리가 '발산하는' 인상이다. 우리가 주는 인상은 말투나 신체 언어와 같이 (거의) 통제할 수 있는 반면, 우리가 '발산하는' 인상은 거의 잠재의식적이며 통제할 수 없다. 우리가 '주는' 인상이 반드시 허구인 것은 아니지만, 그것들은 우리가 통제할 수 있기 때문에 왜곡되거나 과장될 수 있다. 우리 자신에 관해 스스로에게 하는 이야기는, 말하자면 우리가 '주는' 이야기이다. 언제나 사실인 우리 자신에 관한 이야기는 우리가 '발산하는' 이야기이며, 왜곡이나 과장에 의해 제약되지 않는다.

해설

(A) 우리는 우리가 '주는' 인상과 '발산하는' 인상 두 가지에 의해 자신의 인상을 만들어 나간다는 맥락이므로, '형성'을 의미하는 formation이 문맥상 적절하다.
(B) 우리가 '발산하는' 인상은 통제할 수 없고 언제나 사실이므로, '잠재의식적인'을 의미하는 subconscious가 문맥상 적절하다.
(C) 우리가 스스로에게 말하는 이야기는 '발산하는' 인상이고 그것은 우리 자신에 의해 왜곡되거나 과장되지 않는다는 맥락이므로, '제약되지 않다'를 의미하는 unconstrained가 문맥상 적절하다.

TEXT FLOW

도입	우리는 우리 자신에 관해 스스로에게 하는 이야기와 진실된 우리 자신에 관한 이야기의 방식으로 인생을 바라봄
전개	인상에는 우리가 '주는' 인상과 우리가 '발산하는' 인상이 있음
부연	우리가 '주는' 인상은 통제할 수 있지만, '발산하는' 인상은 잠재의식적이며 통제할 수 없음
결론	우리 자신에 관해 스스로에게 하는 이야기는 우리가 '주는' 이야기이고, 진실된 우리 자신에 관한 이야기는 우리가 '발산하는' 이야기임

구문

• The stories about ourselves [that are invariably true] are the ones [we "give off,"] [unconstrained by distortion or exaggeration].
: 첫 번째 [ ]는 The stories about ourselves를 수식하는 관계절이고, 두 번째 [ ]는 the stories about ourselves를 대신하는 the ones를 수식하는 관계절이다. 세 번째 [ ]는 앞의 내용 전체를 부연 설명하는 분사구문이다.

05
정답 ①

일부 사상가들은 전쟁이나 전투의 목표가 자신의 모든 적을 죽이는 것이라고 가정한다. 철학자 Elaine Scarry가 자신의 사색이 깊은 책 'The Body in Pain'에서 설명한 것처럼, 그것은 잘못 알고 있는 것이다. 전쟁은 양립할 수 없는 생각에서 비롯된다. 국경을 어디에 그어야 하는지, 또는 그들이 서로를 어떻게 대해야 하는지, 또는 어느 나라가 최고의 정치적, 경제적, 또는 종교적 시스템을 가지고 있는지에 대해 두 나라의 생각이 서로 다르다. 불일치에 직면할 때, 그들은 상대 나라가 동의하도록 강제하기 위해, 자국민의 생명과 신체 그리고 그들 재산의 일부를 기꺼이 위험에 처하게 할 것이다. 마찬가지로 상대방도 논쟁에서 이기기 위해 자국민과 그들의 자원 일부를 차라리 위태롭게 하겠다고 생각한다. 전투 중에 양측은 자신들이 선호하는 생각을 위해 사람들과 다른 자원(일반적인 문구로 생명과 재산)을 잃는다. 한쪽이 완전히 전멸할 때까지 추구되는 전투나 전쟁은 거의 없다. 오히려, 어느 시점에서, 한쪽이 생명과 재산을 더 이상 잃는 것보다는 자신들의 생각 일부를 포기하겠다고 결정한다. 그것은 항복한다.

해설

서로 생각이 다른 두 나라는 자신의 생각에 상대방이 동의하도록 하기 위해 전투나 전쟁을 하는데, 그 와중에 생명과 재산을 잃기도 하지만, 어느 순간 한쪽이 생명과 재산을 더 이상 잃는 것보다는 생각을 일부 포기하겠다고 하면 전쟁이 끝난다는 흐름이므로, 빈칸에 들어갈 말로 가장 적절한 것은 ① '항복하다'이다.
② 공표되다 ③ 계속하다 ④ 대립하다 ⑤ 지배하다

TEXT FLOW

도입	일부 사상가들은 전쟁이 모든 적을 죽이는 것이라고 하지만 이는 잘못된 생각임
전개 1	불일치에 직면하면, 상대 나라가 동의하도록 강제하기 위해 자국민의 생명과 재산의 일부를 위험에 처하게 함
전개 2	전투 중에 양측은 자신들의 생각을 위해 사람과 자원을 잃음
결론	한쪽이 완전히 전멸하기 전, 자신들의 생각 일부를 포기하겠다고 결정하여 항복함

구문

• Rather, at some point, one side decides [that it **would rather** give up on some of its ideas **than** lose any more of its lives and wealth].

: [ ]는 문장의 동사 decides의 목적어 역할을 하는 명사절로, 'B하기보다는 차라리 A하겠다'는 의미의 「would rather A than B」가 사용되었다. 이때 than 다음에 동사원형이 오는 것에 유의한다.

06 정답 ①

우리에게 과부하가 걸리는 바로 그 순간에, 이메일은 업무 진행을 돕고, 조직의 경향을 평가하고, 동료 직원의 의견, 제안, 아이디어를 받는 데 유용하다. 이러한 이점을 유지하면서 나 자신의 생산성을 높이기 위해 나는 화면에 여러 개의 '누름 버튼'을 만들었다. 내가 버튼을 클릭하면, 그것이 수신자에게 내 결론이나 질문을 알려 주는 미리 설정된 메모를 삽입하고, 주석이 달린 메시지를 내 비서나 내게 메시지를 이메일로 보낸 사람에게 전송하며, 수신 메시지 목록에서 메일을 삭제하는데, 모든 작업은 한 번의 클릭으로 이루어진다. 나에게는 '네, 제가 할게요.', '아니요.', '당신이 처리하세요.', '대화합시다.' 등의 말이 적절하게 표시된 각기 다른 버튼이 있다. 나는 이러한 누름 버튼을 통해 메시지 당 평균 응답 시간을 1분 미만으로 줄일 수 있을 정도로 충분한 메시지에 회신할 수 있었다. 의심의 여지없이, 미래의 이메일 소프트웨어에는 우리의 이메일 부하를 줄이는 데 도움이 될 이러한 기능이 포함될 것이다. 물론, 이 기술이 근본적인 문제를 제거하지는 못한다. 그것은 단지 그것의 시작을 지연시킬 뿐이다.

해설

이메일의 이점을 유지하면서 생산성을 높이기 위해 필자는 미리 기능이나 메시지를 설정해 놓은 여러 개의 누름 버튼을 만들어 놓고, 필요한 버튼만 누름으로써 시간을 단축하여 많은 이메일에 회신할 수 있었다는 내용의 글이다. 따라서 빈칸에 들어갈 말로 가장 적절한 것은 ① '우리의 이메일 부하를 줄이는'이다.
② 이메일의 긴급성을 판단하는
③ 대인 관계를 늘리는
④ 우리의 실시간 예측 속도를 향상시키는
⑤ 알 수 없는 발송자에게서 온 메일을 차단하는

TEXT FLOW

도입	이메일은 업무에 있어서 유용함
전개	생산성을 높이기 위해 화면에 여러 개의 '누름 버튼'을 만들었음
부연	미리 설정된 메모, 메시지, 메일 삭제 기능의 버튼이 있어서 시간을 단축할 수 있음
결론	미래의 이메일 소프트웨어에는 이러한 이메일 부하를 줄일 기능이 포함될 것임

구문

• When I click on a button, it **inserts** a preset note [informing the recipient of my conclusion or question], **forwards** the annotated message to my assistant or the person [who emailed me the message], and **removes** the mail from the incoming message list — all with one click.

: inserts, forwards, removes가 and에 의해 병렬 구조를 이루고 있다. 첫 번째 [ ]는 a preset note를 수식하는 현재분사구이고, 두 번째 [ ]는 the person을 수식하는 관계절이다.

07 정답 ②

주자로서, 우리가 명심해야 할 것이 하나 있다. 우리가 장기적으로 투자하지 않을 때, 일정에 행사가 없으면 스스로 동기를 부여하기 어렵다고 느낄 수도 있다. 우리의 훈련은 주자로서 그리고 인간으로서 우리의 장기적인 성장을 희생하면서 경주 당일의 요구에 지나치게 집중될 수도 있다. 우리는 우리의 인식된 가장 큰 약점을 극복하는 데 (병적으로) 집착하기 때문에 도움이 되거나 건강에 좋은 것보다 더 많은 장거리 달리기나 수직(수직 고도 상승) 훈련을 밀어 넣으려고 할 수도 있다. 우리는 심지어 그것이 의도적이었다는 것을 마음속 깊이 알고 있을 때, 결백과 의도치 않은 실수를 주장하며 추가 훈련을 집어넣거나 계획을 무시하는 방법을 찾는 지점에 이를 수도 있다. 어떤 퇴보이든지 재앙처럼 느껴진다. 의지할 일관된 훈련 기반이 없다면 뒤로 물러나는 가장 작은 발걸음은 우리를 심각한 퇴보로 몰아넣는다. 우리는 다음 결과를 달성하면 우리가 이러한 행동을 멈출 것이라고 스스로에게 말할 수도 있지만, 그것들은 중독성이 생겨서 멈추기 어려울 수 있다.

해설

장기적인 훈련 계획에 근거하여 훈련하지 않을 때 일정에 행사가 없으면 스스로 동기를 부여하기 어려울 수도 있으며, 훈련이 단기적인 성취에 지나치게 집중되고 어떤 퇴보라도 마치 재앙처럼 느끼면서 지나친 훈련을 하게 될 수도 있다는 내용이므로, 빈칸에 들어갈 말로 가장 적절한 것은 ② '장기적으로 투자하지 않을'이다.
① 우리의 약점을 극복하지 못할
③ 예상치 못한 방해를 맞닥뜨릴
④ 사소한 좌절을 너무 자주 겪을
⑤ 교육 일정을 변경하려고 하지 않을

⊗ 매력적인 오답 주의!

④ 글 전체의 의미를 이해하기보다 weakness, mistakes, The smallest steps backward make us sink into serious regression 등의 단편적인 어휘나 표현을 근거로 선택한 것으로 보인다. [선택률 25%]

TEXT FLOW

주제	장기적으로 투자하지 않을 때, 일정에 행사가 없으면 스스로 동기를 부여하기 어려움
부연 1	장기적인 성장을 방해하는 경주 당일의 요구에 집중하거나 힘든 훈련을 넣음
부연 2	의지할 일관된 훈련 기반이 없다면 우리를 퇴보로 몰아넣음

구문

• We may try to cram in **more** long runs or vert (vertical elevation gain) [**than** is helpful or healthy] because we are fixated on overcoming our perceived biggest weakness.

: [ ]는 선행사 more long runs or vert를 수식하는 관계절이다. than이 관계대명사의 역할을 하며, 이때 선행사에 보통 비교급 표현이 쓰인다.

08 정답 ⑤

인류가 처음에는 로봇으로, 그다음에는 동물로, 그리고 마침내는 인간으로 자신의 존재를 우주로 확장하기 시작한 것은 불과 50년 전이었다. (C) 다른 세계를 향한 우리 종(種)의 이러한 시험적인 확장은 기술의 발달에 의해 가능해졌는데, 그것은 마침내 우리의 상상력과 탐험 욕구를 보완하고 뒷받침할 수 있는 수준에 도달하기 시작했다. (B) 그러나 우주의 크기와 여러 세계에서 제법 생명체가 바싹 파고들 만한 장소라고 기대되는 곳의 수가 증가하고 있는 것을 고려할 때, 탐색은 겨우 시작되었다. 우리가 마침내 다른 세계에서 생명체를 발견하게 되면, 그리고 우리는 그럴 것인데, 그것은 인류 역사상 가장 중요한 문화적 사건 중 하나가 될 것이며 우리의 기원에 대한 질문에 지대한 영향을 끼칠 것이다. (A) 그러므로 그러한 가능성이 문자 기록을 가지고 있었던 그 먼 옛날부터 원시적이든 선진적이든 모든 인류 문명과 문화에 의해 논의되어 왔음을 아는 것은 놀랄 일이 아니다. 이러한 생각에 이름이 붙여지기 전에 조차도, 외계에 대한 그런 호기심은 신화, 동굴 벽화, 허구 문학, 음악과 시, 그리고 나중에는 영화와 TV 프로그램을 통해 그 배출구를 찾았다.

해설

인류가 자신의 존재를 점차 확장해 가기 시작한 것이 불과 50년 전이었다는 내용의 주어진 글 다음에는, 그 내용을 This tentative expansion of our species towards other worlds로 받아서 글을 이어 가는 (C)가 온 다음, However로 시작하여 그런 탐색이 겨우 시작된 것인데, 다른 세계에서 생명체를 발견하면 그것은 인류 역사상 가장 중요한 문화적 사건 중 하나가 될 것이라는 내용의 (B)가 온 후, 마지막으로 therefore와 such possibilities로 (B)의 내용을 이어 가는 (A)가 오는 것이 글의 순서로 가장 적절하다.

TEXT FLOW

도입	인류가 자신의 존재를 우주로 확장하기 시작한 것은 불과 50년 전임
부연 1	이는 우리의 상상력과 탐험 욕구를 뒷받침할 수 있는 기술의 발달에 의해 가능해짐
부연 2	탐색은 겨우 시작되었고, 외계에서 생명체를 발견하면 인류 역사상 가장 중요한 문화적 사건이 될 것임
부연 3	그 가능성은 문자 기록을 가지고 있던 먼 옛날부터 논의되어 왔었음

구문

• However, **considering** the size of the universe and the growing number of promising sites on many worlds [where life might quite like to snuggle up], the search has barely begun.
: considering은 '~을 고려할 때'의 의미를 갖는 전치사이다. [ ]는 many worlds를 수식하는 관계절이다.

09
정답 ⑤

지저귀는 새에 있어 뇌의 좌우 기능 분화는 다른 새들이 부르는 친숙한 노래를 인식하고 자신들의 노래를 만드는 능력의 필수적인 부분인 것처럼 보인다. 비록 지저귀는 새의 뇌 양쪽 반구에 노래를 담당하는 동일한 핵의 집합이 존재하지만, 오직 좌반구에 있는 노래를 담당하는 핵의 집합만이 노래 부르는 것을 조절한다. 노래 조절에 대한 좌반구의 이러한 우위는 금화조를 제외한 지금까지 연구된 모든 지저귀는 새의 종에서 발견되었다. 이 종에서는 우반구가 노래를 만드는 데 더 큰 역할을 하기는 하지만, 좌반구 또한 어떤 역할을 지니고 있다. 노래를 담당하는 핵은 노래를 만드는 데뿐만 아니라 노래를 인식하는 데도 쓰이고, 이러한 노래에 대한 인식은 좌우 반구에서 다르다. 금화조는 자신이 듣고 있는 노래의 개별 음절에 있는 배음에 대한 정보를 처리하기 위해 우반구를 사용하고, 좌반구는 노래 전체에 대한 정보를 처리하기 위해 사용한다. 즉 우반구는 노래의 세부 사항을 처리하는 반면, 좌반구는 노래 전체를 듣고 그렇게 함으로써 친숙한 노래와 낯선 노래를 구별하는 데 사용된다.

해설

주어진 문장은 금화조가 노래의 개별 음절에 있는 배음에 대한 정보 처리를 위해서는 우반구를 사용하고, 노래 전체에 대한 정보 처리를 위해서는 좌반구를 사용한다는 내용이다. 이 문장의 앞에는 뇌의 좌우 반구가 하는 일이 다르다는 내용이, 뒤에는 이 문장을 부연 설명하는 문장이 와야 자연스러운 흐름이 되므로, 주어진 문장이 들어갈 가장 적절한 곳은 ⑤이다.

⑦ WHY 고난도

각 문장이 새가 노래를 인식하고 만드는 데 있어 뇌의 좌우 기능이 다르다는 진술을 반복하고 있어 문장 간의 논리적 흐름이 부자연스러운 곳을 찾기가 쉽지 않은 고난도 문제이다.

TEXT FLOW

도입	지저귀는 새에 있어 뇌의 좌우 기능 분화는 노래를 인식하고 노래를 만드는 능력의 필수적인 부분임
전개 1	금화조를 제외한 모든 새는 좌반구에서 노래 부르는 것을 조절함
전개 2	금화조는 노래의 개별 음정을 처리하기 위해 우반구를 쓰고, 노래 전체에 대한 정보를 처리하기 위해 좌반구를 씀

구문

• **Lateralization** of the brain in songbirds **seems** to be an essential part of their ability [to recognize familiar songs {sung by other birds}] and [to produce their own songs].
: 주어의 핵이 Lateralization이므로 단수 동사 seems가 쓰였다. 두 개의 [ ]는 their ability를 수식하는 형용사적 용법의 to부정사구로 and에 의해 병렬 구조를 이루고 있다. { }는 familiar songs를 수식하는 과거분사구이다.

10
정답 ④

예언의 목적이 미래에 대한 불확실성을 없애고자 하는 것이긴 하지만, 무작위의 형태를 띤 불확실성은 자주 예언을 만들어 내는 데 사용되는 기제이다. 찻잎과 서양톱풀의 줄기가 떨어지는 무작위의 방식은 이것을 분명히 보여 준다. 그것은 마치 무작위성이 '정보'를 알려 주는 힘으로 가는 입구로 작용하는 것 같다. Théphile Gautier는 그것을 설명하는 멋진 방식을 가지고 있었다. 그는 "아마도 우연은 신이 서명하고 싶지 않을 때(자신을 알리고 싶지 않을 때) 사용하는 신의 필명인 것 같다."라고 말했다. 찻잎과 서양톱풀 줄기의 예는 또한 초자연적인 메시지를 해석하기 위해서는 자주 특별한 종류의 지식이 필요하다는 것을 보여 준다. 사실상, 신비주의자, 사제, 예언자, 그리고 제사장은 부분적으로 신으로부터 전달된 메시지를 이해할 수 있는 유일한 인간으로서의 독특한 중간자 역할 때문에 사회에서 자신의 지위를 유지하는 것이다. Tacitus 시대의 게르만 사제들이 룬 문자가 새겨진 나무껍질 줄기를 무작위로 골라 선택했을 때, 그리고 유대인들이 제비를 뽑아서 중요한 결정을 했을 때, 그 무작위의 과정은 우월한 존재의 의지가 자신을 나타낼 수 있는 기회를 주는 것 같아 보였다. 성경에 이르기를, "뽑은 제비는 무릎에 떨어지지만, 그것의 모든 결정은 신으로부터 나온다."

➡ 무작위한 일들에서 신의 메시지를 해석하는 특별한 지식을 소유하는 것은 몇몇 선택된 개인들이 사회에서 그들의 지위를 유지하도록 해 주었다.

해설

세상의 불확실성은 그것을 이해하고 미래를 예측하고자 하는 욕구로 이어지며, 예언자들이 특별한 지식을 가진 해석자의 역할을 맡아 신의 의지가 표현되는 방식을 설명했다는 내용의 글이다. 따라서 요약문의 빈칸 (A), (B)에 들어갈 말로는 ④ 'divine(신의) - hold(유지하다)'가 가장 적절하다.

① 조작된 - 유지하다
② 조작된 - 거절하다
③ 고대의 - 변하다
⑤ 신의 - 변하다

TEXT FLOW

도입	무작위의 형태를 띤 불확실성은 예언을 만들어 내는 데 사용되는 기제임
부연 1	이 무작위성은 신이 정보를 알려 주는 힘으로 작용함
부연 2	예언자들은 신으로부터 전달된 메시지를 이해하는 중간자 역할로 사회에서 자신의 지위를 유지함

구문

• Although the aim of a prophecy is [to remove uncertainty about the future], uncertainty in the form of randomness is frequently the mechanism [used to generate prophecies].
: 첫 번째 [ ]는 주격 보어 역할을 하는 to부정사구이고, 두 번째 [ ]는 the mechanism을 수식하는 과거분사구이다.

11-12

정답 11 ③   12 ②

타인의 고통에서 기쁨을 경험하는 'Schadenfreude'는 여러 연구에서 보여 주었듯이 명백히 시샘과 관련이 있다. 우리가 누군가를 시샘할 때, 그들이 좌절을 겪거나 어떤 식으로 괴로워하면 우리는 신이 나거나 기쁨까지도 느끼는 경향이 있다. 그러나 그보다는 그 정반대를 실행하는 것이 현명할 것인데, 그것은 철학자인 Friedrich Nietzsche가 'Mitfreude'라고 부른 것으로, '함께 기뻐하는 것'이다. 그가 썼듯이, "우리를 무는 뱀은 우리를 다치게 할 의도이고, 그렇게 할 때 그것이 기뻐하는데, 가장 하등인 동물도 다른 사람의 고통을 상상할 수 있다. 그러나 타인의 기쁨을 상상하고 그것에 기뻐하는 것은 가장 고등인 동물들의 최고 특권이다."
이것은 하기 쉽고 쉽게 잊히는 것으로 사람들의 행운을 그저 축하하는 것 대신, 공감의 한 형태로, 적극적으로 그들의 기쁨을 느끼려고 노력해야 한다는 것을 의미한다. 이것은 우리의 첫 번째 성향이 시샘의 고통을 느끼는 것이기 때문에 다소 자연스러울(→ 부자연스러울) 수 있지만, 다른 사람들이 스스로의 행복이나 만족감을 경험하는 것이 그들에게 어떻게 느껴질 것임에 틀림없는지 상상하도록 우리는 스스로를 훈련시킬 수 있다. 이것은 우리의 뇌에서 추한 시샘을 깨끗하게 없앨 뿐만 아니라 또한 흔치 않은 형태의 친밀한 관계를 만든다. 우리가 'Mitfreude'의 대상이 된다면, 우리는 단지 말을 듣는 것 대신에, 우리의 행운에 대해 상대방의 진정한 흥분을 느끼고, 이는 우리가 그들에 대해 똑같이 느끼도록 유도한다. 그것은 워낙 드문 일이기 때문에 그것에는 사람을 결속시키는 큰 힘이 담겨 있다. 그리고 다른 사람의 기쁨을 내면화할 때 우리 자신의 경험과 관련하여 이 감정을 느낄 수 있는 우리 자신의 능력을 늘린다.

해설

11 다른 사람의 고통에 대해 기쁨을 느끼는 것은 상대방에 대한 시샘에 바탕을 둔 감정이 우리의 첫 번째 성향이기 때문에 흔히 있는 일일 수 있지만, 그보다는 타인의 기쁨에 대해 함께 기뻐할 수 있도록 자신을 훈련하라는 내용의 글이므로, 글의 제목으로 가장 적절한 것은 ③ '타인의 고통이 아니라 타인의 기쁨에서 기쁨을 느껴라'이다.
① 공감은 진정으로 학습할 수 있을까?

② 부러움은 영감이나 갈등의 원천인가?
④ 감정 공유: 동물과 인간의 차이
⑤ 인간관계의 기반으로서 협력이 아닌 경쟁

12 우리의 첫 번째 성향이 시샘의 고통을 느끼는 것이기 때문에 다른 사람의 기쁨을 공감의 형태로 적극적으로 느끼는 것은 다소 부자연스러울 수 있지만 훈련을 통해 타인의 기쁨을 경험하도록 상상할 수 있다는 맥락이 되어야 하므로, ②의 'natural(자연스러운)'을 'unnatural(부자연스러운)'과 같은 낱말로 바꾸어야 한다.

TEXT FLOW

도입	우리는 타인의 고통에서 기쁨을 느끼는 경향이 있음
전개 1	함께 기뻐하는 것을 실행하는 것이 더 현명하고, 고등 동물들의 최고 특권임
전개 2	이것은 공감의 한 형태로 노력하고 훈련해야 함
전개 3	흔치 않은 형태의 친밀한 관계를 만들고, 사람을 결속시키는 힘이 있음

구문

• But it would be wise to practice instead the opposite, [what the philosopher Friedrich Nietzsche called *Mitfreude*] — "joying with."
: [ ]는 the opposite의 구체적인 내용을 설명하는 동격절이고 "joying with"는 *Mitfreude*의 의미를 설명하고 있다.

고난도 모의고사 13회

01 ②	02 ①	03 ④	04 ①	05 ④	06 ⑤
07 ④	08 ④	09 ②	10 ⑤	11 ②	12 ⑤

01

정답 ②

고통이 심한데 의미 있는 부상은 발생하지 않았다면 어떻게 될까? 그 고통은 진짜인가? '부상이 곧 발생할 것'이라는 고통이 하는 역할의 이런 진실성의 모순이 바로 침을 쏘는 곤충들이 이용하는 것이다. 누군가 벌을 밟을 때, 이 벌이 발바닥에 쏜 침은 고통을 유발하고, 발을 드는 것이 벌에게 이로운 반응이다. 이 침 쏘기로 의미 있는 신체적 부상이 그 사람에게 유발되었는가? 흔히 그 대답은 '아니요'이다. 침을 쏘는 곤충은 고통 신호의 정직함 속에서 이 약점을 자기에게 이롭게 이용하는 데 명수이다. 침을 쏘는 곤충에게, 우리는 단지 속임수에 속아 넘어가는 바보일지도 모른다. 우리에게는 확실한 것보다 <u>안전한 것</u>이 더 나은데, 그런 까닭에 우리는 그 (고통) 신호가 정말이라고 믿는다. 부상이 사실인 경우에, 그 부정적인 손실(부상)은 그 고통을 무시함으로써 얻게 되는 그 어떤 편익보다 훨씬 더 클 수 있다. (부상의) 위험을 왜 무릅쓰겠는가? 생명의 위험-편익 방정식에서 (부상의) 그 위험은 흔히 그 어떤 잠재적 이득도 축소한다. 여기에서 고통의 심리가 성립한다. 동물이나 인간이 고통의 저편에서 이로움이라는 무지개가 기다리고 있다는 것을 알 수 없다면, 자연스러운 심리는 무지개를 좇지 말라고 지시한다.

해설

우리는 고통이 가져오는 부상이 진짜인 경우에 그 부정적인 손실이 고통을 무시함으로써 얻게 되는 이익보다 훨씬 크기 때문에 고통이 신체적 부상을 정말로 가져온다고 쉽게 속아 넘어간다는 고통의 심리에 관한 글이다. 따라서 고통의 심리에 대한 이유를 설명하는 밑줄 친 부분이 의미하는 바로 가장 적절한 것은 ② '고통이 손실로 이어질 것임을 가정하는 것'이다.
① 고통 신호의 정직성을 의심하는 것
③ 고통의 진실성을 맹목적으로 받아들이지 않는 것
④ 고통을 무시함으로써 이익을 극대화하는 것
⑤ 고통을 이용하는 곤충의 속임수에 넘어가지 않는 것

TEXT FLOW

도입	부상이 발생할 것이라는 고통이 하는 역할의 진실성의 모순이 침을 쏘는 곤충들이 이용하는 것임
전개 1	침을 쏘는 곤충은 고통 신호의 정직함을 자기에게 이롭게 이용하고 있음
전개 2	우리는 확실한 것보다 안전한 것이 더 나으므로 고통 신호가 사실이라고 믿음
전개 3	부상이 진짜인 경우 그 손실이 고통을 무시함으로써 얻는 이익보다 더 클 수 있음

구문

• **If** the damage **were** real, the downside cost **could** far **outweigh** any benefit [obtained by ignoring the pain].
: 「If+주어+were ~, 주어+could+동사원형 ....」의 가정법 과거 구문으로 현재 사실에 반대되는 가정을 하고 있다. [ ]는 any benefit을 수식하는 과거분사구이다.

02

정답 ①

연구는 반대자들이 '숨겨진' 영향력을 가지고 있다는 것을 반복적으로 보여준다. 일반적으로, 그들은 공개적인 곳보다는 사적인 곳에서 더 많이 태도를 변화시킨다. 그들은 다수의 사람이 그 영향력을 깨닫지 못하거나 인정하지 않더라도 마음을 변화시킨다. 우리는 모의 배심원단 심의를 이용하는 우리의 많은 연구에서 이러한 패턴을 본다. 반대자가 타협하지 않으면 합의에 좀처럼 도달되지 않는다. 대다수는 의견을 바꾸지 않을 것이다. 그들은 단지 짜증을 낼 뿐이다. 하지만 반복되는 패턴은 심의 중 불과 10분 후에 그리고 아무런 움직임이 없음에도 불구하고 태도에서 변화가 있다. 참가자들은 흔히 이러한 변화를 직접적으로 인식하지 못하지만, 연구자가 질문의 문구를 바꾸면 그들의 반응은 자신들의 태도 변화를 반영한다. 연구자는 "원고가 두 배의 금액을 요구했다면 어떨까요?"와 같은 무수한 '가정'의 질문을 할 수 있다. 이를 통해 다수가 보호되는데, 그들은 반대자에게 설득당했다는 것을 인정하지 않고도 마음을 바꿀 수 있다.

해설

반대자들은 다수의 사람들이 깨닫지 못하거나 인정하지 않더라도 사람들의 마음을 바꾸게 하는, 숨겨진 영향력을 가지고 있다는 내용의 글이다. 따라서 글의 제목으로 가장 적절한 것은 ① '반대의 영향력: 보이는 것 이상'이다.
② 다수결 원칙에 관한 숨겨진 가정
③ 반대가 소용없는 이유: 완고한 다수
④ 반대자가 많을 때만 발생하는 갈등
⑤ 효과적인 문제 해결 도구로서의 타협

TEXT FLOW

도입	반대자들이 숨겨진 영향력을 가지고 있음
전개	그들은 다수의 사람들이 깨닫지 못하거나 인정하지 않더라도 그들의 마음을 변화시킴
예시	모의 배심원단 심의에서 반대자가 타협하지 않으면 합의에 좀처럼 도달되지 않음
부연	반복되는 패턴으로 다수의 사람들은 인식하지 못하지만 태도에서 변화가 생김

구문

• This gives the majority cover: [they can change their minds without acknowledging **having been persuaded** by the dissenter].
: [ ]는 앞 문장의 내용을 구체적으로 설명하는 동격절이다. having been persuaded의 완료 동명사를 사용한 것은 인정하는 것은 현재이고 설득당한 것은 과거에 일어난 일이기 때문이다. 동명사의 시제가 주절의 시제보다 한 시제 앞설 때는 「having+p.p.」 형태의 완료 동명사를 사용한다.

03

정답 ④

아마도 다른 어떤 종보다도, 인간들은 놀랍도록 긴 시간 동안 그야말로 서로를 사랑한다. 그들은 다른 사람들에게 시간과 에너지, 심지어 자신의 생명까지 줄 정도로 사랑한다. 사람들이 자신의 친족이 아니고 아마도 개인적으로 그들을 도울 수 없는 사람들을 돕기 위해 자신들의 자산, 그리고 그들의 지위로부터 얻는 그 어떤 영향력이든지 사용하는 것을 보는 것은 흔한 일이다. 과학자들은 이제 이러한 종류의 이타적인 사랑에 대한 설명을 제공한다. 그들은 집단들이 대체로 이타적인 구성원들이 있을 때 매우 자주 더 잘 생존한다는 것을 보여 주었다. 오래 전에는 이타적인 행동, 즉 모두가 생존하도록 돕는 행동은 자신의 고기를 나누는 것을 의미했다. 오늘날 집단적인 생존은 직장에서의 팀워크와 가정에서의 가족에 대한 충실이 가장 중요하다. 이타주의는 유전적으로나 문화적으로 도덕적 가치로 전승될 수 있지만, 그것이 어떻게 발생하든 간에, 그것은 생존을 돕는다. 무임승차자나 지위에 집착하는 사람들로만 전적으로 구성된 집단들은 다음 세대까지 도달할 가능성이 더 낮다.

해설

④ 뒤에 이어지는 절이 문장의 필수 요소를 모두 갖추고 있으므로 복합관계대명사 whatever를 써서는 안 되고 복합관계부사인 however로 바꿔야 한다.

① to see ~ resources와 and로 대등하게 연결된 to부정사구를 유도하므로 to help를 쓰는 것은 적절하다.

② 형용사인 altruistic을 수식하므로 부사인 mostly를 쓰는 것은 적절하다.

③ behavior를 수식하는 관계절을 유도하며 관계절에서 주어 역할을 하므로, 관계대명사 that을 쓰는 것은 적절하다.

⑤ Groups를 수식하는 분사구를 유도하며 수동의 의미이므로, 과거분사인 made를 쓰는 것은 적절하다.

TEXT FLOW

도입	인간은 이타적인 사랑을 함
부연	과학자들은 집단에서 이타적인 구성원들이 있을 때 더 잘 생존한다고 함
예시	예전에는 자신의 고기를 나눠주는 행동으로, 오늘날은 직장에서의 팀워크와 가정에서의 가족에 대한 충성으로 나타남
결론	이타주의는 생존을 도움

04 정답 ①

만성적인 스트레스는 뇌가 위협을 처리하는 방식에 영향을 미친다. 사람의 공포 반응은 환경에서 눈에 띄는 위협을 감지하고 공포와 불안감을 유발하는 데 도움을 주는 편도체와 사람의 반응을 현실에 맞게 조정하는 전두엽 피질 및 기타 뇌피질부를 포함하여 다수의 뇌 부위를 수반한다. 사람이 감정 조절 상태에 있을 때 이러한 반응은 균형 잡힌 상태이다. 그러나 장기간의 스트레스는 편도체의 활동을 증가시켜 이 부위의 뉴런 성장을 촉진하는 한편 전두엽 피질의 힘을 감소시킨다. 이것은 사람의 감정 조절 능력을 없앤다. 두려움은 치안 유지에 역할을 하지만(범죄자의 총격 사건 현장에 처음 도착했을 때 두려움을 느끼는 것은 당연한 일이다), 만성적으로 스트레스를 받는 경찰관은 두려움을 느끼고 이에 대응하는 데 더 빠를 수도 있다. 편도체 활동이 증가하고 전두엽 피질의 반응이 약해지는 것은 공격성과도 관련이 있으므로, 그 경찰관은 또한 폭력에 더 취약할 수 있다.

해설

(A) 사람의 공포 반응과 관련된 편도체에 대한 설명으로 뒤에 공포와 불안감을 유발한다는 내용이 이어지므로, '감지하다'의 의미인 detect가 문맥상 적절하다.

(B) 사람이 감정 조절 상태에 있을 때 편도체와 전두엽 피질 및 기타 뇌피질부의 반응은 균형 잡힌 상태일 것이므로, '균형 잡힌'의 의미인 balanced가 문맥상 적절하다.

(C) 스트레스를 받으면 눈에 띄는 위협을 감지하고 공포와 불안감을 유발하는 편도체의 활동을 증가시켜 공포감을 조절하는 능력이 감소된다고 하였으므로, '더 빠른'의 의미인 faster가 문맥상 적절하다.

TEXT FLOW

주제	만성적인 스트레스는 뇌가 위협을 처리하는 방식에 영향을 미침
부연	장기간의 스트레스는 편도체의 활동을 증가시키고, 전두엽 피질의 힘을 감소시켜 감정 조절 능력을 없앰
예시	만성적으로 스트레스를 받은 경찰관은 두려움을 느끼고 이에 대응하는 데 더 빠를 수도 있음

구문

• A person's fear response involves multiple parts of the brain, including **the amygdala**, [which helps detect noticeable threats in the environment and generate feelings of fear and anxiety], and **the prefrontal cortex and other areas**, [which modulate a person's reaction to bring it in line with reality].

: the amygdala와 the prefrontal cortex and other areas는 전치사 including의 목적어이고, 두 개의 [ ]는 각각 앞의 목적어에 대해 부연 설명하는 계속적 용법의 관계절이다.

05 정답 ④

모든 조직이 그것의 지배적인 견해, 가치, 그리고 규범을 형성하고 가르치는 것은 바로 언어를 통해서이다. 견해는 학습된 언어 내의 단어에서 만들어진다. 언어에서의 강조는 견해에서의 강조를 만들어 낸다. 따라서 자본주의 사회에서 우리는 '경쟁', '자유 기업', '이익', '개인의 노력', '사유 재산', 그리고 '시장' 같은 특정한 단어들을 반복해서 사용하기 쉽다. 이 단어들을 중심으로 반복해서 강화되는 일련의 견해들이 증가할 것이다. 우리가 사회주의에 관한 견해를 가질 수는 있지만, 물론 그것들이 자본주의에 대한 우리의 헌신과 관련해서 부정적으로 사용되지 않는 한 그런 견해들은 덜 강화된다. 정치 지도자들은 단어의 사용이 사람들의 사고에 영향을 미치는 중요한 방식이라는 것을 알고 있으며, 지지를 얻기 위해 단어들은 신중하게 선택된다. '테러와의 전쟁', '악한 집단', '선제적 전쟁'은 모두 우리가 싸우고자 하는 대상을 향한 정책을 우리가 '이해'하고 지지하도록 돕기 위해 지도자들이 사용하는 어구들이다. '상속세', '세속주의자', '파시즘 신봉자', '자유주의 교수', 그리고 '진화론자'는 매우 복잡한 문제에 대한 단순한 설명을 의심 없이 받아들이도록 우리에게 영향을 미치기 위해 사용되는 어구들이다.

해설

어떤 면을 강조하기 위한 단어를 선택해서 사용하면 특정한 견해가 강조된다는 내용의 글이다. 정치 지도자들이 지지를 얻기 위해 단어들을 신중하게 선택한다는 내용에 대한 사례 다음에 빈칸이 이어지고 있으므로, 빈칸에 들어갈 말로 가장 적절한 것은 ④ '매우 복잡한 문제에 대한 단순한 설명을 의심 없이 받아들이도록 우리에게 영향을 미치기'이다.

① 정치인들이 사실에 근거하여 정책을 만드는 것이 얼마나 중요한지 보여주기

② 정치 지도자들이 사회의 공동 이익을 위해 일하는 것을 격려하기

③ 타협이 항상 정치에 있어 생산성의 핵심이라는 것을 증명하기

⑤ 사회의 불공정하고 불평등한 기회의 분배를 비판하기

TEXT FLOW

도입	모든 조직이 견해, 가치, 규범을 형성하고 가르치는 것은 언어를 통해서임
전개 1	언어에서의 강조는 견해에서의 강조를 만들어 냄
전개 2	정치 지도자들은 이를 알고, 지지를 얻기 위해 단어들을 신중하게 선택함

구문
• Around these words will grow [a set of ideas {that are reinforced over and over}].
: Around these words가 강조를 위해 문장 앞에 쓰여서, 주어 [ ]와 동사 will grow가 도치되었다. { }는 a set of ideas를 수식하는 관계절이다.

06
정답 ⑤

대도시와 시골 지역의 구분은 전 세계의 민주국가들을 재편하고 있는 문화적, 정치적 갈등의 핵심이다. 여기서 경제적 요인들이 중요하지만(주요 대도시들은 성장의 동력이 되었던 반면에, 작은 도시들과 시골 지역들은 분투 중이다), 인식이 어떻게 배분되는지에 대해서는 거의 틀림없이 더 중요한 분열이 있다. 대도시 중심지로부터 멀리 떨어져 있는 지역 사회는 말할 만한 어떤 흥미로운 것도 없다고 여겨지는 것이 너무나 흔한 일이다. 그들의 지식과 문화는 주요 매스컴, 대학교, 또는 전문 기관에 의해 가치 있게 여겨진 것이 아니라 오히려 유인물과 정보의 수동적인 수신자였다. 생태학적 비상사태와 인류세의 여명은 이것을 잠재적으로 변화시킨다. 즉 멀리서 자연에 관한 사실과 이론을 모으기보다는, 자연과 함께 살고 일하는 사람들은 자연이 더 정치적으로 문제가 되어 감에 따라 점점 더 가치 있어질 수 있는 노하우를 가지고 있다. '시민 과학'과 병행하여, 시골 인구 전체에 흩어져 있는 비전문 지식을 활용하는 것이 필요하기도 하고 정치적으로 유익하기도 할 것이다.

해설
대도시는 경제적으로 성장하는 반면에, 작은 도시와 시골 지역들은 경제적, 문화적으로 대도시에서 소외될 뿐만 아니라 대도시 제공 정보의 수동적 수신자로 여겨져 왔지만, 생태학적 비상사태와 인류세의 여명을 통해 자연과 함께 살고 일하는 사람들이 가진 노하우의 가치가 점점 인정받고 있다는 내용의 글이다. 따라서 빈칸에 들어갈 말로 가장 적절한 것은 ⑤ '시골 인구 전체에 흩어져 있는 비전문 지식을 활용하는 것'이다.
① 대다수의 도시 시민들을 농촌 문화에 노출시키는 것
② 대도시와 농촌 사이의 경계를 흐리거나 지우는 것
③ 더 많은 사람들이 도시를 떠나 농촌에 살도록 장려하는 것
④ 도시들이 그들의 문제를 해결하기 위해 기술을 어떻게 사용하는지 알아내는 것

ⓧ 매력적인 오답 주의!
② 글 중간에 언급된 '자연과 함께 살고 일하는 사람들이 가진 노하우가 가치 있어진다'는 반전을 명확하게 이해하지 못하고, 앞부분에서 언급되었던 '대도시와 농촌 지역의 구분'에 초점을 두어 선택한 것으로 보인다. [선택률 31%]

TEXT FLOW

도입	대도시와 시골 지역의 구분 중 인식이 어떻게 배분되는지에 대해 분열이 있음
전개	작은 도시와 시골 지역들의 지식과 문화는 소외되었고, 대도시 제공 정보의 수동적인 수신자였음
반전	생태학적 비상사태와 인류세의 여명으로 이것은 변화되고 있음
결론	자연과 함께 살고 일하는 사람들의 노하우가 점점 더 가치 있어질 수 있음

구문
• Their knowledge and culture have **not** been valued by major media outlets, universities, or expert institutions, **but rather** they've been passive recipients of handouts and information.
: 'A가 아니라 오히려 B'를 의미하는 「not A but rather B」 구문이 사용되었다.

07
정답 ④

세계가 점점 더 연결되어 감에 따라, 인류학의 중요성 역시 증가한다. 예를 들어, 최근에 인류학자들은 전염병, 자연재해, 그리고 내전으로 고통받고 있는 사람들을 돕는 데 중요한 기여를 해 올 수 있었다. 그들은 도움을 제공하고자 하는 사람들을 교육하는 것뿐만 아니라 고통받는 사람들을 돕는 데 문화적 지식을 사용하는 것을 포함하여 다양한 방식으로 이것을 한다. 예를 들어, 이것은 토착 부족들이 현대 의약품과 의료 시설을 불신하거나 이해하지 못할 수도 있는 지역 그리고 그 부족이 정부나 외국인에 대한 전반적인 불신을 가지고 있을 수도 있는 지역에서 특히 중요하다. 인류학자들은 도움을 제공하는 사람들과 도움을 받는 사람들 사이에서 교육하거나 중재자로서 역할을 하면서 일할 수 있다. (그들은 인간 생물학과 인간 문화 양쪽 모두에 대한 포괄적인 이해에 영장류의 진화 및 인간이 아닌 영장류의 행동에 대한 지식이 포함된다는 것을 알고 있다.) 인류학자들은 잠재적인 오해를 완화할 수 있고, 그들은 또한 전체론적 관점을 통해 긴급 지원조차도 문화의 다른 측면에 심오한 영향을 미칠 수 있다는 것을 인식한다.

해설
세계가 점점 더 연결되어 감에 따라, 인류학의 중요성 역시 증가하여 도움을 제공하고자 하는 사람들을 교육할 뿐만 아니라 고통받는 사람들을 돕는 데 문화적 지식이 사용된다는 내용의 글이므로, 인류학자들은 인간 생물학과 인간 문화에 대한 포괄적인 이해에 영장류의 진화와 인간이 아닌 영장류의 행동에 대한 지식이 포함된다는 것을 알고 있다는 내용의 ④는 글의 전체 흐름과 관계가 없다.

TEXT FLOW

도입	세계가 점점 더 연결되어 감에 따라 인류학의 중요성도 커지고 있음
부연	인류학자들은 사람들을 교육하고, 고통받는 사람들을 돕는 데 문화적 지식을 사용함
예시	특히 불신이 있는 지역에서 그들은 중재자로서 역할을 할 수 있음
결론	그들은 잠재적인 오해를 완화하고, 문화의 다른 측면에 영향을 미칠 수 있음

구문
• For example, in recent times, anthropologists have been able to make important contributions to [helping people {suffering from epidemics, natural disasters, and conflict}].
: [ ]는 전치사 to의 목적어인 동명사구이고, 그 안의 { }는 people을 수식하는 현재분사구이다.

08
정답 ④

화제가 무의식적인 정신으로 바뀌면 프로이트적 사고와 다윈적 사고 사이의 차이는 지속되고, 그 차이의 일부는 고통의 기능을 중심으로 돌아간다. (C) 다윈의 '황금률'을 떠올려 보라. 즉 자신의 이론과 불일치한 것처럼 보이는 모든 관찰 결과를 즉시 기록하는 것인데, "그 이유는 경험을 통해 나는 그러한

사실과 사고가 호의적인 것들에 비해 기억에서 빠져나가기가 훨씬 더 쉽다는 것을 알았기 때문이다." (A) 프로이트는 이 말을 '불쾌한 것을 기억으로부터 멀리하려는' 프로이트적 경향의 증거로 인용했다. 이러한 경향은 프로이트에게 정신적으로 건강한 사람들과 병든 사람들 사이에서 똑같이 발견되고 무의식적인 정신의 역학에 중심적인 넓고 일반적인 경향이었다. (B) 그러나 이러한 일반론으로 여겨지는 것에 한 가지 문제가 있는데, 때로는 고통스러운 기억은 잊기 가장 어렵다는 것이다. 실제로 프로이트는 다윈의 황금률을 인용한 후 불과 몇 문장 지나지 않아 사람들이 그에게 이것을 언급했다는 사실을 인정하면서 특히 고통스러울 정도로 끈질긴 불만이나 굴욕의 기억을 강조했다.

해설
무의식적인 정신에 관해 프로이트적 사고와 다윈적 사고 사이의 차이가 주로 고통의 기능에 관해서라는 내용의 주어진 글 다음에, 다윈의 '황금률'을 언급하면서 자신의 이론과 일치하지 않는 관찰 결과일수록 기억나지 않게 된다는 내용인 (C)가 온 다음, 프로이트가 다윈의 이 말을 인용하면서 불유쾌한 것을 기억에서 멀어지게 하려는 일반적인 경향이 있다고 설명했다는 내용인 (A)가 온다. 마지막으로 이런 일반론에 문제가 하나 있다고 하면서 때로는 불만과 굴욕 같은 고통스러운 기억은 잊기 가장 어렵다는 것을 프로이트가 인정하고 강조했다는 내용인 (B)가 오는 것이 글의 순서로 가장 적절하다.

⑦ WHY 고난도
글의 소재가 추상적이고 각 단락 간의 논리적인 관계를 추론할 수 있는 직접적인 연결 고리가 없어, 글의 주제를 정확히 파악한 후 이를 바탕으로 전개될 내용을 논리적으로 추론해야 하는 고난도 문제이다.

TEXT FLOW

도입	무의식적인 정신에 대해 프로이트적 사고와 다윈적 사고의 차이가 고통의 기능임
전개 1	다윈의 '황금률'에 따르면 자신의 이론과 불일치한 관찰 결과일수록 기억나지 않게 됨
전개 2	프로이트는 이를 불쾌한 것을 기억에서 멀어지게 하려는 일반적인 경향이 있다고 함
부연	그러나 프로이트는 동시에 고통스러운 기억은 잊기 어렵다는 것을 인정함

구문
• This tendency was for Freud a broad and general **one**, [found among the mentally healthy and ill alike], and [central to the dynamics of the unconscious mind].
: one은 tendency를 받는 부정대명사이다. 두 개의 [ ]는 a broad and general one을 수식하고 있는데, 첫 번째 [ ]는 과거분사구이고, 두 번째 [ ]는 형용사구이다.

09 　　　　　　　　　　　　　　　　　　정답 ②

음악적 판단은 절대로 완전히 격리된 채 이루어지지 않는다. '취향 문화'의 형성은 항상 사회적으로 정의되어 왔다. 특정 장르의 음악에 참여하는 것은 역사적으로 순전히 독립된 미적 선택에 의해서가 아니라, 개인의 사회적 위치에 의해 결정되었다. 실제로, 사회학적 관점에서, 취향은 미적인 범주라기보다는 항상 사회적 범주이며, 그것은 우리가 우리의 사회적 위치를 나타내기 위해 문화적 판단을 사회적 '통화'로 사용하는 방식을 의미한다. 이것은 오늘날 덜 분명할 수도 있는데, 그 이유는 현대 사회의 특징은 더 오래된 취향 문

화의 해체와 새로운 취향 문화의 확산이기 때문이다. 이런 상황에서 문화 거래는 점점 빠르게 일어나며, 이런 이유로 문화 경제가 가열되고 신제품의 회전율이 빨라지고 있다. 취향 문화 자체가 변화하고 있을 뿐만 아니라, 사람들은 이제 그것들 사이에서 매우 더 쉽게 이동하는 경향도 있다. 이 요인들은 각각의 모든 것의 위치가 상대적이라는 느낌을 일으킨다. 현대의 음악적 선택은 전에 없이 다양하며, 그 다양성의 효과는 필연적으로 음악적 판단의 문제에서 개인이 유일한 권위자일 수 있다는 것을 확인하는 것이다.

해설
오래된 취향 문화의 해체와 새로운 취향 문화의 확산이라는 현대 사회의 특징을 설명하는 주어진 문장이 없으면, In this context로 시작하여 현대 사회의 특징이 기술되는 ② 다음 문장과 사회적 범주에서 취향이 결정되었다는 ② 앞 문장 사이에 내용상 단절이 일어난다. 또한 주어진 문장의 This may be less clear today의 This는 ② 앞에 있는 내용을 나타내므로, 주어진 문장이 들어가기에 가장 적절한 곳은 ②이다.

TEXT FLOW

도입	'취향 문화'의 형성은 격리된 것이 아니라 개인의 사회적 위치에 의해 결정됨
전개	이것은 오늘날 더 오래된 취향 문화의 해체와 새로운 취향 문화의 확산으로 덜 분명할 수 있음
부연	현대 사회는 취향 문화가 빠르게 변화하고 사람들은 그것들 사이에서 쉽게 이동함

구문
• **Not only** are taste cultures **themselves** shifting, but people now tend to move between them with greater ease.
: 부정어구 Not only가 문장 앞에 나와서 주어 taste cultures themselves와 동사 are가 도치된 형태이다. themselves는 taste cultures를 강조하는 재귀대명사이다.

10 　　　　　　　　　　　　　　　　　　정답 ⑤

Berkeley 대학의 연구자인 Mary Main은 '성인 애착 인터뷰'라는 인터뷰를 개발했다. 이 인터뷰에서 Main은 사람들이 자신의 어린 시절 이야기를 어떻게 말했는지, 그리고 이 어린 시절이 고통스럽고 충격이 컸는지 아닌지에 대해 점수를 매겼다. 그녀는 이야기의 내용보다 이야기가 어떻게 말로 표현되는지에 대해 더 관심이 있었다. 자신의 매우 충격적인 어린 시절에 관해 일관성 있는 이야기를 할 수 있었던 사람들은 같은 양의 어린 시절의 충격적인 경험을 가지고 있지만 어쩐지 그것을 마무리하지 못했던 사람들과는 매우 다른 종류의 부모가 된 것으로 관찰되었다. 그들은 이러한 어린 시절의 사건들에 관한 자신의 설명에서 불안하거나, 정신이 팔려 있거나, 일축하거나, 전혀 일관성이 없었다. 이 두 유형의 부모들의 아기들을 연구할 때, Mary Main은 놀라운 결과를 발견했다. 어떻게든 충격적인 경험을 마무리했고, 그것에 관해 일관된 이야기를 할 수 있었으며 그 이야기를 하는 동안 흐트러지지 않고 감정이 복받치지 않은 사람들에게는 안정적인 애착을 가진 유아들이 있었다. 반면 충격적인 경험이 마무리되지 않았고, 그것에 관해 일관된 이야기를 할 수 없었으며, 그 이야기를 하는 동안 정리되지 않고 감정이 복받쳤던 사람들에게는 불안하게 애착을 가진 유아들이 있었다.

➡ Mary Main은 부모들이 어린 시절의 충격적인 경험을 극복했는지의 여부가 유아들이 그들의 부모에 대한 애착에서 느낀 안도감 수준에 영향을 미쳤다는 것을 알아냈다.

어린 시절의 충격적인 경험이 정리가 되어 일관된 이야기를 할 수 있었고 그 이야기를 할 때 흐트러지거나 감정이 북받치지 않았던 사람들에게는 안정적인 애착 관계를 가진 유아가 있었던 반면, 그렇지 못한 사람에게는 불안정한 애착 관계를 가진 유아가 있었다는 내용이므로, 요약문의 빈칸 (A), (B)에 들어갈 말로는 ⑤ 'overcame(극복했다) – security(안도감)'가 가장 적절하다.

① 경험했다 – 안도감　　　② 경험했다 – 성숙함
③ 잊었다 – 책임감　　　④ 극복했다 – 책임감

TEXT FLOW

연구	Main은 인터뷰를 통해 어린 시절 이야기가 어떻게 말로 표현되는지 보았음
결과	어린 시절에 대해 일관성 있게 이야기를 한 사람과 그것을 마무리하지 못했던 사람들은 매우 다른 종류의 부모가 된 것으로 관찰됨
부연	일관된 이야기를 할 수 있었던 사람들에게는 안정적인 애착을 가진 유아들이 있었고, 마무리하지 못한 사람들에게는 불안정 애착을 가진 유아들이 있었음

구문

• People [who were able to tell coherent stories about their traumatic childhood] were observed to be very **different** kinds of parents **than** people [who had the same amount of childhood trauma but were somehow not done with it].
: 두 개의 [ ]는 각각 People과 people을 수식하는 관계절이다. different than은 different from과 같은 의미로 미국식 영어에서 사용된다.

11-12

정답11 ② 12 ⑤

인간은 보통 변화하는 데 엄청난 양의 노력이 필요할 나쁜 패턴에 갇혀 있다. 조직도 같은 문제를 가지고 있다. 나는 고군분투 중이던 역사가 긴 회사를 알고 있다. 문제들이 일시적이고 시장은 결국 회복할 것이라는 데 동의했지만, 단기적으로 그 회사는 재앙에 직면해 있었다. 영향력 있는 한 임원은 해답은 해고라고 확신했다. 그는 그것을 사용해야 할 필요성에 대해 명확하고 설득력이 있었다. 그 이하의 것은 뭔든 용기와 뛰어난 사업 감각이 부족한 것이었다. 마구 해를 입히는 선택이 선견지명 있고 대담한 것의 동의어로 등장하기 시작했다.

하지만 또 다른 임원은 이런 견해에 근심해서 회사가 과거에 어떻게 역경에 대처했는지 추적해 달라고 인사과에 요청했다. 그들은 대공황의 기록으로 되돌아가서, 그 기간 내내 회사는 단 한 명의 직원도 해고하지 않았다는 것을 알게 되었다. 그들은 급여를 줄였고, 근무 시간을 줄였으며, 수당을 낮추었지만, 실직하는 사람은 아무도 없었다. 이것이 제시되었을 때, 그때까지 침묵했던 몇몇 관리자들이 말을 했다. 대공황 이야기는 회사로서 그들이 어떤 존재였는지에 대해, 그리고 그들이 역경 속에서 직원들과 함께 일한 긴 역사를 가지고 있다는 것을 그들에게 상기시켰다. 자신들의 역사와 전통에 연결됨으로써, 그들은 해고가 유일한 선택이라고 생각하는 패턴에서 벗어날 수 있었다. 그러나 그들은 반대자가 자신들이 나쁜 패턴에 있다는 것을 지적하지 않았다면 그렇게 할 수 없었을 것이다. 때때로 의견 불일치(→ 의견 일치)가 조직의 주요 문제이다.

해설

11 긴 역사를 가지고 있던 회사가 당장의 어려운 상황에 대처하는 방법으로

해고라는 전형적인 해결 패턴을 따르려다가, 이 해결책에 반대하는 다른 임원이 확인을 요청해서 대공황 시기에 회사가 단 한 명의 직원도 해고하지 않았다는 것을 알게 되고, 그에 따라 나쁜 해결 패턴에서 벗어나 새로운 방식으로 문제 해결이 가능했다는 내용의 글이다. 따라서 글의 제목으로 가장 적절한 것은 ② '문제 해결을 위해서는 나쁜 패턴에서 벗어나라'이다.
① 기업의 쟁점: 고용과 해고
③ 리더십의 형태로서 직원 권한 부여
④ 조직의 원동력: 상호 동의
⑤ 성공을 위한 신속한 의사 결정 기술을 개발하라

12 해고만이 문제 해결이라고 생각했던 한 영향력 있는 임원의 의견에 반대하는 다른 임원의 요청으로 회사의 역사를 알아본 결과, 대공황 시기 내내 회사가 해고가 아닌 협력적인 방식으로 역경을 극복했다는 것을 알고 나서 새로운 문제 해결 방식을 찾아낸 것이므로, 만약 그들의 의견이 일치했다면 기존의 전형적인 패턴에서 벗어나지 못했을 것이라는 맥락이 되어야 한다. 따라서 ⑤의 'disagreement(의견 불일치)'를 'agreement(의견 일치)'와 같은 낱말로 바꾸어야 한다.

TEXT FLOW

도입	긴 역사를 가진 회사의 한 임원은 당장 어려운 상황에서의 해답은 해고라고 확신했음
전개	이 해결책에 근심한 다른 임원은 대공황의 시기조차 단 한 명의 직원도 해고하지 않았다는 것을 알게 됨
결론	이를 제시하여, 해고가 유일한 선택지라고 생각하는 패턴에서 벗어날 수 있었음

구문

• The Depression story reminded them of [who they were as a company], [that they had a long tradition of {working with their employees through adversity}].
: 첫 번째 [ ]는 전치사 of의 목적어이고 두 번째 [ ]는 reminded의 직접목적어이다. { }는 a long tradition의 내용을 구체적으로 설명하는 동격 어구이다.

고난도 모의고사 14회

01 ⑤	02 ③	03 ③	04 ⑤	05 ④	06 ①
07 ②	08 ③	09 ②	10 ④	11 ⑤	12 ④

01
정답 ⑤

내가 가장 하고 싶은 일 중 하나는 신경 윤리학 논의에서 '미끄러운 비탈길' 주장을 없애는 것이다. 이것은 협회의 각종 보고서에서 많은 논쟁의 중심이 되어 왔다. 미끄러운 비탈길이 우리를 데려갈 극단을 주장함으로써 윤리학자들은 대중의 두려움을 이용하며, 우리가 과학자들에게 1인치를 주면 그들은 1마일을 가져갈 것이라고 말한다. 사실, 이런 주장들의 대부분은 공상 과학 소설의 소재이다. '인간 침팬지', 다시 말해 과학자들이 현대의 유전자 조작술을 사용하여 인간과 침팬지를 이종 교배할 것이라는 두려움을 예로 들어 보자. 여러분이 인간 침팬지를 가능성으로 제시하자, 갑자기 모든 사람이 파킨슨병, 알츠하이머병, 그리고 다른 질병들을 치료할 수 있는 연구, 즉 생쥐에게 인간 줄기세포를 배양하도록 과학자들을 내버려두는 것을 두려워한다. 그러나 '인간 침팬지'는 근거로 들기에는 상식을 벗어나고 시대에 뒤떨어진 하찮은 논의이며, 학계에서든 그 밖의 다른 분야에서든 간에, 인정받는 논평자가 신경 과학의 발전이 이 사례와 아주 조금 유사한 것을 얻으려고 노력해야 한다고 제안하는 것을 발견하기는 어렵다.

해설
신경 윤리학 연구를 바라보는 관점에 대한 내용으로, '인간 침팬지'의 사례처럼 어떤 것에 대한 극단적 결과를 주장하며 대중의 두려움을 이용하는 윤리학자들이 있지만, 실제로 이것은 일종의 '미끄러운 비탈길' 주장이며, 근거로 들기에는 상식을 벗어나고 시대에 뒤떨어지며 없어져야 할 논의라고 주장하는 글이다. 따라서 밑줄 친 부분이 글에서 의미하는 바로 가장 적절한 것은 ⑤ '무언가가 좋지 않은 결과를 가져올 것이라는 과장된 주장'이다.
① 감정에 대한 호소에 근거한 오류
② 곧 밝혀질 것 같은 일련의 미지의 진리들
③ 현대 과학자들에 의해 거부된 교육 이론
④ 대다수의 지시를 받는 논쟁적이지만 반론의 여지가 없는 의견

TEXT FLOW
도입	신경 윤리학 논의에서 '미끄러운 비탈길' 주장은 없어져야 함
부연	'미끄러운 비탈길'은 극단을 주장하여 대중의 두려움을 이용함
예시	과학자들이 유전자 조작술을 이용하여 '인간 침팬지'를 만들 것이라는 두려움이 있음
결론	이는 상식에 벗어나고 시대에 뒤떨어지며 없어져야 할 논의임

구문
• [One of the things I would most like to do] is [eliminate the "slippery slope" argument from neuroethical discussions].
: 첫 번째 [ ]가 주어이고, 두 번째 [ ]는 주격 보어 역할을 하는 to부정사구에서 to가 생략된 형태이다.

02
정답 ③

우리가 세상에서 상호 작용하는 방식은 현실에 대한 두 가지 시각, 즉 우리가

정신에 대한 주의 집중이라고 부르는 정신에 대한 시각과 사물로 이루어진 세계의 물리적 특성에 대한 또 하나의 시각으로 나뉠 수 있다. 현대의 삶은 정신적인 내적 시각을 존중하기보다는 물리적인 시각에 자주 의존한다. 내적인 주관적 세계에 대한 이러한 집중의 부족은 걱정거리인데 정신을 보지 않는 것은 사람들이 존중이나 연민을 갖지 않고 다른 사람들을 대하도록 유도할 수 있기 때문이다. 우리가 가족이나 친구들과 집에서, 선생님과 또래와 학교에서, 그리고 문화와 사회의 더 큰 사회적인 세상과의 상호 작용에서 가지는 경험이 우리의 실체를 형성하므로, 우리가 그러한 경험에 주의를 기울이는 방식은 정신에 대한 주의 집중을 촉진하거나 좌절시킬 수 있다. 그러므로 이러한 경험 대부분이 외적으로 집중되어 물리적인 사물에 대한 우리의 인식 체계만 활용한다면, 우리는 우리 자신의 내적 삶과 대인 관계의 삶의 개인적인 세상을 보고 형성할 기술을 개발할 수 없을 것이다.

해설
정신적인 내적 시각과 주관적인 세계에 대해 주의 집중을 하지 않고 외적으로 집중된 물리적인 사물에 대한 인식 체계만 활용한다면, 우리의 내적 삶과 대인 관계의 삶의 개인적인 세상을 보고 형성할 기술을 개발할 수 없을 것이라는 내용이므로, 글의 주제로 가장 적절한 것은 ③ '우리의 주관적인 정신적 경험에 집중하지 않는 것의 위험성'이다.
① 우리의 내적 세계를 형성하는 데 있어 사회적 경험의 역할
② 자신의 이미지를 사회 규범과 일치시키지 않는 이유
④ 사회적 상호 작용의 산물로서의 존중과 연민
⑤ 내적 세계와 외적 세계의 차이로 인해 발생하는 좌절감

TEXT FLOW
도입	우리는 정신에 대한 시각과 물리적 특성에 대한 시각으로 세상과 상호 작용함
전개	현대의 삶은 정신적인 내적 시각보다는 물리적인 시각에 의존함
부연	정신을 보지 않으면 존중이나 연민을 갖지 않고 다른 사람을 대할 수 있음
결론	물리적인 인식 체계만 활용하면, 내적 삶과 대인 관계의 삶의 개인적인 세상을 보고 형성할 기술을 개발할 수 없을 것임

구문
• [This lack of focus on the inner subjective world] is a concern because [not seeing the mind] can lead to [people treating others without respect or compassion].
: 첫 번째 [ ]는 주절의 주어이고, 두 번째 [ ]는 부사절의 주어이다. 세 번째 [ ]는 전치사 to의 목적어 역할을 하는 동명사구이고, people은 동명사구의 의미상의 주어이다.

03
정답 ③

뇌에 있어, 모든 것은 처음에는 잡음이다. 그런 다음 뇌는 잡음의 패턴을 알아차리고 한 수준 위로 이동하여 그러한 패턴이 상호 작용하는 방식의 패턴을 알아차린다. 그런 다음 그것들은 한 수준 더 위로 이동하고 계속 그것은 이어진다. 보다 단순한 층의 위에 세워지는 패턴 인식의 층은 우리 주변의 세상으로부터 무엇을 예상할지에 대한 대략의 이해가 되며, 그것들의 상호 작용은 우리의 인과 관계에 대한 감각이 된다. 공의 둥긂, 탁자의 단단한 가장자리, 봉제 인형의 부드러운 팔꿈치, 각각의 물건은 다른 경로 말고 특정한 신경의 경로를 흥분시키며 각각의 노출은 뇌가 세상의 그러한 요소들을 예측하게 되고 그것들을 맥락 안에서 더 잘 이해하게 될 때까지 그것들의 연결을 강화한다. 이와 비슷하게, 원인은 대개 결과로 이어지므로, 우리의 내재된 패턴 인식은 내가 밤에 울면 엄마가 오실 것이다, 으깬 감자는 나를 행복하게

할 것이다, 벌은 쏘면 아프다와 같이 알아차리고 예측을 형성한다. 우리는 예측할 수 없는 혼돈으로 가득한 삶을 시작하지만, 우리의 규칙적인 인식은 우리가 그 혼돈을 예측할 수 있는 질서로 바꾸기 위해 사용하는 예측이 된다.

해설
③ making sense of의 동작 주체는 the brain이며 대상은 those elements of the world이므로, 주체와 대상이 같지 않다. 따라서 재귀대명사 themselves는 them으로 고쳐야 한다.
① 문장의 동사가 notice와 move up이고, 주절의 주어인 brains와 능동 관계이므로 주절의 내용을 보충하는 분사구문의 현재분사 noticing은 어법상 적절하다.
② 주어는 Layers ~ layers이며, 주어의 핵은 Layers이므로, 이와 연결되는 술어 동사로 become은 어법상 적절하다.
④ 동사 lead를 수식하므로 부사인 regularly는 어법상 적절하다.
⑤ 목적(~하기 위해)을 나타내는 to부정사구 to turn은 어법상 적절하다.

TEXT FLOW
도입	뇌는 처음에는 잡음이었던 패턴을 알아차리고, 그 패턴이 상호 작용하는 방식의 패턴을 알아차림
전개 1	패턴 인식의 층은 이해가 되고, 그것들의 상호 작용은 인과 관계에 대한 감각이 됨
전개 2	내재된 패턴 인식은 예측을 형성함
결론	혼돈으로 삶을 시작하지만, 규칙적인 인식은 혼돈을 질서로 바꾸기 위해 사용하는 예측이 됨

04
정답 ⑤

1960년대, 철학자 Hubert Dreyfus는 '컴퓨터가 지능적이기 위해서는 몸이 필요하다'라고 주장했다. 이 입장은 당연한 귀결을 가지는데, 기계가 무슨 지능을 성취할 수 있는지 간에, 기계에 주어지는 어떤 몸도 인간의 몸이 아닐 것이기 때문에, 그것은 결코 사람이 가지고 있는 것과 같지 않을 것이다. 그러므로 기계의 지능은 그것이 아무리 흥미롭다 할지라도 생경할 것이다. 신경 과학자인 Antonio Damasio는 다른 연구 전통에서 이 주장을 이어간다. Damasio에게는, 모든 사고와 모든 감정이 합체되어 있다. 우리는 말 그대로 우리의 느낌과 함께 사고하기 때문에 감정의 부재는 합리성의 범위를 축소시킨다. Damasio는 심신 이원론은 없으며, 사고와 감정 사이에 어떤 분리도 없다고 주장한다. 우리가 결정을 내려야 할 때, 우리의 신체에 의해 형성되는 뇌 과정은 우리의 즐거움과 고통을 기억함으로써 우리의 추론을 인도한다. 이것은 왜 로봇이 인간과 같은 지능을 결코 가지지 못할 것인지에 대한 논거로 거부될(→ 받아들여질) 수 있다. 즉 그들에게는 신체적 느낌도 감정에 대한 느낌도 없다.

해설
인간에게는 몸이 있어 느낌과 감정이 있고 그에 따라 지능도 있는데, 컴퓨터는 몸이 없기 때문에 인간과 같은 지능을 가질 수 없다는 내용이므로, ⑤의 'rejected(거부되다)'를 'taken(받아들여지다)'과 같은 낱말로 바꾸어야 한다.

TEXT FLOW
도입	한 철학자는 컴퓨터가 지능적이기 위해서는 몸이 필요하다고 주장하였음
부연	기계의 지능은 결코 사람이 가지고 있는 것과 같지 않을 것임
전개	한 신경 과학자는 모든 사고와 감정은 합체되어 있다고 주장함

결론	로봇이 감정이 없다는 것은 인간과 같은 지능을 가질 수 없는 것에 대한 논거로 받아들여질 수 있음

구문
• When we have to make a decision, [brain processes {that are shaped by our body}] guide our reasoning by remembering our pleasures and pains.
: [ ]는 주절의 주어이고, 그 안의 { }는 brain processes를 수식하는 관계절이다.

05
정답 ④

유전자 특허에 대해 많은 비평가들에 의해 제기되는 주요 우려는 생명체의 요소를 다루는 특허가 인간 개인과 인간 사회에 대한 크게 확대된 힘을 개인, 기업 및 정부에게 줄 수도 있다는 것이다. 예를 들어, 한 농부가 단순히 그의 이웃과 경쟁하고 독자 생존 가능한 농부로 남아 있기 위해서 최고의 작물에 접근하기를 원하고 사실상 최고의 작물을 필요로 하며, 그 작물들은 모두 회사가 소유한 특허에 의해 보호된다면, 그는 작물이 훨씬 더 적은 법적 제한에 의해 보장되었던 시절에 비해 경제적으로 더 약해졌는가? 일부 비평가들은 기술적으로 발달하고 특허가 지배하는 지역의 농민들처럼 상대적으로 가난하고 약한 많은 사람들의 상황이 중세 세계의 농노들의 상황과 비슷하다고 시사한다. 그들은 자신들의 보잘것없는 작은 땅으로 연명할 수 있도록 허용되기 위해 영주 권위자에게 완전히 의존한다. 그들에게 더 유용한 도구를 주기보다는, 특허로 통제되는 혁신은 그들이 독립할 수 있는 거의 모든 능력을 앗아간다. 이러한 비평가들에게 특허란 농부와 같은 사람들로 하여금 살아남기 위해 체제 안에서 겨우 충족될 만큼만의 이익을 허용하지만 번창할 정도로 충분하지 않은 수익을 허용할 회사에의 종속으로 몰아넣을 수 있다.

해설
많은 비평가들이 유전자 특허는 개인, 기업 및 정부에게 인간 개인과 인간 사회에 대해 확대된 힘을 줄 수도 있다고 우려하는데, 그것은 마치 중세 세계의 농노가 보잘것없는 작은 땅으로 연명하기 위해 영주 권위자에게 의존해야 했던 것과 비슷한 상황으로 이해할 수 있다는 내용의 글이다. 특히 특허로 통제되는 혁신이 어떤 역할을 하는지는 마지막 문장에서 더 자세히 기술되는데, 사람들이 살아남기 위해 체제 안에서 겨우 충족될 만큼만의 이익을 허용하지만 번창할 정도로 충분하지 않은 수익을 허용할 회사에 종속된다는 내용이다. 따라서 빈칸에 들어갈 말로 가장 적절한 것은 ④ '그들이 독립할 수 있는 거의 모든 능력을 앗아간다'이다.
① 그들이 자신들의 환경에 급격한 변화를 만들도록 동기를 부여한다
② 특정 문제에 대해 근본적인 해결책을 제공한다
③ 그들의 우려를 실제 공간이 아닌 가상 공간으로 제한한다
⑤ 생존하기 어려운 가혹한 환경을 견딘다

TEXT FLOW
도입	비평가들은 유전자 특허는 개인, 기업 및 정부에게 인간 개인과 인간 사회에 대해 확대된 힘을 줄 수 있음을 우려함
전개 1	기술적으로 발달하고 특허가 지배하는 지역의 농민들은 중세 세계의 농노들과 상황이 비슷함
전개 2	특허로 통제되는 혁신은 그들이 독립할 수 있는 능력을 앗아감
결론	그들에게 살아남기에 겨우 충족될 만큼의 이익은 허용하지만 충분하지는 않은 수익을 허용할 회사에의 종속으로 몰아넣을 수 있음

• A major concern expressed by many critics of genetic patenting is [that {patents ⟨covering elements of life forms⟩} may give {individuals, companies, or governments} {greatly expanded powers over human individuals and human societies}].

: [ ]는 동사 is의 주격 보어 역할을 하는 명사절이다. 첫 번째 { }는 that절의 주어이고, 그 안의 ⟨ ⟩는 patents를 수식하는 현재분사구이다. 두 번째 { }와 세 번째 { }는 각각 give의 간접목적어와 직접목적어이다.

06 정답 ①

우리가 의미나 지칭을 가진 단어의 배열에 의해서라기보다는 하나의 물체로서 구성된 시 한 편에 대해 해설을 제공할 때, 우리는 일종의 해석을 하는 것인데, 그 이유는 우리가 그 시에 암시되어 있는 것을 해설의 명시성으로 번역하고 있기 때문이다. 그러한 해설은 대개 한 시대와 장소의 특정한 관심사와 어휘에 연결되어 있다. 시를 그것의 용어와 목적으로 전환하려는 가장 최근의 가장 유행하는 각 (학문) 분야의 경향을 넘어서기 위해, 문학 비평은 그 자체의 가설을 필요로 하는데, 그것은 아마도 독자적인 비평 언어로 이어질 것이다. 이것은 문학이 다른 상징적 표현 체계와 연관이 없다는 의미가 아니다. 그것은 그것들과 어떠한 종류의 관계도 맺을 수 있지만, 하나의 체계로서의 문학은 비평의 가설적인 창작물로 남는다. Northrop Frye가 설명하는 비유는 수학인데, 그것은 항상 그 자체의 용어를 가지고 다른 체계와 관계를 맺는 자체 완결적인 체계이다.

해설

시를 해설하는 것은 일종의 해석이며 그러한 해설은 시간과 장소의 영향 하에 있으므로, 문학 비평이 이것을 넘어서려면 일종의 독자적인 상징 체계가 필요하고, 이것은 Northrop Frye가 수학의 비유를 들어 말했듯이, 자체적으로 완결된 체계여야 한다는 내용이다. 따라서 빈칸에 들어갈 말로 가장 적절한 것은 ① '아마도 독자적인 비평 언어로 이어질 것이다'이다.
② 필연적으로 작품에 대한 면밀한 분석으로 증명되어야 한다
③ 결국 현대적인 해석에 영향을 미칠 수 있다
④ 반드시 역사적 권위가 함께 제시되어야 한다
⑤ 종종 다른 비평가들의 해설에 의존한다

⊗ 매력적인 오답 주의!

③ 글의 전체적인 맥락을 파악하여 빈칸이 포함된 문장 뒤로 이어지는 정보에 근거하지 않고, 주로 앞부분에서 언급됐던 commentary, interpretation, translating 등의 단편적인 어휘를 통해 추론하여 선택한 것으로 보인다. [선택률 27%]

TEXT FLOW

도입	시 한 편에 대해 해설을 제공하는 것은 일종의 해석을 하는 것임
전개 1	해설은 한 시대와 장소의 특정한 관심사와 어휘에 연결되어 있음
전개 2	이를 넘어서기 위해서 문학 비평은 독자적인 비평 언어가 필요하고, 하나의 체계로서 문학은 비평의 창작물로 남을 수 있음

구문

• [When we offer a commentary upon a poem, {which has been constructed as an object rather than by an arrangement of words with meanings or referents}], we produce ~.

: [ ]는 시간을 나타내는 부사절이고, 그 안의 { }는 선행사 a poem을 부연 설명하는 계속적 용법의 관계절이다.

07 정답 ②

일부 정책 프로그램에 대한 자격은 개인의 측정 가능한 특성이 특정 기준점보다 높은지 낮은지의 여부에 따라 결정된다. (B) 예를 들어, 정부는 연소득이 2만 달러 미만인 가구에 대해서만 공공 의료 보험을 제공할 수 있다. 공공 의료 보험을 받은 사람들과 받지 못한 사람들의 건강 결과를 비교한 관찰 연구는 두 집단이 여러 면에서 다르므로 편향될 가능성이 있을 것이다. (A) 그러나 소득이 2만 달러가 넘는 모든 사람의 건강을 2만 달러 미만인 모든 사람의 건강과 비교하는 대신, 그 프로그램 자격을 '간신히' 갖춘 사람과 '간신히' 놓친 사람의 결과를 비교한다고 가정해 보라. 2만 달러가 훨씬 넘는 가구와 2만 달러 훨씬 미만인 가구는 서로 다르지만, 2만 1달러를 버는 가구는 1만 9천 999달러를 버는 가구와 유사할 가능성이 높으므로 이것은 매력적인 전략이다. (C) 이러한 접근 방식은 회귀-불연속 분석이라고 불린다. 실험을 되풀이하기 위해 이 접근 방식이 충족해야 하는 근본적인 가정은 자격을 간신히 놓친 사람의 특성이 자격을 간신히 획득한 사람들과 평균적으로 동일하다는 것이다.

해설

일부 정책 프로그램에 대한 자격은 개인의 측정 가능한 특성이 기준점보다 높은지 낮은지의 여부에 의해 결정된다는 내용의 주어진 글 다음에는, 이러한 기준점을 소득 2만 달러에 맞춘 공공 의료 보험 정책을 예로 들어 공공 의료 보험을 받는 사람들과 아닌 사람들의 건강 결과 비교는 편향될 수 있다는 내용의 (B)가 와야 한다. 그다음에는 이러한 편향된 결과를 피할 수 있는 전략을 제시하는 (A)가 오고, 이 접근법을 회귀-불연속 분석으로 정의하여 설명하는 (C)가 오는 것이 글의 순서로 가장 적절하다.

TEXT FLOW

도입	정책 프로그램에 대한 자격은 개인의 측정 가능한 특성이 기준점보다 높은지 낮은지의 여부에 따라 결정됨
예시	정부는 연소득이 2만 달러 미만인 가구에 대해서만 공공 의료 보험을 제공함
부연	공공 의료 보험을 받는 사람과 아닌 사람들의 건강 결과 비교는 편향될 수 있음
결론	프로그램 자격을 '간신히' 갖춘 사람과 '간신히' 놓친 사람의 결과를 비교하는 회귀-불연속 분석이 매력적인 전략임

구문

• Suppose, though, [that {instead of **comparing** the health of everyone above $20,000 **with** the health of everyone below $20,000}, {we **compare** the outcomes for those who were just barely eligible **to** those who just barely missed ⟨being eligible for the program⟩}.]

: [ ]는 Suppose의 목적어 역할을 하는 명사절이다. 그 안의 첫 번째 { }는 전치사구로 뒤에 동명사구가 이어지며, 「compare A with B」의 구조가 사용되었다. 두 번째 { }는 주절이며, 「compare A to B」의 구조가 사용되었고, 그 안의 ⟨ ⟩는 missed의 목적어 역할을 하는 동명사구이다.

08

설문 조사의 대상 모집단이 넓은 지리적 영역을 포괄하는 경우에, 단순 무작위 표본은 그 나라의 여러 매우 다른 지역의 응답자를 선택했을 수 있다. 데이터를 수집하기 위해 사용되는 방법이 대면 면접 유형이라면, 분명히 많은 이동이 수반될 수 있다. (B) 이 문제를 극복하기 위해 조사할 지역을 더 작은 지역으로 나누고, 많은 이러한 더 작은 지역들이 무작위로 선택한다. 원한다면, 선택된 그 더 작은 지역들 자체를 더 작은 구역으로 나누고 이런 구역들의 수를 무작위로 선택할 수 있다. (C) 이런 절차는 단순 무작위 표본(이나 층화 표본)이 선택될 정도로 면적이 작아질 때까지 계속된다. 최종 표본은 소수의 지역에 집중된 응답자로 구성되어야 한다. (A) 각 지역에서 선택된 무작위 최종 표본은 모집단의 비율과 동일한 것이 중요한데, 그렇지 않으면 특정 지역을 향한 치우침이 생길 수 있다. 현 상황에서는, 동일 지역 내의 사람들이 하는 응답의 유사성으로 인해 치우침이 발생할 가능성이 있지만, 이는 줄어든 이동 시간에 대해 지불하는 대가이다.

해설
설문 조사의 대상 모집단이 넓은 지리적 영역을 포괄할 때 단순 무작위 표본이 수반하는 많은 이동의 문제를 언급한 주어진 글 뒤에는, 그 문제의 해결 방안으로 조사 지역을 더 작은 지역으로 나누어 무작위로 선택하는 것을 제시한 (B)가 이어진 후, 조사 지역을 더 작은 지역으로 계속 나누어 최종 표본을 선택하는 절차를 언급한 (C)가 온 다음, 마지막으로 무작위 최종 표본이 모집단의 비율과 동일하지 않을 경우에 생기는 문제를 언급한 (A)가 오는 것이 글의 순서로 가장 적절하다.

TEXT FLOW

도입	설문 조사의 대상 모집단이 넓은 지리적 영역을 포괄하면, 단순 무작위 표본은 많은 이동이 수반됨
전개 1	이를 극복하고자 조사할 지역을 더 작은 지역으로 나누어 무작위로 선택함
전개 2	최종 표본은 소수의 지역에 집중된 응답자로 구성되고, 모집단의 비율과 동일해야 함

구문
• [If desired], the smaller areas **chosen** could themselves be divided into smaller districts and [a random number of these selected].
  : 첫 번째 [ ]는 If it is desired에서 it is가 생략된 형태이다. chosen은 the smaller areas를 수식하는 과거분사이다. 두 번째 [ ]는 a random number of these could be selected에서 반복되는 could be가 생략된 형태이다.

09

여러분이 이 문장들을 읽는 데 의식적인 주의를 집중하면, 시각적 유입을 통제하는 무의식적 부분들은 여러분의 의식적인 의도가 자신들의 감각의 관문이 좁아지는 것을 무시할 수 있게 해 준다. 그것은 들어오는 정보를 평상시처럼 통제하려고 더는 활동하지 않는다. 그 결과 이 페이지의 단어들은 독자적인 개체로서 눈에 띄기 시작한다. 반면에 여러분이 우연히 지나가면서 무심코 탁자 위에 놓인 신문을 보게 된다면, 그 신문이 단어들로 가득한 것을 볼 수도 있겠지만, 단어들 자체를 반드시 알아차리지는 못할 것이다. 무의식의 수준에서 여러분은 그것들을 들어오지 못하게 통제해 왔다. 마찬가지로, 여러분이 무심코 책 한 권을 펴서 어떤 페이지를 대충 훑어본다면, 여러분은 단

어들을 '볼' 수는 있겠지만, 반드시 개체로서의 단어들이나 그 속의 의미에 적극적으로 주의를 기울이지는 않을 것이다. 들어오는 시각적 메시지, 즉 이 경우에는 단어와 문장 속의 의미는 '통제되는데', 이것은 여러분의 무의식적인 부분이 시간상 그 순간에 주의를 기울일 만큼 그것들이 중요하지 않다고 결정했기 때문이다. 이것은 여러분을 계속 눈에 보이는 세계의 표면에만 적응하게 한다.

해설
on the other hand가 포함된 주어진 문장은 ②의 앞 문장과는 달리 무의식이 시각 정보의 유입을 통제하는 상황을 언급하며 내용상 반전이 이루어지는 부분이다. ② 다음에 무의식이 시각 정보의 유입을 통제하는 상황에 대한 내용이 계속 이어지므로, 주어진 문장이 들어가기에 가장 적절한 곳은 ②이다.

⊘ WHY 고난도
② 앞의 문장에 the words가 있어서 ② 다음 문장의 대명사 them은 문제를 푸는 단서가 될 수 없기 때문에 have gated them out이 의미하는 바를 정확히 파악해야 풀 수 있는 고난도 문제이다.

TEXT FLOW

도입	문장을 읽는 데 의식적인 주의를 기울이면 시각적 유입을 통제하는 것을 중단시킬 수 있음
전환	무심코 놓인 신문에 단어가 가득한 것은 보이지만, 단어들 자체는 알아차릴 수 없음
결론	이 경우 단어와 문장 속 의미는 통제되는데, 무의식이 그것들이 중요하지 않다고 결정했기 때문임

구문
• Similarly, **if** you casually **opened** a book and **glanced** at a page, though you **might** "see" the words, you **would** not necessarily be actively attentive [to them as individuals] or [to the meanings inside them].
  : 「If+주어+과거 동사 ~, 주어+might/would+동사원형 ....」의 가정법 과거 구문으로 현재 사실에 반대되는 가정을 하고 있다. 두 개의 [ ]는 or로 연결되어 attentive에 이어진다.

10

풍력 발전기를 생각해 보자. 미국에서 그것들은 매년 최소한 4만 5천 마리의 새와 박쥐를 죽이는 것으로 추산되어 왔다. 그것은 많은 새와 박쥐인 것처럼 들린다. 그 숫자를 전체적인 시야로 보려면, 주인의 집을 들락날락하도록 허용된 반려 고양이가 고양이 한 마리당 1년에 평균 300마리가 넘는 새를 죽이는 것으로 측정되어 왔다는 점을 생각해 보라. 만일 밖에서 사는 고양이의 미국 개체수가 약 1억 마리라고 추산된다면, 고양이는 풍력 발전기에 의해 매년 죽임을 당하는 고작 4만 5천 마리에 비해 미국에서 최소한 매년 3백억 마리의 새를 죽인다는 계산이 나올 수 있다. 그러한 풍력 발전기의 대가는 불과 150마리의 고양이가 하는 일과 동일하다. 따라서 우리가 미국의 새와 박쥐에 대해 진심으로 우려한다면 풍력 발전기보다 오히려 고양이에 주안점을 두어야 한다고 주장할 수도 있을 것이다. 고양이보다 풍력 발전기를 더욱 변호하자면, 고양이들은 에너지, 오염되지 않은 공기, 그리고 지구 온난화의 완화를 제공하여 우리의 새들에게 가하는 해를 보상하지 않지만 풍력 발전기들은 그러한 모든 것들을 정말 제공한다는 점을 숙고해 보라.

➡ 반려 고양이에 비해, 풍력 발전기는 새와 박쥐에 대한 훨씬 덜 상당한 영향의 정도를 갖는다.

해설

풍력 발전기가 많은 새를 죽이는 것 같지만 반려 고양이가 죽이는 새의 수와 비교해 보면 사실상 그리 많은 수가 아니라는 내용이므로, 요약문의 빈칸 (A), (B)에 들어갈 말로는 ④ 'level(정도) – significant(상당한)'가 가장 적절하다.

① 다양성 – 측정 가능한
② 다양성 – 지속 가능한
③ 기간 – 상당한
⑤ 정도 – 지속 가능한

TEXT FLOW

도입	풍력 발전기가 매년 최소한 4만 5천 마리의 새와 박쥐를 죽이는 것으로 추산되어 옴
반론	고양이는 한 마리당 1년에 평균 300마리가 넘는 새를 죽이는 것으로 측정되어 옴
부연 1	풍력 발전기의 대가는 불과 150마리의 고양이가 하는 일과 동일함
부연 2	고양이는 새에게 가하는 해를 보상하지 않지만, 풍력 발전기는 오염되지 않은 공기와 지구 온난화를 제공함

구문

• [To place that number in perspective], consider [that pet cats {that are allowed to wander in and out of their owners' houses} have been measured to kill an average of more than 300 birds per year per cat.
: 첫 번째 [ ]는 목적을 나타내는 부사적 용법의 to부정사구이다. 두 번째 [ ]는 consider의 목적어 역할을 하는 명사절이고, 그 안의 { }는 pet cats를 수식하는 관계절이다.

11~12

정답 11 ⑤ 12 ④

미국의 추수 감사절 휴일을 생각할 때 어떤 이미지가 떠오르는가? 순례자들, 아메리카 원주민들, Macy의 추수 감사절 행진, 그리고 미식축구가 두드러지게 중요한 부분이겠지만, 곁들이는 모든 음식과 함께하는 칠면조가 많은 사람에게 떠오른다. 풍성한 음식은 미국의 추수 감사절 이야기에 바탕을 두고 있다. 전통에 따르면, 1621년의 겨울은 플리머스 식민지의 순례자들에게는 아주 지독했다. 자신들의 음식, 사냥 방법, 지역 음식과 재배 기법에 대한 지식을 공유한 아메리카 원주민들이 없었다면, 순례자들은 목숨을 잃었을 것이다. 성공적인 가을 수확 후에, 순례자들은 만찬을 함께하고 신에게 감사함으로써 아메리카 원주민 친구들과 같이 축하했다. 그러나 이 이야기는 역사학자, 사회학자, 식품학자들이 설명하듯이, 현실이라기보다는 근거 없는 믿음이다. 더 정확하게, 추수 감사절 전통은 남북 전쟁 이후에 미국의 국가적 결속을 증진하기 위해 만들어졌다.

Siskind에 따르면, 추수 감사절 의식에 참여하는 것은 '이민자 집단을 그 나라의 '건국'으로 이어지는 문화 역사에 연결시킴으로써 미국인들로 변화시킨다'. 순례자와 아메리카 원주민들이 만찬에서 풍성한 수확을 함께했다고 생각되는 이 건국 설화는 대체로 만들어진 것으로, 즉 그 전통은 첫 번째 추수 감사절이 문화적으로 구성되고 이상화된 형태에 근거를 두고 있다. 이처럼 만들어진 전통은 적어도 세 가지 중요한 목적을 간과한다(→ 목적에 부합한다). 첫째, 그것은 사회적 응집력을 상징하며 강한 집단적 정체성을 만들어낸다. 둘째, 만들어진 전통은 새로운 사회적 제도를 확립하고 기존의 제도를 합법화한다. 마지막으로, 만들어진 전통은 공유된 규범과 가치를 실천하는 집단의 공유된 그 규범과 가치로 개인들을 사회화한다. 추수 감사절은 만들어진 과거에 현재의 근거를 두고, 국가적 통합을 상징하며, 가족 제도에 기초한 뚜렷한 국가적 정체성을 재확인하는 중요한 만들어진 전통이다.

해설

11 미국의 추수 감사절 휴일은 남북 전쟁 이후에 미국의 국가적 결속, 즉 국가적 정체성을 증진하기 위해 만들어진 전통이라는 내용의 글이다. 따라서 글의 제목으로 가장 적절한 것은 ⑤ '추수 감사절 휴일: 국가적 정체성을 위해 만들어진 전통'이다.
① 미국인들이 추수 감사절에 주로 하는 일
② 추수 감사절 전통의 많은 변화
③ 아메리카 원주민에게 있어 추수 감사절의 의미
④ 추수 감사절 의식이 점점 간소화되는 이유

12 추수 감사절 휴일이 문화적으로 구성되고 이상화된 견해에 근거를 두었으며, 이처럼 만들어진 전통은 이어지는 세 가지 주요 목적을 위한 것이라는 맥락이 되어야 하므로, ④의 'defeat(간과한다)'를 'serve(부합한다)'와 같은 낱말로 바꾸어야 한다.

TEXT FLOW

도입	미국 추수 감사절을 떠올리면, 추수 감사절 이야기에 바탕을 둔 풍성한 음식이 떠오름
전개 1	이 이야기는 근거 없는 믿음이고, 남북 전쟁 이후 국가적 결속을 위해 만들어진 추수 감사절 전통임
전개 2	이 전통은 집단적 정체성을 만들고, 사회적 제도 확립 및 제도 합법화, 개인의 사회화 목적에 부합함
결론	추수 감사절은 국가적 정체성을 확인하는 만들어진 전통임

구문

• Thanksgiving is an important invented tradition [grounding the present in an invented past], [symbolizing national unity], and [reaffirming a distinct national identity {based on the institution of the family}].
: 세 개의 [ ]는 an important invented tradition을 수식하는 현재분사구로 and에 의해 병렬 구조를 이루고 있다. 세 번째 [ ] 안의 { }는 a distinct national identity를 수식하는 과거분사구이다.

고난도 모의고사 15회

01 ①	02 ①	03 ③	04 ⑤	05 ④	06 ④
07 ②	08 ⑤	09 ③	10 ②	11 ④	12 ⑤

01

정답 ①

우리는 무엇을 하라는 말을 듣는 것을 좋아하지 않는다. 우리는 자신의 삶을 즐기고 싶고, 정정당당하게 그것을 즐기고 싶다. 그 평형 상태를 어지럽히는 사람들은 우리를 불편하게 만들고, 그래서 도덕주의자들은 종종 축제에 초대받지 않은 손님이며, 우리는 그들에 대한 수많은 방어책을 가지고 있다. 유사하게, 일부 사람들은 열악한 물리적 환경으로부터 스스로를 한동안 분리시킬 수 있다. 어떤 것을 만들어 냄으로써 그들은 이익을 얻을 수 있다. (공장의) 주인은 자신의 화학 공장 쪽에서 불어오는 바람과 반대 방향에서 살 수 있고, 벌목꾼은 자신이 죽을 때까지는 나무가 동이 나지 않을 것을 알고 있을지도 모른다. 마찬가지로, 사람들은 열악한 도덕적 환경으로부터 스스로를 분리시킬 수 있고, 혹은 그것으로부터 이익을 얻을 수 있다. 일부 나무가 다른 나무로부터 영양분이나 빛을 빼앗음으로써 잘 자라는 것과 꼭 마찬가지로, 일부 사람들은 다른 사람들에게서 그들의 몫을 빼앗아 번성한다. 서양의 백인 남성은 비서양인, 혹은 비백인, 아니면 여성의 열등한 경제적 또는 사회적 지위 때문에 번성할지도 모른다. 우리가 그와 같은 한, 우리는 <u>뚜껑이 들어올려지는 것을 원하지 않을 것이다.</u>

해설

현재의 삶을 유지하려고 노력하면서 물리적으로나 도덕적으로 열악한 환경으로부터 <u>스스로를 분리시키는</u> 일부 사람들이 다른 사람의 몫을 빼앗아 번성한다는 내용이다. 밑줄 친 '뚜껑이 들어올려지는 것을 원하지 않는다'는 말은 남들의 몫을 빼앗아 번성하는 그 사람들과 같이 우리도 현재의 상태가 바뀌는 것을 원하지 않는다는 의미, 즉 현재 누리고 있는 기득권을 놓지 않기 위해서는 자신들의 도덕적인 결함이 드러나길 원하지 않거나 피한다는 뜻이므로, 밑줄 친 부분이 의미하는 바로 가장 적절한 것은 ① '자신들의 도덕적인 결함이 드러나는 것을 피한다'이다.
② 남을 탓하기보다 자기 자신을 되돌아본다
③ 우리가 무시당하는 느낌을 싫어한다
④ 사회적 균형을 약화시키는 행동을 비판한다
⑤ 자신들의 행동 부족을 정당화할 이유를 찾는다

ⓦ WHY 고난도

명확한 주제문이 없어 전체 글의 내용을 종합하여 중심 내용을 추론해야 하는데, 첫 두 문장이 함축적인 의미를 담고 있어서 독해의 방향을 정하기도 쉽지 않고 핵심어인 equilibrium 또한 추상적 개념이어서 지문의 내용을 파악하기 어려운 고난도 문제이다.

TEXT FLOW

도입	사람들은 자신들을 불편하게 만드는 사람들에 대한 방어책을 가지고 있음
전개 1	그들은 열악한 물리적 환경으로부터 <u>스스로를 분리시킬 수 있</u>고, 어떤 것을 만들어 내서 이익을 얻을 수 있음
전개 2	그들은 열악한 도덕적 환경으로부터 스스로를 분리시켜 그것으로부터 이익을 얻을 수 있음

02

정답 ①

여러 해 동안 매일 퇴근 후 특정한 도로를 이용해 집으로 돌아가는데 어느 날 여러분의 집으로 가는 도로가 붕괴되어 더 이상 그 길을 이용할 수 없게 되었다고 상상해 보라. 오랜 시간에 걸쳐 많은 도로가 건설된 지역에 살고 있다면, 다른 경로를 통해 집에 도착할 수 있기 때문에 한 도로가 붕괴되어도 여러분은 목적지에 도달하는 데 지장이 없을 것이다. 그러나 그것만이 집까지 가는 유일한 길이거나 여러분이 아는 유일한 길이라면, 여러분은 문제를 겪는다. 마찬가지로 뇌의 한 경로가 쇠퇴해 더 이상 기억이나 정보에 접근할 수 없는 경우, 다국어 사용자는 다른 언어, 또는 두 개 이상의 언어에서 축적된 단어, 기억, 경험 간의 연결로 인해 시간이 지남에 따라 구축된 다른 경로를 가지고 있다.

해설

매일 퇴근길에 이용하던 도로가 붕괴되었을 때 다른 도로가 있다면 다른 경로를 통해 집으로 갈 수 있는 것처럼, 뇌의 한 경로가 쇠퇴해 더 이상 기억이나 정보에 접근할 수 없을 때 다국어 사용자는 다른 인지적 경로를 사용할 수 있다는 내용이므로, 글의 제목으로 가장 적절한 것은 ① '인지적인 경로를 다양화시키는 다국어 사용의 힘'이다.
② 많은 경로의 장점: 혼잡을 방지하는 보험
③ 사용 중인 언어 간의 격차를 해소하는 데 필요한 기술
④ 익숙한 경로의 붕괴: 통근의 어려움
⑤ 다국어 두뇌: 의사소통을 할 너무 많은 방법

TEXT FLOW

도입	매일 퇴근 후 이용하는 도로가 붕괴되어 그 길을 이용할 수 없게 되었다고 상상함
전개 1	다른 경로가 있다면 목적지에 도착하는 데 지장이 없었을 것임
전개 2	뇌의 한 경로가 쇠퇴한 경우 다국어 사용자는 다른 인지적 경로를 사용할 수 있음

구문

• In the same way, [if one pathway in the brain has decayed and is no longer available for accessing memories or information], a multilingual has other pathways [that have been built over time as a result of the links between words, memories, and experiences {accumulated in the other languages or across two or more languages}].
: 첫 번째 [ ]는 조건을 나타내는 부사절이다. 두 번째 [ ]는 other pathways를 수식하는 관계절이고, 그 안의 { }는 words, memories, and experiences를 수식하는 과거분사구이다.

03

정답 ③

자신의 저작물 전체, 특히 저서 'The Feeling of What Happens'에서 그가 하는 설명의 풍부함과 깊이에도 불구하고, Damasio는 의식이 어떻게 발생하는지와 감정이 그 발생에서 담당하는 중심적인 역할을 설명하려는 자신의 시도에서 고군분투한다. 그 고군분투는 대체로 우리에게 이 현상의 특수성을 개념화할 수 있는 언어가 없다는 사실에 기인하는데, 언어를 초월하는 것을 표현할 수 있는 언어의 단점을 고려할 때 아마도 우리는 결코 그것을 갖지 못할지도 모른다. 우리의 경험에 있는 모든 것이 결국 언어, 즉 음악 교육자들과 다른 예술의 교육자들이 대단히 잘 알고 있는 것에 의해 정확하게 표현될 수 있는 것은 아니다. 우리는 음악을 확실히 경험하는 것처럼 느낌

과 의식을 경험한다. 그러한 경험들을 언어가 전달할 수 있는 표현으로 제시하는 것은 언어와 느껴지고 알고 있는 경험 사이의 차이 때문에 매우 좌절스럽고 불만족스러울 수 있다. 그럼에도 불구하고 Damasio가 자신의 뇌 연구에서 제시하는 몇몇 통찰은 음악이 어떻게 작동하고 우리가 그것을 가르치는 데 어떻게 더 효과적일 수 있는지를 명확하게 한다.

해설

③ something을 수식하는 관계절 안에서 music educators, and educators in the other arts가 주어인 동사 자리이므로 knowing은 복수 동사 know로 고쳐야 한다.
① his attempts를 수식하는 형용사적 용법의 to부정사 to explain은 어법상 적절하다.
② is의 주어 역할을 하면서 express의 목적어 역할을 하는 명사절이 필요하므로 관계대명사 what은 어법상 적절하다.
④ 뒤에 명사구가 나오므로 전치사구 because of는 어법상 적절하다.
⑤ several insights를 수식하는 관계절을 이끌고 있으므로 관계대명사 that은 어법상 적절하다.

TEXT FLOW

도입	Damasio는 의식이 어떻게 발생하는지와 감정의 중심적인 역할을 설명하려는 시도에서 고군분투함
부연	이 현상의 특수성을 개념화할 수 있는 언어가 없다는 사실에 기인함
전개	우리의 경험에 있는 것이 언어에 의해 정확하게 표현될 수 있는 것은 아님
부연	언어와 느껴지는 경험 사이의 차이 때문에 불만족스러울 수 있음

구문

• [Putting those experiences into the representations {language is capable of mediating}] can be very frustrating and unsatisfying [because of the disparities **between** language **and** felt, aware experience].
: 첫 번째 [ ]는 문장의 주어이고, 그 안의 { }는 the representations를 수식하는 관계절이다. 두 번째 [ ]는 because of가 이끄는 부사구이고, 그 안에 'A와 B 사이에'라는 의미의 「between A and B」가 쓰였다.

04 정답 ⑤

야구공을 치거나 악기를 연주하는 것은 일련의 단계 속에서 복잡한 작업을 수행하는 근육의 복잡한 조절을 필요로 한다. 그러나 그것들은 숙련된 수행자에게서, 인식 바깥에서 자동적으로 일어난다. 이런 과업들은 우리가 완전히 인식할 수 없긴 하지만 여전히 사고와 행동에 중대한 영향을 미치는 정신의 부분을 필요로 한다. 창의성은 또한 무의식적인 정신 작용에서 비롯되는 것으로 보이는데, 어려운 문제에 대한 해결책은 무의식에서 잠복기를 거친 후에 '갑자기 튀어나오는' 것처럼 보일 수도 있기 때문이다. 직관적인 느낌이나 예감은 통례적인 추론 없이 무언가를 감지하는 무의식에 근거하는 것처럼 보인다. 타당한 이유 없이 행동하는 것은 의심스러운 인생 전략처럼 보일 수도 있지만, 우리는 매우 제한된 정보로 선택해야 하는 많은 애매한 상황에 직면한다. 만약 우리 직관의 원천이 실제로 숙련된 무의식이라면, 예감을 따르는 것은 무작위의 선택보다 훨씬 더 열등한(→ 우월한) 전략을 구성하는 것으로 보인다.

해설

직관의 원천은 숙련된 무의식이기 때문에 예감을 따르는 것은 무작위

의 선택보다 더 나은 전략이 될 것이다. 따라서 ⑤의 'inferior(열등한)'를 'superior(우월한)'와 같은 낱말로 바꾸어야 한다.

⊗ 매력적인 오답 주의!

②, ③ 글의 주제를 반대로 파악했거나, the idea of objective truth의 의미를 반대로 해석하여 선택한 것으로 보인다. [선택률 20%, 24%]

TEXT FLOW

도입	야구공을 치거나 악기를 연주하는 것은 숙련된 수행자에게서 무의식적으로 일어남
전개	창의성, 직관적인 느낌, 예감도 무의식적인 정신 작용에서 비롯되는 것으로 보임
결론	직관의 원천이 숙련된 무의식이라면, 예감을 따르는 것은 우월한 전략이 될 것임

구문

• These tasks require a part of the mind [that we cannot be fully aware of], but **one** [that still exerts critical influence on thoughts and actions].
: 두 개의 [ ]는 각각 선행사 a part of the mind, one을 수식하는 관계절이며, one은 the mind를 받는 부정대명사이다.

05 정답 ④

사람들이 때때로 진리의 객관설보다 상대주의, 심지어 단순한 상대주의를 선호하는 한 가지 이유는 상대주의가 더 큰 관용을 장려한다는 느낌 때문이다. 그야말로 '단 하나의 진리'가 있다는 생각은 어떤 사람은 진리에 대한 특권적 접근권이 있고 다른 사람은 그런 것이 없다는 확신과 흔히 함께 작동한다고 상대주의자들은 지적한다. 바로 이러한 정서가 19세기 서구 식민주의의 특징이었는데, 당시 선교사들은 식민지 정부의 군대 및 경찰과 함께 일하며 사람들로 하여금 식민주의자들이 믿기를 원하는 것을 믿도록, 또는 적어도 믿는다고 말하도록 강요했다. 그러나 객관적 진리 같은 것이 없다면, 진리에 대한 특권적인 위치를 지닌 사람은 아무도 없다. 우리는 더 이상 우리가 진리를 알고 있고 그들은 그렇지 못하다고 말함으로써 우리의 신을 사람들이 믿도록 강요하는 것을 정당화할 수 없다. 객관적 진리라는 생각을 버리는 것이 더 관대한 인생관을 장려하는 것처럼 보인다.

해설

19세기 서구 식민주의는 자신들만이 객관적 진리를 가지고 있고 다른 사람은 그것이 없기 때문에 자신들이 믿는 것을 사람들이 믿도록 할 수 있었지만, 진리에 대한 그와 같은 특권적 접근법을 버리고 상대주의를 취해야 삶에 대한 더 큰 관용을 가질 수 있다는 내용의 글이다. 따라서 빈칸에 들어갈 말로 가장 적절한 것은 ④ '버리는 것'이다.
① 시험하는 것　　　　　　② 반기는 것
③ 개발하는 것　　　　　　⑤ 기억하는 것

TEXT FLOW

주제	사람들이 상대주의를 선호하는 이유는 더 큰 관용을 장려한다는 느낌 때문임
부연 1	19세기 서구 식민주의는 자신들이 가지고 있는 객관적 진리를 다른 사람들에게도 믿으라고 함
부연 2	객관적 진리가 없으면 그에 대한 특권적인 위치도 없고, 사람들을 믿도록 강요하는 것도 정당화할 수 없음

• One reason [that people sometimes favor relativism—even simple relativism—over objective theories of truth] is the sense [that relativism encourages greater tolerance].
: 첫 번째 [ ]는 One reason을 수식하는 관계절이고, 이때 that은 why 대신에 사용된 관계부사이다. 두 번째 [ ]는 the sense와 동격의 명사절이다.

06
정답 ④

우리가 인류의 생물학적 하위 집단으로 간주할 수 있을 만큼 동질적인 어떤 인간 집단을 확인할 수 있다고 가정해 보라. 반드시, 그 집단 내 사람들 간의 차이는 그 집단과 다른 인간 집단 간의 차이를 크게 초과한다. 논란이 많았던 미국의 흑인과 백인의 IQ 차이를 살펴보자. '평균' 성적은 아프리카계 미국인이 유럽 혈통의 미국인보다 떨어질 수도 있겠지만, 그렇다고 하더라도 각 하위 집단 내의 IQ 점수의 범위가 매우 넓어서 수백만 명의 백인들은 수백만 명의 흑인들보다 지적으로 열등할 것이다. 극단적인 예를 들자면, 그 평균 차이는 IQ 200을 가진 순수 아프리카계의 9세 소녀가 1930년대에 출현하는 것을 막지 못했다. 그것은 99%를 초과하는 그녀 세대의 백인 아이들보다 더 나은 것이었다. 게다가 그녀는 자라면서 미국 흑인들이 직면해야 했던 위협적인 불리한 조건에도 불구하고 이 점수를 획득했다.

해설

각 하위 집단 내의 IQ 점수의 범위는 매우 넓어서 수백만 명의 백인들이 수백만 명의 흑인들보다 지적으로 열등할 것이라는 사례에 비추어 볼 때, 한 집단 내 사람들 간의 차이는 그 집단과 다른 집단 간의 차이보다 더 클 것이다. 따라서 빈칸에 들어갈 말로 가장 적절한 것은 ④ '그 집단과 다른 인간 집단 간의 차이를 크게 초과한다'이다.
① 그 인구 구성원들의 성별 구성을 거의 반영하지 않는다
② 교육이 집단 전체에 영향력을 확장함에 따라 점차 사라진다
③ 생물학적 요인보다는 사회적인 요인과 관련이 있는 것으로 밝혀진다
⑤ 다른 생물학적 하위 집단 간의 차이에 비해 상대적으로 작다

TEXT FLOW

도입	인간 집단 내 사람들 간의 차이는 그 집단과 다른 인간 집단 간의 차이를 크게 초과함
부연 1	미국의 흑인과 백인의 IQ 차이에서 평균 성적은 백인이 높게 나옴
부연 2	그러나 각 하위 집단 내의 IQ 점수의 범위가 매우 넓어서 수백만 명의 백인들은 수백만 명의 흑인들보다 지적으로 열등할 것임
예시	IQ 200을 가진 아프리카 소녀는 99%를 초과하는 그녀 세대의 백인 아이들보다 나은 것임

구문

• ~; even so, [the range in IQ scores within each subpopulation] is **so** wide **that** millions of whites will be intellectually inferior to millions of blacks.
: [ ]가 문장의 주어이고, 동사는 is이다. '너무 ~해서 …하다'를 의미하는 「so ~ that ….」 구문이 쓰였다.

07
정답 ②

아이러니하게도, 과학은 감각의 정보에 호소하기도 하고 동시에 그것들을 신뢰할 수 없는 것으로 거부하기도 한다. 우선 감각 정보가 측정된다. (B) 따라서 측정할 수 있는 감각 경험만이 과학에 포함된다. 측정이 불가능한 것, 본질적으로 정성적인 것은 단지 주관적인 감각으로 여겨진다. 측정이 가능한 특성에는 감각과 무관하다고 추정되는 객관적인 실재가 부여된다. (A) 그러나 우리는 측정이 가능한 것들의 인식은 색채를 보는 것만큼 불가분하게 감각에 예속된다는 것을 보여 주었다. 사실, 측정이 가능한 특성은 어떤 면에서 감각 중에서 가장 개인적으로 규제된 것에 근거하고 있다. (C) 그것들은 우리에게 우리 자신의 몸에 대해 말해 주는 것이다. 우리가 우리의 감각을 통해 세상에 대해 알게 되는 것을 근거로, 우리는 과학을 측정할 수 있는 그런 경험으로만 한정하기로 선택하는 것은 감각 경험의 본질이라는 틀 내에서 내린 완전히 자의적인 선택이라는 것을 이해할 수 있다.

해설

감각 정보의 측정에 대해 언급한 주어진 글 다음에는, 측정 가능한 감각 경험만이 과학에 포함된다는 내용의 (B)가 온 후, 측정이 가능한 것은 감각에 예속되고 그런 이유로 가장 개인적으로 규제되는 한계를 가진다는 문제점을 지적하는 (A)가 온 다음, 마지막으로 과학을 측정이 가능한 경험만으로 한정하는 것은 완전히 자의적인 선택이라고 결론짓는 (C)가 오는 것이 글의 순서로 가장 적절하다.

TEXT FLOW

도입	과학은 감각 정보를 측정하고, 측정 불가능한 것은 주관적인 감각으로 받아들임
부연	측정이 가능한 것은 감각에 예속되고, 감각 중에서 가장 개인적으로 규제된 것에 근거함
결론	과학을 측정할 수 있는 경험으로만 한정하는 것은 자의적인 선택임

구문

• However, we have shown that knowledge of measurables is **as** inextricably bound to the senses [**as** is seeing color].
: [ ]는 as seeing color is bound to the senses에서 bound to the senses가 생략되고 주어 seeing color와 동사 is가 도치된 형태이다. '~만큼 …한/하게'를 의미하는 「as+형용사/부사+as」 구문이 쓰였다.

08
정답 ⑤

높은 지위 집단 구성원의 의무와 책임은 본질적으로 사회적일 수 있는데, 예를 들어 그들은 흔히 자신들의 집단에 영감을 주고, 구성원들 사이에 평화를 유지하고, 개인들 사이의 의사소통을 용이하게 할 것으로 기대된다. 그러나 대부분의 집단 환경에서 그들은 또한 그 집단이 직면하는 기술적 문제도 이해해야 한다. 업무에 유능한 사람에게 책임을 맡기는 것은 집단이 더 잘 수행하도록 돕는다. 그러므로 많은 집단은 영향력을 할당할 때 사교적 기술과 같은 다른 요인들보다는 업무 역량을 우선시한다. 예를 들어, 엔지니어 팀에서는 기술적 능력이 의사소통 능력보다 더 중요하게 여겨질 것이다. 그러나 집단은 흔히 그들의 지위 계층 구조를 업무 역량 차이에 근거를 두지 못한다. 예를 들어, '지위 특성 이론' 전통의 많은 연구는 집단 구성원들이 지위 할당을 성별, 인종, 사회적 계층, 그리고 신체적 매력과 같은 특징에 근거를 두며, 이러한 특징이 그렇지 않은데도 일반적인 역량과 관련되어 있다고 생각한다는 것을 발견한다. 마찬가지로, 자신감이 더 높은 개인은 자신감이 실제

능력을 크게 예측하는 것이 아닌데도, 리더로 선택될 가능성이 더 높을 수도 있다.

해설

For example로 시작하는 주어진 문장은 '지위 특성 이론' 전통의 많은 연구에 따르면, 집단 구성원들이 지위 할당을 성별, 인종, 사회적 계층, 그리고 신체적 매력과 같은 특징에 근거를 두며, 이러한 특징이 그렇지 않을 때조차도 일반적인 역량과 관련되어 있다고 생각한다는 것을 발견한다는 내용으로, 이 문장 앞에는 집단은 지위 계층 구조를 업무 역량의 차이에 근거를 두지 못한다는 내용이 있어야 하고, 이 문장 뒤에는 Similarly로 주어진 문장의 내용에 대한 부연 설명을 이어가는 내용이 나와야 한다. 따라서 주어진 문장이 들어가기에 가장 적절한 곳은 ⑤이다.

TEXT FLOW

도입	높은 지위 집단 구성원의 의무와 책임은 사회적이지만, 그들은 기술적 문제도 직면함
전개	집단은 그들의 지위 계층 구조를 업무 역량 차이에 근거를 두지 못함
부연	집단 구성원들은 지위 할당을 성별, 인종 등의 특징에 근거를 두어, 그것이 역량과 관련되어 있다고 생각함

구문

• Therefore, many groups **prioritize** task competence **over** other factors like social skills [when allocating influence].
  : 'B보다 A를 우선시하다'를 의미하는 「prioritize A over B」가 쓰였다. [ ]는 분사구문으로 의미를 명확하게 하기 위해 접속사 when이 생략되지 않고 쓰였다.

09 정답 ③

도시에서 더 빠른 속도를 달성하는 것은 기후 변화 적응을 촉진할 것인데, 사람들이 (살) 지역에 대한 더 많은 선택권을 가질 것이기 때문이다. 만약 Mary가 편도로 30분 동안 통근할 의향이 있고 시속 40마일로 이동할 수 있다면, 그녀는 그녀의 직장 주변 반경 20마일 안에서 살 곳을 찾을 수 있다. 반지름이 20마일인 원의 면적은 3.14×400, 즉 1,200제곱마일이 넘는다! 그렇게 큰 면적은 Mary가 자신의 요구에 맞는 지역을 찾을 충분한 기회를 제공한다. 이 점을 이해하기 위해서는 혼잡한 도시에서 Mary가 단지 시속 15마일의 속도로 통근하기를 기대할 수 있다고 가정해 보라. 통근 시간이 30분이면, 그녀는 직장이 있는 곳에서 반경 7.5마일 내에서만 집을 구할수 있을 것이고, 이 원의 면적은 3.14×7.5×7.5=176제곱마일과 같다. 이것은 찾아다니기에 훨씬 더 작은 면적이다. 더 많은 주거 기회를 가짐으로써, 각각의 가정은 기후 회복력이 있는 지역을 찾을 더 큰 기회를 갖게 될 것이다.

해설

주어진 문장은 혼잡한 도시에서 Mary가 시속 15마일의 속도로 통근하기를 기대할 수 있다고 가정하는 내용으로, 뒤에는 이 가정에 관련된 시속 15마일의 속도로 통근할 경우에 대한 자세한 내용이 와야 하므로, 주어진 문장이 들어가기에 가장 적절한 곳은 ③이다.

TEXT FLOW

도입	도시에서 더 빠른 속도를 달성하는 것은 기후 변화 적응을 촉진하고, 사람들이 살 지역에 더 많은 선택권을 줌
예시	Mary가 통근 시간이 30분이고 시속 40마일로 이동하면 직장 주변 반경 20마일 안에서 살 수 있지만, 시속 15마일로 이동하면 반경 7.5마일 안에서 살 수 있음
결론	더 많은 주거 기회를 가질수록, 가정은 기후 회복력이 있는 지역을 찾을 더 큰 기회를 가지게 됨

구문

• Such a huge area provides ample opportunities [{for Mary} to find the neighborhood {that matches her desires}].
  : [ ]는 ample opportunities를 수식하는 to부정사구이고, 그 안의 첫 번째 { }는 to부정사구의 의미상의 주어이며, 두 번째 { }는 the neighborhood를 수식하는 관계절이다.

10 정답 ②

역사학자는 과거 시제를 선호하지만, 동사의 시제는 흔히 약간 혼란스러운 주제이다. 이것은 대체로 문학에 관해 글을 쓰는 학자들이 일련의 서로 다른 관행을 가지고 있기 때문이다. 한 문학 평론가는 "'Black Boy'에서 Richard Wright는 미국의 인종 차별주의와 자본주의에 반대하여 유창하고 강력하게 말한다."라고 쓸 수도 있다. Wright의 말은 1937년에 그가 그것을 썼을 때 그랬던 것처럼 오늘날에도 진짜인 것처럼 들린다. 문학에 관한 글쓰기의 목적으로, 현재 시제는 작가의 생각이 오늘날에도 여전히 유효하다는 것을 전달한다. 고전 문학은 오늘날 독자에게 강력한 영향을 미치지만, 역사학자는 Wright의 소설을 그의 삶과 시대의 상황 안에 두기를 원한다. Wright는 오늘날 실제로 말하지 않으며, 1960년에 사망했다. 그는 대공황 시기 동안 'Black Boy'를 썼다. 그 당시에 독자들은 Wright의 작품을 오늘날과는 다르게 해석했다. 현재 시제를 사용하는 것은 Wright의 삶과 시대의 연대기를 혼란스럽게 하는 반면에, 과거 시제를 사용하는 것은 작가가 한 사건을 다른 사건과 관련하여 배열할 수 있게 한다.

➡ 문학 비평가는 작가의 생각에 즉시성의 느낌을 주기 때문에 현재 시제를 선호하는 반면, 역사학자는 사건의 순서에 중점을 두기 때문에 과거 시제를 선호한다.

해설

한 문학 평론가는 Richard Wright가 1937년에 'Black Boy'를 썼을 때처럼 현재 시제를 통해 작가의 생각이 오늘날에도 여전히 유효하다는 것을 전달하는 반면, 역사학자는 한 사건을 다른 사건과 관련지어 연대기로 배열하기 때문에 과거 시제를 쓴다는 내용의 글이다. 따라서 요약문의 빈칸 (A), (B)에 들어갈 말로는 ② 'immediacy(즉시성) – sequence(순서)'가 가장 적절하다.

① 통제 – 중요성	③ 즉시성 – 중요성
④ 실현 – 기원	⑤ 실현 – 순서

TEXT FLOW

도입	역사학자는 과거 시제를 선호하지만, 문학에 관해 글을 쓰는 학자들은 서로 다른 관행을 가지고 있음
부연 1	문학 평론가는 작가의 생각이 오늘날에도 유효하다는 것을 전달하기 위해 현재 시제를 씀
부연 2	역사학자는 한 사건을 다른 사건과 관련하여 연대기로 배열하기 때문에 과거 시제를 씀

• Wright's words ring just **as** true today **as** they **did** in 1937 when he wrote them.
  : '~만큼 …한/하게'를 의미하는 「as+형용사/부사+as」 구문이 쓰였다. did는 rang true를 받는 대동사이다.

• A good deal of empirical evidence supports the view [that emotions, whether positive or negative, tend to be socially shared], and [that the social sharing of emotions results in a strong emotional impact on the exposed person].
  : 두 개의 [ ]는 the view와 동격 관계를 나타내는 명사절이다.

11-12

정답 11 ④ 12 ⑤

많은 양의 경험적 증거는, 긍정적인 것이든 부정적인 것이든, 감정이 사회적으로 공유되는 경향이 있고 감정의 사회적 공유는 (그 감정을) 접한 사람에게 강력한 감정적 영향을 초래한다는 견해를 뒷받침한다. 감정적 경험은 한 사람이 그 경험에 대해 다른 사람과 이야기하도록 자극하는데, 영향을 받은 사람들은 자신들의 경험에 대해 더 많이 이해하고 알려고 하기 때문이다. 개인적 감정이 더 강렬할수록, 우리가 그것을 다른 사람들과 공유할 가능성이 더 높다. 어떤 사건에 대해 이야기하는 것은 기억에 도움이 될지도 모르는 예행연습의 한 형태인데, 왜냐하면, 기억을 안내하는 사회적 메커니즘으로 여겨지는, 경험을 말하거나 언어로 옮기는 것은 사람들의 마음속에서 그 사건을 조직화하고 완전히 이해하는 것을 도울 수 있기 때문이다. 따라서 개인의 기억의 틀을 규정하는 주요한 상징체계로서의 언어는 '감정적 격변 후의 중요한 인지적, 학습 과정의 매개체'이다. 사건이 감정을 더 많이 자극할수록, 그것은 사회적 공유와 그 사건에 대한 명백히 생생하고 정확하며 구체적인 기억을 더 많이 이끌어 낸다. 섬광 기억이라고 알려진 이런 종류의 기억은 보통의 기억과는 질적으로 다르며 시간의 측면에서 우월하다고 여겨지는데, 이런 유형의 기억은 다른 기억보다 더 선명하고 시간에 의해 영향을 더(→ 덜) 받는다고 추정되기 때문이다. 놀랍고 감정적으로 강렬한 사건의 결과이기 때문에, 섬광 기억은 오래 지속될 가능성이 높다.

해설

11 감정은 사회적으로 공유되는 경향이 있는데, 감정이 더 강렬할수록 우리가 그것을 다른 사람들과 공유할 가능성이 더 높으며, 감정적 경험에 대해 말로 이야기하는 것은 아주 생생하고 정확하며 구체적인 기억을 이끌어 내는 등 기억에 도움이 된다는 내용의 글이므로, 글의 제목으로 가장 적절한 것은 ④ '기억의 활성제로서의 사회적으로 공유된 감정'이다.
① 과거의 경험이 우리의 성격을 형성한다
② 언어의 힘: 그것이 현실을 형성하는 법
③ 섬광 기억: 정확한 역사 기록이 아니다
⑤ 새로운 언어를 배우는 데 있어 감정의 이점

12 섬광 기억은 보통의 기억과는 달리 시간의 측면에서 우월하다고 여겨진다고 했는데, 이는 강렬한 사건의 결과로서 기억이 오래 지속된다는 것이며 시간의 영향을 덜 받는다는 것이므로, ⑤의 'more(더)'를 반의어인 'less(덜)'로 바꾸어야 한다.

TEXT FLOW

도입	감정은 사회적으로 공유되는 경향이 있고, 그 공유는 접한 사람에게 감정적 영향을 초래함
부연 1	개인적 감정이 더 강렬할수록 그것을 다른 사람들과 공유할 가능성이 더 높음
부연 2	이야기하는 것은 마음속에서 그 사건을 조직화하고 이해하도록 돕고, 생생하고 구체적인 기억을 더 많이 이끌어 냄
결론	섬광 기억은 놀랍고 감정적으로 강렬한 사건의 결과이기 때문에 오래 지속될 가능성이 높음

본문 102쪽

REVIEW 모의고사 **01 회**

| 01 ② | 02 ⑤ | 03 ⑤ | 04 ① | 05 ① | 06 ② |
| 07 ③ | 08 ⑤ | 09 ④ | 10 ③ | 11 ④ | 12 ③ |

01 정답 ②

전시 디자이너, 미술관 큐레이터와 마찬가지로 사진작가들도 관람객이 사물을 특정한 관점을 따라 특정한 비교를 하도록 촉진하여 특별한 기분을 만들어 내기를 바라는 명확한 배열 속에서 보기를 원한다. 그들은 단일 이미지가 불확실하며 '그것이 무엇에 관한 것인지'를 쉽게 그리고 모호하지 않게 드러내지 않는다는 점을 알고 있다. 사진작가들이 뉴스와 광고 같은 다른 목적을 위해 사진을 제작할 때는, 대체로 모든 '관련 없는' 세부 사항, 즉 그들이 주의를 끌기를 원하는 뉴스 이야기의 '핵심'이나 제품의 특징을 제외한 모든 것을 전부 배제하도록 사진을 구성한다. 그들은 그 이야기의 핵심적인 아이디어를 강조하거나 그 제품의 매력을 향상하기 위해 요점과 밀접한 관련이 있는 세부 사항을 주의 깊게 선택한다. 과학적인 목적을 위해 제작된 사진들도 이와 비슷하게 제작자(대체로 그 과학 논문의 저자)가 사용자들이 알기를 바라는 점에 그 사진의 내용물을 제한하고 그 목적과 관련 없는 것은 무엇이든지 엄격히 배제한다.

해설
사진작가들은 자신들이 원하는 방식의 특정한 배열로 사진을 만들어서 특정한 비교를 유도하고 특정한 분위기를 형성하려고 핵심적인 아이디어를 강조하거나 요점과 관련이 있는 세부 사항을 주의 깊게 선택한다는 내용이므로, 글의 주제로 가장 적절한 것은 ② '사진에서 시각적 내용의 의도적 배열'이다.
① 광고 및 그래픽 디자인에서 사진의 힘
③ 뉴스 기사 또는 제품 특집에서 사진작가의 역할
④ 이야기를 구성하기 위한 사진 배열의 기술적 어려움
⑤ 자연 환경 사진을 보는 감정적 효과

02 정답 ⑤

우리는 신중함이 필요하다. 인간의 미덕은 다층적이다. 자연이 인격을 형성한다는 것은 절반의 진실에 불과하고, 그것을 전부라고 받아들이면 어리석은 것이다. 그것은 모든 시민적 덕성을 제외할 것인데, 그것 없이 우리는 인간일 수 없을 것이다. 인격은 자연과 문화의 변증법에서 발달된다. "인간은 본래 정치적 동물이다." 인간은 스스로 도시 국가인 도시를 세우고 그 안에서 사회화하는 것을 좋아하는 동물이다. "인간은 인위적이 되는 것이 자연스러운 동물이다." '호모 사피엔스'는 '타고난 이방인'이다. 인간이 자연과 만날 때 '자연스럽게' 하는 것은 자신을 자연과 구별하는 문화를 만드는 것이다. 농업, 상업, 그리고 산업이 그들의 진정한 천직이다. 미덕은 '함양되고,' '키워져야' 한다. 향수를 불러일으키는 소박함과 검소함 속에서 야생적인 자연과 함께 산다는 것은, 인간의 비범한 재능이 얼마나 많이 자연으로부터의 이탈 및 수완 좋은 자연의 변형에서 발견되는지를 망각하는 낭만적이고 터무니없는 생각이라고 이러한 '인문주의자들'은 말할 것이다. 이것에 대한 현대어는 "개발하라!"이다.

해설
⑤ 문장의 동사는 is이고, 주어를 이끌어야 하므로, 동사 Live를 동명사 Living 또는 To live로 고쳐야 한다.
① if절의 주어 it(= That nature builds character)과 동사 is가 생략되어 있으므로, 과거분사 taken은 어법상 적절하다.
② 두 개의 절을 연결하고 선행사인 all the civic virtues를 수식하고 있으므로, 관계대명사 which는 어법상 적절하다.
③ build의 주어인 animals가 다시 목적어로 사용되고 있으므로, 재귀대명사 themselves는 어법상 적절하다.
④ 선행사를 포함한 관계대명사 What이 이끄는 절이 주어이고, 동사가 필요하므로 is는 어법성 적절하다.

03 정답 ⑤

어떤 것을 가치 있게 여기는 것은 그것이 가치 있다고 믿고 그것에 '관심을 갖는' 것이다. 관심을 갖지 않으면 어떤 것을 가치 있게 여기지 않는다. 불행하게도, 관심의 본질은 이해의 개념만큼이나 거의 모호하다. 그러나 적어도 한 가지는 분명한데, 관심은 그것이 감정과 갖는 관계를 떠나서는 정의될 수 없다는 것이다. 심지어 관심을 감정에 대한 단순한 성향이라고 생각할 수도 있다. 나는 이것이 오류라고 생각한다. 관심을 가지는 것이 다양한 다른 감정, 행동, 생각을 낳기 때문에, 그것은 감정을 과장되게 드러내는 단순한 성향으로 환원될 수 없다. 내가 자신 있게 단언할 수 있는 것은 우리의 감정은 우리가 무엇에 관심을 가지느냐에 달려 있다는 것이다. 예를 들어, 우리는 우리가 관심을 가지고 있는 것에 대해서만 두려워한다. 일반적으로, 보통의 감정은 우리가 관심을 가지고 있는 어떤 것이 영향을 받을 것 같거나, 영향을 받아온 방식에 대한 평가를 본질적으로 포함한다. 그러나 누군가가 어떤 것에 관해 관심을 가질 수 있으면서 그것이 위협을 받을 때 두려움을 느끼지 않거나 그것이 번성할 것 같을 때 희망을 느끼지 않는 경향이 있을 수 있다고 생각하는 것은 일관성이 없는 일이다. 따라서 우리의 관심사가 때때로 우리의 감정적인 반응에 의해 우리에게 드러난다는 것을 말하는 것은 논란의 여지가 있다(→ 논란의 여지가 없다).

해설
앞 문장에서 누군가가 어떤 것에 관해 관심을 가질 수 있으면서 그것이 위협을 받을 때 두려움을 느끼지 않거나 그것이 번성할 것 같을 때 희망을 느끼지 않는 경향이 있을 수 있다고 생각하는 것은 일관성이 없는 일이라고 말하고 있으므로, 우리의 관심사가 때때로 우리의 감정적인 반응에 의해 우리에게 드러난다는 것을 말하는 것은 논란의 여지가 없다고 해야 내용이 자연스럽다. 따라서 ⑤ 'controversial(논란의 여지가 있는)'을 'uncontroversial(논란의 여지가 없는)'과 같은 낱말로 바꾸어야 한다.

04 정답 ①

13년 동안 영국 의학 저널의 책임자인 Richard Smith는 자신의 저서에서, 각각의 기고자가 각각의 소논문에서 어떤 부분의 일을 수행했는지를 명백하게 설명해 주는 방법 없이는 과학이 잘 작동될 수 없다고 말한다. Smith는 공동 저자들의 목록이 그들의 전기 및 그들이 각 연구에 기고한 내용과 함께 저널에 포함되어야 한다고 제안한다. 이 관계는 논문 저자 당사자들에 의해 전개되고 동의되어야 한다. 그러나 이 생각은 과학의 위대한 세계 지도자들을 설득하지 못하는데, 그들은 자신들에게 그 지도력을 제공해 온 것이 바로 그 기고 시스템이기 때문에 그 시스템에 매우 만족해한다. 그러나 그것[기고 시스템]은 재능 있는 젊은이들이 그것에 참여하는 것을 단념시킨다. 현재의 과학자는 연구가 자기 자신의 것이라고 느끼지 않는다. 그 과학자는 자신의 이름이 쓰인 과학 문헌을 만들지만, 많은 경우 심지어 그 글을 쓴 적도 없거나 그 글의 일부도 쓰지 않았다. 사실, 힘 있는 연구 집단이 과학자들이 데이터를 넘기는 전문 작가, 즉 젊은 박사들을 고용하는 것이 점점 더 흔해지고 있다.

해설

Richard Smith는 각각의 기고자가 소논문에서 어떤 일을 수행했는지 설명해야 한다고 주장하고, 세계 지도자들은 자신들에게 지도력을 제공한 지금의 기고 시스템에 만족하지만, 지금의 기고 시스템은 재능 있는 젊은이들이 참여하는 것을 단념시키고, 과학자는 자신의 이름이 쓰인 과학 문헌을 만들지만, 많은 경우 심지어 그 글을 쓴 적도 없거나 그 글의 일부도 쓰지 않았다는 내용이므로, 빈칸에 들어갈 말로 가장 적절한 것은 ① '연구가 자기 자신의 것이다'이다.
② 그 보상이 충분하다
③ 지도자들이 그들과 협력한다
④ 공동체가 협업을 중시한다
⑤ 주제가 자신들의 전문 분야와 관련 있다

05
정답 ①

완전히 건설되어 시험되기 전까지는 쉽게 검증될 수 없는 종류의 큰 것이 있다. 이것은 댐, 터널, 건물, 다리와 같은 토목 공학 프로젝트들인데, 그것들은 규모가 너무나 크고 비용이 너무나 거대하며, 디자인이 그 장소에 너무나 특화되어 있어서 그 건축물은 고유하다. 그것이 공장에서 만들어지는 것이 아니라 한 장소에 건설되는 유일한 것이어서, 검사할 만한 1회용 표본이 없다. 이론을 실험하거나 대안적인 설계를 비교하기 위해 축소판 모델이 사용될 수도 있지만, 어떠한 모델도 지어진 실제 건축물의 조건을 절대 완전히 복제하지 못할 것이다. 이론의 여지없이 의미 있는 모델들이 가능하다 해도, 그 건축물이 영향을 받을 미래의 지진, 폭풍, 그와 유사한 것들이 가진 자연력을 완전히 모델링하는 것은 불가능하다. 요컨대, 거대한 토목 공학 건축물을 명확하게 검증하는 유일한 방법은 자연이 그것을 어떻게 시험할 것인지를 예상하며 건설하고 자연이 그렇게 하도록 내버려 두는 것이다. 거대한 규모의 토목 공학 공사에 대한 이러한 사실은 <u>주의 깊고, 사전 대책을 강구하는 실패 분석</u>을 필요로 한다.

해설

거대한 건축물들은 어떠한 수학적 모델이나 모형으로도 미리 쉽게 검증하고 분석하기 어렵고, 축소판 모델을 사용해도 자연력을 완전히 모델링하는 것은 불가능하므로, 그 디자인의 유효성을 검사하려면 자연이 그것을 어떻게 시험할 것인지를 예상하며 건설하고 자연이 그렇게 하도록 내버려 두는 것이라는 내용이다. 따라서 빈칸에 들어갈 말로 가장 적절한 것은 ① '주의 깊고, 사전 대책을 강구하는 실패 분석'이다.
② 보관 시설의 충분한 공간
③ 실제 사용 전 현실 사회 실험
④ 안전 기능이 포함된 사전 제작 모델
⑤ 협력적이고 지속적인 자금 지원 자원

06
정답 ②

여러분이 이 문장들을 읽는 데 의식적인 주의를 집중하면, 시각적 유입을 통제하는 무의식적 부분들은 여러분의 의식적인 의도가 자신들의 감각의 관문이 좁아지는 것을 무시할 수 있게 해 준다. 그것은 들어오는 정보를 평상시처럼 통제하려고 더는 활동하지 않는다. 그 결과 이 페이지의 단어들은 독자적인 개체로서 눈에 띄기 시작한다. 반면에 여러분이 우연히 지나가면서 무심코 탁자 위에 놓인 신문을 보게 된다면, 그 신문이 단어들로 가득한 것을 볼 수도 있겠지만, 단어들 자체를 반드시 알아차리지는 못할 것이다. 무의식의 수준에서 여러분은 그것들을 들어오지 못하게 통제해 왔다. 마찬가지로, 여러분이 무심코 책 한 권을 펴서 어떤 페이지를 대충 훑어본다면, 여러분은 단어들을 '볼' 수는 있겠지만, 반드시 개체로서의 단어들이나 그 속의 의미에 적극적으로 주의를 기울이지는 않을 것이다. 들어오는 시각적 메시지, 즉 이 경우에는 단어와 문장 속의 의미는 '통제되는데', 이것은 여러분의 무의식적인 부분이 시간상 그 순간에 주의를 기울일 만큼 그것들이 중요하지 않다고 결정했기 때문이다. 이것은 <u>여러분을 계속 눈에 보이는 세계의 표면에만 적응하게 한다.</u>

해설

무심코 탁자 위에 놓인 신문을 보게 된다면, 그 신문이 단어들로 가득한 것을 볼 수도 있겠지만 단어들 자체를 반드시 알아차리지는 못할 것이고, 무심코 책 한 권의 어떤 페이지를 훑어본다면, 단어들을 볼 수는 있겠지만 단어들의 의미에 적극적인 주의를 기울이지 않을 것인데, 이는 무의식이 시각 정보의 유입을 통제하기 때문이라는 내용이므로, 빈칸에 들어갈 말로 가장 적절한 것은 ② '여러분을 계속 눈에 보이는 세계의 표면에만 적응하게 한다'이다.
① 무의식적인 시각적 단서에 대한 여러분의 인식을 높인다
③ 여러분의 의식의 초점을 주변 세부 사항으로부터 분산한다
④ 시각적 자극에 대한 고조된 감정적 반응을 유발한다
⑤ 여러 단계에서 시각적 입력의 신경 처리를 촉진한다

07
정답 ③

18세기 부와 교육의 증가는 예술 시장의 성장과 공공 전시회 및 박물관의 출현에 반영된 것처럼 예술에 대한 대중 관심의 확장을 동반했다. 공개 판매와 경매는 예술품에 굶주린 대중을 위한 초창기 장이 되었고, 딜러들은 상점 창문, 신문 광고, 판매 카탈로그 등 새로운 마케팅 전략을 사용하여 새로운 부유층을 수집의 즐거움과 사회적 이점으로 유혹했다. 판화는 고급 예술의 범위를 크게 확장했고 그림 수집이 유행했지만 그림과 조각품을 소유하려면 큰돈이 필요했다. (하지만 서양에서 18세기 중반에 회화와 조각을 위한 예술원의 발달은 고도로 기능적인 작품이 '예술'이라는 인식을 확립했다.) 자신만의 수집품이 없는 사람들을 대변하여, 비평가들은 예술에 대한 대중의 더 큰 접근성을 요구했고, 세기 중반부터 그들의 요구가 받아들여졌다. 예술원은 회원들의 작품을 정기적으로 전시하는 전시회를 후원했는데, 가장 잘 알려진 전시회는 파리의 '살롱'(1737년부터)과 런던의 왕립 예술원 전시회(1768년부터)였다.

해설

18세기 부와 교육의 증가로 인해 예술에 대한 확장된 대중의 관심은 공개 판매 및 경매, 예술품 수집, 대중의 접근성을 높인 전시회 출현 등 일련의 과정을 통해 충족되었음을 설명하는 글이므로, 18세기 중반에 회화와 조각을 위한 예술원의 발달은 고도로 기능적인 작품이 '예술'이라는 인식을 확립했다는 내용의 ③은 글의 전체 흐름과 관계가 없다.

우리는 일을 하지 않으면 우리의 규율이 약화되고 우리의 마음이 방황하는 경우가 아주 많다. 우리는 월급을 쓰면서 재미있게 놀기 시작할 수 있도록 근무일이 끝나기를 갈망할 수도 있지만, 우리 대부분은 여가 시간을 조금씩 허비해 버린다. (C) 우리는 힘든 일을 피하며, 도전적인 취미에 참여하는 경우는 매우 드물다. 그 대신에 우리는 TV를 보거나 쇼핑몰에 가거나 페이스북에 접속한다. 우리는 게을러진다. 그리고 나서 우리는 지루해하고 초조해한다. 우리의 주의는 외부로의 집중에서 벗어나 내부로 향하고, 우리는 결국 Emerson이 자의식의 감옥이라고 말한 것에 감금된다. (B) Csikszentmihalyi는 심지어 형편없는 일자리조차도 '자신의 일에 몰두하고, 자신을 그 일에 집중하고 몰입하도록 부추기는' '내재된' 목표와 과제를 가지고 있기 때문에, '실제로 여가 시간보다 더 즐기기 쉽다'고 말한다. (A) 하지만 그것은 우리의 기만하는 마음이 우리가 믿기를 원하는 바가 아니다. 기회가 주어지면, 우리는 간절히 자신에게서 노동의 고됨을 덜어낼 것이다. 우리는 자신에게 나태를 선고할 것이다.

해설

우리는 일을 하지 않으면 우리의 규율이 약화되고, 여가 시간을 조금씩 허비해 버린다는 내용의 주어진 글 다음에는, 힘든 일을 피하고 도전적인 취미에 참여하는 대신에 게을러져서 자의식의 감옥에 감금된다는 내용의 (C)가 와야 한다. (C)의 내용의 결과로 일자리는 실제로 여가 시간보다 더 즐기기 쉽다는 Csikszentmihalyi의 말을 인용하는 (B)가 온 다음, But과 (B)의 내용을 가리키는 that으로 시작하여 우리는 간절히 자신에게서 노동의 고됨을 덜어낼 것이라며 (B)의 내용을 반박하는 내용의 (A)가 마지막에 오는 것이 글의 순서로 가장 자연스럽다.

사회생활은 인간의 본능에서 비롯된다. 인간의 본능은 인간화된 본능과 비인간화된 본능을 포함한다. 인간화된 본능은 원래 인간적인 것과 관련되어 이용된다. 비인간화된 본능은 원래 비인간적인 것과 관련되어 이용된다. (C) 사회적 동물 사이에서는 같은 종의 동물에게 다른 종의 동물에게와 다르게 행동하는 것이 꽤 흔한 일이다. 예를 들어, 식인 풍습과 같은 종의 동물들 사이의 살상은 심지어 같은 종들 간에 싸우는 중에도 사회적 동물에는 드문 일이다. (A) 지배의 목적으로 같은 종의 동물들 간에 싸우는 것은 의례적인 경우가 흔하고 심각한 부상을 입히지 않는다. 같은 종의 동물들로 인한 동물들의 새끼에 대한 해악은 잦은 일이 아니다. (B) 반면에, 포식자로서 동물은 주저 없이 다른 종의 먹잇감을 죽인다. 먹잇감으로서 동물은 다른 종의 포식자로부터 탈출하기 위해 교묘하게 다루는 전략을 세운다. 동물은 다른 종의 동물과 같은 종의 동물 사이를 분명하게 구별한다.

해설

인간화된 본능은 원래 인간적인 것과 관련되어 이용되고, 비인간화된 본능은 원래 비인간적인 것과 관련되어 이용된다는 내용의 주어진 글 다음에는, 인간화된 본능과 관련된 내용인 사회적 동물 사이에서의 같은 종의 싸움에 관한 내용인 (C)가 와야 한다. 이어서 같은 종의 싸움에 대해 추가로 제시하는 내용의 (A)가 온 다음, On the other hand로 시작해 (C), (A)와 상반되는 내용인 다른 종의 싸움에 관한 내용을 언급하며, 동물은 다른 종의 동물과 같은 종의 동물 사이를 분명하게 구별한다는 내용의 (B)가 오는 것이 글의 순서로 가장 적절하다.

나는 전에 여전히 살아 있는 아주 오래된 나무 그루터기 잔해를 우연히 발견했다. 그런데 어떻게 그 잔해는 그렇게 오랜 시간 삶을 붙잡고 있을 수 있었을까? 나무에 살아 있는 세포는 당분의 형태로 식량을 가지고 있어야 하고, 숨을 쉬어야 하며, 적어도 조금은 자라야 한다. 하지만 잎이 없이는, 그래서 광합성이 없이는 그것은 불가능하다. 지구상에 존재하는 어떤 생명체도 수세기 동안 단식을 유지할 수 없으며, 심지어 나무의 잔해조차도 그렇지 못하며, 스스로 살아남아야 했던 그루터기도 분명 그렇지 못하다. 이 그루터기에 뭔가 다른 일이 일어나고 있는 것이 분명했다. 그것은 이웃 나무들, 특히 그들의 뿌리에서 도움을 받고 있는 것이 틀림없다. 유사한 상황을 조사 중인 과학자들은 나무 사이의 영양소 교환을 용이하게 하는 뿌리 끝 주변의 균 네트워크에 의해 원격으로 지원이 전달될 수 있거나 뿌리 자체가 상호 연결될 수도 있다는 것을 발견했다. 내가 우연히 발견한 그루터기의 경우, 오래된 그루터기 둘레를 파서 그것을 다치게 하고 싶지 않았기 때문에, 나는 무슨 일이 일어나고 있는지 알 수 없었지만, 한 가지는 분명했으니, 그것은 주변의 나무들이 그루터기가 살아남게 하려고 그 그루터기에게 당분을 퍼붓고 있었다는 것이다.

해설

나무 세포는 당분 식량을 가지고 있어야 하고, 숨을 쉬고, 자라야 해서 잎이 없이는 불가능한데, 주어진 문장의 this stump는 여전히 살아 있는 아주 오래된 나무 그루터기이므로, 이 그루터기를 살아 있게 하는 다른 어떤 일이 주어진 문장 다음에 이어져야 한다. 따라서 주어진 문장이 들어가기에 가장 적절한 곳은 그것(this stump)은 뿌리에서 도움을 받고 있는 것이 틀림없다는 내용 앞인 ③이다.

구조적 지도자들은 자신들의 조직을 위해 구조, 전략 및 환경의 관계에 대한 새로운 모델을 개발한다. 그들은 이행에 초점을 맞춘다. 정답은 그것이 이행될 수 있을 경우에만 도움이 될 뿐이다. 이러한 지도자들은 합리성, 분석, 논리, 사실, 자료를 강조한다. 그들은 분명한 구조와 잘 개발된 관리 시스템의 중요성을 강하게 믿을 가능성이 높다. 훌륭한 지도자는 명료하게 생각하고, 현명한 결정을 내리며, 좋은 분석 기술을 가지고, 일을 완수할 수 있는 구조와 시스템을 만들 수 있는 사람이다. 구조적 지도자들은 자신들의 설계를 제자리에 놓는 것의 어려움을 오판하기 때문에 때때로 실패한다. 그들은 그것이 만들어 낼 저항을 흔히 과소평가하고 자신들의 혁신에 대한 지지 기반을 구축하기 위한 조치를 취하지 않는다. 요약하면, 그들은 인적 자원, 정치적, 상징적 고려 사항 때문에 흔히 실패하게 된다. 구조적 지도자들은 지속적으로 실험하고 평가하며 적응하지만, 자신들이 위치한 전체 환경을 고려하지 못하기 때문에 때때로 그들은 비효율적이다.

해설

주어진 문장의 They는 structural leaders(구조적 지도자들)를 가리키고, the resistance that it will generate의 it은 ④ 앞의 putting their designs in place를 가리킨다. 또한 자신들의 혁신에 대한 지지 기반을 구축하기 위한 조치를 취하지 않는다는 내용은 구조적 지도자들이 실패하는 원인이 되므로, 주어진 문장이 들어가기에 가장 적절한 곳은 ④이다.

호주 원주민 수렵 채집인들은 가내 생산 방식의 표본인데, 이 방식에서는 최소의 외부 압력으로 가구 수준에서 생산 결정이 내려진다. 호주 원주민들은 노동, 기술, 자원을 그것들의 생산 가능한 최대한도까지 사용하지 않고, 그 대신 순전히 물질적인 관심사보다 자신들의 여가, 공유, 의례 활동을 극대화하기로 선택했다. 그들의 수렵 채집 체계의 상대적 일관성과 영속성은 호주 원주민들이 의도적이든 아니든 지속 가능한 성장 없는 문화를 고안해 냈다는 것을 말한다. 호주 원주민들은 잉여 생산물을 더 많은 인구를 부양하거나 경제적 생산을 증대하는 데 '투자'하지 않고, 그 대신 그것을 또한 사회 전체의 이익이 되고 문화의 재생산에 기여하는 방식으로 사람들이 자신들의 사회 문화 자본을 구축하게 돕는 활동으로 돌렸다. 식량 공유, 의례상의 축제, 그리고 여가는 성장을 줄이는 효과를 제공했고, 호주 원주민들이 인구 증가와 부양 증대의 끝없는 순환의 딜레마를 피하는 데 도움이 되었다. 사람들이 식량을 공유했을 때는, 자신들의 당면한 필요를 제외하고는 생산하게 하는 유인이 거의 없었다.

➡ 호주 원주민 수렵 채집인들은 성장을 강조하지 않는 문화를 실천하면서 잉여 생산물을 사회적, 문화적 자본을 구축하는 데 사용했고, 필요 이상을 생산하는 생산 방식을 피했다.

해설
호주 원주민 수렵 채집인들은 여가, 공유, 의례 활동을 극대화하고 의도적이든 아니든 지속 가능한 성장 없는 문화를 고안하여 실행했으며, 자신들의 당면한 필요를 초과해서 생산하게 하는 유인을 갖지 않았다는 내용의 글이므로, 요약문의 빈칸 (A), (B)에 들어갈 말로는 ③ 'practicing(실천하다) – avoiding(피하다)'이 가장 적절하다.
① 상상하다 – 피하다
② 실행하다 – 발전시키다
④ 거부하다 – 발전시키다
⑤ 거부하다 – 의문을 제기하다

REVIEW 모의고사　02회

01　　　　　　　　　　　　　　　　　　　　　정답 ④

자신의 직속 선임자들과 매우 비슷하게, Carl von Clausewitz는 자신이 전투에 이기는 기술이라 부른 전술과 전쟁의 목적을 달성하기 위해 전투를 활용하는 기술이라고 정의한 전략을 구별했다. 그러나 더욱 근본적으로, 전쟁이란 두 명의 독립된 인간 사이의 결투였다. 그것의 상호 작용적인 본성은 그것을 다른 활동들과 뚜렷이 구분 지었다. 다른 말로 나타내면, (생명이 없는 물질에 행동을 가하는 것만이 수반되는) 검을 만드는 것과 누군가의 찌르기를 받아넘기고 자신의 찌르기로 응수할 수 있는 다른 검투사에게 대항해 그것을 사용하는 것은 전혀 별개의 일이었다. 전쟁의 이론에 관한 간결하지만 명석한 논의에서, Clausewitz는 자신의 선임자 각각에 의해 제안된 체제는 사실의 일부 요소를 포함하고 있었다는 점을 인정한다. 그러나 어떠한 체제도 전쟁은 싸움으로 구성되며, 그 싸움, 다시 말해 전투가 전쟁의 결과를 결정한다는 근본적인 사실을 가리도록 허용되어서는 안 된다. 크고도 날카로운 검으로 뒷받침되지 않는다면 환상적인 조종이 아무리 많아도 전혀 효력을 발휘할 수 없을 것이다.

해설
전투에 이기는 기술이라 부른 전술과 전쟁의 목적을 달성하기 위해 전투를 활용하는 기술이라고 정의한 전략에 관한 내용으로, 밑줄 친 부분이 있는 문장의 fancy maneuvering(환상적인 조종)은 전투에서 다른 검투사에게 대항해 검을 사용하는 것을 뜻하고, a big, sharp sword(크고도 날카로운 검)는 전투하기 위해 만들어진 검을 의미한다고 볼 수 있다. 따라서 밑줄 친 부분이 의미하는 바로는 ④ '강하고 효과적인 군사력 또는 능력'이 가장 적절하다.
① 지역에 대한 방대하고 광대한 통제력
② 정교하고 발전된 저장 시설
③ 교활하고 전략적인 전장 지휘관
⑤ 공격할 수 있는 높고 유리한 지대

02　　　　　　　　　　　　　　　　　　　　　정답 ④

채집자의 사회적인 조직에 대한 이견에도 불구하고, 핵심적인 인구 통계적 사실은 논란의 여지가 없다. 야생 식량 자원의 낮은 밀도는 대부분의 현대 채집자들이 대개 가까운 친척인 2명에서 8명으로 이루어진 매우 작은 집단 안에서 자신들의 시간의 대부분을 보낸다는 것을 의미한다. 그러나 모든 사람들은 최소한 500명으로 이루어진 훨씬 더 큰 집단에 속해야 하는데, 이러한 집단만이 독자적으로 생존 가능한 번식 집단을 제공하기 때문이다. 그렇게 많은 채집자들이 물리적으로 모이는 것은 드문 일이지만, 아무리 가장 작은 집단이라도 아마도 50명이 넘는 사람들로 이루어진 더 큰 모임이나 캠프에서 주기적으로 모이며 이러한 모임/캠프 네트워크는 요구되는 크기의 유전자 풀을 만든다. 풍요로운 환경에서는 사람들은 이러한 더 큰 집단 안에서 연중 더 많은 시간을 보내고, 가혹한 환경에서는 연중 더 적은 시간을 보낸다. 그러나 정말 풍요로운 환경, 특히 해양 자원이 풍부한 환경에서만, 채집자들은 수십 명, 간혹 수백 명에 달하는 집단으로 영구적으로 살아갈 수 있다. 남 캘리포니아의 Chumash로부터 알래스카의 좁고 길게 다른 주로 뻗어 있는 지역의 Tlingit에 이르기까지, 북아메리카 태평양 연안의 오래된 채집자 마을이 가장 잘 알려진 사례이다.

해설
야생 식량 자원의 낮은 밀도는 채집자들이 작은 집단에서 자신들의 시간을 대부분 보내고, 더 큰 집단만이 독자적으로 생존 가능한 번식 집단을 제공하며, 풍요로운 환경에서 사람들이 더 큰 집단 안에서 더 많은 시간을 보내고, 가혹한 환경에서는 더 적은 시간을 보낸다는 내용이므로, 글의 주제로 가장 적절한 것은 ④ '채집자 사회의 사회적 구성과 인구 통계적 특징'이다.
① 현대의 채집인이 직면한 경제적, 사회적 도전 과제
② 채집 기술의 변화를 설명하는 환경적 요인
③ 환경 및 인구 통계학적 요인이 채집 사회에 미치는 영향
⑤ 고대 채집 사회와 현대 채집 사회의 구조의 차이

03 정답 ④

풍력 발전기를 생각해 보자. 미국에서 그것들은 매년 최소한 4만 5천 마리의 새와 박쥐를 죽이는 것으로 추산되어 왔다. 그것은 많은 새와 박쥐인 것처럼 들린다. 그 숫자를 전체적인 시야로 보려면, 주인의 집을 들락날락하도록 허용된 반려 고양이가 고양이 한 마리당 1년에 평균 300마리가 넘는 새를 죽이는 것으로 측정되어 왔다는 점을 생각해 보라. 만일 밖에서 사는 고양이의 미국 개체수가 약 1억 마리라고 추산된다면, 고양이는 풍력 발전기에 의해 매년 죽임을 당하는 고작 4만 5천 마리에 비해 미국에서 최소한 매년 3백억 마리의 새를 죽인다는 계산이 나올 수 있다. 그러한 풍력 발전기의 대가는 불과 150마리의 고양이가 하는 일과 동일하다. 따라서 우리가 미국의 새와 박쥐에 대해 진심으로 우려한다면 풍력 발전기보다 오히려 고양이에 주안점을 두어야 한다고 주장할 수도 있을 것이다. 고양이보다 풍력 발전기를 더욱 변호하자면, 고양이들은 에너지, 오염되지 않은 공기, 그리고 지구 온난화의 완화를 제공하여 우리의 새들에게 가하는 해를 보상하지 않지만 풍력 발전기들은 그러한 모든 것들을 정말 제공한다는 점을 숙고해 보라.

해설
풍력 발전기가 많은 새를 죽이는 것 같지만 반려 고양이가 죽이는 새의 수와 비교해 보면 사실상 그리 많은 수가 아니며, 풍력 발전기는 고양이보다 에너지, 오염되지 않은 공기, 지구 온난화의 완화를 제공하여 새와 박쥐에게 가하는 영향보다 더 가치가 있다는 내용의 글이므로, 글의 제목으로 가장 적절한 것은 ④ '풍력 발전기: 새와 박쥐에게 미치는 영향 이상의 가치'이다.
① 반려 고양이와 새를 기르는 것: 위험한 상황
② 고양이와 풍력 터빈: 새의 두 가지 가장 큰 두려움
③ 새와 박쥐: 강력한 풍력 발전기의 최근 희생자
⑤ 보존: 자연과 기술 사이의 균형 있는 활동

04 정답 ⑤

인간의 가장 기본적인 본능은 자기 보존을 위한 본능이다. 형법은 이러한 충동을 인정하고 정당방위의 원칙을 통해 사법 제도에서 그것의 사용을 허용한다. 정당방위를 주장하는 개인이 합리적으로 행동할 때, 그는 다수의 범죄에 대해 완전하게 방어하게 되는 이점을 얻을 것이다. 대부분의 경우, 피고가 무력 사용이 필요하다는 합리적인 믿음을 가질 경우에만 정당방위가 성공할 것이다. 그러므로 문화적 방어 사건에서 중요한 문제는 누군가가 그러한 '합리적' 믿음을 가지고 있는지를 어떻게 판단하는지가 될 것이다. 정당방위의 또 다른 특징은 피고인이 필요하고 비례적인 대응을 행사했다는 것을 입증할 수 있어야만 그 전략이 이긴다는 것이다. 비례의 원칙 요건이 문화적 방어 사건

의 피고에 대한 그것의 효용을 제한할 가능성이 있다. 이에 대한 이유는 무엇이 비례적 대응에 해당하는지에 대한 판단은 평가를 하는 사람의 문화적 배경에 따라 다를 것이기 때문이다. 짐작건대, 피고의 문화계 구성원들이 그것이 그렇다고 동의할지라도, 지배 문화권 출신의 판사는 그 행위를 비례적 대응으로 보지 않을 수 있을 것이다.

해설
⑤ it은 the act를 가리키고, 앞에 나오는 was a proportionate response를 대신하므로, 대동사 did를 was로 고쳐야 한다.
① 앞의 the instinct for self-preservation을 대신하고 뒤의 명사를 수식하므로, it의 소유격 its는 어법상 적절하다.
② 앞의 동사 acts를 수식하므로 부사 reasonably는 어법상 적절하다.
③ 뒤에 완전한 절 the strategy only wins가 이어지므로 명사절을 이끄는 접속사 that은 어법상 적절하다. 뒤의 provided ~ proportional response는 부사절이다.
④ 앞의 the person을 수식하는 분사구를 이끌고 있으므로, 현재분사 making은 어법상 적절하다.

05 정답 ⑤

스포츠 텍스트에는 많은 형태, 기능, 독자층이 있다. 전통적인 스포츠 보도는 현장에 참석하지 않은 사람들을 위해 일어난 일을 증언하기 위한 것이다. 가장 기본적이고 외연적인 수준에서, 예를 들어 Gresty Road Ground에서 2,816명의 춥고 비에 젖은 관중이 지켜보는 가운데, 영국 축구 3부 리그에서 Crewe Alexandra가 Burnley와 0대 0으로 비겼다는 것은 논란의 여지가 없는 진술이다. 여기에는 사람의 개입이 많이 필요하지 않다. 즉, 몇 단위의 데이터가 '유선으로 전송'되거나 컴퓨터 데이터베이스에 입력되어, 해운이나 주식 시장 보고서보다 더 문화적 반향(反響)이 거의 없는 텍스트를 생성한다. 다만, 그러한 익명의 정보 단위가 그것에 생계를 의존하는 선원이나 '사무직원'에게는 훨씬 더 중요하고 깊은 의미를 갖는 것처럼, 관련 스포츠 팬은 이러한 사실에 의미를 부여할 뿐만 아니라 더 많은 정보를 기대할 것이다. 따라서 많은 스포츠 추종자들이 단순한 뉴스 요약 형식에 오랫동안 만족할 것 같을(→ 할 것 같지 않을) 것이다.

해설
익명의 정보 단위가 그것에 생계를 의존하는 선원이나 '사무직원'에게는 훨씬 더 중요하고 깊은 의미를 갖는 것처럼, 스포츠 텍스트에 관련된 스포츠 팬은 정보 단위에 의미를 부여할 뿐만 아니라 더 많은 정보를 기대할 것이라는 앞의 내용으로 미루어, 많은 스포츠 추종자들이 단순한 뉴스 요약 형식에 오랫동안 만족할 것 같지는 않을 것이라고 해야 내용이 자연스럽다. 따라서 ⑤ 'likely(할 것 같은)'를 'unlikely(할 것 같지 않은)'와 같은 낱말로 바꾸어야 한다.

06 정답 ⑤

1968년, Vermont 주의 관련 공무원들은 고속도로를 따라 펼쳐진 삼림과 목초지의 아름다운 경관을 보호하려는 시도를 했는데, 당시 고속도로는 식당과 기타 업체들의 간판과 보기 흉한 광고판에 의해 훼손되고 있었다. 주 의회 의원들은 간단한 해결책을 가지고 있었는데 그것은 일정한 크기 이상의 모든 광고판과 간판을 금지하는 법이었다. 길에는 곧 간판의 수가 더 적어지고 크기도 더 작아졌기 때문에 어떤 의미에서 그것은 효과가 있었지만, 또한 다른 무엇인가가, 즉 이상하고 거대한 조각품이 많아지는 일이 자연스럽게 발생했다. 자신의 사업에 대한 관심을 끌기 위해, 한 자동차 판매상은 진

짜 Volkswagen Beetle을 움켜쥔 12피트 16톤의 고릴라를 세웠다. 이에 뒤질세라, 양탄자 가게 주인은 김이 나오는 거대한 도자기 찻주전자와 그 찻주전자에서 나와 겨드랑이에 양탄자 한 롤을 끼고 있는 거대한 지니를 세웠다. 이런 구조물들은 어떤 종류의 메시지도 표시하지 않고 있었기 때문에, 법이 적용되지 않았다. 입법 기관은 사회적 세계의 악명 높은 원칙, 즉 <u>의도하지 않은 결과</u>의 법칙을 완전히 이해하지 못했던 것이다.

해설

Vermont 주에서 경관 보호 차원으로 일정한 크기 이상의 광고판과 간판을 금지하자, 간판의 수는 더 적어지고 크기는 더 작아졌지만, 자동차 판매상은 차를 움켜쥔 고릴라를 세우고 양탄자 가게 주인은 거대한 지니를 세우는 등의 이상하고 거대한 조각품이 많아지는 일이 발생하였으므로, 이러한 결과는 입법 기관이 의도하지 않은 결과일 것이다. 따라서 빈칸에 들어갈 말로 가장 적절한 것은 ⑤ '의도하지 않은 결과'이다.
① 고의적 행위
② 입법적 감독
③ 비례적 대응
④ 규제의 준수

07
정답 ②

재촬영은 시간이 어떻게 원래 장면을 변화시켰는지 보여 주기 위해 사진작가가 이전에 찍었던 피사체로 돌아가 똑같은 사진을 다시 만들려고 시도하는 때이다. 돌아가는 사진작가가 원래 장면을 더 쉽게 복제할 수 있도록 정확한 기록이 유지된다. 원본 사진과 새로운 사진은 비교하기 쉽도록 보통 서로 나란히 전시된다. 또 다른 형태의 재촬영에서 사진작가는 일정 기간 동안 똑같은 피사체로 돌아온다. 이것의 예는 일주일 동안 매일 여러분 자신의 사진을 찍는 것에서부터 수십 년에 걸쳐 Georgia O'Keeffe를 찍은 Alfred Stieglitz의 사진에 이르기까지 다양할 것이다. 사진작가와 피사체의 관계는 일정 기간 동안 추구된다. 그 결과는 느낌, 빛, 분위기의 변화로 인해 이 조합에서 생길 수 있는 <u>광범위한 시각적 가능성을 나타낼</u> 것이다.

해설

재촬영은 원본 사진과 새로운 사진이 비교하기 쉽게 나란히 전시되고 사진작가는 일정 기간 동안 똑같은 피사체로 돌아오는데, 일주일 동안 매일 여러분 자신의 사진을 찍는 것에서부터 수십 년에 걸쳐 Georgia O'Keeffe를 찍은 Alfred Stieglitz의 사진에 이르기까지 다양할 것이라는 내용의 글이므로, 빈칸에 들어갈 말로 가장 적절한 것은 ② '광범위한 시각적 가능성을 나타낼'이다.
① 일관된 시각적 정체를 드러낼
③ 피사체의 미래 자질과 관점을 강조할
④ 기술 정보의 정적 변화를 전달할
⑤ 관련 없는 환경에 대한 다양한 의문을 제기할

08
정답 ③

의사 결정의 한 가지 특징은 뇌의 구조와 관련이 있다. '뇌는 선입관 없이는 문제를 분석할 수 없다.' 누군가 한 가지 문제나 질문에 직면했을 때, 선입관은 때로는 질문이 표현되거나 정보가 제시되는 방식에 기초하고 의존하여 즉시 사용된다. 따라서 회복 가능성이 80%라는 의사의 예후에 대한 환자의 반응은 평생 아픈 채로 있을 확률이 20%라는 소식에 대한 그의 반응과 다르다. 이성적인 사고는 80%의 성공 확률과 20%의 실패 확률을 동일하게 인식할 것이다. 진화적으로 이성적인 방식으로만 행동하는 정신은 동등함을 인

식하지 못할 것이다. 그러한 인식은 모든 경우에 사실을 비교하고 분석하는 데 필요한 노력의 가치가 없으므로 우리는 <u>이미 뇌에 존재하는 개념과 태도를 고수한다</u>. 선입관 없이 우리가 질문을 검토할 수 있다는 일반적인 믿음은 잘못된 것이다.

해설

뇌는 선입관 없이는 문제를 분석할 수 없고, 진화적으로 이성적인 방식으로만 행동하는 정신은 동등함을 인식하지 못할 것이어서, 이런 인식은 모든 경우에 사실을 비교하고 분석하는 데 노력을 할 필요가 없으며, 선입관 없이 우리가 질문을 검토할 수 있다는 믿음은 잘못된 것이라는 내용의 글이므로, 빈칸에 들어갈 말로 가장 적절한 것은 ③ '이미 뇌에 존재하는 개념과 태도를 고수한다'이다.
① 주관적인 선입관보다 객관적인 분석에 우선순위를 둔다
② 외부 요소가 의사 결정에 미치는 영향을 간과한다
④ 의사 결정 과정에서 직관의 역할을 최소화한다
⑤ 순전히 이성적인 의사 결정의 한계를 인정한다

09
정답 ③

정치인, 특히 전국적인 주목을 받는 정치인은 흔히 농담 삼아 나르시시스트라는 이유로 비난을 받지만, 진정으로, 그들의 직업이 특히 이 파괴적인 성격 특성에 기여한다. (B) 예를 들면, 성공적인 후보가 되기 위해, 여러분은 심지어 패배가 있을 것 같음에도 불구하고 이상할 정도로 낙관적이어야 하며 (정치인에게는) 일상이 된 지속적인 비난에도 불구하고 높은 수준의 자존감을 지니고 있어야 한다. (C) 게다가, 여러분은 비록 성공이 부분적으로 많은 보좌관과 조력자의 노력에 의해 성취된 것임에도 불구하고 성공에 대한 인정을 계속 혼자 받는다. 마지막으로, 여러분은 끊임없이 사람들이 여러분에게 의지하고, 여러분을 믿으며, 어떤 대의명분의 유일한 대표로서 여러분에게 책임을 묻게 한다. (A) 이 모든 힘은 어떤 사람들이 세상이 자신을 중심으로 돌아간다고 믿게 하는, 과장된 자만심으로 이어질 수 있다. 바로 그때 자신들의 통제 불능의 행동은 합리화하기가 더 쉬워진다.

해설

정치인은 나르시시스트라는 이유로 비난을 받지만, 직업이 이 성격 특성에 기여한다는 주어진 글 다음에, 이 특성의 예시로 성공적인 후보자는 항상 낙관적이어야 하고, 지속적인 비난에도 높은 수준의 자존감을 지녀야 한다는 내용의 (B)가 와야 한다. 성공이 보좌관과 조력자의 노력에 의한 것임에도 인정은 혼자 받고, 대의명분의 유일한 대표로서 여러분에게 책임을 묻게 한다는 특성을 추가 예로 제시하는 내용의 (C)가 온 다음, 앞의 내용을 All of this power로 받아서, 모든 것이 자신을 중심으로 돌아간다고 믿게 하는 과장된 자만심을 가질 수 있다는 단점을 언급하는 내용의 (A)가 오는 것이 글의 순서로 가장 적절하다.

10
정답 ②

동부 아프리카의 일부 개체군의 침팬지는 작고 가는 막대기로 흰개미 둔덕을 탐지하여 흰개미를 낚는다. 그러나 서부 아프리카의 일부 다른 침팬지 개체군은 큰 막대기로 흰개미 둔덕을 파괴하여 그 곤충을 한 움큼 퍼내려고 시도한다. (B) Boesch와 McGrew 같은 현장 연구자들은 이와 같은 특정한 도구 사용 관행이 다양한 군집의 개체 사이에서 '문화적으로 전수된'다고 주장했다. 하지만 또한 꽤 그럴듯한 상충하는 설명이 있다. (A) 사실은 서부 아프리카의 흰개미 둔덕이 더 많은 양의 비로 인해 동부 아프리카의 흰개미 둔덕보다 훨씬 더 부드럽다는 것이다. 따라서 큰 막대기로 둔덕을 파괴하는 전략

은 서부 개체군에서만 이용 가능하다. (C) 그러므로 이 가설에 따르면, 표면적으로는 인간의 문화적 차이와 비슷하지만, 어떤 유형의 사회적 학습도 전혀 개입되지 않은, 행동의 집단적 차이가 존재할 것이다. 그러한 경우에 '문화'는 단순히 서로 다른 개체군의 서로 다른 지역 생태에 의해 주도되는 개별 학습의 결과일 뿐이다.

해설
동부 아프리카 침팬지는 작고 가는 막대기로 흰개미를 잡고, 서부 침팬지는 큰 막대기로 흰개미를 잡는다는 주어진 글 다음에, 이와 같은 특정한 도구 사용 관행은 문화적으로 전수된다고 주장하지만 상충하는 설명이 있다는 내용의 (B)가 와야 한다. 즉 서부 아프리카의 흰개미 둔덕이 동부 아프리카의 둔덕보다 많은 양의 비로 더 부드러운데, 큰 막대기로 둔덕을 파괴하는 전략은 서부 개체군에서만 이용 가능하다는 내용의 (A)가 온 다음, 행동의 집단적 차이는 서부 다른 개체군의 다른 지역 생태에 의해 주도되는 개별 학습의 결과라는 내용의 (C)가 오는 것이 글의 순서로 가장 적절하다.

11 정답 ③

17세기와 18세기에 아일랜드는 잉글랜드의 식민지였다. 이것은 잉글랜드가 모든 아일랜드의 자원을 통제했다는 것을 의미했다. 그중 많은 수가 영국령이었던 많은 다른 식민지의 상황에서처럼, 잉글랜드는 잉글랜드 자체가 식민지 권력이 되는 일을 하지 않았다. 중개인은 식민화의 효과적인 도구였다. '비국교도들'은 영국인 아래에 있었지만 아일랜드 가톨릭교도 위에 있었다. '대개 장로교 농부, 기술자, 그리고 소규모 소매상인'이던 이 비가톨릭교도인 아일랜드 비국교도들은 영국에 의해 강요된 억압적인 위계질서를 유지하는 것을 도왔다. 그들은 종종 비교적 거의 아무것도 대가로 받지 않고 잉글랜드인들이 노동과 골칫거리를 면하게 해 주었다. 그들은 자신들의 사회적 지위로부터 아주 중요한 한 가지 혜택을 받았다. 아일랜드 가톨릭교도처럼, 그들 자신도 가혹한 환경에서 살아갈 수도 있었지만, 개신교도로서, 그들은 최소한 자신이 지배적인, 즉 더 나은 민족이라고 여길 수 있었다. 다시 말해, 그들이 생각하는 '민족'이라는 관점에서 모든 개신교도는 영국인이 강요한 위계질서로부터 혜택을 받았다. 아무리 가난할지라도, 개신교도는 가톨릭교도가 아니라 아일랜드 개신교도가 되는 것으로부터 정신적인 힘을 얻었다.

해설
주어진 문장은 아일랜드 비국교도들이 사회적 지위를 얻었고 이것으로부터 중요한 한 가지 혜택을 받았다는 내용이므로, 앞에는 아일랜드 비국교도들은 잉글랜드 지배의 중개인 역할을 했다는 내용이 제시되고, 뒤에는 개신교도로서 아일랜드 가톨릭교도보다 자신들을 더 나은 민족이라고 여길 수 있는 정신적인 힘을 얻었다는 내용이 언급되는 ③에 들어가는 것이 가장 적절하다.

12 정답 ④

우리는 흔히 너무 빨리 선택해서 그 행동에 관련된 모든 요소들을 거의 구별할 수 없다. 우리가 시간이나 공간, 또는 그 둘 모두에서 우리와 멀리 떨어져 있는 대체물이나 행동 방침 각각의 장점을 평가할 때, 우리는 선택에 관여하는 모든 요소들을 알게 될 가능성이 더 많다. 우선, 우리는 미래를, 그리고 특히 각각의 대체 행동이 우리에게 어떻게 영향을 미칠지 예측하려고 한다. 이러한 노력에서 우리는 비슷한 상황의 과거 경험에 대한 기억에 크게 의존하는데, 왜냐하면 과거에 대한 지식과 본성의 한결같음에 대한 신뢰가 없다면 우리는 미래를 예측하기가 막막할 것이기 때문이다. 심사숙고된 상황에 우리 자신을 투영할 때, 우리는 무엇보다도 그것이 우리에게 즐거움이나 고통, 기쁨이나 슬픔, 만족이나 혐오감 어느 것을 가져다주든, 그것이 우리의 감정에 어떻게 영향을 미칠지에 관심이 있다. 그리고 물론, 우리가 숙고하는 이런 단계에서도, 우리는 비슷한 정서의 회상에 의해 인도된다. 따라서 정신의 합리적 기능 못지않은 정서적 기능이 우리가 하는 각각의 중요한 선택에서 중요한 역할을 한다.

해설
주어진 문장은 우리는 심사숙고된 상황이 감정에 어떻게 영향을 미칠지 관심이 있다는 내용이므로, 주어진 문장 앞에 심사숙고하는 내용이 있어야 하는데, 그것은 우리는 비슷한 상황의 과거 경험에 대한 기억에 의존하여 미래를 예측하고자 한다는 내용이므로, 주어진 문장이 들어가기에 가장 적절한 곳은 ④이다. 또한 ④ 다음의 '비슷한 정서'는 주어진 문장의 '즐거움이나 고통, 기쁨이나 슬픔, 만족이나 혐오감'을 나타낸다.

REVIEW 모의고사　03회

| 01 ② | 02 ② | 03 ④ | 04 ② | 05 ① | 06 ① |
| 07 ④ | 08 ② | 09 ② | 10 ④ | 11 ⑤ | 12 ② |

01　정답 ②

더 많은 혁신이 반드시 더 좋은 것은 아니라는 것을 명심하라. 일부 혁신 지지자들은 혁신에 대한 자신들의 분명한 열의에 도취되었는데, 그들은 모든 기업이 상당하고 지속적인 양의 혁신, 특히 급진적이며 판도를 바꾸는 혁신을 얻으려고 노력해야 한다고 권고해 왔다. 이것은 전혀 사실이 아니다. 제품 수명 주기가 두 번 지난 이후에도 생존하고자 하는 모든 조직은 건전한 혁신의 주입이 필요하고, 그것을 얻기 위해 투자해야 한다. 하지만 이것은 조직이 끊임없는 블록버스터급이거나 획기적인 혁신을 필요로 한다는 것을 의미하는 것은 아니다. 획기적이고 급진적인 혁신의 지속적인 공급을 효과적으로 활용할 수 있는 조직을 상상하기는 어려운데, 그런 혁신은 각각 그 조직의 사업과 기술 기반에 상당한 변화를 초래할 것이다. 그런 수준의 변화는 경쟁사를 괴롭힐 수도 있지만, 그것은 또한 지속적이고 급진적인 변화로 인해 조직에서 발생하는 엄청난 긴장 및 불안정과 더불어, 그런 혁신의 흐름을 개발하는 데 드는 막대한 비용을 고려할 때, 혁신하는 조직의 근간을 무너뜨릴 것이다.

해설
모든 기업이 상당하고 지속적인 양의 혁신, 특히 급진적이며 판도를 바꾸는 혁신을 얻으려고 노력해야 한다는 것은 사실이 아니며, 지속적이고 급진적인 변화로 인해 발생하는 엄청난 긴장, 불안정, 막대한 비용으로 조직의 근간이 무너질 수 있다는 내용의 글이므로, 글의 주제로 가장 적절한 것은 ② '성공을 위한 지속적인 급진적 혁신에 대한 오해'이다.
① 점진적 혁신과 급진적 혁신의 차이점
③ 조직에서 지속적인 혁신을 관리하기 위한 전략
④ 지속적인 급진적 혁신의 재정적 및 관리상의 이점
⑤ 급진적 혁신을 지속해서 구현하는 데 필요한 자원

02　정답 ②

겉보기에는 자동인 것 같은 인간의 사회적인 본성에 대한 가장 흥미로운 증거 가운데 하나는 한 직사각형의 주위를 도는 두 개의 삼각형과 한 개의 원을 다룬 Fritz Heider와 Marianne Simmel의 1944년의 유명한 만화 영화에서 나온다. 그 만화 영화는 그저 모양들만을 묘사하지만, 사람들은 이러한 물체들을 인간 배우로 이해하고 그것들의 움직임을 중심으로 하여 사회적인 드라마를 구성하지 않는 것이 거의 불가능하다고 느낀다. 그 비디오를 더 면밀히 보고, 그 현상을 묘사하는 Heider와 Simmel의 소논문을 더 면밀히 읽으면, 이 모양들을 사회적인 방식으로 지각하는 것은 자동적인 것이 아니고 자극과 상황의 특징에 의해 환기된 것임에 틀림없다는 것을 시사한다. 이러한 모양들은 사회적인 행동을 구체적으로 모방하는 궤적으로 움직이도록 고안되었다. 만일 그 모양들의 움직임이 변화되거나 뒤바뀌면, 그것들은 같은 수준의 사회적인 반응을 이끌어내지 못한다. 게다가 이 만화 영화의 원래 연구의 참가자들은 그 모양을 실험자들이 사용하는 언어와 지시에 의해 사회적인 방식으로 묘사하도록 유도되었다. 인간은 사회적인 렌즈를 통해 세상을 볼 준비가 되어 있고 기꺼이 그렇게 할 수도 있지만, 그들은 자동으로 그렇게 하지는 않는다.

해설
② 문장의 주어는 A closer look ~ article describing the phenomenon이고 목적어는 명사절 that the perception of these shapes ~ and situation이므로 문장의 동사가 필요하다. 따라서 분사 suggesting을 동사 suggests로 고쳐야 한다.
① 「find + 가목적어(it) + 목적격 보어(nearly impossible) + 진목적어(not to interpret ~ their movements)」 구문이므로, it은 어법상 적절하다.
③ 관계대명사의 선행사가 복수 명사 trajectories이므로 복수 동사 mimic은 어법상 적절하다.
④ the language and instructions를 선행사로 하고 used의 목적어 역할을 하는 관계대명사 that은 어법상 적절하다.
⑤ view the world through a social lens를 do so로 대신하고 있으므로, so는 어법상 적절하다.

03　정답 ④

항공 운송은 눈보라가 항공 운수에 폭포 효과를 미칠 수 있는 겨울 동안과 같은 기상 장애에 특히 취약하다. 지구의 바람 패턴에는 계절성이 있다. 제트 기류 또한 국제 항공사들이 고려해야 하는 주요 물리적 요소이다. 항공기에 있어서, 바람의 속도는 이동 시간과 비용에 영향을 미칠 수 있다. 대륙 간 비행에 있어서 뒤바람이 부는 조건은 예정된 비행시간을 1시간까지 단축할 수 있다. 예를 들어, 겨울철의 강한 제트 기류 조건 때문에, 미국 동부 해안과 유럽 간 대서양 횡단 비행은 동쪽으로 가는 비행에 있어 예정된 것보다 30분에서 45분 더 일찍 도착할 수 있다. 그러나 서쪽으로 가는 비행에 있어서, 비정상적으로 강한 제트 기류 조건은 비행시간을 단축시킬(→ 연장시킬) 것이고 때로 항공편이 어쩔 수 없이 Gander(Newfoundland)나 Bangor(Maine) 같은 기착지 공항에서 예정에 없던 연료 보급 착륙을 하도록 할 수 있다. 기후 변화는 북대서양 제트 기류의 강도를 높일 것이며 북미와 유럽 간의 서쪽으로 가는 비행시간을 연장할 수 있을 것으로 예상된다.

해설
서쪽으로 가는 비행에 있어서, 비정상적으로 강한 제트 기류 조건은 Gander(Newfoundland)나 Bangor(Maine) 같은 기착지 공항에서 예정에 없던 연료 보급 착륙을 하도록 할 수 있다는 내용으로 보아, 비행시간을 단축시키는 것이 아니라 연장시킨다는 내용이 되어야 하므로, ④ 'shorten(단축시키다)'을 'lengthen(연장시키다)'과 같은 낱말로 바꾸어야 한다.

04　정답 ②

아이러니하게도, 과학은 감각의 정보에 호소하기도 하고 동시에 그것들을 신뢰할 수 없는 것으로 거부하기도 한다. 우선 감각 정보가 측정된다. 따라서 측정할 수 있는 감각 경험만이 과학에 포함된다. 측정이 불가능한 것, 본질적으로 정성적인 것은 단지 주관적인 감각으로 여겨진다. 측정이 가능한 특성에는 감각과 무관하다고 추정되는 객관적인 실체가 부여된다. 그러나 우리는 측정이 가능한 것들의 인식은 색채를 보는 것만큼 불가분하게 감각에 예속된다는 것을 보여 주었다. 사실, 측정이 가능한 특성은 어떤 면에서 감각 중에서 가장 개인적으로 규제된 것에 근거하고 있다. 그것들은 우리에게 우리 자신의 몸에 대해 말해 주는 것이다. 우리가 우리의 감각을 통해 세상에 대해 알게 되는 것을 근거로, 우리는 과학을 측정할 수 있는 그런 경험으로만 한정하기로 선택하는 것은 감각 경험의 본질이라는 틀 내에서 내린 완전히 자의적인 선택이라는 것을 이해할 수 있다.

측정이 가능한 것들의 인식은 색채를 보는 것처럼 불가분하게 감각에 예속된다는 것을 보여 주었고, 측정이 가능한 특성은 어떤 면에서는 감각 중에서 가장 개인적으로 규제된 것에 근거하고 있다고 했으므로, 빈칸에 들어갈 말로 가장 적절한 것은 ② '자의적인'이다.
① 이성적인   ③ 의식적인   ④ 목적이 있는   ⑤ 경제적인

05   정답 ①

맥락의 중요성을 무시하는 윤리학 이론가들의 반복되는 경향에 반대하여 최근 도덕 철학에서 다수의 목소리가 울려 나오고 있다. 예를 들어, 단순성과 질서에 대한 애정 때문에 도덕적 환경의 풍부한 다양성을 보지 못하는 이론가들에 대해 이의가 제기되고 있다. 이러한 목소리로, 이론이 모든 것을 몇 개의 선호되는 부류로 한정해서는 안 된다는 것을, 너무 과격하게 윤리학의 설명적인 개념을 가지치기하고 강화하는 제안들이 결국 중요한 현상들을 제외하거나 혹은 그것들을 인식할 수 없게 만들 것이라는 점이 우리에게 상기된다. 단순히 도덕적 이론을 소유한 것이 도덕적인 지식으로서 충분하다는 오만함에 대해 다른 이의가 제기되어 왔다. 일련의 도덕적인 원칙이 아무리 적절할지라도, 결국 한 상황에서 무엇이 가장 중요한지 인식하지 못하는 사람은 그 원칙을 어디에 적용할지 알 수 없을 것이다. 도덕적인 지식이 없는 사람은, 비싸긴 하지만, 길을 찾기에는 보잘것없는 장비를 갖추었다는 것을 알게 되는 GPS를 장착한 초보 등산객처럼, 무턱대고 여기저기 발을 헛디딜 것이다. 여러분의 지도가 아무리 좋아도, 여러분이 어디에 있는지 모른다면 그것은 여러분이 길을 잃는 것을 막아 줄 수 없다.

단순성과 질서에 대한 애정 때문에 도덕적 환경의 풍부한 다양성을 보지 못하는 것에 이의를 제기하고, 일련의 도덕적인 원칙이 아무리 적절할지라도, 결국 한 상황에서 무엇이 가장 중요한지 인식하지 못하는 사람은 그 원칙을 어디에 적용할지 알 수 없을 것이라는 내용의 글이므로, 빈칸에 들어갈 말로 가장 적절한 것은 ① '맥락의 중요성을 무시하는'이다.
② 현대 도덕 이론을 정당화하는
③ 도덕적 딜레마의 미묘한 차이를 반영하는
④ 윤리적 문제의 복잡성을 강조하는
⑤ 개인적 관점의 영향을 불신하는

06   정답 ①

고통이 심한데 의미 있는 부상은 발생하지 않았다면 어떻게 될까? 그 고통은 진짜인가? '부상이 곧 발생할 것'이라는 고통이 하는 역할의 이런 진실성의 모순이 바로 침을 쏘는 곤충들이 이용하는 것이다. 누군가 벌을 밟을 때, 이 벌이 발바닥에 쏜 침은 고통을 유발하고, 발을 드는 것이 벌에게 이로운 반응이다. 이 침 쏘기로 의미 있는 신체적 부상이 그 사람에게 유발되었는가? 흔히 그 대답은 '아니요'이다. 침을 쏘는 곤충은 고통 신호의 정직함 속에서 이 약점을 자기에게 이롭게 이용하는 데 명수이다. 침을 쏘는 곤충에게, 우리는 단지 속임수에 속아 넘어가는 바보일지도 모른다. 우리에게는 확실한 것보다 안전한 것이 더 나은데, 그런 까닭에 우리는 그 (고통) 신호가 정말이라고 믿는다. 부상이 사실인 경우에, 그 부정적인 손실(부상)은 그 고통을 무시함으로써 얻게 되는 그 어떤 편익보다 훨씬 더 클 수 있다. (부상의) 위험을 왜 무릅쓰겠는가? 생명의 위험–편익 방정식에서 (부상의) 그 위험은 흔히 그 어떤 잠재적 이득도 축소한다. 여기에서 고통의 심리가 성립한다. 동물이나 인간이 고통의 저편에서 이로움이라는 무지개가 기다리고 있다는 것을 알 수 없다면, 자연스러운 심리는 무지개를 좇지 말라고 지시한다.

우리는 확실한 것보다는 안전한 것이 더 낫기 때문에 고통 신호가 정말이라고 믿고, 고통이 가져오는 부상이 사실인 경우에 그 부정적인 손실이 고통을 무시함으로써 얻게 되는 이익보다 훨씬 클 수 있다는 내용의 글이므로, 빈칸에 들어갈 말로 가장 적절한 것은 ① '단지 속임수에 속아 넘어가는 바보일지도 모른다'이다.
② 우리 자신이 그것들의 전술에 무관심하다고 생각한다
③ 통증 지각의 복잡성을 이해한다
④ 그것들의 교활한 전략을 마비시키는 것으로 보일 수 있다
⑤ 그것들의 위협을 감지하는 센서가 장착되어 있다

07   정답 ④

친숙한 속담의 사례를 주어진 상황에서 인식하는 행동은 그 상황의 새로운 이해에 도움을 줄 수 있다. 그것은 상황의 피상적인 세부 사항을 훨씬 넘어서는 신선하고, 추상적이며, 자명하지 않은 관점을 제공한다. 속담은 다소 미묘하고 복잡한 범주의 표지이므로, 속담을 상황에 적용하는 것은 그렇지 않으면 숨겨져 있을 수도 있는 측면을 끌어내는 방법이다. 비록 어쩌면 편향된 종류의 이해일지라도, 속담을 표지로 이용하는 것은 보고 있는 것을 이해하는 방식이다. 갓 마주한 상황에 속담을 적용하면 순전히 논리적인 분석이 아니라 보는 것을 속담의 렌즈를 통해 걸러내는 데서 나오는 일종의 통찰력을 얻게 된다. (차이점은 속담이 고정된 표현인 반면에, 속담 어구는 문맥의 문법에 맞게 변경을 허용한다는 것이다.) 요약하자면, 속담은 서로 비유로 모두 연결되어 있는 과거, 현재, 미래, 가상 등 일련의 매우 다양한 상황에 대한 편리하고도 간결한 표지이다.

친숙한 속담의 사례를 주어진 상황에서 인식하는 것은 보고 있는 것을 속담의 렌즈를 통해 걸러내는 데서 나오는 일종의 통찰력을 주며 상황을 심층적으로 이해하는 데 도움이 된다는 내용의 글이다. 따라서 속담과 속담 어구의 차이점을 설명하는 ④는 글의 전체 흐름과 관계가 없다.

08   정답 ②

기체 형태의 질소는 다른, 더 반응성이 있는 대기 가스가 가까이 오지 못하게 하는 것이 중요한 상황에서 자주 사용된다. (B) 예를 들어, 그것은 생산 또는 보관 중인 전자 부품 같은 재료를 보호하는 데 있어 블랭킷 가스로서 산업에 도움이 된다. 포도주의 산화를 막기 위해 포도주병은 코르크가 제거된 후에 자주 질소로 채워진다. (A) 최근에 질소는 또한 과일을 딴 후에 부패로부터 보호하기 위해 과일을 뒤덮는 데 사용되어 왔다. 예를 들어 사과는 공기가 질소로만 된 곳에서 낮은 온도로 유지되면 30개월까지 저장될 수 있다. (C) 이런 활용 이외에 질소는 원유 생산에도 사용되는데, 원유를 표면에 올라오게 하기 위해 압축된 형태로 펌프를 통해 질소를 땅속으로 보낸다. 보통의 공기는 이 목적으로 사용될 수 없는데, 이는 공기를 구성하는 기체들 중 일부가 원유와 반응하여 원하지 않는 부산물을 만들어 낼 것이기 때문이다.

질소는 더 반응성 있는 대기 가스가 가까이 오지 못하게 하는 상황에서 사용된다는 주어진 글 다음에, 이 예시로 전자부품을 보호하는 블랭킷 가스로서 산업에 도움이 되며, 포도주의 산화를 막는 용도로 사용된다는 내용의 (B)가 와야 한다. 이어서 최근에는 또한 과일 부패를 막는 용도로 사용된다는 내용과 이에 대한 예시를 제시하는 내용의 (A)가 온 다음, In addition to these applications로 시작하며, 앞에서 언급한 질소의 용도에 덧붙여, 질

소가 원유 생산에도 사용된다는 내용의 (C)가 오는 것이 글의 순서로 가장 적절하다.

09

정답 ②

모든 조직이 그것의 지배적인 견해, 가치, 그리고 규범을 형성하고 가르치는 것은 바로 언어를 통해서이다. 견해는 학습된 언어 내의 단어에서 만들어진다. 언어에서의 강조는 견해에서의 강조를 만들어 낸다. (B) 따라서 자본주의 사회에서 우리는 '경쟁', '자유 기업', '이익', '개인의 노력', '사유 재산', 그리고 '시장' 같은 특정한 단어들을 반복해서 사용하기 쉽다. 이 단어들을 중심으로 반복해서 강화되는 일련의 견해들이 증가할 것이다. (A) 우리가 사회주의에 관한 견해를 가질 수는 있지만, 물론 그것들이 자본주의에 대한 우리의 헌신과 관련해서 부정적으로 사용되지 않는 한 그런 견해들은 덜 강화된다. 정치 지도자들은 단어의 사용이 사람들의 사고에 영향을 미치는 중요한 방식이라는 것을 알고 있으며, 지지를 얻기 위해 단어들은 신중하게 선택된다. (C) '테러와의 전쟁', '악한 집단', '선제적 전쟁'은 모두 우리가 싸우고자 하는 대상을 향한 정책을 우리가 '이해'하고 지지하도록 돕기 위해 지도자들이 사용하는 어구들이다. '상속세', '세속주의자', '파시즘 신봉자', '자유주의 교수', 그리고 '진화론자'는 매우 복잡한 문제에 대한 단순한 설명을 의심 없이 받아들이도록 우리에게 영향을 미치기 위해 사용되는 어구들이다.

해설
언어를 통해서 모든 조직이 지배적인 견해, 가치, 규범을 형성하고 가르치며, 언어에서의 강조는 견해의 강조를 만들어 낸다는 주어진 글 다음에, 자본주의 사회에서 반복해서 사용되는 단어 중심으로 반복해서 강화되는 일련의 견해들이 증가할 것이라는 내용의 (B)가 와야 한다. 사회주의에 관한 견해가 자본주의에 대한 우리의 헌신과 관련해서 부정적으로 사용되지 않는 한 그런 견해들은 덜 강화되며, 정치 지도자들은 단어들을 신중하게 선택한다는 내용의 (A)가 온 다음, 정치 지도자들이 신중하게 단어들을 선택하는 예시를 들어 설명하는 내용의 (C)가 오는 것이 글의 순서로 가장 적절하다.

10

정답 ④

하향식 포트폴리오 구성은 자산 배분으로 시작된다. 예를 들어, 현재 자신의 모든 돈을 은행 계좌에 보유한 사람은 전체 포트폴리오의 어느 정도가 주식, 채권 등으로 이동되어야 하는지를 먼저 결정할 것이다. 이런 방식으로, 포트폴리오의 전반적인 특징이 수립된다. 예를 들어, 1926년부터 대기업의 보통주식의 평균 연간 수익률은 1년에 11퍼센트보다 더 높았던 반면, 미국 재무부 단기 채권의 평균 수익은 4퍼센트 미만이었다. 반면, 주식은 범위가 −46퍼센트만큼이나 낮고 55퍼센트만큼이나 높았던 연 수익률 때문에 훨씬 더 위험스럽다. 이와 대조적으로, 재무부 증권은 실질적으로 위험이 없는데, 여러분은 그것을 살 때 얼마의 이자를 벌어들일지 안다. 따라서 투자금을 주식 시장이나 재무부 증권이 거래되는 화폐 시장에 배분하는 결정은 여러분의 포트폴리오의 위험과 수익 둘 다에 큰 영향을 미칠 것이다. 하향식 투자자는 먼저 이것과 기타 매우 중요한 자산 배분 결정을 내린다.

해설
In contrast로 시작하여, 재무부 증권은 실질적으로 위험이 없다는 주어진 문장의 내용으로 보아, 주어진 문장 앞에는 수익률이 위험한 자산 배분에 관한 설명이 있어야 하는데, 주식은 범위가 −46퍼센트만큼이나 낮고 55퍼센트만큼이나 높았던 연 수익률 때문에 훨씬 더 위험스럽다는 내용이 이에 해당한다. 따라서 투자금 배분 결정은 포트폴리오의 위험과 수익 둘 다에 영향을 미친다고 결론을 내리는 ④ 앞에 주어진 문장이 들어가는 것이 가장 적절하다.

11

정답 ⑤

Berkeley 대학의 연구자인 Mary Main은 '성인 애착 인터뷰'라는 인터뷰를 개발했다. 이 인터뷰에서 Main은 사람들이 자신의 어린 시절 이야기를 어떻게 말했는지, 그리고 이 어린 시절이 고통스럽고 충격이 컸는지 아닌지에 대해 점수를 매겼다. 그녀는 이야기의 내용보다 이야기가 어떻게 말로 표현되는지에 대해 더 관심이 있었다. 자신의 매우 충격적인 어린 시절에 관해 일관성 있는 이야기를 할 수 있었던 사람들은 같은 양의 어린 시절의 충격적인 경험을 가지고 있지만 어쩐지 그것을 마무리하지 못했던 사람들과는 매우 다른 종류의 부모가 된 것으로 관찰되었다. 그들은 이러한 어린 시절의 사건들에 관한 자신의 설명에서 불안거나, 정신이 팔려 있거나, 일축하거나, 전혀 일관성이 없었다. 이 두 유형의 부모들의 아기들을 연구할 때, Mary Main은 놀라운 결과를 발견했다. 어떻게든 충격적인 경험을 마무리했고, 그것에 관해 일관된 이야기를 할 수 있었으며 그 이야기를 하는 동안 흐트러지지 않고 감정이 북받치지 않은 사람들에게는 안정적인 애착을 가진 유아들이 있었다. 반면 충격적인 경험이 마무리되지 않았고, 그것에 관해 일관된 이야기를 할 수 없었으며, 그 이야기를 하는 동안 정리되지 않고 감정이 북받쳤던 사람들에게는 불안하게 애착을 가진 유아들이 있었다.

해설
어린 시절의 충격적인 경험을 정리해서 일관된 이야기를 할 수 있었고 그 이야기를 할 때 흐트러지거나 감정이 북받치지 않았던 사람들에게는 안정적인 애착 관계를 가진 유아가 있었다는 내용과, 그렇지 못한 사람에게는 불안정한 애착 관계를 가진 유아가 있었다는 내용이 대조적으로 이어져야 하므로, 주어진 문장이 들어가기에 가장 적절한 곳은 ⑤이다.

12

정답 ②

아이가 서너 살이 되기 전까지는 세는 능력이 습득되지 못한다는 사실이 그 특징이 타고나는 것이 아니라는 것을 반드시 증명하는 것은 아니다. Piaget의 실험을 포함하는 많은 관찰에서, 세기와 산수는 의사 소통하는 능력 및 대체로 모국어인 주어진 언어를 사용하는 능력과 함께 습득되었다. 주어진 언어로 의사소통하는 것이 타고난 속성이 아니고 학습된 것이라는 것은 놀랄 일이 아니다. 언어를 배우는 능력은 타고난 특징이지만 그 언어 자체를 습득하는 것에는 여러 해가 걸린다. 다양한 실험에서 보이듯, 어린이가 언어를 배우기 전에, 그의 산수 능력은 작동하기 시작하지 않는다. 아이의 세는 능력 부족이 장애가 아니라 그가 몇 년 동안의 연습을 더 하기 전까지는 그가 이해하지 못하는 질문에 대답해야 한다든가, 혹은 기대되는 대답이 무엇인지를 그가 깨닫지 못한다는 사실이다. 질문을 이해하는 것이 결과를 분석하는 데 중요한 역할을 한다는 것을 보여 주는 검사를 고안하는 것은 쉽다.

➡ 세는 능력의 지연은 타고난 능력의 부족이 아니라 산수 과업을 완전히 이해하기 위한 언어 발달의 필요성에 기인한다.

해설
아이가 서너 살이 되기 전까지는 세는 능력이 습득되지 못하는 것이 타고나는 것이 아니라, 세기와 산수는 의사소통하는 능력 및 모국어 사용 능력과 함께 습득되는 언어를 습득하는 것에 서너 해가 걸리고, 언어를 배우기 전에 산수 능력은 작동하지 않으며, 세는 능력 부족이 아니라 질문을 이해하지 못해 대답을 못하기 때문이라는 내용의 글이므로, 요약문의 빈칸 (A), (B)에 들어갈 말로는 ② 'delay(지연) - comprehend(이해하다)'가 가장 적절하다.
① 지연 – 피하다
③ 변화 – 기대하다
④ 차이 – 이해하다
⑤ 차이 – 기대하다

REVIEW 모의고사 [04회]

01 ②	02 ④	03 ⑤	04 ⑤	05 ③	06 ②
07 ③	08 ③	09 ⑤	10 ③	11 ⑤	12 ④

01

정답 ②

유전자 특허에 대해 많은 비평가들에 의해 제기되는 주요 우려는 생명체의 요소를 다루는 특허가 인간 개인과 인간 사회에 대한 크게 확대된 힘을 개인, 기업 및 정부에게 줄 수도 있다는 것이다. 예를 들어, 한 농부가 단순히 그의 이웃과 경쟁하고 독자 생존 가능한 농부로 남아 있기 위해서 최고의 작물에 접근하기를 원하고 사실상 최고의 작물을 필요로 하며, 그 작물들은 모두 회사가 소유한 특허에 의해 보호된다면, 그는 작물이 훨씬 더 적은 법적 제한에 의해 보장되었던 시절에 비해 경제적으로 더 약해졌는가? 일부 비평가들은 기술적으로 발달하고 특허가 지배하는 지역의 농민들처럼 상대적으로 가난하고 약한 많은 사람들의 상황이 중세 세계의 농노들의 상황과 비슷하다고 시사한다. 그들은 자신들의 보잘것없는 작은 땅으로 연명할 수 있도록 허용되기 위해 영주 권위자에게 완전히 의존한다. 그들에게 더 유용한 도구를 주기보다는, 특허로 통제되는 혁신은 그들이 독립할 수 있는 거의 모든 능력을 앗아간다. 이러한 비평가들에게 특허란 농부와 같은 사람들로 하여금 살아남기 위해 체제 안에서 겨우 충족될 만큼만의 이익을 허용하지만 번창할 정도로 충분하지 않은 수익을 허용할 회사에의 종속으로 몰아넣을 수 있다.

해설
많은 비평가들이 유전자 특허는 개인, 기업 및 정부에게 인간 개인과 인간 사회에 대해 확대된 힘을 줄 수도 있다고 우려하는데, 그것은 마치 중세 세계의 농노가 보잘것없는 작은 땅으로 연명하기 위해 영주 권위자에게 의존해야 했던 것과 비슷한 상황으로 이해할 수 있다는 내용의 글이다. 특히 특허로 통제되는 혁신이 어떤 역할을 하는지는 마지막 문장에서 더 자세하게 기술되는데, 사람들이 살아남기 위해 체제 안에서 겨우 충족될 만큼만의 이익을 허용하지만 번창할 정도로 충분하지 않은 수익을 허용할 회사에 종속된다는 내용이므로, 글의 주제로 가장 적절한 것은 ② '가난하고 약한 사람들을 종속시키는 유전자 특허'이다.
① 유전자 특허 분야의 법적이고 정책적인 조치
③ 농부들이 특허로 통제되는 혁신을 탐색하기 위한 전략
④ 유전자 특허가 사회적 및 경제적인 힘에 미치는 영향
⑤ 중소기업을 위한 유전자 특허의 혜택

02

정답 ④

뇌에 있어, 모든 것은 처음에는 잡음이다. 그런 다음 뇌는 잡음의 패턴을 알아차리고 한 수준 위로 이동하여 그러한 패턴이 상호 작용하는 방식의 패턴을 알아차린다. 그런 다음 그것들은 한 수준 더 위로 이동하고 계속 그것은 이어진다. 보다 단순한 층의 위에 세워지는 패턴 인식의 층은 우리 주변의 세상으로부터 무엇을 예상할지에 대한 대략의 이해가 되며, 그것들의 상호 작용은 우리의 인과 관계에 대한 감각이 된다. 공의 둥긂, 탁자의 단단한 가장자리, 봉제 인형의 부드러운 팔꿈치, 각각의 물건은 다른 경로 말고 특정한 신경의 경로를 흥분시키며 각각의 노출은 뇌가 세상의 그러한 요소들을 예측하게 되고 그것들을 맥락 안에서 더 잘 이해하게 될 때까지 그것들의 연결을 강화한다. 이와 비슷하게, 원인은 대개 결과로 이어지므로, 우리의 내재된 패턴 인식, 즉 내가 밤에 울면 엄마가 오실 것이다, 으깬 감자는 나를 행복하게

할 것이다, 벌은 쏘면 아프다와 같이 알아차리고 예측을 형성한다. 우리는 예측할 수 없는 혼돈으로 가득한 삶을 시작하지만, 우리의 규칙적인 인식은 우리가 그 혼돈을 예측할 수 있는 질서로 바꾸기 위해 사용하는 예측이 된다.

해설
뇌에 있어 모든 것이 처음에는 잡음이고, 그다음에 뇌가 잡음의 패턴을 알아차린 다음, 패턴 인식의 층은 우리 주변의 세상으로부터 무엇을 예상할지에 대한 대략의 이해가 되며, 우리의 규칙적인 인식은 우리가 그 혼돈을 예측할 수 있는 질서로 바꾸기 위해 사용하는 예측이 된다는 내용의 글이므로, 글의 제목으로 가장 적절한 것은 ④ '혼돈에서 질서로: 뇌의 예측하는 춤'이다.
① 뇌 적응의 메커니즘 분석하기
② 인지적 해석의 깊이 탐구하기
③ 야생 길들이기: 우리 마음이 패턴을 찾는 방법
⑤ 문제 해결하기: 규칙적인 뇌 패턴 해독하기

03

정답 ⑤

예언의 목적이 미래에 대한 불확실성을 없애고자 하는 것이긴 하지만, 무작위의 형태를 띤 불확실성은 자주 예언을 만들어 내는 데 사용되는 기제이다. 찻잎과 서양톱풀의 줄기가 떨어지는 무작위의 방식은 이것을 분명히 보여 준다. 그것은 마치 무작위성이 '정보'를 알려 주는 힘으로 가는 입구로 작용하는 것 같다. Théphile Gautier는 그것을 설명하는 멋진 방식을 가지고 있었다. 그는 "아마도 우연은 신이 서명하고 싶지 않을 때(자신을 알리고 싶지 않을 때) 사용하는 신의 필명인 것 같다."라고 말했다. 찻잎과 서양톱풀 줄기의 예는 또한 초자연적인 메시지를 해석하기 위해서는 자주 특별한 종류의 지식이 필요하다는 것을 보여 준다. 사실상, 신비주의자, 사제, 예언자, 그리고 제사장은 부분적으로 신으로부터 전달된 메시지를 이해할 수 있는 유일한 인간으로서의 독특한 중간자 역할 때문에 사회에서 자신의 지위를 유지하는 것이다. Tacitus 시대의 게르만 사제들이 룬 문자가 새겨진 나무껍질 줄기를 무작위로 골라 선택했을 때, 그리고 유대인들이 제비를 뽑아서 중요한 결정을 했을 때, 그 무작위의 과정은 우월한 존재의 의지가 자신을 나타낼 수 있는 기회를 주는 것 같아 보였다. 성경에 이르기를, "뽑은 제비는 무릎에 떨어지지만, 그것의 모든 결정은 신으로부터 나온다."

해설
⑤ to부정사구 to manifest의 의미상의 주어인 the will of the superior being을 대신하는 것은 재귀대명사이므로 it을 itself로 고쳐야 한다.
① 뒤에 이어지는 절이 주어(tea leaves and yarrow stalks)와 완전자동사(fall)로 이루어진 완전한 절이므로 in which는 어법상 적절하다.
② as if가 이끄는 절에 동사 serves가 있으므로, the powers를 수식하는 현재분사 divulging은 어법상 적절하다.
③ 주어인 a special type of knowledge가 동사 require의 동작의 대상이므로, 수동형 is required는 어법상 적절하다.
④ 전치사 as가 이끄는 전치사구에서 명사구 the only people을 수식하고 있으므로 형용사 able은 어법상 적절하다.

04

정답 ⑤

영화는 흔히 장소에 대한 이상화된 묘사를 구성하는데, 이러한 장소에 대한 우리의 진정한 이해를 왜곡할 수 있는 흥미를 돋우는 이야기를 엮어 낸다. 영화의 이러한 묘사는 이러한 목적지의 매우 색다른 측면을 증폭시켜, 현실 세계의 미묘하고 다면적인 현실을 반영하지 않는 일차원적인 시각을 조장하는 경향이 있다. 그 결과, 관람객은 이러한 묘사를 해당 장소의 진정한 모습으로

그대로 받아들여 자신도 모르게 지나치게 낙관적이거나 비관적인 인상을 갖게 될 수도 있다. 이로 인해 사람들은 부풀려지거나 정당하지 않은 기대감을 가지고 목적지에 도착했다가 자신들이 마주하는 더 불완전한 현실에 직면할 수 있다. 마찬가지로, 영화는 자주 창의적인 자유를 발휘하여 특정 장소를 위험, 범죄 또는 기타 불리한 특성이 가득한 곳으로 묘사하여, 사람들이 이러한 장소를 방문하는 것에 대해 부당한 우려나 두려움을 갖게 한다. 따라서 영화의 렌즈는 스토리텔링을 위한 흥미를 돋우는 매체이지만, 때때로 허구와 현실의 경계를 명료하게 만들어(→ 모호하게 만들어), 크레디트가 올라가고 나서도 오랫동안 지속되는, 장소에 대한 잘못된 인상의 씨앗을 심을 수 있다.

해설
영화는 흔히 어떤 장소를 지나치게 낙관적이거나 비관적으로 표현하여, 관람객이나 실제 방문객이 그 장소에 대한 잘못된 인상을 가지게 할 수 있다는 내용의 글이다. 따라서 영화의 렌즈는 스토리텔링을 위한 흥미를 돋우는 매체이지만, 때때로 허구와 현실의 경계를 모호하게 만든다는 내용이 자연스러우므로 ⑤ 'clarify(명료하게 만들다)'를 'blur(모호하게 만들다)'와 같은 낱말로 바꾸어야 한다.

05
정답 ③

높은 지위 집단 구성원의 의무와 책임은 본질적으로 사회적일 수 있는데, 예를 들어 그들은 흔히 자신들의 집단에 영감을 주고, 구성원들 사이에 평화를 유지하고, 개인들 사이의 의사소통을 용이하게 할 것으로 기대된다. 그러나 대부분의 집단 환경에서 그들은 또한 그 집단이 직면하는 기술적 문제도 이해해야 한다. 업무에 유능한 사람에게 책임을 맡기는 것은 집단이 더 잘 수행하도록 돕는다. 그러므로 많은 집단은 영향력을 할당할 때 사교적 기술과 같은 다른 요인들보다는 업무 역량을 우선시한다. 예를 들어, 엔지니어 팀에서는 기술적 능력이 의사소통 능력보다 더 중요하게 여겨질 것이다. 그러나 집단은 흔히 그들의 지위 계층 구조를 업무 역량 차이에 근거를 두지 못한다. 예를 들어, '지위 특성 이론' 전통의 많은 연구는 집단 구성원들이 지위 할당을 성별, 인종, 사회적 계층, 그리고 신체적 매력과 같은 특징에 근거를 두며, 이러한 특징이 그렇지 않은데도 일반적인 역량과 관련되어 있다고 생각한다는 것을 발견한다. 마찬가지로, 자신감이 더 높은 개인은 자신감이 실제 능력을 크게 예측하는 것이 아닌데도, 리더로 선택될 가능성이 더 높을 수도 있다.

해설
높은 지위 집단 구성원의 의무와 책임은 본질적으로 사회적일 수 있어서, 엔지니어 팀에서는 기술적 능력이 의사소통 능력보다 더 중요하게 여겨질 가능성이 더 높을 것이지만, 집단은 흔히 그들의 지위 계층 구조를 업무 역량 차이에 근거를 두지 못하고 그 외 개인의 특징이나 성향도 일반적 역량에 관련 지어 생각한다는 내용이므로, 빈칸에 들어갈 말로 가장 적절한 것은 ③ '영향력을 할당할'이다.
① 전문성의 순위를 매길 ② 적성을 평가할
④ 숙련도를 측정할 ⑤ 협업을 촉진할

06
정답 ②

진보에 대한 개념에 대해 자주 선언되는 위기의 결과 중 하나는 미래는 문제적이 되고 현재가 절대적인 것이 된다는 것이다. 우리는 현재가 군주이자 주인인 역사성의 체제에 우리 자신이 있다는 것을 발견한다. 이것은 현 입법 기관, 단기, 소비 지상주의, 우리 세대, 근접성 등의 억압적인 힘이다. 이것은 금융 부문에, 투자보다는 수익에, 회사의 화합보다는 비용 절감에 특권을 주는 경제이다. 우리는 더는 공간과 관련이 없고 시간과 관련이 있는 제국주의, 즉

모든 것을 식민지화하는 현재의 제국주의를 실천한다. 스스로를 희생하는 삶으로 이루어진 미래에 대한 식민지화와 그 미래를 흡수해 그것을 기생적으로 먹고 사는 현재의 제국주의가 있다. Bertman은 그것을 '지금의 힘', 즉 시간의 어떤 다른 차원에 투자되지 않는 현재의 힘이라고 부른다. 이러한 현재가 장기를 단기로, 지속성을 즉각성으로, 영구성을 일시성으로, 기억을 감각으로, 비전을 충동으로 대체한다.

해설
진보에 대한 생각의 위기에 따른 결과 중 하나는 현재가 절대적인 것이며 현 입법 기관, 단기, 소비 지상주의, 우리 세대, 근접성 등의 억압적인 힘이 되고 장기를 단기로, 지속성을 즉각성으로, 영구성을 일시성으로, 기억을 감각으로, 비전을 충동으로 대체하는 미래에 대한 식민지화를 한다는 내용의 글이므로, 빈칸에 들어갈 말로 가장 적절한 것은 ② '그 미래를 흡수해 그것을 기생적으로 먹고 사는'이다.
① 긍정적 변화의 가능성에서 눈을 멀게 하는
③ 과거를 되찾아 미래를 변화시키는
④ 우리의 미래를 가치 있고 번영하며 성공하게 만드는
⑤ 과거와 동화되어 공생적으로 번영하는

07
정답 ③

만성적인 스트레스는 뇌가 위협을 처리하는 방식에 영향을 미친다. 사람의 공포 반응은 환경에서 눈에 띄는 위협을 감지하고 공포와 불안감을 유발하는 데 도움을 주는 편도체와 사람의 반응을 현실에 맞게 조정하는 전두엽 피질 및 기타 뇌피질부를 포함하여 다수의 뇌 부위를 수반한다. 사람이 감정 조절 상태에 있을 때 이러한 반응은 균형 잡힌 상태이다. 그러나 장기간의 스트레스는 편도체의 활동을 증가시켜 이 부위의 뉴런 성장을 촉진하는 한편 전두엽 피질의 힘을 감소시킨다. 이것은 사람의 감정 조절 능력을 없앤다. 두려움은 치안 유지에 역할을 하지만(범죄자의 총격 사건 현장에 처음 도착했을 때 두려움을 느끼는 것은 당연한 일이다), 만성적으로 스트레스를 받는 경찰관은 두려움을 느끼고 이에 대응하는 데 더 빠를 수도 있다. 편도체 활동이 증가하고 전두엽 피질의 반응이 약해지는 것은 공격성과도 관련이 있으므로, 그 경찰관은 또한 폭력에 더 취약할 수 있다.

해설
사람의 공포 반응은 환경에서 눈에 띄는 위협을 감지하고 공포와 불안감을 유발하는데, 장기간의 스트레스는 사람의 감정 조절 능력을 없애고, 만성적으로 스트레스를 받는 경찰관은 두려움을 느끼고 이에 대응하는 데 더 빠를 수도 있다고 했으므로, 빈칸에 들어갈 말로 가장 적절한 것은 ③ '또한 폭력에 더 취약할 수 있다'이다.
① 나중에 자신의 행동을 정당화할 가능성이 있다
② 갈등을 더 잘 해결할 가능성이 있다
④ 허용 범위를 초과할 수 있다
⑤ 상호 공감 능력이 높아질 수 있다.

08
정답 ③

때때로, 가장 작은 에너지 제품인 배터리가 그러하듯이, 작은 것들이 큰 문제를 일으킬 수 있다. 수명이 다하면, 배터리는 쓸모없고, 가치 없고, 독성이 있는 불행한 조합이 된다. 배터리의 복잡한 화학 성분은 분리하기 어려울 수 있고, 아무런 처리 없이 그것을 매립지에 버리는 것은 독성 화학 물질을 자연 환경으로 방출할 수 있다. 배터리를 재활용하는 것은 그것을 매립지에 묻는 것보다 적어도 10배가 넘는 비용이 든다. (몇 가지 단점이 있지만 배터리를

재활용하면 그것들이 토양과 수원을 오염시키고 납, 니켈, 카드뮴과 같은 독소로 야생 동물에게 해를 끼치는 것을 방지하는 데 도움이 된다.) 배터리 폐기물의 독성 때문에, 많은 정부가 재활용을 강제하기 위해 소비자 수준에서 그것들의 처리를 규제해 왔다. 예를 들어, 캘리포니아가 가정용 쓰레기에 배터리를 버리는 것을 금지한다는 사실에도 불구하고, 캘리포니아 사람들은 자신들이 구입하는 배터리의 5퍼센트 미만을 재활용한다.

해설
배터리 폐기물의 독성은 자연 환경에 치명적이어서 많은 정부가 재활용을 강제하기 위해 소비자 수준에서 그것들의 처리를 규제해 왔다는 내용의 글이다. 따라서 몇 가지 단점에도 불구하고 배터리를 재활용하면 야생 동물에게 해를 끼치는 것을 방지하는 데 도움이 된다는 내용의 ③은 글의 전체 흐름과 관계가 없다.

09 정답 ⑤

대부분의 운동선수들은 그날그날의 상황이나, 심지어 낮은 수준의 경쟁 경기에서도 잘 기능할 수 있을 정도의 충분한 핵심 정신력을 개발해 왔다. 그러나 더 부담이 크고 압박감이 가득한 상황에 직면하게 되면, 그들은 실패할 수도 있다. (C) 이는 운동선수와 그들의 코치들에게 매우 좌절감을 줄 수 있는데, 왜냐하면 그들은 자신들이 좋은 성적을 낼 잠재력을 가지고 있다는 것을 알고 있기 때문이다. 경기력의 문제가 정신적인 능력 부족 때문이라는 것을 인식하지 못한 채, 코치들은 운동선수들이 자신의 신체 능력을 훨씬 더 열심히 연마하도록 다그칠 수도 있다. (B) 체조 선수는 기구에서 추가적인 시간을 보낼 수도 있다. 농구 선수는 연습 후에 자유투를 쏘는 데 추가적인 시간을 보낼 수도 있다. 장거리 달리기 선수들은 때로 과훈련이라고 할 수 있을 정도까지 훨씬 더 격렬하게 뛸 수도 있다. (A) 실제로, 일부 경기력 문제는 형편없는 훈련이나 생체 역학과 같은 신체적 문제에서 비롯될 수도 있다. 그러나 많은 경우에 부적절한 정신력이 그 원인일 수 있다.

해설
운동선수들은 정신력을 개발해 왔지만, 더 부담이 크고 압박감이 가득한 상황에 직면하게 되면 실패할 수도 있다는 주어진 글 다음에, 이 실패가 운동선수와 그들의 코치에게 좌절감을 줄 수 있고 코치들은 운동선수들이 자신의 신체 능력을 훨씬 더 열심히 연마하도록 다그칠 수도 있다는 내용의 (C)가 와야 한다. 이어서 그 예로 연마하도록 코치가 다그치는 것에 체조 선수, 농구 선수, 장거리 달리기 선수는 과훈련을 할 수도 있다는 내용의 (B)가 온 다음, 일부 경기력 문제가 훈련이나 신체적 문제가 아니라 부적절한 정신력일 수 있다고 결론을 내리는 내용의 (A)가 오는 것이 글의 순서로 가장 적절하다.

10 정답 ③

인종, 언어, 종교, 관습, 과학 문화 등의 공통성과 같이 매우 다양한 특성을 가질 수 있는 사회적 유사성은 통합의 힘으로 작용한다. 즉 '유유상종'은 정확히 사회 법칙이다. (B) 민족의 구성에서 인종의 공통성은 근본적인 힘이며, 그것은 다른 유사성, 즉 종교나 일반 문화의 공통성에 의해서만 때때로 이의가 제기될 수 있다. 한 사람을 사회로 진입하게 하는 공감의 본능은 유사성과 밀접하게 결부되어 있다. (C) 이 명백한 사실은 더 설명의 여지가 거의 없는데, 그것은 기본적이고, 더는 줄일 수 없으며, 영구적인 사실이다. 그러나 그 결과, 유사성에 근거한 결속은 노동의 분업에 근거한 결속보다 우리에게 훨씬 더 수용 가능한 것으로 나타나는데, 그것은 의무 대신 공감이라는 생각을 불러일으키기 때문이다. (A) 우정과 공손함의 관계, 박애적 제안, 자선 사업을 불

러일으키는 것이 바로 이것이다. 그것은 자신의 본분을 수행할 필요성을 보여 주기보다 다른 사람의 도덕적 충동을 지속하는 수단을 우리에게 제공한다.

해설
인종, 언어, 종교, 관습, 과학 문화 등의 다양한 사회적 유사성은 통합의 힘으로 작용한다는 주어진 글 다음에, 민족의 구성에서 인종의 공통성은 근본적인 힘이며 공감의 본능은 유사성과 밀접하게 결부되어 있다는 내용의 (B)가 와야 한다. 이러한 유사성에 근거한 결속은 훨씬 더 수용 가능한데, 이는 의무 대신 공감이라는 생각을 불러일으키기 때문이라는 내용의 (C)가 온 다음, 우정과 공손함의 관계, 박애적 제안, 자선 사업을 불러일으키는 것이 공감이라는 내용의 (A)가 오는 것이 글의 순서로 가장 적절하다.

11 정답 ⑤

왜 어떤 사람들은 음모론적 사고를 하는데 다른 사람들은 그렇지 않을까? 부풀려진 자신감이나 낮은 자존감 같은 요인과 관련된 다양한 심리적인 이론이 제시되어 왔다. 음모론은 몇몇 사람이 거대하고도 혼란스럽게 하는 사건에 직면하여 불안과 통제력 상실의 느낌을 다루기 위해 사용하는 대처 메커니즘이라는 것이 더 대중적인 합의인 것 같다. 인간의 뇌는 무작위적인 사건을 좋아하지 않는데, 그것은 우리가 그것으로부터 배울 수 없고 따라서 그것을 계획할 수 없기 때문이다. (이해 부족, 사건의 규모, 그것의 개인적 영향 또는 우리의 사회적 지위로 인해) 우리가 무력감을 느낄 때, 우리는 우리가 맞설 수 있는 적을 정의하는 설명에 마음이 끌릴 수 있다. 이것은 이성적인 과정이 아니며, 음모론을 연구한 연구자들은 '직감을 따르는' 경향이 있는 사람들이 음모론에 기반한 사고를 할 가능성이 가장 높다고 지적한다. 이것이 바로 무지가 음모론에 대한 믿음과 매우 관련되어 있는 이유이다. 우리가 자신의 분석적인 능력에 기반하여 무언가를 이해할 수 있는 능력이 더 적으면, 우리는 그것에 의해 더 큰 위협을 느낄 수도 있다.

해설
주어진 문장의 'This(이것)는 무지가 음모론에 대한 믿음과 매우 관련되어 있는 이유이다'라는 내용으로 보아 This는 ⑤ 앞의 '직감을 따르는' 경향이 있는 사람들이 음모론에 기반한 사고를 할 가능성이 가장 높다는 내용을 가리키고, ⑤ 다음 문장의 '자신의 분석적인 능력에 기반하여 무언가를 이해할 수 있는 능력이 더 적다는 것'은 무지에 해당한다. 따라서 주어진 문장은 ⑤에 들어가는 것이 가장 적절하다.

12 정답 ④

학생 평가에서 수집된 데이터의 품질과 도출된 결론 및 추론은 조사에 참여하는 교사의 인식과 가치관에 의해 영향을 받는다. 학생의 문화적 배경을 조사하려면 어느 정도의 객관성이 필요하다. 데이터 수집 시 자기중심적이거나 민족 중심적인 관점은 역효과를 낳는다. 자신의 개인적 또는 문화적 경험에 근거하여 가치 판단을 내리지 않고 학생의 문화를 조사할 수 있어야 한다. 학생의 배경과 경험에 대한 데이터를 수집하는 유일하게 정당한 이유는 교실 수업을 개선하기 위해서이다. 자신의 수업이 일부 학생 집단에 잘 맞지 않는데도 그것이 적절하고 변경해서는 안 된다고 확신하고, 수업 실패의 원인을 학생이나 학생의 생활 환경 탓으로 돌리는 교사는 학생에 대한 데이터를 수집하는 것이 아마 도움이 되지 않을 것이다. 이러한 교사에게는 데이터 수집이 자신의 학생에 대한 부정적인 믿음을 강화할 가능성이 있다.

해설

주어진 문장의 '학생의 배경과 경험에 대한 데이터를 수집한다'는 내용으로 보아, 주어진 문장의 앞에는 학생에 관한 데이터 수집과 관련된 내용이 있어야 하고, 주어진 문장의 '교실 수업을 개선하는 것이 데이터를 수집하는 정당한 이유'라는 내용으로 보아, 주어진 문장 다음에는 수집된 데이터의 실제 사용에 관한 내용이 있어야 한다. 따라서 주어진 문장은 ④에 들어가는 것이 가장 적절하다.

REVIEW 모의고사 05회

01 ⑤	02 ③	03 ③	04 ④	05 ①	06 ④
07 ④	08 ②	09 ④	10 ②	11 ④	12 ⑤

01 정답 ⑤

Steven Johnson은 2005년에 낸 자신의 저서 'Everything Bad Is Good for You'에서 컴퓨터 사용자들의 뇌에서 보이는 광범위한 풍부한 신경 활동을 책을 읽는 사람들의 뇌에서 분명하게 보이는 훨씬 더 조용한 활동과 대조했다. 그 비교는 그로 하여금 컴퓨터 사용이 독서보다 정신에 대한 더 집중적인 자극을 제공한다고 말하게 만들었다. 그는 신경에서 보이는 증거에 의하면 심지어 '독서는 오랜 시간에 걸쳐 감각을 덜 자극한다'라는 결론을 내리도록 이끌 수도 있다고 썼다. 그러나 비록 Johnson의 진단이 정확하기는 하지만, 서로 다른 뇌의 활동에 대한 그의 해석은 오해의 소지가 있다. 그 활동을 그토록 지적으로 도움이 되게 만들어 주는 것은 독서가 '감각을 덜 자극한다'는 바로 그 사실이다. 우리가 산만하게 하는 것들을 거르고 전두엽의 문제 해결 기능을 진정시키도록 해 줌으로써, 깊은 독서는 깊은 사색의 한 형태가 된다. 경험이 많은 독서가의 정신은 고요한 정신이며 시끄러운 것이 아니다. 우리의 뉴런 발화에 관한 한, 더 많은 것이 더 좋다고 추정하는 것은 오류이다.

해설

Steven Johnson의 견해와는 달리, 독서의 약한 자극이 전두엽의 문제 해결 기능을 진정시킴으로써 깊은 사색을 가능하게 하기 때문에 지적으로 도움이 된다는 내용이므로, 글의 제목으로 가장 적절한 것은 ⑤ '책 읽기에서 덜 자극된 감각이 주는 지적 보상'이다.
① 강렬한 정신 자극의 신경학적 이점
② 정신적 관여에 대해 다시 생각하기: 깊은 사고의 가치
③ 전자책 대 실제 책 읽기: 서로 다른 정서적 효과
④ 과도한 자극의 함정: 두뇌 활동 자세히 살펴보기

02 정답 ③

미국교육학회의 전 회장 Larry Cuban이 지적하듯이, 학교는 선진 세계의 '교육'에 대해 우리가 생각하는 방식을 사실상 거의 아무것도 바꾸지 못한 기술에 수년간 수십억 달러를 써 왔다. 자주, 우리는 디지털 도구가 학교 밖의 학습자와 창작자에게 제공하는 힘과 자유를 그들이 똑같은 그 도구를 (학교) 건물 내로 가져올 때는 박탈해 버린다. 우리 대부분이 그것의 결과물인 학교 교육 체제는 우리가 인터넷에서 배우고, 창작하고, 연결할 수 있는 더 다루기 힘들고, 덜 1차원적이고, 더 자기 조직적인 방법들과 잘 어울리지 않는 일련의 구조와 효율성에 바탕을 두고 있다. 사실, 그 체제는 학교에서 디지털 기술을 거의 부지불식간에 하찮은 존재로 만든다. 우리는 그것들을 실험실이나 도서관으로 밀쳐 버리는데, 다시 말해 학생들의 손에 맡기면, 그것들은 교과서 읽기, 문서 만들기, 혹은 평가받기와 같은 별개의 한정된 목적에만 사용된다. 오늘날의 학교에서 우리가 기술을 개인적인 학습 도구가 아니라 주로 제도적인 교육 도구로 간주한다고 주장하는 사람이 거의 없을 것이다.

해설

③ The system of schooling을 수식하는 관계절의 동사는 are이고, 문장의 주어는 The system of schooling that most of us are products of이므로, 문장의 동사가 필요하다. 따라서 동명사 being을 is 로 고쳐야 한다.

① 뒤에 이어지는 절에 주어(we)와 think about의 목적어(an "education" in the developed world)가 있으므로, 명사절을 이끄는 how는 어법상 적절하다.

② 관계절의 주어가 복수 digital tools이므로 복수 동사 give는 어법상 적절하다.

④ they're의 they는 digital technologies를 대신하고 동사 use의 동작 의 대상이 되므로 수동형을 이루는 과거분사 used는 어법상 적절하다.

⑤ 뒤의 부사구 as an institutional teaching tool을 수식하므로, 부사 primarily는 어법상 적절하다.

03   정답 ③

우리는 우리의 건설된 풍경을 대체로 무시하는데 왜냐하면 사실상 우리가 그 것들의 생성에 명백한 지분이나 영향력이 전혀 없기 때문이다. 이것은 우리 의 일상 경험과 필요의 다른 영역에 대한 우리의 접근 방식과 일치하여, 의학 적 도움을 위해서는 의사에게 가고, 차를 수리하기 위해서는 자동차 정비사 를 방문한다. 우리 대부분은 암시적으로든 명시적으로든, 건설된 환경에 대 한 통제권을 포기하고, 그것들에 대한 의사 결정권을 시 의회 의원, 부동산 개발업자, 건설업자와 토건업자, 제품 제조업자, 그리고 설계사와 같은 전문 가들에게 맡겨 왔다. 우리 대부분은 건설된 환경에 변화를 가져오는 데 자신 들이 도움이 된다(→ 무력하다)고 인식한다. 바로 이런 무력감은 역설적인 상 황을 초래한다. 즉 부동산 개발업자들은 소비자들이 원하는 것이라 믿는 것 을 기반으로 새로운 프로젝트를 구성하는데, 그들은 그것을 주로 이전 소비 자들이 무엇을 구입했는지 살펴봄으로써 평가한다. 그러나 건설된 환경에 관 한 한, 소비자들은 전통적인 디자인에 대해 별로 생각하지 않고 그것에 끌린 다. 그러므로 개발업자들은 사람들이 원한다고 생각하는 것을 계속해서 건설 한다. 무엇이 사람들에게 더 나을지, 사람들이 무엇을 좋아할 수 있을지, 혹 은 그들이 실제로 무엇을 필요로 할지 한발 물러나 생각해 보는 사람은 아무 도 없다.

해설
우리는 의사나 자동차 수리공에게 의료와 수리를 맡기듯, 건설된 풍경에 대 한 통제권을 전문가들에게 맡겨 왔다는 내용과 이런 무력감이 역설적 인 상황을 초래한다는 내용으로 보아, 우리 대부분은 건설된 환경에 변화 를 가져오는 데 자신들이 무력하다고 인식한다는 내용이 자연스러우므로 ③ 'helpful(도움이 되는)'을 'helpless(무력한)'와 같은 낱말로 바꾸어야 한다.

04   정답 ④

한 fMRI(기능성 자기 공명 영상) 연구에서, 피실험자들은 세 가지 차원(색 상, 모양, 또는 패턴) 중 하나에 대한 자극을 분류하도록 요청받았다. 행동 측 면에서, 한 가지 연구 결과는 피실험자들은 머무름 실험에 비해 전환 실험에 서 자극을 분류하는 데 더 오래 걸린다는 것이었다. 뇌의 측면에서, 전두두정 골(前頭頭頂骨) 영역이 머무름 실험보다 전환 실험 동안 더 반응적이었다. 사 실, 다중 작업이 신경 인지적 요구를 높인다는 견해와 일관되게, 피실험자가 같은 과제에 머무를 때보다 새로운 과제로 전환할 때 제어 회로망의 과제 표 현 강도가 더 컸다. 이것은 우리가 하나의 과제에서 다른 과제로 전환할 때 더 많은 신경 처리가 요구되는데, 그 이유는 우리가 새로운 과제의 표현을 다 시 머리에 상기시킨 다음 그것을 이용하여 새로운 과제를 수행하기 위해 관 련된 정보에 주의력을 할당해야 하기 때문이다. 그 결과, 과제 사이를 전환할

때, 우리는 단일 작업에 집중력을 유지하는 데서 오는 자동성과 효율성의 이 점을 잃는다.

해설
다중 작업이 신경 인지적 요구를 높이는 것과 마찬가지로, 피실험자가 같은 과제에 머무를 때보다 새로운 과제로 전환할 때 제어 회로망의 과제 표현 강 도가 더 컸는데, 이는 하나의 과제에서 다른 과제로 전환할 때 더 많은 신경 처리가 요구된다는 내용의 글이므로, 빈칸에 들어갈 말로 가장 적절한 것은 ④ '자동성과 효율성'이다.

① 규제와 안정성

② 명료성과 투명성

③ 유연성과 적응성

⑤ 통합과 유지

05   정답 ①

규범적 믿음은 일반적으로 사회적 상호 작용에서 비롯되는 것으로 여겨진다. 실제로, 규범의 사회적 영향에 대한 초기 연구의 많은 부분은 규범에 대한 정 보를 전달하기 위해 연출된 환경에서 실제 인물을 이용했다. 예를 들어, 자동 운동 효과에 관한 Sherif의 연구는 한 과제에 대한 그들의 평가 결과가 다른 참가자들에게 공개되는 (보통 3명의) 참가자 집단을 이용했다. 마찬가지로, Asch는 자신의 순응성 연구에서 규범적 정보를 전달하기 위해 공모자를 이 용했는데, 그것은 Latané와 Darleyin이 다원적 무지에 대한 연구에서 그 랬던 것과 마찬가지였다. 이러한 전통적 방법이 여전히 사용되고 (그리고 규 범의 사회적 영향에 대한 '유일한' 접근법으로 널리 인용되고) 있지만, 규범적 정보가 비사회적 경로를 통해 전달되는 다른 절차들이 채택되어 왔다. 즉, 다 른 사람들이 행동하는 것을 보는 것이 특정한 맥락에서 사회적 규범에 관한 정보를 명확하게 제공할 수 있지만, 사회적 상호 작용은 요구되지 않는다. 개 인은 다른 이들의 행동에 관한 추론을 이끌어 내기 위해 사회적, 비사회적인 다양한 신호를 이용한다.

해설
규범적 믿음에 대한 초기 연구 대부분은 연출된 환경에서 실제 인물을 이용 했고 규범적 정보가 비사회적 경로를 통해서도 전달되는 절차들이 채택되어 왔으며, 개인은 다른 이들의 행동에 관한 추론을 끌어내기 위해 사회적, 비사 회적 신호를 모두 이용한다는 내용이므로, 빈칸에 들어갈 말로 가장 적절한 것은 ① '다른 사람들이 행동하는 것을 보는 것'이다.

② 역사적 자료를 분석하는 것

③ 문화적 상징을 해석하는 것

④ 소셜 미디어 동향을 관찰하는 것

⑤ 공개적 발표문을 모니터링하는 것

06   정답 ④

사람들은 시간과 돈이 잘 먹는 데 가장 큰 장애물로 인식된다고 말한다. 대 부분의 경우, 둘 다 진정한 장애물이 아니다. 미국인들은 화면 앞에서 하루에 여덟 시간을 보낸다. 평균적으로, 우리 각각은 하루에 두 시간을 인터넷에 쓰 는데, 그것은 20년 전에는 존재하지조차 않았던 것이다! 그렇지만 우리가 가 족을 위해 계획을 세우고, 장을 보고, 요리를 할 시간은 낼 수 없는 것인가? 가공된 정크 푸드와 패스트푸드를 먹는 것보다 신선한 육류, 생선, 그리고 농 산물을 사는 데는 돈이 약간 더 들 것이라는 것은 사실이다. 하지만 그럴 필 요는 없다. 사실, 연구들은 진정한 식품을 먹는 것이 가공식품을 먹는 것보다 더 비싸지 않다는 것을 보여 주었다. 여러분은 풀을 먹인 스테이크를 사야 할

필요는 없다(비록 그것이 이상적일지라도). 여러분은 더 적은 돈으로 잘 먹을 수 있다. 전체적인 시야로 보면, 유럽인들은 소득의 20퍼센트 정도를 음식에 사용하고, 미국인들은 9퍼센트만 사용한다. 초반에 쓰지 않는 것을 우리는 말미에 약국과 병원에서 지불한다.

해설
미국인들은 양질의 음식을 준비하기 위해 응당 사용해야 할 시간과 돈을 사용하지 않고 정크 푸드와 패스트푸드를 먹는데, 결국 건강을 해쳐서 약국과 병원에서 그만큼의 시간과 돈을 사용한다는 내용의 글이므로, 빈칸에 들어갈 말로 가장 적절한 것은 ④ '진정한 식품을 먹는 것이 가공식품을 먹는 것보다 더 비싸지 않다'이다.
① 균형 잡힌 식단은 많은 사람에게 부족한 요리 기술이 필요하다
② 건강한 식단을 유지하는 것은 일반적인 약보다 비용이 많이 든다
③ 한두 가지 특별한 재료로 요리를 준비하는 것이 좋다
⑤ 신선한 재료는 가공된 재료보다 맛이 더 좋다

07
정답 ④

서양의 사회 과학은 과학자로서 사회 과학자들이 '이론적인 태도', 즉 거리를 두고 과학적으로 심사숙고하는 태도를 채택해야 한다는 생각을 대체로 지지한다. 이론의 창시자로서 사회 과학자는 사회·정치적 세계에 대해 사심 없는 관찰자가 되어야 하며, 그런 의미에서 사회로부터 떨어져 있어야 한다. 사회 과학자는 사회의 활동을 냉정하게 연구해야 하며, 세계가 존재하는 방식에 대한 이론적 설명을 개발하고 시험하는 것만을 목표로 두어야 한다. 이런 사고방식에서, 전통적으로 생각되었던 사회·정치적 삶을 이론화하는 활동은 사회적 삶의 활동의 나머지 밖에 존재한다. 사회·정치적 세계가 존재해야 하는 방식에 관한 판단은 다른 사람들이 결정할 수 있도록 맡겨져야 한다. (따라서 이렇게 모델링된 사회 세계는 사회 정치적 세계인데, 개인과 계층은 경쟁과 협력에 많은 시간과 에너지를 소비한다.) 사회 과학의 일과 개별적인 사회 과학자는 가치 판단의 영향을 받지 않아야 한다. 즉 우리가 사회에서 인간으로서 어떻게 살거나 행동해야 할지에 관한 결정과 관련하여 중립적이어야 한다.

해설
서양의 사회 과학자는 사회·정치 세계에 대해 사심 없는 관찰자가 되어 사회로부터 떨어져 있는 상태로 연구에 임해야 한다는 내용의 글이다. 따라서 모델링된 사회 세계는 개인과 계층이 경쟁과 협력에 많은 시간과 에너지를 소비하는 사회 정치적 세계라는 내용의 ④는 글의 전체 흐름과 관계가 없다.

08
정답 ②

운이 조금이라도 있다면, 우리는 폐기물을 만드는 것이 우리가 풀어야 할 문제가 아니라는 것을 깨달을 것이다. 만약 살아 있는 어떤 종이 폐기물을 발생시키지 않는다면, 그것은 아마도 죽은 것이거나 적어도 매우 아픈 것이다. (B) 우리에게 있고 우리가 다뤄야 할 문제는 우리가 만들어 내는 폐기물을 허비한다는 것이다. 폐기물을 영양분으로 변환하는 것은 에너지를 필요로 하기도 하고 발생시키기도 한다는 것을 생각해 보라. 우리는 항상 상업용 및 가정용 기기를 위한 에너지원을 찾고 있지만, 생태계는 결코 전선을 연결할 필요가 없다. (A) 생태계의 어느 구성원도 생산물을 내기 위해 화석 연료나 배전망 연결을 필요로 하지 않고, 자연 체계에서는 또한 폐기물이 결과물도 아니다. 자연에서는, 한 공정의 폐기물은 항상 다른 공정을 위한 영양분, 재료, 혹은 에너지원이다. 모든 것이 영양분 흐름 속에 머문다. (C) 따라서 오염의 환경 문제뿐만 아니라 희소성의 경제 문제에 대한 해결책은 자연 생태계에서

관찰할 수 있는 모델의 적용에서 찾을 수 있을 것이다. 어쩌면 우리는 우리의 관점을 넓히고 폐기물의 개념을 버림으로써 난제를 해결책으로 바꿀 수 있다.

해설
폐기물을 만드는 것이 우리가 풀어야 할 문제가 아니라는 주어진 글 다음에, 우리가 다루어야 할 문제는 우리가 만들어 낸 폐기물을 허비하고 있는 것이며, 우리는 항상 상업용 및 가정용 기기를 위한 에너지원을 찾고 있지만, 생태계는 결코 전선을 연결할 필요가 없다는 내용의 (B)가 와야 한다. 자연에서는 모든 것이 영양분 흐름 속에 머문다고 하며 (B)를 부연하는 내용의 (A)가 온 다음, 생태계의 모델을 적용하여 환경과 경제의 문제를 해결할 수 있다고 결론을 내리는 (C)가 오는 것이 글의 순서로 가장 적절하다.

09
정답 ④

분리 독립을 지지하는 서아프리카에서의 내전은 비교적 쉽게 이해할 수 있는데, 이곳에서 민족 집단은 자신의 새로운 국가를 개척하기 위해 싸운다. (C) 대의명분이 없는 서아프리카의 반군들은 이해하기가 더 어려운데, 이들은 국가 규모의 쿠데타에서처럼, 정해진 이념적 강령 없이 국가 정부를 장악하고 싶어 한다. 반군들은 자신의 목표가 더 청렴하고 더 공정한 정부를 도입하는 것이라고 주장하지만, 그들 자신의 지도자들이 너무 자주 명백하게 부패해 있기 때문에 그러한 주장은 타당하지 않아 보인다. (A) 하지만 추종자들과 함께한 우리의 인터뷰는 그들이 합리적인 내기를 하고 있다는 것을 암시한다. 즉, 더 공평하게 전리품을 나눔으로써 모든 사람이 이익을 얻거나, 그들의 편이 권력을 얻어서 전리품을 그들 방식으로 관리할 것이기 때문에 적어도 그들 자신이 이익을 얻을 것이다. (B) 많은 이들은 그저 자신의 고향 마을을 지키기 위해 반란군에 가담한다. 반군들은 굉장히 지역적인 관점을 가지고 있다. 그들은 수도에서 국가 정부를 장악하는 것을 목표로 하는데, 왜냐하면 이것이 여전히 전리품의 분배를 통제하는 방법이기 때문이다. 이념으로서 훌륭한 통치는 국가적 공평, 혹은 그저 일련의 새로운 승리자들을 의미할지도 모른다.

해설
분리 독립을 지지하는 서아프리카에서의 민족 집단은 자신의 새로운 국가를 개척하기 위해 싸운다는 주어진 글 다음에, 서아프리카의 반군들은 자신의 목표가 공정한 정부를 도입하는 것이라고 주장하지만, 자신의 지도자들이 너무 부패해 있기 때문에 그 주장은 타당하지 않다는 내용의 (C)가 와야 한다. 이어서 실제로는 더 공평하게 전리품을 나누어 자신들의 편이 권력을 얻고 이익을 얻기 위함이라는 내용의 (A)가 온 다음, 많은 이들이 굉장히 지역적인 관점을 가지고 있고 전리품의 분배를 통제하는 방법으로 국가 정부를 장악하는 것을 목표로 한다는 내용의 (B)가 오는 것이 글의 순서로 가장 적절하다.

10
정답 ②

언어적으로 생각하는 것의 한 가지 이점은 언어가 지금 여기에서 여러분을 자유롭게 해 준다는 것이다. 언어와 의미 덕분에, 여러분은 가능한 미래의 사건에 관해, 멀리 떨어져 있는 사람들에 관해, 먼 과거에 했던 약속에 관해 생각할 수 있다. 쥐나 곤충은 본질적으로 즉각적인 현재에 살고 있으며, 그것이 보고 듣고 맛볼 수 있는 것에 기초해서만 대응할 수 있다. 언어는 사람들이 한 번도 일어나지 않았던 가능한 사건들을 상상할 수 있게 해 준다. 이 기능은 매우 도움이 되고 자유롭게 해 준다. 단 하나의 예로, 언어가 없는 동물들은 올해 수확물의 일부를 내년에 심기 위해 남겨 두어야 한다는 것을 도저히 이해할 수 없어서, 배가 고파지면 자신들의 씨앗용 옥수수를 먹을 것이다. 그들은 단기적으로는 기분이 좋아지겠지만, 내년에는 심을 것이 없어 농작물이

전혀 없을 것이다. 아주 많은 종들이 식물을 먹기는 하겠지만, 우리 종이 땅을 경작해 수확물을 거두는 유일한 종이라는 것은 거의 우연이 아니다.

해설

언어는 사람들이 한 번도 일어나지 않았던 가능한 사건들을 상상할 수 있게 해 준다고 말하는 주어진 문장이 없으면, This facility로 시작하여 이 기능이 매우 도움이 되고 자유롭게 해 준다는 ② 다음 문장과 쥐나 곤충은 본질적으로 즉각적인 현재에 살고 있으며, 그것이 보고 듣고 맛볼 수 있는 것에 기초해서만 대응할 수 있다는 ② 앞 문장 사이에 내용상 단절이 일어난다. 또한 주어진 문장의 This facility는 ② 앞에 있는 내용, 즉 언어의 기능을 나타내므로, 주어진 문장이 들어가기에 가장 적절한 곳은 ②이다.

11 정답 ④

컴퓨터 기반의 검색 도구는 의심의 여지없이 유용하여, 'Current Contents'는 여러분이 관심 있는 저널의 최근 출판물을 빠르게 살펴볼 수 있게 해 주고, 'Web of Science'(그리고 이와 유사한 도구)는 저자, 키워드, 또는 인용구 추적으로 문헌을 신속하게 검색하게 해 준다. 검색 엔진을 사용할 수 있기 전에는 우리는 어떻게 그것을 했을까? 나는 가령 지난 5년간 해당 주제를 발표한 주요 저널을 대강 훑어보며 관련된 논문은 무엇이나 복사하는 것으로 시작할 것이다. 그런 다음에 나는 더 오래된 문헌을 찾아 내기 위해 이들 논문 속의 인용문들을 검토하고, 그 인용문들에 대한 참조 문헌의 빈도와 성향으로부터 중요한 자료를 유추할 것이다. 이 방법의 큰 장점은 그 분야의 인용 구조를 제공하고 상황이 어떻게 발전해 왔는지 어느 정도 감을 잡을 수 있게 해 준다는 것이다. 한 가지 관련된 기법은 반대 방향으로 검색하는데, 이 부분에서 검색 엔진이 큰 도움이 된다. 가령 20년 전에 발표된 해당 주제에 대한 핵심 논문을 찾고 나서 이 논문을 인용하는, 그때 이후로 발표된 논문을 살펴보라. 때로는 그것들이 특이한 장소에서 발표되었거나 명백하게 연관된 키워드나 제목이 없기 때문에, 그렇게 하지 않으면 놓칠 수 있을 논문을 획득하게 된다.

해설

주어진 문장은 한 가지 관련된 기법은 반대 방향으로 검색하는데, 이 부분에서 검색 엔진이 큰 도움이 된다는 내용이므로, 예시로 제시한 20년 전에 발표된 해당 주제에 대한 핵심 논문을 찾고 나서 이 논문을 인용하는, 즉 그때 이후로 발표된 논문을 살펴보면 놓칠 수 있을 논문을 획득하게 된다는 내용 앞인 ④에 들어가는 것이 가장 적절하다.

12 정답 ⑤

자신들에게 집중할 때, 사람들은 (불안한 감정과 이미지 같은) 내적인 정보를 인식하게 되는데, 그들은 그것들을 자신들의 최악의 공포에 대한 충분한 증거라고 잘못 받아들인다. 가장 흔한 공포 중 하나는 여러분이 불안하다는 것을 사람들이 알게 될 거라는 것이다. 사회적 불안 장애를 가진 사람들은 그들이 느끼는 것보다 훨씬 덜 불안해 보이지만, 그들은 자신들의 감정이 자신들이 어떻게 보이는지에 대한 좋은 지표라고 믿는 경향이 있다. 이미지 또한 두드러진 역할을 한다. 특히 불안할 때 사회적 불안 장애를 가진 사람들은 마치 관찰자의 시각에서 보듯 자신들의 마음속 눈으로 스스로를 본다고 보고한다. 유감스럽게도, 그들이 보는 것은 관찰자가 사실상 보는 것이 아니라 대신에 자신들의 최악의 공포가 시각화된 것이다. 그러므로 얼굴이 붉어지는 것에 대해 우려하는 사람은 실제로 약간 분홍빛이 되었을 지도 모르지만, 그들의 마음속 눈에서는 자신들이 비트 같은 붉은색이며 자신들의 이마로부터 큰 땀방울이 뚝뚝 떨어지고 있는 것으로 보일 것이다.

➡ 사회 불안 장애를 가진 사람들은 자신의 내적 감각과 이미지를 자주 <u>과대평가하는</u>데, 이는 그들을 다른 사람들이 자신을 실제 보이는 것보다 더 불안하게 인식한다고 <u>믿도록</u> 한다.

해설

자신에게 집중할 때, 사람들은 내적 정보를 인지하면서 그것들을 공포에 대한 충분한 증거라고 잘못 받아들이게 되고, 자신의 내적인 정보를 과대평가하여 자신이 불안하다는 것을 다른 사람들이 실제 보이는 것보다 더 불안하게 인식하게 될 것이라고 믿게 만든다는 내용의 글이므로, 요약문의 빈칸 (A), (B)에 들어갈 말로는 ⑤ 'overestimate(과대평가하다) – believe(믿다)'가 가장 적절하다.

① 피하다 – 증명하다
② 피하다 – 의심하다
③ 간과하다 – 믿다
④ 과대평가하다 – 의심하다

부록 WORDS REVIEW

고난도 모의고사 01회

A

01 인위적인 02 버리다 03 대피 04 구별하다 05 깊이 생각하다 06 반사적인 07 발휘하다, 행사하다 08 구별 09 이로운 10 보도[방송] 11 대기의 12 검소함

B

01 opponents 02 correlation 03 subjective
04 relevant 05 linger

C

01 uncontroversial / 화석 연료의 사용이 환경 악화와 기후 변화에 기여한다는 것은 논란의 여지가 없는 발언이다.
02 anonymous / 소셜 미디어 플랫폼은 표현의 자유와 프라이버시를 제공하면서 사용자가 익명으로 유지할 수 있도록 한다.

고난도 모의고사 02회

A

01 조명 02 조정하다, 중재하다 03 장애물 04 가공하지 않은 05 흥미를 돋우는, 설득력 있는 06 허가하다 07 추상적인 08 조장하다 09 모호하게 만들다 10 단언하다 11 버리다, 폐기하다 12 통합하다

B

01 specify 02 oppressive 03 distort
04 impractical 05 incoherent

C

01 ambiguous / 그림의 모호한 색상과 모양은 다양한 해석을 가능하게 했고, 미술 비평가들 사이에 활발한 논쟁을 불러일으켰다.
02 amplified / 관중들의 환호성이 경기장의 에너지를 증폭시키며 경기장 전체에 퍼져 나가는 강렬한 흥분을 불러일으켰다.

고난도 모의고사 03회

A

01 제공, 공급 02 타협하다 03 무너뜨리다, 침식하다 04 미적인 05 궁극적인 06 숙고하다 07 위신 08 제약 09 정당한 10 상관관계 11 의식화하다 12 역량

B

01 run counter to 02 in the face of 03 Compared to

04 accused of 05 with no regard for

C

01 sudden / 고온에서 저온으로의 갑작스러운 변화는 즉각적인 수리가 필요한 파열과 누출을 일으킬 수 있다.
02 Constructive / 멘토나 상사의 건설적인 피드백은 직원들이 기술을 다듬고 직장에서 성과를 높이는 데 도움이 될 수 있다.

고난도 모의고사 04회

A

01 분별 있는 02 대륙 간의 03 변환, 전환 04 지루한 05 거래 06 두드러진 07 자율적인 08 지표 09 적응력 10 주장 11 탐지하다, 조사하다 12 관점, 차원

B

01 collapse 02 imminent 03 fundamental
04 substantiate 05 contradiction

C

01 scarcity / 빗물 수집 시스템의 구현은 미래에 사용할 강우량을 저장함으로써 일부 지역 사회에서 물 부족을 완화하는 데 도움이 되어 왔다.
02 sustainable / 신재생 에너지 공학 분야는 세계의 증가하는 에너지 수요를 충족시키기 위해 태양열, 풍력, 지열과 같은 지속 가능한 에너지원을 개발하는 데 중점을 둔다.

고난도 모의고사 05회

A

01 설득력 있는 02 현대의 03 출현 04 인구 변동 05 영역, 영토 06 시각, 관점 07 돌파구 08 속성 09 강화하다 10 전문 기술 11 화폐의 12 조립

B

01 calls into question 02 Speaking on behalf of
03 compensated for 04 come into play

C

01 explicitly / 약병의 경고 라벨에는 가능한 부작용과 자세한 용량 지침이 명시적으로 나열되어 있어야 한다.
02 innate / 과학자는 철새의 선천적 행동이 조상으로부터 물려받은 유전적 성향에 영향을 받는다는 가설을 세웠다.

A

01 예민한   02 개성   03 뒤집다   04 상쇄하다   05 지각의
06 (사실임을) 입증하다, 증명하다   07 친밀한   08 옹호하다   09 직
면시키다   10 변수   11 하찮은 존재로 만들다, 무시하다   12 한결같음,
균일성

B

01 immense   02 divergent   03 discrete
04 intrinsic   05 depleting

C

01 inadequate / 그의 최선의 의도에도 불구하고, 복잡한 이론에 대한 그
의 설명은 부적절했고 청중들을 혼란스럽게 만들었다.
02 theoretical / 수학에서 무한과 허수와 같은 이론적 개념은 유형적인
양을 넘어 추상적인 개념을 탐구할 수 있게 해 준다.

A

01 할당하다   02 ~ 덕분에   03 유사성   04 궁극적으로   05 자연스
러운, 자발적인   06 절차   07 공감   08 그럴듯하게   09 ~을 이용하
다   10 언어적으로, 말로   11 대안   12 자선의

B

01 distributes   02 manipulated   03 furnishes
04 conceived   05 cultivate

C

01 disclosure / 의료 시설은 환자 정보의 프라이버시를 보장하고 무단 공
개를 방지하기 위해 엄격한 기밀 유지 방침을 유지한다.
02 invaluable / 박물관의 희귀 유물 소장품은 귀중하고 다른 곳에서는 찾
아볼 수 없는 역사를 엿볼 수 있다.

A

01 연장시키다   02 나타내다   03 1회용의, 마음대로 쓰고 버리는
04 수정 가능성   05 묘사하다   06 풍부한   07 가정의   08 통치 (방
식), 관리(법)   09 사전 대책을 강구하는   10 이끌어 내다   11 연방의
12 우선시하다

B

01 vulnerable   02 deterioration   03 facilitate
04 implausible   05 replicate

C

01 automatic / 자동 반려견 사료 공급기는 예정된 간격으로 음식을 분배
하여 내가 부재중일 때도 내 반려견에게 먹이를 잘 주었다.
02 discrimination / 차별에 맞서 싸우려는 입법 노력에도 불구하고, 미묘
한 편견은 여전히 사람들을 고용하는 방식에 영향을 미치며, 일부 집단에
게 동등한 고용 기회를 주지 않는다.

A

01 오랜 시간에 걸쳐, 만성적으로   02 비교   03 합의   04 표현
05 (권력·권위를) 행사하다   06 격앙시키다   07 체제   08 구성
09 피상적인   10 통합   11 독점적인   12 식민지화하다

B

01 deviation   02 exploitation   03 cohesion
04 inspiration   05 distractions

C

01 concise / 그 책의 첫머리에 있는 간결한 요약은 독자들에게 명확한 로
드맵을 제공했고, 말의 바다에서 길을 잃지 않고 핵심 사항을 파악할 수 있게
해 주었다.
02 Conversely / 그 회사는 자사 직원의 복지를 우선시한다. 반대로, 그
회사의 경쟁사는 어떤 비용을 치르더라도 생산성을 극대화하는 것을 우선시
한다.

A

01 영역   02 박해하다   03 이성적인   04 유혹하는 것, 미끼   05 자
의적으로   06 ~을 막다   07 유산   08 구별하다   09 육성하다
10 받아들이다   11 지배   12 직설적으로

B

01 seasoned   02 obscure   03 dissuade
04 dictated   05 distances

C

01 virtuous / 그 경찰관의 덕망 있는 행동은 사법 제도에 대한 믿음을 회
복시키고 국민의 감탄을 자아냈다.
02 consent / 새로운 정책을 시행하기 전에, 그 회사는 모든 직원의 서면
동의를 요구했다.

A

01 기만하다, 속이다   02 반복해서 일어나는   03 관용   04 신생의   05 순응하다   06 일관성   07 정통의   08 긴밀하게 관련짓다   09 ~와 일치하다   10 부족한, 희귀한   11 결정적이지 않은   12 맡기다

B

01 articulated   02 consolidate   03 Disengaged
04 embedded   05 undermined

C

01 overestimate / 시장 수요를 과대평가하는 임원의 성향은 과잉 생산과 과잉 재고로 이어져 궁극적으로 회사의 수익에 타격을 입혔다.
02 sacred / 그 제사장이 성스러운 의식을 수행할 때, 사람들은 의식적인 몸짓의 심오한 의미를 감지하면서 경외심을 가지고 지켜보았다.

A

01 피로, 긴장, 부담   02 획기적인   03 양립할 수 없는   04 (병적으로) 집착하게 하다   05 새기다   06 음절   07 강화하다, 심화시키다   08 최적으로   09 불안정   10 언제나   11 수직의   12 예언

B

01 infusions   02 addictive   03 arguably
04 dominance   05 supernatural

C

01 proponents / 역사를 통틀어, 많은 위대한 지도자들이 폭력보다는 외교를 통해 갈등을 해결하기 위해 노력하며 평화의 지지자로 등장했다.
02 primitive / 고고학자들은 수천 년 전의 원시적인 도구들을 발견함으로써 초기 인류 문명을 밝혀냈다.

A

01 부정적인   02 해체, 단편화   03 애착   04 선견지명 있는   05 기억   06 역경의   07 심한, 강렬한   08 장기간의   09 필연적으로   10 조정하다   11 생태적인   12 활용[이용]하다

B

01 indigenous   02 deliberation   03 recipients
04 coherent   05 epidemics

C

01 diminished / 부지런한 물리 치료와 재활 덕분에, 하루가 지날수록 부

상의 고통이 줄어들었다.
02 Altruistic / 이타적인 개인은 종종 지역 사회에서 자선 사업을 지원하기 위해 시간과 자원을 자발적으로 제공한다.

A

01 중세   02 무시하다, 중단시키다   03 소멸하다, 죽다   04 두드러지게   05 연민, 동정심   06 지칭, 지시 대상   07 해설   08 비율   09 전환하다   10 풍성한   11 사용하다   12 (근거로 인물·예 등을) 들다[언급하다]

B

01 comparable   02 rationality   03 explanatory
04 subordination   05 solidarity

C

01 eligible / 농부들은 자격이 있다면 농업 생산성과 지속 가능성을 높이는 데 도움이 되는 보조금을 신청할 수 있다.
02 Restrictions / 정치 불안으로 인한 특정 지역 여행 제한은 관광 산업과 지역 생계에 부정적인 경제적 영향을 미쳤다.

A

01 유창하게   02 전달하다   03 반드시   04 구체적인   05 평균의   06 부여하다   07 유사하게   08 미치다, 발휘하다   09 격리[분리]시키다   10 주거의   11 이끌어 내다   12 위협적인

B

01 decayed   02 conceptualize   03 arbitrary
04 assimilate   05 intricate

C

01 resilient / 그 소년은 회복력 있는 면역 체계 덕분에 예상보다 훨씬 빨리 병에서 회복했다.
02 inferior / 그 제품의 열등한 품질은 고객 불만 증가와 그에 따른 매출 감소에 직접적인 책임이 있었다.